Colonial Spanish America

Colonial Spanish America

A Documentary History

Edited by

KENNETH MILLS
Assistant Professor of History
Princeton University

and

WILLIAM B. TAYLOR
Edmund and Louise Kahn Professor of History
Southern Methodist University

A Scholarly Resources Inc. Imprint
Wilmington, Delaware

First published 1998
Printed and bound in the United States of America

Scholarly Resources Inc.
104 Greenhill Avenue
Wilmington, DE 19805-1897

Library of Congress Cataloging-in-Publication Data

Colonial Spanish America : a documentary history / edited by Kenneth Mills and William B. Taylor.
p. cm.
Includes index.
ISBN 0-8420-2572-3 (cloth : alk. paper). — ISBN 0-8420-2573-1 (pbk. : alk. paper)
1. Latin America—History—To 1830. 2. Latin America—History—To 1830—Sources.
I. Mills, Kenneth (Kenneth R.) II. Taylor, William B.
F1412.C642 1998
980'.01—dc21 97-44250
CIP

∞ The paper used in this publication meets the minimum requirements of the American National Standard for permanence of paper for printed library materials, Z39.48, 1984.

ACKNOWLEDGMENTS

The editors express their special thanks to the following people and institutions who have helped make this project a pleasure.

William Taylor is indebted to E. William Jowdy for his generous interest and bracing criticism of many introductions to selections. He also thanks Thomas B. F. Cummins for collaborating on short notice in an appraisal of the enigmatic portrait of the three gentlemen from Esmeraldas; Karin E. Taylor for redrawing the plan of the Huejotzingo altarpiece and sending her father off to read Italo Calvino; Daniel Slive for advice about colonial engravings; and James Early for sharing slides from his splendid collection on colonial Mexican architecture. The Edmund and Louise Kahn Chair fund at Southern Methodist University helped cover editorial costs.

Kenneth Mills thanks Roger Highfield for the way he speaks about the place of primary sources in teaching and David Church Johnson for his teaching in practice; Elizabeth Mills for her timely criticism and suggestions; Peter Lake for his comments on a few of the selections used in our comparative seminar; and Peter Brown, Robert Connor, and J. Paul Hunter, among others, for advice and encouragement along the way. He is grateful for support of this project from the John Carter Brown Library at Brown University, as well as the University Committee for Research in the Humanities and Social Sciences, the Program in Latin American Studies, and the Department of History, all at Princeton University.

John Blazejewski, Richard Hurley, and Andrew Reisberg expertly photographed the previously published images. Margaret Case read a late version of the manuscript, and her careful and creative eye, along with the expertise of Linda Pote Musumeci of Scholarly Resources, did much to establish its final form. Finally, both editors want to acknowledge the students in their respective classes who, usually without knowing it, have partaken of a number of teaching experiments and contributed both to what appears in, and what has been shed from, this book.

CONTENTS

PART II *The Americas as New Worlds for All?*

PART III *Spanish American Baroque in a Long Seventeenth Century*

PART IV Bourbon Rules and American Practices in a Short Eighteenth Century

EDITORS' NOTE

This collection is made up of selections, and by this term we refer both to written and visual sources and to the introductions which precede them. Due to pressures of space, we have excerpted portions of a few of our written selections and omitted the scholarly notes from previously published secondary and primary sources. When information contained in these notes has seemed crucial to the understanding or integrity of the selection, this information has been included or summarized within square brackets in the body of the text. Readers wishing to read these works as their authors first intended them to appear are urged toward the Notes on Selections and Sources section at the end of the volume. Information on each source is collected there, with references to scholarly work that has particularly informed or assisted the editors in introducing a selection, or to which we wish to draw readers' attention.

Foreign words and phrases are set in italics at first appearance, with a short definition. An independent Glossary of key terms and foreign words used in more than one selection is also provided. The translations of archival and published documentary material originally not in English are the work of the editors unless otherwise indicated in the Notes on Selections and Sources. We have made the following adjustments in the written selections: spelling conforms to United States English; typographical errors have been corrected; on rare occasions, we have altered punctuation to assist clarity; certain words have been capitalized and other small changes in spelling have been made to conform to the style used throughout the book; and ellipses mark parts of a text that we have left out. Our occasional glosses, additions, and interjections appear in brackets, as do the similar interventions of any previous editors.

LIST OF ILLUSTRATIONS

INTRODUCTION

Texts and Images for Colonial History

Exploration is not so much a covering of surface distance as a study in depth: a fleeting episode, a fragment of landscape, or a remark overheard may provide the only means of understanding and interpreting areas which would otherwise remain barren of meaning.

—Claude Lévi-Strauss, *Tristes tropiques (1984)*

We may distinguish between two types of imaginative process: the one that starts with the word and arrives at the visual image, and the one that starts with the visual image and arrives at its verbal expression.

—Italo Calvino, *Six Memos for the Next Millennium (1988)*

This book of readings and images on the history of colonial Spanish America is intended for students and teachers as well as for scholars and general readers. Through a variety of documents, both written and visual, it aims to provide more than a conventional treatment of the "great themes" associated with the study of the colonial period. These include exploration; military and spiritual conquest; the formation, consolidation, reform, and collapse of colonial institutions of government, and Church, and the accompanying changes in the economy and labor; and the relations between American-born Creoles and *peninsulares* (people from the Iberian Peninsula). Our sources bear on these themes, among others, but through a focus on religion and society as a way to a more integral history.

Mesoamerica (the highlands of central and southern Mexico and Central America) and Peru (the vast western portion of South America) receive special attention because these two areas held the great indigenous state societies and silver deposits that attracted Spanish interests; they became the principal colonial heartlands. For two centuries the administrative reach of their viceregal capitals at Mexico City and Lima extended to the limits of Spanish territory in America. Mesoamerica and Peru are also the regions best known to historians of the colonial period, thanks to their unusually rich documentary record. Other regions appear here in several texts and images—the Caribbean imagined in an illustration for Amerigo Vespucci's letters; the coast of Ecuador in a striking portrait of three Mulatto gentlemen; Paraguay in a letter from a Guaraní chief and the plan of his mission settlement; and frontiers of southern South America and Mexico in Concolorcorvo's travel account, the story of the Black settlement of Amapa, and Argentina's Declaration of Independence. But the emphases and absences arise from our wish to delve into some matters and areas in depth, rather than labor to cover a bit of almost everything.

The majority of the readings are primary documents, a number of which are translated into English for the first time. In addition, images made during the colonial period are presented as primary visual documents, records of life and thought in colonial times that redirect as well as amplify the themes and changes that will be met in the written selections and in wider reading and discussion. Among the primary sources are not only letters, sermons, exhortations, reports, travel accounts, portions of treatises, speeches, decrees, pronouncements, and literary productions, but also carved stones, textiles, altarpieces, the upper reaches of church interiors, maps, portraits, and inscriptions on monuments and public works. The preponderance of primary material among the selections represents the choice of two teachers, largely in answer to their own students' enthusiasm for the immediacy and insight that the study of contemporary sources can bring. For similar reasons, the selections emphasize people at various levels of society in their places and times, rather than as solitary thinkers or faceless masses, their backs turned toward us. Eight secondary sources—essays written about colonial history by later scholars—have also been included to ask and underscore provocative questions, and to demonstrate the act and influence of historical interpretation.

Each document, either written or visual, is accompanied by an introduction composed in the spirit of invitation as much as direction. To increase the accessibility of the selections and suggest how they can be read together, these introductions supply information about the image or text and place it within wider contexts, identifying points of special interest, posing problems and queries, and, in particular, encouraging readers toward their own understandings. The introductions are meant to develop briefly one line of interpretation and to open discussion, rather than to have the last word about a document. Since the selections and introductions are points of entry as well as points of view, the pages of this book are meant to be turned in both directions. Once met, they will need to be reviewed in light of their neighbors and other sources that suggest related themes. History, in E. P. Thompson's words and practice, is "the restless discipline of context." The introductions supply some of the immediate context for a source and suggest several connections to other sources that are good for thinking about a fuller history—and about what was changing or not changing. But this is open-ended work. Much of the challenge of contextualization calls for ingenuity, adjustment, and some "exact imagining" from readers.

Within this book, readers will encounter coincidences and the challenge of holding apparently contradictory ideas—paradoxes—in mind rather than moving directly to one or the other as "true" or typical. Certain texts and images are juxtaposed for the ways in which they might be related to each other and illuminate wider issues. Thus, for instance, a testimony telling of the life of Santa Rosa of Lima and a letter written by Mexican nun and scholar-poet Sor Juana Inés de la Cruz, along with two posthumous portraits of these women, are paired for comparison. Then, thinking across other sources, readers can consider the life of Santa Rosa in terms of a description of seventeenth-century Lima, the weighty insistence of Francisco de Avila's sermon for Christmas Eve, the campaigns to stamp out native Andean religious error, fear of incursions by seafaring Protestant adversaries, and the decoration of a Rosary chapel that emerge out of the same intellectual and political climate, as well as a provocative secondary source that celebrates the seventeenth century as a golden age. Thus, the selections are not meant to file in and out of the reader's mind, one by one. A historical vision of colonial Spanish America that aims to be broad and deep depends on reconsideration of sources and ideas in light of subsequent study, prompted not only by messages in this book but also by other readings and reckonings that will become a study of colonial Latin America.

Although the selections for the most part are arranged chronologically and set in four broad parts, we have resisted the temptation to impose a single periodization on the book on the grounds that it would distract unnecessarily from the associations that can be made between selections at long as well as short range, and leave the impression that certain dates are inevitable benchmarks and need not be questioned. Of course, the collection cannot magically escape the influence of the periodizations that have guided and organized the study of colonial Latin American history in the past, even if we wanted it to. Composing a sourcebook on the colonial period in itself involves a choice about periodization. It is important to ask when and how basic structures of society, government, material life, and ideas changed. But, extending Olivia Harris's argument (Selection 6), periodization from a Spanish perspective alone, or from the history of political institutions, runs the risk of relegating certain changes and continuities to a distant background and making others appear unduly formative. A fixed sequence of chronological turning points risks a narrative that determines our expectations and our very manner of addressing the past. In offering more than an institutional perspective, the selections often blur the familiar temporal and territorial boundaries of this colonial history.

In many general surveys of colonial Spanish America, the military conquests of the early sixteenth century and the independence movements of the early nineteenth century have seemed to be the great events, as if bracketing three centuries of inertia with sudden action. Especially for Spaniards, conquest and insurgency do represent compelling beginnings and endings, but they were only the most dramatic events, not the only important ones. In the introductions and choice of sources—such as the Inka's tunics, the Aztec Stone of the Five Eras, the Texupa map of 1579, and the testimony of Francisco Poma y Altas Caldeas before an ecclesiastical judge in 1657—we mean to remind readers of the variety and complexity of Amerindian societies before the Spaniards' arrival, and to suggest that they would persist and be profoundly affected, not simply be erased or replaced (however gradually), by the military defeats and capitulations of their significant political centers. The difficulty for historical interpretation posed by the fact that much of the existing evidence on the indigenous peoples of the Americas comes from post-Conquest records is presented with an invitation to consider the various cultures that found expression in colonial times as clues to a past as well as to a present and future. "Indians" (people descended from indigenous groups living under Spanish rule)—like Africans brought originally to the Americas as slaves, Spaniards and other Europeans, and people of the racial and cultural combinations that resulted—are not viewed as growing less "authentic" in their transformations during the colonial period. Rather, they are seen as living not so much within separate spheres of action as within a common ground that, despite restrictions and pressures, contributed to the development of complex and rich colonial cultures. We view this common ground of sixteenth-century conflicts and confusion, collaboration and reconceptualization, as a "new world" for Africans and indigenous peoples as much as for Spaniards.

The placement of some images is meant to draw attention to overlapping "long" and "short" centuries of change without fixing a beginning or an end. Most images owe their position to a particular written source or group of sources—the Inka's tunics and the Aztec Stone of the Five Eras are set next to readings that relate to pre-Hispanic Peru and Mexico, Felipe Guaman Poma de Ayala's sketches of Catholic priests are juxtaposed with his words about them, and so on. But there are four clusters of images—easily identified by the gray borders on their pages—that both mark transitions between parts of the book and reflect back on issues and subjects introduced in earlier selections:

The first cluster (Selections 9–11)—consisting of early European depictions of native Americans and a Morisco (new convert to Christianity from Islam) mother and daughter in Spain—appears at the end of Part I. It both enlarges the subject of contact and discoveries and opens Part II's consideration of indigenous and European expectations, intentions, and fears in the course of the sixteenth century.

The second cluster (Selections 20–24)—from the Codex Osuna and Codex Sierra, Diego Valadés's ideal churchyard, the Huejotzingo altarpiece, and the portrait of three Mulatto gentlemen from Esmeraldas—and the readings that precede it in Part II concern the unfinished formation of a colonial order of institutions and social relationships in the sixteenth and early seventeenth centuries.

The third cluster (Selections 36–37)—the Dominicans' Rosary chapel in Puebla, Mexico, and paintings of a Corpus Christi procession in Cusco, Peru—completes what we are calling a long seventeenth century. These images at the end of Part III reflect on the meaning of Baroque Catholicism and society often associated with the seventeenth century, but not readily distinguished from social and cultural patterns in the late sixteenth or eighteenth century. Colonial circumstances heightened the troubling inequalities, contradictions, and nostalgia for a lost golden age that are identified with Baroque culture in Catholic Europe, but the seventeenth century is no longer so easily described as an interlude of uneventful retrenchment, decadence, superstition, and economic depression. Stretched beyond the years 1600 and 1700, the long seventeenth century in Spanish America shares a distinctive elaboration of customary relationships, a flowering of providential American holiness expressed in hugely popular pilgrimage sites and religious art and literature, a shrunken but dynamic native American population, and counterpoints of increasing production for regional consumption, world markets, and contraband trade with the English, Dutch, and French, who were establishing their own American colonies. All of these developments happened in a time of weakened imperial control as Spanish fortunes declined in Europe.

Images in the fourth cluster from the late eighteenth century (Selections 45–48)—two paintings of Mexican *castas* (racial and cultural mixture), inscriptions on fountains and monuments in Mexico City, the portrait of a famous sixteenth-century Inka rebel, and a Peruvian allegory of America—bear on the emerging Bourbon vision of a second "conquest" and some long continuities with which it clashed or sought to connect. In choosing readings and images for Part IV that date from the second half of the eighteenth century and beyond, we are not suggesting that the first half of the century is of little importance to colonial history or understandable only as an extension on a long seventeenth century. Old patterns continued, but the early decades of the eighteenth century witnessed the only extended time of real economic growth in the late colonial period and a foreshadowing of impressive development in the old peripheries of Cuba, Puerto Rico, Venezuela, and Argentina, and the initiatives of the new Bourbon dynasty in Spain (from 1700) to rejuvenate its empire in America with monopolistic trading companies and more administration. A new historical consciousness and vogue of neoclassicism and efficiency marked Bourbon times without simply replacing customary practices and what are usually regarded as Baroque tastes. But the eighteenth-century "conquest" would not be like its sixteenth-century counterpart. Many American subjects now spoke the imperial language in their own way, shared a religious culture and body of law, and were not so divided among themselves. They had a more refined sense of their rights and often focused political resentment on privileged newcomers from Spain and representatives from colonial administrative centers. And Spanish imperial initiatives in the eighteenth century were increasingly blocked by other nations with American interests, as a succession of European wars with New World theaters demonstrated. This short eighteenth century led to the loss of Spain's mainland American empire rather than its new conquest.

Another departure from the usual categories in colonial Spanish American history is our presentation of the often separated histories of the Spanish kingdoms in the Iberian Peninsula and America in this era. Historians of colonial Spanish America often say that the Christian Spanish experience of Jewish and Muslim peoples (not to mention their contacts with the Guanches of the Canary Islands) shaped the way that Spaniards would conceive of and interact with the indigenous peoples of the Americas. Yet, of what did this shaping consist, and how long did it last? With some notable exceptions, these histories remain virtually separate endeavors of Hispanists and Latin Americanists. The image of an intermittent Christian crusade to reconquer the Iberian Peninsula from increasingly fragmented Muslim rule, culminating in the capitulation of the last Islamic kingdom of Granada in 1492, has long afforded an "Iberian background" for Latin American history. The "reconquest" of Granada in particular provides a dramatic Old World backdrop and a helpful prelude to further crusades and conquests that, thanks to Columbus's voyage into the Atlantic that same year, would continue in the Americas. And the "reconquest" has provided a neat label that has given meaning to the mentality and spirit of the conquistador. As the story goes, the late medieval Spanish adventurer-conqueror, embodying the centuries-old struggle with the forces of Islam and influenced by the heroic feats recounted in the popular chivalric romances of his day, took ship to new fields of battle and wonder.

Knowledge of pre-1492 Iberian history has obvious benefits for an understanding of the Spaniards' ways of seeing America and its peoples, as a reading of the letters of the conqueror of the Aztecs, Hernán Cortés, or the chronicle written by one of his most observant footsoldiers, Bernal Díaz del Castillo, makes abundantly clear. But a fixation on Iberia-as-prelude and on the background of reconquest, with its accompanying images of dramatic defeat and the abrupt repudiation of a medieval coexistence between peoples of cultural and religious differences, misses the ways in which Spain and America share an interlocking history after 1492, a history consisting of more than the relationship between metropole and colony. To encourage some wider transatlantic thinking, we include images and texts related to Spanish Moriscos during a "long sixteenth century" that, in Iberian terms, can be said to begin with the final stages of the war waged by Ferdinand and Isabella against Granada in the 1480s and to end with the expulsion of the Moriscos, mostly to North Africa, from 1609 to 1614. In some striking ways their experience of Spanish Christian rule compares with that of many Amerindian peoples in the early colonial period.

Comparing contemporaneous developments in Spain also works to remind readers of the relevance of a wider European scene between the late fifteenth and early nineteenth centuries. The repercussions of the Protestant Reformation sparked by Martin Luther's challenges to the Catholic center of Christendom, and the Roman Church's own reforms in response, especially those associated with the Council of Trent (1545–1563), as well as wars among European states and the expansion of international trade and empires throughout the period, are important to this wider context for the study of colonial Latin America. The study of efforts to evangelize Indian peoples in Mexico or Peru, for instance, can benefit from being viewed as part of considerably broader Spanish ambitions at the time. As contemporary churchmen were fond of observing in Spain itself, in southern Italy, in other parts of Catholic Europe, and in the Philippines archipelago, there were great and varied expanses of "other Indies" at seemingly every turn, and not only among new converts from Islam. Particularly in the small towns and in the countryside, there were Europeans who, though nominally Christian and not, strictly speaking, members of an entirely alien culture, were thought to practice unacceptable forms of religion and to be greatly in need of instruction. In the minds of many missionaries and parish priests, who themselves are among the most important bridges between the histories of Europe and America, the real differences between the ministries among Christian rustics, the Spanish Moriscos, or native American peoples diminished before the immensity of their task.

The opening words of the *Recopilación de leyes de los reynos de las Indias,* the great compilation of Spanish-American law published in 1681, made explicit the inevitable links among religion, politics, and society. The king acknowledged that "God Our Lord by His infinite mercy and goodness, has bestowed upon us, without our deserving it, a great share of the dominion of this world. . . . Consequently, we find ourselves with a greater obligation than other princes to strive to serve Him and the glory of His Holy Name, and to employ all the power He has given us to see that His name is known and worshiped throughout the world as the true God." The obligations between Christian king and new American subjects expressed in this soaring statement of legitimacy and mission are reciprocal, but with a clear warning:

> Desiring this glory of Our God and Lord, happily have we succeeded in bringing into the fold of the Holy Roman Catholic Church the innumerable peoples and nations who inhabit the Western Indies, islands, and mainland of the Ocean Sea, and other places subject to our dominion. And so that everyone, throughout the world, may enjoy the inestimable benefit of Redemption through the Blood of Our Lord Jesus Christ, we beg and we charge the natives of our Indies to receive and listen kindly to the Teachers and Preachers we send them, and give credence to their teachings. . . . And if, with a stubborn and obstinate spirit, they err and refuse to accept and believe what the Holy Mother Church teaches, they are to be punished according to law and in the cases prescribed by law.

Few would deny that religion merits an important place in the study of colonial Latin America, but it is worth considering what this place has most often been, and what it might be. This collection offers a basis for studying colonial history without cordoning off religion from other aspects of life, and without assigning it a predetermined role either as a totalitarian and repressive force (principally a ready justification and vehicle for colonial domination) or as an essentially private or selfless activity (little more than the province of shaded cloisters, home altars, and busy church deacons). Here, religion is not conceived of as a subject separate from the Catholic Church, nor do we mean to equate church and religion and pursue only accounts of bishops' tenures or the evangelizing record of one religious order or another. Our selections feature religion in ways that display its pervasive but often elusive presence in daily life and thought, and in the exercise of colonial power and habits of conception.

Like many other subjects when viewed in a more searching and connecting fashion, colonial religion contains and changes too much to be compressed into a narrow definition. It is here treated as the means by which people expressed and lived their allegiance to an order that transcends human power and promises well-being. Religion is lived and experienced, not just imposed and prescribed. For the most part, colonial religious beliefs and practices were dynamic rather than timeless, capable of adaptation and reformulation in different intellectual climates, capable of being used both to justify and question colonial authority, and capable of being compassionate, demanding, and punitive.

A number of the selections demonstrate that Indian religious life in colonial times was not simply a story of loss and impoverishment, nor did it tend inexorably toward a crystallized state. A protean Catholicism was as central to the sixteenth-century thought-world of Spanish theologian Francisco de Vitoria, a troubled Morisco Jesuit, or of native Andean chronicler Felipe Guaman Poma de Ayala as it was to Guaraní spokesman Nicolás Ñenguirú in the 1750s, leader of a runaway slave community Fernando Manuel in the 1760s, Indian parishioners of Ozoloapan in the 1770s, or parish priest José María Morelos in early nineteenth-century Mexico, on the eve of independence from Spain.

Religion can serve as a nexus for much of what is generally treated as political, social, economic, and cultural history. Colonial Spanish America was what Natalie Zemon Davis, a historian of western Europe in the same centuries, has called a "religious culture." Religion became the principal expression of authority and social order in most of Spanish America. Colonial administrators and spokesmen during the sixteenth and seventeenth centuries viewed the parts of a growing empire as building blocks of a universal Christian state ascending in pyramid fashion to an all-seeing monarch subject only to God. These blocks were parts of a larger plan, the contours of which can be perceived in urban designs and descriptions, whether in Lima, one of the great colonial cities during its early seventeenth-century prime, or in tiny Amapa, with its brand-new church in late colonial times, or in a depiction of a great arm reaching out from Mexico City to the Indian pueblo of Texupa in the 1560s.

Many of the selections from different times and places in colonial history feature the imagination and organization of space, providing another set of records about intersections of the political and religious in daily life. The ideal church courtyard, a native artist's elaborate map of an Indian parish and a district governor's plan for a Black township, the plan of a Jesuit mission and the layout of a capital city, the erection of public works (with their commemorations inscribed upon them)—in each case, aims were projected onto space. The artistic and architectural forms of imperial Rome set something of an ideal for Spanish projections of political and religious power in the American colonies. This ideal was held during early Hapsburg times in the sixteenth century, when the Spanish Christian monarchy was striving toward a universal empire that would unite the diverse parts of the earth and not only emulate but also surpass Rome's achievement. And it was accented under Bourbon rule, when neoclassical styles were selected to express the restrained and "enlightened" grandeur of an order-seeking and rationalized eighteenth-century empire.

Spanish notions of civility and effective colonization stressed nothing so much as the superiority of urban living over all other forms of society. And no settlement—whether a small pueblo, provincial city, or viceregal capital—was complete until churches had been built and regular services were held. Yet, how would these reorderings of space and settlement be viewed? Here, as in most cultural matters, continuity and local pride were a vital part of changing spatial arrangements. A district governor's authoritative report on Texupa, New Spain, in 1579 describes a reconstituted "landscape," a restructured, potentially bountiful place beneath the superimposed design of Christianity and Spanish authority. Yet an Indian's pictorial representation of Texupa that accompanied the district governor's report suggests more complicated local understandings of the same landscape and emerging realities. His depiction gives special importance to familiar surroundings, teeming with sacred life that seems to be enhanced by the new Christian church complex, more than it dwells on the destruction of old ways and the reordering of the community by the ideal grid plan for a town.

The colonial parish was a nucleus of administration, organized in close relation to civil districts, and parish priests were appointees of the Spanish Crown. Like many members of religious orders and the small host of secular officials, they were relied upon for routine administration, support of royal initiatives, and local information that might be of use to the Crown. People inhabited a religious landscape in which churches, especially parish churches, were significant places. Families were ordered to live within earshot of the bells, which rang out emergencies and punctuated the day with calls to devotion just as the cycle of feast days and holy seasons marked out the year with pertinent lessons.

This colonial society, marked by great inequalities, consisted of people with needs and experiences that differed dramatically, but their beliefs and practices nonetheless intertwined. Within densely populated areas, and often in regions considerably beyond, people of all kinds developed a relationship with Christianity, even if simply as nominal converts or participants who took the state religion largely on their own terms. Similarly, a steadily more varied society developed under the same broad system of law and political authority. The presence and observance of Spanish law and political and religious authority was not the same everywhere, but it conferred a kind of membership and association.

People were identified, and they identified themselves, according to certain legal categories and interpersonal obligations, often within relationships dependent on kin, community, ethnic group, or patron. Such relationships were not always mutually agreed upon or beneficial, but they could foster a sense of mutual responsibilities and localized social arrangements that lent substance to the metaphors about protection and instruction that often described them. At the same time, people were placed into an elaborate set of political, social, racial, commercial, and religious hierarchies, a number of which were mainly hypothetical. Like the meanings in the upper reaches of the sixteenth-century altarpiece at Huejotzingo, the higher echelons of these elaborations of privilege and power were distant for many people. But they may well not have been so mysterious and abstract when intermediaries were as close as a regional magistrate, an itinerant seller of foreign wares, a multilingual interpreter, or a friendly little figure of Saint Anne, dwarfed by her throne, leaning forward the better to hear the troubles of her devotees.

Each of the documents in the collection connects to the wider community from which its author draws and into which it feeds, and many of them expand standard notions of the viable and imaginable in colonial times. Parts of this book tell an undeniable story of physical and cultural violence, destruction, and dislocation; indeed, Flemish Franciscan Pedro de Gante, Andean chronicler Felipe Guaman Poma de Ayala, Guaraní mission leader Nicolás Ñenguirú, and royal postal inspector Alonso Carrió de la Vandera (alias Concolorcorvo) all wrote, in part, to record and warn against the abuses and injustices they observed. But the collection also offers connecting stories of survival and readjustments within the colonial regime. In this way, the selections qualify the metaphor of "conquest," either military or spiritual, that heralds abrupt destruction and presents colonial settings as simply arenas for the struggle of opposing worlds, classes, or other social groups. Despite the best efforts of spokesmen such as Vespucci's German illustrator in the early sixteenth century, or the late eighteenth-century minister of the Indies, José de Gálvez, it is the impure, incomplete, and paradoxical that come through time and again.

Politics has often been described as the art of the possible, and it appears thus in a number of the selections. In spite of its ideal representations, power in precolonial and colonial times was not so much handed down from on high or decreed from some oracular center—as if the Aztec Stone of the Five Eras could stand for the scores of small states and hundreds of Mesoamerican communities whose people also saw themselves as belonging to central places—as it was contested, negotiated, and renegotiated between aspiring rulers and subjects, not to mention a number of crucial intermediaries. Power, with its concomitant expectations and obligations, was not expressed only in words, proclamations, and formal laws. Indeed, an overt show of force was often "bad politics" and detrimental to what might be more constructively coaxed through subtle and regular expressions of solidarity and consensus. In spite of such encouragement, however, political and religious cultures in colonial Latin America were rarely harmonious. And yet there were many ways in which colonial culture might be more than stage-managed by a governing elite, and might be shared and unifying.

The constant interplay between ideals and realities is another recurring theme in the selections. Just as the Inka's manner of dress and the symbolic messages it conveyed depended on his audience, a colonial social order had to be carefully composed. Spanish Christians, as much in the Iberian Peninsula as in America, faced the challenges both of understanding and of living in a social order that comprised a variety of multiethnic settings. Certainly, official arguments for a peaceful and well-ordered society might often be used to establish tighter control. But a colonial order had many supporters, who included many who were outside official circles. Visions of seventeenth- and eighteenth-century Baroque Catholicism as a transcendent unity despite the potent contradictions and inequities in nearly all facets of life come through in paintings, church interiors, and formal reports, not to mention in Mariano Cuevas's retrospective from the late 1920s (Selection 29). The selections inevitably feature the conflict and competition that were inherent in colonial lives, but these are not the only or even the most remarkable aspects in a long and complex history. Many of the images and readings offer opportunities to consider colonial contexts as settings in which people and ideas interacted by design and circumstance. Survival was in many cases a process of transformation and reformulation more than simple resistance and accommodation.

Many colonial subjects who could not claim Spanish ancestry suffered horribly under Spanish rule, whereas others successfully challenged the terms of their subjugation and carved out advantageous situations for themselves and their companions within the constraints and pressures that they faced. In commissioning paintings and altarpieces, Indian officials took part in the creation and modification of images of themselves as participants in a common, negotiated colonial culture. A Christian Indian's cooperation with his parish priest in the seventeenth-century central Andes did not win him approval from religious leaders of his community who were intent on countering and reinterpreting Christianity, but it also did not preclude him from sympathetic participation in a colonial Andean religion and culture that was changing. Spanish Christians, whether governors, landowners, mine bosses, or churchmen, were not alone in perpetually pursuing choices and situations within the colonial system that favored them and those whom they represented. From early colonial times they were joined by many others who, despite precarious and discouraging circumstances, discovered opportunities and niches that, in an extension of Waud Kracke's phrase, "made the found world their own" and responded as that "found world" continued to change. The selections in this book illustrate how—through negotiation, competition, and sometimes violent confrontation—diverse individuals and groups in colonial society arrived at common understandings, if not shared values, and ways of making do.

In studying this colonial history, it is hard to avoid feelings of distaste or outrage at the often noisy, high-handed behavior and biases of Spanish Christian governors, churchmen, scribes, and travelers upon whom we often rely for information about subject peoples. For, just as the historian Robert Muchembled has remarked about a similar predicament in the study of early modern France, "we have to ask repression to recount the history of what it is repressing." Yet a number of the selections also reveal what repression thought it was repressing, not to mention the ways in which it was frustrated and fell short of its mark. Grounded in an ample context of time and place, the often tidy narratives presented in colonial records can become points of entry into situations that they meant to obscure or eradicate.

Cracks in the armor and ideology of empire were widely noticed, even if this knowledge was concentrated locally and gathered little political momentum before the late eighteenth century. Runaway slaves settled into the new town of Amapa in 1769 with banners of colonial legitimacy flying in all directions, but the suspicion lingered that Amapa was merely a convenient "castle" for further assaults on the colonial order by these new subjects, and that they would return to the mountains if called to account. Túpac Amaru, the last of a series of sixteenth-century Inkas who resisted Spanish domination for almost forty years from a base in Vilcabamba, Peru, was remembered centuries after his death by a multi-ethnic population in the Andes for the injustice thought to have been visited upon him by an overreaching peninsular Spanish viceroy. Some of the most withering critiques of colonial practices were mounted by privileged Creoles, including priests, who saw evils in the practice of colonialism while still exercising power over others in the service of the Crown.

As a number of our selections show, colonial expressions of authority and hierarchy frequently contained a basis for denying Spanish Christian legitimacy, challenging impositions in the name of the king or even God, and reformulating prescribed ideas and practices. Thus, Francisco de Avila's mid-seventeenth-century sermon before a native Andean congregation, inculcating Christian practices and warning against non-Christian ones, could be seen as more than a narrow-minded polemic. It also provides a vantage point from which to view a purposeful dialogue being attempted between an indigenous past and an Indian present, as the techniques of evangelization changed. A series of paintings celebrating colonial social order and participation in Cusco's Corpus Christi festivities features both paternalistic direction and a variety of people taking part in the year's greatest religious and civic procession. Even the heroic missionary narrative, anticipated in the instructions to the Franciscan "Twelve" and expressed in Fray Pedro de Gante's spirited defense of Indian neophytes near Mexico City—usually so adept at turning obstacles into surmountable or edifying difficulties—cannot entirely muffle the voice of an errant pupil.

K.M. kenmills@princeton.edu
W.B.T. wtaylor@mail.smu.edu

PART I

Old Worlds and the Time of Discoveries

 1

The Ancestors of the People Called Indians
A View from Huarochirí, Peru
(ca. 1598–1608)

In the 1570s and and 1580s over one hundred small Andean settlements (*llactas*) in the colonial province of Huarochirí were resettled into hamlets, villages, and towns by Spanish officials to ease labor exaction and facilitate evangelization. Among the native peoples affected were the Checas, from whom came the native recorders and editors of an extraordinary assemblage of oral traditions and sacred histories in the Quechua language—the Huarochirí Manuscript (ca. 1598–1608)—from which this selection derives; it recorded the worldview of these Andean people in a time of momentous change.

The new province of Huarochirí (Huaro Cheri in the following source), a mountainous area to the southeast of Lima, had been carved out of the populous northern portion of the province known to its previous rulers, the Inkas, as Yauyos. The Inkas, like the Aztecs in central Mexico, were latecomers to widespread power in pre-Hispanic times. Before the principal period of Inka ascendancy outside the Cusco Valley (which came after 1400), there had been a period of some four hundred years in which local and regional cultures of the central Andes had flourished without much interference from larger states. Incorporation in the Inkas' Tawantinsuyu—in the Quechua language, the land of the four quarters—brought to the region a number of political, economic, cultural, and religious impositions, but it did not mean the demise of local Andean traditions. What we understand of Inkaic imperialism suggests that although Inka expansion had devastating effects on some peoples and regions, the undeniable coercion in their project of empire was in places leavened by deft diplomacy and by very generous treatment for groups who were held in imperial favor. Troops made up of loyal peoples were ready to stamp out opponents and rebels, but the Inkas of the Andes were by custom incorporative and reciprocal—that is, they sought to consume, be nourished by, and repay many of the cultures they came to control rather than obliterate and replace them. The region of Huarochirí, within the Inkaic province of Yauyos, appears to have been one of those on good terms with Cusco, and here Inka political arrangements did not strip away existing patterns of settlement or ethnic divisions.

Under the Inkas, local and regional religious systems—often focused on one or a group of ancestor beings, *huacas* (sometimes spelled *wak'as* or *guacas*) and *malquis* (or *mallquis*)—continued within a larger system of Inka-influenced religious cults that were at least broadly similar and ancestral in emphasis. According to Andean traditions, in ancient times, long before the years of Inka expansion or the arrival of the Spanish invaders, the land was inhabited by a succession of powerful warring beings or god-men and god-women called huacas. Although the translation is imperfect, huacas were perhaps the foremost among a host of other lineage and personal sources of sacred power and energy that can be called "gods" and "divinities" in English, although in thinking of them one should abandon the fundamental Judeo-Christian separation between the natural and the supernatural. Huacas were (and still are) places and physical objects of special, sacred significance—often outcroppings of rock, remarkable peaks, or springs.

In the region of Huarochirí, the principal huacas were the highlander Paria Caca, a male being associated with a twin-peaked snowcapped mountain visible on the eastern horizon, and the coastal Chaupi Ñamca, his sister or female counterpart, associated with a five-armed crag of rock. This symbolic union of a highland and a coastal divinity seems to have made sense of the Yauyos highlanders' victory over the Yuncas lowlanders as a coming together into one family (Selection 35 from Cajatambo, Peru, features a similar explanation of coexistence).

Other huacas of greater and lesser importance were also part of a set of sacred traditions that connected a number of neighboring peoples. One of the more important divinities was a coastal trickster named Cuni Raya Vira Cocha (sometimes simply Cuni Raya or Vira Cocha in seeming acknowledgment of two coinciding pan-Andean gods), who is featured in this selection. Cuni Raya is associated with water and irrigation, the media through which he, in the course of his entertaining adventures and buffoonery, is continually making and remaking an imperfect world. After a certain point in these ancient times, ordinary men and women existed as well, although their lives were much affected by the powerful, roaming huacas and by *villcas*, the demigodlike humans whom the huacas held in particular favor. The Huarochirí narratives make it clear that in this time the divine shaping of earthly affairs was a fact of life in what Frank Salomon calls the "mythic landscape": entire landforms were raised from dust, irrigation and agricultural systems were cut out of the sides of mountains, unjust men were ruined and put to shame, beautiful virgins were seduced, and whole worlds were washed into the sea only to be reconstituted anew.

From the point of view of the Checas and other native Andean groups, most of whom by the last quarter of the sixteenth century had come to live in the resettled villages and towns and within parish networks, religious life was changing. But the huacas who had once lived in these lands and carried out their various feats were still present. They had been the organizers of the known world, and thus the world could be both explained and managed. The physical surroundings, local agricultural traits and preferences, and the order of social arrangements and various rivalries were all grounded in the huacas' initiatory actions and guiding influence. The landscape displayed what amounted to living proof. When the huacas' exploits were completed, when their particular deeds had been accomplished, or when, as we shall see, they had been superseded by huacas more crafty or powerful than themselves, it was common for them to turn to stone, either in their own shapes or in those of animals. This divine lithomorphosis did not spell the end of their power over the lives of their "children," the generations of men and women who would inhabit the land in their wake and gaze upon them every day; on the contrary, lithomorphosis made their power everlasting. The huaca ancestors represented stability and permanence, but they were simultaneously vital and integrated into the colonial conditions of their people.

Of equal importance to Andean peoples were the malquis, a number of whom were also significant to the people of Cajatambo (Selection 35). Malquis were more recent ancestors whose bodies were carefully preserved and wrapped (effectively mummified), and who commonly resided in resting places or cave tombs often near the huacas, and who were nourished, consulted, and cared for in similar ways. The Andean social, ritual, and territorial units called *ayllus,* as well as smaller lineage groups, had networks of ministers and guardians of traditions who attended to these different kinds of gods, and who were joined by a number of ritual specialists skilled in the arts of healing, love, hate, divination, and dream interpretation, among other things.

The assemblage of oral traditions and sacred histories that has been called the Huarochirí Manuscript demonstrates that local and regional ways of making sense of the world retained their vitality and ability to transform themselves through Inkaic times and into the colonial era. The style of the Huarochirí narratives is meandering; there are stories within stories, and lots of doubling back. They are deceptively simple, with arresting silences, repetitions of key phrases, and a cadence that suggests the style of the natural storytellers whose words informed the text created by native writers and editors.

The marginal comments that were scrawled on the original manuscript in Spanish and Quechua offer important hints about the possible genesis of the work and remind us that this was not a simple production. A number of these annotations seem to have been the work of Francisco de Avila (1573?–1647), the parish priest of San Damián de Checa after 1597 and one of the principal campaigners to investigate and repress suspect Andean religiosity and alleged perversions of Catholicism (see Selection 34). The marginalia in Spanish seem obsessed with identifying place names and specific information about persistent worship of huacas. Avila sought out evidence of Andean gods and religious practices from Indian ministers in San Damián, San Pedro de Mama, and other communities in the region. By June 1609 he had convinced the rector of the Jesuit college in Lima of the need for two padres to assist him in his labors. The mass of testimonial, narrative, and physical evidence that Avila, his native Andean supporters and associates, and Jesuit assistants managed to compile about colonial Andean religion fueled his own efforts to "extirpate" idolatry, and helped him to persuade the archbishop of Lima and other officials to support an even wider campaign of extirpation in other regions. The Huarochirí Manuscript, perhaps the single most important collection of material on pre-Hispanic Andean and colonial religion from native Andean tellers and writers, came out of this priest-extirpator's project.

Avila was knowledgeable about Andean traditions, yet the extent of his role in the creation and editing of much of the work is not clear. And, in any event, the manuscript is considerably more than simply a "tainted" source on Andean traditions or a blind servant of repression. Salomon contends that "because it was composed [by native Andeans] in relative independence from Spanish conceptions about native religion, it has in the end provided a uniquely authentic monument of the very beliefs Avila meant to destroy." Is such a text, then, collected and written in colonial times, essential to the preservation of knowledge of the lives lived by "the ancestors of the people called Indians," as the recorders and editors claim in the first line of this reading?

The text selected comes from the preface and early chapters of the book and is chosen to show native categories of thought and a regional vision of ancient Peruvian times before the Inkas and Spaniards. Even in this passage, the narratives inevitably tell us about the colonial times out of which they emerged, principally because of the complicated voices of the native Andean recorders and editors. These writers make an effort to render their work in terms that they think would appeal to a Christian mentality, although this effort is best described as uneven. Furthermore, they want to merge the traditions they collect and commit to writing with a Christian history, in ways that remind us of the chronicle attributed to the contemporary Andean Christian writer, Felipe Guaman Poma de Ayala (Selection 25). What is to be made of the allusions to Christianity in the text and, at times, the seeming resemblance of described events to biblical happenings? Are these allusions and resemblances evidence of these native Andeans' desire to please the priest Avila, whom they could expect to check some or all of their lines? Or might they also be something else?

Interventions by the recorders-editors occur on a number of occasions, as when sexually explicit passages (usually stated plainly in Quechua) seem softened through the choice of Quechua terms that revolve around "shame." More directly, in their presentation of the time "the ocean overflowed" and only one man survived, the editors state that "we Christians believe it refers to the time of the Flood." In writing of the story in this way, they open their own interpretation of the traditions to question, not least by implying that they have opponents in their midst. There seems to be a set of native Andeans, not very clearly defined, who believe in what the huacas had done and can do. These opponents to the Andean Christians are said not to think that this story of watery cataclysm refers to the Christian God's particular vengeance or an Andean Noah taking refuge from the Flood on a peak or in his ark equivalent. "They," the recorders-editors report, "believe it was Villca Coto mountain that saved them." The death of Jesus also had powerfully ambiguous implications to the authors of the Huarochirí Manuscript. They transport an interpretation based on the darkness described in Luke 23: 44–45 into the relation as a possible explanation for the darkness and chaos (llamas driving men, inanimate objects coming to life in order to revolt, and so on) that was said to have fallen on the land after the death of the Sun in ancient times. Again, we see the phrase, "Here's what we Christians think about it." Yet the passage relating the death of the Sun to the death of the Son ends, "Maybe that's what it was."

Are doubts, and perhaps even a collective smile, visible here? Are there other points in the selection in which the recorders-editors are not differentiating so clearly between Andean traditions and what seem to be the traces of Christianity? Does the splitting of colonial Andean society implied by the occasional use of "us" and "them"—"we" who accept Christianity and "they" who still reject it—reflect the exclusivist dichotomies (Christian/Andean, good/evil, accommodating/resistant, and so on) that were expressed in Christian doctrine classes and in sermons? Or perhaps the neat polarized factions delineate extremes in society while obscuring the contours of a more complicated coexistence of huaca worship (and other Andean beliefs and practices) with Christianity.

There is a real possibility that Christian notions were shaping parts of this narrative in fundamental ways. Yet there may be a trap in following this interpretative line too closely, in sifting through the text in search either of pre-Hispanic Andean survivals or of Christian influence. How far does one go? In the reading there is, for instance, a glorification of the huaca who appears as a "little guy," the poor and friendless beggar. This motif recurs in the collection of narratives. Does one suppose that it reflects the influence on native Andeans of Christian notions of poverty learned, say, from visiting missionaries or wandering holy men? Or perhaps the motif of the little guy achieving victory in the end is a convention of Andean oral tradition, not to mention a wider human story-telling inclination. The prototypical huaca hero is not only humble and poor; he or she is also a devious trickster. The traditions explain how the visible world and its people came into being; but, along the way, the reader or hearer seems called upon to root for the clever huaca little guy and the modest people with whom the gods often interact.

This text, collected in the late sixteenth and early seventeenth centuries, need not be simply one or the other. As the historian Inga Clendinnen has written of Indian "religion" in early colonial Mexico, the Huarochirí Manuscript tells of an emerging and vital colonial religious culture in the central Andes that seems to be understood less well, not better, when it is dissected into persistent purities and Christian assimilations.

[Preface]

If the ancestors of the people called Indians had known writing in earlier times, then the lives they lived would not have faded from view until now.
As the mighty past of the Spanish Vira Cochas is visible until now, so, too, would theirs be.
But since things are as they are, and since nothing has been written until now,
I set forth here the lives of the ancestors of the Huaro Cheri people, who all descend from one forefather:
What faith they held, how they live up until now, those things and more;
Village by village it will be written down: how they lived from their dawning age onward.

Chapter 1
How the Idols of Old Were, and How They Warred among Themselves, and How the Natives Existed at That Time

In very ancient times, there were huacas named Yana Ñamca and Tuta Ñamca.
Later on another huaca named Huallallo Caruincho defeated them.
After he defeated them, he ordered the people to bear two children and no more.
He would eat one of them himself.
The parents would raise the other, whichever one was loved best.
Although people did die in those times, they came back to life on the fifth day exactly.
And as for their foodstuffs, they ripened exactly five days after being planted.
These villages and all the others like them were full of Yunca.

[margin, in Quechua: full of Yunca]

When a great number of people had filled the land, they lived really miserably, scratching and digging the rock faces and ledges to make terraced fields.
These fields, some small, others large, are still visible today on all the rocky heights.
And all the birds of that age were perfectly beautiful, parrots and toucans all yellow and red.

Later, at the time when another huaca named Paria Caca appeared, these beings and all their works were cast out to the hot Anti lands by Paria Caca's actions.
Further on we'll speak of Paria Caca's emergence and of his victories.

Also, as we know, there was another huaca named Cuni Raya.
Regarding him, we're not sure whether he existed before Paria Caca or maybe after him.

[margin, in Spanish: Find out whether he says that it isn't known if he was before or after Caruincho or Paria Caca.]

However, Cuni Raya's essential nature almost matches Vira Cocha's. For when people worshiped this huaca, they would invoke him, saying,

Cuni Raya Vira Cocha,
You who animate mankind,
Who charge the world with being,
All things are yours!
Yours the fields and yours the people.

And so, long ago, when beginning anything difficult, the ancients, even though they couldn't see Vira Cocha, used to throw coca leaves to the ground, talk to him, and worship him before all others, saying,

Help me remember how,
Help me work it out,
Cuni Raya Vira Cocha!

And the master weaver would worship and call on him whenever it was hard for him to weave.

For that reason, we'll write first about this huaca and about his life, and later on about Paria Caca.

Chapter 2
How Cuni Raya Vira Cocha Acted in His Own Age. The Life of Cuni Raya Vira Cocha. How Caui Llaca Gave Birth to His Child, and What Followed

[margin, crossed out, in Spanish: Note that it isn't known whether this was before or after Caruincho.]

A long, long time ago, Cuni Raya Vira Cocha used to go around posing as a miserably poor and friendless man, with his cloak and tunic all ripped and tattered. Some people who didn't recognize him for who he was yelled, "You poor lousy wretch!"

Yet it was this man who fashioned all the villages. Just by speaking he made the fields, and finished the terraces with walls of fine masonry. As for the irrigation canals, he channeled them out from their sources just by tossing down the flower of a reed called pupuna.

After that, he went around performing all kinds of wonders, putting some of the local huacas to shame with his cleverness.

Once there was a female huaca named Caui Llaca.

Caui Llaca had always remained a virgin. Since she was very beautiful, every one of the huacas and villcas longed for her. "I've got to sleep with her!" they thought.

But she never consented.

Once this woman, who had never allowed any male to fondle her, was weaving beneath a lúcuma tree.

Cuni Raya, in his cleverness, turned himself into a bird and climbed into the lúcuma.

He put his semen into a fruit that had ripened there and dropped it next to the woman.

The woman swallowed it down delightedly.
Thus she got pregnant even though she remained untouched by man.
In her ninth month, virgin though she was, she gave birth just as other women give birth.
And so, too, for one year she nursed her child at her breast, wondering, "Whose child could this be?"

In the fullness of the year, when the youngster was crawling around on all fours, she summoned all the huacas and villcas to find out who was the child's father.
When the huacas heard the message, they were overjoyed, and they all came dressed in their best clothes, each saying to himself, "It's me!" "It's me she'll love!"

This gathering took place at Anchi Cocha, where the woman lived.

[margin, in Spanish: The gathering was in Anchi Cocha.]

When all the huacas and villcas had taken their seats there, that woman addressed them:
"Behold, gentlemen and lords. Acknowledge this child. Which of you made me pregnant?" One by one she asked each of them:
"Was it you?"
"Was it you?"
But nobody answered, "The child is mine."

The one called Cuni Raya Vira Cocha had taken his seat at the edge of the gathering. Since he looked like a friendless beggar sitting there, and since so many handsome men were present, she spurned him and didn't question him. She thought, "How could my baby possibly be the child of that beggar?"
Since no one had said, "The child is mine," she first warned the huacas, "If the baby is yours, it'll crawl up to you," and then addressed the child:
"Go, identify your father yourself!"

The child began at one end of the group and crawled along on all fours without climbing up on anyone, until reaching the other end, where its father sat.
On reaching him, the baby instantly brightened up and climbed onto its father's knee.
When its mother saw this, she got all indignant: "Atatay, what a disgrace! How could I have given birth to the child of a beggar like that?" she said. And taking along only her child, she headed straight for the ocean.
And then, while all the local huacas stood in awe, Cuni Raya Vira Cocha put on his golden garment. He started to chase her at once, thinking to himself, "She'll be overcome by sudden desire for me."
"Sister Caui Llaca!" he called after her. "Here, look at me! Now I'm really beautiful!" he said, and he stood there making his garment glitter.

Caui Llaca didn't even turn her face back to him.
"Because I've given birth to the child of such a ruffian, such a mangy beggar, I'll just disappear into the ocean," she said. She headed straight out into the deep sea near Pacha Camac, out there where even now two stones that clearly look like people stand.
And when she arrived at what is today her dwelling, she turned to stone.

Yet Cuni Raya Vira Cocha thought, "She'll see me anyway, she'll come to look at me!"
He followed her at a distance, shouting and calling out to her over and over.

First, he met up with a condor.
"Brother, where did you run into that woman?" he asked him.
"Right near here. Soon you'll find her," replied the condor.
Cuni Raya Vira Cocha spoke to him and said,
"You'll live a long life. You alone will eat any dead animal from the wild mountain slopes, both guanacos and vicuñas, of any kind and in any number. And if anybody should kill you, he'll die himself, too."

Farther on, he met up with a skunk.
"Sister, where did you meet that woman?" he asked.
"You'll never find her now. She's gone way far away," replied the skunk.
When she said this, he cursed her very hatefully, saying,
"As for you, because of what you've just told me, you'll never go around in the daytime. You'll only walk at night, stinking disgustingly. People will be revolted by you."

Next he met up with a puma.
"She just passed this way. She's still nearby. You'll soon reach her," the puma told him.
Cuni Raya Vira Cocha spoke to him, saying,
"You'll be well loved. You'll eat llamas, especially the llamas of people who bear guilt. Although people may kill you, they'll wear you on their heads during a great festival and set you to dancing. And then when they bring you out annually, they'll sacrifice a llama first and then set you to dancing."

Then he met up with a fox.
"She's already gone way far away. You'll never find her now," that fox told him.
When the fox said this, he replied,
"As for you, even when you skulk around keeping your distance, people will thoroughly despise you and say, 'That fox is a sneak thief.' When they kill you, they'll just carelessly throw you away, and your skin, too."

[A marginal addition in Quechua begins here.]

Likewise he met up with a falcon.
"She's just passed this way. You'll soon find her," said the falcon.
He replied,
"You're greatly blessed. When you eat, you'll eat the hummingbird first, then all the other birds. When people kill you, the man who has slain you will have you mourned with the sacrifice of a llama. And when they dance, they'll put you on their heads so you can sit there shining with beauty."

And then he met up with some parakeets.
"She's already gone way far away. You'll never find her now," the parakeets told him.
"As for you, you'll travel around shrieking raucously," replied Cuni Raya Vira Cocha. "Although you may say, 'I'll spoil your crops!' when people hear your screaming they'll chase you away at once. You'll live in great misery amidst the hatred of humans."

[The marginal addition ends here.]

And so he traveled on. Whenever he met anyone who gave him good news, he conferred on him good fortune. But he went along viciously cursing those who gave him bad news.

When he reached the seashore, [crossed out in original manuscript: he went straight over it. Today people say, "He was headed for Castile," but in the old days people said, "He went to another land."] he turned back toward Pacha Camac.

He arrived at the place where Pacha Camac's two daughters lived, guarded by a snake.

Just before this, the two girls' mother had gone into the deep sea to visit Caui Llaca. Her name was Urpay Huachac.

While Urpay Huachac was away, Cuni Raya Vira Cocha seduced one girl, her older daughter.

When he sought to sleep with the other sister, she turned into a dove and darted away.

That's why her mother's name means "Gives Birth to Doves."

At that time there wasn't a single fish in the ocean.

Only Urpay Huachac used to breed them, at her home, in a small pond.

It was these fish, all of them, that Cuni Raya angrily scattered into the ocean, saying, "For what did she go off and visit Caui Llaca, the woman of the ocean depths?"

Ever since then, fish have filled the sea.

Then Cuni Raya Vira Cocha fled along the seashore.

When Urpay Huachac's daughters told her how he'd seduced them, she got furious and chased him.

As she followed him, calling him again and again, he waited for her and said, "Yes?"

"Cuni, I'm just going to remove your lice," she said, and she picked them off.

While she picked his lice, she caused a huge abyss to open up next to him, thinking to herself, "I'll knock Cuni Raya down into it."

But Cuni Raya in his cleverness realized this; just by saying, "Sister, I've got to go off for a moment to relieve myself," he made his getaway to these villages.

He traveled around this area for a long, long time, tricking lots of local huacas and people, too.

[marginal note, in Spanish, crossed out: n.b. This huaca's end will be told below.]

Chapter 3
What Happened to the Indians in Ancient Times When the Ocean Overflowed

Now we'll return to what is said of very early people.

The story goes like this.

In ancient times, this world wanted to come to an end.

A llama buck, aware that the ocean was about to overflow, was behaving like somebody who's deep in sadness. Even though its [father] owner let it rest in a patch of excellent pasture, it cried and said, "In, in," and wouldn't eat.

The llama's [father] owner got really angry, and he threw the cob from some maize he had just eaten at the llama.

"Eat, dog! This is some fine grass I'm letting you rest in!" he said.
Then the llama began speaking like a human being.
"You simpleton, whatever could you be thinking about? Soon, in five days, the ocean will overflow. It's a certainty. And the whole world will come to an end," it said.

The man got good and scared. "What's going to happen to us? Where can we go to save ourselves?" he said.
The llama replied, "Let's go to Villca Coto mountain.

[margin, in Spanish: This is a mountain that is between Huanri and Surco.]

There we'll be saved. Take along five days' food for yourself."
So the man went out from there in a great hurry, and himself carried both the llama buck and its load.
When they arrived at Villca Coto mountain, all sorts of animals had already filled it up: pumas, foxes, guanacos, condors, all kinds of animals in great numbers.
And as soon as that man had arrived there, the ocean overflowed.
They stayed there huddling tightly together.

The waters covered all those mountains and it was only Villca Coto mountain, or rather its very peak, that was not covered by water.
Water soaked the fox's tail.
That's how it turned black.
Five days later, the waters descended and began to dry up.

The drying waters caused the ocean to retreat all the way down again and exterminate all the people.
Afterward, that man began to multiply once more.
That's the reason there are people until today.
Regarding this story, we Christians believe it refers to the time of the Flood.
But they believe it was Villca Coto mountain that saved them.

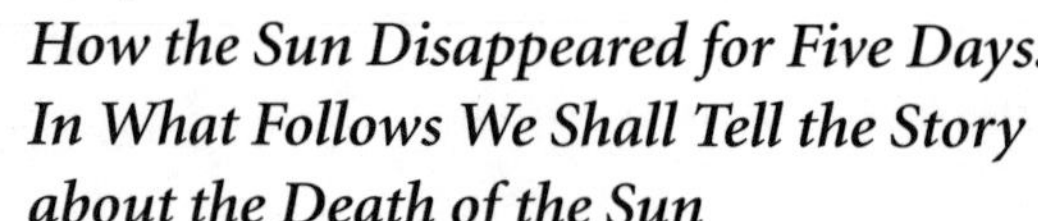

Chapter 4

How the Sun Disappeared for Five Days. In What Follows We Shall Tell the Story about the Death of the Sun

In ancient times the Sun died.
Because of his death it was night for five days.
Rocks banged against each other.
Mortars and grindstones began to eat people.
Buck llamas started to drive men.
Here's what we Christians think about it: We think these stories tell of the darkness following the death of Our Lord Jesus Christ.
Maybe that's what it was.

Chapter 5

How in Ancient Times Paria Caca Appeared on a Mountain Named Condor Coto in the Form of Five Eggs, and What Followed. Here Will Begin the Account of Paria Caca's Emergence

In the four preceding chapters we have already recounted the lives lived in ancient times.

Nevertheless, we don't know the origins of the people of those days, nor where it was they emerged from.

These people, the ones who lived in that era, used to spend their lives warring on each other and conquering each other. For their leaders, they recognized only the strong and the rich.

We speak of them as the Purum Runa, "people of desolation."

It was at this time that the one called Paria Caca was born in the form of five eggs on Condor Coto mountain.

A certain man, and a poor friendless one at that, was the first to see and know the fact of his birth; he was called Huatya Curi, but was also known as Paria Caca's son.

Now we'll speak of this discovery of his, and of the many wonders he performed. . . .

 2

The Inka's Tunics

(fifteenth to sixteenth centuries)

Both coastal and highland peoples of pre-Hispanic Peru excelled in textile making. An indigenous weaving tradition still flourishes today, especially in the Andes mountains. To a certain extent, skills in the two major available fibers (a hardy cotton: *Gossypium barbadense,* and wool from the native camelids: llamas, alpacas, and vicuñas) developed out of a need for warm clothing, particularly in the high Andes where temperatures can fluctuate sharply both by day and by season. Yet, although woven blankets, clothing, sacks, saddlebags, and pouches for carrying coca leaves were items of necessity, textiles might also function as forms of cultural and political expression. Andean techniques and patterns were many, and a startling number of colors was produced by the dyes from local plants and the secretions of shellfish and insects (on the use of red from the cochineal beetle in another region, see Selection 13). The elaborate textiles created by the Paracas peoples of the central Peruvian coast during the first millennium B.C. are perhaps the most celebrated examples of these ancient Andean arts, although expert textile making was widespread down to the last and best-known Andean state before the Spanish arrival, that of the Inkas, and continued through colonial times.

Figures 1 and 2 are examples from this tradition of meaningful fabrics in the form of *uncus*—Quechua for sleeveless tunics. The first garment (Figure 1), an Inka key checkerboard tunic, is from Inka times, and the second (Figure 2), a royal tunic, may be from the early colonial period. Of all the distinctive accoutrements and apparel of the Inka royalty—the crown or ornamented headgear (*masca paycha*), a colorful feather collar (*huallca*), the scepter (*suntur paucar*), the halberd (*tupa yauri*) and the golden beaker (*tupa cusi*), or the club (*champi*)—the uncu may have said the most about its wearer to his viewers. The abstract patterns and designs on the uncus conveyed complex symbolic information about order in the Andes and the universe. The unique king and son of the Sun, the Sapa Inka, wore a number of tunics that told of his exalted position within an elaborate set of social and political relationships. An uncu might also set out an interpretation of history, with its precise iconography establishing a living ruler's special identification with an ancestral king. A ruling Inka's tunics changed with the calendar and to meet the needs of feasts (*raymi*) or other occasions.

The checkerboard effect created by numerous abstract, square design units (*tucapu* or

Figure 1. An Inka key checkerboard tunic (fifteenth–sixteenth centuries). Courtesy of the Textile Museum, Washington, DC.

t'oqapu) was called the *collcapata* motif, and it was one of the standardized types in surviving pre-Hispanic tunics. The squares might be a striking black and white; or, as in the upper two-thirds of the first uncu, each square might alternate in color and contain a standard pattern that John Howland Rowe has called the "Inka key." (The lower one-third of this tunic features six bold stripes in alternating red and blue.) The collcapata design is thought to suggest the rows of stone storehouses (*collca* or *colca*) to which agricultural tribute flowed from the four quarters of the empire (Tawantinsuyu, or Land of the Four Quarters). The collca were the particular attributes of Andean farmers—non-Inkas such as the peoples from Huarochirí, whose traditions were encountered in Selection 1—and many others throughout Tawantinsuyu. The collcapata seems to have expressed concepts of commonality and, ultimately, unity of all ranks of people, representing a careful kind of foundation upon which the structure of Inkaic universalism was built.

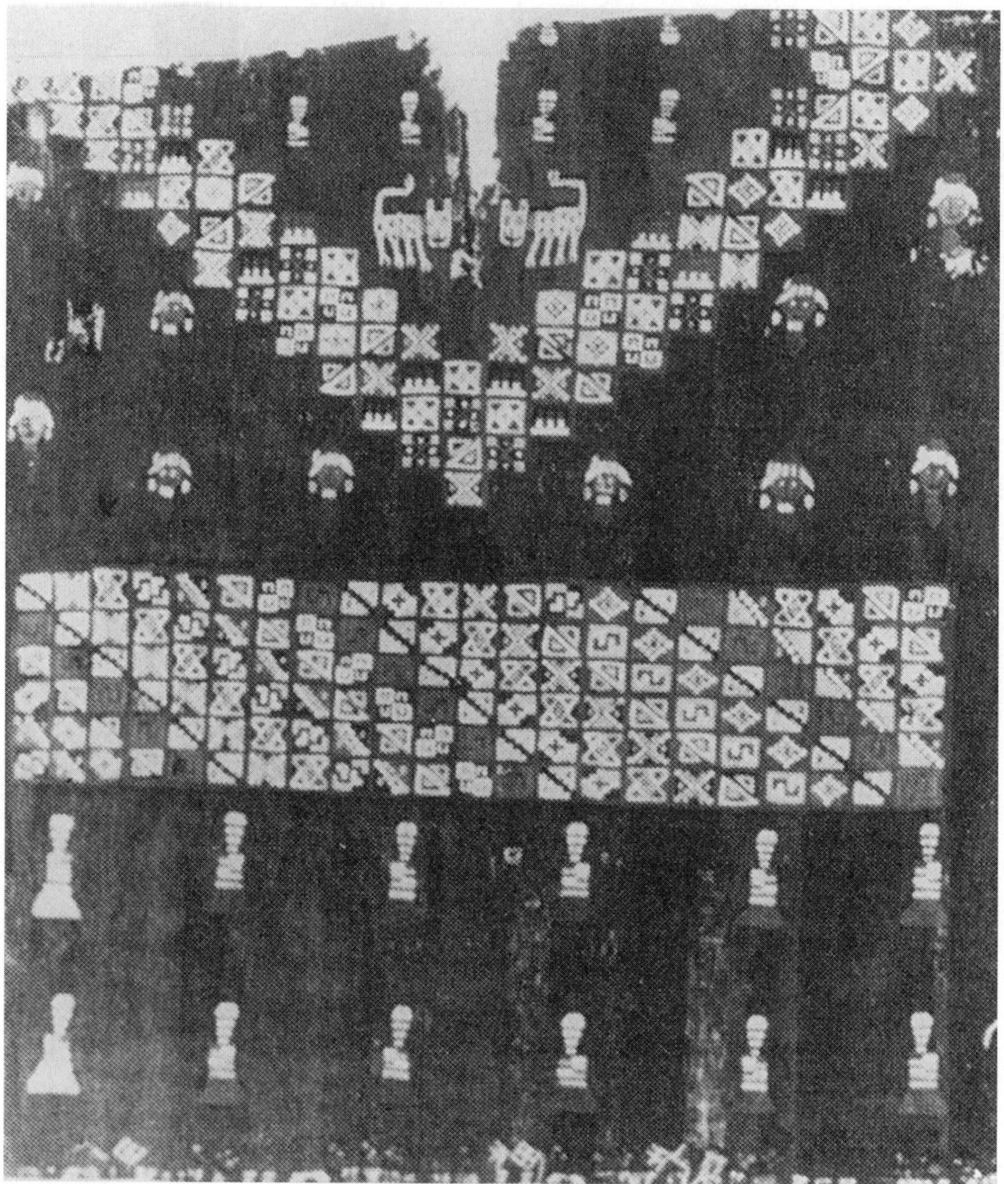

Figure 2. A royal tunic (the "Poli uncu") (sixteenth century).

A tunic with a collcapata design was worn by the Inka when he attended one of the three principal feasts of the year to which all kinds of people came, the Inka *raymi* in May. The Collcapata was also worn when the Sapa Inka and his noble retinue left the Valley of Cusco and toured the provinces. On these occasions the royal uncu featured neither of the two kinds of royal borders around the ruler's neck—the *ahuaqui*, a V-shaped yoke design of woven squares, or the huallca collar. Such a border is not present in our first uncu, but in the second one it is there in the form of an ahuaqui yoke (in this example, there are four rows of exquisite tucapus on either side of the tunic's neck opening). Since the border signified the separation of the divine Inka from his subjects, stressing the grandeur of the political head, such symbols were absent on popular and inclusive occasions. The Inka also wore another type of tunic featuring a *casana* design—a large square frame with four smaller squares within, woven into the lower half of the tunic—particularly in the foot-plowing and planting season, August and September, with which it was most associated. Its political message seems to have been a nuanced one about hierarchy and integration: the casana was often worn in combination with an ahuaqui neck border and might also be juxtaposed with the collcapata motif.

Just as surely as the Inka's uncu and other attributes could project a message of measured inclusion and alliance to peoples beyond the Inka royalty and notables or in the outlying provinces, the uncu could also communicate details of power and succession to those at the political center. At the festival of Capac raymi, attended only by the Inka, the royal relatives, and the Cusqueño elite, a so-called royal uncu was worn. According to Rowe, our second tunic is probably an heirloom of a noble family woven in the Inka style in early colonial times; it possesses the distinctive features of royalty also present in the few surviving pre-Hispanic examples of its kind. R. Tom Zuidema describes the second tunic's background color as "blue or purple." It features an elaborate ahuaqui yoke design, a red field within a border that consists of squares filled with seven kinds of tucapus. The two felines, each a mirror image of the other, within the border and close to the neckline, are another indication of Andean royalty, as were the many "extra" designs that would not be present on the tunic (or drinking vessel, for that matter) of an ordinary person.

These extras seem set off by a wide waistband of many differently colored rows of tucapus running diagonally, acting as a frame. Beneath the waistband are two rows of six crowns or royal headgear, each with its three intricate parts (two feathers or a small scepter, above a square golden plaque, and a lower fringe). Five of the crowns in each row have red fringes, while one is yellow. Two sixteenth-century chroniclers, Pedro Cieza de León and Martín de Murúa, claimed that each red thread in this lower fringe represented one of the Inka's enemies slain in battle. And El Inca Garcilaso de la Vega, writing in the early seventeenth century, informs us that an Inkaic crown prince wore a yellow fringe to symbolize his status as an initiate and to indicate that he had not yet killed an enemy. Working constructively from these fragments of information, Zuidema suggests that the five red-fringed crowns in two rows in the lower half of the second uncu may relate to the two arrangements of five trophy heads to either side of the ahuaqui yoke in the royal tunic's upper half. "Thinking of the probable use of this uncu," Zuidema writes, "I propose that the ten red masca paychas on each side represented the ten *panacas* [lineage branches of the Inka nobility] of the organization of Cusco and the two yellow ones the noble initiates at the time of Capac raymi."

When the Spaniards arrived in Peru and began to investigate Inkaic and non-Inkaic Andean societies, perhaps their most repeated early impression concerned the Andeans' apparent lack of a written language. Yet a more expansive definition of what "written" communication might be would allow room not only for the sophisticated pictographic expression of Mesoamerican peoples but also for the iconography of Andean cultures. Zuidema writes of an expressive tradition of lordship in the Andes in which "the iconographic whole was the lord, including his royal paraphernalia, body decorations, and tunic." Spanish Christians would bring an array of powerful symbols of prestige and messages of lineage and authority on their persons and in their creations, but such symbols and messages arrived in lands already exquisitely familiar with such means of expression and expectation. To employ a phrase that Zuidema himself borrows from Roland Barthes, the Inka's "written garments" in the years before the Spanish arrival are but one example of a means through which the rulers of a vast and dynamic pre-Hispanic Andean state could communicate alliance and distinctions, and political and social hierarchy, as well as ritual roles.

3

The Lords and Holy Men of Tenochtitlan Reply to the Franciscans, 1524

(1564)

The following two chapters of a *coloquio*, or exchange of speeches, between lords and holy men from the Aztec capital of Tenochtitlan and "the Twelve" (the first group of Franciscan evangelizers in central Mexico; see Selection 7), purports to be the Indians' reply to the friars' explanation of their mission in 1524, three years after Cortés had captured the city. It was written out in parallel Nahuatl and Spanish texts in 1564 by or for Bernardino de Sahagún (1500–1590), the famous Spanish Franciscan linguist and missionary who, with the collaboration of surviving elders and young Indian nobles who studied with him in the school of Santiago Tlatelolco on the outskirts of Mexico City, composed the monumental work about beliefs and practices in Aztec society known as the Florentine Codex.

This coloquio is not a literal transcription of what the friars and Indians said to each other on a single occasion. Sahagún could not have witnessed such an encounter, since he did not reach Mexico until 1529. But several early Spanish chroniclers who were there by 1523 refer to such formal exchanges, and Sahagún reportedly drew upon an accumulation of notes and conversations with Indian informants and members of "the Twelve" in his 1564 composition. It is, then, a literary reworking into one scene of the fragmentary recollections of several such encounters. Sahagún's stated intention in his studies and writings was to understand Indian life and religion more thoroughly, the better to make converts. This intention undoubtedly shaped his presentation of Aztec culture (including the silences) in ways that remain obscure to us, but his deep interest in native life and thought led to the inclusion of much that was tangential, if not irrelevant, to his stated purpose. Miguel León-Portilla, a leading student of Aztec culture and Nahuatl sources, concludes that this coloquio was crafted as an instrument of evangelization, but it also offers an authentic glimpse of the Aztec religion and vision of the world and response to Spanish colonization.

If so, what is glimpsed? The words attributed to the Aztec lords convey a feeling of profound but not altogether incompatible differences between their vision of divinity and human destiny and that of the friars. They accept, even welcome as providential, the arrival of the Spaniards and their king as rulers, but are reluctant to substitute the newcomers' religious doctrines for their own.

They are impressed by the majesty of the Christian God and accept the Bible as a "book of celestial and divine words." They accept the friars as bearers of divine riches, as God's representatives sent by "our great Emperor," Charles V; and they are prepared to consider their teachings, and adopt them in good time, but they are not persuaded by the friars' assertions that "we do not know the One who gives us life and being . . . that [the gods] we worship are not gods." They fear the wrath of their ancestral gods, omnipresent in the landscape, and the creative and destructive forces of nature, hungry for propitiation, if they were to neglect or forsake them. Their ceremonies and sacrifices, they assure the friars, are not empty gestures, easily abandoned. The Aztec interlocutors convey a profound veneration for their forebears—ancestor worship, a Spaniard might have called it—and a way of thinking about divine power that blurred basic dichotomies and boundaries of Christian thought, such as natural/supernatural, heaven/earth, and good/evil. Acceptance of Christianity does not strike them as an all-or-nothing proposition. Speaking in a convivial way as one elite group to another, they warn of popular rebellions rooted in desperation should the Spaniards force such a choice.

Chapter 6
How the Indian Lords Responded to the Twelve

After the twelve priests had finished their first speech to the lords and nobles of Mexico [Tenochtitlan], one of them arose and most courteously and urbanely replied in the following way:

"Dear Sirs, you are most welcome among us. Your coming to our city gives us pleasure. We are at your service and offer you all that we have. We know that you come from among the clouds and mist in the sky. That, along with your persons and way of speaking which we ourselves have seen and heard, makes your arrival unique and marvelous. Altogether, it seems like a celestial event, as if you had opened in our presence a chest of divine riches from the Lord of the sky, and of riches from the great priest who is Lord of the earth, riches that are sent to us by our great Emperor. You showed us all sorts of precious stones—most pure, resplendent, flawless, big and round, sapphires, emeralds, rubies, and pearls. You showed us new kinds of feathers, rich ones of great value. What gives us anguish now is that our wise men who were prudent and skillful in our kind of speech and who were in charge of the principality [the territory controlled by Tenochtitlan], are now dead. If they had heard from your mouths what we have heard, you would hear in return a most agreeable salutation and reply. But we who are inferior and less wise, what can we say? Even though, in truth, we are the leaders of the kingdom and republic, we lack their knowledge and prudence, and it does not seem just to us that the customs and rites that our forebears passed down to us, which they considered good and worthy of safekeeping, should be lightly set aside and destroyed by us.

"Besides this you should know, our lords, that we have priests who guide us and prepare us in the culture and service of our gods. There are also many others with distinct names who serve in the temples day and night, who are wise and knowledgable about the movement of the heavenly bodies as well as about our ancient customs. They have the books of our forebears which they study and peruse day and night. These guide us and prepare us in counting the years, days, months, and feasts of our gods, which are celebrated every twenty days. These same priests are in charge of the histories of our gods and the rules about serving them, because we are in charge only of warfare, collection of tribute, and justice. We will gather them together and tell them what we have heard of the words of God. It is well that they answer and contradict, for they know and it falls to them by their office."

Having finished speaking, the lords took their leave of the twelve. That same day, the principal lords and priests of the idols gathered and the lords recounted all that had happened, giving a full account of what the twelve had said. They remained a long time discussing this matter.

Having understood the reasoning and speech of the twelve, the principal lords and priests of the idols became greatly agitated and fell into a great sadness and fear, offering no response. Some time later they began to speak again and decided among themselves to go together the following day to see, hear, and speak to the twelve. Once the following day dawned, they all gathered and went directly to where the twelve were. Upon arrival, all greeted them and spoke to them affectionately. And the lords said [to the twelve]: "Our Lords, here before you are our principal lords and priests. They have come. We have told them all you said to us yesterday. Here they are. Let them respond. And so that they may be fully satisfied [that they understand what you said], please tell them again from the beginning all that you said to us yesterday, though we know it is tedious for you to do so." Then one of the twelve, using the interpreter, repeated everything that they had said to the lords the day before. Having heard this, one of the principal lords arose, asked the indulgence of the twelve, then began to speak and made the following long speech.

Chapter 7
In Which the Reply of the Principal Holy Men to the Twelve Is Found

"Our lords, leading personages of much esteem, you are very welcome to our lands and towns. We ourselves, being inferior and base, are unworthy of looking upon the faces of such valiant personages. God, Our Lord, has brought you to rule us. We do not know where you come from or where our lords and gods dwell because you have come by sea, through the clouds and mist, a route we have never known. God sends you among us as His own eyes, ears, and mouth. He who is invisible and spiritual becomes visible in you. And we hear His words with our own ears through you, His representatives. We have heard the words that you have brought us of the One who gives us life and being. And we have heard with admiration the words of the Lord of the World which he has sent here for love of us, and also you have brought us the book of celestial and divine words.

"You have told us that we do not know the One who gives us life and being, who is Lord of the heavens and of the earth. You also say that those we worship are not gods. This way of speaking is entirely new to us, and very scandalous. We are frightened by this way of speaking because our forebears who engendered and governed us never said anything like this. On the contrary, they left us this our custom of worshiping our gods, in which they believed and which they worshiped all the time that they lived here on earth. They taught us how to honor them. And they taught us all the ceremonies and sacrifices that we make. They told us that through them [our gods] we live and are, and that we were beholden to them, to be theirs and to serve countless centuries before the sun began to shine and before there was daytime. They said that these gods that we worship give us everything we need for our physical existence: maize, beans, chia seeds, etc. We appeal to them for the rain to make the things of the earth grow.

"These our gods are the source of great riches and delights, all of which belong to them. They live in very delightful places where there are always flowers, vegetation, and great freshness, a place unknown to mere mortals, called Tlalocan, where there is never hunger, poverty, or illness. It is they who bestow honors, property, titles, and kingdoms, gold and silver, precious feathers, and gemstones.

"There has never been a time remembered when they were not worshiped, honored, and esteemed. Perhaps it is a century or two since this began; it is a time beyond counting. Who can remember when or how those celebrated and sacred places came into being, where miracles occurred and answers were given, called Tulan Vapalcalco, Xuchatlapan, Tamoancham, Yoalliycham, Teutiuacam? The inhabitants of these aforementioned places reigned and ruled everywhere, so honored, so famous, such kingdoms and glory and lordship.

"It would be a fickle, foolish thing for us to destroy the most ancient laws and customs left by the first inhabitants of this land, who were the chichimecas, the tulanos, those from Colhua, the tepanecas, for the worship, faith, and service of the abovementioned [gods], in which we were born and raised. And we are accustomed to them and we have them impressed on our hearts.

"Oh, our lords and leaders! You should take great care not to do anything to stir up or incite your vassals to some evil deed. How could you leave the poor elderly among us bereft of that in which they have been raised throughout their lives? Watch out that we do not incur the wrath of our gods. Watch out that the common people do not rise up against us if we were to tell them that the gods they have always understood to be such are not gods at all.

"It is best, our lords, to act on this matter very slowly, with great deliberation. We are not satisfied or convinced by what you have told us, nor do we understand or give credit to what has been said of our gods. It gives us anguish, lords and fathers, to speak in this way. Here present are the lords charged with governing the kingdom and republics of this world. All of us together feel that it is enough to have lost, enough that the power and royal jurisdiction have been taken from us. As for our gods, we will die before giving up serving and worshiping them. This is our determination; do what you will. This will serve in reply and contradiction to what you have said. We have no more to say, lords."

 4

The Aztec Stone of the Five Eras
(late fifteenth century)

This famous stone monument from the ritual precinct of the Aztec capital of Tenochtitlan, over which the Spaniards built their own capital city of Mexico, was unearthed during a street-paving project near the end of the colonial period. Measuring nearly twelve feet across, it has long been called the Sun Stone or the Calendar Stone: "Sun Stone" on the assumption that it depicts the face or mask of a sun god, Tonatiuh, at the center and served as an object of sun worship; "Calendar Stone" because time is a dominant feature, if not the main point (one of the circular bands records the signs for the twenty days of a month, and the motifs at the center of the stone depict the Aztecs' conception of five historical ages). Whatever it is called, this mysterious object is packed with messages, irreducibly from another place, combining time and space in ways that are hard to fathom in our words. Still, it provokes speculation about Mesoamerican views regarding time, space, and destiny in comparison with those of Spaniards and colonial subjects. Some of the similarities and differences would have contributed to successful Spanish colonization of native American state societies. (Consider the view of time and order expressed in the Huejotzingo altarpiece, Figures 16 and 17).

The detailed drawing of the stone (on which we point out the main elements) was first published in a long, learned treatise by Antonio de León y Gama in 1792, two years after it was discovered. León y Gama recognized both the cult-object and calendrical possibilities in the design, although his schooling in math and science led him to focus on the astronomical connections and chronology of Aztec history that he found in it. His keen scientific interest in the stone and his observation that prominent families of Mexico City had begun to keep such pre-Hispanic objects in their homes as curiosities will be worth recalling in connection with other readings and images from the eighteenth century that appear later in this sourcebook.

An alternative to Sun Stone/Calendar Stone ways of interpreting this great disk, put forward recently by Richard Townsend, fits well with the remarkable discoveries made by archaeologists since 1978 at the adjoining site of the Aztecs' principal temple (Templo Mayor). If Townsend is correct, the face or mask in the center of the stone represents the Earth Monster, Tlaltecuhtli, rather than a sun god. It would then follow that the three inner circles represent the disk of the Earth, expressed in time as well as circular space, bathed in a great field

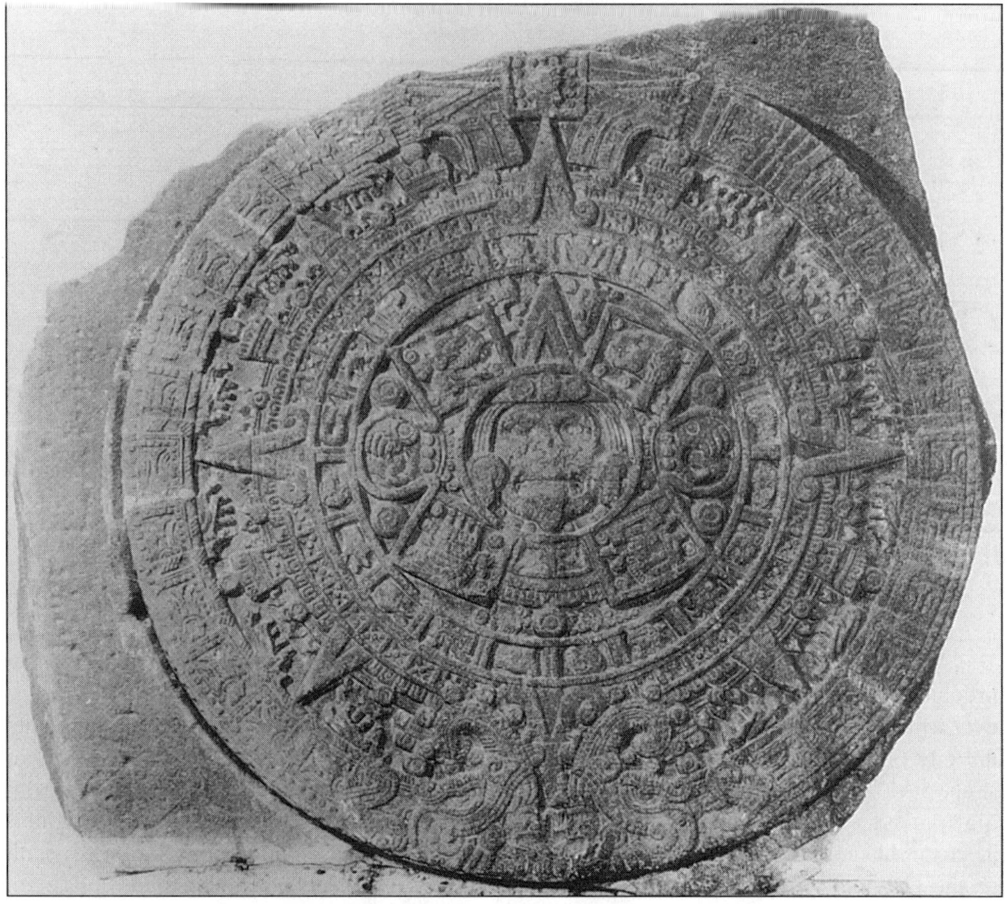

Figure 3. Aztec Stone of the Five Eras (late fifteenth century).

of daylight and fire. The face's prominent tongue is said to be a flint knife, symbol of war, and the two lobes on either side of the face contain claws that grasp human hearts. The Earth Monster is often depicted in Aztec inscriptions as a gaping, toothy mouth at the center of the Earth, consuming blood sacrifices. The face, combined with the four boxes arrayed around it, depict the five historical eras. In the box on the upper right is the first era when giants roamed the Earth, living on wild fruits and roots. Like the time of darkness and chaos in the Andean Huarochirí Manuscript (Selection 1), this was an imperfect era; it ended when a jaguar devoured the giants. Moving counterclockwise, the second era was destroyed by hurricanes that turned people into monkeys. The third one ended in a rain of fire and its people perished or were changed into birds. The fourth era ended in floods that turned people into fish. In the fifth and present era the sun, moon, and humans appeared. The face at the center and the four boxes combine to form the symbol of this era, "Ollin" or movement, auguring destruction by earthquake. This arrangement suggests the necessity of sacrifice and combat for the Aztecs to fulfill their destiny at the center of the cosmos.

The pattern of circles continues. The band of twenty day signs that constitute a month surrounds this central image. Beyond it are four bands that are thought to express the awesome power of the sun: first, a band of precious

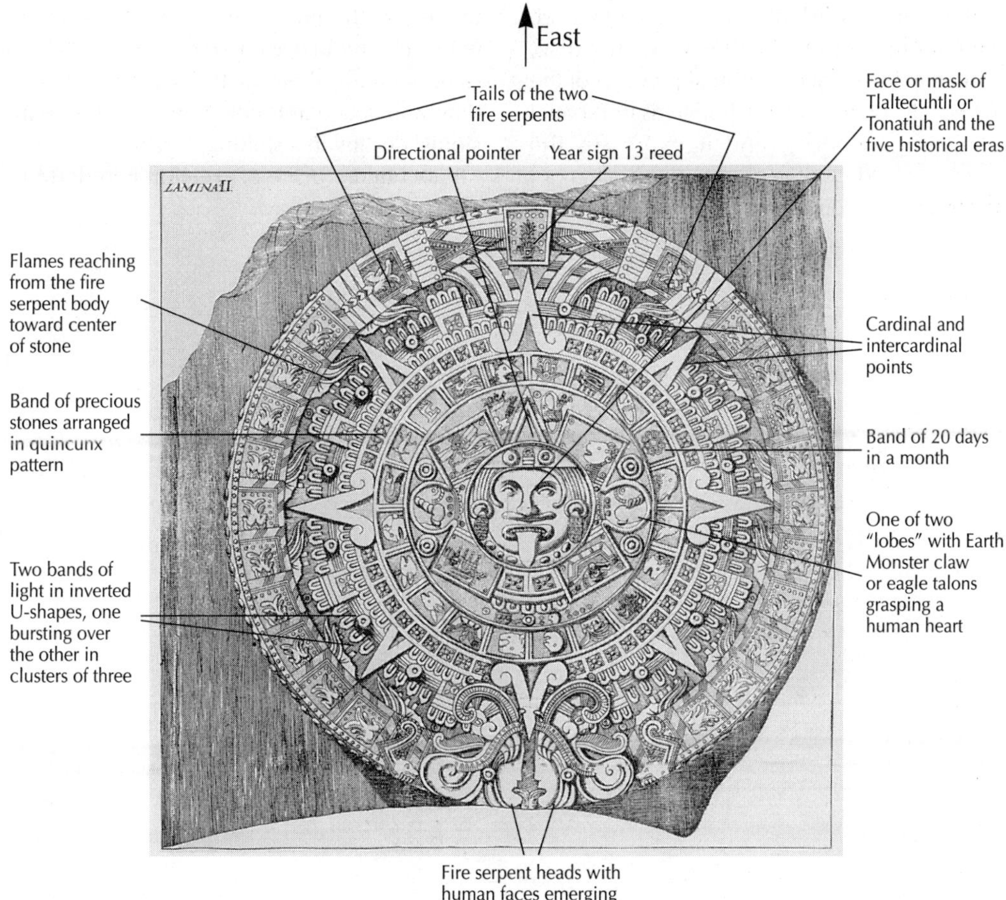

Figure 4. Drawing of the Aztec Stone of the Five Eras, 1792.

turquoises or jades arranged in a quincunx pattern (a familiar Mesoamerican way of indicating sacred space and direction, with four corner points and a center point, or fifth direction; another quincunx arrangement on this stone combines the central face with the four previous eras in one instance and the four cardinal points in another); then two bands of inverted U's separated by a band of four lines with circles interspersed. Between the cardinal and intercardinal points, clusters of three of the inverted U's above more quincunxes burst through the band of lines and the outer ring of U's. The wide band at the edge of the stone is formed by two fire serpents that meet at the bottom of the stone with human faces emerging from the heads, flames reaching out from them toward the center. The direction "up" is emphasized by a pointer directly above the central face. It indicates the place where the fire serpents began their journey across the sky; that is, east, the source of the rising sun. At that point of special emphasis is a year glyph, 13 reed, which Townsend suggests stands both for the distant beginning of the present era and for the year that corresponds to 1427 in the Christian calendar, when expansion of the Aztec tribute empire began in earnest and an ambitious building phase at the Templo Mayor was undertaken.

Whether the face at the center represents the Earth Monster or a sun god, the image as a whole seems to express the sense of a sacred center within concentric circles—a center that is thirsty for nourishment from human blood, sanctioning warfare. Either way, this disk, placed in the great ceremonial precinct of the Aztec city, points to Tenochtitlan as the spatial center of authority, and it expresses the demands and creative/destructive powers of divine forces. More than a cult object dedicated to the sun, this great stone seems to be a kind of city charter that asserted the Aztecs' right to rule, situating them at the sacred center of time and space and celebrating their expansionist destiny in a shifting, threatened world. "Tenochtitlan, place of creation and destruction," it seems to say.

 5

Coexistence in the Medieval Spanish Kingdoms
(ninth to twelfth centuries)

In the early eighth century, Arab and Berber invaders from what is today Morocco and the Maghrib in North Africa consolidated a rapid series of military victories and took decisive political control over much of the Iberian Peninsula, calling their territory al-Andalus. From a height of power in the tenth century, when caliphs ruled at Córdoba, Muslim rule fragmented into six large states (or party kingdoms) and a number of smaller ones. Al-Andalus was once again dominated briefly by two groups of Muslim Berber invaders and reformists, the Almoravids and the Almohads, who crossed the Straits of Gibraltar in succession in the eleventh and twelfth centuries. But the Almohad domain was dramatically reduced within a little more than a half-century by separate onslaughts from three Christian powers in the north—the kingdoms of León-Castile, Portugal, and Aragón-Catalonia. Toledo fell permanently to the Christians in 1085, Córdoba in 1236, Valencia in 1238, and Seville in 1248, effectively confining al-Andalus to the southern emirate of Granada, ruled by the Nasrid dynasty from 1231 to 1492.

The three short passages that form the next reading offer Muslim points of view on the history of Iberia before 1492, and they also suggest several ways in which colonial situations brought about by Spanish expansion thereafter can be studied. They were composed in Arabic by different Muslim authors between the ninth and early twelfth centuries, during the ascendance of al-Andalus, in places where Christians appear as a minority population or a savage enemy in the northern distance. These passages illuminate habits of mind toward subject populations and peoples with different religions and customs of living. And they provide substance for thinking about what is often called *convivencia*—a Spanish word loosely translated as the "coexistence" of Muslims, Christians, and Jews within medieval Iberian society.

The historian Ramón Menéndez Pidal originally employed the idea of convivencia in his study of the origins of the Spanish language. He used it to denote the existence of variant forms in early peninsular Romance languages (a "convivencia of norms"), but his student Américo Castro was the first to apply it more broadly to cultural matters. Generally speaking, Castro's convivencia stressed the creative interaction between groups and the roles that this interaction played in the shaping of Spanish culture, which he considered mainly in terms of literary sources. Seen too idealistically, the notion of coexistence conjures up a harmonious intercultural marketplace in medieval Spain that downplays or glides past bitter tension and eruptions of violent conflict. Used with caution, however, the idea of coexistence can shed light on a history of interaction that produced a gradual conversion of an indigenous Hispano-Roman majority to Islam, centuries of miscegenation between Muslims and other groups, and patterns of negotiation and economic interdependence. But irrefutable evidence of cultural intermixture and proximity between peoples neither eliminated strong concepts of pollution nor lifted a prevailing atmosphere of fear, distrust, sectarian prejudices, and the potential for vicious expressions of hatred. To further complicate the story, such rivalries, suspicions, and ethnic exclusivity among peoples living together in medieval Iberian cities under Muslim or Christian rule may actually have contributed to a certain stability in the social order. Tension and distance between peoples became as customary as selective intercultural borrowing in matters of dress, diet, language, and comportment.

The behavior of Spanish Muslim rulers and commoners alike frequently attracted the censure of Muslim jurists and religious scholars, especially after the mid-ninth century when, in al-Andalus, these jurists and scholars generally adhered to a rigorous and conservative school of Islamic law called Maliki after its founder, Malik b. Anas (ca. 710–796). Such jurists and scholars were routinely questioned on points of doctrine and practice, and they would deliver rulings and opinions, usually citing religious authorities and precedents, not unlike their Christian counterparts (see especially Selection 8 from a later Dominican theologian and professor). The Muslim jurists' rulings reveal concern over the blurring of what were meant to be strict religious boundary lines between Muslims and Christians—a response to the twin facts that Spanish Islam had developed for centuries in an environment at a substantial geographical remove from its region of origin, and in a land in which Christianity and Christians remained an influence. The cities of al-Andalus, in particular, afforded many opportunities for contact between Muslims and Mozárabes (Christians living under Muslim rule). The contact often was of an unspectacular day-to-day variety, but these passages suggest that concerns were developing about more substantial mingling and even official tolerance of religious laxity, including Muslim attendance and participation in Christian religious festivals and the failure of rulers to curb such "popular" behavior.

In part 1, one of these jurists—probably Abu'l-Asbagh 'Isa b. Muhammad al-Tamili, identified in the opening line—questions the legality of Muslims' observance of, and participation in, the practices of festivals held by Christian subjects. According to Islamic law, a Muslim's actions and beliefs might be placed in five categories that ranged from greatly praiseworthy to absolutely forbidden. Any innovation—a belief or practice without precedent in the Qur'an or the Sunna (the body of examples set by the Prophet Muhammad)—was worried over and ruled upon, as one sees in Abu'l-Asbagh's text. The jurist finds such innovations in al-Andalus repugnant and forbidden. His ruling identifies women as the principal offenders, who lead other Muslims into gift-giving, preparing special food, and taking holidays, thus "imitating" Christians and becoming corrupted. For Muslims, days off work were to be limited to the two main Islamic festivals: the completion of the fast of Ramadan (*id al-fitr*) and the feast of sacrifice to mark the end of a pilgrimage (*id al-adha*).

Traditions of information and misinformation about different groups of people burgeoned within the heterogeneous societies of medieval Iberia, as in other places and times (not least in Spanish America in colonial times). Polemics—in the medieval Iberian context, aggressive and controversial arguments against other religions, opinions, and customs—were among the most explicit media for these traditions. They were notable for their venom more than their ingenuity, and certain predominant motifs can be traced through many texts. These polemical traditions frequently spilled over into written works that were ostensibly descriptions of others and their practices. Thus, when some Spanish Christian authors surveyed Islam or the life and teachings of the Prophet Muhammad, they routinely saw and emphasized bellicosity, brutishness, materialism, and unbridled sexuality. Muslim baths, presented as places of barely imaginable iniquity, were the feature perhaps most commonly remarked upon by Christians who wished to accent the self-indulgence of Muslims. (The Aztecs of Mexico were similarly condemned by Spanish Christian commentators for their addiction to cleanliness and sensual pleasures.)

Part 2 of the reading—an excerpt from the work of al-Bakri (d. 1094), the son of a Muslim ruler of the southern Spanish town of Saltes—offers a short "description" of Christian Spain that allows the consideration of these matters from another side, particularly with regard to comments on customs of washing. Al-Bakri's text is thought to draw from an earlier tenth-century work, and it may reflect more than purely a Muslim commentator's point of view; a source to whom al-Bakri refers, Ibrahim b. Ya'qub al-Isra'ili al-Turtushi, was a Jew from Tortosa who is thought to have composed a travel account in the 960s for the Caliph al-Hakam II (d. 976).

The three commentators featured in part 3 are similarly concerned with describing "Christians"—this time not the northern marauders, but rather the Mozárabes living among Muslims in the centers of al-Andalus, celebrating their own festivals, paying their taxes, and often Arabized in many of their customs and more or less integrated into society. These selections derive from *hisba* manuals, sets of regulations in which jurists set out the offenses against the Holy Law of Islam. The regulations concern urban morals, including offenses against public morality and standards among traders and consumers in marketplaces monitored by an inspecting official called the *muhtasib*. Ibn 'Abdun, who composed his bans in early twelfth-century Seville, is concerned with inappropriate contact and working relationships; the predations of lustful Christian priests, who "have made what is lawful unlawful, and . . . what is unlawful lawful"; and the sale of medical and scientific books to Christians who might claim Muslim intellectual achievements for themselves. The dates of the compositions of the final two jurists are not certain, but their concerns complement each other and add to what Ibn 'Abdun established. Ibn 'Abd al-Ra'uf, carefully citing Malik and a number of his disciples, and 'Umar al-Jarsifi are here preoccupied with meat and drink and with the commercial transactions that Muslims might face with Jews and Christians. These two non-Muslim peoples (*ahl al-kitab*, those who possessed holy scriptures before Islam was revealed) are referred to by their legal status as *dhimmis* (those protected, but also kept separate, by a pact or *dhimma* within a Muslim state).

1
Muslims Celebrate Christian Festivals in the Mid-Ninth Century

The celebration of the beginning of the Christian year.

Abu'l-Asbagh 'Isa b. Muhammad al-Tamili was asked about the eve of January, which the people call the Birth [of Jesus], for which they work so hard over the preparations, and which they consider one of the great feast days. They give each other different foods, various presents and novelties exchanged by way of gifts, and men and women abandon their work that morning because of the importance they attach to the day. They consider it to be the first day of the year. [The text of the question is:]

"Do you think (may God be generous to you!) that it is a forbidden innovation, which a Muslim cannot be permitted to follow, and that he should not agree to [accept] from any of his relatives and in-laws any of the food that they prepared for [the celebration]? Is it disapproved of, without being unambiguously forbidden? Or is it absolutely [forbidden]? There are traditions handed down from the Prophet of God (may God bless him and grant him salvation!) concerning those of his community who imitated the Christians in their [celebration] of Nauruz [Nawrūz, the first day of the Persian solar year] and Mihrajan [Mihragān, a festival around the autumn equinox, traditionally dedicated to Mithra, a chief god of the ancient Persians, surviving into the Islamic period and spreading with Muslim expansion], to the effect that they would be mustered with the Christians on the Day of Judgment. It is also reported that he said, "Whoever imitates a people, is one of them." So explain to us—may God be generous to you!—what you consider correct in this matter, if God wills."

He answered: "I have read this letter of yours and have understood what you are asking about. It is forbidden to do everything that you have mentioned in your letter, according to the ʿulama [scholars of religious learning]." I have cited the traditions that you mentioned to emphasize that, and I have also cited Yahya b. Yahya al-Laithi [d. 849, a famous Berber jurist and one of the founders of Maliki law in al-Andalus], who said, "[Receiving] presents at Christmas from a Christian or from a Muslim is not allowed, neither is accepting invitations on that day, nor is making preparations for it." It should be regarded as the same as any other day. He produced a *hadith* [a relation of the words or deeds of Muhammad and a source of authority for Islamic law] on this subject going back to the Prophet (may God bless him and grant him salvation!), who one day said to his Companions, "You will become settled among the non-Arabs; whoever imitates them in their [celebration] of Nauruz and Mihrajan will be mustered with them." Yahya also said, I asked Ibn Kinana about that, and informed him about the situation in our country, and he disapproved and denounced it. He said, Our firm opinion about that, is that it is *makruh* (repugnant). Similarly, I have heard Malik say, in the words of the Prophet, may God bless him and grant him salvation, "Whoever imitates a people, will be mustered with them."

Yahya b. Yahya said, "It is similar to racing horses and holding tournaments on al-ʿAnsara (Midsummer's Day)"; that is, not permitted, likewise what women do to decorate their houses on Midsummer's Day. That is an act of pre-Islamic ignorance, as is the way they take out their clothes at night to be soaked by the dew. Abandoning their work on that day is also disapproved of, as is preparing cabbage leaves and greens [vegetarian food]. That women should wash themselves in water on that day is absolutely forbidden, unless it is for [normal reasons such as] a ritual impurity.

Yahya b. Yahya said, "Whoever does this has shared in [spilling] the blood of Zakaria (Zacharias)" [the father of John the Baptist]. It is related that the Prophet, may God bless him and grant him salvation, said, "Whoever multiplies the number of a people is one of them." Whoever is content with an act is a partner of the person who did it. If this is so for someone who approved but did not perform an action, what about the person who did it and made it his custom?! We ask God for success.

2
A Description of Christian Spain from the Tenth Century

Early authorities divided Jilliqiyya [León and Castile, Christian kingdoms in the north of the Iberian Peninsula] into four parts; the first part is that which lies to the west and faces to the north. Its inhabitants are the Galicians [Leonese] and their territory is Galicia [León]. They [are found] around the city of Braqara (Braga), which is in the middle west.

The city of Braga is one of the first cities founded by the Christians and [one of] their capitals. The localities in this country are like Mérida in the skillful way in which they are built and in the construction of their walls. Nowadays it is ruined and almost empty; the Muslims destroyed it and drove away its inhabitants.

The second division is the one called "the district of Ashturish" (Asturias), so-called because of the river there called Ashtru, which waters all their country.

The third division is the south and west of León, whose inhabitants are called the Burtuqalish (Portuguese).

The fourth division is to the south and east and is called Qashtilat al-quswa and Qashtilat al-dunya (Outer and Inner Castile). Its nearest castles [to Muslim territory] are Gharnun (Grañón), al-Qusair (Alcocero), Burghush (Burgos), and Amaya.

Ibrahim (al-Turtushi) said: "The whole of Jilliqiyya is flat and most of the land is covered in sand. Their foodstuffs are mainly millet and sorghum and their normal drinks are apple cider and bushka, which is a drink made with flour (meal). The inhabitants are a treacherous people of depraved morals, who do not keep themselves clean and only wash once or twice a year in cold water. They do not wash their clothes once they have put them on until they fall to pieces on them, and assert that the filth that covers them, thanks to their sweat, is good for their bodies and keeps them healthy. Their clothes are very tight-fitting and have wide openings, through which most of their bodies show. They have great courage and do not contemplate flight when battle is joined, but rather consider death a lesser evil."

3
Rules for the Christians from the Early Twelfth Century

a. Ibn ʿAbdun

A Muslim should not rub down a Jew, nor a Christian [in the baths], neither should he throw out their refuse nor cleanse their lavatories; the Jews and Christians are more suitable for such a job, which is a task for the meanest. A Muslim should not work with the animals of a Jew, nor of a Christian, neither should he ride in their company, nor grasp their stirrup. If [the *muhtasib,* the official charged with maintaining public morals and standards and punishing offenses against the Holy Law of Islam, the Shariʿa] gets to know of this, the perpetrator will be censured.

Muslim women must be prevented from entering disgusting churches, for the priests are fornicators, adulterers, and pederasts. Frankish women [probably meaning any western European Christian women who were not Mozárabes] [too] should be forbidden to enter churches except on days of particular merit or festivals, for they eat and drink and fornicate with the priests: there is not one of them who does not keep two or more of these women, spending the night with them. This has become a regular custom with them, for they have made what is lawful unlawful, and made what is unlawful lawful. The priests must be made to marry, as they do in the east; if they wanted to, they would.

No woman, old or otherwise, should be left in the house of a priest if he has refused to marry. They [the priests] should be forced into circumcision, as al-Mu'tamid 'Abbad made them do. According to their assertions, they follow the path of Jesus (God bless him and grant him salvation!), and Jesus was circumcised; with them, the day of his circumcision [January 1] is a festival which they hold in great regard, [but] they themselves abandon [this practice]!

One must not sell a scientific book to the Jews, nor to the Christians, unless it deals with their own law; for they translate books of science, and attribute them to their own people and to their bishops, when they are [really] the works of the Muslims. It would be best if no Jewish or Christian doctor were left to treat the Muslims; for they have no concern for the welfare of a Muslim, but only for the medical treatment of their co-religionists. How could one trust [one's] lifeblood with someone who has no concern for what is best for a Muslim?

b. Ibn 'Abd al-Ra'uf

Muslims are forbidden to buy meat intentionally from the butcheries of the dhimmis [Christians and Jews]. Malik abhorred this, and [the caliph] 'Umar [b. al-Khattab]—may God be pleased with him—ordered them to be expelled from the Muslims' markets. Ibn Habib [d. ca. 853, jurist, disciple of Malik, and *mufti,* or jurisprudent competent to proclaim a religious opinion (*fatwa*) of Córdoba] said, "There is no objection to them having a butchery isolated from the others, and being forbidden to sell to Muslims. Any Muslim who buys from them will not have his purchase invalidated, but he will be a bad man." In the *Wadiha* [Ibn Habib's work] [he says]: Mutarrif [d. 835, pupil and nephew of Malik] and Ibn al-Majishun [d. 818, another pupil of Malik and mufti of Medina] said that if the meat the Muslim buys from them is the sort they do not eat themselves, such as *tarif* (non-kosher) and suchlike, the purchase is invalidated, and the same for fat. God Almighty said, "We have made unlawful for them [the Jews] the fat of cattle and sheep" (Qur'an 6: 147); such are the undiluted and pure fats such as the intestines, the fat of the kidneys and that which attaches to the stomach and suchlike. God says, "except what their backs carry, or the entrails, or what is mixed with the bone" (Qur'an, loc. cit.). All fat that is in this category becomes an exception. It is specifically not lawful for us either to eat or to trade in any of these fats that are forbidden to them from the animals they have slaughtered. Whatever is not forbidden to them of their slaughtered animals by Revelation, but is only forbidden by their religious law, such as tarif and suchlike, consumption of this, trading in it are frowned on [but not illegal], because it is not their lawful meat. This is the opinion of Malik and some of his disciples.

In the *Wadiha* [it says]: Any meat the Christians slaughter for their churches, or in the name of the Messiah or the Cross or suchlike, corresponds with the word of Almighty God, "what has been consecrated for someone other than God" (Qur'an

2: 168), and is frowned on for us, but not forbidden, because God Almighty has made lawful for us what they [the Christians] slaughter, for he is better informed about what they are saying and intending by this, and [also] about what they slaughter for their festivals and for their misguided purposes. Having nothing to do with it is preferable, because to eat it is to show great regard for their polytheistic ways. Malik and his disciples never ceased to show their abhorrence for that. Malik (may God have mercy on him!) was asked about the food that is prepared for their funerals and which [the Christians] give as alms; he replied, "It is not appropriate for a Muslim to take it or eat it, because they prepared it to glorify their polytheism." Ibn al-Qasim said, about a Christian who willed that some of his property should be sold on behalf of a church, that it was not lawful for a Muslim to buy it, and that any Muslim who bought it would be a bad Muslim.

If a Muslim buys wine from a Christian, whatever wine is found in his possession will be destroyed. If the Christian has already received the price, this will be left to him, but if he has not received it, it will not be settled in his favor. If the wine is no longer in the Muslim's hands, and he has not paid for it, the price will be taken from him and given as alms, and both of them will be punished. If a Muslim destroys wine belonging to a dhimmi, he will be punished. Malik has conflicting opinions on the question of the payment of damages for its value: in one place he says, no fine is imposed on him, and none is lawful, because God had made his price unlawful; elsewhere, he says the price is incumbent on him. He [Malik] abhorred traveling with them [dhimmis] in ships, because of the fear of divine wrath descending on them.

c. 'Umar al-Jarsifi

The dhimmis must be prevented from having houses that overlook Muslims, and from spying on them, and from exhibiting wine and pork in the Muslims' markets, from riding horses with saddles and wearing the costumes of Muslims or anything ostentatious. They must be made to display a sign that will distinguish them from Muslims, such as the *shakla* (piece of yellow cloth) in the case of men and a bell in the case of women. Muslims must be forbidden from undertaking everything that entails baseness and humiliation for the Muslims, such as removing garbage, transporting equipment connected with wine, looking after pigs and suchlike, because this involves the elevation of unbelief above Islam; whoever does such things will be punished.

 6

The Coming of the White People

Reflections on the Mythologization of History in Latin America

OLIVIA HARRIS

Olivia Harris of Goldsmiths' College at the University of London is an anthropologist who has researched and written about an Aymara-speaking people of the Andes among whom a native past is very much present. From this base, Harris's interests have ranged widely, from indigenous participation in market economies to conceptions of death and "the end of the world," kinship, ritual, and gender symbolism. Among other things, her work is characterized by a subtle scrutiny of historical time and close attention to the meanings and effects of the words, assumptions, and boundaries employed both by her subjects and the scholars who have followed. This scrutiny and attention are featured in the reading which follows, an essay in which Harris explores the "almost transcendental status" that "the coming of the White people" is often afforded in our imagining of Latin American history.

As an essay about beginnings of colonial Latin American history, "The Coming of the White People" fits chronologically among the opening sources in this collection, but there is another good reason to consider it early. Harris asks fundamental questions about the points at which historical narratives begin and about the functions that history serves. Such questions seem intended to unsettle and defy definitive answers about the past, affecting the way we think about historical matters and how stories are told—about history as representations of the past.

Harris distrusts the view that native calendrical systems and deep traditions of messianic expectation and prophesy, in particular, inclined a number of indigenous peoples to view the first Europeans arriving in their lands as gods. The appearance of European travelers and warriors would cause more than alarm and wonder, she proposes. It was met also by pragmatic and strategic responses that explode the notion of the native thinker as "tradition-bound," unable to read unfamiliar "signs." From this point she launches a broader discussion of periodization—the practice of setting beginnings and ends and determining "periods" that break up the past into units and, sometimes, stages. Why are certain events treated as epochal, as dawns or as turning points? Why is one aspect pre- and another post-, or one dimension salient and another of fleeting significance? Certain choices and emphases, upon inspection, may seem entirely justified, but this does not remove the need to recognize and revisit our assumptions. If events in colonial Latin American history that are established as important have tended to be identified with Europeans, what are the effects? Who and what are viewed as dynamic, and why?

Harris wonders about the evidence that some Europeans were predisposed to be treated as gods, and about the suggestions that such predispositions were reinforced by local political tensions in early sixteenth-century central Mexico and the Andes. In lands where conquest states were not new to local societies, one needs to consider a range of sources that illuminate how Europeans and their impositions were seen, how they fitted or did not fit into what Harris calls "existing categories of alien and exotic powers." The essay resonates with the great Aztec stone from the ritual precinct in Tenochtitlan (Figures 3 and 4) as well as the sacred histories from Huarochirí (Selection 1) and several sixteenth-century images (Figures 5 through 9), all fragments of pre-Hispanic vision and evidence of early colonial reckoning with a past of which Europeans had become a part. And a number of upcoming readings relate to Harris's fundamental point that indigenous peoples did not think alike, as if in unison. The Spaniards' arrival and the events surrounding the military subjugation of political and religious centers were not always viewed or remembered in the same way.

"The Coming of the White People" challenges us to examine the "naturalness" of our assumptions about momentous events and to determine for whom they were, and have become, significant. She suggests that searchers for a balance to be redressed on behalf of indigenous peoples might profit from considering just what they themselves are contributing to changing visions of the past. Scholarly and political concentration on "the contact situation" or the "evils of Conquest" by Spaniards also imposes a beginning and a rupture, not to mention a period or a process, that may not have existed in the same ways for many of the indigenous peoples whose ancestors experienced it and whose "side" and past are ostensibly being corrected.

1

The Coming of the White People

My point of departure in the paper is the experience of doing anthropological fieldwork in Northern Potosí, Bolivia. Over time I became aware that the Aymara-speaking peasants of the ayllus where I had lived did not periodize the past in the way that I took for granted. In particular, they did not give the same saliency to the moment of the coming of the Spanish or their conquest of the Andean region. This has led me to reflect more generally on the way particular views of the past are constituted; the Columbus quincentenary further led me to ask what are the forces which encourage this fetishization of the moment of the coming of the White people.

Most of us probably remember learning history at school at least in part as a losing struggle against an avalanche of dates. Dates often seemed arbitrary and mathematical, having no intrinsic connection to the narratives of heroism and defeat, death or empire that they were there to order and classify. Yet, there are some dates that are so hedged about with mystique, so fetishized, that we retain them without effort. For the English it is 1066 [the Norman Conquest of England]; for the Scottish, probably it is the pairing of the '15 and '45 [the failed Highlands-based uprisings of 1715 and 1745 in support of Scottish claimants to the throne]. Such dates are usually at the heart of the narratives of nationalist historiography: the moments of defeat, of resistance, of liberation.

The year 1492 is another such date. Its status in Europe is all the more striking since it is not, except for Spain, tied to nationhood in the same way. The 1992 celebration and/or commemoration of Columbus's first voyage to the Caribbean made this process of mythologization abundantly clear. Leif Eriksson may have been the first European to set foot in the Americas but he did not discover the New World in the sense that Columbus did, because he created no enduring myth, and because the changes that resulted were insignificant. Everything we know about Columbus indicates what a self-publicist he was, how conscious he was of the resonances of his actions in the unfolding cosmography of the early Renaissance Mediterranean world. He was well aware, for example, of the significance that his great voyage took place the same year as the Reconquest of Granada and the expulsion of the Jews. His *Book of Prophesies* locates him in a series of cosmic events the predestined nature of which does nothing to undermine the novelty and daring of his enterprise.

When Adam Smith wrote in *The Wealth of Nations* that the discovery of America was one of "the two greatest and most important events in the history of mankind," he was referring to its economic consequences. Two hundred years later the periodization has become more generalized: today many argue that 1492 heralds the dawning of modernity, and even of modern European identity. Thus, Tzvetan Todorov writes in *The Conquest of America* (a book hailed as a classic in many quarters but viewed with scepticism by Americanists):

> The discovery of America . . . is certainly the most astonishing encounter of our history. We do not have the same sense of radical difference in the "discovery" of other continents and other peoples. . . . The conquest of America . . . heralds and establishes our present identity even if every date that permits us to separate any two periods is arbitrary, none is more suitable in order to mark the beginning of the modern era than the year 1492. . . . We are all direct descendants of Columbus, it is with him that our genealogy begins, insofar as the word *beginning* has a meaning.

This uninhibited proclamation has the merit of articulating very explicitly the mythological grounding for modern European identity. Even a more nuanced view of the same event such as that of Steve Stern, which recognizes that 1492 "did not really constitute the decisive or leading 'cause' of this vast configuration of world history," has to start from the premise that this is what it "symbolizes" for us.

What is clear is that the discovery of America functions as an organizing moment for European historical periodization from many distinct perspectives. Still more does it do so in American history, and of course Columbus Day is a national holiday in many parts of the continent. In Mexico and in the Andean region, however, more attention is given in national historiographies to the Spanish Conquest which was effected in the early decades of the sixteenth century. A standard periodization of the past is found throughout Latin America: I recall the daughter of a Bolivian friend of mine stuck over her homework, asking her father what was meant by historical periods. "Easy," he replied, "there are three periods. First, there is before the Spanish (pre-Hispanic), then there is colonial (i.e., the period of Spanish rule), and now is the republican period" (i.e., after independence from Spain).

It is this very obviousness that I wish to question. In my experience of doing fieldwork in the Bolivian Andes, the ways that Aymara-speaking peasants conceptualize the past do not fit in any straightforward sense into this mold. The decisive events which are thought to separate one period from another are rarely phrased in terms of the Spanish. Recognition of this lack of fit has led me to think more generally about the issue of periodization.

There have been many revisionist accounts by historians questioning the givenness of particular periodizations, as in those based, for example, on the English or French "revolutions." However, there has been very little in the way of general discussion of periodization by historians: to what degree are periodizations intrinsic to the body of data itself, and to what degree ad hoc, depending on the particular perspective adopted? Are they fundamental to the historians' craft? Are they an innate function of the way that human beings conceptualize and give meaning to the past?

Among anthropologists there seems to be no discussion at all of this issue. It is by now generally accepted in the discipline that our starting point has been the other of European modernism, the exotic which is constructed in opposition to the concepts of modernist rationality and order. Not only were the characteristic themes of anthropological research those which contrasted most cleanly with the self-image of Europeans themselves, but also anthropologists tended to ignore the impact of colonialism on the non-European populations they studied. As Bernard Cohn put it in his state-of-the-art account of the relations between anthropology and history a decade ago, in studies of colonial contact historians begin at the moment of discovery, while anthropologists typically end with the coming of the destructive other—the Europeans. For both, the moment of discovery is constitutive of their disciplinary orientations.

In recent decades there has of course been a fundamental shift of emphasis, and many anthropologists and historians have turned to the study of colonialism and its impact. This shift of attention has been motivated by a number of factors, an epistemological and political critique of the previous silence as well as the more pragmatic consideration that it was the fact of colonial government that generated a substantial corpus of written documents in many parts of the world. However, there is also something more at work: this is the fascination with the changes wrought by expansionist Europe on the rest of the world that treats these changes as qualitatively different from any other historical process. Eric Wolf's *Europe and the People without History* is a case in point. The narrative is decisively organized around the coming of the Europeans, showing time and again how this process integrated peripheral or autonomous populations into the European world system.

It would appear that periodization is often seen to be given by the material itself, particularly since so much of anthropology is concerned with areas of the world colonized by Europe. As a result, periodization frequently falls naturally into a pre-colonial, a colonial, and a post-colonial matrix without further debate.

To use colonial rule as the axis on which ideas about the past are organized may seem so obvious, so right, that any further discussion is redundant. The coming of the White people has an almost transcendental status in the way the past is conceptualized. However, I think that we need to adopt a more agnostic stance as regards the historical salience of this event, if indeed it should in all cases be treated as an "event." At the very least we need to enquire whether it has the same salience for all colonized peoples as it does for the Europeans themselves.

2

History and Apotheosis

Columbus may be the most mythologized of European "discoverers" of unknown lands and peoples, but there are many others. A salient figure of comparable stature is Captain [James] Cook, who also set sail into the unknown, and with his sailors and crew encountered populations that had no previous experience of White people. According to both academic and popular accounts, Captain Cook was a brilliant navigator, a humanist, and dedicated to exploration, to the advance of civilization and the frontiers of knowledge. He was killed through the ignorance and error of the Hawaiians. These events have been made well known to anthropologists through the influential but controversial interpretations made of them by Marshall Sahlins.

Columbus is often seen as heralding the dawning of the Renaissance; Cook, by contrast, typifies Enlightenment Man. In both cases their historical salience derives in part from the fact that their exploits and achievements exemplify a new spirit, the dawning of a new age. These metaphors of course flow naturally from the concepts of Renaissance ("rebirth") and Enlightenment (dawning).

Recently, Gananath Obeyesekere has published a critique of the work of both Sahlins and Todorov. His particular concern is the way that they accept uncritically the well-known story that the Europeans, whether in Hawaii or in the Americas, were believed to be gods. At the same time, they implicitly accept the enduring European idea that identifies history with the Europeans, and relegates the nonliterate world to the domain of myth. Todorov quite unashamedly invokes a Lévi-Straussian opposition between a Europe oriented to the present, to improvisation and pragmatics, and a non-European world oriented to the past and dominated by tradition.

Obeyesekere's critique is aimed mainly at those who perpetuate the myth of "Europeans as gods" in the late twentieth century. This myth is more entrenched than we might be aware. The godlike status of White explorers and conquerors is a common trope in, for example, the increasingly popular use of primitives as a cinematic theme, by means of which the superior knowledge, understanding, moral stature, or power of the Whites can be delineated (Herzog's *Aguirre, The Wrath of God*, Joffé's *The Mission*, and Boorman's *The Emerald Forest* are obvious examples). However, it also needs unpicking in terms of the original historical context in which it is supposedly enacted.

In the case of Cook's death, his identification by the Hawaiians with their deity Lono is used to evoke their naïveté and shocking error in killing him. In other words, in European narratives at least, the figure of pathos is Cook himself. By contrast, in the narratives of the "discovery" and "conquest" of the Americas, the story focuses more frequently on the pathos and the tragic consequences for the Americans of their lack of comprehension in identifying the White people with gods. The incomprehension is contrasted with the cunning and resourcefulness of the Europeans, thus insinuating that the Europeans did understand what was going on, and what they had "discovered." But it is clear from many clues that the Europeans were predisposed to find the natives treating them as gods. Already in his first voyage, Columbus speculated in his journal whether the Caribbean natives might not have mistaken the seafarers for gods. The theme is fully elaborated in the familiar tale of the conquest of Mexico in which Cortés's arrival [in 1519] was said to be the fulfillment of a prophesy concerning the return of the god Quetzalcóatl, and which Cortés seems to have made good use of, and actively encouraged.

According to many historical accounts, the same theme was repeated thirteen years later in 1532, in which today seems like an uncanny reenactment, in the encounter of Pizarro and his band of Spanish adventurers with King Atahuallpa and the massed Inka armies. Let us look at this case in a little more detail. The story is told by a number of late sixteenth-century chroniclers; for example, [Pedro] Sarmiento writes: "When Atahuallpa heard this [of the arrival of the Spanish] he was delighted, believing that it was Viracocha who had come, just as he had promised them when he went away. . . . And he gave thanks to Viracocha because he was coming at the appointed time."

[José de] Acosta adds a biblical comparison to illustrate the identification of the Christians with pagan gods. This reminds us that there were examples with which the Spanish would have been familiar to reinforce the strength of the association: "They called the Spanish viracochas because they believed they were the children of heaven and deities, just as other peoples once attributed divine status to Paul and Barnabas, calling them Jupiter and Mercury respectively and trying to offer them sacrifices as though they were gods."

Already, by 1560, the equation of Spanish and the god Viracocha was so generally accepted that Domingo de Santo Tomás, in the first Quechua dictionary, translated viracocha as "Christian." And it is still commonplace in the Andean region today for White men and those of high status to be called viracochas. I, too, in line with my androgynous status as an anthropologist, have been addressed as *wiraquchi* on numerous occasions in highland Bolivia.

In recent years, doubts have increasingly been voiced regarding the authenticity of this story. In particular, the Polish ethnohistorians, Marcin Mroz and Mariusz Ziolkowski, have argued that it requires serious qualification. Mroz points out that the earliest accounts of the conquest of Peru make no reference to the identification of the Spanish with Viracocha. It took some time for the confused events of the 1530s to settle into an agreed narrative, and the first version that identifies the bearded White men with Viracocha is that of [Pedro] Cieza de León (1553). Cieza mentions the myth that the god Viracocha had gone away across the sea, but is sceptical about the belief (which he also mentions) that the Spanish are called Viracocha because they came from the sea.

Mroz suggests that it was the Spanish themselves who presented themselves as gods to the Indians. The success of the same idea in the conquest of Mexico would undoubtedly have influenced them. In addition, the ruling classes of Cusco may have endorsed this identification as part of their own local power struggles, in which the Spanish were themselves caught up. Further doubt on the plausibility of the myth is cast by Mariusz Ziolkowski. He points out that the Inkas certainly knew something about the Spanish before the arrival of Pizarro, because four members of an earlier expedition had been taken to the presence of the Inka Wayna Qhapaq [or Huayna Capac] and then killed. We can be sure, then, that the ruling elite knew that the Spanish were not gods but mortal, even if the common people may have had doubts on this score. Ziolkowski also poses the question of translation. Felipillo, the young man captured by the Europeans who served as their interpreter, had to create a means of translating the term "Christians" into Quechua. Since "the sons of god" was a common form of self-designation for the Christians, it seems plausible that Felipillo might have used the phrase "sons of Viracocha." In this case the identification of the Christians with the god Viracocha would be explained as a question of translation, rather than naïveté of mythological structures on the part of the native Americans. In other words, the identification of the Spanish with gods is thoroughly overdetermined, and it seems increasingly likely that it derived from a variety of quite pragmatic considerations, rather than from an absolute propensity of the natives to interpret the coming of the Europeans in terms of their gods.

The evidence for the Andean version of the myth of "White people as gods" supports Obeyesekere's general scepticism and appears to provide further illustration of what is a well-established anthropological theme familiar from Malinowski on: the natives, far from being tradition-bound and governed by an irrational adherence to myth and religion, use the same sorts of pragmatic considerations as Europeans. However, the process of demystification cannot be left there.

There is more to be said on the subject of what is involved in identifying White people with deities. The English or Spanish distinction between "god" and "man" is not the same as that made in other parts of the world. The Judaeo-Christian theological tradition is unusual in the degree to which a radical discontinuity is postulated between divinity and humanity. By contrast, other theologies see connectedness and gradations between them, and in the Americas the concept of "man-god" has been extensively explored, especially for Central Mexico.

Quite apart from such theological considerations, there are many different ways in which an identification between humans and deities can be made. Few deities in the world's religions have the unambiguously high moral standing and ontological transcendence of the god of the Semitic religions. Spirits may be worshiped almost as equals; they may be feared, negotiated with, even ridiculed. The use of distinctive features of White people in identifying and portraying deities may be based on analogy rather than ontological identity. It does not, therefore, necessarily entail that the Whites themselves are thought to be transcendent or surrounded by an extraordinary aura.

For example, in many regions of the Andes, the mountain deities are represented as *gringos* [foreigners] wearing high leather boots with large spurs. There are also mountain deities identified with lawyers, priests, and policemen. In the argument of John Earls this identification is derived analogically: it is the similarity of their power over the common people that leads to their merging.

Colonial rulers were of course in a position to insist on respect from their subordinates. There are many examples from twentieth-century history which reveal how intolerant White people were of any realist portrayal of themselves by colonized peoples which put them in a less than flattering light. What to later eyes seems like mimesis was condemned as caricature and parody. A notorious, if extreme, case was that of Julius Lips, who in the late 1920s as director of the Rautenstrauch-Joest Museum in Cologne assembled a collection of photos of often skilled and imaginative portrayals of Europeans in a realistic or less than glorious light from ethnographic museums across the world. He was denounced to the Nazis by some of his students for shaming the master race and was forced to flee Germany in 1933. He eventually published his material in the United States in 1937 as *The Savage Hits Back*—a title which makes clear the provocative quality the images were perceived to have.

3

Event as Myth

The godlike status of White explorers and conquerors is only one particularly evocative and strongly grounded instance of the more general process of mythologization, in which the coming of the Europeans to other parts of the globe in general attains an almost transcendental status in the way the past is conceptualized. The theme of the presumed divinity of the White outsiders emphasizes their uniqueness, their superior knowledge and powers, the idea that the coming of the Europeans constitutes a significant rupture and discontinuity. Many researchers have assumed that this idea of radical discontinuity would be manifest in indigenous historiographies as much as in those of Europe. Such a view is implicit or explicit in much of what anthropologists and ethnohistorians have written concerning indigenous histories in the Americas.

I wish to suggest that periodizations which derive from this postulate of absolute rupture associated with the coming of the White people are mythologized, in the sense that they derive from a set of criteria which go far beyond the historical data themselves as regards the explanatory power they have. The way that all of us who are not professional historians conceptualize the past is an intersection of the mythical and the empirical.

Furthermore, if it is useful to identify as myth the moments of the transition from one epoch to another, then we must also modify the widely held notion that myth is associated with timelessness. This view is expressed particularly clearly in the influential writings of [Mircea] Eliade. It is true that much of what is conventionally referred to as myth involves a prehistorical world lacking in transformative events. And modern interpretations of the semantics of mythology such as that of Roland Barthes also argue that myths naturalize history and thereby render it timeless.

However, even the most past-oriented, tradition-dominated worlds include some concept of before and after a cataclysm. Myth cannot simply be associated with the static, the timeless, the past-oriented, but may also invoke archetypal moments of rupture, a contrast between before and after, the sense of a beginning. This is the myth of Columbus, especially, as we have seen. It is the way that the historiography of the colonized world has generally been written, although whether the "before" is seen as utopian or as uncivilized and barbarous will obviously depend on the perspective of the writer. However, it is not obvious that the coming of the White people is the means for establishing mythologically the moment of rupture and the beginning of the present era in all social environments.

If this is the case, then clearly the opposition cannot be sustained between mythological, past-oriented, "cold" social orders and historical, change-oriented, "hot" societies which is not only beloved by structuralists, but also underlines most of the ideologies that contrast the world of modernity with that of the primitives. The widespread assumption that mythological thought is concerned with repetition, with timelessness, or with the cyclical does not take into account that the unique event is typically itself "mythologized." Myth includes moments of rupture, of a change of temporality as much as of continuities.

4

The Multiplicity of the Others

One consequence of the increased attention paid to colonial history has been a growing reflexive interest in how the coming of the White people was viewed by the non-European world, both at the time it occurred and later in historical and mythical categories and narratives. There is now a wealth of texts exploring the advent of the Europeans from the "native point of view.". . . The ways Europeans and their culture have been interpreted and incorporated depend on previously existing categories of otherness and ways of representing the alien and exotic. This might be epitomized by wilderness, or by neighboring tribes.

This interpretation seems much more productive than either the simple equation of Europeans with gods or the equally simple denial of this equation. It starts from the necessary assumption that all human societies have means of conceptualizing self and other, the familiar and the foreign, and that they do so largely in terms of images. Any new phenomenon is likely to be interpreted in the first instance in terms of existing images and categories—and this is obviously every bit as true for Europeans confronting the non-European world as vice versa.

There are a number of paradigms within which the coming of the White people can be interpreted. In addition to the mythopraxis in treating Europeans as gods, and their coming as the definitive rupture with a mythical past, we can add the idea that the image of White people as gods derives from pragmatic and mythological considerations on the part of the Europeans themselves, and may be further reinforced by local power struggles, as in the Andean case. Furthermore, insofar as whites are frequently classified in terms of existing categories of alien and exotic powers, their coming may more properly be conceived as one more addition to the mythico-historical world constructed by every human society, rather than as the definitive moment of rupture.

The "naturalness" by which we assume that events which were of momentous significance for European historiography and the construction of the European identity have the same status in the historical imagination of those conquered and subjugated by these same Europeans, needs to be unpicked. It is, therefore, salutary to bear in mind that in some instances indigenous peoples seem to have expressed indifference or at least evinced very little surprise at the arrival of the Europeans. For example, the Selden Codex of the Mixteca includes a detailed chronological sequence, covering the years of the Spanish arrival in Mexico, and their increasing penetration of the south, but fails to mention it.

It might be argued that a case like this reflects merely the failure of communication, or the gaps in Mixtec chronological record keeping. However, a later case, also from Mexico, suggests also that the Spanish Conquest is not the defining feature of all periodizations. In an illuminating study of Nahua (Central Mexico) land titles from the end of the colonial period—an invaluable source for indigenous historical ideas, since claims to land were supported by reference to the past—Stephanie Wood argues that there is very little reference to the Conquest, and that "the Christian victory is ultimately a cause for celebration among at least community leaders." Moreover, the titleholders barely mention the epidemic and do not connect the devastating diseases of the sixteenth century with the arrival of the Europeans.

One could go on citing examples. A final quote from Kay Warren's excellent ethnography of the western highlands of Guatemala makes the point very clearly. "The Trixanos," she writes, "rephrase the creation mythology so that it *omits* mention of the Conquest." In other words, the assumption is clear. Any *accurate* mythology would necessarily have to give the Conquest a prominent place. Failure to mention it constitutes a "rephrasing," an omission, in other words, a distortion of the past. As far as I know, no other historical event is treated in this way in the analysis of indigenous mythology.

5
The "Dance of the Conquest"

There is one example that anyone familiar with the ethnography of highland Latin America would probably see as a significant counter-example to the argument presented so far. This is the so-called "dance of the conquest." In the Andes it takes the form of a ritual reenactment of the encounter between Pizarro and Atahuallpa performed during religious feast days in some regions. These enactments have been used as evidence of the enduring nature of the trauma of the Conquest, and are popular with documentary filmmakers since they are a vivid indigenous representation of the coming of the Europeans.

In recent years a debate has developed as to how to interpret these performances. In 1988 the Peruvian historian, Manuel Burga, published a book in which he argued that the enactment of the encounter between the Inka and Spanish was a transformed version of earlier rituals portraying the antagonistic encounter between insiders and outsiders, wife givers and wife takers: "The enactment of the Inka and the Captain was surely the permitted form taken by Andean rituals in order to survive, retaining the structure and functions that they had before the conquest." In other words, he provides another version of the argument described already, in which the coming of the Europeans is incorporated into preexisting native categories, and becomes an extension or instantiation of a well-established theme. Thierry Saignes published a critique of this position in which he argued that the ritual enactments of the "dance of the conquest" probably derived far more of their impetus from the Spanish Church, in particular the Jesuits, and their attempts to instill the meaning of evangelization into their flocks through theatrical pieces which reenacted the process of conversion to Christianity (drawing analogies with the familiar Andalusian rituals of the battles of the Moors and Christians).

Saignes's position emphasized the European genesis of these myths and enactments, which thereby demonstrate in his view just how far the Conquest and consequent conversion were accepted and internalized by the Andean populations. His argument has in turn been roundly criticized by the Bolivian actor, Orlando Huanca. In stressing the European origins of these theatrical representations, Saignes underplays the agency of the Andean peoples themselves, and the changing contexts in which these dances or dramas have been played out and reenacted to the present day.

Historians such as Saignes and Burga have imposed a unitary meaning, derived from one historical moment, on these dance-dramas of the Conquest. Insofar as they continue to be performed throughout the Andes in changing historical conditions, their meaning is undoubtedly polysemic and capable of reinterpretation. In the context of my previous argument there are two points to be made. First, that . . . these enactments must be placed in the context of a broader field of mimetic art, which in the Andean region today is found in most expressive form in ritual dance. In these dances, all manner of alien powers and beings are enacted, from priests, to bears, to half-naked "jungle" Indians, to devils, or to Che Guevara. Insofar as the "dance of the conquest" forms part of this semantic field, it must be seen as yet one more instantiation of embodying the power and identity of the alien through mimetic dance. In other words, to focus on the "dance of the conquest" is potentially a Eurocentric way of singling out and giving unique status to one particular case of this widespread genre of dances.

The second point in a way contradicts the first, and leads me toward my conclusion. It is that where these dance-dramas are performed as historical commemoration, we should pay careful attention to the social and semantic context. In the Bolivian highlands, these dances are found frequently in urban settings, sometimes with elaborate Quechua scripts. The earliest reference to a performance of the defeat of Atahuallpa, along with representations of other feats and legends of Inka kings, comes from 1555, where it was performed before the Indian nobles in Potosí, and undoubtedly had direct political resonances for the Indian ruling class who were struggling to retain their aristocratic prerogatives under the new regime, and to extend their power. Today one well-known enactment in Bolivia is in the mining town of Oruro, where it is performed by Mestizo town dwellers. In this instance the drama has an immediate salience as an allegory of Bolivian nationalism. In nearby peasant communities, the same story evokes the long struggle with their Creole-Mestizo rulers over rights to their land. In short, where the dance-drama of the conquest does not form part of a wider mimesis of alien beings, its enactment as a self-contained piece of theater very probably expresses an overtly political project or statement.

6
Conclusion

My argument is not that we should dismiss the coming of the Whites in historical analysis, but recognize that usually this moment is treated not as a historical fact with consequences that must be investigated inductively, but as a transcendental event upon whose axis history is created, a rupture from which fundamental categories of periodization and identity are derived. The move to a recognition of the importance of colonialism over the past twenty to twenty-five years has paradoxically reinforced the self-importance of Europeans.

Alongside the perennial fascination among Europeans with the idea that they are treated as gods, there is a more recent interest in seeing ourselves reflected back from the eyes of those others, no longer necessarily as gods, sometimes as demons, sometimes merely with acute mimetic realism, no doubt part of the "culture of narcissism" to which writers such as Christopher Lasch have drawn attention. We have moved from a convention of the invisible observer, the authoritative voice of objectivity, to a new more reflexive position, one that takes pleasure in the otherness of ourselves, the Europeans, as seen through the eyes of exotic observers.

Despite the wealth of new historical and ethnographic research, the strength of the implicit belief persists that until the arrival of "us," there was no history. This is part of what accounts for the commonplace choice of the coming of the White people, or the Europeans, as the paradigm of history. It is yet another instance of the power of implicit categories in the face of empirical evidence. The pragmatic fact that it is only with the coming of the Whites that written records begin in many parts of the world is not sufficient to justify or explain the strength of this assumption. From the point of view of academic historiography we can agree that the arrival of White people was of the greatest historical significance, but we also have to recognize both that factors other than objective historiography enter into this evaluation, and that not all indigenous, colonized peoples give the same centrality to the coming of the Europeans, or certainly to the moment of contact.

However, alongside this new form of Eurocentrism, there is another reason why the coming of the White people occupies such a central place in historical periodizations. It is that the prevailing political and moral context for the study of history is nationalism. The typical narrative form taken by nationalist historiography is that of a prior state of autonomy, followed by fragmentation, defeat, and subjection to an alien power. The conclusion/dénouement to this narrative, realized in some instances, hoped for in others, is liberation from the oppressor and reconstitution of the independent nation.

In the Latin American context, it is in nationalist history that the standard three-part periodization of pre-Spanish, Spanish colonial, and post-Spanish republican is found. In the narrative of the emergence of the Bolivian, or the Mexican, or the Colombian nation, the Spanish Conquest plays a crucial role indeed, initiating the period of subjugation to European rule from which the nation was eventually able to construct itself by opposition. On a somewhat different basis, contemporary Indian movements and indigenous nationalisms also ground their narratives on the moment of Spanish Conquest.

In saying this, I merely wish to draw attention to the fact that apart from the factual basis, or not, of historical narratives, they are also generally formed by a set of structural principles of which periodization is an important one. Periodization, in turn, is frequently grounded in myths which posit a sharp break in the flow of events according to criteria which are themselves derived from ethical and political concerns. There is no doubt that the coming of the White people to colonize other parts of the world operates as one of these mythical markers of rupture. There is also no doubt that it is not universal among colonized peoples, and that its increased salience derives from a political context in which indigenous leaders are seeking to understand the sources of their own powerlessness.

 7

Orders Given to "the Twelve"

(1523)

On the eve of their departure from Spain, the "apostolic twelve" Franciscan friars who accompanied their superior Martín de Valencia received the following *obediencia* (exhortation and instructions) in Latin from their minister general, Francisco de los Angeles. They carried a copy of this document, along with an *instrucción* in Spanish, when they arrived in Mexico in 1524. Although "the Twelve" had been preceded by a few other churchmen, including Mercedarian friar Bartolomé de Olmedo and Franciscan lay brother Pedro de Gante (see Selection 12), it is with them that the organized effort to evangelize the native peoples of Mexico began.

The metaphorical language and preoccupations of de los Angeles allow insight into the expectations and intentions of these missionary friars and the first generation or two of their brethren in New Spain. These Franciscans revived a belief that had developed among early members of their order in the thirteenth century, a belief that they were a divinely inspired force working for the benefit and salvation of souls in the last days of the world. Thus, de los Angeles insists upon the urgency of his call to action, to deeds over words. "Hurry down now to the active life," he writes, and do not be afraid to shock the world with a zeal that some will see as madness. It is the eleventh hour in the struggle for salvation, he warns. There is an invitation to relentless hardships in this life "without promise of reward" and to death in the line of holy duty—in the *obediencia* such a death is called "the palm of martyrdom"; in the *instrucción,* there is an assurance that "even if you do not convert the infidel . . . you have done your duty and God will do His." De los Angeles presents the Devil as a palpable, menacing force in the world, and the Franciscans are to regard themselves as soldiers waging a spiritual war against him. New Spain, the battleground, is simultaneously the vineyard to which God has summoned the friars to labor among new plants as Judgment Day approaches. Native peoples are depicted as unbelievers powerlessly awaiting a redemption of which they are completely ignorant, "held fast [as they are] in the blindness of idolatry under the yoke of the satanic thrall." They are a far cry from the Aztec lords and holy men with whom "the Twelve" converse in Bernardino de Sahagún's 1564 depiction (Selection 3).

These ardent conceptions of themselves and of the evangelization of Indians spring in part from the special situation of the Franciscans (or, as they called themselves, the Order of the Friars Minor, or Minorites) in the Iberian Peninsula in the years after the conquest of Muslim Granada and the expulsion of the Jews in 1492. Virtually from the order's beginnings in the early thirteenth century, there had existed an internal tension over whether to adhere strictly to an original rule of austerity, simplicity, and renunciation of property (as "Observants," in later parlance) or to lead more material lives as a way to exert greater influence in the world (as "Conventuals"). Branches of both tendencies emerged in Iberia in the late fourteenth and early fifteenth centuries. After numerous failed attempts to reunite the many branches and heal the fundamental division between Observants and Conventuals, two bulls were issued by Pope Leo X in 1517. First, he made formal the separation of the Franciscan Order into two independent bodies; and second, he brought about a temporary union of the Observant groups—many of them quite new, having emerged only in the late fifteenth century. (The separation between the Conventual and Observant Franciscans hardened, although many Conventuals joined the more numerous and influential Observants at this time. The Observants' own union did not last, and they soon divided into four groups: Barefoot, or Discalced; Recollects; Reformed; and Capuchins.)

Following their interpretations of the priorities of Saint Francis of Assisi (d. 1226), Observant Franciscans in the fifteenth and sixteenth centuries maintained that the example of a holy and moral spiritual life offered the most powerful incentive in the conversion of others. Generally speaking, this fundamental point distinguished the Franciscans from the Dominican Order (the Order of the Friars Preacher), which was founded by Saint Francis's contemporary, Saint Dominic (d. 1221), and which developed over the same period as the Order of the Friars Minor. The Dominicans favored programs of doctrinal preaching and philosophical arguments with religious opponents as the most effective means of conversion. Once they had attained spiritual maturity and obedience, Franciscans, too, were called on to preach as missionaries in the world. Early Franciscans were known for simple sermons delivered among the poor and lepers, and for their regular withdrawals to secluded places. They preached also among infidels (principally Muslims), but were instructed to avoid entering into complex disputes such as the formal exchanges held with Aztec holy men by their successors. Deeds over words, again; as Saint Francis himself emphasized in his founding rules of the order, *Regula prima,* "All brothers . . . preach by their works."

One of the strictest of the Observant groups in early sixteenth-century Spain would supply many of the early Franciscans in Mexico, including members of "the Twelve." Their interpretation of the original rule stressed that, in the course of the simple preaching of the Word among non-Christians, missionaries should exhibit God's love and thus urge unbelievers toward baptism and becoming Christian. Known as the Minorites of the Blessed Juan de Puebla and the Minorites of the Holy Gospel, they practiced extreme poverty, a rigorous regimen of flagellation, and silent spiritual retreats. These Minorites had also undertaken a short-lived preaching mission among Moriscos (new converts to Christianity from Islam) in the mountains of southern Spain in an effort to promote a simple, austere Christianity among these new and potential converts to the faith. They emerged from the ruling of Leo X with their own Province of San Gabriel, founded in 1518.

The first provincial of San Gabriel was Martín de Valencia, already legendary within the Observant ranks for his humility and practices of penance. He is said to have attracted many fervent religious to the new province. According to Motolinía (Toribio de Benavente), one of these religious, it was during a personal inspection of the province by Minister General Francisco de los Angeles in 1523 that Valencia learned of a plan to send him and twelve companions to begin the evangelization of the indigenous peoples of Mexico. The orders composed by de los Angeles must have emerged from this meeting.

Valencia and his companions were famous in their own time and long afterward. Colonial paintings glorify the moment of their reception in Mexico by Hernán Cortés, with the conqueror typically represented in symbolic self-abasement before their holy purpose and Indian observers absorbing the edifying scene. "The Twelve," as mentioned above, are also the Christian interlocutors in the *coloquios* from which Selection 3 is drawn. And they appear as the bearers of "the church" in Diego Valadés's 1579 depiction of the ideal churchyard-as-schoolroom in Figure 15.

Fray Francisco de los Angeles, minister general and servant of the whole Order of the Friars Minor, to the venerable and his very dear fathers in Christ: Fr. Martín de Valencia, confessor and learned preacher, and to the other twelve friars of the Order of Minors, who under his obedience are to be sent to the places of the infidels who dwell in the lands of Yucatán; that is to say: Fr. Francisco de Soto, Fr. Martín de la Coruña, Fr. José de la Coruña, Fr. Juan Xuárez, Fr. Antonio de Ciudad Rodrigo, and Fr. Toribio Benavente, preachers and confessors; Fr. García de Cisneros and Fr. Luis de Fuensalida, preachers; Fr. Juan de Ribas and Fr. Francisco Ximénez, priests; and to the Brothers Fr. Andrés de Córdoba and Fr. Bernardino de la Torre, devoted lay religious; and to all the others who there shall be received or in the future should be sent, sempiternal health and peace in the Lord.

Among the continuous cares and affairs which daily present themselves to me and occupy my mind, this one presses, worries, and afflicts me first of all, as to how with all the cunning of my bowels and continual sighs of my heart, I might labor with the apostolic man and father of ours, Saint Francis, toward liberating and snatching away from the maw of the dragon the souls redeemed with the most precious Blood of Our Lord Jesus Christ, deceived by satanic wiles, dwelling in the shadow of death, held in the vain cult of idols—and bring them to fight under the banner of the Cross and to place their neck into the yoke of Christ, through you, my dearest brothers, with the favor of the Most High; because otherwise I shall not be able to escape the zeal of Saint Francis athirst for the welfare of souls, pounding day and night with unceasing knocking at the door of my heart. And that which I yearned for with the passing of many days, namely, of being made one of your number, and did not deserve to obtain from the superiors (thus, Father, because such was your pleasure), I confidently hope to attain in your persons through His favor.

For, indeed, the bounty of the Eternal Father chose the same seraphic standard-bearer of Christ to exalt the glory of His Name and procure the salvation of souls, and to forestall the ruin which threatened the Church (and should she fall, save her and raise her to her primitive state), from among many persons endowed and placed in His Holy Church with divine aids and favors—together with his sons, namely, outstanding men who, contemplating and considering the life and merits of the most blessed Saint Paul, glory solely in the Cross of the Lord by spurning worldly delights and consolations for the delights and riches of Paradise.

For the same man of God, not oblivious of his vocation and calling, and ever raising his desire toward the love of heavenly things, sought through the Church Militant both the faithful and the infidels. And even until now do they herald and make manifest unceasingly throughout the whole world the power of the Divine

Name; in spreading the honor and service of the Christian religion, they labor with great vigilance. And what else can be said? For certainly, in chasing away heresies and in destroying other pestiferous and deadly plagues, they willingly offered themselves to contempt. Desiring to shed their own blood, burning with the fire of Christ's love, and thirsting for the palm of martyrdom, the said father with some of his sons went over various parts of the world.

But now that the dawn is far spent and passing away, which is the eleventh hour of which the Gospel speaks, you are called by the head of the family to go forth into his vineyard; not hired for a price like the others, but rather like true sons of such a father, not seeking your own interests, but those of Jesus Christ without promise of pay or reward; may you run like sons following your father to the vineyard—he who desiring to be the last among men did so attain it, and wished that you his true sons should be the last among the rest, treading and trampling upon the glory of the world, despised for littleness and idiocy, possessing the sublimest poverty, and in such a way that the world should regard you with mockery and contempt, and the very picture of contempt and derision, and should consider your life as madness, and your end without honor. For, thus become madmen to the world, you might convert the world by the foolishness of your preaching. Neither should you be disturbed because you are not hired, but rather sent forth without promise of reward; because the man of God, enlightened by an interior inspiration of the Father of Light, foresaw then, not with a clouded eye but with the firm certainty of the sublime, that from the last he would make you the first.

To you, therefore, O sons, with the last end of the world at hand, I your father cry out and bestir your minds that you defend the King's army already falling and presently fleeing from the foe, and, taking up the victorious contest of the heavenly Victor, you preach by word and work unto the enemy. And if up to now, with Zacchaeus up in the figberry tree sucking the sap of the Cross, you sought to see who Jesus might be, hurry down now to the active life. And if you should have cheated anyone from among the souls of men by solely contemplating the mysteries of the Cross, pay back your neighbor fourfold with the active life together with the contemplative, the shedding of your very blood for the Name of Christ and for their salvation—which He regards and weighs fourfold compared with contemplation alone—and then you will see who Jesus is; when, distrusting yourselves while accomplishing this, you shall receive Him with joy into your hearts. He will see to it that while you are small in stature, you will triumph over the enemy. Run therefore thus with such speed as to gain the victory. It follows hence that you, whom the zeal for souls has eaten up according to the sublimity of your profession, and who desire to run in the fragrance of the ointments of those who followed the footsteps of Christ and shed their blood for His love—for this reason you begged me with great importunity, according to the spirit of our Rule, to send you to infidel parts, so that fighting there for Christ in their conversion, you might save the souls of your neighbor and your own, prepared to go to prison and to death for His sake and for their salvation.

Wherefore, having knowledge of your good life and proof of your goodness, and having learned and known from your deeds that you are worthy of the banner of the King of Glory, which you want to raise up in faraway places, and hold up and sustain, flourish and defend even unto death—therefore, confiding in the divine bounty, I send you to convert with words and example the people who do not know Jesus Christ Our Lord, who are held fast in the blindness of idolatry under the yoke of the satanic thrall, who live and dwell in the Indies which are commonly called Yucatán or New Spain or Tierra Firme. With the authority of my office, in the name of the Father and of the Son and of the Holy Spirit, I charge and command you with the merit of holy obedience, so that you may go forth and bear fruit and your fruit may endure.

And to you, venerable father, Friar Martín de Valencia, and to your successors in office, I subject the twelve friars named, and whichever others who in time to come should join themselves to your fold, as to their true pastor and superior; and you I constitute as their true superior, and likewise your successors in office according to the instruction that I intend to give you concerning the mode of your life and conversation; and you I call and constitute for their custos [director of a subprovincial unit of Franciscans], and I wish and order that you be so addressed; and I place and subject you to myself alone and my obedience, and that of my successors in office (according to the instructions that I intend to give you), and also to that of the Commissary of Spain in those things concerning which you alone or your successors, with the majority of the friars, should have recourse by your letters, until you or your successors learn otherwise from the mandates of our general chapter.

Further than this, I charge and command you the twelve through the merit of holy obedience, and the rest who in the future should join your company, and every single person, both you and them—that you will have to obey the said friar Martín de Valencia as your true and indubitable prelate and custos, and his successors in office, in all these things in which you are obliged to obey the minister general and the rest of your prelates according to the tenor of the Rule. And because I am obligated to bring subjects and superior, according to the burden of the office imposed upon me (and which I unworthily fill), and since in the course of time many matters and problems could arise concerning the custody entrusted to you, which might pertain to my office and for the providing and remedying of which my presence should of necessity be required, it follows from this that to you the said friar Martín de Valencia (in whose fervent zeal, religious observance, and laudable maturity, learning, essential discretion, and general ability, I fully confide in the Lord), and to whomsoever of your successors in the office by the tenor of the letters present, I most fully commit all my powers regarding all your subjects, who are as of now and in time should be, and regarding all and whichever friaries, if there are some now of our Order, and those which in the future should exist in New Spain, or the land of Yucatán—giving to you and to them all fullest authority and faculties in one and the other forum, in the external judicial one as well as the internal one of conscience, together with the ordinary one which belongs to me through my office, and even also the apostolic indults and privileges granted to me, with the power of subdelegating; that is to say, publicly and privately to visit, admonish, correct, punish, establish, disestablish, ordain, prohibit and dispose, bind and absolve and dispense from whatsoever penalties, irregularities, and defects, and against whatsoever statutes of the Order, and regarding whatsoever precepts and mandates with which I myself am empowered with regard to either forum; and also by ecclesiastical censures and other canonical penalties to constrain, obstruct, and compel, to interpret and to resolve doubts. Likewise all those things and whichever one of them that in whatsoever manner concern or pertain to my office of minister general, especially in having them performed and carried out as though I myself personally, both by my ordinary power and by my apostolic commission, would perform and accomplish them; and even though the problems were such that, for being so difficult, they needed special and particular declarations. All of these things, and each one of them, I desire to be regarded as sufficiently expressed by the tenor of these presents, excepting two cases which I reserve to myself.

The first: about admitting women, virgins, widowed, or married, into the Order and obedience of Saint Clare, whether from the first or from the second category, or to the Third Order, which [Second and Third Orders] our most blessed father Saint Francis is known to have founded [besides the Friars Minor, the First Order of men]. The second case is: to absolve from the bond of excommunication those who, because of their contumacious disobedience, I should happen to excommunicate by word or in writing. Beyond that, you can depute these my powers and authority, either in whole or in part, either to one or to many, as often as you deem it fitting or consider it proper to entrust these to them, and once entrusted to recall them at your will.

And because you will for a long time endure such great hardships and continuous vigils and cares in carrying out and executing such a great commission and trust, do not let them weaken or exhaust your spirit, but rather find it relaxed and every day more renewed and more completely and fully availing itself of merit. By virtue of the Holy Spirit, and with greater emphasis under obedience, I enjoin you to exercise faithfully and diligently the aforesaid office of pastoral commission and trust, and to carry it out according to the grace which God has given you, and which He will henceforth give and amplify.

Go, therefore, my much beloved sons, with the blessing of your father, to carry out what I have commanded you; and armed with the shield of faith and with the breastplate of justice, with the blade of the spirit of salvation, with the helmet and lance of perseverance, struggle with the ancient serpent which seeks and hastens to lord himself over, and gain the victory over, the souls redeemed with the most precious Blood of Christ. And win them for that Christ in such a manner that among all Catholics an increase of faith, hope, and love may result; and to the perfidious infidels a road may be opened for them and pointed out; and the madness of heretical evil may fall apart and come to nothing; and the foolishness of the gentiles may be made manifest to them, and the light of the Catholic faith may shine forth in their hearts. And you shall receive the eternal kingdom.

Fare ye well, remain with Christ Jesus, and pray for me.

Given in the friary of Santa María de los Angeles on October 30th of the year 1523. Under my signature and with the major seal of my office. Fr. Francisco Angelorum, minister general and servant.

8

Francisco de Vitoria on the Evangelization of Unbelievers, Salamanca, Spain

(1534–35)

The succession of bulls (proclamations) issued by Pope Alexander VI in 1493 grandly, if vaguely, ceded to Ferdinand and Isabella of Spain the right to occupy "such islands and lands . . . as you have discovered or are about to discover." And the Treaty of Tordesillas between the monarchs of Spain and Portugal in the following year, once again adjudicated by the pope, effectively granted the two Iberian neighbors rights over territories (and peoples) then mostly unknown to them. This late fifteenth-century "papal donation" would prove invaluable to the Spanish monarchs in particular, and to a succession of thinkers who pondered the legitimacy of Spain's power over others for centuries to come.

Such claims to potential bounty attracted many challengers beyond the Portuguese. Vocal protests against Spanish territorial claims issued from awakening rivals in western Europe, especially France and England; and the increase in piracy and the flouting of Spanish economic and territorial monopolies in the Indies were more practical expressions of international rivalry (later effects in the Viceroyalty of Peru are discussed in Selection 26). Yet some of the most rigorous intellectual scrutiny of Spain's emerging American claims and their papal legitimation came from within. While reports of the immensity and seemingly limitless potential offered in "the kingdoms of the Indies" were reaching Emperor Charles V, theologians and jurists were pondering the moment in the cloisters and lecture halls of Spain's most hallowed university at Salamanca.

The foremost of this group was Francisco de Vitoria (ca. 1485–1546), who delivered the lecture upon which this reading is based. He is thought to have entered the Dominican Order in about 1506 in Burgos in northern Spain. He pursued courses in the arts and theology in Paris, where he also taught and received his doctorate in theology in 1522, having studied especially under the Flemish Dominican Peter Crockaert (d. 1514). Professors of theology in the early sixteenth century customarily lectured on portions of a standard medieval text for theological studies, the *Sentences* (*Sententiae*) by Peter Lombard, an early twelfth-century theologian at Paris. But, following a gradual shift that had originated in Germany and spread to Paris, Crockaert in 1509 also began lecturing on the *Summary of Theology* (*Summa Theologica*) by Saint Thomas Aquinas (ca. 1225–1274). In Salamanca, Vitoria would later do the same for large parts of his courses, as would others in Spain and Italy. Together, Crockaert and Vitoria coedited an edition of the *Summa* (Paris, 1512), and were influential players in an intellectual movement often called "Second Thomism"—the systematic attempt by a number of sixteenth-century thinkers, many of them Dominicans, to revive the study of, and extend, the conclusions of Saint Thomas Aquinas (as well as the spirit of his thirteenth-century synthesis of the writings of the ancient Greek philosopher Aristotle and Christianity) and to relate them to the problems and needs of their own day.

Vitoria's thinking developed in Paris and in the years of his first academic appointments in Spain. From Paris, he became professor of theology at Valladolid in 1523, before being elected as Prime Professor of Theology at the University of Salamanca in 1526, a position he held until his death twenty years later. Vitoria, along with a number of his students (Domingo de Soto [1494–1560], the Dominican theologian who would become confessor to Charles V and a delegate at the Council of Trent, was perhaps the most famous) and several other later theologians and jurists (notably, Francisco Suárez [1548–1617], the Jesuit theologian and author of a widely read treatise on natural law) are often dubbed the "School of Salamanca" by historians. They did not work and write at precisely the same time, nor were they as uniform in their thinking as the notion of a "school of thought" implies. Yet, generally speaking, Vitoria's students and other later commentators carried on much of the work that he had begun, not least in the further examination of the foundations of Spanish rule in America.

Vitoria never traveled to America, but the place pressed in on him as an intellectual challenge with dramatic practical repercussions—arguably, one of the most significant issues that a contemporary theologian could face. He lived in and contributed to an era in which the Spanish Crown and an array of advisers and experts in theology and jurisprudence started to think over the ramifications of having come upon, assumed control of, and begun to colonize the Indies. From his study in Paris, the young Vitoria must have learned of, and perhaps even followed, the great meeting of theologians and jurists held in Burgos in 1512–13, which discussed the legitimacy of Spanish dominion in the Indies and the treatment of indigenous populations and which also drafted the Laws of Burgos. These were issues to which he would return as a teacher.

Vitoria's attitude to Spanish rule in America has often been treated superficially and rather romantically by students eager to find in him an internal critic of Spain's or the Roman Catholic Church's pretensions and actions—a professorial version of the slightly younger Dominican, Bartolomé de Las Casas, who would campaign so strongly against Spanish maltreatment of the Indians and the *encomienda* regime [a grant of labor and tribute rights from the Crown to a Spanish individual over specified indigenous groups]. But Vitoria, in the words of the Jesuit José de Acosta, who will be met later in this book (Selection 18), preferred to argue as a "moderate lawyer." Vitoria was a brave thinker who decried false claims and abuses of power, but he wove these positions into larger, complex arguments that were not designed to undermine Spanish imperialism. His significant and often critical engagements with Spain's early modern deeds and predicaments profit from being seen within a tradition of what Anthony Pagden calls, in his introduction to Vitoria's work, the "ritual legitimation which the kings of Castile had, since the Middle Ages, regularly enacted when confronted by uncertain moral issues." By establishing that peoples who did not share the Spaniards' belief and value systems could not automatically either be called enemies or be dispossessed of their property and territory, Vitoria and the thinkers whom he influenced spoke directly to the engine of Spanish expansion even if they did not cause it to change much. From Salamanca, the professor of theology thought and commented and provoked, but as part of the process by which the Castilian Crown secured its own authority.

For Vitoria, nothing in the world—no text, no argument, no current event—was unconnected to the restless interpretation and reinterpretation of the social, moral, and political principles of Saint Thomas. These foundations led Vitoria and others to lay the groundwork for a system of thought that may best be described as Spanish Christian universalism. This system of thought was urged forward by the circumstances that Vitoria saw around him; the consolidation of rule by the Spanish Crown in Iberia and America meant that he was arguing for an ethics of Empire.

In doing so, of course, Vitoria and other Thomists stepped into an intellectual and moral minefield in which a number of positions had already been staked out. Among these, the Thomists saw serious errors in the views of humanists (classical scholars) such as Juan Ginés de Sepúlveda (1490–1573), who had justified Spanish domination of native American peoples because he found them to be inferior human beings, living crudely and with no knowledge of Christianity. In terms borrowed from Aristotle's *Politics,* Amerindians were "slaves by nature (*natura servus*)" and might be treated accordingly by a civilized people such as the Spanish. In contrast, he explored the moral foundations for such political rights. Drawing on Saint Thomas's vision of an entire universe governed by a hierarchy of laws, Vitoria visualized a universal (or international) human society in the world into which any number of independent states might fit and foster relationships. In the interests of this universal society made possible by Vitoria's Thomism, a systematic set of laws and principles—an ethical framework—might be discerned which both pleased God and respected the "common good," that is, the rights of all concerned.

On these subjects and others, Vitoria became known not for what he wrote, but for what he said in his lectures. He published nothing in his lifetime, allegedly remarking that his students already had more than enough to read. But his lectures on the *Summary of Theology* and Lombard's *Sentences* were assiduously copied and distributed by a number of his students. The selection that follows is an extract taken from notes made by an anonymous student. (According to accepted practices as well as Salamancan university statutes for which Vitoria and his Parisian training were partly responsible, contemporary lecturers were required to speak slowly and clearly so that this process of dictation and copying could take place.) Thus, many of Vitoria's ideas reached a wider audience indirectly—often channeled, as Pagden observes, into his students' published works.

Some of Vitoria's conclusions about Spain in America struck at the issue of the pope's authority in matters of politics and territorial claims. Vitoria challenged the authority of the Alexandrine donations to the Spanish monarchs, arguing that the papacy could not automatically exercise rights over non-Christian peoples and the lands over which they rightfully ruled. Based on what was known of the indigenous societies in America by the mid-1530s, Vitoria asserted, there existed no legitimate grounds for pretending that these territories were vacant, essentially unoccupied or even ill used (as, later, English and, to a lesser extent, French thinkers would argue.) Vitoria is said to have been dismayed by news of the circumstances surrounding the execution of the Inka Atahuallpa in Peru. On the evidence he had seen, this was a fresh example of illegitimate Spanish action. (Concern with the justice of such acts continued, as Figure 35 [Selection 47] from the late eighteenth century attests.) More generally and just as memorably, Vitoria pointed out the absurdity of a common claim in his day, namely, that the Spaniards gained property rights over American territories because they had been the first to "discover" them. He maintained that discovery "of itself . . . provides no support for possession of these lands, any more than it would if they had discovered us."

As already mentioned, the Thomist understanding of law as divided into a hierarchy of categories underpinned Vitoria's views and arguments. The first was a composite of two: eternal and divine law. It came from God Himself and encompassed all others. Almost as fundamental for Vitoria was the law of nature or "natural law," defined by Aquinas as a set of first principles (*prima praecepta*) granted by God and understood by all "rational creatures," or, as Suárez later put it, "written in our minds (*scriptam in mentibus*)" by God. Vitoria's (and Aquinas's) notion of a natural law upon which all peoples were in agreement grew from a number of assumptions about the essential truth of Judeo-Christianity. The idea of a natural law assumed the universal applicability of the Christian Gospels and accepted the Ten Commandments—especially the fundamental injunction, "Do unto others as you would have them do unto you"—as a "natural" code of conduct and moral framework for all human beings (see also their later importance for Juan Francisco Domínguez in Selection 44). Compilations of Roman law, and the social and political conventions of western Europe in his day, were viewed by Vitoria as accretions upon these "natural" foundations, as Pagden puts it—"the inescapable conclusions of the rational mind drawing upon certain self-evident first principles." These accretions were the third kind of law, human (or sometimes "positive") law, those laws conceived and enacted by human beings; they might vary between the nations and communities of the world, and they were only binding if they grew out of and confirmed the supposedly common principles of natural law. Finally, there was a "law of nations" poised somewhere between natural and human law. The idea of a law of nations is what made the conception of a universal human society possible. Because observance of the law of nature was thought to be required of all people, it could be assumed further that a certain body of universal human laws might be found and respected in any conceivable place or time, even amid the alien practices of non-Christians.

The last point about the legitimacy of certain shared laws and ways in all places, combined with Vitoria's further elaboration of seven "unjust titles" or claims that Spain could not in good faith advance to justify conquests in the Americas, seem, at a glance, to challenge seriously Spain's right to rule indigenous American peoples who possessed their own laws and codes of conduct. But Vitoria did not leave the argument there. He was bound by the rigor of his method (if nothing else) also to investigate a set of "just titles"—arguments drawn from this assumed law of nations by which the Spanish Crown might gather legitimate claims to political and spiritual jurisdiction in America. Seen from the points of view of indigenous societies confronting the Spanish presence, here were the ways in which they might be judged by a Dominican theologian in Salamanca to have forfeited their right to their own dominion.

Vitoria accepted the existence of a natural right of society and communication which all people were bound to respect. Thus, if native American peoples resisted or hindered the Spaniards' desire to "travel" in their territories, the Indians could be judged as violators of an inalienable human right. War might legitimately be made on them. Vitoria asserted that there existed a similarly inalienable right to trade; a right to protect innocents from rulers judged to be tyrants; even a right to protect other peoples from themselves (that is, from the crimes they were alleged to be committing against nature, especially cannibalism and human sacrifice); and a right to preach the Gospel unhindered in any land.

"On the Evangelization of Unbelievers" sits deep within Vitoria's exploration of these unjust and just Spanish claims to dominion (*dominium*) and activity in America. He considers a key question posed by Aquinas (*Summa Theologica* II-II.10.8) and applies it to his time, asking whether a Christian prince (such as Charles V) has the right to convert non-Christians to the faith "by violence and the sword." This "right," along with the other rights or "just titles" described above, pertain to Spain's situation in the Indies, and Vitoria even makes this connection explicit on occasion. Yet he was also thinking of other matters, of fronts on which there were other kinds of unbelievers with whom Spain and the Catholic Church were simultaneously entwined and preoccupied because of the Christian imperatives to evangelize all peoples and maintain the faith in those to whom it had been given. The "modern heretics," the Lutherans, were among those people on Vitoria's mind when he spoke of a Catholic missionary's right to travel and preach, and when he argued that "no one can be good unless he is Christian and accepts our faith."

More fundamentally, Vitoria divides his lecture in two, treating his problem first among peoples who are subjects of the Crown, and second among those who are not. The examples he raises and to which he returns are instructive. In the first category, Vitoria carries in mind principally Mudéjares (Muslims living under Christian rule) and Moriscos (new converts to Christianity from Islam) in the Spanish kingdoms. He collects these historical and contemporary peoples under one Latin term common in medieval times, *Saraceni*, or Saracens. In the second category are the indigenous peoples of America, his "islanders" (*insulani*) and "barbarians" (*barbari*). Yet, as Vitoria would have been well aware by the late 1530s, the two categories of unbelievers do not remain separate. One might argue about precisely when, but the distinction blurs once certain native peoples in the Indies become consolidated beneath Spanish rule. Like other sixteenth-century churchmen (see Selections 15 and 18, for example), Vitoria has both Moriscos and Indians in mind, raising questions and problems that bear directly on the evangelization and colonial conditions of both subject peoples.

Francisco de Vitoria focuses on the role and effects of coercion in matters of religion. He finds religious coercion to be evil and likely to yield results opposite to those intended by the Catholic Church among most unbelievers. "For myself," he emphasizes in discussion of the situation involving Mudéjares and Moriscos, "I have little doubt that more of them could be converted by greater leniency; and they would be likely to remain firmer in the faith." Here and elsewhere in the text, Vitoria's words are loaded as carefully as his target is chosen, and his most potent critical remarks are stated in hypothetical terms. "If, for example, all the Saracens in Spain were to be forcibly converted . . . ," begins one cautionary passage. He lectured in the years of a generally worsening relationship between Spanish Christian rulers and their Muslim and formerly Muslim minorities: after 1492 there was a succession of contraventions of the capitulation agreement that had ended Muslim rule in Granada, many baptisms were forced, and copies of the Qur'an and other Arabic books deemed religious in content were publicly burned, finally provoking a violent and spreading uprising between 1499 and 1501; in 1502 a decree by the Castilian Crown demanded the expulsion of all Muslims who did not accept baptism and convert to Christianity (almost all chose baptism), and two decades later the same "option" was presented to Muslims in the Kingdom of Aragón; and in 1526, as if in confirmation of the problems which arose from such "conversions," Charles V extended the jurisdiction of the Holy Office of the Inquisition to include Morisco religious offenders in the Kingdom of Granada.

Vitoria was trained as a humanist as well as a theologian and, as always, he treats his problem as multisided. He reflects at some length on the occasions when a Christian prince would be just in his use of force against unbelievers, even in matters of religion. Most notable in this regard is his attitude toward apostasy—a convert's backsliding from Christianity to old errors. Having accepted baptism of one's own will, there was no option but Christianity. Vitoria sees the specter of apostasy in terms of natural law, quoting Saint Thomas: "Whoever accepts the law of Christ can be compelled to keep it." Yet Vitoria has a knack for presenting one side of an argument as indisputable, only to allow his emphasis ultimately to fall the other way. Thus, he lays out the conditions which make different kinds of religious coercion legitimate, yet favors conquest "by faith"—setting a virtuous example and persuading people to abandon their old ways and turn Christian. Similarly, while the smashing of idols and other acts of extirpation of religious error are viewed as legitimate and benevolent actions that assist ignorant or misguided sinners, Vitoria advises care and restraint: "This [idol-smashing] ought not to be done on every occasion, primarily because it may provoke their [the new or prospective converts'] fierce indignation, and destroy any kind feelings toward us which they may happen to have."

Vitoria's words on the evangelization of unbelievers seem designed to summon questions and reflection from his students and contemporaries. What had been the nature of the Moriscos' evangelization to date, and where was that evangelization headed? Was the spiritual enterprise among the Moriscos affected by, or affecting, the ways in which the evangelization of Indians in America was being approached? What was the impact of different evangelization methods on new Christians? And finally, with what, precisely, was the Christian faith becoming associated?

Should Unbelievers Be Forcibly Converted?

§1 Aquinas replies by establishing a preliminary distinction, namely, that the unbelievers in question are *those who have never taken the faith*. These *should not be forcibly converted*; but a second conclusion is that they may be *forcibly restrained from hindering the missionaries of the faith*, and from insulting Christ and Christians; this is clear, because everyone has the right to defend himself and his temporal interests, and therefore also his spiritual interests. And his third conclusion is that those who have received the faith may be forced back to the faith; see the explicit testimonies he adduces.

The first conclusion is the determination of the decretal [an authoritative papal decision on a matter of doctrine or ecclesiastical law] *Maiores* (X.3.42.3) and the canon [a provision of Church law] *De Iudaeis* (*Decretum* D.45.5), on the Jews; and of the decretal *Sicut ait* (X.5.7.8) and the canon *Qui sincera* (*Decretum* D.45.3), on heretics. And this is the common opinion of the doctors on Lombard's *Sentences* [1285] IV.4, of Durandus of Saint-Pourçain [1270/5–1334, Dominican theologian], *ad loc.* 6, and Richard of Middleton [d. ca. 1305, Franciscan, Scholastic theologian at Oxford and Paris], in IV.6.3.

A DOUBT ARISES by what law it is prohibited to forcibly convert unbelievers? To harm another is prohibited by natural law; but to force these people to believe is not to harm them, but to help them; *ergo*. The reply is that it is prohibited in many passages of human law; therefore this is no objection, because positive law cannot forbid anything unless it is prohibited in divine law. I conclude that it is prohibited in divine law.

A doubt then arises as to where this prohibition is to be found? Not in Scripture, because if it was there Saint Thomas would have cited it among his authorities, being always a most careful researcher in this respect. I reply that there are no unequivocal authorities to this effect, but that there are some passages from which it may be inferred, though not clearly, at least by deduction. This is as much to say, it comes not from positive divine law but from natural law; and the arguments for proving it depend on natural reason. But whereas Duns Scotus [ca. 1265–1308, Franciscan theologian and teacher] holds that a convincing argument from reason can be made against the conclusion (in *Sentences* IV.4.9), Durandus of Saint-Pourçain, in the passage cited above, constructs a rational argument for the conclusion. I do not know whether it is valid, judge for yourselves, since it is clear enough. Thomist theologians also advance the following proof for the conclusion: Evil means are not justified even by good ends. But to apply coercion to anyone is evil; therefore, unbelievers cannot lawfully be compelled to believe. This argument, however, perhaps involves a *petitio principii.*

ON THIS BASIS, one could construct an *a posteriori* proof of Saint Thomas's conclusion: namely, that *more harm than good follows from forcible conversion, which is therefore unlawful*:

1. In the first place, forcible conversion would cause great provocation and unrest (*scandulum*) among the heathen. If, for example, all the Saracens [Muslims] in Spain were to be forcibly converted, this would cause unrest in [Muslim] Africa, because the Africans would think that Christianity had always been preached and imposed by force throughout the world; whereas, on the contrary, our strongest argument against them is that they have never conquered any land with their faith, as we have with ours. *Ergo.*

2. The second bad effect is that, instead of the benevolent and proper affection required for belief, forcible conversion would generate immense hate in them, and that in turn would give rise to pretense and hypocrisy. We could never be sure whether or not they truly believed in their hearts; there would be nothing to move them to have faith, only intimidation and threats. Their conversion would be empty and ineffective. Again, as Richard of Middleton says, no one can believe unless he wills; but the will cannot be compelled, *ergo*. Besides, license to compel men in this way would be harmful, because if anyone could forcibly convert men to their own religion, the more powerful would drag many more into following their own evil heresies.

§2 NEVERTHELESS, Duns Scotus, in the passage cited above, holds that the opposing argument is, if not true, at least more probable; that is, that *if precautions are taken to ensure that these evil and undesirable consequences are avoided, a prince may forcibly convert pagans who live in his own kingdom*:

1. His proof begins with the canon *De Iudaeis* (*Decretum* D.45.5), which praises Sisebut, king of the Visigoths in Spain [612–621], for his decree ordering the conversion of all Jews. This edict was later revoked by the Council of Toledo [633–634] (*Concilium IV Toletanum* canon 57), but the words of the canon call Sisebut "most pious prince" and remark that the edict "would not have been revoked were it not for the undesirable consequences." *Ergo,* such a decree is lawful.

2. Consequently, assuming for the sake of argument that such an enactment is properly promulgated and published, all are obliged to believe in Christ, and they commit a sin if they refuse to accept the Christian religion.

3. The prince is empowered to punish and coerce those who commit this sin, just as he is for any other sin; further, by thus coercing them, the prince does not harm them, but benefits them; therefore he can coerce them.

4. "Ignorance makes an act involuntary," as is clear from Aristotle's *Nicomachean Ethics* 1110b 17–24; hence there is no injury (*iniuria*) to our Saracen because he *would* accept Christianity if he knew it was better, but in fact he is

ignorant of the faith. Hence his conversion is not involuntary; formally it may be so, but effectively it is voluntary. In the same way, in giving medicine to a patient who does not know that it is good for him, the doctor does no injury (*iniuria*) to the sick man; the latter takes the medicine without formally wishing to do so, to be sure, but in effect he does so willingly.

5. Again, if someone wished to commit suicide, I should be obliged to prevent him from doing so if I could by confiscating his weapons; I am therefore all the more obliged to prevent him from committing spiritual suicide.

6. Furthermore, the commonwealth has the authority to enact laws not only in civil matters, but also in matters of religion; this is part of natural law. Hence every Christian commonwealth has this power to use forcible conversion; *ergo*, any Christian king or commonwealth may lawfully compel their subjects to accept the Christian faith.

7. Their own priests have the power by natural law to instruct them and enact laws in religious matters, and their subjects are bound to obey them under pain of mortal sin, if the law is good. Hence a Christian prince may also compel his own subjects to accept his faith.

[From all this Gabriel Biel (1410–1495) accepts Scotus's opinion as probable, and goes no further than that (in *Sentences* IV.6).]

BUT ON THE OTHER HAND we must reply to this question by going back to our distinction. Some unbelievers are subjects of Christian princes, such as the Saracens who have settled in Spain; but *others are not subjects.*

I REPLY by asserting, first, that to compel those who are subjects is not intrinsically evil, like perjuring an oath; that is, it is not so evil that it cannot sometimes be a good deed. "It is evil," as Saint Thomas says, "but not so evil that it can never be good"; the proof being that it is not by definition so evil as to involve an inevitable breach of charity toward God or one's neighbor. It is not contrary to God's interest; indeed, it is clearly a great advancement of the Christian religion. Nor is it against our neighbor's interest, since it is to his benefit. The confirmation is that when we say something is "lawful," we are not obliged to prove the assertion until contrary proof is offered that it is harmful, according to the decretals *Sicut noxius* (X.2.23.1, and X.1.12.1). In the question under consideration, forcible conversion is in itself lawful, or at least not unlawful, and I am therefore not bound to prove that it is lawful.

Second, I assert that Christian princes have the authority to compel their subjects to believe; that is, if it be lawful to compel unbelievers. Christian princes may compel their own subjects not only in civil matters but also in religious ones; the commonwealth holds both civil and religious authority over its own subjects by natural law, and the prince has the same authority as the commonwealth over his subjects, be they pagans or not. Therefore, that the prince may not so compel them must be due not to lack of power, but to the expediency or otherwise of the policy.

Third, I agree with Saint Thomas that forcible conversion is evil. This is clear from the proof of the reply to the second argument, in the canon *De Iudaeis* (*Decretum* D.45.5).

Fourth, I assert that even if it is not evil *per se*, it is evil because of the evil consequences which it entrains. The proof that it is evil *per se* is that if faith must be received voluntarily, no one can receive it by coercion. And the undesirable consequences mentioned above need no further comment. They are confirmed by experience; we see that Saracens never become Christians; no, indeed, they are as much Moors as ever they were (*tan moros son agora como antes*).

Fifth, if all the evils and undesirable consequences are tolerable, Scotus's opinion is tenable. And this is what Scotus means when he says "if precautions are taken to ensure that evil and undesirable consequences are avoided." To do so, however, is difficult. Nevertheless, if the consequences can be avoided, it will be lawful to use forcible conversion, as Scotus says. The confirmation is to be found in Saint Thomas, *Summa Theologica* I-II.92.1, where he enquires what is the purpose of civil, that is, royal, power and replies that it is not only to preserve peace and good neighborliness, but also to make the citizens good and happy. But no one can be good unless he is Christian and accepts our faith; *ergo*. This is further confirmed by the fact that, from the standpoint of natural law, a prince or commonwealth is empowered to use coercion on them; hence a Christian prince to whom they are subject (may use coercion to convert them).

Sixth, I affirm that Saint Thomas's reply is more convincing than Scotus's, because he addresses the general question and the most usual circumstances, even though a different consequence may sometimes come about by particular circumstances (*per accidens*). The rule which Scotus sets up against Saint Thomas is, if you like, the exception to Saint Thomas's rule. This is confirmed by the traditional custom of the Church; the primitive Church in the times of Augustine [354–430] and Jerome [ca. 342–420] [see Figures 16 and 17 and their introduction] not only did not use coercion, but even refused to grant immediate acceptance to those catechumens who came to the faith of their own accord, making them wait so that they would later be constant in the faith. This is how it should be done.

TO THE FIRST, concerning Duns Scotus's argument concerning King Sisebut, I reply that the king is praised for his zeal and piety, but not for the deed itself, which indeed earned him a rebuke for breaking the strict prohibition against any forcible baptism of unbelievers. And the text of the canon also adduces the argument that God "hath mercy on whom He will have mercy, and whom He will be hardeneth" (Romans 9:18), for faith is a gift from God. All the same, Sisebut was a most pious king, and was perhaps counselled by his bishops to use force in that way.

TO THE SECOND, even granting that they are obliged to receive the faith, this argument implies only that forcible baptism is lawful, and hence that if there are no undesirable consequences they may be coerced. But this does not contradict Saint Thomas.

TO THE THIRD we may reply in the same way. In addition, I assert that an injustice (*iniuria*) is done them, because their liberty is taken away. If a king were to force someone to take a rich and beautiful woman to wife, even a princess, although he might be obliged to marry her and might even find it hard to make a better match, he would nevertheless be wronged if he was coerced.

TO THE FOURTH, that those who are unwilling through ignorance are not in effect being coerced at all, the reply is that this argument proves only that forcible baptism would be lawful if there were no undesirable consequences; but that is all. In addition, I assert that a wrong is done to them, and that they are indeed acting under compulsion "formally speaking"—just like the man who is compelled to marry a wife who is good, but of whom he himself is invincibly ignorant.

TO THE FIFTH I reply that it remains dangerous to coerce anyone in matters of religion, however advisable it may be in other cases. Therefore the analogy is valid.

TO THE SIXTH I concede the premise entirely; but only so long as no undesirable consequences or other evils ensue.

T0 THE SEVENTH I reply that Saracen priests have their authority to coerce subjects because the Saracens themselves have given them the power to teach them in matters of religion. Hence they would commit a sin not merely by refusing to listen to their teaching, but even by not obeying it. In the same way, if the majority of their commonwealth were to accept the Christian faith, the minority who refused to accept it could be compelled to do so by the majority, so long as the faith was sufficiently preached.

THIS CONCLUDES WHAT I HAVE TO SAY about unbelievers who are subjects.

§3 IT MAY BE ASKED, however, regarding the other kind who are not subjects, *whether Christian princes can convert them by violence and the sword, if no scandal or undesirable consequences ensue*? The reply is that they cannot, because the king of Spain has no greater power over them than I do over my fellow citizens; but I cannot compel a fellow citizen to hear Mass; *ergo*.

A DOUBT ARISES whether, given that these unbelievers cannot be compelled to keep the Christian law in this way, *whether they can be compelled to keep the law of nature, which is common to all*? Some reply that they can; that our king can compel these barbarians to keep the law of nature just as I can compel someone not to commit suicide. They prove this by saying that all men profess the law of nature; and, as Saint Thomas puts it, "Whoever accepts the law of Christ can be compelled to keep it."

The reply to this is that there are some sins against nature which are harmful to our neighbors, such as cannibalism or euthanasia of the old and senile, which is practiced in Terra Firma [evidently the American mainlands]; and since the defense of our neighbors is the rightful concern of each of us, even for private persons and even if it involves shedding blood, it is beyond doubt that any Christian prince can compel them not to do these things. By this title alone the emperor is empowered to coerce the Caribbean Indians (*insulani*).

Second, I assert that princes can compel unbelievers who are their temporal subjects to abandon their sins against the commonwealth, because they are subject in temporal matters to their kings. And since the emperor is empowered to make laws for the utility of the commonwealth, if there are any sins against the temporal and human good of the commonwealth, he can compel them to abandon them.

Third, I assert that the faithful cannot compel unbelievers to keep an obvious law of nature, unless it is necessary for the good and peace of the Christian commonwealth, or unless its breach harms a neighbor in the way I have explained.

This I think is most certain. Nor do they have any right to act against the infidels solely on the grounds that the latter do not observe the law of nature. If they did have such a right, a Christian king could also compel them to abandon their idols, and that would mean leaving them without any law. That is false; *ergo*.

A DOUBT ARISES whether it is lawful to smash down the idols of these barbarians, once the faith has been preached to them and they have refused to accept it? It seems that it is lawful because it does them no harm or wrong. The reply is that it is not evil *per se* to do so, being against neither the honor of God nor the good of a neighbor, since it does not harm them. But I say that this ought not to be done on every occasion, primarily because it may provoke their fierce indignation, and destroy any kind feelings toward us which they may happen to have. Among peoples where the majority have been converted, however, or where it is to be hoped they may be converted by such actions, it will be quite lawful. I say the same of their temples; they should not be thrown down, because this is an injury (*iniuria*) to their rights, and because even after they are thrown down, they will rebuild them.

§4 A FURTHER DOUBT ARISES *whether unbelievers may at least be indirectly coerced*, for instance, by taxes and levies by which they may be encouraged to become converts to the faith? The compiler of the *Decretales Gregorii IX*, Raymond of Peñafort [ca. 1175–1275, General of the Dominican Order and friend of Aquinas], wrote elsewhere (*Summa de poenitentia*) that this would be laudable if it were customary, but that it ought not to be introduced as a novelty because of the provocation it would cause, which we ought always to avoid for fear of giving "occasion of stumbling," as Paul makes clear in 1 Corinthians 10:23–33 and 2 Corinthians 6:3. Therefore, it would be a good thing only if laws were passed on this matter; and he cites the canon *Non debet* (*Decretum* C.11.3.64). From this I deduce that Raymond's decision was that it ought not to be done.

IN THIS REGARD, it should be noted that "taxes (*tributum*) and levies (*exactio*)" are of two kinds. One kind may justly be imposed on unbelievers even without their being converted to the faith, such as tributes appropriate to the time and place raised at the outbreak of war, which even unbelievers can understand to be just; the proof is that such tributes could be imposed on them even if they were Christians, and may therefore be imposed on them while they are still unbelievers (I am talking, of course, of unbelievers who live in Christian lands and are subjects of Christian princes). Indeed, they may be required to pay tributes from which Christians are exempted, so long as their fiscal burden is moderate and not increased by the fact that Christians are exempted.

Second, I assert that if the tribute is unjust and immoderate, it cannot be demanded of them. From this it follows that the king can justly order the expulsion of the Saracens from our country if they pose a probable threat of subverting the faithful or overturning the homeland. He may legitimately do this because, even if he knows that it may cause them to be converted to the faith, they are not thereby forced to convert. He could not do it, perhaps with the actual intention of using the fear of exile, which affects even the most strong-minded of men, to effect their conversion; but, as long as that intention is absent, he is empowered to use his rights, whatever the consequences. If he cannot exercise direct compulsion over them, he can make a law ordering the exile from his kingdom of anyone who refuses to become a Christian. That this is lawful is proved by the fact that in other matters where compulsion is unlawful, he may employ the same device. For instance, the law states that any Saracen who sleeps with a Christian woman is punishable by death. If one were caught doing so, the king is empowered to put him to death, whether he sticks to his perfidious creed or whether he becomes a Christian; but he also has the power to pardon him from the death penalty if he is willing to become a Christian, even though his conversion would have come about under fear of death. This would be perfectly fair, because the king would be using his rights.

But as for tributes which cannot also be demanded of the faithful, I assert that they cannot be demanded of unbelievers with the intention of making them convert. Unbelievers cannot be deprived of their goods on the grounds of their unbelief, any more than other Christians, because they possess true right of ownership (*dominium rerum*) over their own property. By the same token, it is clear that they cannot be burdened with greater fiscal obligations than are lawful in the case of the faithful. In saying this, I mean that such impositions are unlawful *per se*, that is, in the absence of any additional cause, such as a crime perpetrated by the unbelievers, or some previous pact; because of Saracens, Jews, or other unbelievers who, either through some criminal action of their own or by the law of war, were in a position to be killed or despoiled of their goods, were to be burdened by heavier taxes than the Christian part of the population, this would not be unjust. For example, if the Saracens were to petition for the right to live among us Christians on the agreement that they pay double tribute, no wrong would be done them if we were then to demand such tribute. Therefore, such exactions could justly be levied upon them by our princes for that purpose.

For that purpose, yes; but could they impose heavier taxes on them to force them to convert? This is still in doubt, since we agree that it is not lawful to use fear and violence to convert them. For myself, I have little doubt that more of them could be converted by greater leniency; and they would be likely to remain firmer in the faith. See Saint Thomas's *Opusculum XXI ad ducissam Brabantiae*, where he explains all this: how the prince may impose heavier taxes on them than on Christians, but not excessive ones, and many other useful remarks on the subject.

§5 IT IS ARGUED, nevertheless, that they can be directly compelled, because Saint Thomas says that they can be compelled *for blasphemy*. But all unbelievers blaspheme continually; therefore it is always lawful to compel them, because they hinder our faith with their blasphemies.

The reply is that unbelievers may blaspheme in two ways. The first is if their blasphemies are an injury (*iniuria*) or impediment to Christians, for instance, if they were to send us a letter full of blasphemies. In this case we may set aside any question of faith; we may go to war against them solely on the grounds that they have done us injury (*iniuria*). But if they keep their blasphemies to themselves, we cannot use this alone as grounds for declaring war against them. We are well aware that both Jews and heathens blaspheme the name of Christ among themselves, but we cannot for this reason alone go to war with them.

A DOUBT ARISES whether princes may lawfully coerce them with threats and intimidation? It seems that they can, because Christ forced Paul to believe by casting him to the ground and blinding him (Acts 9:3–9); therefore the same can be done to unbelievers. The reply is that it is not lawful for all of us to do everything which God is permitted to do, because we are not the masters of mankind as Christ is. Hence, Christ could coerce not only Paul, but the whole world, and He could have left this power to the Church; but He did not. Second, I reply that if it were in our power to move hearts, as Christ could, then it would be lawful for us to behave in this way; but He made Paul believe, not by intimidation but by divine inspiration. It is clear from this that masters, contrary to their own belief, do not have the power to put their infidel servants to death, nor to inflict unjust punishments on them. It is lawful, on the other hand, to give preferential treatment to those of their slaves who are Christians, as opposed to those who are not, as Nicolaus de Tudeschis [1386–1445, canon lawyer and archbishop of Palermo] says of the Jews in his commentary on the decretal *Nouit* (X.2.1.13), where he also holds that unbelievers can be compelled to observe the whole of natural law, because they can be restrained from committing homicide, and also from usury, as stated in the decretal *Usurarum* (*Sext* 5.5.1). But it will not always be lawful to compel them in every matter to do with natural law; they cannot be forcibly compelled to abandon polygamy, for example, or other such practices. In fact, Nicolaus de Tudeschis's examples only serve to prove what I have already said, namely, that they can be forced not to upset the commonwealth, and not to harm their Christian neighbors.

A FINAL DOUBT ARISES whether unbelievers who have not themselves received the faith, but whose parents were converts who have since apostatized, can be forcibly baptized? In other words, can someone who is not baptized but whose father was baptized be compelled to accept baptism? The question is raised by Pierre de la Palu [ca. 1270/1280–1342, a Dominican and titular patriarch of Jerusalem] in his commentary on Lombard's *Sentences* IV.4.4. He comes to no firm decision, but seems to be saying that they can be compelled because the Church has the right to enforce baptism on the children of Christians even against their own or their parents' will, and there is no apparent reason why it should have lost this right in the present case; therefore the Church can use compulsion. I believe that in this case they should indeed be compelled. But against this, it would follow that the Christians can compel Saracens any of whose forefathers were baptized. For example, let us suppose for the argument that the present-day Saracens are separated from these forefathers by ten generations; the argument then runs that the Church had the right to baptize the children of their forefather nine generations back, and hence the children of their forefather eight generations back, and so on down to the present generation; *ergo*. In reply, one may say that if it could be established beyond doubt that these Saracens were the distant descendants of Christians, and if they could be forcibly converted without provocation, then it ought to be done. But the Church does not do so, because it cannot be established, and also because of the inevitable unrest which would ensue.

 9

Two Woodcuts Accompanying a 1509 German Translation of Amerigo Vespucci's Letter to Pietro Soderini

(1504)

The rights and obligations set down by the Catholic monarchs for Christopher Columbus on the eve of his first voyage into the "Ocean Sea" were specific on matters of trade and political possession, but the document is tellingly vague about the destination of the voyage. One learns only from other sources that Columbus and many of his contemporaries expected outer islands and eventually Asia to appear over the horizon. Greater certainty was not soon in coming. The humanist courtier, Peter Martyr of Anghiera (1457–1526), sifted through the first accounts of the islands and mainlands in the Ocean Sea and wrote cautiously of a "new world"—new, that is, from his own perspective and those of his ancient and medieval predecessors. The lands discovered by the westward voyagers, Martyr informed his readers, appeared not to be part of the continent formed by Africa, Asia, and Europe. And yet if they did turn out to be part of one of these, it would have to be Asia. Martyr's caution in the face of the information he was receiving is instructive. He could conceive of a new world, one outside the bounds of what was known in the old, but he did so without abandoning an intellectual tradition and worldview that also influenced his seagoing contemporaries. One of these contemporaries was the Genoese, Columbus, and another was Amerigo Vespucci (1454–1512) of Florence.

Vespucci was educated by his uncle, the scholarly Dominican friar Giorgio Antonio Vespucci, who was also a tutor to Pietro Soderini, who would rise to become head of the Florentine republic (1502–1512). It was to Soderini that Vespucci would later address a long letter describing his four voyages to the Indies. Amerigo's route to the sea came through the business of banking. As a young man he became a clerk in the banking house of the powerful Medici family in Florence, and found a patron in Lorenzo di Pier Francesco de Medici, another eventual recipient of his letters on the Indies. In 1492, Medici dispatched Vespucci to supervise business dealings in Seville's port of Cádiz in southern Spain. After his commission for the banking house was completed, Vespucci remained in Cádiz as an independent trader and speculator and thus was in the perfect spot to learn of events transpiring on the Ocean Sea and to get himself involved. He joined an expedition of reconnaissance to the Indies sponsored by King Ferdinand in 1497–98, probably serving as an astronomer or cartographer. Also in the service of Spain, Vespucci returned to the Indies in 1499–1500 as a ship's pilot. He sailed twice more to the Indies, in 1501–02 and 1503–04, as ship's captain in the service of the Portuguese Crown.

Vespucci is most famous for his *Mundus Novus* ("New World"), a Latin translation of a lost original letter to his Medici patron in 1502. It first appeared in Paris in 1503 and was endlessly translated and adapted thereafter. Vespucci's accounts of his explorations of American coastlines made him an instant rival to Columbus, both as an explorer and as an authority on geography. Historians have often credited Vespucci with having recognized that the shores and islands of the Caribbean were not part of a gateway to Asia, as Columbus believed, but lands then unknown to Europeans. However, any such recognition on his part seems to have had little immediate impact, at least in the interested Spanish circles. Of considerably more lasting influence were his descriptions of foreign peoples and lands. Like the information to appear in Columbus's journal, Vespucci's sometimes fantastical observations drew inspiration and details from an array of descriptive models in European classical and medieval literature—Herodotus, the Irish Saint Brendan, the Venetian Marco Polo, and the travels of the fictitious knight Sir John Mandeville, among them—and would themselves find echoes in many later accounts of Indians and America, including the eighteenth-century travel account by Concolorcorvo (see Selection 41). Well into the 1530s, rumors about unknown American regions and their strange inhabitants persisted, despite a steady succession of exploratory and military enterprises.

Vespucci's "Letter to Soderini," written on September 4, 1504, and published in 1505 or 1506 in Florence, excited as much interest as had his previous missive. As before, translations of the letter into other western European vernacular languages and Latin promptly appeared, sometimes altering the original in order to amplify Vespucci's most fabulous points. And not only the texts were altered in translation and adaptation: the versions were rarely accompanied by the same illustrations. As was also the case with Columbus's earlier descriptions, pictures were left to individual printers and artists. Figures 5 and 6 are the elaborate woodcuts from a 1509 German edition of the "Letter to Soderini" printed by Johannes Grüninger in Strassburg.

The artist who created these images had never been to a Caribbean island or an American coastline, so the woodcuts prompt many questions about the impact of the earliest reports from America on contemporary European minds. What images would be spurred by the mixture of the artist's own notions with Vespucci's words? How would the lands and peoples ostensibly described in the letter be represented? Which depictive norms would prove "naturally" useful and which would have to be invented? And how would one render the first moments of encounter between peoples hitherto unknown to one another? The two images, like the early written account they illustrated, were parts of an atmosphere of mounting speculation and uncertainty about the nature of the Indies and their peoples. They were meant to excite the interest of patrons and general audiences alike. They were meant to fire imagination and ambition.

Projecting from what he had read or heard, it was the artist's task to render peoples and landscape. The written descriptions of Columbus and Vespucci (not to mention later ones by Cortés and others) are purposeful and aimed at further sponsorship: bizarre customs and other deficiencies demanded correction. In his journal, Columbus wrote that the Taíno Indians had nothing he could call religion. On one occasion, he came upon "a beautiful house"; and although he "thought it was a temple" and "made signs to ask if they said prayers in it," the people told him it was not as he guessed. Communication faltered as opportunity beckoned. Once their language is properly learned, wrote Columbus to his sovereigns, returning to his theme in his entry for November 27, 1492, "it will be easy [to convert these people to Christianity], for they have no faith and do not worship idols; Your Majesties will have a city and a fort built here and these lands will be converted."

Vespucci's text, the woodcut artist's principal cue in the images being considered here, often recalls Columbus's absolute statements in allegedly describing Amerindian life. Vespucci admires Caribbean peoples for their physical skills such as running and swimming. But, as Columbus was wont to do, he remarks that they are completely shameless about their nakedness; they have no possessions beyond a few colored feathers and necklaces featuring fishbones and small stones; they have no guiding rhythm to their lives, no order, no trade, nothing to obey; they have no set mealtimes and would rather eat off the ground whenever they please, and they do not seem ever to want to cut their hair; there is no marriage practised among them; they have no justice, not even to discipline their children. This new world emerges as a place of deficiency and "barbaric" customs. Civilization, to a contemporary European reader and viewer, is turned on its head.

In the first image four Indians of both sexes are grouped in the foreground. The man seated in the center, with his head in one hand, is the picture of tedium. His boredom

Figure 5. Illustration from a German translation of Amerigo Vespucci's letter to Pietro Soderini, Strassburg, 1509.

sets the stage. To either side of him, a woman casually dandles her child and a second man tends to his bow. The turn of their heads and the man's gesture with his free hand suggest a domestic chat, but all around this relaxing scene there are surprises. Just behind them, taking a direct prompt from Vespucci's letter, a man shows no inhibition about urinating in public. In his letter describing his first voyage along Caribbean coastlines and beginning up the Atlantic coast of North America, Vespucci remarks that although the Indians were discreet in defecating, they made water wherever and whenever they pleased, even "while standing speaking to us." Farther in the background, in front of some strangely shaped dwellings, a butcher and his mate matter-of-factly chop up human limbs. Faithful to his text, the artist maximizes the shock to his viewer by integrating the startling and peculiar as familiar in the Indians' daily life.

In the portion of the letter describing his third voyage down the Atlantic coast of South America, Vespucci tells of an encounter between a member of his crew and a group of native women who were perhaps Guaraní. The Europeans had come ashore in small boats and were waiting to pick up two crewmen who had gone inland a few days before, seeking knowledge of the land—its riches, spices, and peoples. One young sailor went among the Indians who had come down from a hill, while the other Europeans remained in their boats "to reassure them." According to Vespucci, a group of women surrounded the man, "touching him and gazing at him in wonder." Encircled as he was, the man did not see another woman descend from a hill behind him and raise a club to deliver a blow to his head. The man dropped dead among the women, who dragged him by his feet toward the hill, while the Indian men rushed to the beach firing arrows at the boats. A few gunshots from the Europeans in the boats had little effect beyond frightening the Indians back up the hill, Vespucci laments, and their admiral forbade the crew to mount an attack and avenge the death. The author reports that he and his companions watched in horror as the women cut their victim into bits, "roasting him before our eyes, holding up several pieces toward us and eating them," and leaving few doubts as to the fate of the two other seamen.

Our second image has been drawn from the description of this incident. The scene is of a beach near a rocky hill. In the right foreground a naked woman is about to club a clothed European from behind. A trio of naked women with long, wild hair seems to welcome and caress the man. The juxtaposition sets established European notions of femininity beside barbarism and brute violence. On the hill behind, a woman embraces a man and looks up at him smiling; another man with his hands clasped in front of his chest gazes calmly to the side. Yet, for the European eye, there are more surprises in store. In addition to the woman with the club in the foreground, within the normality of the group on the hill a person is seen heading into a cave on hands and knees.

For the author, the unfamiliar had to be rendered to excite interest but also to be understandable and convincing. Vespucci, echoing Columbus, asks for evidence of an indigenous religious or moral code of conduct to help him understand. He asks for a parallel between the Indians and familiar non-Christian peoples in Europe's present and past. He asks for things that might be called offerings, sacrifices, or a church. But instead of similitude he turned up differences. "We did not learn that they had any law, nor can they be called Moors or Jews," he writes, "and [they are] worse than pagans: because we did not observe that they offered any sacrifice; nor even had they a house of prayer." The woodcut artist drew from similar cultural wells. His depictions of Vespucci's sylvan landscape populated by naked peoples with long, unkempt hair met what many contemporaries were predisposed to see, borrowing from long-established images of heathen and "wild people."

But what else was conveyed in these woodcuts produced in Germany, where Vespucci's accounts were so often reprinted, adapted, and illustrated? What would the images inspire in their viewers? Wonder?

Figure 6. Illustration from a German translation of Amerigo Vespucci's letter to Pietro Soderini, Strassburg, 1509.

Revulsion? Perhaps fear? Both Columbus's and Vespucci's descriptions of first contact emphasized the Indians' fear. The naked people ran for the hills at the sight of the Europeans and their ships. Vespucci opined that one group of Indians was terrified and rejected gestures of friendliness and peace on seeing the newcomers to be clothed and so different in appearance from themselves. Have the Europeans and Indians reversed roles in the Grüninger woodcuts of 1509? The pictorial new world seems a tempting place in which Europeans might lose not only their lives but also their cultural bearings. Regardless of the inaccuracies and exaggerations in the artist's depictions, to Europeans contemplating these images the Indians appear at home and free to behave in their startling ways. Arguably, it is the Indians and their environment that inspire fear. They are powerful, like the woman's raised club or a rumor of cannibalism. Theirs might be a power poised to threaten degeneration and death as much as to invite domination and desire.

10

Christoph Weiditz's Drawing of an Indian Woman of Mexico

(1529)

In 1528 the conqueror of Tenochtitlan, Hernán Cortés, returned home in order to defend himself before Charles V (both king of Spain and Holy Roman Emperor) against allegations of rebellion while in Mexico. The numerous "treasures" he brought from the lands formerly ruled by the Aztecs included human specimens. Like the letters from Mexico written to Charles V by Cortés, such "treasures" from hitherto unknown civilizations across the seas helped to justify his overstepping of the rules. They also excited imperial support for more ventures in the most alluring "kingdom" yet stumbled upon in the Indies. One sign of the conqueror's rehabilitation in official eyes was an arresting medallion portrait struck by a young German medalist named Christoph Weiditz, for which Cortés almost certainly sat in 1529.

Weiditz, who practiced his craft in Augsburg, had traveled to Spain that year as part of a small group of artists from southern Germany summoned to the roving court of Charles V. In Toledo, Weiditz must have met not only Cortés but also the human "treasures" from Mexico, a number of whom became the subjects of the thirteen drawings of Indians that the German executed. These drawings form one of a number of subgroups within the body of his 154 sketches of diverse subjects and regional peoples in Spain and the Netherlands in the space of the next three years (his drawing of the Morisco woman and her daughter, Figure 8 in Selection 11, is part of another such subgroup). The bold lines and shading in the drawings may indicate that Weiditz intended them as bases for later woodcuts, yet his *Trachtenbuch* (costume book) of colored drawings remained unpublished until 1927.

Seven of the thirteen drawings of Indians depict men with grayish-brown skin and thick, shoulder-length black hair playing games with stones and a ball, or else juggling and tossing a log with their feet. These active figures wear very little, although jewels set in the skin of their cheeks, foreheads, and lips, single earrings, feathered belts, and anklets are prominent adornments. These Indians performed in Toledo before Charles V and a larger audience that probably included Weiditz. Cortés also sent the jugglers on to Rome in the same year to appear before Pope Clement VII, who was said to have "thanked God that such countries had been discovered in these days." Along with Weiditz, the Indians from Mexico may even have accompanied the court to the Netherlands in 1530–31.

Figure 7. Drawing of an Indian woman of Mexico by Christoph Weiditz, 1529.
Courtesy of Dover Publications, New York.

Weiditz did not sketch the seven native Mexican men in repose, but rather chose to depict them performing. The inscriptions on the first two—probably written later by a scribe, though perhaps based on Weiditz's own scribblings from the time—stress the curiosity of the games and actions. "These are the Indian people whom Ferdinand Cortez brought to His Imperial Majesty from India and they have played before His Imperial Majesty with wood and ball," the first one announces. And the second, reflecting on a Mediterranean parallel in the street game of *mora,* states that "with their fingers they gamble like the Italians."

Less active, but perhaps even more curious and novel to the artist, was the Indian woman of Figure 7. She is one of six women whom Weiditz portrayed standing alone (several hold "exotic" accoutrements such as a decorated drinking jug, a feather sunshade and colorful parrot, and an elaborate spear and shield). What might her gaze and stance mean? She looks away from the viewer; her demeanor, while not subdued, seems, more than anything, posed. She is isolated from her social context and makes no gesture. Yet is she not as much a displaced "performer" as the ball players and log jugglers? Was this even her clothing, festive or otherwise? She was brought from Mexico and then draped and adorned in order to be seen by an emperor and, after him, by many crowds, among which must have been Christoph Weiditz, who recorded her thus. She stands simply—barefoot, covered by a fine garment of feathers with colored borders, an elegant headdress falling to her left shoulder, and a golden necklace with a red stone at the center at her throat—like a museum piece.

11

Christoph Weiditz's Drawing of a Morisco Woman and Her Daughter at Home

(1529)

Although his many drawings of baggage carts, wagons, and people on horseback suggest that Christoph Weiditz accompanied the imperial court through Castile to Catalonia in 1529, it is not known for certain if the artist from Augsburg ever traveled to the southern kingdom of Granada during his time in Spain. Although the vividness of his set of eleven scenes of Granadine Moriscos (new converts to Christianity from Islam) dancing and working, at home and traveling, might suggest the experience of a keen observer who walked the city streets and countryside and quickly sketched what he saw, one cannot be sure of this experience. Weiditz would have known the contemporary genre of costume books. He may have drawn inspiration and details of Morisco costume and general appearance from existing pictorial sources and perceptions gained from his Spanish Christian hosts.

The German's interest in the Moriscos of Granada, as opposed to the Moriscos living in Valencia, for instance (people virtually in the path of the court in 1529), may have come from their recent conquest by Castilian Christians (1492) and their apparently greater preservation of Muslim traditions. It was not as if the Arabic language and numerous non-Christian customs and practices were not retained by Moriscos in the Kingdom of Aragon, particularly in certain small communities and rural regions, for they certainly were (see Selection 15, a letter from Fray Juan Izquierdo on the subject of the Moriscos of Valencia). But by the end of the third decade of the sixteenth century, many other Aragonese Moriscos were highly "Spanish" and "Christian" in comportment and appearance. Moreover, even though a royal decree requiring that Aragonese Moriscos be baptized was not issued until 1526 (twenty-two years after the decree demanding the baptisms of the Moriscos of Castile, with the Granadine population foremost among them), the Aragonese and the Valencian Moriscos were more familiar, albeit marginalized, inhabitants of a land subsumed beneath Spanish Christian overlordship almost three centuries before. (Valencia was taken by James I of Aragon, "the Conqueror," in 1238.) For the early sixteenth-century traveler in the Spanish kingdoms, the concentrations of more northerly Moriscos would not have possessed the lure and reputation of the peoples of Granada.

Somewhat like the Mexican Indians drawn by Weiditz in the same year, the Moriscos of

Granada would have offered a vision of a recently conquered people, still "exotic" in costume and custom. In the drawing reproduced in Figure 8, the curiosity of the home dress of a Morisco woman and her daughter is emphasized. "In this manner the Morisco women [of Granada] dress in their house with their children," the inscription reads. Weiditz's choice of the Granadine subjects seems to affirm a belief that only from Granada—or at least from the sources that he consulted or copied—might expressions of such difference be gained and considered.

By the end of the third decade of the sixteenth century, when Weiditz was in Spain, the newly converted of Granada were increasingly being perceived by Spanish authorities as the stubborn remnants of the last Muslim stronghold in western Europe. Only three years before, after a crucial *junta* in Granada presided over by Charles V himself, these Moriscos were declared subject to the authority of the Holy Office of the Inquisition, the ultimate policing body of Catholic Christian orthodoxy. Although a tradition of negotiated delays in the implementation of full-blown inquisitorial persecution of Moriscos would continue even after the pronouncements of this *junta* in 1526, the decision is an early sign of the demands on the newly converted from Islam that would only harden and be reiterated as the sixteenth century proceeded. Morisco practices involving the preparation of food, regular bathing, and dress were only the most notorious among customs once permitted by Spanish Christian officialdom, but increasingly found intolerable. Certain Moriscos argued eloquently that the conversions to Christianity of many of their number were genuine, and that their surviving manners of dress, Arabic names, and numerous other daily practices were now regional expressions divested of religious, and certainly of seditious, meaning. Nonetheless, a growing share of Morisco culture was seen as suspect, part of what was responsible for the perceived nonassimilation of the Morisco population and all the danger it could seem to represent for Old Christians at a time when a Muslim menace was perceived from without (from Turks as well as Barbary pirates) as well as from within.

The official demands made on Spanish Morisco society (and not just in the Kingdom of Granada) are comparable to what was experienced by many indigenous societies in the Americas in early colonial times. The jostle of evangelization strategies, debates over the appropriate jurisdictions of the Holy Office, and the constant interplay between optimism and pessimism in the evangelization settings of America are of a piece with developments among the Moriscos before their expulsion (mostly to North Africa) between 1609 and 1614.

Weiditz's image of a Morisca and her daughter at home invites such a comparison, especially with respect to dress and to the representation of cultural and religious "others." Granadine Morisco clothing underwent changes comparable to transformations seen in Amerindian societies in the core areas of Spanish-Indian interaction in contemporary Spanish America. Generally speaking, the subject populations' dress altered more in the cities than in the countryside, and men took on more Hispanicized garments (and economic pursuits) than women. In the case of Granada, Moriscas who walked in the streets had been required to abandon their traditional covering of the face. But they had substituted a wide mantle, like the one worn by the girl in this picture, which was nearly as effective a concealment. At home, of course, modest covering was of less importance, as Weiditz's drawing conveys.

Four of Weiditz's depictions of Moriscos could be described as lacking social context, in the manner of the Indian woman of Figure 7 (Selection 10). The others, however, capture people engaged in real activities: sweeping a floor, spinning, carrying bread, dancing in a group accompanied by musicians, traveling with their families through the countryside with a horse, or simply walking and gesturing.

The woman in Figure 8 is accompanied by a female child (one assumes it is her

Figure 8. Drawing of a Morisco woman and her daughter at home by Christoph Weiditz, 1529.
Courtesy of Dover Publications, New York.

daughter), whom she is either pointing out (or perhaps disciplining) while pulling her closer by the wrist. As we have noted, it is unclear whether Weiditz was ever in Granada, let alone taken to the home of a Morisco family. Yet it is a credit to the artist's mind and hand that in looking at this drawing one can imagine a domestic situation intruded upon by a foreign visitor expressing an interest in family members and their clothing. The dress is elaborate, suggesting perhaps noble lineage or considerable wealth. One interpretation of the woman's gesture would tell of her pride in her daughter's fine costume (although one cannot see its colors in our reproduction): a green, gold, and white striped mantle with golden edges, worn over a red-and-silver-embossed dress lined in blue, with gold buttons, along with purple stockings.

If Weiditz himself did not visit the home of a Morisco family in Granada, then the Spanish sources from which he drew shared with him an intimate knowledge of (or at least the appearance of) some of Granada's Moriscos. Does the familiarity in the gestures and action of the Morisco mother and child lessen the exoticism of the exotic, creating pictorial space for subjects who are better known to the Spanish Christian than indigenous peoples of the Americas and, thus, more than museum pieces? What are the ramifications of seeming to be better known to one's conqueror and, alternatively, to being hitherto unknown in all but reinterpreted legend? Christoph Weiditz's drawing of the Moriscas challenges the viewer to reinvestigate the drawing of the Mexican woman—the one who had been brought to Europe—by the same artist in the same year, and to think over what the study of Spanish Christians, Moriscos, and Indians might contribute to the interlocking history of the Spanish world.

PART II

The Americas as New Worlds for All?

12

Fray Pedro de Gante's Letter to Charles V, Mexico City

(1552)

This letter to the king about the dangers to the Christian evangelization of Mexico, and the abuse of Indians and threats to their spiritual and temporal survival near Mexico City in the first decades of colonial rule, must have caught the attention of its recipient. The author, Fray Pedro de Gante (Peter of Ghent), reputedly a bastard son of the Holy Roman Emperor, Frederick III, or of his son Maximilian (and therefore a kinsman of Charles V), was a near-legendary figure to early Spanish and Indian chroniclers. He arrived in New Spain in 1523, nine months before Martín de Valencia and "the Twelve" were sent out with their orders from Fray Francisco de los Angeles (see Selection 7), and he began the long, exhausting labor of evangelization and instruction that earned him the reputation of a beloved "soul of iron."

Gante was known for his austerity. He repeatedly refused ordination and a bishopric, preferring the humble title of *lego*, or lay brother. He was tirelessly committed to teaching and founded as many as one hundred churches and Indian schools by 1529. The first school, San José de los Naturales, was situated in the courtyard of the main Franciscan church in Mexico City, where Moctezuma's fantastic aviary had been located. It remained his home base to the end of his long life in 1572. There, having learned Nahuatl, he taught Christian doctrine, arithmetic, music, various trades, and the rudiments of reading and writing Castilian and Latin to as many as six hundred Indian boys at a time. Alonso de Montúfar, the second archbishop of Mexico, reportedly said, "I am not the real archbishop because that person is a lay brother, Pedro de Gante." In 1529, Gante succinctly described his life in Mexico: "In the daytime I teach reading, writing, and singing; at night I read the catechism and preach."

This blunt letter highlights a festering dilemma in the Spanish colonial enterprise: the repeated intention that Indians must have the opportunity to know God and be saved; and the inevitable, indispensable requirement that they serve the Spaniards, both the king and colonists. To Gante in 1552, these two purposes were not simply in tension; overwork, mistreatment, frivolous litigation, and other abuses threatened to overwhelm a declining Indian population and prevent them from becoming true Christians.

There is a message of impending crisis. Gante warns that Indians might simply disappear due to illness and overwork. They now had no time to attend classes or even Sunday

Mass. Indians of Mexico City had lost their hospital, and Gante's pupils no longer had the resources needed to pursue their studies. He was concerned, too, about the declining authority of the friars. "Until recently, we friars resolved their [Indians'] disputes," he says in describing the growing influence of lawyers and courts. Another preoccupation was the likely substitution of diocesan priests for friars in the pastoral work.

Gante was not like Dominican friar Bartolomé de Las Casas, the most famous voice of protest over the Spaniards' mistreatment of Indians in the sixteenth century, who, in old age, became a thundering opponent of the entire colonial enterprise apart from evangelization. Like Las Casas, however, Gante understood that "it is the struggle for their salvation that justifies their discovery." He could be a fierce critic of abusive Spanish conduct and yearned for an order to society that kept spiritual ends clearly in view. At the same time, Gante urged a balance of interests: a moderation of the Crown's tribute tax and the endless appetite for Indian labor in Mexico City, which would give Indians time to provide for their families and the opportunity to become good Christians. Indians emerge here as people in need of places of "consolation," separate places for their spiritual growth, but always in the company of the friars. He regarded the people of central Mexico as able children in need of closer tutelage and paternal care—not, as for Las Casas, as equals of Europeans. He continually appealed for more friars as well as for Indians' relief from tax and labor demands.

The ways of the veteran mentor appear on every page of the letter. He skillfully cajoles his royal interlocutor, reminding him of their shared Flemish roots and personal acquaintance, pointing out the friars' decades of self-abnegation and vital service to God and Crown in this faraway land, pointing out the heavy weight of the king's moral responsibility, and reminding him that he is accountable to God. Last, he offers practical solutions, emphasizing and repeating his key points for effect ("above all," "I firmly believe," he keeps saying) and expressing paternal concern for his Indian flock. This text has the special immediacy and credibility of an elderly man famous for his relentless integrity who spent his energies for the cause he proclaims, but who knows that he will never be able to discuss these urgent matters in person with the king. Gante does not want to give in, "to see the early achievements reduced to nothing."

May the very high Emperor of the Heavens, whose place you occupy on Earth, extend your life and protect your Royal person in His holy service so that your vassals and clergymen may benefit as you favor the poor. And after your blessed journey has been completed, may you go on to glory. Amen.

I am a member of the order of the blessed Saint Francis, native of the city of Ghent, and chaplain in Your Majesty's service. I came from the aforementioned city to the kingdoms of Spain with the armada in which Your Majesty traveled. I accompanied your confessor, Father Clupion, who disembarked at Santander, on the same boat in which Fray Joan de Teta, guardian of the Franciscan monastery of Ghent, also traveled by your order. Along with another friar, he and I went to New Spain at your behest, and we were the first members of a religious order to go there. And Our Lord chose to take Fray Juan de Teta and our other companion to Him almost as soon as we arrived because they died during the discovery of Honduras with the marqués [Fernando Cortés, Marqués del Valle]. I was left alone to do what I could by the Lord's inspiration to try to bring these natives to the faith. Soon another twelve Franciscans arrived, sent by Your Majesty.

I sometimes intended to write an account to Your Majesty as the first to come among these natives and to have had contact with them and worked with them so long. But I did not do so, thinking that one day I would return to kiss your Royal feet and tell it all to you in person. Seeing this possibility delayed, that I was not given license to leave, and that I was now old and near death, I wanted to write this letter to you, brief though it is, because if God decides to take me, I will at least have discharged my conscience with Your Majesty, pleading with you, as to a vicar of Christ, for a remedy for these recently converted souls, that they may receive your favor, that their instruction and conversion may go forward, and that Your Majesty may have the prize of such a multitude of souls converted to God. And so I appeal to your piety to come to their aid and not allow them to be destroyed, which is where they are heading if a solution is not forthcoming.

These Indian people of New Spain are vassals of Your Majesty; therefore it is a just thing that they be favored by you as such. Since members of the religious orders are in this land for their conversion and assistance, and Your Majesty wishes it so, I dare to plead with you for a remedy because, for their people to be saved, they are in great need of relief in order to devote themselves at least somewhat to matters of the Faith. After all, it is the struggle for their salvation that justifies their discovery. Given the way they are going now, this is an impossibility because they do not even have time to look after their subsistence. So they die of hunger and leave their communities because of too much work.

I firmly believe that if the decrees Your Majesty sent here for their benefit were implemented, and if the governors and judges did more than pretend to do so, great good would have come to these people. Even more firmly I believe that Your Majesty's intention is that they be saved and that they know God. For this to happen, they must have some relief, so that with the moderate labor needed to meet their tribute obligation, they can still give themselves wholeheartedly to our teachings and whatever else to which their souls are suited. Otherwise, God will have good reason to complain, for Spaniards came to this land and have taken their property for their own benefit, and Your Majesty has extracted great benefit from them, too. And they may be going to Hell just like before; and where they were many, they are now less than a few.

What is in the past cannot be remedied, but it is just that a remedy be found for the future and that Your Majesty ensure that the decrees issued about personal service be followed because this is one of the main reasons for the destruction of these people. Your Majesty, Most Serene Lord, should know that the Indians who are required to labor for a master in Mexico City in domestic service and bring firewood, fodder, and chickens leave their pueblo for a month at a time, especially those who live a considerable distance from the city. And the poor Indians often have to buy these things because they are not to be found in their pueblos, leaving them in a desperate state looking for these things day and night because the order regarding service is that every day they perform service in the encomendero's house. Thus, they have to buy these things every day, and are always away from their homes and sorely mistreated by the people they must deal with, including slaves, free blacks, and servants of the encomenderos. Instead of feeding them, they mistreat them physically and verbally, causing them to flee and go off to the mountains. Your Majesty should know that Indians in service are like slaves of the blacks, who order them around and punish them as if they were the master.

There is a long history to this, and I do not want my account to be overlong, but I know for certain that if it is not stopped, they will soon be gone, for they are diminishing like the bread that is consumed each day. For the love of Our Lord, may Your Majesty take pity on them and consider what is happening to the poor Indian woman who is in her house with no one to support her and her children, for her husband is hard pressed simply to meet his tribute requirement. She has to go, leaving the home and her husband, perhaps even leaving the children to destruction. Nowhere in the world were men such as these, who had nothing, required to pay tribute; thus, having to find a way to pay it outside [their pueblo], they never have time to rest.

Finally, as a servant of Your Majesty and one who better than anyone knows them and deals with them, I advise you that if Your Majesty does not establish that, as in Spain, they be required to pay tribute only from what they have, within thirty years these parts will be as deserted as the [Caribbean] islands, and so many souls will be lost and Your Majesty's tender conscience. They should be regarded as free individuals and not required to [pay tribute] from what their pueblo has, for Spaniards were never required to do so. They should give tribute to their master from what they produce, and no more, without having to kill themselves trying to make the payment and serving personally. In this way, things will change, and they will become imbued with the Articles of Faith, and their souls will be saved because they will be able to attend the lessons and sermons and will not have any reason to miss them, and tribute will not be the cause of their souls going to Hell because they did not know God and did not confess and did not hear Mass or the lessons of the Faith.

But with thirty or forty more years of service, [the Spaniards] will lose this land forever, for without Indians it is worthless. Your Majesty will certainly understand how the friars who came to convert these souls will feel, for they came here so long ago and saw so many people here to convert. Instead of continually multiplying, there will be no one left; and instead of growing day by day, there will be fewer, and places will be deserted. Certainly it has been the cause of great despair among them.

I turn now to plead with Your Majesty to act as a good shepherd with your sheep and consider that Christ Our Redeemer did not come to spill His precious blood for tribute, but for souls; for a single soul saved is worth more than all the worldly possessions. You are most Christian, and I do believe you will find a remedy and will see that it is the good zeal of a friar and servant of yours that moves me. It has been a great sadness for my soul to see the early achievements reduced to nothing, where once the churches were overflowing with people, now they are not even half full. This is because even on Sundays and other holy days they must find a way to pay their tribute. This is credible because these people are so poor that many of them do not even have decent food, only roots and greens.

One thing that could well destroy them completely is the recently reissued order that these Indians hire themselves out against their will. This order calls for pueblos within a ten-league radius [of Mexico City] to send Indians for hire for all the plots of land held by officials and others. The salary designated for common people is twelve maravedies a day, and I do not know how much for others. So the Indian comes when he is required to serve, comes from ten leagues away, a two-day trip, leaving his wife and children dying of hunger. Once in Mexico City he waits for someone to hire him, selling the shirt off his back in order to survive because it may take three or four days before he is hired. Then he is paid twelve maravedies a day and it costs him ten or the entire amount to eat, so he serves without pay because he must spend this amount just to survive. It gives me such pain to speak of this that I do not want to go on at length, except to tell Your Majesty that an Indian having been away from his home for a month working without pay and having sold his clothes and lost time needed in his fields and his children and wife suffering the loss, returns to the demand for tribute when he does not have even enough to eat. Then comes the personal service, and having been unable to work his fields he can take no more, so he leaves, with his household in ruins. May Your Majesty consider how this man can be a Christian. I believe that if he had been, he would turn into a Moor out of despair.

I leave aside the many acts of mistreatment they receive. I do not want to talk about them because there would be no end; a kick, a hair pulling, or a clubbing is never lacking. Your Majesty, for the love of God, do not allow such great inhumanity to continue. Make them free, and if someone wants to hire himself out, whether he is a dignitary or not, it should be of his own free will, and he should come to an agreement with the Spaniard and not be forced or have the wage set arbitrarily. And they should not go into debt [to the employer] because it destroys them—if the Indian becomes indebted, it is his livelihood that is at stake. The Indian who hires himself out voluntarily does so to support himself; but if he is forced to do so, it is the cause of communities being abandoned.

It has also been ordered that every Indian from every pueblo within the ten-league radius bring a load of firewood to the city. This is a great burden because it takes two days to cut the wood and bring it to Mexico and another day or two to return home. He returns exhausted and nearly dead to find that what little there was in his house has been eaten, and he has only been paid half a real when it cost him a full real just to eat, and his work went unpaid. Oh, how cruel! Don Antonio de Mendoza [Viceroy of New Spain, 1535–1550] certainly understood this, for he is said to have observed that this could not last long or the place would be destroyed. And he was certainly right in the end, for within a year and a half where this went on, there are fewer people in every pueblo. They are Your Majesty's vassals; they cost the blood of Christ; their property has been taken away; they have lost their lands in exchange for souls. There is good reason to cry out for them.

In making this report to Your Majesty, I fulfill my duty to God. To speak more precisely, in numbers, would require a long time. May Your Majesty, most Christian as you are, remedy the situation, preventing personal service altogether and not allowing the hiring [of Indians] against their will or the collection of tribute from community property. There is no other solution.

What has been ordered thus far with regard to slaves in the mines should go forward, and miners should not be allowed to keep them locked away so that they cannot come to ask for their liberty. And whoever makes such a request should have justice done expeditiously, without giving rise to routine lawsuits with them; a judge should be appointed to give them justice expeditiously, going to the mines and putting their situation to rights.

And Your Majesty should not allow lawsuits among Indians, for there is already corruption in this. Now they know nothing but lawsuits, and the notaries are very busy with such business because the Indians press lawsuits for no reason at all, over a bit of worthless land. They spend the tribute and community property in lawsuits and carry them on for three or four years. There is great destruction in this for the Indians. It is unbelievable how they have become such avid litigators, spending what they have on agents, lawyers, notaries, and interpreters. Worst of all, it comes out of the sweat of the Indian commoners, whose belongings are sold in order to litigate. Until recently, we friars resolved their disputes. They did not allow differences among themselves, and in a single day they would accept the resolution, and were content. After Spaniards put into their heads that lawsuits are better, they destroy them and deceive them. Under the guise of doing them a favor, they take advantage of them. And there are disputes among pueblos, and they spend what they have because their leaders, on the pretext of litigating, eat and drink and spend the community's wealth and the sweat of the commoners, robbing them, and everything is lost.

And I attest to Your Majesty that it has happened that a Spaniard will join with Indians who are in conflict with other Indians. To take advantage of them, he will inquire into their reasons for litigating and tell them that their cause is just and they will get what they request without any complications. They make the Indians serve them and work in their homes, and spend their money; and the Indians are left without anything. Your Majesty should see the conscience with which they do this. To remedy this situation, lawsuits among Indians by any means should not be permitted; rather, the friars should get them to agree, as has been done heretofore, with no cost to their property or having to miss their spiritual lessons or leave home, and, above all, without their bringing forward new lawsuits every day and killing themselves as a result. May Your Majesty remedy this situation instead of allowing it or doing anything to encourage it, so that the conservation and peace of these natives will be sought in every way possible, and that they may be favored and not be used so inhumanly, and that they be treated as if they were our next of kin.

I firmly believe that one of the things in this land that most needs a remedy is this city of Mexico. Those who were once lords of the whole land are now slaves, and even worse than slaves. And since they serve the entire city—dignitaries and lesser folk alike, especially in the homes of those who govern—their women suffer deprivation because an Indian is away in service to the Spaniard for a month or two, especially in the houses of those who govern in Your Majesty's name. The woman must seek to feed herself, her husband, and their children, and also to pay the tribute. And what her husband ordinarily would do, she must do; and she goes out to bring back firewood and greens because her husband is obligated to personal service and cannot do this. May Your Majesty consider whether this work is tolerable. With regard to sustenance and rest, dogs lead a better life than Indians because dogs are fed while Indians are made to work for others without being fed. Considering that the Indians of this city of Mexico are so poor, having no lands or resources other than their labor, you will understand how they must suffer. And above all, even if the Indian is an official or a dignitary, he must do the labor service like anyone else. And it is a shame that Indian children ten or twelve years old must travel eight or ten leagues in search of maize and go carrying heavy loads with their mothers in order to support themselves and their fathers and find the means to pay the tribute every eighty days. And lacking lands to plant, they must buy it with the toil of their hands in order to eat and provide for their parents and pay the tribute. For the love of God, Your Majesty should provide that in no way, under no circumstances, should anyone make use of them in this way, that such services be completely stopped, and that they be left to be Christians, for even on the high holy days of Christmas, Candlemas, and Easter they are not allowed to rest.

In this city of Mexico, in the patio of the church of San Francisco there is a chapel called Saint Joseph. There I have worked with [the Indians] day and night for more than thirty years, being with them constantly in a school that is adjacent to this chapel, where I have taught them to read and play musical instruments and taught them their spiritual lessons, and I have always taken charge of them and looked out for them. And they have rebuilt this chapel of Saint Joseph, good and strong, in order to celebrate with fitting solemnity the Divine Offices. There, in fact, they are celebrated, and the Indians are confessed and preached to and baptized and treated with all charity. I believe Your Majesty knows what the Franciscan friars have done in this regard, seeking God's honor and the salvation of [the Indians'] souls wherever [we have] monasteries among these people. And because of the great poverty that exists among their poor Indians, the schooling does not advance for lack of essentials, even food. And this is such an essential activity, being where the Indian children and youths learn their spiritual lessons and are taught to read and write and sing and play instruments, and the reason why the Divine Offices are celebrated devoutly is because they serve at Mass.

In order that improvements be made and the said school does not come to an end, Your Majesty, merciful person that you are, should make grants to these Indians and the said school of some assistance for the maintenance of the natives and so that they will help me there, as they have done up to now, that they will have the means to eat and pay their tribute, so that the spiritual instruction of one and all may go forward and what has been lost will be restored. May Your Majesty grant them 500 or 600 pesos annually, considering the many people who could be taught. It would be a great consolation to the natives, considering the plight of these Indians of Mexico, for they have no lands, nor any means of providing for themselves except laboring for their masters. May your deputies make the money available in the manner that seems best to Your Majesty. It is certain that, without this support, the effort will fail because, lacking subsistence and having to pay the tribute, they will leave the school and spiritual lessons behind. It would certainly be a great service to God in terms of good learning, for, seeing the support, those yet to be born or who are now children would make an extra effort, and a grand thing and great service to God would result. I cannot specify for certain the great service that would result and will result from it, except that it will be forthcoming. And since I am the one undertaking the work and have worked so much with them and intend to continue teaching them until I die, it is a just thing that I receive the grant.

I dare to approach Your Majesty about this, being your fellow countryman and because what I request is in the service of God and for the honor and benefit of Your Majesty. Therefore, for the love of God, please grant what I have asked for the benefit of the Indians' salvation and spiritual education. And please order that some indulgences from His Holiness be sent for the said chapel of Saint Joseph, and permission for some kind of special celebration there (especially an annual celebration and indulgences for this chapel like His Holiness granted to the Colegio de los Niños of this city, thanks to your intercession), so that, with such acts of support, they may go forward and know Your Majesty's favor.

May you order also that under no circumstances can bishops or other prelates act to take away the said chapel and other churches that [the Indians] have in their parishes, where they find consolation; nor can the secular priests take them over in order to become vicars, because for the preservation of these natives, members of the orders are needed, as Don Antonio de Mendoza ordered. Nor should the Indians be divided up, but left as they are; to do otherwise would be to destroy them. In all of this, Your Majesty, being most Christian, will do as you think best, for you know that the Indians have grown up with the friars.

These Indians had a hospital in this city where sick Indians were treated, which they built at their own cost. And there the sick Indians were treated and found consolation. Then it was taken away for the Colegio de los Niños, with an order that another one, just as good, be made for them. It has now been two years, and neither has another one been started nor the original hospital returned, to the detriment of those who are sick. This is an essential matter. In reverence to God, may you order the hospital returned or a new one built as soon as possible so that those who are sick do not die for lack of a place to be treated. May you also make a gift of some amount to the said hospital for maintenence and treatment, and grant a special sum for these poor little ones. May Your Majesty thereby become the patron of this hospital, for the consolation of these Indians, that they may know your favors and know that Your Majesty loves them and looks out for them, as I hope for the great mercy you will extend them.

I have here given an account and made my entreaties, as a servant to his master. What remains is the equipment needed for the job and the officials to undertake its construction. For this work, the friars are indispensable, and we are short of them—there are houses [evangelizing centers] among these natives that have only two or three friars. For this, Your Majesty should order that workers be sent for Jesus Christ's project—many of them, and soon. May some of them be from Flanders and Ghent because if the Indians see that people from my homeland remain among them, they will not feel that I have left them bereft when I die. And because this is so essential—as essential as bread for sustenance—I shall stop here and submit myself to Your Majesty's mercy and magnificence, reminding you to send shepherds for your sheep. Also, do not forget what you have ordered about Indians settling together and not spilling out over the mountains where they will not know God. This is most necessary to complete the conversion of these people and for the friars to keep track of them without having to go looking for them in the mountains. In the mountains there is nothing but idolatry, while, when they live together and can be supervised, Christianity and benefit to their souls and body are advanced, and they do not die without faith and baptism and knowledge of God. This is one of the main ingredients in their salvation, I firmly believe, since it contributes to their well-being in every sense. Your Majesty will know how to deal with this.

Our Lord, Most Serene person and of Royal state, whose hands I kiss, may Our Lord guard you and extend your life in His holy service, as we your subjects and clergymen do desire. Amen. From the Franciscan monastery in Mexico City, February 15, 1552.

13

The Evils of Cochineal, Tlaxcala, Mexico (1553)

This record of the city of Tlaxcala's municipal council (*cabildo*) three decades after Tlaxcalan lords allied with Cortés to destroy the Aztec state reveals some striking changes in life there under Spanish rule. Composed in Nahuatl (the language of much of central Mexico at the time of the Conquest) with Roman script and translated into English by James Lockhart, the writing itself is evidence of both change and continuity. The document reveals a traditional hereditary elite making the transition to the Spanish colonial regime as elected officeholders in a municipal council system linked to the Spanish district governor appointed by the Crown (here the *corregidor* is Alonso de Galdós) and a central administration in Mexico City.

In some ways, Tlaxcalan leaders and communities enjoyed a privileged place in the colonial order as the most important native allies of Cortés. Their political and property rights were confirmed early; their native capital received the unusual status of "city" by 1535; they succeeded, as colonial law provided, in keeping civilian Spaniards from living among them during the sixteenth century; they lobbied, with less success, for relief from the tribute and labor demands that weighed heavily as the population declined in early waves of epidemic diseases; and groups of Tlaxcalans were invited to join Spanish colonizing expeditions on the frontiers of New Spain. In this document, one of the Tlaxcalan leaders is away serving as a kind of circuit judge in the Valley of Mexico district of Coyoacan.

The Indians of early colonial Tlaxcala enjoyed considerable prosperity, easing some of the adjustments to a new state system and religion and to changes in diet, language, dress, labor service, and production. Much of the initial Spanish influence in the province of Tlaxcala filtered in through the top—through the provincial Indian nobles who received coats of arms from the Spanish Crown, learned to read and write Spanish and sometimes Latin, and were among the first to accept Christian baptism and instruction. After the 1560s the hardships of epidemic disease, state demands for tax payments and labor, the mixed blessings of European livestock, and migration out of the province for residence and work in Puebla or in the new colonial settlements far to the north were more apparent at all levels of Tlaxcalan society. Still, Tlaxcalans continued to survive and adapt to new conditions.

In this record of their *cabildo* deliberations of March 3, 1553—during that early period of prosperity—the lords of Tlaxcala express concern about the increasing production of cochineal, a small insect that thrives on the native nopal cactus of central and southern Mexico. The females of this cactus mite were collected, dried, and crushed into a deep red dyestuff that was coveted in Europe, as well as in Indian America, before chemical dyes. The elected leaders' concerns suggest a new level of commercialization of cochineal, grown in many new places, absorbing the energies of people and land previously devoted to food crops; new patterns of local consumption (*cacao,* or chocolate, which was not grown locally, and the fermented beverage, *pulque,* get special attention here); a knowledge of Christian teachings; and challenges to the customary powers, habits of consumption, and social standing of these lords. But notice that, in spite of the rulers' laments about disorder and moral decay, the changes were not simply in the direction of destruction, dissipation, and demoralization. Remember that great changes are described in this document from the vantage point of a hereditary elite working to protect its position under new colonial circumstances.

In the loyal city of Tlaxcala on Friday, the third day of the month of March of the year 1553, there assembled in the cabildo the magnificent lord Alonso de Galdós, corregidor in the province of Tlaxcala for His Majesty, with Miguel Cardenel, Spaniard, as interpreter; and it was in the presence of the very honorable lords Don Domingo de Angulo, governor; and the alcaldes ordinarios [members of the cabildo exercising judicial authority] Don Diego de Paredes, Félix Mejía, Alonso Gómez, and Don Diego de Guzmán; and of the four rulers, Don Juan Maxixcatzin, Don Julián Motolinía—Don Juan Xicotencatl is sick—; it was in the presence of Don Francisco de Mendoza; and the regidores [secondary members of the cabildo] Don Julián de la Rosa, Buenaventura Oñate, Antonio del Pedroso, Antonio Téllez, Hernando Tecepotzin, Don Juan de Paz, Baltasar Cortés, Pablo de Galicia, Pedro Díaz, and Tadeo de Niza; not (done) before Don Domingo de Silva, who is sick, and Lucas García, acting as judge in Coyoacan; it was done before us, Fabián Rodríguez, Diego de Soto, and Sancho de Rozas, notaries of the cabildo of Tlaxcala. They deliberated about how the cochineal cactus, from which cochineal comes, is being planted all over Tlaxcala. Everyone does nothing but take care of cochineal cactus; no longer is care taken that maize and other edibles are planted. For food—maize, chilis, and beans—and other things that people need were once not expensive in Tlaxcala. It is because of this (neglect), the cabildo members considered, that all the foods are becoming expensive. The owners of cochineal cactus merely buy maize, chilis, etc., and are very occupied only with their cochineal, by which their money, cacao beans, and cloth are acquired. They no longer want to cultivate their fields, but idly neglect them. Because of this, now many fields are going to grass, and famine truly impends. Things are no longer as they were long ago, for the cochineal cactus is making people lazy. And it is excessive how sins are committed against Our Lord God: These cochineal owners devote themselves to their cochineal on Sundays and holy days; no longer do they go to church to hear Mass as the Holy Church commands us, but look only to getting their sustenance and their cacao, which makes them proud. And then later they buy pulque and then get drunk; all of the cochineal owners gather together. If they buy a turkey, they give it away for less than its price, and pulque, too; they lightly give away their money and cacao. Not remembering how Our Lord God mercifully granted them whatever wealth is theirs, they vainly squander it. And he who belonged to someone no longer respects whoever was his lord and master, because he is seen to have gold and cacao. That makes them proud and swells them up, whereby it is fully evident that they esteem themselves only through wealth. And also the cochineal dealers, some of them noblemen, some commoners, and some women, line up here in the Tlaxcala marketplace and there await the cochineal. When they are not collecting cochineal quickly, then they go to the various homes of the cochineal owners, entering the houses. And there many things happen; they make the women drunk there, and there some commit sins. They go entering the homes of anyone who has cochineal plants; they already know those from whom they customarily buy dye, and sometimes they also go on Sundays and holy days, whereby they miss attending Mass and hearing the sermon, but go only wanting to get drunk. And these cochineal dealers act as if the women who gather dye have been made their relatives. Some of the men hire themselves out to Spaniards to gather dye for them, and they give them money and cacao. And later they distribute the women to them, making them like their relatives; to some they assign seven or eight (women), or thereabouts, to gather dye for them. Because of this, many improper things are done. And of those who hire themselves out, many are likewise ruined, because some act as slaves in the hands of the Spaniards. If it were not for cochineal, they would not become such. And both the cactus owners and the cochineal dealers so act that for little reason they begin to pair with each other, or take one another as co-godparents, or just feed one another, gathering and collecting together with their wives. They feed one another, however many of them there are; they give one another a great deal of food, and the chocolate they drink is very thick, with plenty of cacao in it. When they find the chocolate just a little watery, then it is not to their liking and they do not want to drink it. Some pour it on the ground, whereby whoever has given his very good cacao to someone is affronted, but they imagine themselves very grand because of it. And so then they buy pulque or Castilian wine; even though it is very expensive, they pay no heed, but give (the price) to the person selling it. And then they become entirely inebriated and senseless, together with their wives; they fall down one at a time where they are congregated, entirely drunk. Many sins are committed there, and it all comes from cochineal. Also these cochineal dealers no longer want to cultivate the soil; though some of them own fields, they no longer want to cultivate; they do nothing but look for cochineal. And both the cactus owners and the cochineal dealers, some of them, sleep on cotton mats, and their wives wear great skirts, and they have much money, cacao, and clothing. The wealth they have only makes them proud and swaggering. For before cochineal was known and everyone planted cochineal cactus, it was not this way. There were some people of whom it was clearly evident that they lived in knowledge of their humility, but just because of the cochineal now there is much drunkenness and swaggering; it is very clear that cochineal has been making people idle in the last eight or nine years. But in the old days there was a time of much care in cultivation and planting; everyone cultivated the soil and planted. Because of this, the cabildo members said it is necessary that the cochineal cactus decrease and not so much be planted, since it causes idleness. It is greatly urged that everyone cultivate and plant; let much maize, chilis, beans, and all edible plants be grown, because if Our Lord God should wish that famine come, and if there were in people's possession much money, cacao, and cloth, will those things be eaten? Will there be salvation through them? It cannot be. Money, cacao, and cloth do not fill up one. But if people have much food, through it they will save themselves, since no one will (starve); no one will die being wealthy. Therefore two or three times the lord viceroy who presides in Mexico City, Don Luis de Velasco, has been told and it has been brought to his attention how the dye brings affliction, and he has been informed of all the harm done. And after that the lord viceroy gave orders in reply, ordering the lord corregidor that in his presence there be consultation here in the cabildo to approve how many plantings of cochineal cactus are to be kept by each person; it is to be a definite number, and no longer will there be planting at whim. And in consulting, some of the cabildo members said that five plantings of cochineal cactus should be kept (by each person), and others said that fifteen should be kept. But when the discussion was complete, everyone approved keeping ten plantings of cactus, and the lord corregidor also approved it. No one is to exceed (the number). And the women who gather dye in the marketplace are to gather dye no more. Nevertheless, it is first to be put before the lord viceroy; what he should order in reply will then be made public. Then in the cabildo were appointed those who will go to Mexico City to set before the lord viceroy what was discussed as said above. Those who will go are Alonso Gómez, alcalde, and the regidores Antonio del Pedroso, Pablo de Galicia, and Pedro Díaz, with the notary of the cabildo Fabián Rodríguez. It is by order of the cabildo that they will go to Mexico City. The most illustrious lord viceroy will decide how to reply; then it will be announced all over Tlaxcala in what manner cochineal cactus is to be kept.

[There follow eighteen of the names found at the beginning of the document, with other rubrics.]

Done before us, notaries of the cabildo. Fabián Rodríguez, notary. Diego de Soto. Sancho de Rozas.

14

The Indian Pueblo of Texupa in Sixteenth-Century Mexico

(1579)

Hundreds of thousands of Spaniards went to America during the colonial period, but no Spanish king ever paid a visit, nor did more than a few of the leading royal councilors who passed judgment on American affairs. Yet America was quite extensively, sometimes minutely, governed from Spain, and Spaniards were great consumers of news and information about "the Indies." The vast collection of documents in Seville's Archivo General de Indias testifies to this thirst for information and will to administer. Especially valuable to historians are the reports submitted in response to royal questionnaires that periodically blanketed the colonies, calling for details about places, resources, and life among the king's subjects across the Ocean Sea.

Philip II, who reigned from 1556 to 1598, was an avid gatherer of such information. His long questionnaire of 1577 elicited a particularly rich set of reports, or *relaciones geográficas,* from local districts in New Spain (167 of the 208 reports received were for New Spain). The questionnaire called for precise information about location, natural resources, economic activity, political jurisdictions, boundaries, native languages, pre-Hispanic institutions, modes of war, historical traditions, house types, religious practices, and more. In addition to the written report, the king's instructions called for a *pintura* (picture or map) of the area.

An intriguing report (Selection 14) and accompanying pintura (Figure 9) were received from the town of Texupa, Oaxaca, in southern Mexico, on the road from the colonial city of Antequera (the modern city of Oaxaca) to Puebla and the viceregal capital. The written report was prepared by the Spanish *corregidor* for Texupa with the help of two Dominican pastors from testimony by unnamed local Indians. To all appearances, the map was prepared by one of the Indian informants, not by the district governor or the Dominicans. In counterpoint, the pintura and the report complement each other as perceptions of Texupa and its vicinity at the end of the great epidemic that swept through New Spain in the late 1570s.

In its matter-of-fact answers to the king's questionnaire, the report identifies some notable changes in material life for the people of Texupa: new clothes, new food, new economic activities (animal husbandry and the cultivation of silk, in particular), tile roofs, and silver currency. It recognizes the drastic decline in population since the Spaniards arrived. People are not as healthy as they used to be, the report states, but it does not

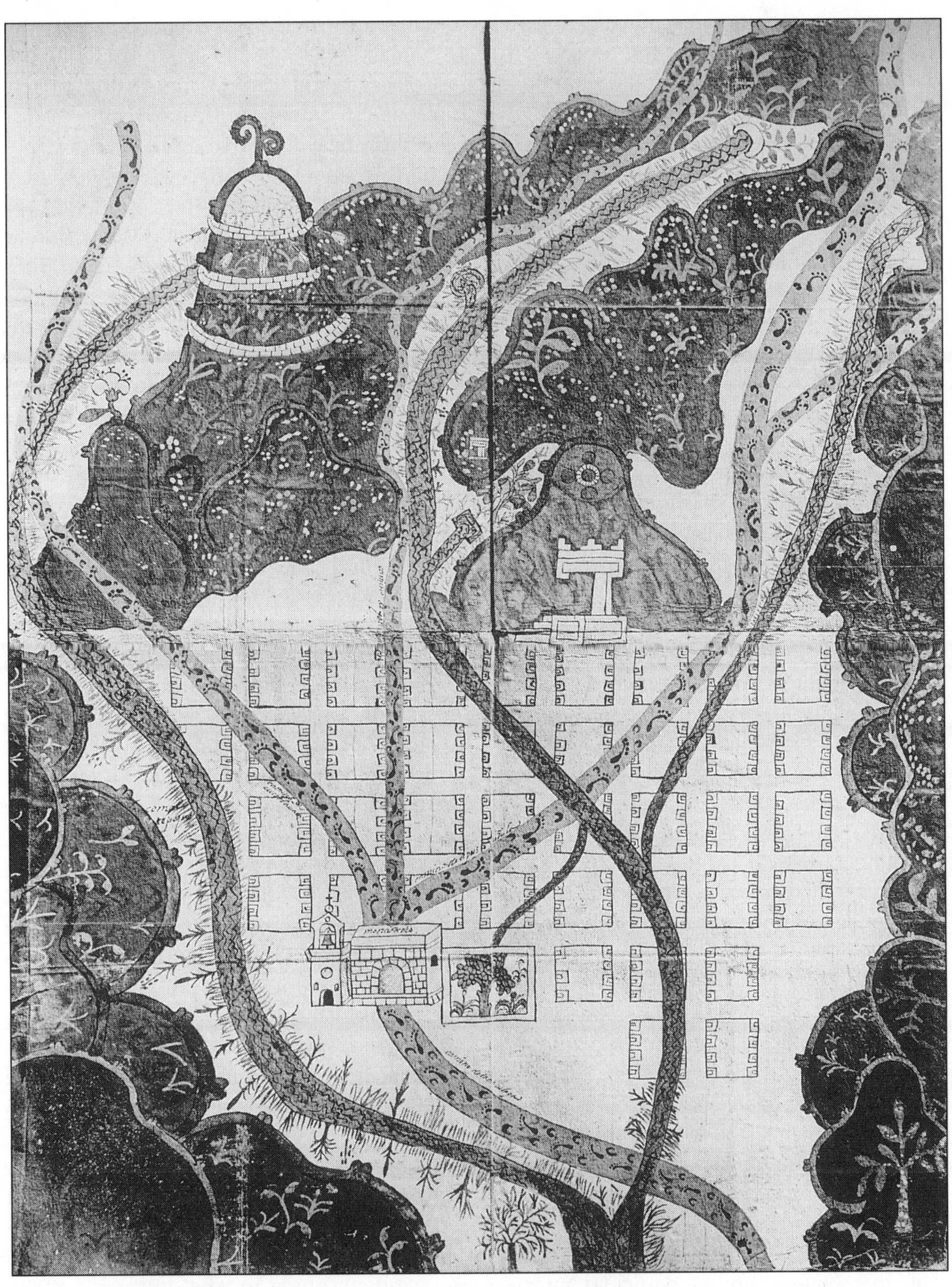

Figure 9. Map of Texupa, Mexico, 1579. *Pintura* accompanying the Texupa *relación geográfica*. East is at the top, with its sacred hills, shrines, arroyos, streams, and paths coming into town, the paths converging on the Dominican church and compound. The west side of Texupa is "the entrance to the pueblo . . . more open . . . a fertile depression a little less than one-fourth of a league wide."

mention epidemic diseases introduced from Europe as a cause. Rather, the great dying was attributed to diet—too much eating and richer foods. Even though the report is filtered by the corregidor's determination to answer only the questions at hand and his disgust with pre-Hispanic religious practices, there are hints of local pride in the descriptions of warrior garb and the orderly government of former times that undoubtedly were provided by his Indian informants.

The pintura (Figure 9) illustrates two great changes in early colonial Texupa: the physical reorganization of the community according to the standard Spanish colonial grid plan; and the advent of Christianity, as represented by the church-monastery-orchard compound. But the composition and its living landscape also suggest important continuities in the artist's conception of his community that muffle the sense of transformation of local life under Spanish rule. Like a pre-Hispanic screenfold or "picture book," its story is told almost exclusively in stylized color drawings. The few words on the map identify Comaltepeque (one of the hills mentioned in the report), the Dominicans' monastery ("monasterio"), and the road from the town of Tamaçulapa ("camino de tamaçulapa"). Like some pre-Hispanic Mixtec records, it represents real space, locating prominent physical features of the landscape in ways that were understood by viewers. The conventions for representing the important features of the landscape—especially hills, temples, roads, and sources of water—are similar, too, and there is the same sense of human settlement identified by its surroundings more than by the place itself. However, the way of representing that sense of place and landscape has changed. Whereas pre-Hispanic records from the Mixteca located the viewer in the landscape by way of a meandering string of place glyphs (especially of hills, mountains, and temples) that could be seen in only this sequence from a particular vantage point, the 1579 pintura offers a more European notion of mapping and landscape in which physical features are arranged according to compass directions and a bird's-eye view.

A section of the pre-Hispanic Codex Vindobonensis studied by archaeologists John Pohl and Bruce Byland can illustrate this change. They found that the meandering line of places reproduced in Figure 10 (top left) represents an actual landscape visible from a location near the town of Tilantongo. They call this sequence of places "The View from Red and White Bundle." The meandering line of places begins with Red and White Bundle (the bundle-like form in the lower right). Then comes a fretted temple with a serpent emerging, which is the town of Tilantongo; then the Hill of the Wasp, Hill of the Enclosure, Hill of Flints, and so on, ending with Jaguar Rock and a variant form of Red and White Bundle above the "rock." In Figure 10 (bottom left), Pohl and Byland depict the same landscape from a European perspective, with Red and White Bundle as the point of reference and the various hills and other places visible from it in a clockwise order. In this depiction it would be appropriate to fill in the intervening spaces as they appear to the photographic eye.

In the 1579 pintura of Texupa, east (the place of the rising sun) rather than north is "up," with its concentration of sacred hills and shrines, but the pintura situates the streambeds, hills, and fertile depression in relationship to the town by the cardinal directions in a European way and offers a more illusionistic landscape. The rows of hills and mountains that surround the town in the 1579 depiction more closely approximate a bird's-eye view than does the pre-Hispanic landscape from the Codex Vindobonensis. The effect of a range of hills is achieved by overlapping the native symbol for hill used in the Codex. But the luxuriant vegetation perhaps has less to do with a photographic approximation of the surroundings than with an idealized depiction of promontories and depressions that seem to ripple with life and provide an abundance of running water, a precious resource in what today is a stark, dry, eroded area during the eight or nine months between rainy seasons.

This colonial pintura is too complex in its combination of old and new forms and its

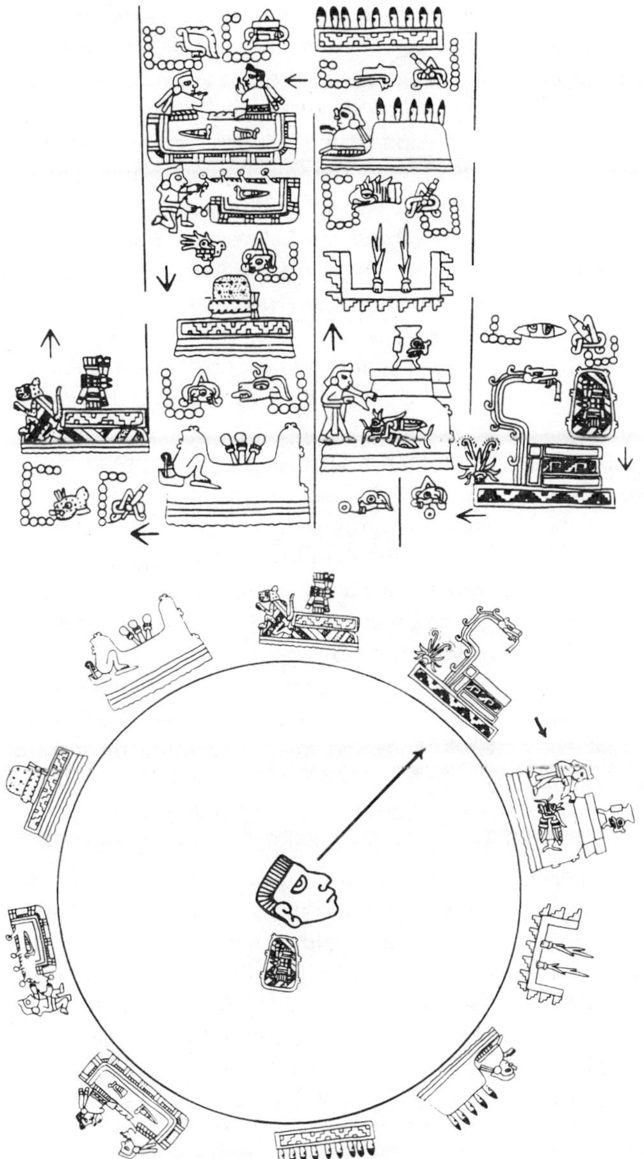

Figure 10. "The View from Red and White Bundle": A Mixtec landscape discovered by John Pohl and Bruce Byland. The image at top left is redrawn in black and white from the Codex Vindobonensis, a manuscript made in the Mixteca Alta region near Texupa before the arrival of the Spaniards. Arrows have been added to show the sequence of figures. In the image at bottom left, Pohl and Byland imagine the same landscape, in a bird's-eye view. Courtesy of Cambridge University Press.

ways of depicting the landscape for one neat interpretation to satisfy all viewers who would engage its complexity by emphasizing one feature or another. Is it mainly about oppositions? About native identity versus colonial organization? Does it represent a repudiation of, or indifference toward, Spanish rule and colonial transformations? Do the organic shapes and muted colors of the landscape menace the apparition-like colonial settlement? Do the curving lines of streambeds and old roads that overlap the grid plan of the town somehow subvert the grid and colonial organization, tearing it open or crossing it out, as one scholar suspects? The roads are not mentioned in the written report, and they do seem to suggest more important pathways than the straight streets of the new town.

If we accept this way of interpreting the overlay of forms on the pintura, one colonial form is not covered over or canceled: it is the monastery and church with its walled garden of abundant new fruits and other plants. It appears on top of the ancient roadways and streambed that cross the town, all three of which converge at the site, lending additional importance to it ("all roads lead here" may be the message). The only other man-made structure that seems to have the same importance as the church complex is the pre-Hispanic temple at the base of the hill on the eastern edge of town. The prominence and rough equivalence of these two structures suggests a reverence for the sacred and its institutions that makes no sharp distinction between past and present.

Another, perhaps more promising, interpretation of the Texupa pintura that would also emphasize the landscape (on which the maker lavished such care and to which he gave such scope) does not interpret the overlay of roads and streambeds on the colonial town plan as a repudiation of colonial rule. The depiction of the landscape is seen less as being about competition with the town than it is about a pre-Hispanic concept of space in which human settlements were regarded as temporary and located by their enclosures—that is, by the permanent features and sacred places that surround them—more than as permanent, freestanding places in their own right. Much as the depictions of landscape in most of the surviving ancient Mixtec records were political maps in which ruling elites were shown inheriting and exercising territorial power, the 1579 pintura seems to make a political statement, celebrating Texupa as a central place. If so, it is a grand statement that continues long-standing local claims to authority more than it confronts and challenges colonial power. If not the world's navel (as the Aztec Stone of the Five Eras seems to assert for Tenochtitlán; see Selection 4), Texupa at least appears as a center of things, *the* town, surrounded by places that teem with plant life and spiritual power, a community not obviously subordinate to any political order imposed from outside.

As a glimpse of how colonial reorderings could be viewed by native subjects during the sixteenth century, the Texupa pintura expresses more than a Spanish conquest of the landscape. As in most cultural matters involving colonial Indians in central and southern Mexico, local pride and attachment to place were a vital part of changing spatial and political arrangements. The Spanish corregidor's report describes a more colonized landscape—a restructured, potentially productive place beneath the superimposed design of Christianity and Spanish authority. The Indian painter's representation of Texupa suggests a rather different understanding of the place and emerging colonial realities. In its luxuriant hills, meandering paths, and straight lines, his depiction of home gives special importance to familiar idealized surroundings teeming with sacred life. That life seems to be augmented by the new Christian church complex more than it dwells on the reshaping of the community into the Spanish ideal for an urban settlement.

Relación Geográfica of Texupa, 1579

In the pueblo of Texupa this twentieth day of October 1579, I, Diego de Avendaño, His Majesty's corregidor of said pueblo, have been ordered by the Most Excellent Viceroy and His Majesty's Governor of this New Spain, Don Martín Enríquez, to report in the interests of the good government of this New Spain. Here I, the said corregidor, do so in the company of the very reverend fathers, Fray Antonio de la Serna, pastor of the monastery of said pueblo of Texupa, and Fray Pasqual de la Anunciación, resident of the monastery. Below I answer each of the questions in the viceroy's circular.

The pueblo of Texupa in the Mixteca Alta stands alone, without any subordinate settlements. It is fifty-eight leagues east of Mexico City, almost entirely over very rough roads, although the leagues here are said to be not as long as those in Spain. It is thirty-eight leagues of rough road east of the city of Puebla and twenty-two leagues west of the city of Antequera in the Valley of Oaxaca through both rough and flat terrain. Texupa is in the diocese for which Antequera, with its cathedral, is the capital.

The pueblo of Texupa is situated on a plain between two hills. The western part is more open than the part bathed by the afternoon sun. The hill nearer the pueblo is called Comaltepeque in the Mexican language [Nahuatl], and the other hill Miagualtepeque, also in the Mexican language. It has a fertile depression a little less than one-fourth of a league wide, running west of the pueblo for about one league. Above the pueblo two little arroyos originate. One goes through the center of the pueblo and the other across the northern edge. They join at the entrance to the pueblo and form a depression below it.

This pueblo has a monastery of friars of the Dominican Order, with two friars in residence for the instruction of the natives. His Majesty pays for their maintenance since the pueblo belongs to the royal Crown [rather than being assigned in *encomienda*].

Pueblos in the vicinity are Yanguitlan, four leagues to the east, some of it rough terrain and some flat. To the east is another pueblo called Tonaltepeque, two leagues by rough road. Another pueblo called Cuestlavaca is to the north three leagues by very rough road. To the west is another pueblo called Tamaçulapa, one and one-half leagues over flat ground. The pueblo of Teposcolula is to the south three leagues by rough road over hills. (Recall that the leagues are not as long as in Spain.)

In this pueblo the Indians speak two languages, Mixtec and Chocho. The more widely spoken is Mixtec. The Mixtec name for Texupa is Ñundaa, which in Spanish means "blue land," or "Texupa" in the Mexican language. Why it is called by this name could not be determined.

The lord and cacique in the time of their infidelity when the Marquis [Hernán Cortés] arrived was Yesa Huyya. He and his wife, named Yaanicuin, and their descendants were subjects of King Motecçuma for many years before then. They paid tribute to their King Motecçuma with slaves, parrot feathers, and a little cochineal. They gave the cacique copal [an incense from tree resin] and whatever else was needed for their rites and the devil's house [temple] where they performed their sacrifices.

The devil [god] they worshiped was called Yaguizi; another one was called Yanacuu. In Spanish the word for the latter devil means "wind" and the former means "lizard." They offered these devils dogs, quail, green feathers, many insects, and Indians for sacrifice. Their customs used to be very bad and abominable.

This cacique nobleman appointed another noble as governor of the Indians. He, in turn, appointed someone in each neighborhood to govern the Indians there. They were at war with an upstart Chocho lord who defeated them. In battle they wore quilted cotton down to the navel as a sort of breastplate. They made their hair stand on end and were armed with shields and clubs studded with obsidian blades.

They used to dress in "gicoles," a sort of Turkish costume open in front, dyed in the color that the wearer preferred. Now they wear Castilian-style clothing, hats, shirts, shoes, and breeches. Others wear jackets and loose blankets knotted at the shoulder.

Formerly their diet generally consisted of dry tortillas, chili peppers, insects, mice, lizards, and snakes. In their celebrations the nobles ate native chickens, venison, human flesh, dogs, and insects. Now the common folk usually eat tortillas, chili peppers, and many other types of vegetables; and the nobles eat chickens, venison, beef, mutton, and other things, and those who can obtain it eat wheat bread. They used to be healthier than they are now. It is not known why this should be, but it is thought that by eating less and eating less rich foods they lived longer.

In the said pueblo many mulberry bushes grow. They are used for silkworms, but little silk is produced here. The reason is that when the Marquis came to conquer, there were more than 12,000 Indians in this pueblo, and now there are fewer than 750. There are also some productive fruit trees called cherries; also white zapotes [native fruit], and fruit from the nopal cactus. Spanish trees grow here: pears, apples, and peaches. These types of fruit do well. Lettuce, radishes, cabbage, broad beans, chick-peas, and onions also do well.

Maize is grown in this pueblo, and a little wheat. A little silk is produced, but no cochineal, wine, or olive oil.

In this pueblo there are a few sheep and goats, and some pigs. With a little effort they would multiply greatly because the land is well suited to it. Some of the Indians have mules and horses to help them in their work.

There are no salt deposits in this pueblo. They get their salt from the Indians of Teposcolula and elsewhere. They obtain the wool and cotton for their clothing outside the pueblo.

There are some stone and clay houses in this pueblo, with their tiled roofs and roof terraces.

The trade and produce of the natives of this pueblo amount to the cultivation of their fields. Each married Indian pays a silver peso and one-half fanega [about three-quarters of a bushel] of maize in tribute to Your Majesty. And they benefit from the production of silk.

The pueblo of Texupa enjoys a good climate in a healthy location. The winds generally come out of the north and usually are moderate.

There is moderate rainfall beginning at the end of April and ending at the end of September. The pueblo has a temperate climate, more cold than hot.

I, the said corregidor, carried out the said inquiry recorded here, without discovering anything more. In the presence of the said friars, and Gobernador Don Joseph de Sandoval, Don Gregorio de Lara the cacique, alcaldes Don Gabriel de Mendoça, Gabriel Rodríguez, and Francisco Sánchez, Indian nobles and natives of the said pueblo of Texupa.

15

Fray Juan Izquierdo's Letter and Report to Charles V, Barcelona, Spain

(1552)

The diffuse nature of the political and religious power structure within Spain and through its overseas empire accentuated the importance of advisers to the Crown, whether informal, appointed for a particular purpose, or as members of permanent councils. As noted in Selection 14 and Figure 9, the Crown grew adept at encouraging reports and commanding information from a variety of people in strategic positions. Another such adviser was the friar Juan Izquierdo, who wrote from Barcelona on August 10, 1552, on the subject of the "conversion and reduction" of the Moriscos (new converts to Christianity from Islam) of Valencia, Spain.

In the letter that prefaces his report, Izquierdo demonstrates his feeling for the wider aims of religious reform in his day. Like Francisco de Vitoria in his lecture on the evangelization of unbelievers (Selection 8), Izquierdo discusses Spanish Moriscos as interconnected with the confusion of "so many important affairs" and the current "increase of kingdoms and of the faith." He refers to the threats posed to Catholic Spain by "the infection of the Lutheran heresy" and the various "enemies" of Catholic Christianity, but also—held implicitly in the notion of Catholic "increase"—the challenges of evangelization in America. Religious error was a problem to be confronted everywhere, with respect to the peoples brought into the diverse and emerging "unity" of the Spanish world who were improperly indoctrinated and, worse yet, to false Christians, who might be seen as representing political as well as religious threats. Valencian Moriscos hostile to both Christianity and the increasing demands upon them by the Spanish state might seek alliance over the Pyrenees with the French or across the Mediterranean with the Turks, rather as unsubjugated or rebellious Indians on the frontiers of Spanish control in America might welcome strategic negotiations with Dutch or British privateers and, eventually, settlers.

Izquierdo's report suggests "a remedy," a set of practical actions that, properly implemented, could "heal" the malady of an imperfectly Christianized population within Spanish society. His ambivalent priorities and the coexistence within his report of seemingly contradictory positions resemble the intermittent debates of authorities over the appropriate measures to take among the "newly converted" peoples in Spanish America. On the one hand, Izquierdo advises that Moriscos ought ideally to be subject to the pope and, more particularly, to the full authority of the Holy Office of the Inquisition. Yet, on the other hand, he notes that, "except in the gravest and most serious cases," the Moriscos of Valencia are sufficiently new to the faith to require more moderate treatment than that normally extended to "heretics who are descended from Old Christians." Impatience with the Moriscos is evident here, but there is also a concern not to discourage them from voluntary participation.

Like the Indians in their first generations under Spanish Christian domination, the Moriscos are not yet expected to "know better." Yet the period of grace to be enjoyed by Moriscos—the baptized descendants of longtime Muslim "neighbors" and "rivals"—on the strength of their continued ignorance seems to be shorter (and, arguably, much more bitter) than that afforded to peoples in the Indies (recall Selections 10 and 11 as well as 8). In both Spain and America, increasing demands for conformity from subject populations sharpened the definitions of what would be allowed under Spanish Christian rule (and probably made their integration less possible), but they did not necessarily mean that the commitment to bring about the new subjects' inclusion was lessening.

Mirroring some of the concerns of the Jesuit José de Acosta a few decades later in America (Selection 18), Izquierdo is as concerned about the propriety and diligence of the representatives of the Christian faith (the rectors, or pastors in parish churches) among the newly converted as he is about the Moriscos themselves. And, from this friar's point of view, the attention to the power of good examples and of the obstructions in the path of the full conversion and integration of the Valencian Moriscos might also extend beyond the clerical realm to secular forces. As in many Spanish American situations, some "lords" (estate owners and landholders whose rough equivalents in sixteenth-century America are the *encomenderos*), who ought to be protecting their Morisco dependents from abuses of authority and nurturing them in the new faith, are accused of thinking primarily of their own interests and of working against the local pastors.

In mid-sixteenth-century Valencia, Izquierdo uncovered for Charles V a number of matters that were also evident in contemporary Spanish America, not least that the effective teaching of the faith to a body of new converts was only the most obvious challenge in a contemporary evangelization setting.

Esteemed and Powerful Sir,

In Your Majesty's letter, I have seen your holy desire to advance the divine cult of Our Holy Catholic faith and the well-being of the religious orders. I see also that you command me to advise on matters concerning the conversion and reduction of new converts in the Kingdom of Valencia, to ensure that the infection of the Lutheran heresy does not enter through this principality, and to look to the reform of the monasteries. In undertaking these tasks, my spirit receives no small amount of happiness, Most Christian Prince, proving to me what Your Majesty already understands, namely, that in the midst of so many important affairs in your states and kingdoms, and in this age when young men grow accustomed to having their attention diverted from God, Your Majesty gives such close attention to things touching the faith and service thereto. Thus, I have true hope in God that through the work of your hands, the kingdoms possessed by the infidels who were formerly Christians will be recovered, so that heresy will end, and that you will be given victory over your enemies and will be guided in your affairs, taking example from the Holy Scripture which tells of the kings who understood how to devote themselves to the divine cult and to extirpate the idolatry in their realms, just as Your Majesty is doing.

With the report that I send, you will understand that I do not want to bring sorrow to Your Majesty. Even though some of the provisions concerning the new converts cannot be put into practice immediately, Your Majesty can draw up orders for when the Cortes [assembly of government] meets, even if the execution of the same must come with time, which I hope God will enable you to accomplish soon. Meanwhile, an order can be drawn up for what is needed from Rome, may Our Lord increase its [Rome's] life with the increase of kingdoms and of the faith, as I and this His house do entreat, where a special prayer for Your Majesty is always said. Barcelona, August 10, 1552. From your perpetual prayer-maker and servant, Fray Johan Izquierdo.

[the following document is appended]

What seems fitting as a remedy for the newly converted people in the Kingdom of Valencia is the following:

1. First, that the Prince, our lord, arrange with the pope for a bull that will commend the charge of all the newly converted in the Kingdom of Valencia either to the current inquisitors, or to a person in whom Your Majesty trusts in all that touches the things of the faith. This should be done in order that they might be taught and instructed in the Christian religion with full authority for several years to absolve them, exorcise them, and make special dispensations for consanguineous marriages, and to oversee their marriages and mediate their difficulties, which are neither few nor simple, and to punish them with penalties of abjuration, reconciliation, and relaxation to the secular arm as heretics, if necessary.

2. That, because they are new to the faith, one should not proceed against them with the full rigor that one is accustomed to apply against heretics who are descended from Old Christians, except in the gravest and most serious cases.

3. That for a period of twenty years or some other space of time set down by Your Majesty, even though they might be fined and receive the lightest punishments, their property should not be confiscated lest it seem that they are being punished with such ends in mind, and that this not be the ruin of the lords.

4. That the inquisitor(s) can order the rectors [pastors] of the churches of the new converts to maintain permanent residence in them, and that those who are absent or who are not competent in the teaching of the new converts or the administration of the sacraments to them should be removed from their rectories, which are to be assigned to others who are able, because it has been so decreed and because there have been some very ugly and scandalous cases. There are rectors in charge of small settlements in Valencia who do not say four Masses in a year, and through such pastoral negligence souls perish.

5. That the one who pays the rectors should not have the power to appoint them, so that he should not be in a position to choose whoever may suit him.

6. Among the new converts, one should dispense with the observance of many of the feasts demanded by the Church. It is enough that they observe Sundays and the feasts of the Incarnation, Christmas, the Circumcision, the Magi, Easter, the Ascension, Whitsuntide, the Conception of Our Lady, the Purification and the

Assumption, Saint John the Baptist, Saint Peter, and All Saints, because having to pay so much to their lords and the tithe to the Church, they cannot sustain themselves, especially those with lords to whom each person is accustomed to pay sixteen arrobas of passa [about 440 pounds, or 200 kilograms, of dried fruit]. Now that they are Christians, each must pay four arrobas [about 110 pounds, or fifty kilograms], along with other heavy charges.

7. It is very necessary that Your Majesty order the lords of new converts, under threat of grave penalties, not to accept on their lands the vassals of other lords, because if a lord is a Christian and he wants his vassals to live as Christians and presses them in this way, they will go to the lands of other lords, who will defend them and permit them to live in their sect [as Muslims]. Whereby, they do not dare to compel them to live as Christians because they do not wish to depopulate their lands.

8. The lords should be ordered to assist the rectors in matters which concern the instruction of the new converts, and not to bother and hinder them. Many lords favor their vassals so much that they threaten and maltreat the rectors, who then abandon their posts or fail to compel the new converts to hear Mass or confess their sins, or fail to baptize their children or bury their dead as Christians. With regard to disarming the new Christians and other temporal things, Your Majesty will know what to do, and when.

16

Alonso Ortiz's Letter to His Wife, Mexico City (1574?)

Alonso Ortiz's letter from Mexico City to his wife, Leonor González, in Zafra, Spain, offers a rare glimpse into the life and concerns of one of the two hundred fifty to three hundred thousand people who left Castile for the New World in the sixteenth century. Ortiz's principal interest lay in making money, and it was for this end that he left for America. Yet, for the student of history, this surviving letter, probably written on March 8, 1574, makes him more than a name on a list of ship's passengers or a name on an inventory of stock in a warehouse. Ortiz emerges from this document as an individual with his own dilemmas and dreams, who seeks to maintain strong connections with his family in Spain.

The letter has a number of motifs. One of these is Ortiz's stress on the value of perseverance. Life has not been easy for him, not that he seems to have expected ease. He alludes to "difficulties" endured in Spain, where his family's movements might still be hindered by creditors waiting to be paid. Even in Mexico, he has clearly shifted occupations before taking up the tanning of animal hides and venturing a small business with a partner. He works hard and lives frugally, and advertises these facts to his wife. As Ortiz is well aware, for people like him, America habitually shattered more dreams than it fulfilled.

Related to his views on perseverance is Ortiz's stoical blend of longing for home and family with enthusiasm for his commercial ventures. For him, life seems to be a mixture prepared and stirred by an all-knowing God. Ortiz sees God's will in all that happens to him; God guided him to Mexico, led him to become a tanner, brought him a compassionate business partner, provides him with good health and the capacity to take advantage of it. "God does no harm," he reminds his wife, "and . . . even a leaf on a tree does not move without His will." Mexico, for Ortiz, is a place where one endures a number of personal privations in order to acquire wealth that would be barely imaginable for him in Zafra. "I do suffer," he informs his wife, but "I also earn very abundantly." Communication between Mexico and Spain seems slow and unreliable. Ortiz reveals that letters sent sometimes never arrived. One senses his frustration at the lack of news from home and at seeing a number of his personal connections there fading away in his absence.

With only the remote prospect of a reunion in America, his family has been left behind. They receive letters like this one, telling of his loneliness, his accomplishments, and the survival and transformation of his hopes. Perhaps now, he writes, a new source of financial support and a plan of action will bring his wife and children to him. Yet, even here, Ortiz seems braced for disappointment and the need for adjustment. At one point, he states bluntly that he will remain in Mexico, the place to which God has guided him and in which his business prospects are looking up. At another, he mentions that he has kept open a condition in his latest business contract that would allow an eventual return to Castile. The family reunion in Mexico planned and proposed by Alonso Ortiz depends ultimately on Leonor González's decision, her disposition toward travel and a life in New Spain for her family. One wonders whether the couple had spoken and written of this matter earlier.

His letter includes one paragraph in which the correspondent sets out to tell his wife "about things here." For him, this means money, that is, the amount and kind of rent he has paid on the house and tannery in which he now lives and strives. Tanning was one of the most unpleasant and least prestigious trades, and Ortiz gives his wife little notion of what the work was like. His attitudes toward his "between six and eight" Indian workers are almost as veiled, although there may be hints of meaning in their manner of mention. At least from the evidence in this letter, Alonso Ortiz, on the subject of Indian laborers, is no Pedro de Gante (see Selection 12). Each Indian brings in an amount of money for Ortiz, and he keeps track. There is a great range in the profitability of the Indians' activity, with some bringing in thirty pesos and others only ten. His words on the subject end curtly: "About them [the Indian workers] I will not say more than that I pay them each week for what they do." Otherwise, Ortiz's letter is like most letters between husband and wife—personal and centered on the correspondent's own situation.

My lady,

Juan López Sayago gave me some of your letters, and I have others from a sailor who told me he got them from a certain de la Parra, who died at sea. From both sets of letters, I was most pleased to learn that you and all my children are well. Also, I was very happy to find among the letters given to me by Sayago a missive from my compadre Leonis de la Parra, because even though he wrote in his letter of having sent me others, none of them reached me. I will write to him with this fleet, and you can tell him for me that I have been negligent in not writing and that I ask his pardon. Up to now I have simply not been able to write. But be assured that in all I have done, I have asked God and His Blessed Mother to grant me health and, even more, the ability to take advantage of this time and my good health. Thus I have gone on, seeking first the things for which I have prayed; second, the tears that He has seen flow from my eyes; and finally—and most important—all that you, my lady, have prayed for, knowing as I do that I have not been forgotten, that you will have commended me to God and His Blessed Mother. And so they have done these things for me, and I also trust that they will have done as much—and more—for you and the children. Because, over here, even though it seems that one suffers much work and tribulation, one knows that God does no harm and that even a leaf on a tree does not move without His will.

I endured difficulties before God guided me here, to the place where I am and will remain. And all that I have suffered since coming is nothing to me because the troubles that you and my children have endured are what give me great sadness and torment, as well as those of your father and mother, and your brothers and sisters.

And I now feel it more than ever because God has led me to become a tanner, and there is no better position than this over here. Moreover, the great expectations which I brought, I still have. In order that I will make good use of the health with which God has blessed me, and that this time not be lost, I have worked, and I continue to work, with great care; I try not to spend money wastefully, and I earn much more than I need to make ends meet. There is, in all this, only one thing wrong, and this is that I do not have you and the children with me, because if I did have you here, and if God granted me health, saving even a thousand Castilian ducados each year would mean little to me.

To show you what I mean about things here, I have rented a house and tannery from April 1, 1573, until the end of March 1574. This has cost me ninety pesos de tipuzque, which are eight reales [one silver peso] each, and this I paid four months before the terminal date. And now, from April 1, 1574, I have rented another house for one hundred pesos de minas, which are thirteen and one-quarter reales for each peso, which I must pay in advance. In addition, I have between six and eight Indians who work with me, and each one that I have brings in thirty pesos, twenty, fifteen, or some only ten. About them I will not say more than that I pay them each week for what they do. I tell you all this so that you might consider that here, where I do suffer, I also earn very abundantly.

God has also brought me a partner so that I may not lose more time. He saw immediately my situation, and saw the distress I have over my wife and children, and he understands how much this afflicts me. And when I formed the partnership with him, I made no other condition than that if I wanted to depart for Castile within the three years of our contract, I could do so. He, who will not be leaving because he sees that much profit can be made in the long term, agreed to send 150 pesos to Seville with a merchant friend of his, a sum which is meant entirely for you, that you and the children may come. These pesos are meant to feed you, to pay for the preparation of your belongings and provisions for the trip, and for all other related business, and the money is yours from him. My partner tells me that he wants to provide for you from his house, and that the sum of money is to be understood as yours from him, so that certain people do not suggest that I sent it and that they neither hinder nor interfere with your coming, because your arrival would bring me great joy. So, if you decide to come, send your letter by the advance ship preceding the fleet on which you will sail. And to those men to whom I am indebted, you may say that on another fleet I will send one hundred hides that will be worth enough for everyone to be paid. With these letters will go also my power of attorney in order that you may act on my behalf, and that you can put me under obligation for the shipping costs, even if they amount to 200 Castilian ducats, that I shall pay upon your arrival. Dated in Mexico City on the eighth of March,

Alonso Ortiz

 17

Jerónimo de Benarcama's Letter to Francisco de Borja, Granada, Spain (1566)

The Society of Jesus was founded by Ignatius de Loyola (1491–1556), a Basque of military experience, under the authority of Pope Paul III in 1539–40. The Jesuits established seminaries and schools attached to their colleges throughout Catholic Europe. The motivation to convey Catholic Christianity to places and peoples beyond Reformation Europe was always part of Jesuit thinking, growing out of the early desire of Ignatius and a number of his companions to work in the Holy Land. In the years after 1540, their attention was drawn especially to non-Christian peoples contacted and, in some cases, ruled by Portugal and Spain. Francisco Xavier (1506–1552) sailed from Lisbon, Portugal, in 1541 for India and the coasts and islands then called the "Indies of the East," where he baptized people and preached in the hope of laying the foundation for the Christianization of Japan and China. The Jesuits arrived in the Americas in 1565, first in Brazil and Florida, and then in Peru in 1568 and New Spain in 1570. José de Acosta, the author of the reading (Selection 18) that follows the present one, was among the Jesuits who reached Spanish America at a point (1572) when the order's mission to the Moriscos in the Kingdom of Granada had fallen victim to the climate of distrust which spread with the Alpujarras rebellion and its bitter aftermath.

About a decade before these hostilities, in the late 1550s, the Jesuits' attention had been drawn to a large sector of Granada called the Albaicín, which stood off on the second hill that divided the city proper from the hill dominated by the great palace of the Alhambra. Here, according to one Jesuit correspondent in 1559, "more than 8,000 citizens," almost all of them Moriscos, dwelt. With encouragement from members of the new Christian nobility in the Albaicín, and from the coffers of Archbishop Pedro de Guerrero (1546–1576), Jesuits of the newly founded college at Granada and a few other Andalusian *colegios* established a satellite "house of doctrine" in the heart of this neighborhood. Thus began the most systematic episode of evangelization among the Moriscos of Granada, and perhaps the Moriscos in Spain as a whole. During its more than a decade of existence (1559–1570), the house's complement of Jesuit *padres* (fathers) and *hermanos* (brothers) fluctuated between seven and twelve (within some thirty-five Jesuits at the College of Granada in 1559 and forty-seven in 1569). Padres administered sacraments and were licensed to preach, while hermanos worked as assistants who heard confession and taught the basics of Christian doctrine.

Whereas schools among the native people of Granada had been of limited appeal, underfunded and generally short-lived in the early sixteenth century, the Jesuits' apparent successes prompted much early optimism. Pedro Navarro reported to Rome in August 1559 that "already" the house of doctrine served "some 200 students . . . and every day [the number] is increasing." The student body would rise to as many as 550 in 1560, although by that time the Jesuits' school was both attracting and admitting an increasing number of non-native Old Christian children. In that year, a group of "350 Morisquitos" (little Moriscos) shared their teachers with 200 Old Christian children.

From their home base, the Jesuits would venture into the squares and winding streets of the Albaicín. They were busiest on Sundays and feast days, inquiring as to why people were not in church hearing Mass. In their own accounts of these forays, it was a rare thing if a Jesuit preacher did not manage to lead a group of negligent Moriscos back to the church and participation in the day's devotions.

Small companies of missionaries also spread out to the communities of Moriscos living in the surrounding countryside, particularly in the Alpujarras mountains south of Granada. It was in these settings that the more promising Morisco students from the Albaicín, some of them already Jesuits-in-training, were thought most valuable. Although a few of the non-Morisco Jesuits of the Albaicín had learned the local Arabic dialect of *algarabía* well enough to deliver a sermon and hear confession, the select Morisco youths were often the adepts—native speakers who could facilitate deeper instruction. Moreover, their very presence was designed to encourage the urban and rural folk to see their own potential and that of their children in these young Christian models.

The Jesuits' mission work in the Albaicín and environs followed patterns established not only by Archbishop Hernando de Talavera (1492–1507) in immediate post-reconquest Granada but also, for that matter, by successive purveyors of the Gospel since early Christian times. Relevant lessons, ideas, and techniques also flowed back to evangelization settings in Spain from colonized Atlantic islands (especially the Canaries) and from newly conquered regions of the Americas, not to mention the East Indies. Reports and letters, as well as missionary personnel, channeled information and inspiration between the parts of what was increasingly being presented as a larger Spanish Christian unity.

A comparison with pedagogical efforts in early New Spain offers a good example of how educational efforts traveled as a central feature of evangelization. In the years directly following Cortés's military victories in the Valley of Mexico, a school was established at Texcoco by three Flemish Franciscans, one of them Pedro de Gante (the author of Selection 12). Their initiatives were followed up after 1524 by members of "the Twelve" Franciscan apostles and their successors, as seen in the schools at Tlatelolco-Mexico City, Tlaxcala, and Huejotzingo, among others. Later educational initiatives often reflected altered aims and perspectives, but the schools were not only the product of the first Franciscans in Mexico. After their arrival in Peru in 1568 and New Spain in 1570, for instance, the Jesuits established similar schools along with their residences and centers for study and training. In the last decades of the sixteenth century, and into the seventeenth, these institutions became familiar home bases for itinerant missions into the hinterlands. Educating the children of the indigenous elite in the regional schools was as central to the program of evangelization in Spanish America as it was to those which spread from the Albaicín into the communities in the Alpujarras mountains.

The Jesuit instructors in their schools throughout the Spanish world received careful directives from their superiors on many points of procedure, not least in the early identification of the young candidates best suited for clerical training. These boys became assistants in language acquisition. At best, they might mature into a native clergy, or, if expectations were lowered, at least a devoted band of catechists with a valuable store of local knowledge. This selection of the most promising among the Indian or Morisco student bodies did not diminish the importance of reaching the students who were not to be educated as potential priests or even formal catechists. It was a signal hope of the generation of Catholic churchmen whose aims were influenced by the atmosphere (if not the actual decrees) of the Council of Trent that all individuals would finally receive enough fundamental education to become good Christians. Reformative "missions" (the word is of this era) among a vast laity in western Europe deemed much in need of doctrine are part of the context in which the evangelization of former Spanish Muslims and adherents of native American religious systems was pursued. In all settings, but perhaps most urgently in "colonial" circumstances, the Jesuits sought good examples, a new Christian generation of women and men who would teach and personify Christian values and practices at home, in the presence of their own children and other relatives.

In sixteenth-century Spanish America, some Indians and people of mixed race (including those of African descent) followed up their years of education by living and working in convents and churches, dressing in habits, and associating themselves with churchmen and their religious orders or parishes. Their duties ranged from those of servants and manual laborers to those of scholars and research assistants, who shared the lives of the friars in almost every respect save that of official status. Yet however well educated and committed these native and mixed-race Christian assistants and scholars of early Spanish America appeared, very few were admitted to religious orders or ordained as secular priests. Despite substantial and sustained early efforts at instruction in central Mexico, for instance, native collegians were ultimately found unfit for ordination not so much for a perceived lack of intellectual capacity as for the presumed strength of their attachment to worldliness, to sensual living, and to value systems that made them ill suited to become Franciscan friars. In the curt estimation of the first bishop of Mexico, Juan de Zumárraga, writing to Charles V in 1540, the Indian students "tend toward marriage rather than toward continence."

A roughly analogous but also suggestively different situation occurred in sixteenth-century Granada. More young men who were the offspring of Morisco mothers and Spanish fathers appear to have become diocesan clergy (secular priests not attached to religious orders) serving in sixteenth-century parishes of Moriscos in the kingdom than was the case with Mestizos in contemporary Spanish America. And although the number of men perceived as "full-blooded" Moriscos who took the habit of a religious order and/or were ordained as priests was still small, their relative number appears to have been greater than that of Indians from a much more numerous population (even after the greatest ravages of disease) in the Indies. In the case of the Morisco Jesuits, identification is difficult and research has not been exhaustive. Yet it is certain that at least six Moriscos (or young males with at least one Morisco parent) who had been students of schools in Granada, Gandía, and Murcia (and five or six other strong possibilities, two of whom were denied admisssion) were accepted by the Society of Jesus as novices and hermanos in this period. These cases invite comparison with the more isolated American ones not only of Indian but also of Mestizo and Mulatto student-candidates in the sixteenth century and later: among others, Diego Valadés, the multilingual Mestizo Franciscan and author of the *Rhetorica Christiana* (1579) (see Selection 22), who had studied under Pedro de Gante in Mexico; Blas Valera (1544–1597), the Mestizo Jesuit scholar from Chachapoyas, Peru, assistant to the Third Provincial Council of Lima, and chronicler of the Inkas—at least before his fall from the Society's favor, on account of the theological and practical implications of his views on the sacred potential of the Quechua language and Inka religious concepts in the ongoing evangelization of native Andeans; and Santa Rosa's contemporary in Lima, the Mulatto Dominican, Martín de Porras (1579–1639).

How do these new Christians' experiences compare? Were the new converts from Islam regarded as an order of people higher than native Americans (or Tagalog speakers in the Philippines archipelago, for that matter) by Spanish Old Christians? From the points of view of not a few Old Christian authors who expressed some optimism about the assimilation of Moriscos, former Muslims were a not-so-distant people "of the Book" who had been deceived by a false prophet and were now being gathered back into the fold. Among the descendants of militant enemies of Christianity from whom the Kingdom of Granada had been reconquered, perhaps there was added incentive to teach and ordain more young models for conversion.

Jerónimo de Benarcama (1548–?), the author of the letter that follows, was one of the Morisco children who went beyond the period of intensive education and followed his Jesuit teachers around the Albaicín reciting the Christian doctrine. By the age of ten or eleven, Jerónimo was said to have dressed in religious robes, and his teachers clearly hoped that he might join the select rank of Moriscos led by a celebrated contemporary in Granada, a Morisco Jesuit padre named Juan de Albotodo (1527–1578). Albotodo, to whom Jesuit correspondents regularly referred as the "apostle to the Moriscos," was an ordained priest who preached and taught the Christian doctrine in algarabía in the Albaicín and in the surrounding communities of the Alpujarras in the 1550s and 1560s. The fruits of his pastoral work were much praised within the Jesuits' reports from Granada. Other evidence suggesting that Albotodo and a few of his Morisco assistants drew a decidedly mixed response from the heterogeneous Morisco population of his region is deemphasized by almost all Jesuit reports of him. Writers took care not to dislodge the image of a "solid" convert who obeyed, a tireless preacher, and a model native Jesuit who committed himself totally to his ministry and to the local glory of Christianity.

If Albotodo emerges as a polished embodiment of the Morisco new order sought by Old Christians active in this ministry and by their converts, then Jerónimo de Benarcama is a rough edge—the less made-to-order and more precarious face of the new Christian in a contemporary evangelization setting. The figure of Albotodo arguably plays a part as protagonist in a steadily advancing Christianizing narrative, while Benarcama's complicated self represents a detour, an unfortunate complication that cannot quite be repressed by Jesuit participant-tellers. The figure of Albotodo rises almost entirely out of glowing accounts written by others who were eager to see in him (and in any other new convert who would offer the opportunity) an embodied edifying story. The novice Jesuit Benarcama, in contrast, brought trouble, threatening to present an unedifying narrative and ambiguous example to all.

Benarcama knew that a flurry of correspondence about him had been passing between his superiors in the Jesuit province of Andalusia, and that Francisco de Borja (1510–1572), the third Father General of the Society in Rome, had already been duly informed of the matter concerning Brother Benarcama. You will already have heard tell of me, of how I came to enter the order, and other things, Benarcama self-consciously began his letter, while at the same time implying strongly that there was so much more than his notoriety to understand. This Jesuit Father General would read the letter with knowledge, if not much sympathy. Before pursuing his religious education and admission to the Society, Borja had been duke of Gandía (near Valencia). He had supported a significant educational effort among the Moriscos there, founding a school which, among other goals, had sought to educate a Morisco novitiate to assist evangelization in that region.

Written on September 25, 1566, Benarcama's letter delves straight into the complex Granada of his day, examining barriers, points of contact, and traditions of misrepresentation between social groups. Benarcama points at "good" and "bad" in both the Old and new Christian communities. He manages to be insightful without being particularly endearing. Given the vow of Jesuit obedience that he has taken, he emerges as a proud, at times even manipulative young man, and it is not difficult to imagine how he irritated his superiors. He as much as asks the Father General to pause and imagine the repercussions if he, the Morisco novice whom everyone knows, were to leave the Jesuits because of his "indisposition." And Benarcama knows just where to strike for effect. He refers to himself and to Albotodo as the Granadine Moriscos' examples, and their only protectors and defenders. Did Benarcama have an inflated idea of his own importance? (It certainly served his interests to be significant.) Or was he, as a potential Albotodo, a genuinely critical agent and symbol for a number of parties in the Granada of the 1560s?

Benarcama's aptitude was quickly noticed after he entered the Jesuit Order in 1562 at age fourteen, but reports claimed that his health declined rapidly over his next four years in the novitiate. After a series of illnesses remarked upon by his superiors, he was sent to convalesce in the *colegio* at Granada, which he soon left for the refuge of his mother's house in the Albaicín quarter. It was at first claimed by his Jesuit superiors that he hoped to recover his strength and return to his studies and the service of God. Yet the problem of "ill health" might have meant a number of things within the contemporary Society of Jesus: ill health was sometimes a code for any number of difficulties emerging between a novice or Jesuit and his superiors, often an indication, in John O'Malley's words, of "a growing sense of incompatibility on one side or the other, or both." In Granada there were mounting signs that Benarcama's "indisposition" was more than simply physical. In the meantime, his father, a prominent and demonstratively Christian post-Conquest noble, died. In the young Jesuit's words, his father's death left his mother and siblings "so poor that if bread was not given to them as alms, they would not eat." What was more, like their Morisco neighbors, Benarcama would later state, his family members endured the abuses and financial demands that plagued "the poor people" of this place. His feeling of responsibility for his family, along with his outrage at the conditions suffered by "the people of his nation," come into sharper relief in the letters he wrote after the one excerpted below, especially as it became increasingly clear that his college rector and provincial had lost patience with his special requests for solitude and more time to study.

In his letter to Borja, Benarcama seems motivated by contradictory impulses that express his complicated position and those of others like him. There is a raging sense of injustice within this Morisco novice who feels the conditions of his family and relatives. Yet he also feels an anxious need to belong as a Christian and to live up to his assumed role as a pathbreaker in difficult times. His words suggest that he felt immense pressure as one of the privileged boys who had been chosen and educated by the fathers, and who was now depended upon—as much by certain Moriscos as by other Jesuits—to be an agent in the assimilation of others. Here was a new convert from Islam who had accepted membership within a Christian community, who was anxious about his immortal soul, and who was facing some culminating vows. Would he be another Padre Albotodo? His strong inclination toward his studies (as opposed to preaching in the Alpujarras, for instance) seems to be a sign that this was not to be. Perhaps he was also pestered by doubts that his efforts as Christianizer would do anything to better the Granadine Moriscos' conditions.

Benarcama clearly chafed within the controls of the order, and yet he seeks (at this point) to retain his place and to serve God. He wants Christianity and to be a Jesuit, but he also wants these things his way. A proud and angst-ridden young man who feels so many eyes upon him never quite disappears beneath the apologetic language expected of someone in his position writing to the Father General, and even more so from one with such a mixed history. His promises to reform notwithstanding,

there is in this letter a hint of his later decision that his return to the fold would only come if he could make his studies the center of his life, perhaps at the University of Alcalá, where many of his teachers had studied, and where he might also put his learning to use.

There is in Benarcama an interesting opportunity to consider what membership or association in a religious order, not to mention the issue of ordination, was like from the position of a member of the native nobility. Benarcama in Granada begs comparison with indigenous collegians, native scholars, and artists trained in European traditions and techniques in early colonial Spanish America, for whom similar choices and challenges appeared. In Benarcama's case, the young Morisco, who was to have abandoned the matters of the world and the ties of his relatives in preference for complete obedience to his superior and to God, was drawn instead toward an ultimate responsibility to his own desires, to his family, and perhaps also to his people as a local leader. His early decision to be a Jesuit comes to seem a bitter mistake. An amazing series of interviews in his mother's home, increasing disobedience of his superior's entreaties, captures, and jail breaks ensue, all related from the point of view of his disgruntled Jesuit superiors.

Yet of what precisely did Benarcama's resistance consist? There is no evidence to suggest that his commitment to Christianity had diminished, although his faith may have been less rigorous than that demanded of a would-be native missionary and more closely connected to the situation of his family and respectful of the needs of the Morisco community. Just as Jerónimo de Benarcama disappeared from view behind the outbreak of the Morisco rebellion in the Alpujarras in 1568 and the pressing nature of his superiors' other concerns (among them, the arrival of the first Jesuits in Peru in that year), there surfaced a rumor of his wish to marry a cousin, with whom he might presumably raise a family.

[Benarcama's letter to the Father General is joined close to its mid-point]

Your Honor should know that I am a native of this kingdom of Granada of the Moriscos. That is, I am a grandson of the man who was once the Moorish lord or magistrate of the city of Guadix (I say this even though it seems immodest because it seems relevant to what I am about to say), and as such I am as well known by the leaders and notables as by the general population throughout this kingdom. . . .

[It is necessary that we establish a few other truths.] The first is that in the whole of this kingdom there is neither a leader, nor a member of the nobility, nor a prelate who does not have his eyes fixed on me, as does the Count of Tendilla, the president of the audiencia [regional governing body and court], the archbishop of this city [Granada], the bishops of Guadix and Almería, the deans [of the cathedrals], and so on. So much so that I am terrified and overwhelmed by what is expected of me, and about this I speak frankly. The second [truth] is that all of the natives of this kingdom are much persecuted by the Old Christians, and they [the Moriscos] have no one to protect and defend them except for Father Albotodo and myself. Many of them have told me that it [Albotodo's and my presence and ministry] cheers them greatly and that because of it they want to enroll their children in school so that they can grow up to be churchmen. And [further,] there is not a Morisco nobleman who has not expressed his hope that, through me (even though I am a vile and feeble instrument), God will work wonders among them. The third [truth] is that I am so well known by them that if the newly converted of this kingdom number

200,000 or 300,000 souls, not 100 could be found who do not know me, as I already said, because I am from the nobility, as well as for other reasons.

With these things established, then, if I left the Society [of Jesus], the news would go out across the whole kingdom that would be so sad for the virtuous and so joyful for the evil. Sad for the good Old Christians because they would lose hope and at once despair at the worth of this people [the Moriscos], seeing that one [of those whom] they had their eyes on did not persevere. And sad for the good ones among the natives because their guard would have dropped, and it is disheartening [to think that] they would then have no one to defend them against the words of their detractors. Happy for the bad Old Christians because they would truly get their desired occasion to grumble, and happy for the bad natives because seeing me unable to carry on would confirm their cherished opinions that this generation has neither the ability nor the [intellectual] wherewithal for the tenets of Christianity. Judge for yourself, then, Father, if my leaving would be more an offense to God, a pleasure to the Enemy [the Devil], and an unedifying example to the people, than [an act] in the interests of the glory of God and the edification of all.

The other difficult matter that stirs me still more is the danger to my soul, for I am certain that if I were to leave the Society I would see the inferno open for me and that my soul would be lost to the flames of Hell. . . . If I leave the Society . . . with health and freedom and other circumstances of which I will not speak so as not to defame anyone, I do not know what will become of my soul.

I have summarized the difficulties about which I wrote to the Father Provincial [and have written] of my feelings about leaving, but his response has not yet arrived.

My view on this matter [of abandoning] is stated in these terms, with which, even though unworthy, I now earnestly and humbly ask Your Honor for the love of that so merciful Lord for whom I prepare with such a special vocation and who, by such an indirect route and without my deserving it, brought me to be in this holy Society. . . . I trust that I do not have to be cheated of my hope and then that I will never lose my place, for which, not without reason, God now gives me my health, so much so that I am [privately] carrying my studies forward. And I do all that is asked and commanded of me with a great desire to live all the days of my life in obedience in the Society of Jesus, so much is my pain and repentance and intention to make amends for all the mistakes I have made and for all my carelessness up to now. Time does not allow me to say more. . . .

Your unworthy son and servant in the Lord,

Geronimo de Benarcama

18

José de Acosta on the Salvation of the Indians (1588)

José de Acosta was born in the Castilian city of Medina del Campo in 1540. Following a path that was also traversed by four of his five brothers, he entered the Jesuit Order in Salamanca at the precocious age of nine. At twenty, in a letter to a superior, Acosta reflected that as a young novice he had studied and performed the Spiritual Exercises—a series of meditations undertaken by all prospective Jesuits—for some three weeks, "even though," he complained of his supervisors, "they would not allow me to spend the entire day shut up inside because I was a child." He set out as a preacher and a teacher of theology in a succession of the Jesuit colleges that had sprung up in the Iberian Peninsula. A good writer with an excellent command of Latin, Acosta frequently composed letters to Rome on behalf of his college rectors, particularly from Segovia and Alcalá. He was ordained in 1566 while at Alcalá, where, unlike his contemporary Jerónimo de Benarcama (in Selection 17), he was allowed time for study, focusing on courses in philosophy and theology at the university. The effects of conventional as well as Renaissance humanist learning at Alcalá would be put to good use by Acosta in his later writings, most of which were stimulated by his assignment to the new Jesuit province of Peru.

He arrived in Lima in April 1572 in the company of two other fathers, part of a small, third group of Jesuit arrivals to the southern Viceroyalty of Spain's American possessions (seven Jesuits had disembarked in 1568, and another twelve in 1569). Acosta picked up where he had left off in Spain, initially teaching theology at the Jesuit College of San Pablo in Lima. Some exceptional abilities must have been quickly noted, because in the next year his provincial sent him on a sixteen-month tour of the central and southern parts of the Andean region. The Jesuits were eager to expand their new missionary base in the south-central Andes, and Acosta's assignment was to determine how this goal might best be accomplished. He was to examine the prevailing conditions and prospects for missions in Cusco, Arequipa, Potosí, Chuquisaca, and La Paz (all of which would come to have Jesuit fathers and colleges). Part of Acosta's research tour coincided with an ambitious general visitation of the realm then being made by Viceroy Francisco de Toledo (1515–1582), whom the Jesuit seems to have impressed. Acosta would also have benefited from the opportunity to compare notes with the viceroy's advisers and assistants, among them the lawyer and keen observer of mid-sixteenth-century native Andean culture, Juan Polo de Ondegardo.

Back in Lima, Acosta was promoted on Toledo's recommendation to a professorship in theology at the University of San Marcos, a position he held for only a short time before taking on a five-year term as the Jesuits' second provincial of Peru (1576–1581). Reflecting the growing respect he commanded in ecclesiastical and political circles, Acosta served as principal theologian and adviser to the Third Provincial Council of Lima (1582–83), convened by Archbishop of Lima (and later saint) Toribio Alfonso de Mogrovejo (1581–1606). In addition to his influence in the conception of the pivotal council that would reflect the concerns of the Church's general Council of Trent to South America, Acosta helped shape and draft its acts and decrees. He also assembled the third council's pastoral complements, including texts by Polo de Ondegardo on the Indians' "errors" and "superstitions," a confessor's manual, thirty-one sermon texts, and two catechisms for Indians that Acosta himself edited and that others would translate into the principal indigenous languages of Quechua and Aymara. The trilingual results, the *Christian Doctrine* and *Catechism for the Instruction of Indians,* were published in Lima in 1584 and 1585.

Acosta's experiences and study of the pastoral situation in one of the great Indian heartlands of the Americas provided inspiration for two books that he was already writing in the 1570s and 1580s. He left Peru in 1586 for a year in Mexico in order to confer with people there and to collect additional information for his writings. After a time in Rome, gaining papal approval for the decrees of the Third Provincial Council and discussing American evangelization with the general of his order, Acosta was back in Spain. His remaining years were spent writing and publishing his books, teaching theology, and occasionally advising the Crown on American matters. Acosta's best-known work, the ambitious *Natural and Moral History of the Indies* (*Historia natural y moral de las Indias*) (Seville, 1590), was a Spanish translation of the first of two Latin tracts that he had published two years before in Salamanca (*De natura Novi Orbis libri duo, et de promulgatione evangelii, apud barbaros, sive de procuranda Indorum salute libri sex*). This history was quickly translated into English and other western European languages. Acosta died in 1600 at the age of sixty.

Less widely known outside circles frequented by churchmen and students of evangelization is the second tract in Latin, a guide for Christian priests serving among Indian peoples. Though published in 1588, Acosta makes clear in the selection which follows that he was writing it in Peru as early as 1576. *How to Provide for the Salvation of the Indians* (*De Procuranda Indorum Salute*) is a missionary masterpiece that highlights Acosta's erudition and considerable abilities as a writer. The work combines a fervent immediacy drawn from personal experiences in the spiritual plane with a subtle application of Christian theology and missionary practice that is somehow both learned and accessible. In *De Procuranda,* Acosta confronts a number of vital issues related to Indian peoples and their relationship with Catholic Christianity at a late sixteenth-century moment that he presents as critical for the Indians, as well as for the Church and the Spanish monarchy. Writing in provocative, general terms to his mostly clerical audience, Acosta observes that the Indians' attachment to Christianity is not forming at the expense of their ancestral religious beliefs and practices. Virtuous living and habits of devotion seem an external gloss on many Indians' lives, a dutiful shine that dulls without the scrutiny and urging of assiduous priests and judges. A number of salvations seem to hang in the balance.

Acosta wrote *De Procuranda* at a time when missionary enchantment with the prospects for Christianity in the "New Jerusalem" to be built among the indigenous peoples of Latin America is often said to have been uniformly on the wane. Histories of the evangelization of Indians in colonial Spanish America tend to pocket efforts at understanding and persuasion in the sixteenth century, a slide to pessimism and coercion in the seventeenth century, and an atmosphere of resignation and increasing indifference in the eighteenth century. By Acosta's time, the optimism and sympathy so characteristic of the evangelization of early New Spain is often said to have made way for lowered expectations, distrust, and cold practicality. Indeed, there is a certain reserve to Acosta's missionary hope in an American future. He prefers to argue, he says—thinly cloaking a criticism of the style of his Dominican predecessor, Bartolomé de Las Casas—in the manner of "a moderate lawyer" rather than "an uncritical enthusiast." Acosta perceives complications in the evangelization of Indians, but is he accurately described as disillusioned with them, as hardened or narrow in vision?

One might argue that his words are a caution to anyone who would seal off an early colonial "era of missionary optimism and patience" from a subsequent "era of disillusionment and pessimism" that is usually said to begin in the late sixteenth century, around the time of the Third Provincial Councils in Lima and, a few years later, in Mexico City (1585). In its fervor and imagery, the following passage recalls the exhortation to the twelve Franciscan apostles on their way to Mexico (Selection 7) and the letter from Pedro de Gante (Selection 12). Reminiscent of the writings of Las Casas himself, Acosta's text aggressively counters the arguments of the Indians' "detractors," defending the new converts and offering up remedies for the future. Especially in the Andes, where civil wars, determined Inka rebels, and difficult terrain had delayed Spanish religious and political consolidation before the 1560s and 1570s, the arrival of members of the religious order that had risen so quickly to prominence in Catholic Europe was a kind of new beginning.

Acosta's *De Procuranda* reflects the Jesuit ascent and the sense of occasion. It demonstrates the Society's concern with pedagogical excellence, exemplary virtue, and missionary feats that might equal those of Saint Francis Xavier in distant corners of what would have seemed to a sixteenth-century missionary as an exhilarating, widening Spanish world much in need of the word of God. Within this expanding world, attention might shift between various constituencies judged to be in need of mission, indoctrination, or reform. For Acosta, Catholicism was becoming more portable, more committed to, and even defined by its traveling translocal program of evangelization. Jesuits in the New World, as in the old, echoed the sentiment of one late sixteenth-century Spanish correspondent to Rome who enthusiastically predicted that wherever there was a square or a crowd in a street, there would be a Jesuit father preaching.

Intensive experiences in America and Europe had, by the last quarter of the sixteenth century, thus required the adjustment of dreams but not their disappearance. *De Procuranda*'s pastoral optimism is a tower steadied by realism. Acosta and his generation of Jesuits expected to win souls in the world, but to win them gradually and not without surmounting sizeable obstacles. Some of the American obstacles are judged by Acosta to be intrinsic to the lands and their peoples. According to his evolutionary scale, some Indian groups were more capable of receiving an Hispanic brand of Christian civilization than others. But other obstacles were placed by Spanish Christians themselves. As late sixteenth-century Jesuits were discovering at virtually the same time among "newly converted" *naturales* (natives) in Valencia, Granada, Florida, Brazil, Mexico, Peru, and so on, missionary endeavors were precarious and reversible. In this age of reform, missions were vulnerable enough in contemporary Europe among the many who were ostensibly of the same faith, but they were especially so among neophyte peoples such as Indians and Moriscos—peoples who fell beneath even heavier official scrutiny and a changing hierarchy of demands, needs, and fears.

Jesuit pedagogy blended classical ethics and decorum with a Christian moral tradition, with the result that emulation and edification became the principal aims of the constructive relationship that was to mature between teachers and pupils, missionaries and new converts. A student, moved by the merits of the good example before him, was to be inspired to similar virtue. Reflecting on these aims, Acosta seems acutely aware of how close missionary reverses were in the New World and of where he should apportion the blame. His hope for the Indians' salvation is bound to an acutely critical appraisal of his fellow Spanish Christians. In *De Procuranda,* he does not let his readers forget the ultimate importance of the Indians' will and determination in their own Christianization, a process that—again, like Las Casas—he sees as having crept along, often in spite of Spanish Christian behavior. The faith and its new contexts are a tender plant for Acosta; and, in his view, Christianity had grown its roots in late sixteenth-century Indian soil principally because "men who have suffered serious wrongs from Christians still have not cast Christ aside." For those Spanish Christians who take advantage of Indians and live as poor examples among populations assumed to be impressionable, Acosta serves up a cool reminder of Judgment Day: "God does not distinguish between them and us."

In marked contrast to the problems encountered in assuring the Indians' salvation, he features Jesuit advances. Fruits are measured in a number of ways, not least by the "companions in this happy dawn of the Gospel," the indigenous lay assistants and local equivalents of a Valadés or an Albotodo (see Selections 22 and 17, respectively), who were won to God's side and chose to assist the fathers' ministry among their people. The native peoples, in Acosta's mind, become not foes aligned in defensive positions and needing to be overcome so much as the Jesuits' principal allies, the coveted reward for the Society's exhibitions of virtue, patience, and energy. Presaging the seventeenth-century accounts from Mexico featured in a later selection by Mariano Cuevas (Selection 29), Acosta emphasizes a mutual respect developing between itinerant Jesuit fathers and the Indian people who sought them out as confessors of sins and preachers on Sundays and festivals.

Like the Franciscan superior instructing Valencia and "the Twelve" over half a century earlier, and like Francisco de Vitoria lecturing about the place of coercion in evangelization (Selections 7 and 8), Acosta connects missionary deeds and aspirations in America to those of the first apostles of Christianity. He universalizes the American evangelization settings, making their Christianizers aspirants to the same praise and metaphors as the faith's founders: farm workers prepare the soil, sow seeds, tend fragile plants, destroy weeds, await the harvest, and reap bountiful rewards, while shepherds guard flocks from danger, their own bad judgment, and the temptation to stray. Acosta, as artfully as any clerical participant-teller in his day, builds upon pregnant allusions to the primitive church and the biblical analogies (principally to Samaria) by comparing Indian peoples with "pagans" from Europe's past. On an obvious and practical level, such thinking had, for almost a century by Acosta's time, made Indians more intelligible to Europeans and the Europeanized in America. Further, the transhistorical analogy, like the translocal commitment noted above, seemed to promise a Christianized future, a great goal for which to strive. The parallels allowed some Spanish Christians to counter the diminished hopes of other contemporary missionaries for the evangelization of Indians. Acosta and others reduced Indians to a few categories (not just one) in ways that strengthened changing notions of Spain's providential role in the unification of all humankind under Christian rule. Acosta suggested that vigorous self-reform would have to accompany renewed effort if evangelization was to advance.

Chapter 14
The Christianity in Which the Majority of the Indian Peoples Live

1. The Indians' situation appears to me very similar to that of the Samaritans of ancient times of whom we read in the fourth book of Kings [II Kings]: wounded by terror and fear of the lions who wreaked havoc among them, the settlers asked God for a priest who would teach them the divine law. "One of the priests," reads the Scripture, "deported from Samaria, was then to establish himself in Betel, and he taught them [the settlers] how to worship the Lord." And there followed an enumeration of various of their superstitions, after which was added: "So they worshiped the Lord and served their gods at the same time, in keeping with the religion of the country from which they came to Samaria. They come, observing their ancient rites, right up to today. They do not venerate the Lord, nor do they live according to His commandments and rules, but instead follow the law and norms already stated," etc. The Scripture concludes: "Thus, that people honored the Lord and gave worship to their idols. And up to today their descendants continue doing the same as their ancestors did."

I do not believe that one needs to describe in greater richness of detail and elegance all that is our Indians' way of life and religiosity. They give worship to Christ and they serve their gods, they revere the Lord and they do not revere Him; the two extremes are confirmed by Holy Scripture. They venerate Him only in word, they venerate Him as long as the priest or judge urges, they venerate Him, in short, only with the appearance of Christianity. They do not venerate Him from deep inside, they do not give true worship nor hold the faith in their hearts as is truly required. What use is there to carry on? The [pre-Hispanic Indians'] descendants continue doing the same as their ancestors did.

Chapter 15
Despite This, There are Great Hopes that the Indians Will Receive the True Faith and Salvation; To Imagine Otherwise Is Contrary to the Spirit of God

1. Consider the Samaria of our own time, a place which Christ occupies together with Succoth-Benoth of Babylon, Nergal of Cuth, Ashima [of the people of Hamath], Nibhaz and Tartak [of the people of Avva], Andrammelech and Anammelech [of the people of Sepharvaim], and other monstrous gods. It is not so much that one worships Christ along with others as much as it is that, in a certain way, one obliges Him to suffer that insult and affront against Him, in being associated with demons and showering them with honors through His participation. But that does not mean we should reject our Samaritans and give up all hope in them. The Lord will remember Samaria, too. And the time will come when it [our Samaria] will receive the word of God and listen to Philip after rejecting Simon, and be worthy of having Peter and John as its preachers. The time will come when [our Samaritans] will say: we, too, believe that He [Christ] is truly the Savior of the world.

Also, Christ will make the Samaritans surrender themselves and show His disciples golden fields ready for harvesting, for He proclaims a successful harvest and promises bountiful fruit for eternal life. Why, then, should we lose hope? Why do we command with Jewish arrogance that the Samaritans go far away? Would it not be much better to proclaim the Gospel to them in imitation of the Lord and His apostles? We believe the seed that grows and bears fruit over the whole world will, in the end, also yield its bounty in this arid and inhospitable land. That which is parched will become a spring, because rocks have smashed in the desert and been moved by rivers.

It will come, Samaria's time will come, and those who earlier had received the order, "Neither go to the land of the pagans nor enter the cities of Samaria," then will hear the precept of the Lord: "Receive strength, [for] the Holy Spirit will descend over you, and you will be my witnesses not only in Judaea, but also in Samaria and to the ends of the earth." I have arrived at a firm conviction, and it is impossible for me to think in another way, that, although it may yet be a while and it may perhaps [require] more effort and prudence at the beginning, the time will come when, by the kindness of the Holy Spirit, the Indian peoples will be much enriched through the grace of the Gospel, and the Lord of all that is holy will be presented with abundant fruit.

2. The only difficulties I fear are the great shortage of ministers [who are] sensible and faithful in Christ, together, of course, with a surfeit of mercenaries and others who are looking out for their own interests rather than those of Jesus Christ. Because if the unfit pastors were merely useless, they would be tolerable. But the fact is that they are doing much damage and scattering Christ's flock, and all this causes us pain and occurs without courageous objection from us.

Therefore, if the Lord would dispatch real workers to His ripe fields, and I mean irreproachable workers who proceed with respect for the word of God, and who see in these peoples not personal gain but the peoples' interests; who gladly put aside wealth only for the good of their children and are, moreover, completely willing to wear themselves out for the salvation of their souls; who will love their spiritual children so much that they will wish to give to them not only the Gospel of Christ but also their own lives; who, trying to please God, speak in ways that [show they] do not look to ingratiate themselves with men, but only to win over God (who knows the hearts of men), whose words are neither characterized by flattery nor encouraged by greed—workers, in short, who with the greatest sincerity seek not their own glory but that of God—at that time, with their sheaves replete, the barrenness will come to an end and the most bountiful fields of grain will spring up and be harvested for eternal life. Meanwhile we must be patient and pray fervently to God to send His workers.

3. Let no one think that I have said this thoughtlessly: experience itself is more than enough proof. There are men of God—and although, I admit, they are few, they exist—[men] who have observed for themselves that the Indians' malice does not arise from their nature. Those [Indians] who have had reliable, diligent, and wise priests and guides sense very well the power of the divine doctrine; and they respond, little by little, by setting an example with their lives, naturally, of course, as

happens in everything; but, they receive the seed and yield a harvest on their own: first, [there] is a shoot, that is to say, the external practices of the religion; then, the sprig of understanding and a variety of emotional attachments; finally, the wheat at the height of its maturity, that is, the faith now fully working through love, with acts worthy of God. One cannot insist on the maximum growth right away, in only one day.

If the decrees that have emanated from the Catholic King and his Council [of the Indies], by the great zeal that they have for the Christian religion and the concern that they have for the Indians' salvation, and which so wisely keep an eye on their [the Indians'] interests and well-being, will be carried into effect with as much diligence and loyalty as the gravity of the situation that led to their promulgation, before long the task of saving the Indians will not only be simple and pleasant but even very fruitful. In spite of everything, [and] whatever the situation is at the moment, it is not so bad that many thousands of Indians have not been won for Christ. And whereas some zealous persons moan excessively that all the Indian peoples are going back to their Baal, and cry that they all maintain their huacas and serve their Supay [an ambiguous Andean force ill-advisedly pressed into service by some sixteenth-century evangelizers and lexicographers as a synonym for the Devil], the Lord keeps for Himself more than seven thousand who do not bend a knee before Baal, and there is even an Obadiah enriched with the gift of prophecy. "The Lord knows His own; all peoples will serve Him." In these circumstances it is not the Christian way, indeed it is very contrary to the spirit of Christ, to keep the people away from our ministry and to dissuade them from the enterprise, [or to say that] because the difficulties will be great they cannot have over them the rule of God and His grace; and with the harvest being very meager, the fruits of the souls cannot fail to be abundant and the rewards before God immense.

[Acosta continues along related lines in Chapters 16 and 17. He is confident about the conversion of many Indians, arguing that their "internal religiosity" should not always be doubted. And he returns to the theme of how essential able, sensible, and dignified priests are to the maintenance of the faith in its new lands in the Spanish world. Acosta invokes the authority of his personal experiences, and he finds the Indians eager to imitate good examples, capable of receiving the faith and abandoning their non-Christian ways; he finds them naturally obedient and respectful of people in power. He underscores his points with further examples from the Bible and from the histories of early Christian missionaries among the pagans of Europe (missions to Ireland and Britain are the examples that occur to him), the twists and morals of which he knows so well and relates exquisitely. Acosta's purpose is clear: America is part of the Christian revelation. Friars and priests and Indians are playing their parts in a divinely sanctioned story that will cost much toil and many lives. Doubts and regrets will flourish in even the strongest of missionaries. But there is a magnificent ending even in this most barbarous of lands. The Jesuit's principal messages build up an exhortation aimed at his fellows: we Christians in the Indies must not lose heart in our venture to win the Indians over to God's side. We can learn and gain strength from the "patience," "perseverance" (these words are repeated by Acosta), and "apostolic industry" of the "soldiers of Christ" who have gone before us in other barren lands. We should be cheered by the evidence of bountiful crops of millions of souls reaped by our holy predecessors. In the same manner, one day we shall harvest. But, first, great effort (by good teachers and healthy doctrine) is required. "A plant comes to nothing," the Jesuit writes, playing on 1 Corinthians 3:7–9 to make a confident return to his metaphor, "if it is not watered."]

Chapter 18

Not Only Is There Hope for the Future, There Also Exists Evidence of Great Results in the Present

1. The problems I have examined to this point are expressed as if I myself held a low opinion of the Indian peoples who are to be led to the truth of the Gospel and as if I had no confidence that notable results might come from these apostolic labors. Although what I have said about these peoples, for whom I feel a deep fondness, is, as some of our own [Spanish Christians] pointed out well enough, not only a little dishonorable but positively unjust and damaging. Still, I allow myself to do it, because in the defense of the Indian cause I prefer to act as a moderate lawyer rather than as an uncritical enthusiast.

Most of the mercenaries slanderously claim that these peoples surrounded by the great ocean were barbarous, irrational, inhuman, thankless, superficial, coarse, and, in the end, unsuited to understand the Gospel and the whole spiritual enterprise. Still, unless we set aside the objectivity of the facts, what has been achieved with them up to now is sure proof that in a way we should not give up hope for the salvation of so many peoples. So, if the detractors of the Indians' chance of salvation were right in their allegations, they will in no way achieve what they so much desire.

If I am to say what I sincerely feel, I do not doubt for a moment that there is no reason to call into question the character and nature of these peoples with respect to the cause of the Gospel. And I am fully certain that if the Gospel had been introduced into these regions in the way in which the Gospel's founder intended, the gains made would equal those about which we read in the primitive apostolic church. Because if, in spite of such depravity [among] our men [Spaniards], with their immense chasms of greed, their violent pillage and servitude, and their outrageous instances of cruelty, men who have suffered serious wrongs from Christians still have not cast Christ aside, and when a little more well-behaved instructor or reformer of their ways comes to them, they listen with admirable attention and respect, show themselves to be more malleable than wax, and strain to imitate any honest and decent gesture they see. Think what might have been—Holy God!—if from the very beginning of the evangelization they could have glimpsed the beautiful feet of the heralds of peace, if they had learned for themselves by deed and word, and not out of our self-interest, that they were being sought for Christ!

2. Of course, the fathers of our modest Society [of Jesus], who have already spent eight years in these regions of Peru and who know from experience the customs of these peoples, through having set out on many extensive missions, through the administration of their own parishes, or through frequent dealings with them even when they have not held the position of parish priest, affirm with great sincerity that they have met with better results than they expected in all places, placing their lives on the line with God as a witness if what they say is not true.

Moreover, some of our most serious and prudent fathers assure us in the letters they write that nowhere have they seen an easier or better field for evangelization.

And those recently arrived from Spain have held on to the common opinion, that is, the opposite view, [but] in the end they jettisoned it completely after contrasting it with [what they learned from] years of experience. For they had seen that these Indians are intelligent, gentle, humble, obedient, devoted to the good priests, they despise pomp and luxury (a thing some find hard to believe), and once they have accepted the religion and virtue willingly and with sincerity, they stand firm in their resolve. It is easy for me to tend toward this opinion, when we see them so committed to the Inkaic religion or so absorbed by the superstition of their huacas that, in order to conceal some useless idols with which they have been entrusted or a hidden treasure, they often die willingly, giving up their fortunes and their own lives rather than the secrets of their parents' superstition.

Who is not aware that Indians were frequently flogged with lashes by Spaniards and burnt by fire set beneath them, and that in the midst of these tortures, they uttered not a single word against their convictions? Why, then, should we think that the Devil is more bold in his own defense than Christ? Or that these peoples, who have been created and redeemed by God, are going to be more steadfast in the preservation of their pernicious falsehoods than saving truths? One thing is certain: give me apostolic men among the Indians that I shall repay you in Indians' souls.

Perhaps because they have seen in us of the Society some kind of life that is honest and removed of all ambition, they come to us, often from far away, and with great enthusiasm and after having traveled thirty or eighty leagues, they make their confessions. We have seen them attend the sermons with such frequency that they seemed gripped by an insatiable hunger for the word of God, going from one to the next until [they have heard] four and five in the same day, and [they do] this every Sunday and feast day. Anyone seeing the endless crowd of those who ask for and receive the sacrament of confession and absolution would think themselves witness to a jubilee or the celebration of Holy Week.

They ask that weighty penances will be imposed on them; and if those which are set are not as heavy as they wish, they place them on themselves, driving themselves to tears and bitter pain. They encourage each other to penance with such passion that our fathers cannot satisfy them all and grumble that they are overwhelmed by inappropriate requests. They are so constant in their intentions to reform that one learns of some women (these being of the weaker sex) who, without entreaties, threats, nor [even] a sword drawn and held to their necks, could not be persuaded to go back to their old lovers.

They gladly give up all of their possessions; they hunger most eagerly for the body of Christ, and those to whom it is permitted [through Holy Communion] receive it with great purity of soul, maintaining it [their cleansed state] with devotion and declaring that once they have taken Communion there is no room [in their lives] for criminal acts. We heard of an Indian who felt such anger at himself for once failing in his intention that [only] with great difficulty could he be restrained from strangling himself like an ungodly and sacrilegious traitor to the body of the Lord. It is known that some are so full of devotion to God that they attain an extremely wise and exalted sense of the sacred, to the point that sometimes they have the heavenly prescience to foretell the future.

Many will consider all that I am saying to be exaggerations which exceed all limits, or they may even smile as if these are stories. But I speak of sure and proven facts. And no matter what those who consider themselves the only Christians say, the grace of God has also been spread among these peoples, purifying their hearts with faith, and God does not distinguish between them and us. And there are those who, already won over by the facts themselves, realize that they had never seen or expected such a thing from these Indian peoples; and so they are amazed and give thanks to God the Greatest Father of the orphans. Some even choose to join us [Jesuits], as companions in this happy dawn of the Gospel.

There are very many who, out of envy, are furiously against us and keep on attacking us, [but] one must rejoice at the salvation of brothers and warmly congratulate one's collaborators. What our [Jesuit] fathers have begun, more than completed, is small enough and is deserving of no more special tribute than that which could be made to any minister of the Gospel who is not unskilled or unfaithful to his mission. These same fellow Jesuits who have taken up the ministry of the Indians' salvation are very few; and, also, they are not endowed with the qualities needed for an undertaking of such importance.

3. From all that I have said, one can now easily understand the excellent and abundant results that will follow if the Lord of such ripe grain decides to send numerous workers possessed of suitable strength and talents to work in this field. And even though we reckon that many other Indian groups are able to receive the Gospel in the form we have described here, and such is without a doubt the experience we have of the Peruvians, in the remaining parts of this book we will observe [a certain] moderation and not speak so broadly of the matters of Indians, [in order] not to give the impression either that we have overlooked other Indian peoples [or] that we are unaware that they are less able.

Because although we have mostly our Indians, the ones we know, before our eyes, if it proves possible, we want what is written [here] to be of wider value for the salvation of all. We know for a fact that even among those barbarous peoples whom we classify in the last place [in a non-Christian hierarchy that ranks nomadic hunter-gatherers very low], the Gospel's grace is reaping magnificent and copious fruit. One certainly knows that the Brazilian Indians are second to none in their ferocity and hideous customs, and yet we have learned from the letters of our fellow Jesuits that thanks, above all, to the Society of Jesus, they have become tame and molded to divine and human laws, [and] learned to be men and good Christians at the same time.

Now, also, the faith is enjoying its first fruits among the pagans, and the Gospel's harvest among the peoples is better than could be expected. Our great plea must be that Christ Our Lord will make us worthy ministers of the New Testament, for who could be qualified for such a ministry?

Up to now we have shown how the preaching of the Gospel among barbarous peoples, though extremely difficult, is necessary and highly fruitful. In the following part we will explain how to do it.

 19

Miguel Hernández, Master of Mule Trains

JOHN C. SUPER

Explorers, conquerors, viceroys, missionaries, saints, prelates, poets, merchants, landlords, rebels, criminals, heretics, and others who came under the Inquisition's probing gaze are among the best-known individuals in colonial Spanish American history. We miss the vast majority of people leading less notorious lives with little power over others. John C. Super, professor of Latin American history at the University of West Virginia, describes such a life at the turn of the seventeenth century in the provincial city of Querétaro, a few days' travel north of Mexico City. It is a glimpse of the ordinary experiences of an extraordinary man that invites questions about choices, discrimination, and survival for people of color in early colonial society.

In piecing together the testament and scattered financial records of Miguel Hernández, Mulatto owner and operator of a string of mules hired out to haul goods in central Mexico, Super finds someone who succeeded in his business and established himself as a person of trust and respect among Indian neighbors and some influential Spaniards. Hernández's Querétaro seems to have been a more open and prosperous town than the view of a Spanish American economic depression in the seventeenth century would predict. What might explain Querétaro's apparent prosperity and the opportunities it afforded a man such as Hernández? And how did his identity as a person of mixed African ancestry limit his contacts and opportunities?

Miguel Hernández was a free Mulatto who lived a good, full life in sixteenth-century Mexico. He married, raised a family, and lived to see his children find their own place in the world. He acquired an education and became a community figure in his own way. After years of work and dedication he achieved local economic influence and prominence. Miguel Hernández found success and love during an era of increasing social and racial prejudice. Mexico did not have its social and racial arrangements fully worked out in his day, but increasingly, toward the end of the century, life was difficult for people of mixed blood.

Miguel Hernández is an important man to know. He is one of those people historians too infrequently encounter, who went beyond mere accommodation to create a rich and rewarding life in the face of difficult circumstances. He did so in an orderly and even way, living a relatively prosaic and unassuming life. He was neither a spirited rebel nor an adventurer; he was simply a diligent and persistent man who gradually expanded the horizons of his own world.

Miguel can be recalled today because of his literacy and his knowledge of Spanish legal ways. He was a frequent visitor to the office of several notaries in the town. From the contracts Miguel entered, the will that he wrote, and the contracts and wills written by his friends, it is possible to reconstruct some few aspects of his life. Much of the documentation relating to Miguel would have been impossible to use if he had not been able to sign his name. His signature made it possible to distinguish him from the other Miguel Hernándezes that appear in the notarial records.

Miguel's signature gives us a more direct, personal understanding of the man. In the absence of a portrait, it is the only likeness of him that endures. With the heavy emphasis on form and style in writing in the sixteenth century, his signature does give something of an intellectual portrait. His signature of 1598 is here reproduced.

His hand was steady and sure, with more attention to the careful formation of each letter than to exaggerated embellishment. Like most men of learning, though, he did have concern for stylistic impression, so there is some flourish and grace to his signature. He obviously held a quill comfortably and confidently. The quality of his hand places him closer to the trained professionals than to the marginally literate men who scratched out crude signatures. Miguel's signature implies that he was literate. Literacy was quite common among sixteenth-century Spaniards in Mexico but was unusual among Mulattoes, Blacks, and Indians. His literacy therefore immediately placed him in a select group.

Miguel was born in Mexico City in the middle of the sixteenth century, the legitimate son of Pedro Hernández and Ana Hernández, natives of the same city. He was a second-generation Mexican, a man of the New World who had few ties with Spain or Africa. He married Ana Hernández (no relation to his mother), who was also born in Mexico City; it is likely that some of their children were born there too. Though details are few on Miguel's background, documentation from later years suggests that he used his legitimacy, literacy, and freedom to good advantage. He did some work as a muleteer, became more familiar with the complexities of trade, and developed personal and financial associations with people of wealth.

Miguel's ties to Mexico City were strong but not strong enough to bind him to a life there. The chances of material gain for men of color at the center of the colonial economy had lessened as life became more settled and orderly after the Conquest. Very few Blacks and Mulattoes, whether slave or free, broke through the legal and social barriers to occupy master positions in the more important crafts or to own valuable property. Thus, many of them looked to the provinces for opportunities. Earnest colonists, along with debtors, renegades, and escaped slaves, moved to the provinces to escape the growing rigidity of the social and racial hierarchy of Mexico City.

Miguel Hernández chose the town of Querétaro as his new home. It was a good choice. Querétaro was then a small agricultural and commercial town with a promising future. A man of vision could easily see that the town was on the verge of expansion, though few could have foretold the population growth from about 1,000 in 1590 to over 5,000 in 1630. The key to the town's growth was location. Querétaro straddled the highway connecting Mexico City with the silver mines at Zacatecas and the north. The rich agricultural and pastoral lands of the Bajío spread toward the east, producing crops for distribution to the north and south. Commerce, and the transportation system on which it depended, tied the economy together and linked it to larger population centers. Economic growth generated social opportunity. Race, sex, and background influenced a person's place in Querétaro, but they did not determine it. A free man of color with luck and hard work could build a fine life there.

When Miguel arrived in Querétaro, he automatically joined a special group. Since he was free, literate, and skilled as a muleteer, he became one of the leading Mulatto citizens. The less fortunate lived for the service of others, bound by the debts that they had accumulated. These men and women labored in fields and factories for two or three pesos each month. With debts that might approach 100 pesos (sometimes incurred to obtain release from jail), such people normally faced years of servitude. Less fortunate still were slaves, the largest group of Mulattoes in the town.

Often, Mulattoes lived on the edge of the law. Contemporaries saw them as dangerous and unstable, as troublemakers who caused more harm than good. They committed (or at least were accused of committing) crimes of assault, rape, drunkenness, and theft more often than Spaniards and Indians. Partly for this reason, local officials from time to time tried to enforce the stringent royal legislation restricting the behavior of Mulattoes. In 1597 the town magistrate ordered them to leave the Indian areas because of their corrupting influence. In 1623 the magistrate ordered all free Mulattoes and Blacks to perform service for Spaniards. Even men with money and a good reputation experienced the burden of discrimination. Juan Bautista, a free Mulatto, opened a hatter's shop and was thrown in jail for his efforts on the pretext that he was not a professional hatmaker, and that he did not have a license for his shop. The real reason was that the established merchants and manufacturers could more easily intimidate a man of color who did not have powerful friends.

Miguel Hernández carefully sidestepped many of the traps that ensnared other Mulattoes and Blacks in this society. Like the surefooted mules that he led, he seldom stumbled as he walked through the Spanish world. His ability to contract large debts without being forced into servitude is strong evidence of the standing he achieved in the community. Miguel managed, at least for some practical purposes, to overcome the stigma of his color. He became a Spaniard in his economic activities, and much of the rest of his life personified the opposite of the nasty stereotypes that Spaniards had of mixed-bloods. Subtleties in the notarial records help to illustrate this. Notaries, who knew Miguel well, at times forgot to add the customary remark that he was a Mulatto; at other times they hastily scratched in "free Mulatto" above his name, adding as an afterthought something that was becoming less important.

After moving to Querétaro, Miguel began building his own freighting business. By the end of the 1590s his success allowed him to expand. In March 1599 he bought six mules for 215 pesos; in August he bought two more for 72 pesos. Business was good enough that he could pay these debts in a year, either in cash or by discounting freight charges. By 1604 he had expanded again, buying eight more mules, not yet entirely paid for. This gave him a train of twenty mules, a substantial investment by local standards. Twenty mules with tack might bring a thousand pesos in the very brisk provincial mule market. The same amount could buy a wheat farm with tools and stock, several thousand acres of grazing land, or a flock of two thousand sheep.

The expansion of Miguel's business can be understood only against the background of a rapidly growing provincial economy. With the catastrophic decline of the Indian population in the sixteenth century, Spaniards were forced to turn from a reliance on Indian surplus to a more direct control over economic production. The rise of the Spanish population and the colonization of the far north hurried this development. Querétaro benefited from the changes. By 1600, Querétaro farmers and ranchers sold maize, wheat, and mutton to hungry urban populations; and just as important, local merchants shipped out wool, first in its raw state, then as a manufactured item produced by the town's *obrajes* (woolen factories). With large quantities of bulky goods moving north and south, Querétaro became a transportation center requiring the services of scores of freighters.

Like several other local muleteers at this time, Miguel earned most of his income from hauling wool to the southern markets of Mexico City, Texcoco, and Tlaxcala. For every twenty-five pounds that he hauled, he received about three reales. He supplemented this income with small profits from petty trade. The sale of cloth was a natural consequence of the muleteer's knowledge of prices and markets. Farm workers and artisans owed him a few pesos for rough garments. Here, Miguel was similar to other mixed-bloods and Indians who sold bits of cloth, thread, and foodstuffs for a few extra pesos. He differed from them in that once in a while he carried more valuable cloth on consignment from Mexico City people to the province. His wife even bought a dress from one of these Mexico City sellers for thirty-five pesos. Miguel may also have earned a little money from the collection of the tithe, a tax levied by the Church on economic production. One of his debtors was Luis de Vargas, who owed him twenty bushels of wheat—eight for the sale of a saddle and twelve for the tithe. Since merchants almost monopolized the collection of the tithe, it is likely that Miguel was a subcontractor or an agent for a merchant. Finally, Miguel sold mules. Retailing mules that he bought wholesale or selling those no longer needed for his business brought in cash.

To help finance his business, Miguel turned to local landowners and merchants. By 1604 he had open accounts with the merchants Fulano de Oviedo, Hernando de la Vega, and Francisco Vásquez. He had another account with Luis de Tovar, a sharp businessman and one of the fastest-rising persons in all of Mexico. Tovar had grown up watching his father wheel and deal in the eastern Bajío wool trade and by the 1590s, when he was in his early twenties, had himself begun to invest directly in the trade. Eventually he invested in large tracts of land and became an important political figure in Mexico. Miguel's association with Tovar was probably a short-run boon to his freighting business, although if the association had continued, Miguel might have ended up simply as an employee of Tovar. Other people contributed to the building of Miguel's business, but only in a small and sporadic way.

The facts that survive from the conduct of the business imply that Miguel was an aggressive and enterprising man, not afraid of taking risks. He seized the opportunity for growth, rushing into debt to increase the size of his mule train. Yet he exercised caution and showed sound judgment by not overexpanding or overextending his credit. Miguel's spirited business temperament paid social and economic dividends. By 1604 he had become a *señor de recuas* (master of mule trains), a smart leap from his status as a simple muleteer (*arriero*) in the 1590s. There were other muleteers in Querétaro, but none of them was addressed as *señor*. Miguel had reached an enviable status in the freighting profession, but he had not reached the top. This position belonged to the owners and masters of the heavy carts and wagons that rumbled between Querétaro and Mexico City. These men were exclusively Spaniards and often figured among the most prominent men in local society. With their large wagons they could easily ship more freight than the muleteers, who were increasingly confined to shorter hauls and harder roads. The lives of some muleteers were like the roads they traveled—rough, continually turning, separated from the mainstream of provincial life.

Miguel Hernández was different. While he never reached the top, he did earn enough to buy valuable property in the town. In 1598 he owned a house and garden worth 500 pesos, a large amount for town property in the 1590s. Apparently he had bought a substantial parcel of urban property just to the west of the center of town after arriving in Querétaro. At this time several Indians, Blacks, and Mulattoes lived in the area. He sold a section of the land (about 15 x 20 yards) for seventy-two pesos in 1598. He also owned irrigated property just to the north of town, which he sold for thirty pesos. Miguel was profiting from the fast growth of Querétaro in the 1590s.

Miguel also used his new wealth to buy a Black slave. By doing so, he joined a fairly exclusive group dominated by Europeans. The slave was sick and at 150 pesos may not have been a sensible purchase economically, but the prestige and other social benefits of owning him probably compensated for this.

Miguel had deep ties to Querétaro. His profession made him a man of the road, but his property and his family made him a man of the town. His wife Ana bore four children: Francisco Hernández, Juan Hernández, María Magdalena, and Elvira Martínez de San Miguel. Remarkably, all of them survived and were a part of the family in the 1590s. It is to Ana's credit that the family survived as a unit.

What little is known of Miguel's wife is confused by the existence of another Ana Hernández who lived next door. Miguel said that his wife was a Mexican Indian (probably Aztec), but at times she was referred to as a Mulatto. The other Ana was definitely a Mulatto, who worked as a domestic for two pesos a month in the 1590s. It is probable that Miguel's wife came from a common Indian family. She made no pretenses about her background, and when she married Miguel she brought no material goods into the marriage. She was illiterate but most certainly Spanish-speaking, even though she at times negotiated contracts with the aid of an interpreter. When Miguel died, Ana turned to her son Juan to help her manage her affairs, giving him power of attorney to represent her and her husband's property. Her reliance on Juan was never total. As late as 1622 she appeared in the notary's office to handle family matters.

Miguel's family may have extended beyond his wife and children. Members of a Mulatto family headed by another Miguel Hernández appeared in Querétaro. This Miguel had his interests in land, not in transportation and trade. Blacks and Mulattoes had the chance to own small rural properties (*ranchos* and *labores*) in the province during this time, but they could not expect to become masters of large agricultural and pastoral enterprises (*haciendas* and *estancias*). Miguel raised crops and a few goats, pigs, and horses on a farm to the south of Querétaro. He also had connections in Mexico City, where he still owned a small house worth 150 pesos in 1600. In that year his family appraised his estate at 1,028 pesos. Miguel's estate shows that small farms could provide more than a subsistence living, but they seldom provided as much opportunity for gain as commerce. Unfortunately, there is no direct proof of the two Miguel Hernández families being related by blood or marriage. Extended Mulatto families held together by common social and economic interests may have existed, but they are difficult to document.

There was a woman in Querétaro who has to be considered a member of the family, even though she was not related. She was the widow Ana Enzemoche, an Otomí Indian. Since Ana had no family (as she put it, "not having daughters nor sons, brothers nor sisters, no relatives, nor heirs"), she claimed the Hernández family as hers. She gave María Magdalena a plot of land for her dowry, made both Miguel's daughters heirs to her entire estate, and then appointed Miguel and his wife as executors of her estate. The widow was dear to the Hernández family, as close as any relative could have been.

Miguel's circle of close associations stretched far beyond his family. Many of his friends were his neighbors: Hernando, an Indian singer in the chapel; Cecilia, the Indian wife of a Spaniard; Ana, the Mulatto servant; and the many Mulattoes and Blacks who belonged to Miguel's *cofradía* (confraternity). If this cofradía was similar to others in town, its members met often to plan religious festivals, talk about finances and organization, and provide social and economic assistance to widows, orphans, and the sick. Other friends were outsiders, people whom he had met on the road or old acquaintances from Mexico City. When the free Mulatto Martín Gracia became ill in Querétaro, he immediately sought his friend Miguel to help write his will and organize his papers. He gave Miguel control over some houses he owned in Mexico City and charged him with seeing that his daughter received money for a dowry.

He also claimed Spaniards as friends. His closest Spanish friend was Domingo Correa Falcón, a merchant. Their friendship probably began with a business deal, then assumed more permanence when Correa Falcón became Miguel's *compadre*, the godfather of one of his children. Miguel always referred to Correa Falcón as his compadre and called on him to help set up his estate. Through his membership in the cofradía of the Santísimo Sacramento (this was in addition to his membership in the Black and Mulatto cofradía), Miguel associated with the richest landowners, the most active merchants, the most powerful bureaucrats. Miguel knew them all; and in the last years of his life, when he was a señor, it is not too difficult to imagine that he looked them in the eye as an equal. He spoke their language, wore their clothes, followed their laws, and succeeded in their businesses.

Many of Miguel's relationships crossed racial and social boundaries. The restrictions that often placed Mulattoes and Mestizos much closer to the Indian world did not usually apply to him. His life did not fit into any one level of the complex social and racial hierarchy evolving in Mexico; instead, it bridged many levels of the hierarchy. His ties with Indians and mixed-bloods were warm and personal. After all, Miguel was still married to an Indian commoner, and his children had been raised among Indians. Yet his occupation and interests threw him headlong into the Spanish world, a world in which he eventually moved with ease. He seemed to walk the cultural bridge without anxiety or doubt. Certainly he curried favor with influential Spaniards. This was natural for anyone chasing the good life in early Mexico. While doing so, he did not suppress his own origins or that of his family. Dodging the past was an established art practiced by many in the sixteenth century, but not by Miguel.

Much more of Miguel's life would be understandable if it were possible to reconstruct more fully the lives of his children after they struck out on their own. This was not possible because of their common surname, and because they were no longer Mulattoes. Spanish racial nomenclature was inclusive enough to provide for the offspring of Mulattoes and Indian women, but such artificiality did not exist in the province. Children of Mulatto and Indian unions with a good social and economic background usually escaped derogatory racial labeling.

It is known for certain that one of Miguel's sons did not follow his father's profession. Juan, who earlier may have been a shepherd, joined the artisan ranks in 1599 when he apprenticed with Bartolomé Vásquez, the best blacksmith in town. Juan agreed to serve for a year and a half in return for bed, board, and clothing. After that time he would be a journeyman, allowed to practice his trade anywhere. Juan probably finished his apprenticeship, since his father guaranteed that he would. Blacksmiths led a decent life in the province. Their position fell somewhere between silversmiths and architects at the top and tailors and carpenters at the bottom. Francisco Hernández also may have been a smith; at least there was another blacksmith in town with that name in 1600. It is reasonable to assume that Miguel's sons had joined the lower ranks of Spanish society.

No definite information is available on Miguel's daughters, but with their substantial inheritance from Ana Enzemoche (which included twenty-nine parcels of land), they should not have lacked suitors. Elvira's name suggests that she was already married or had been married previously. If they did marry, it is likely that they married Indians or mixed-bloods of good standing, since even some Spanish women with dowries had a difficult time finding Spanish husbands around 1600. If they did not marry, they probably had enough money to aspire to a comfortable life in the prestigious local Convent of Santa Clara de Jesús.

Miguel Hernández died suddenly in 1604, leaving his wife and children as survivors. Probably struck by disease or the victim of an accident, he only managed to mark his testament with four heavy strokes, whereas a few days before he still had a fine signature. He quickly called on his compadre to help him with his will. Miguel named his children as heirs, each to share equally in his wealth. He then made his peace with the Church, asking that Masses be performed before his special saints. He was anxious to be buried in the Convent of San Francisco, and even before writing his will had made arrangements for this with the guardian of the convent. The guardian readily acknowledged the request because Miguel was a man of substance and virtue. By avoiding the passions that had destroyed many, Miguel had created a life of meaning that was respected by his family and friends.

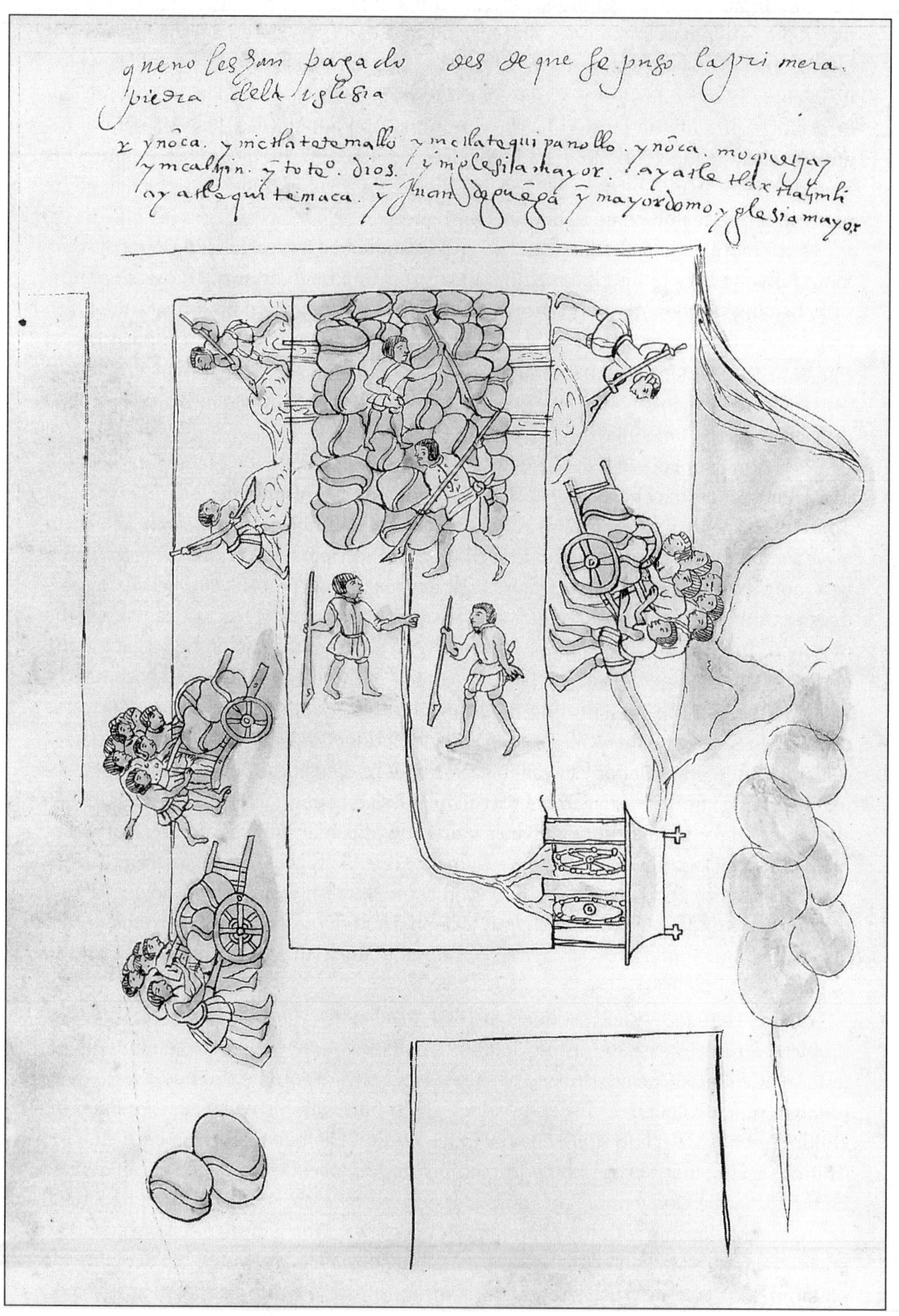

Figure 11. Illustration from the Codex Osuna, Mexico City, 1565.

20

Two Images from the Codex Osuna, Mexico City

(1565)

During a *visita*, or general inspection of local government, in and around Mexico City in 1565, various Indian communities complained strenuously about unjust and uncompensated labor service and other onerous demands for food, fodder, and building materials. Part of the legal record of this visita, known as the Codex Osuna, registered the complaints of Indian communities in the jurisdiction of Mexico City, Tlatelolco and Tacuba (near the city limits), and Tula in the modern state of Hidalgo in a form that combined the pictorial tradition of pre-Hispanic records with a written Nahuatl text in Roman letters and Spanish glosses.

The complaints in the Codex Osuna, including the two images (Figures 11 and 12) and texts given here, echo the grim account and warnings of Pedro de Gante's letter of 1552 to Charles V (Selection 12) that labor demands exceeding those of the Aztecs will ruin these new American subjects if the Crown does not intervene. The rapid decline of the Indian population from epidemic disease made the labor demands all the more onerous. In the first image (Figure 11), Indian men are shown quarrying and moving large blocks of stone by wheeled carts—a European introduction—for construction of a church. The accompanying Nahuatl text identifies the church in question as the "great church" (cathedral) in Mexico City, and adds that not since the work began had Indian laborers received any wages from the overseer, Juan de Cuenca. The short Spanish gloss says simply that "they have not been paid since the first stone of the church was set in place."

The second image (Figure 12) makes a direct connection to Gante, who was still alive. The issue, as the Spanish text reveals, was whether Bachiller Moreno, the archbishop's adviser on Indian affairs, acted on the approval of either the archbishop or the viceroy when he had ordered the Indians of Mexico City to acquire three bells for the church of San Pablo two years earlier. Moreno is shown seated in the upper right corner beneath a church identified as that of "Sanc Pablo," speaking and gesturing with both hands toward three bells. To show that San Pablo was one of the four "barrios," or settlements, in the jurisdiction of the Indian government of Mexico City, the Indian author of the Codex Osuna arrays little churches of the four subordinate settlements of Sanc Pablo, Sanc Juan, Sancta María, and Sanc Sebastián around the larger church for the capital city with its place glyph of a nopal cactus on a pile of stones. Two features of this image are of special interest as an

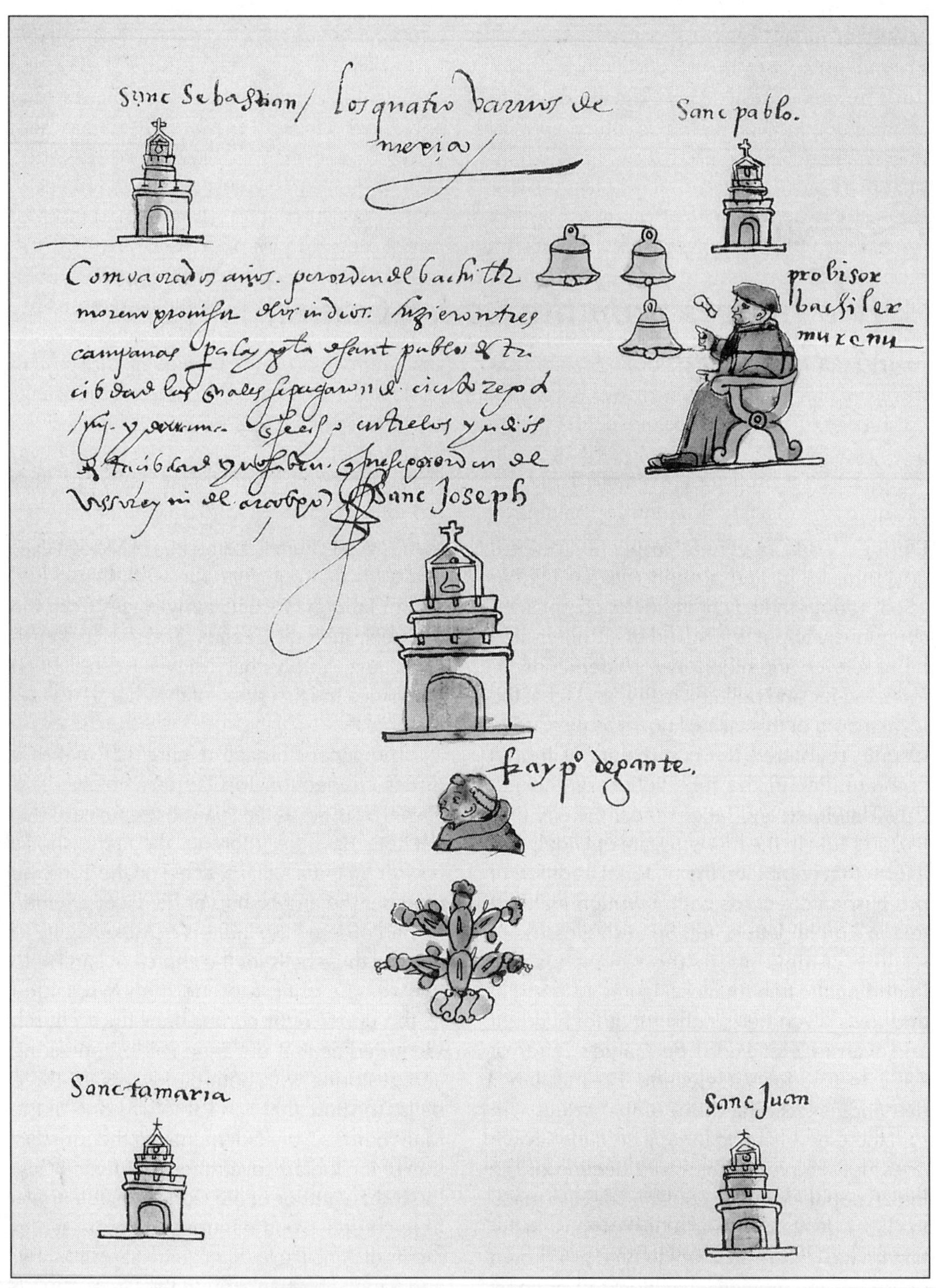

Figure 12. Illustration from the Codex Osuna, Mexico City, 1565.

Indian vision of the space and the subject at hand. First, the configuration of the five places recalls the sense of five directions that pervades pre-Hispanic representations of space: four corners raying out from the paramount fifth direction, the sacred center (see Figures 3, 4). Second, rather than identifying Mexico City with its cathedral, the author shows the chapel of San José de los Naturales ("Sanc Joseph") as the important church at the center. San José was, indeed, where most of the city's Indian neophytes went for instruction, church services, and the sacraments, but it was also a local Indian place in a fuller sense. It was built and maintained by Indians of the vicinity at their own expense and had been accorded some privileges and special indulgences usually reserved for cathedrals. The author goes further, embellishing the representation of the Indian church in Mexico City with a drawing of the head and shoulders of the beloved Pedro de Gante. That his name and person were then synonymous with Christian piety, service, and local pride is suggested also by the popularity of "Pedro de Gante" as the personal name taken by newly baptized Indians in the city. Together these two images from the Codex Osuna provide a suitably mixed sense of the demands made on Indian subjects and the succor offered them by the new church and its Spanish priests.

21

Two Images from the Codex Sierra, Oaxaca, Mexico

(1555, 1561)

An illustrated account booklet from the 1550s and 1560s known as the Codex Sierra enlarges the 1579 Texupa map's representation of early colonial experience in Indian perspective for a part of southern Mexico (see Selection 14 and Figure 9). It records community expenses for a place also called Texupa, perhaps located near the Texupa of the 1579 report or at least in the same Mixteca region that forms an arc from the highlands to the coast in northern and western Oaxaca.

Like the map for the Texupa *relación geográfica,* the images in the Codex Sierra also suggest a colonial Indian viewpoint that drew upon pre-Hispanic knowledge and new forms of expression to represent local activities under Spanish rule. Arranged in European book form rather than the traditional screenfold, it gives a running account of community expenses for the pueblo of Santa Catarina Texupa from 1550 to 1564. The pages of entries in horizontal lines combine the older way of recording events in pictures with written words in Nahuatl using Roman letters. Many of the entries are for church expenses—equipment and supplies for Mass, musical instruments, religious art, food for the priest, and money spent on holy day festivities.

The first entry included here (Figure 13) dates from 1555 and shows a frame containing a stretched cloth on which there is a sleeved arm and hand holding a large key. The writing notes that ten pesos were spent for a painting of Saint Peter. This economical way of depicting a painting of Saint Peter fits with the pre-Hispanic practice of a conceptual more than a visual art, representing figures and events by combining signs rather than attempt-

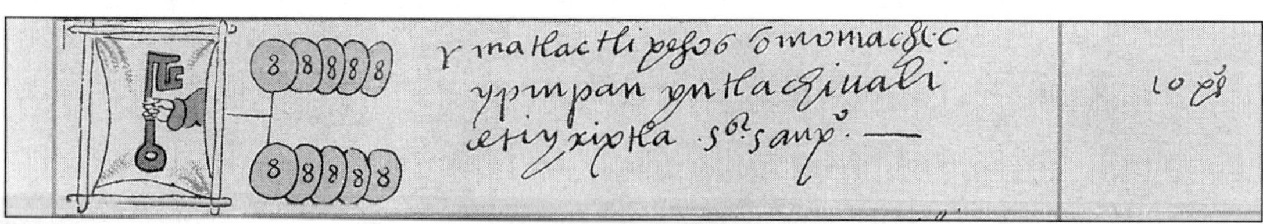

Figure 13. Illustration from the Codex Sierra, Oaxaca, Mexico, 1555. Courtesy of the Marquand Library of Art and Archaeology, Department of Rare Books and Special Collections, Princeton University Libraries.

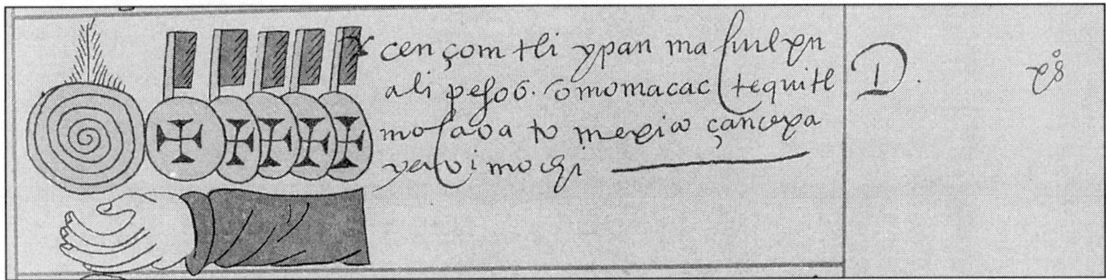

Figure 14. Illustration from the Codex Sierra, Oaxaca, Mexico, 1561. Courtesy of the Marquand Library of Art and Archaeology, Department of Rare Books and Special Collections, Princeton University Libraries.

ing a literal depiction. In pre-Hispanic pictorial records it is the arms and hands of highly stylized human forms that are especially expressive, and here an arm in European dress grasps the key, telling us that someone associated with a key is depicted in a painting. That someone is Saint Peter because the key is his particular symbol as keeper of the heavenly gates.

The second entry (Figure 14), from 1561, also shows a large sleeved arm and hand, but it is more expressive in a European way. The text reads "500 pesos were sent to Mexico City to pay for various things purchased there." Miguel de Unamuno once anatomized Madrid as "a stomach, not a brain," consuming the wealth of the nation rather than providing Spain with intelligent leadership. Here in the Codex Sierra, Mexico City becomes a giant outstretched arm with the palm of the hand cupped upward, awaiting payment.

Taken together with the Texupa *relación geográfica* and its map, the Codex Sierra can serve both to elaborate on and reflect further about Olivia Harris's thought that the Conquest was less the defining historical moment for many indigenous people than it was for Spaniards (Selection 6). Harris's main example of indigenous people expressing indifference, or at least little surprise, at the arrival of Europeans comes from another Mixteca pictorial record produced earlier in the colonial period, known as the Selden Codex. It records in indigenous style events that happened shortly before and after Spaniards entered the region, yet it fails to note the Spanish presence at all. By comparison, the Spaniards' presence is more of a defining feature in the Codex Sierra and the Texupa maps, which were produced later in the sixteenth century.

22

Fray Diego Valadés's Ideal Atrio *and Its Activities*

(1579)

Born in 1533 to a conquistador father and Indian mother, Diego Valadés would become the first recorded Mestizo friar of the Franciscan Order in Mexico. Under the influence of Pedro de Gante, whom he later assisted, Valadés entered the order at an early age, becoming an excellent Latinist and following the Observant tradition. He helped to evangelize hostile Chichimecs of north-central Mexico and assisted Gante at the Indian school of San José de los Naturales in Mexico City before being sent to Rome in 1570 as the Franciscans' agent to the Vatican. There he composed and illustrated the *Rhetorica Christiana,* an extraordinary theological text in Latin, intended to assist preachers of his order among Indians of the New World.

Focused so clearly on America, the *Rhetorica* was also the first printed account of the evangelization of Mexico. Valadés argued for the natural human rights of Indians. He considered them as fully human as Europeans and praised the advanced cultures of pre-Hispanic central Mexico (although he also supported war for "just cause" against "barbaric" Chichimecs who rejected Christ). He regarded Indian converts generally as sincere Christians who repeatedly demonstrated their love of the missionary friars, and he wrote optimistically of the great potential of the young Indian men and women of New Spain.

He was interested in the organization of space in Indian pueblos—town plans, churches, and courtyards for open-air instruction—that would best suit a civil life and the evangelization enterprise. His illustration of the organization and uses of an ideal *atrio* (church courtyard) is at once symbolic and descriptive. The church in the center is not so much a real building as the dwelling place of the Holy Spirit, borne in procession on the shoulders of Saint Francis and Martín de Valencia, the leader of "the Twelve" (see Selection 7), who also appear as bearers in this illustration. Beneath them is the inscription, "The first to bring the Holy Roman Church to the New World of the Indies." The Holy Spirit in the form of a dove reaches the various activities depicted in the atrio with dotted lines. And above the church is God seated in judgment in Heaven, with an angel and the Virgin Mary interceding for the souls of Christians. The activities depicted were inspired by the uses to which Valadés had seen Pedro de Gante put the great chapel and courtyard of San José de los Naturales in Mexico City. He sets Gante

Figure 15. Illustration from Diego Valadés's *Rhetorica Christiana*, 1579.
Courtesy of the John Carter Brown Library at Brown University.

himself into the scene in the upper left—the only named priest—in the act of teaching, and he describes Gante in his text as "a man of singular piety and devotion who taught [the Indians] all of the arts, for none was foreign to him."

Teaching and learning Christian principles and practices are the great activities of this circumscribed space, this place apart. It teems with lessons and rites: group instruction in the Catechism, prayers, the marriage sacrament, the creation of the world, writing, and contrition; a funeral accompanied by Gante's beloved cantors; a marriage ceremony; confessions; a baptism; Mass; Holy Communion; extreme unction; and a judicial proceeding with the priest sitting as magistrate. In the four corners are the unusual chapels found in many early church compounds in Mexico and Peru. Here, friars are giving instruction to separate groups of women, men, girls, and boys. These *posa* (stopping place) chapels served also as processional stations for the solemn Corpus Christi festivities (see Selection 29 and Figures 26 and 27) and instructive displays during Easter and Christmas, and perhaps as meeting places for local confraternities and neighborhoods within the community. The sick are cared for, as an act of Christian charity, along the two outer paths connecting the chapels.

23

The Huejotzingo Altarpiece, Mexico

(1586)

The most costly and esteemed piece of public art in communities of the old central areas of colonial Spanish America was usually the main altarpiece of the local church, whether it was the seat of a parish, a modest chapel in an outlying village, a pilgrimage shrine, the cathedral, or a church of one of the religious orders. Occupying the apse—the often semicircular space at the very front center of the church where the great sacramental rites took place—it was the destination: the grand and glittering, yet remote, form that beckoned viewers from the moment they entered the building.

Such colonial altarpieces, usually large gilded ensembles that gave form to divinity and depicted the life of Christ and the lives of saints, were meant to evoke feelings of awe and devotion and to invite contemplation. They were much in the spirit of "Tridentine Catholicism"—the reforms and practices affirmed by Church leaders who gathered at the Council of Trent between 1545 and 1563 in response to the Protestant Reformation that had begun to divide Christianity irrevocably in the 1520s. Among its many initiatives, the Council of Trent promoted the special importance of saints and images. One Trent decree declared that "images of Christ, the Virgin Mother of God, and the other saints should be set up and kept, particularly in churches, and that due honour and reverence is owed to them, not because some divinity or power is believed to lie in them as reason for the cult, or because anything is to be expected from them . . . , but because the honour showed to them is referred to the original which they represent. . . . The faithful are instructed and strengthened by commemorating and frequently recalling the articles of our faith through the expression in pictures or other likenesses . . . which is a help to uneducated people."

In the spirit of this Tridentine vision of didactic art and the prevailing Spanish conception of Indians as perpetual children, the evangelization and ongoing instruction of native Americans made lavish use of paintings, engravings, and stone and wood carvings. As a seventeenth-century manual for parish priests put it, "Indians are often moved more by examples [including graphic illustrations] than by explanations." In the central areas of the viceroyalties of New Spain and Peru, Indian communities entered enthusiastically into this visual expression of devotion, sometimes vying with each other for the grandest and most beautiful set of religious images, especially on the main altarpiece.

Figure 16. Main altarpiece in Huejotzingo, Mexico, 1586.

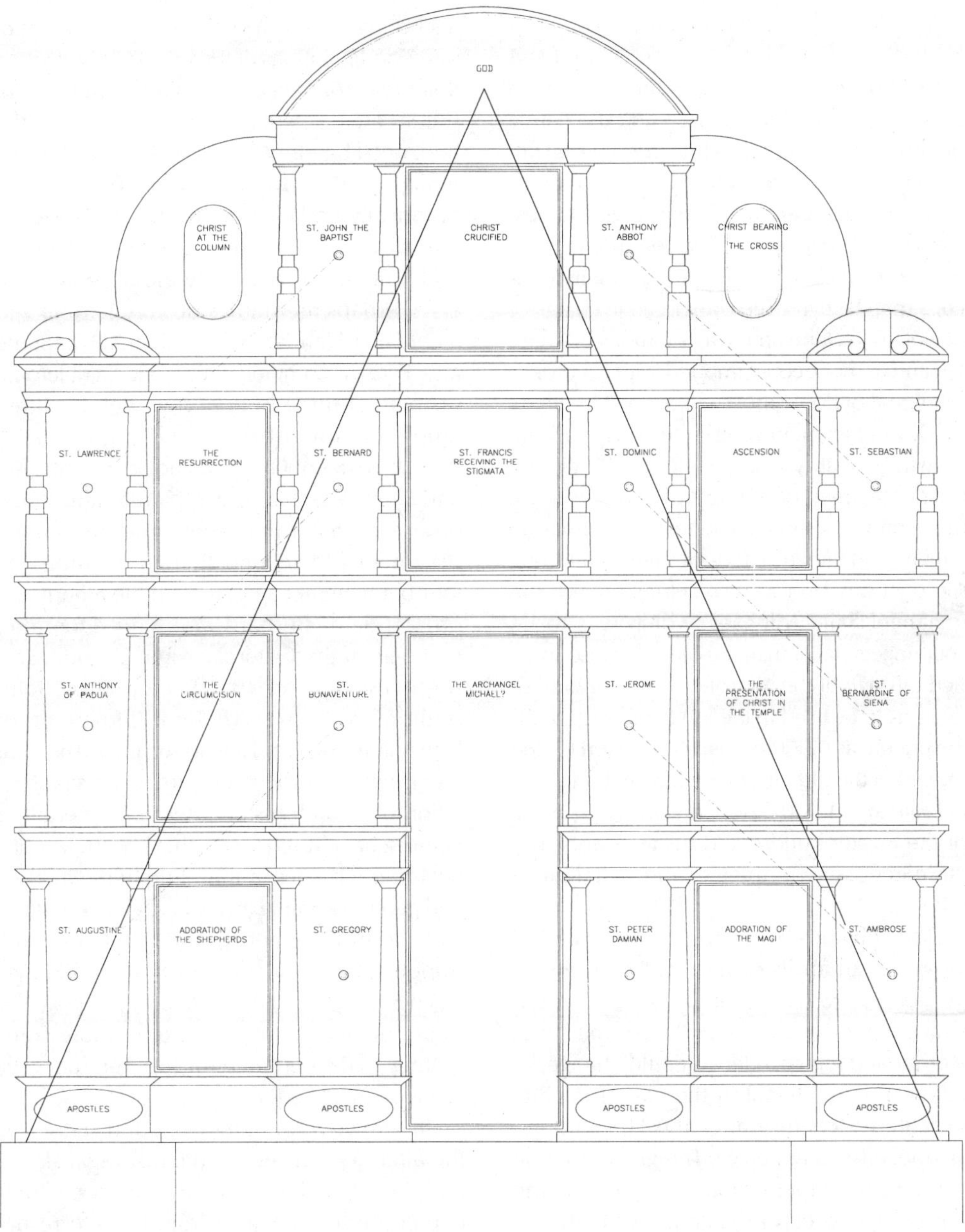

Figure 17. Schematic drawing of the Huejotzingo altarpiece.
Adapted by Karin E. Taylor.

One of the few large altarpieces that survives largely intact from the sixteenth century is in Huejotzingo, an important colonial Indian pueblo near the provincial city of Puebla, not far from Mexico City. It was commissioned by the Indian officials of the pueblo in 1584 "according to the wishes of the Franciscan father in charge of the church and the native Indians." The work, an architectural project in its own right, is a great gilded wood structure with columns, decorated moldings, statues, and paintings (Figure 16). The construction was directed by a Flemish painter residing in Mexico, Simon Pereyns. The Franciscan in charge of Huejotzingo at the time was a famous evangelizer and author deeply imbued with his order's millennial outlook (those expecting to witness the Day of Judgment), Gerónimo de Mendieta. He was probably responsible for the choice and deployment of the statues and paintings. The contract called for a series of paintings by Pereyns and fifteen statues of saints, including one of the patron saint of Huejotzingo, the archangel Saint Michael (which was to be "four fingers" taller than the others). It also specified the size of the altarpiece and the kind of columns to be used in the lower rows of saints. The price was 6,000 pesos, a great sum for the time, plus the old altarpiece (given to Pereyns and valued at 1,000 pesos), and living expenses for the master builder and his assistants. The altarpiece was completed and installed in 1586.

The religious art of the colonial period was never art for its own sake. It was always instructive, always meant to convey a vision of divine order and transcendence. This sense of order and transcendence could change, as did the Rosary chapel in the city of Puebla, dedicated a century after the Huejotzingo altarpiece (see Figure 25). The great ordering theme of the Huejotzingo altarpiece is the providential sweep of Catholic Church history and the life and figure of Christ.

The overall arrangement of this altarpiece displays Christian history with a powerful sense of hierarchical, masculine authority. The basic form of this ordering is a series of triangles, associated with the Trinity (the threefold conception of divinity in the Father, the Son, and the Holy Spirit). One triangle connects the bottom and top of the altarpiece (Figure 17): Christ's twelve apostles in a line of four groups of three at the base and God at the apex, anchoring the seven vertical rows of statues of saints and paintings of the life of Christ. Within this great triangle three smaller triangles of statues are nestled, each spanning two of the horizontal bands of the altarpiece. The bottom triangle, just above the twelve apostles—the historical foundation of Christianity—presents the "doctors" or framers of Church doctrine and liturgy, and two early monastic reformers. (Perhaps the statues of Saint Jerome and Saint Peter Damian were switched sometime after Pereyns completed his work. Saint Jerome fits better on the bottom row with his three fellow doctors of the early Church: Saint Augustine, Saint Gregory, and Saint Ambrose; and Saint Peter Damian is paired more obviously with Saint Bonaventure as a monastic reformer.) The second triangle is traced by four of the great teachers from the mendicant orders: Saint Bernard and Saint Dominic, founders of the Cistercians and Dominicans, respectively; and two Franciscans, Saint Anthony of Padua and Saint Bernardine of Siena. (It is not surprising to see the mendicant orders figuring prominently in such a representation of Church history; this was, after all, a Franciscan church.) The third triangle connects early heroes of the Church: the martyrs and penitents Saint Lawrence, Saint Sebastian, Saint John the Baptist, and Saint Anthony, Abbot. Chronological at its base, the higher reaches of the altarpiece's statuary celebrate the Church's mission and some of its more compelling male heroes with less reference to chronological sequence.

If the wooden framework and statues of the altarpiece represent the historical skeleton of the Church, then the paintings, which depict the life of Christ from birth to resurrection and ascension to Heaven, become its flesh and blood. Another prominent feature of the altarpiece's arrangement and sculpted features that suggests a second organic metaphor for the majestic sweep of Church history and organization is the central panel reaching from the base up to God. Within it are the most important figures of all—a low-relief depiction of Saint Francis receiving the wounds of Christ (flanked by statues of two other founders of religious orders), and the crucified Christ (flanked by statues of a penitential and a martyred hero and by paintings of Christ's suffering at the column and on the road to Calvary). The crucified Christ is no longer in place, and the statue now sited at the top of the panel appears to be another image of Saint Francis. The missing statue of Saint Michael may originally have been located just below Saint Francis. In any event, this central panel suggests a massive tree trunk from which branches of exemplary Church leadership and heroism spread. History in this vision of order is moving in one direction, toward which the apexes of the triangles point: toward a final judgment and day of salvation for the chosen.

We can only guess at the more worldly implications spoken or silently understood by priests and parishioners of Huejotzingo who knew this altarpiece well. But an educated guess is not out of order, since religion was the main expression of colonial ideology in Spanish America before the eighteenth century and provided some of the concrete symbols for social order and authority that appear repeatedly in other kinds of records. The altarpiece suggests both hierarchical order and mediated authority, much as power in colonial Spanish America frequently was exercised by appointment and command, and entreaties were made through intermediaries. On the altarpiece, saints stand between the viewer and God, inviting appeals for intercession. As the Council of Trent recommended, "It is a good and beneficial thing to invoke them [the saints] and to have recourse to their prayers and helpful assistance to obtain blessings from God through His Son Our Lord Jesus Christ." As a vision of history and authority, this early colonial altarpiece invites comparison to that of the Aztec Stone of the Five Eras (Figures 3, 4).

Saints Depicted in the Huejotzingo Altarpiece

Bottom row, left to right:

Saint Augustine (354–430). One of the major early theologians, famous for his *City of God* and *Confessions.* Following his conversion in 386 he led a contemplative life and became bishop of Hippo in 396. He promoted the idea of the Trinity and a just God as neither simply a loving God nor the source of evil in the world.

Saint Gregory (540–604). Another leader of the early Church; the first and greatest of the popes named Gregory and the first monk chosen as pope; a former civil magistrate of Rome who supported the founding of monasteries.

Saint Peter Damian (1007–1072). Theologian and monastic reformer inspired by the early desert monks; a fierce critic of clerical misconduct.

Saint Ambrose (339–397). Bishop of Milan and a famous preacher and theologian who helped establish basic Church liturgy (ritual practices).

Second row:

Saint Anthony of Padua (1195–1231). Portuguese Franciscan missionary in northern Africa, then a hermit in Italy. Known as a gifted preacher with a remarkable knowledge of the Bible.

Saint Bonaventure (1221–1274). "The Seraphic Teacher." Italian Franciscan theologian, reformer, Minister General of the order from 1257–1274, and staunch defender of the mendicant friars. A prolific author known for his personal simplicity.

Saint Jerome (341–420). Famously learned scholar, secretary to the pope (382–385), founder of religious houses, and hermit. He was largely responsible for the Latin version of the New Testament.

Saint Bernardine of Siena (1380–1450). "The People's Preacher." Italian Franciscan preacher and figure in the Observant movement within the order (calling for strict observance of the Franciscan rule).

Third row:

Saint Lawrence (d. 248). An early martyr; one of the seven deacons of Rome; thought to have been put to death by being roasted on a gridiron.

Saint Bernard of Clairvaux (1090–1153). French theologian and charismatic founder and leader of the Cistercians, the followers of the rule of Saint Benedict. A prolific writer, including a treatise on the duties of the pope; a famous preacher against heresy and a promoter of the Second Crusade in France and Germany.

Saint Dominic (1170–1221). Castilian founder of the Dominican Order—the highly educated "Order of Preachers"—who vowed to live in monastic poverty following his service preaching against the Albigensian heresy in southern France. He was known for his deep compassion for every sort of human suffering.

Saint Sebastian (dates unknown). Roman martyr, said to have been an officer of the imperial guard of Diocletian. The traditional story is that he survived being shot with arrows once his conversion to Christianity was discovered, but was then battered to death with cudgels.

Top row:

Saint John the Baptist (d. 29?). The martyred "Herald of Jesus Christ." In about 27 A.D. he appeared as an itinerant preacher announcing "Repent, for the Kingdom of Heaven is at hand." He baptized Christ, and those who confessed their sins, in the waters of the river Jordan.

Saint Anthony, Abbot (ca. 250–355). Ascetic desert monk in Lower Egypt; founder of monasticism in the sense of gathering into loose communities hermits who sought his advice; famous for his heroic struggles against temptation; spent his later years living alone in a cave near the Red Sea.

 24

The Mulatto Gentlemen of Esmeraldas, Ecuador

THOMAS B. F. CUMMINS AND WILLIAM B. TAYLOR

This remarkable group portrait, painted in 1599 by Andrés Sánchez Gallque, is the oldest surviving signed and dated painting from colonial South America. The three nearly life-size figures are clearly identified by name and age, all with the Spanish honorific title of *don*: Don Francisco de Arobe, age 56, in the middle, flanked by his son, Don Pedro, age 22, and another young man, Don Domingo, age 18. Don Francisco was the leader of a previously independent Afro-Indian community in the province of Esmeraldas on the north coast of Ecuador. A 1606 report describes him as the Spanish-speaking Mulatto (of mixed African ancestry; here, presumably, African and Indian) *gobernador*, or governor, of a settlement of thirty-five Mulattoes and 450 Christian Indians, some of them native to the area, others removed from distant coastal areas and governed by the Mulattoes as their subjects. In 1597, following the military and diplomatic efforts of Juan del Barrio de Sepúlveda (a judge on the Audiencia of Quito) and the missionary work of the Mercedarian Diego de Torres, Don Francisco and his community accepted Spanish authority and Christianity.

When these three men visited Quito two years later, Barrio commissioned the portrait and sent it to Spain as a memento of the event, celebrating a favorite imperial story about securing new frontiers and converting barbarians. The three figures are dressed in an ethnically mixed style of courtly attire. The lace collars and sleeves, as well as the satin or silk cloaks, were Spanish fashions. The artist draws attention to the garments by emphasizing the folds and ruffs as well as the rich color and sheen of the cloaks. Beneath his cloak each man wears an Andean-style poncho made of European brocade-like material. Underneath the poncho is a European-style sleeved and buttoned shirt, with a fancy *lechuguilla*, or ruff. The fine cloth and style of dress best suited to the cool highlands add to their appearance of civility and dignity. As Barrio notes in a letter that accompanied the portrait, people from the coast normally wore only a light shirt. In the portrait it is the golden ornaments piercing their faces and the necklaces of white seashells worn over the ponchos that distinguish them as men of the coast. These ornaments have a long

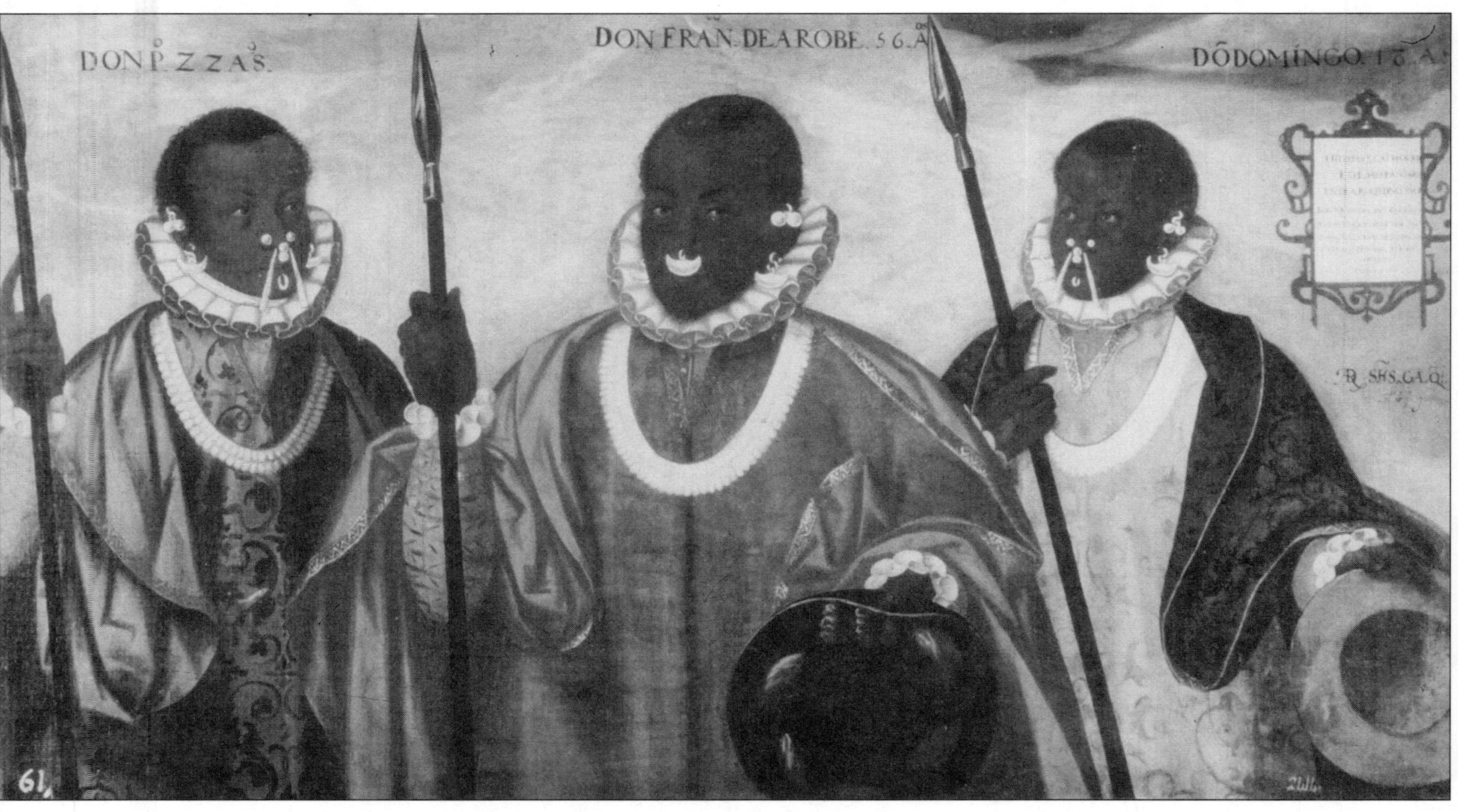

Figure 18. "The Mulatto Gentlemen of Esmeraldas," Ecuador, 1599.
Courtesy of the Museo de América, Madrid.

tradition there, dating back to at least 500 B.C., as seen on Jama-Coaque and La Tolita ceramic figurines.

The three men appear as if standing before the king as his loyal subjects, doffing their hats and holding their new steel-tipped spears as though they were ready to defend the coast against the king's enemies, whether English and Dutch pirates or hostile Indian groups and Mulatto slavers. It was surely intended as a likeness, for it was regarded by its patron, the high court judge, as a document of an American event; only now do we look at it as a freestanding work of art. But something else is going on here, too. In a sense the three black gentlemen are trophies, stuffed and mounted on a wall of blue.

The painting offers little, if anything, about how the three men thought about their attire and the portrait-making event, but it is fair to assume that they did not regard themselves as fixed in their proper place, as we see them here. The 1606 report adds something of their longer view of the event and tells a less triumphant imperial story than does the 1599 painting. In 1605 the province of Esmeraldas was convulsed by raids and bloody battles among rival Mulatto elites and their Indian subjects and allies. Don Francisco and his companions were not accused of participating in the upheaval, but colonial officials were disappointed by his failure to help bring the perpetrators to justice. When reprimanded for their indifference, his son, Don Pedro, reportedly threatened to burn their fields and disappear into the jungle if the Spaniards sent a punitive expedition. The colonial investigator in 1606 complained that Don Francisco and his people were drunkards and not true Christians ("they are not Christians in their hearts"), and he concluded that the money spent in Quito for blankets, jugs of wine, and fine clothing (perhaps the very outfits displayed in the portrait) had been wasted on them.

Whether or not they were Mulattoes in the Spaniards' racial sense, the portrait and the 1606 record show Don Francisco and his young companions as new people in a cultural sense—part African, part Indian, part Spanish Christian, and now American in their particular way, as social categories loosened and were reshaped on the margins of the Spanish empire.

Judge Barrio's selection of the artist to paint the portrait is almost as interesting as the painting itself. Sánchez Gallque was an Indian born in Quito who trained in the European style of painting with Pedro Bedón, a Dominican friar and artist. Along with other native artists, Sánchez Gallque belonged to the Confraternity of the Rosary, established by Bedón with the utopian aim of bringing Spaniards, Indians, and Africans together. In a way, such a wish is expressed in this portrait to which Mulatto, Indian, and Spaniard all contributed. But this resort to pictorial representation as a way of conveying information to royal authorities in Spain also expressed another kind of "Americanization"—an enforced, Spanish one in which colonial subjects were regarded as incompletely Hispanicized, requiring perpetual tutelage and restraint. Combining both expressions, the portrait of these three men becomes as hauntingly familiar and remote as the nineteenth-century photographs of Indian chiefs in U.S. Army officers' uniforms.

PART III

Spanish American Baroque in a Long Seventeenth Century

25

Felipe Guaman Poma de Ayala's Appeal Concerning the Priests, Peru

(ca. 1615)

Felipe Guaman Poma de Ayala was a native Andean from the province of Lucanos in the central Andes in the late sixteenth and early seventeenth centuries. He claimed descent from a line of nobility in his province and also sought a distinctly colonial form of legitimacy. Guaman Poma followed the path of his father, who, he said, had spent his life in the service of God and the king of Spain. He was educated in the Spanish language and western European learning and had become an adherent of a fiery, Old Testament brand of Christianity. Guaman Poma spent many years working as an interpreter in Quechua. In the 1560s he was briefly in the employ of Cristóbal de Albornoz, a general inspector and judge of suspect Andean religion whom Guaman Poma found just and fair. In these activities, Albornoz and Guaman Poma anticipated the more systematic "idolatry" investigations of the seventeenth and early eighteenth centuries (see Selections 34 and 35). Through reading and experience, he became familiar with contemporary Spanish chronicles and Christian devotional and moral texts, and he borrowed and adapted to his own purposes a number of their principles and conventions when he himself began to draw and write.

Guaman Poma composed a remarkable manuscript, the *New Chronicle and [Treatise on] Good Government* (*Nueva corónica y buen gobierno*), a work he is thought to have finished in about 1615. The *Nueva corónica* consists of a massive assemblage of almost 1,200 pages, including nearly 500 drawings, which Guaman Poma meant explicitly for the eyes of King Philip III. In part it is a history of the world from the perspective of the Andean region, encompassing Andean cultures, the Inkas, and the Spanish conquest and colonial rule in Peru. It is part autobiography and travelogue punctuated by the anecdotes and examples that become the vehicles of Guaman Poma's arguments. It is a moral condemnation and stinging critique of the flagrant disobedience of royal laws and colonial ordinances that were supposed to protect Indians and other subjects in the Kingdom of Peru. And it is also an appeal for measures that would assist the survival of native Andean peoples. Figures 19 and 20 are two of his drawings, and the reading that follows is a translated excerpt of two passages from his text. Both the visual and verbal sources come from the section of the *Nueva corónica* that Guaman Poma devoted to the discussion of Catholic priests.

His drawings and writing work together—equally graphic, complementing each other, imprinting themselves on the minds of their viewer/reader and demanding a unified response. Indeed, recalling Italo Calvino's words in the second epigraph to the introduction of this sourcebook, it would be difficult, and probably beside the point, to say whether Guaman Poma intended his viewer/reader to separate the visual and the verbal, to start an imaginative process with either one or the other. As is particularly vivid in Figure 19, Guaman Poma's words of explanation and speech could hardly be more integral to what he has drawn, allowing the visual and the verbal to merge.

Generally speaking, Guaman Poma's treatment of parish priests in the Peru of his day is as critical of some members of the religious orders as it is of the diocesan priests serving in Indian parishes—priests who were not of the orders, and who were subject directly to bishops within dioceses. His ire is carefully aimed, even if at one point he says that he is restraining himself from naming names he knows very well. Sometimes he cannot help himself, exposing in the reading with unforgiving precision the vile deeds of certain individuals, such as Father Juan Bautista Aluadán. Others, and occasionally certain groups, receive notable praise.

In Figure 19, Guaman Poma sketches one of the praiseworthy, one of "the fathers of the Society of Jesus," in action. Apart from concentrations of *padres* in special houses among native Andean peoples in Juli, Chucuito (near Lake Titicaca and what is today Bolivia), and in the Cercado district of Lima, the Jesuits' principal contact with Indians in the late sixteenth and early seventeenth centuries came from itinerant missions into the provinces from the order's urban colleges. The Jesuits are described in Guaman Poma's inscription as "the most holy men in the world, who believe, [show] love, and perform charitable acts and who, moreover, give all that they have to the poor people of this kingdom." The father's gestures are of giving, of effort and approach. He steps forward, about to put a rosary and an assortment of sacramental medallions into the praying hands of a kneeling Indian man.

Guaman Poma imagines the Indian's words at this moment and writes them around the person's head to carry along his story. This Indian is an Andean Christian, tired of suspicion and persecution, and fearful of rejection. "Confess me, Father, of all my sins. Don't ask me about *huacas* and idols, and, for the love of Jesus Christ and His Holy Mother Mary, absolve me [of my sins] and don't throw me out the door. Have mercy on my soul." Another text has been penned just beneath the bottom line that frames the picture. More than simply a further expression of his admiration for the Jesuits, here is part of Guaman Poma's remedy for the ills that afflict the Indians in their parishes: "If the said reverend fathers were teaching the Gospels and preaching on the passions of Jesus Christ, [on] the Virgin Mary, all the saints, the Day of Judgment, and the Holy Scriptures, [then] the Indians would not take flight." Here, as he would have been well aware, Guaman Poma joins his voice to those of other (Spanish) seventeenth-century commentators who maintained that the native Andeans' salvation would be greatly served if the Jesuits could be persuaded to reconsider their customary aversion to parish service.

The Jesuits, however, appear as an all-too-scarce remedy in this portion of the *Nueva corónica,* one of few exceptions to the rule among the priestly cohort perceived by Guaman Poma in the late sixteenth and early seventeenth centuries. In this reading and in Figure 20, the artist/author singles out the diocesan priests for particular condemnation. Guaman Poma compares the priests he has known and seen, and of whom he has heard tell in his travels, with the "blessed friars" of the orders who preceded them. The priests of his own time, including the friars, come off very poorly. The artist/author contends that Christianity was once carried to the Andes and put before native peoples in an appealing and effective manner, but that the spirit of the early friars and a charismatic faith have died in the Peru of Viceroy Toledo's time (1569–1581) and thereafter. Indians are now driven into

Figure 19. Drawing by Felipe Guaman Poma de Ayala, Peru, 1615. Courtesy of Siglo Veintiuno Editores, Mexico City.

the ground by the very people who should be raising them up through their examples and teachings in the faith.

Like the intellectual message of Francisco de Vitoria (Selection 8), the recommendations of Pedro de Gante and Juan Izquierdo (Selections 12 and 15) in different but related contexts, the work of José de Acosta who simultaneously had conditions in Peru specifically in mind (Selection 18), the letter by a Guaraní leader named Nicolás Ñenguirú (Selection 38 and Figure 28), and many others both before and after him, Guaman Poma calls for Spanish Christian responsibility. This native Andean's critique measures Spanish Christians by their own standards, turning the recognizable language and moral guidelines of Christianity against its supposed purveyors among "new Christians." The effects of this appraisal and redirection are biting. These parish priests are scandalous servants of no one except the Devil and themselves. They are exemplary only in their capacity to sin and corrupt others. They seek financial, not spiritual, profit from administering the Holy Sacraments. They employ Indian parishioners in all manners of work for little or no pay, simultaneously using up and repulsing a native Andean population who are left with no energy or desire for Christian lives—even if they knew, or could remember, what those were. Many people, according to Guaman Poma, flee their homes and communities to escape the predations of pastors who live like so many lords of the land. In Guaman Poma's estimation, the priests ultimately suffer in comparison even with the integrity and good examples of pre-Hispanic Andean religious ministers who, in his view, "were Christians in everything but their idolatry."

Guaman Poma wants to expose the behavior of parish priests such as Francisco de Avila in Huarochirí, whom he denounced in one portion of the *Nueva corónica* (and see Selection 34), who seek to conceal their many abuses, reprehensible conduct, and illegitimate children behind their holy office or showy exhibitions of zeal. Guaman Poma repeats that the priests' exploitation of Indians is frequently sexual in nature. It is in his treatment of these matters that he invests the most emotion and moral indignation. He needs to describe and comment upon terrible things in a graphic manner before God and king, and to arouse people to what is occurring in Peru. Parish priests, like other Spaniards, seek out Indian women and men whom they can oppress and mistreat with virtual impunity and hateful hyprocrisy. Through abusive relationships and perversions, Guaman Poma writes, the Indian women become "notorious whores," and a Mestizo population multiplies while the number of native Andeans diminishes.

The corrupt priests do not act alone, and Guaman Poma is at pains to portray visually and textually the disreputable alliances that the churchmen seek with Spanish secular and religious officials. And such priests draw more people into their selfish, profit-making webs than simply Spanish officials. The second image (Figure 20) picks up on a theme that Guaman Poma discusses twice in the written passage, namely, the extravagant and drunken dinners convened by parish priests to impress others and cement their wicked alliances with illicit business partners and relatives of their mistresses, all "at the expense of the poor Indians." The devastating effects of these corrupt cooperatives are many in Guaman Poma's view, not least the opportunities that such alliances allow for "low-bred Indians" to enlist priestly assistance in their selfish displacement of legitimate, "hereditary" Andean lords.

In Figure 20, as in most of his drawings, Guaman Poma has paid attention to the depiction of people. "The father invites the drunks," the title reads, "low-bred Indians, Mestizos, [and] Mulattoes, to take part in the robbing of the poor Indians." A priest in his three-cornered hat and high-buttoned collar sits at the head of his own table. He is unshaven, intent on sipping from the full drinking vessel at his lips. His companions include, as advertised, a Mulatto and a Mestizo or native Andean behind the table, and another native Andean on the far left, seen in profile, having his cup filled. The Mulatto is elaborately dressed, but

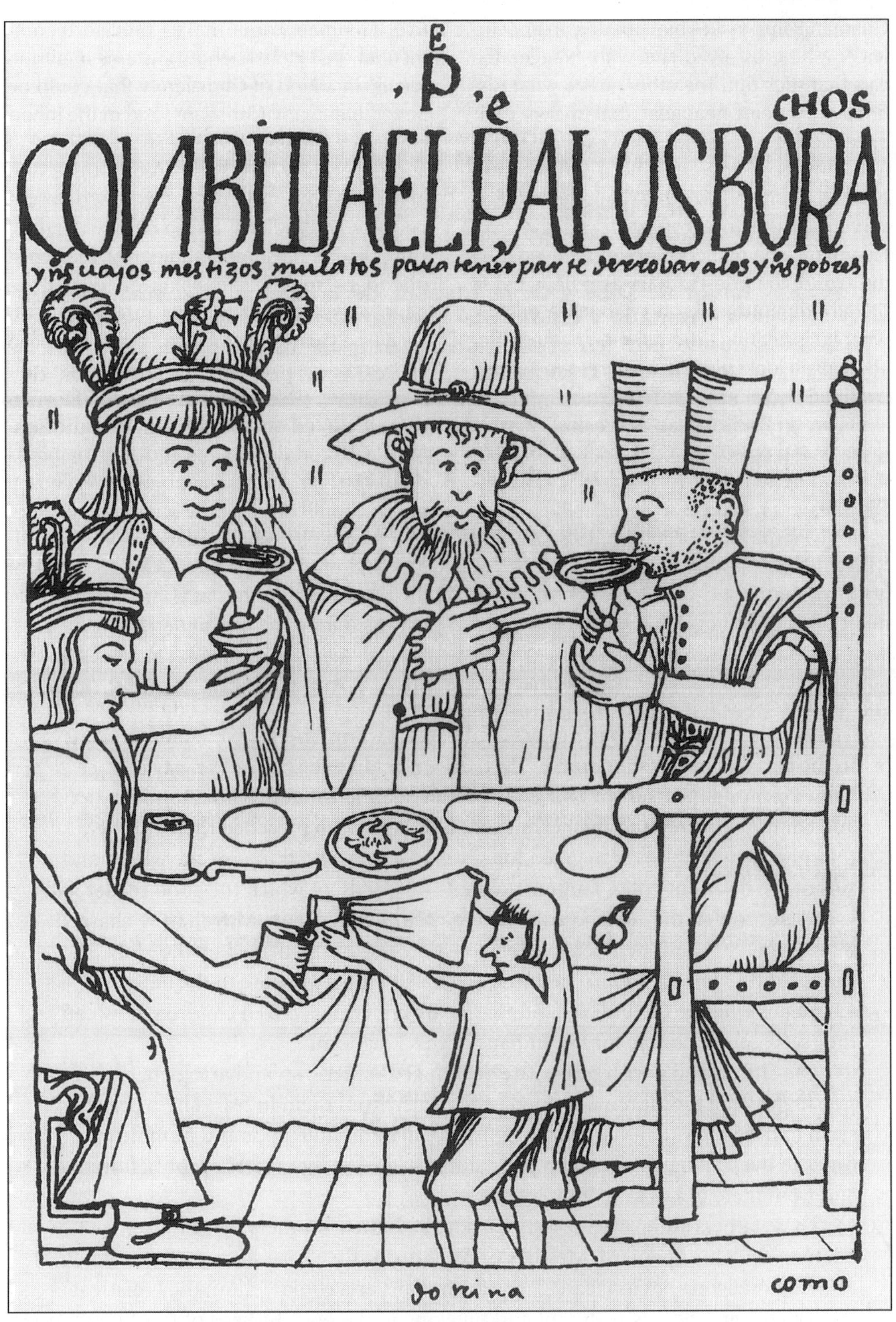

Figure 20. Drawing by Felipe Guaman Poma de Ayala, Peru, 1615.
Courtesy of Siglo Veintiuno Editores, Mexico City.

Guaman Poma makes him ape-like in appearance, a bit cross-eyed and with exaggerated ears that stick out. The other guests wear distinctive Andean headgear that shows their pretension to noble status. Most eyes are on the imbibing host, toward whom the Mulatto points. Despite his size, the diminutive Indian servant in the foreground draws the eye. Guaman Poma renders him shorter even than the arm of the priest's chair, as if he is being literally diminished by his servitude and by what he is hearing from the men at the table. The servant looks glum as he raises the jug and continues to pour.

Guaman Poma repeats a pessimistic refrain in the *Nueva corónica,* and it is not absent from the reading that follows. "There is no remedy," he writes. And yet at places in the work—as in his portrayals of "good priests," among whom are the Jesuits—he clearly preserves hope for the reform of colonial Peru. In the midst of an often tragic and disturbing narrative, Guaman Poma makes precise recommendations. He somehow sustains a faith in ideals, in a kind of Christianity that could be better than many Christians, and in the inherent justice of higher levels of Spanish Christian authority. He writes that "from fatigue and nightmare, the bishops of this kingdom die because we [Indians] are so cruelly treated." He calls for harsh punishment of the worst offenders, for the cleansing effect that he believes such punishments might have on Peru. And Guaman Poma, the Andean Christian and would-be royal adviser, grows more specific. These priests should be at least fifty years old, appointed on an interim basis, and carefully monitored, and the Indians' opinions should be both sought and honored. Moreover, priests should be carefully screened by a succession of able Jesuits and friars for their abilities and preparation as pastors. Usurpers of their holy office, the false priests, must be banished from the Indian parishes.

The aforementioned priests, fathers, and pastors who stand for God and his saints in the parishes of this kingdom of Peru do not act like the blessed priests of Saint Peter and the friars of Our Lady of Mercy, Saint Francis, Saint Dominic, and Saint Augustine, and the hermits of Saint Peter who preceded them. Rather, they give themselves over to greed for silver, clothing, and things of the world, and sins of the flesh, appetites, and unspeakable misdeeds, of which the good reader will learn later so that they can be punished in exemplary fashion. May they be charged by their prelates and members of [religious] orders, and punished by the Holy Inquisition. Their acts do harm to the Spaniards and even more to the new Christians who are the Indians and Blacks. By fathering a dozen children, how can they set a good example for the Indians of this kingdom?

The fathers and parish priests are very angry, imperious, and arrogant, and are so haughty that the aforementioned Indians flee from them in fear. These priests seem to have forgotten that Our Lord Jesus Christ became poor and humble in order to live among and bring in poor sinners, leading them to His Holy Church and from there to His kingdom in Heaven.

These fathers and parish priests consort with their brothers and children or relatives, or some Spaniard, Mestizo, or Mulatto, or they have slave men or women or many yanacona or chinacona [servant] Indians and cooks, whom they mistreat. With all of this, the mistreatment and pillaging of the poor Indians of this kingdom increases.

These parish priests engage in commerce themselves or through a third party, committing wrongs and failing to make payment. And many, many Indians must concern themselves with collecting [from the priests], for which there is no legal recourse in the entire kingdom.

These fathers and pastors demand that women's clothing of fine cloth and ordinary cloth, and sashes for the waist [all] be made for sale, saying it is for their prelates. They order, and deputies oversee, the manufacture of clothing by the poor Indians, who are paid nothing in the entire kingdom.

These fathers and pastors are occupied in demanding that clothing from ordinary cloth, sacks, canopies, bedspreads, tablecloths, sashes for the waist, belts, cords, and other things be made for them for trade and commerce without pay. In pursuit of this, they punish the leaders, the alcaldes [local magistrates], and the fiscales [the pastors' lay assistants]. In the face of such demands many people flee the kingdom.

These fathers and parish priests in this kingdom all keep mita [corvée labor] Indians busy: two Indians in the kitchen, another looking after the horses, another in the garden, another as janitor, another in the kitchen, others to bring firewood and fodder, others as shepherds, harvesters, messengers, field workers, and tenders of chickens, goats, sheep, cows, mares, and pigs. And in other things they insolently put the aforementioned hapless Indian men and women of this kingdom to work without pay. And for this reason they leave their homes.

These parish priests pasture ten mules and others belonging to their friends, which they fatten up at the expense of the Indians and single women who must take care of them. Some have many cows; also a thousand head of goats or sheep and pigs, mares or native mountain sheep, one or two hundred chickens and rabbits; and planted fields. And people are put in charge of all of these things with their corrals and buildings, keeping the poor Indians busy and without pay. And if one is lost, [the person responsible] is charged for one hundred; and they [the workers] are neither paid nor fed. With so much work, they leave.

These fathers and parish priests in this kingdom keep in their kitchens four unmarried women mita workers, cooks, and the head cook who oversees the preparation of meals, [and in addition to] the mita women and women under the priest's supervision, there are beautiful unmarried women. They also keep more than eight boys and overseers, and much equipment, all at the expense of the Indians. These males, plus the servant women, consume a bushel and a half of food daily and they are paid nothing. And these Indian women give birth to Mestizos and become wicked women, whores in this kingdom.

These fathers and parish priests of this kingdom ask for Indians to carry to market their wine, peppers, coca, and maize. Some have Indians bring mountain wine and coca down from the high plains to the hot lowlands. Being highland people, they die from fever and chills. And if the goods are damaged in transit, the Indian is forced to pay for them.

These parish priests have thread spun and woven, oppressing the widows and unmarried women, making them work without pay on the pretext that they were living in illicit unions. And in this the Indian women become notorious whores, and there is no remedy. And they do not wish to marry, staying with the priest or a Spaniard. Consequently, the Indians of this kingdom are not multiplying, only Mestizos, and there is no remedy.

These parish priests take from every pueblo things belonging to the church, hospital, or members of confraternities, saying that they must help them; and they use them up with impunity. They do so with the help of the corregidor or the visitador [administrative inspector, or inspector and judge of idolatry]; and in this way the Indians are robbed of their belongings and community.

These parish priests of this kingdom keep the offerings and alms for the Masses in honor of the departed. For a sung Mass they demand six pesos; if it is ordered, three pesos; for a spoken Mass they demand four pesos; if it is ordered, one peso. Some collect ten or twenty pesos. And they do not perform the said Mass and offering for four reales, which is supposed to be voluntary and suitably returned. Their belongings should be returned to the poor Indians, and these fathers should be punished in this kingdom. [But] there is no remedy for it.

These priests demand five pesos for the banns and candle and offering for a marriage, and four pesos for a baptism, without accepting that Your Majesty pays them a salary. [These collections] should be returned and [the act] punished.

These priests eat at no expense to themselves, paying nothing for their wheat, maize, potatoes, mutton, chicken, eggs, bacon, lard, tallow candles, peppers, salt, dried potatoes, preserved goose, dried maize, choice grain, beans, lima beans, chick-peas, green beans, fish, shrimp, lettuce, cabbage, garlic, onion, cilantro, parsley, mint, and other trifles and foodstuffs and fruits, firewood, and fodder. And they pay nothing for it, or occasionally four reales in order to ease their consciences. And there is no remedy or favor to the poor Indians of this kingdom.

And thus the Indians leave, and their pueblos, [once so] full of labor, are abandoned.

These parish priests do not want to obey or follow what the Holy Council [the Third Provincial Council of Lima, 1582–83] and ordinances and royal decrees of Your Majesty have ordered, to the effect that they are not to have women, whether unmarried or married or widowed, whether old or young, in their house and kitchen. They are not to live together even under the pretext of instruction in Church doctrine, so that the harm and disputes do not multiply and the Indians and their possessions, which serve God and Your Majesty, are not used up; even though they are ordered to serve their [the Indians'] mothers and fathers, [and] go to the communities and sapci [or sapsi, surplus goods held in common] of every province. There is no remedy.

And consequently the number of Mestizos and half-breeds multiplies in this kingdom.

These parish priests clamor to involve themselves too much in judicial matters. Having become secular priests, they want to become assistant pastors, then titular priests, and even corregidor and recklessly order about the alcalde and principal cacique [or *kuraka,* native lord and governor]. As a result they enter into disputes and initiate petitions and are bad examples for the pueblo. They cause destruction for the caciques and other leading Indians, and for the corregidores and encomenderos, and there is no remedy. They treat them so imperiously and thereby destroy the Indians of this kingdom.

Father Juan Bautista Aluadán [whom Guaman Poma isolates as an offender on two other occasions as well] was pastor of the pueblo of San Cristóbal de Pampa

Chire. He was a most imperious, cruel father; the things he did were unspeakable. For example, he took an Indian from this pueblo named Diego Caruas who had not given him a ram and put him on a cross like that of Saint Andrew [that is, in the shape of an X]. He tied him up with leather strips, began to burn him with a tallow candle, applying fire to his anus and private parts, abusing him with many lighted candles. And he opened his buttocks with his hands, and they say he did many other unspeakable things of which God will take note, a great many harmful and evil acts. Thus he tormented the painters he summoned. He did this because the unmarried women of Don Juan Uacrau complained that Father Aluadán stripped his [Uacrau's] daughter naked and examined her anus and genitalia and put in his fingers and gave her four beatings on her bottom. Every morning he did this to all the unmarried women. [The native] governor, Don León Apouasco, tried to oppose this and entered a petition, but the aforementioned Father Aluadán responded by saying that [the governor] hid Indians during the visita [general inspection]. And so he was exiled; from this misfortune, Apouasco died.

Consider, Fathers, whether all of you deserve to be brought before the Holy Office [of the Inquisition]. May you be punished for such arrogance, which you practice on the pretext of being the titular priest and teaching Church doctrine to young women. From fatigue and nightmare, the bishops of this kingdom die because we [Indians] are so cruelly treated.

These parish priests fall from grace by involving themselves so much in judicial matters and commit great offenses and serve as bad examples and are not obeyed and create disputes because they sin publicly with all the unmarried women of the parish who live with them.

These women and their parents and relations cannot confess [to such a priest], nor is the sacrament of confession valid, nor is he worthy of a salary from them. Because how can he confess and absolve someone with whom he sins mortally, a sacrilegious sin with these Indian women?

All of this deserves great punishment; and even more than punishment, such a sin should be made known to the Inquisition. Properly punished, this will be a good example to the faithful Christians of Jesus Christ in the world and in this kingdom.

These fathers hire other priests in the vicinity, because their bad deeds are known among them, to confess these unmarried Indian women on the pretext of saying that they are helping each other. In this way they are a bad example for the Christians and show no fear of God and punish [the women's] parents. And there is no remedy for the poor Indians. And thus they die off and do not multiply.

These parish priests have Indian women in the kitchens or elsewhere who act as their married woman, and others as mistresses, and with them they have twenty children, which is a public and well-known fact. And they call these Mestizo children their nephews and nieces and say that they are the children of their brothers and relatives. In this way many sins mount up, and the Indian women learn them from one another, and thus many little Mestizo boys and girls multiply. This is a bad example to the Christians; every one of these [priests and women] needs to be convicted and punished and exiled from the parish.

And so they [the priests] defend themselves, saying that they are the titular priests, appointed by Your Majesty forever. And they say they are rich, with plenty of silver to use in court. And thus no one raises a hand [against them]. On this pretext they show no fear of God or justice. He makes himself into another bishop and has more leeway for his misdeeds than the king; and thus the entire province is being destroyed.

The ancient [Andean] priests of metals, idols, demons, and gods, high priests of stone according to their law, [these] priests of metals acted devoutly and gave good example, as with the virgins and nuns of the temples. And so the rest submitted to their justice and law. They were Christians in everything but their idolatry.

Now the priests and ministers of the eternal, living God are [as I have described them]. From such a bad father springs a bad child, lost to the things of the true God. From a bad tree comes bad fruit, from a bad foundation comes a bad root. This badness is what God punishes most severely in Hell and in this life.

These fathers and pastors are very fierce. They punish the aforementioned fiscales and sacristans and cantors and schoolchildren. They punish very cruelly, as if they were punishing a Black slave, with such malice and harm and vehemence, and they do not stop. They [the Indians] run away and flee and are put in shackles and stocks. With this, these Indians die, and in this kingdom there is no one who takes their side.

These fathers and pastors, acting as judges but without appointment, have prisons and jails in the sacristy, [the room with the] baptismal font, and bedroom. And they have shackles, chains, handcuffs, irons, and stocks with a lock. With these they abuse the poor people of this kingdom, doing them only harm, taking away the possessions and daughters of the poor Indians.

Their names are not mentioned here so that they will not take offense.

These parish priests puff themselves up like a great lord, become rich, and play the role of benefactor. Accordingly, they invite Spanish strangers, encomenderos, corregidores, and the caciques [to dine and drink with them]. The meal they consume is at the expense of the poor Indians. For this purpose they levy contributions from among the Indians of this kingdom.

The priest should not be allowed to be a shopkeeper or merchant or petty trader on his own account or through anyone else, including his siblings and relatives. When he sells food or clothing, he is already acting like a petty dealer. He does not deserve the name of priest because in this kingdom they [the priests] are shopkeepers and small-time dealers. On the pretext of collecting offerings, he buys and sells, so that every pueblo's offerings are sold to the poor of Jesus Christ, and with the proceeds he furnishes their churches.

And so, my Father, he [the priest] goes about winning souls, distributing alms, and living the life of the saints. The priest with more than a thousand pesos [in income] can apply some to the hospital or for the aforementioned work of the Church in the pueblos, because in his parish he keeps the Church as poor as a stable with his demands, and he wants nothing other than to gather silver and rob the poor Indians of this kingdom. . . .

These fathers and pastors of the said parishes call [some of] the Indian tributaries "Don Juan" or "Don Pedro," or they make a habit of eating and chatting with them, because they do business with them or because their daughters or sisters are their mistresses. And they scorn and cast out and exile the hereditary [Indian] lords. The result is many "dons" and "doñas" [springing up] among the low-bred mitayo Indians. See how Don Juan World-Turned-Upside-Down invites the drunkard! He [the priest] will be a drunkard like the rest of them, dishonoring his priest's table in this kingdom.

Because of so much damage and so many complaints lodged against them, these fathers and pastors should be appointed on an interim basis—for a year at a time if he is good; and if not, may he not remain a single day. He should be at least fifty years old because a child's or young man's follies are not good in the world, nor can they be tolerated; [such younger men] commit blunders that cannot be found out.

They should be proven and tested for academic preparation as well as for humility, charity, love and fear of God and justice, and for knowledge of the Quechua [or] Aymara languages of the Indians, needed to teach them, confess them, and preach the Gospel and sermons [to them].

They should be examined by the reverend fathers of the Jesuit Order; second, by the Franciscan friars; third, by the humble hermits who are most holy fathers; fourth, by those of the Dominican Order who are great scholars and preachers in the world. Those [who pass the examinations] should be sent to Your Lordship and to the lord viceroy for appointment as interim pastors, posting a guaranteed bond. With this they will lose their arrogance; they will obey Your Lordship.

In the time of the conquest of a province there was only a single priest in charge of instruction; and before there was a priest, a poor Spaniard was responsible for teaching [Christian] doctrine in each province of this kingdom. And this teacher of doctrine was called uiczarayco. . . .

And so everyone gathered around the priest from the time of Barchilón [who, in midsixteenth-century Huamanga, began the Hospital of San Juan de Dios, which served the native poor], and they called him uiczarayco because he demanded no silver, only enough to eat. Thus these first ones were exemplary saints. They feared God and justice; [they feared] the pope, the king, and their prelate, and they did not pretend to be a bishop or a magistrate. Thus [the people] converted to God, giving themselves over to peace and to the royal Crown.

And if it were then as it is now, with so much harm, they would have risen up or, if not, the Indians of this kingdom would have been finished off, as they are now being finished off by the priests.

Among these priests there are many who go hungry and are so very poor, and others who are superior scholars and sons of humble gentlemen who are deserving of parish assignments. But there are others who are not deserving, who have usurped parish assignments. There, they have twenty children and do great harm. Claiming to be titular priests, they refuse to leave the parish.

So they should be appointed on an interim basis and post bond; then all will eat well or better. And if [the pastor] is very good, may he, at the Indians' request, die there. [But] if he is a source of great harm and arrogance, may he appear before Your Lordship for punishment or pardon and be removed from his jurisdiction and lordship, even if it be to Rome or Castile. May he again appear before Your Lordship to make restitution to the Indians. And giving him license and a letter of safe passage, if he wishes to go to another diocese in this kingdom, let him do so. In this way such great harm in this kingdom will stop.

May these parish priests not impede the Indian men and women of this kingdom from wearing silks and Castilian cloth as they please, as long as they do not tyrannize the leading caciques. And may they eat at table with tablecloths and dinnerware of silver or gold, rather than of wood or pottery. May they keep clean and be rich so that they may serve God and Your Majesty. If the people are rich, Your Majesty, the encomendero, the corregidor, the priest, and the chief cacique will be rich. Therefore, if the priests or corregidores stand in the way, may they be punished in this kingdom.

26

Pedro de León Portocarrero's Description of Lima, Peru

(early seventeenth century)

After the capture of Atahuallpa and his army at Cajamarca in 1532, the Inka's highland capital of Cusco was occupied by Spanish soldiers. Yet in contrast to New Spain, where the Aztecs' Tenochtitlan became the viceregal capital of Mexico City, Cusco was deprived of its central political and symbolic role after control was wrested from the Inkas in Peru. The Spanish considered establishing a highland capital but ultimately needed the sea and its connection to Europe, via the isthmus at Panama. Pizarro's home base, the City of the Kings—soon known as Lima—was founded on the coast of central Peru in 1535 and soon reoriented the political, religious, and commercial space of western South America. As the capital of the Spanish Hapsburgs' South American viceroyalty, Lima was one of the most remarkable colonial cities by the early seventeenth century, when this selection was written.

Beginning in the mid-sixteenth century, Lima became a magnet for economic opportunists, and many others besides, as did, on a lesser scale, the great silver-mining center of Potosí, the cause of much of the Peruvian "opportunity" after 1545. (Potosí, in the region that is today Bolivia, had a population of 120,000 by 1572, and an astounding 160,000 by 1610. Seville, which had swelled into the largest city in Spain in the course of the sixteenth century, thanks to its role as the gateway for Indies trade and emigration, had about 90,000 inhabitants in 1590. By comparison, Lima had about 13,000 in 1593.) Like Potosí, Lima drew Spaniards from Mesoamerica and the Caribbean islands as well as from the Spanish kingdoms. The city also became a major destination for enslaved Africans brought to work and build the colony's base. Lima drew on neighboring valleys for wheat, maize, livestock, wine, olives, and other goods, but the city's rapidly increasing population was soon dependent for many of its staples (and most of its luxuries) on trade within a steadily widening sphere in Spanish America, Europe, and Asia.

Contemporary population figures must be taken as rough estimates—and some of our sources were not above exaggerating certain elements of the population and magnifying the size and importance of Lima—yet a basic idea of the composition of society in the early seventeenth century helps to imagine the place described by the author of the passage. The viceroy's census of 1614 marked

Lima's population at 25,454 persons, among whom were: 10,386 Africans (5,857 women and 4,529 men); 9,616 Spaniards (5,257 men and 4,359 women); 1,978 native Andeans (1,116 men and 862 women); 744 Mulattoes (418 women and 326 men); and 192 Mestizos (97 men and 95 women). Notably, persons recorded as *negros* (Africans) outnumbered all other groups, and there were more African women and Mulattas than male counterparts. The figures for Mulattoes and Mestizos seem conspicuously low for 1614, suggesting that, in official terms at least, many were being designated as Africans or Indians or else were "passing" as Spaniards (see also Selections 28 and 45, featuring Figures 30 and 31). This is the first census in which the Indian residents of Lima, almost all of whom were migrants, were included in the city's count, perhaps because it seemed significant and possible now that they were concentrated in the sector of the city called the Cercado. As Frederick P. Bowser has observed, an increasing number of slaves brought to Peru from different parts of Asia were not included in the census. The Franciscan Creole Buenaventura de Salinas y Córdova (1592–1653), whose grandfather had been one of the Spanish conquerors of Peru, claimed that the population of his native city climbed substantially from the 1614 figure to 40,000 by 1630.

Its dwellers and visitors looked on the city with different eyes and from different angles. Sometimes their reactions (like their lives) are difficult to trace, as, for example, in the experience of Lima for the thousands of African and Mulatto women who worked principally as domestic slaves and servants (for insights from another region see Selection 28). The center of political and religious authority staggered Felipe Guaman Poma de Ayala, the Hispanicized native Andean author and artist (Selection 25 and Figures 19, 20). Yet that impression did nothing to lessen the danger and corruption he saw in Lima and other sizable cities and towns in Peru—especially for the displaced highland peoples who were brought there by Spaniards to work, or who fled problems or squalor in their depopulated communities and came in search of new livelihoods.

Guaman Poma documented how Indians were mercilessly preyed upon in the provinces but, for him, the city was even worse. He believed that cities ought to be left to the Spaniards, Africans, and people of mixed race, and that native Andeans should return to their home communities, where they might prosper and be guided and protected by Christianized native governors such as himself. Guaman Poma found that Indians lost their bearings and integrity in walled districts, intersecting streets, and teeming squares. Indian women (whose sexual and physical abuse by Spaniards was uncompromisingly investigated by Guaman Poma and is a prominent thread running through his chronicle) slid into habits of brazenness and were lured into prostitution, while honest men became drinkers, idlers, and devotees of petty crime and other forms of degeneracy.

In his *History of the Foundation of Lima* (composed ca. 1639), the Andalusian Jesuit Bernabé Cobo (1580–1657) was bothered by another kind of degeneracy promoted by living in Lima—an ailment, it seems, that affected not Indians but the wealthy sectors of the city. Father Cobo noted Lima's vigorous life of business in approving terms, but he was disgusted by the uses to which most of the financial gains were put. He lamented the "empty pomp" of the culture of plenty and the affluence of the few, and he scorned extravagant expenditure on such items as sumptuous furniture and glittering jewelry.

Yet not a few Creole intellectuals in the first decades of the seventeenth century saw the *peninsular* Cobo's "empty pomp" in quite another way. Exhibitions of the well-planned splendor of their Lima, a New World marvel, were the strings upon which they played a political agenda. A number of Creole authors combined enthusiastic celebrations of their native city and its overflowing wealth with spirited defenses of the abilities of fellow Creoles and condemnations of peninsular Spaniards' prejudices, greed, and exploitation of native Andeans and Creoles alike. Their pride helps explain the extent of the planning, building projects, and religious institutions that dominated the urban landscape in a place that a number of these writers celebrated as one of the urban wonders of the world. Friar Salinas y Córdova acclaimed the city alongside Rome for Lima's impressive ecclesiastical architecture and religious ornamentation, Genoa for its sense of style, Florence for its fair climate, Venice for its wealth, and Salamanca for its learning. The mining of precious metals cost much suffering and many Indians' lives, and this was to be lamented by the Creole commentator (and blamed on the transforming evils of peninsular brutality and indifference), but silver and mercury produced the untold wealth that flowed not only back to coffers in Europe but also into the privileged sectors of Lima's fast-growing population, with some of it transformed into its parks and plazas, buildings and gardens.

The author of the selection that follows did not record his name. However, Guillermo Lohmann Villena has argued convincingly that it was Pedro de León Portocarrero, a man whose life story offers a number of points of entry into the interlocking history of the contemporary European and Atlantic world. León was a *converso*, a new Christian of Portuguese Jewish descent, from Galicia in northwestern Spain. He was investigated by the Inquisition in Toledo in the late sixteenth century for the persistent profession and practice of Judaism. He repented of the alleged offense and was handed a light sentence, ordered to process in an *auto-da-fé* (the Inquisition's public ceremony featuring acts of repentance and sentences of punishment for religious offenders) in Toledo in 1600 and to wear a *sambenito*, a penitential garment that marked a former religious offender. People of Jewish and Moorish descent were prohibited from traveling to the Indies at this time, but many went anyway, attracted by the prospect of lessened notoriety and, often, the opportunities of new lives among relatives already there. They entered secretly, often through the port of Buenos Aires. León was one of these secret Iberian emigrants to South America.

He lived in Peru for about fifteen years (1600–1615), and in Lima itself for a decade. He appears to have composed his description of the city and the other places he visited after he returned to Spain. Yet in only a limited sense can León be called a foreign traveler. He was an insider with an eye for detail, who married a Christian woman and had two children and participated vigorously in the commercial life of early seventeenth-century Lima.

That said, there is possibly even more to the author's tracing of Lima's streets, his noting of the positioning of its palaces and armaments, the locations of surrounding Indian towns, and, in parts of the description not included here, his careful attention to the state of its port and urban defense initiatives. Without arguing that espionage was the only or even the central purpose of León's research and writing, Lohmann Villena places the author within the context of an international contingent of "spies," snooping around and collecting information in the wealthy capital of the southern viceroyalty that would be of great interest to enemy powers—especially to the Dutch, who (like the English and French) already had colonizing designs on the Indies well beyond what they would eventually achieve in northeastern Brazil, the Caribbean, and the Guyanas. A number of people believed to be secret agents were captured by colonial officials in Lima and found to be of Portuguese Jewish descent; some had lived for a time in Holland before arriving in Spanish America.

It is uncertain if spying or assisting a challenge to Spanish control in Peru was our author's intention; if, in another part of his anonymous description, the cool reference to incursions by Dutch "adversaries" (*contrarios*) in the waters off Lima's port of Callao is an example of León's careful adoption of a tone that would not attract attention. But after establishing himself as a successful merchant in Lima, our author fell under suspicion for other reasons. Perhaps anticipating another arrest by the Inquisition on charges of Judaizing—this time, not only an alleged secret adherence to the Jewish faith but also the proselytization of others—León in 1615 took flight for Spain. He left his wife, business interests, and Peru, taking with him his nine-year-old son and six-year-old daughter. He erred in not anticipating diligent communication between the tribunals of the Inquisition in Lima and Seville, for he was promptly arrested and imprisoned when he landed in Seville. Appearing before the Inquisition once again, León admitted his converso lineage but denied the charges of Judaizing and endeavoring to convert Christians to Judaism in Lima. He maintained that he was being framed by enemies who stood to gain by his downfall. The inquisitors seemed to believe him or, at least, they were not sufficiently convinced of his guilt. León was set free with an obligation to pay a fine of 300 ducats.

His description of the city of Lima betrays few signs of the trials and tribulations that interrupted his life. One detects in this piece of writing, if anything, an admiration for the things he describes, many of which were the manifestations of Spanish Christianity. A crypto-Jew's duplicity? A curious infiltrator's artful veil over a useful piece of intelligence? The eloquent product of a few Peruvian years of happiness, curiosity, travel, and business in the life of a new Christian otherwise threatened by suspicion and bouts with the Inquisition? The splendor of his Lima does not seem threatened or about to decline along with the regularity of the shipments of Peruvian silver to Cádiz. The document and its converso author, whose very presence in Peru was a crime, find their place under the rule of a viceroy-poet, Don Juan de Mendoza y Luna, the Marquis of Montesclaros (1606–1614); out of his viceregency came an extraordinary cluster of eventual saints and pious persons (see Selections 30 and 32, with Figure 23, on Santa Rosa), an upsurge in the efforts to eliminate suspect Indian religiosity (Selections 34 and 35), a flourishing of Baroque art and architecture, and an extraordinary number of synthesizing histories from different sources such as José de Acosta (Selection 18) and Felipe Guaman Poma de Ayala (Selection 25 and Figures 19 and 20).

In his city tour, the author comments on many of the same highlights as Salinas y Córdova, reminding us that civic pride was not a Creole preserve. Of particular note is the size and splendor of Lima's religious establishment in the early seventeenth century. Salinas's chronicle from 1630 complements León's mostly physical descriptions with a sense of the human proportions of this religious culture. Salinas maintained that in 1630 there were as many as 400 secular priests in Lima—more, if one counted the port of Callao and other surrounding parishes. And the city seems to have held even greater attraction for members of the religious orders, with about 900 male religious in Lima at this time. Salinas writes of 1,366 nuns in the city, coming mostly from families who could afford the sizeable endowments described by León, served by 899 female slaves. The great Augustinian Convent of the Incarnation took up its own city block, housing 450 nuns, 50 novices, and 276 slaves. There were 210 nuns of the Conception, with 23 novices and 245 slaves; 150 nuns of the Holy Trinity (with 10 novices), served by 130 slaves; 65 Barefoot nuns (and 20 novices) with more than 100 slaves; 197 nuns lived in the Convent of Santa Clara (with 20 novices) and 120 slaves; and in the newly founded (ca. 1623) convent so wished for by Santa Rosa before her death, that of the Dominican nuns of Saint Catherine of Siena, there were already 46 nuns, who kept 38 slaves.

Of 700 Dominican friars in this order's province of Peru, Salinas wrote that 250 lived in Lima. Salinas's own order, the Franciscans, also had some 700 friars in Peru, of whom another 250 were in the city—190 of whom resided in the massive structure featured in Figure 22. Of 500 Augustinians in Peru in 1630, 170 lived in the convent in Lima, with many more in the College of San Ildefonso, and 130 of 330 Mercedarians were similarly based in Lima. The Jesuits had a complement of 250 in Peru at this time, with about 150 members resident in Lima. A good number of the

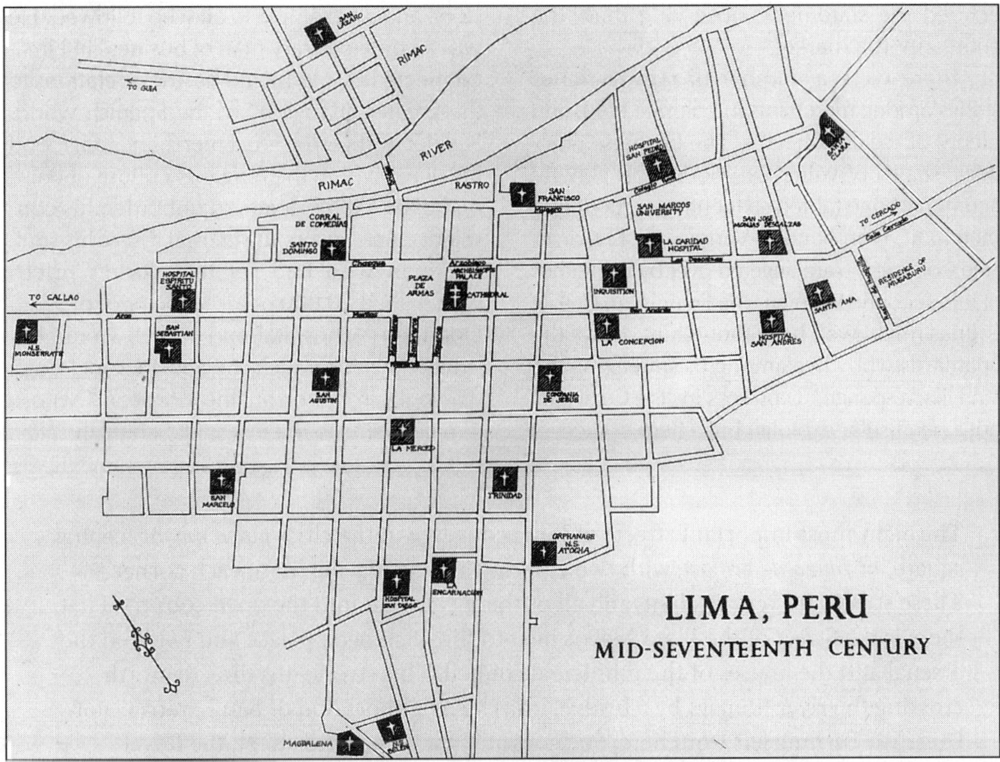

Figure 21. Plan of Lima, Peru, in the mid-seventeenth century. Courtesy of the University of Oklahoma Press.

Society were occupied in teaching a student body of over 180, drawn principally from the children of the city's elite, in two colleges, San Pablo and San Martín. According to Salinas, an alumnus of San Martín from the time when Father Pablo José de Arriaga (the famous proponent and agent of the Extirpation of idolatry) had been rector, 14 Jesuits taught at the college in 1630. Other teachers worked among the 50 novices in the Society's own novitiate. And 6 Jesuits were based in a house of doctrine established among the over 800 Indians who lived in the some two hundred dwellings that made up the Cercado in 1630 (similar to the residence that members of the Society had erected over a half-century earlier among the Moriscos in the Albaicín quarter of Granada; see Selection 17).

León's tour of Lima's religious architecture and general urban landscape contains within it a detailed description of the city's commercial practices. For him, the city's commerce is clearly hard-headed and competitive, but it is also commended in moral terms, described as "the most true, fair, and worry free that one can find in the world." León clearly knew this realm of activity intimately. His description of the market square and the central streets named after the merchants and wares that lined them brings to life a bustling emporium of moving parts. (See the plan of the streets and principal ecclesiastical buildings in Figure 21.) The account puts the lie to the (mostly Protestant-inspired) depiction of the Spaniard as the idle "Mongol of America," a rusty former conquistador whose dignity resided in his shunning of entrepreneurial activity and an utter dependence on native laborers and slaves. "Everyone is involved," León writes, "all have dealings and everyone is a merchant, even if it is through a third party or on the sly." The contemporary Salinas echoed the statement, observing that "the entire city is a market."

There were a number of rags-to-riches stories among merchants in colonial Peru, and plenty of wealthy figures. The business practices, scales of value for goods, and general acumen of one fabled sixteenth-century Lima merchant, Don Nicolás Vargas—or El Corso, "the Corsican"—are lingered over by the author of this account. Whereas the Franciscan Creole Salinas might well have found him one of the Spaniards who "live among us squeezing the land like a sponge," León sees in "the Corsican" not a peninsular exploiter but a hero, a success story, and an example to all who followed. He was a contemporary man of business in Lima, connected by blood and business relations to the greater "Babylon" of the Spanish world, Seville. And yet the great merchant, too, found his place within the religious culture of colonial Lima. At his death, to unburden his conscience and ensure the eternal rest of his soul, the man who had set the world's prices bequeathed 80,000 pesos to the prior of Santo Domingo. A hospital and church were constructed, within which a chapel to Saint Joseph was built in honor of "the Corsican," whose remains came to rest in a vault behind the altar.

The eight most important streets of Lima converge in the city's *plaza mayor* [central square, or *plaza de armas*], with two entering at [and leaving from] each corner. These streets are very straight, and all of them carry on into the open country. First there is the Street of the Plaza Mayor next to the [viceregal] palace and between the arsenal and the houses of the municipal council. This street runs directly north, crossing the river [Rímac] by a bridge, into the neighborhood of San Lázaro [Saint Lazarus]. Turning left from here, one goes along a very grand street, the Royal Highway of the Plains, which passes along the Carabaillo River, and through the cultivated plots of land and countryside, to Chancay by way of the Arena mountain range. Four leagues [about 14 miles] on is Carabaillo, an Indian community. Returning to Lima's bridge [over the Rímac], the street goes straight to the church and hospital of San Lázaro, into which anyone who is afflicted with Saint Lazarus's illness [blindness] is taken. Turning to the right, one arrives opposite the wooded park in between San Lázaro and the Hill of San Cristóbal. It features a great variety of trees, such as cedars and poplars, as well as trees bearing oranges, lemons, olives, apples, and other fruits. It has eight rows of trees interspersed with four fountains whose waters fall into stone basins, and are connected to channels from the river which are used to irrigate. All of these rows run directly to the monastery of the Barefoot Franciscan friars that stands at the foot of the Hill of San Cristóbal. These friars have a well-built house and garden. Upstream near the Hill of San Cristóbal is the road to Lurigancho, an Indian community which lies beyond the hill, one league [about 3 1/2 miles] from Lima. Out here there are many cultivated fields as the road leads up to the mountains.

Another street leaves [the *plaza mayor*] from the east side of the palace and approaches the slaughterhouses, coming out in a square that is next to the Franciscans' monastery, a large and very rich house. Including its garden, it takes up two blocks right next to the river. From there, the street passes by the church of San Pedro and reaches [another] large and rich convent, that of Santa Clara. Next to these nuns' abode, running from north to south, is the city's principal water aqueduct. The street then passes the northern part of the walled district [the

Cercado] of the Indians. From this point a road begins that extends straight to the reservoir, the source of much of the water that courses through pipes into the city's fountains in the squares, in the palace, and in the monasteries and houses of the nobility. This is the water that the people of this city drink, finding it better than the water from the river. This reservoir is in the middle of a green meadow, and [leaving from it] the road passes through many cultivated fields, heading to the Valley of Santa Inés, a beautiful valley bursting with fruit and water. Out here there are many Indians, and the road continues toward the mountains.

Another street leaves from the palace and the houses of the archbishop and proceeds straight to the east, passing the College of Santo Toribio and the houses of the main postal office, and continuing to the square of the Inquisition, some three blocks east from the plaza mayor. The secret jails and their prisoners are here, and here, [too,] the inquisitors live and have their chapel, taking up an entire block on the south side [of the square]. On the east side of this square is the church and House of Charity, in which poor sick women are treated and many poor maidens are sheltered until they leave to be married, and [also] where women who live indecently are taken in. Near to this charitable house, on the north side [of the square of the Inquisition], is the College of the King. From here the street leads into the square of Santana (Santa Ana), in which there is the convent of the Barefoot nuns and the hospital and parish church of Santa Ana. This is the hospital for Indians in which all their illnesses are treated. Its income from rent is 30,000 assayed pesos [monetary unit of 12 reales in value]. The street continues along next to the church of the Barefoot nuns, by the drilled rock and on to the church of the Prado, right next to the gate into the Indians' Cercado. Next to this entrance lies Dr. Franco's small farm, once owned by the author of this account. The road [then] runs perfectly straight to the east, through fields of wheat and alfalfa. To its right, two leagues [about 7 miles] from Lima, sits Late, an Indian town. And from here another road stretches toward Santa Inés and the mountains. Turning back to the Royal Highway, it passes through the area of Late (*la rinconada de Late*), where cucumbers, sweet potatoes, maize fields, and vegetable gardens flourish. [A trip along this road] is a delightful excursion for the people of Lima. The road [the Royal Highway] goes to la Seneguilla, where it resumes its course.

Another street leaves the plaza mayor next to the cathedral and leads to the monastery of the Conception, which houses nuns and is rich and pleasant. It carries on to the hospital of San Andrés, a large and excellent house in which Spaniards are treated when they are ill. It crosses the plaza of Santa Ana and joins the main road that heads to the mountains. Turning back, next to the church of Santa Ana, on its right side, this street proceeds to the lime and brick ovens. The owner of these works is Alonso Sánchez, a lime processor who, in my time there, employed four hundred Black slaves. This road carries on to the open country and to the Royal Highway of the coastal plains, [while] another turns to the east and comes out at the guaquilla of Santa Ana [probably a small mound of pre-Hispanic remains or a shrine to Saint Anne, and possibly both]. Here, there is a large field all around, filled with irrigated gardens adjacent to a large water channel. And from here a road heads southeast to the gunpowder works, where much powder is ground very fine.

Here is their watermill where the work is done, and [also] a separate house where the powder is locked up. This powder house is a quarter of a league from the city, and its road passes on through the fields and the valley of la Seneguilla.

Another street leaves [the *plaza mayor*] by the Clothiers' Street. These shops [more than twenty, according to Salinas] stock clothing for Blacks. This street goes straight south and passes by the side of the Mercedarian friars' monastery and leads directly to the convent of the nuns of the Incarnation, the most renowned [religious] house in Lima, in which there are more than four hundred professed nuns. Many of the rich nobles' daughters come [to stay in this house] to learn good manners, and they leave it [ready] to marry. In this convent there are splendid and intelligent women, endowed with a thousand graces, and all of them, both nuns and [pious] lay women, have Black women slaves to serve them. They [the nuns] make preserves and assortments of sweets of various kinds, and they are so good that one cannot imagine a greater treat. They have a large and comfortable garden, and this convent and its garden extend for two blocks in length and one in width. For any woman who wishes to enter a convent in Lima, the cost of her admission and necessities alone is 6,000 pesos, while for a nun who wants a separate cell, a Black woman to serve her, and 100 pesos of income, the endowment required is 12,000 pesos; for others the cost is [still] more, set in accordance with their wealth: but even they never quite get the best [of everything]. Continuing on from this convent, one arrives at the monastery of the Conventual Dominican friars and heads into the open country and the coastal plains road.

Another street leaves by the main one, [and] that is the Merchants' Street, along which there are always at least forty shops [but Salinas claimed more than twenty warehouses and at least two hundred shops] packed full of assorted merchandise, whatever riches the world has to offer. Here is where all of the important business in Peru transpires, because there are merchants in Lima whose estates are valued at 1 million pesos, with many more at 500,000 or 200,000, and at 100,000 pesos there are very many. Among the ranks of these rich [merchants], few operate shops. [Rather,] they put their money to work in Spain, in Mexico, and in other places. And there are some who have dealings in the great China, and many merchants [also] invest in rent-producing property. Here [on this street], they sell merchandise on credit for at least a year, and, if the orders are large, for two and three years, receiving their payment [in installments] three times a year.

Commerce in Lima is the most true, fair, and worry free that one can find in the world because the order of buying and selling is that which has been practiced for many years, an order set down by "the Corsican" [Don Nicolás Vargas]. He was the principal merchant and the richest man Peru has ever seen. His sons are the marquises of Santillana, both of Seville. "The Corsican" established a scale of value for all goods made anywhere in the world, and all are obliged to pay those prices. On some commodities he set [the estimated price] very high and on others very low, in accordance with their value at the time. And the brokers [even now] follow his practice on merchandise that was produced and named after his time; and this method of appraisal has been preserved up to today.

The order that the merchants observe in buying their goods is that they take the [manifests of] the merchandise that the transporters give them in order to [start with] the same prices they would in Spain or Mexico. Then, they immediately revise the prices of items, with the prices of some goods rising and others falling, according to the current demand and value of the merchandise locally. Thus, the setting of the price is up to date, with each kind [of goods] given the value at which one can sell it at the time of its purchase. And the reckoning and the repricing is made in assayed pesos, and by this the value is determined, and it is made also with [attention to] the running account. These [become] the prices because [at them] the given merchandise can be sold, reflecting the sum of the one account and the other, with both accounts governed by current [financial] conditions. Then one can begin to see if one profits or loses, and the men who sell them set their own refixed prices and accounts; and thus the price rises and falls accordingly, and they buy these goods at so much percent, more or less, of the cost. Later, as they come from Spain, once all is in order, they send the cargo to the buyers' house, supplying everything correctly and accompanied by an account.

In merchandising one must always take into account the damaged goods and additions. "Damaged goods" are things that are broken, stained, or that have become damp or rotten. An "addition" occurs with the kinds of merchandise that one sells of different qualities; for example, saying it is from one master craftsman's shop when it turns out to be from another's, or saying that a piece of cloth is twenty-four [in size] when it is twenty-two, or not to have the advertised brand, and such things. This is what one means by damages and additions; and in order that they be accounted for, a third of each part is chosen and scrutinized. And the ones [who do this] are always merchants of good conscience who remove what they should and discount the value of the merchandise. Because of this [wise and honest practice] the goods are never returned, litigation and grief are avoided, others buy at the current estimated price, and [still] others at so much percent above the cost in Castile or Mexico. And sometimes they buy a variety of loose goods; but with the assorted large shipments, some of which are worth 100,000 pesos, the sales are always by the rate [method].

All the merchants are exceedingly skillful in their buying. A merchant will collect all the manifests of shipments brought to the plaza for sale, and quickly refix their prices, and from there choose and buy whatever seems best to him. This gives an idea of the merchants of Lima. [Everyone] is involved, from the viceroy to the archbishop; all have dealings and everyone is a merchant, even if it is through a third party or on the sly.

Continuing on with [the description of] this sixth street, one reaches the immense and wealthy monastery of the Mercedarian friars, and then passes to the parish church of San Diego, [also] a hospital for convalescents recovering after treatments of their illnesses in the hospital of San Andrés. When their health returns and they can move about, they are sent to this convalescent hospital. There, they receive all they need until they are sufficiently fit to go back to work. From here, the road meets a little square and the Conventual Mercedarians, and goes directly to the countryside and the sea to the south, about three-quarters of a league from Lima passing the Indian community of Magdalena.

From among the arcades [on the *plaza mayor*] where there are four streets and the Merchants' Street [already described], another street leaves, beginning with the

Street of the Mantas [cloaks and coverings of coarse cotton cloth], which is also lined with merchants' shops. This street, like the Merchants' Street, takes up its own block. Along this entire street, proceeding directly west, there are many shops with different specialties: chandlers, confectioners, boilermakers who work with a lot of copper, blacksmiths, and other craftsmen. And it passes next to the Espíritu Santo hospital for sailors who are gathered there and cured when they are ill, [then] under the arch and on to the church of Monserrat. The street heading south from there goes straight toward the road to [Lima's port of] Callao. . . .

The last of the eight streets that leaves the square departs from beside the arsenal in the palace, the houses of the municipal council, and the house of Don Alonso de Carabajal, because in all of the intersections of the plaza there are three corners. This street proceeds straight to the monastery of the Dominican friars, the most wealthy and outstanding [of the male religious houses] in Lima, the north walls of which are washed by the river. And here, in a bit of space not occupied by the friars, sits the theater. The compound consists of two blocks of houses, with seven patios. This street carries on straight to the river. For anyone going south, by turning left from any of these last streets [I have described], one can reach Callao.

One [other] street [worth mentioning, the better to understand the design of Lima], two blocks from the east side of the plaza mayor and running north to south, goes by the church of San Francisco to the house [and church] of the Jesuit fathers, the richest and most powerful residence [of all religious] in Lima. Even the facings of the altars [in the Jesuits' church] are made of finely worked and thick silver. Its memorials they put up during the week of mourning [Holy Week] are all of crimson velvet, all adorned on top in solid silver, with a thousand bows, intricately worked by an artist's chisel, so high that they reach the church's ceiling and so wide that they stretch across high pillars and arches from one wall to the other. They have infinite riches in this monastery and residence.

On another street that runs behind the Jesuits' establishment is the College of San Martín, also belonging to the Society of Jesus; it has more than five hundred students, the sons of notables throughout the kingdom [of Peru] who send them there to study, and who pay the Jesuits an annual fee of 150 ordinary pesos for each one, from which sum the students are fed [as well as instructed]. These Jesuits offer a very elaborate course of studies incorporating many branches of learning. As it continues, the street passes next to the monastery of the Trinity for nuns, and then arrives at the parish church and house for orphans, children abandoned by mothers who did not want their parents to know of their ruinous acts and [thus] gave birth to the children without parental knowledge. Farther along one comes upon another Jesuit convent and house of no small amount of wealth. It was built when I was living in Lima with a gift of 300,000 pesos from the secretary to the Inquisition, Antonio Correa. From such choice morsels many in Peru stuff themselves without choking, because they have the stomach for everything. They [the Jesuits] keep a lovely garden and also have many riches in this house, so that no Jesuit suffers want. The street [then] carries on to Guadalupe, a monastery of the Franciscan friars. Here, the Royal Highway of the coastal plains heads south, the ocean on its right, straight to Pachacama [formerly the site of the great pre-Hispanic divinity, Pacha Camac], an Indian community four leagues from the city.

Extending from east to west, another street passes close to the Jesuits' church and into the Street of the Silversmiths [with more than forty public shops, says Salinas, and over two hundred people trained to work in silver and gold], which runs from the corner of the Street of the Mantas [with more than thirty shops selling clothing mostly to native Andeans] to the corner of the Merchants' Street. Off this Street of the Silversmiths is the Hatters' Alley, [which] leads to the church of San Agustín. In this block there are a great number of apothecaries, and all of them are not more than a block from the [central] plaza. San Agustín is the rich house and church of the Augustinian friars. The street passes to the great and sumptuous parish church of San Sebastián and continues up to the mills of Montserrat, to which a large channel provides water for the milling and irrigation of gardens, turning left for the port of Callao.

Another two streets, heading from east to west, leave from beside the [convent of the] Incarnation and San Diego and pass near to San Marcelo, the principal parish church in Lima. Here, taking up a space on the left side, is the [monastery] of the Conventual Augustinians. Both of these streets lead straight to the road bound for Callao.

These are the highlights of Lima. The city has many other streets, but the ones described here have all the monasteries, churches, and squares, and all that is best about the city, something that the others do not have for our purpose.

27

The Church and Monastery of San Francisco, Lima, Peru

(1673)

This image folds out of a 1675 work celebrating the church and convent of Saint Francis in Lima after its restoration following earthquake damage. The *Temple of Our Great Patriarch, San Francisco, in the Province of the Twelve Apostles of Peru in the City of the Kings, Ruined and Raised to a Grander State by Divine Providence* was published in Lima and "composed by an obedient son of the Province," father and preacher Miguel Suárez de Figueroa. The title shows that central Mexico was not the only place in Spanish America remembered as a recipient of an "apostolic twelve" (see Selections 3 and 7). In other ways, too, this image, and the text that accompanies it, is a glorification of the wealth and power of the Franciscan establishment in the city and in Peru.

Pedro de León Portocarrero noted the Franciscans' monastery and church in the early seventeenth century, either just before or after an earthquake in 1609 (see Selection 26). The structure sat (as a smaller version of it still does) just east of the *plaza de armas*, "a large and very rich house," which, "including its garden . . . takes up two blocks right next to the river." It became an even more impressive part of the city's space after León's time, as this engraving, ostensibly from its moment of reconsecration in 1673, shows. The engraver's angle of view allows one to look beyond the main facade and different entrances, over the walls and around the domes. Inner fountains, as mentioned in León's account, can be seen. And numbers (corresponding to a small legend on the far right) mark the principal sectors of the community, including a long central garden, an infirmary, an area for the novices, and special cloisters and courtyards. The figure depicted in the bottom right corner is Antonio de Somoza, the Franciscans' commissary general for the Indies (among his other offices), to whom Suárez de Figueroa dedicates his book.

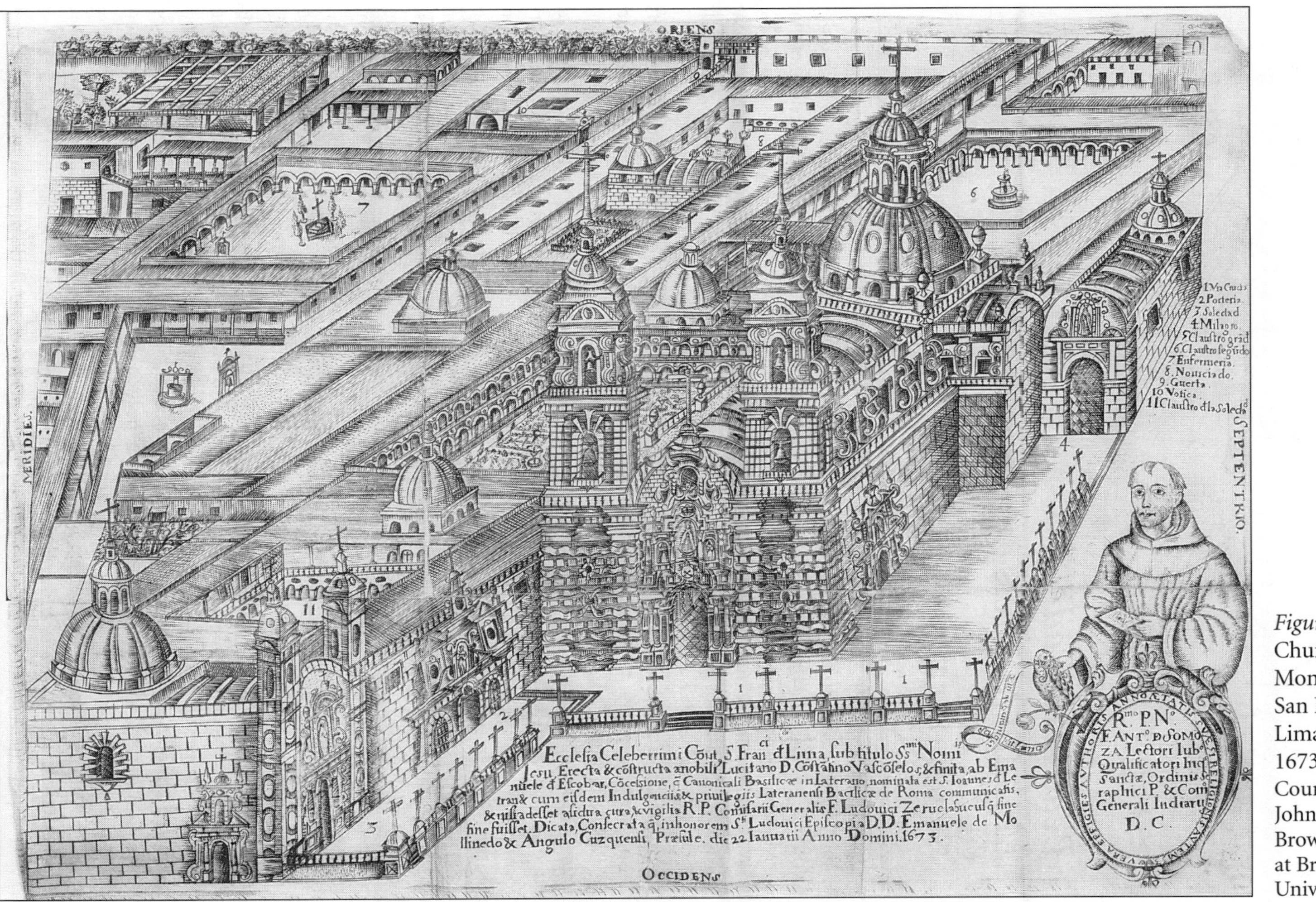

Figure 22. Church and Monastery of San Francisco, Lima, Peru, 1673. Courtesy of the John Carter Brown Library at Brown University.

28

Beatriz de Padilla, Mulatta Mistress and Mother

SOLANGE ALBERRO

In this short essay, Solange Alberro of the Centro de Estudios Históricos, El Colegio de México, employs trial records dating from 1650 from the Tribunal of the Inquisition in Mexico City to describe the eventful life of a woman of color in mid-seventeenth-century New Spain. Alberro finds a fascinating story, of great interest in itself. Beatriz de Padilla's significant place in her hometown, Villa de Lagos, though perhaps never quite secure, was due principally to her own formidable intelligence, ambition, and charms. The circumstances of what Alberro calls her "active and somewhat irregular private life" call for a wider consideration of other women in this colonial society (such as Sor Juana Inés de la Cruz in Selection 31) and "the partial survival represented by the process of genetic and cultural *mestizaje* [miscegenation]."

As Alberro notes, concubinage was a part of life accepted by most people so long as these unions complied with a certain range of expectations. Such relationships were expected to stay behind their thin disguises of propriety and not to be flaunted. Although such "illicit" (from the Christian point of view) relationships outside of wedlock were certainly not the exclusive pursuit of Spanish and Creole men, on the one hand, and women of color, on the other, these kinds of interracial unions were common, founded in part on the cold fact that White men often held power over Africans, Indians, and people of mixed racial descent and took advantage of this power to gratify their sexual and psychological desires.

The case of Beatriz de Padilla reminds us of the hidden understandings, rules, and temptations in relationships between women and men from different stations in colonial society. These relationships might be characterized by more than simple oppression or sexual exploitation. In the present case, a long-standing genuine love and affection between Beatriz de Padilla and a local priest seem to have been the cause of slander and charges of murder-through-sorcery brought against her by jealous members of his family. In considering the verdict of the Tribunal of the Inquisition in the case of Beatriz de Padilla, Alberro wonders whether the woman's straightforward admissions in her own defense, "the recollection that she had been the beloved companion of a brother," combined with her noted and considerable beauty, may have elicited sympathy from clerical interrogators who could not help but reflect on their own lives and desires.

Beatriz de Padilla participates in other kinds of interracial interaction as well. Like her intimate relationships, these do not conform to what might seem the initially expected norms. A rebellious soul, solidarity with other women and men of color was not part of her agenda. She resents the defaming inaccuracy of the racial label, Mulatta (half African); she is lighter skinned than that. She admits to having landed in trouble for beating an Indian woman for no reason, and to treating slaves and domestic servants with brutality. She has clearly "risen" in her own eyes (not to mention the view of those in whom she inspired envy and jealousy) to become a woman of some standing and an heir in a priest's household.

In her analysis of the case, Alberro suggests that, in spite of her marginal position in society, such a colored woman possessed a remarkable degree of "freedom" to act spontaneously, "to walk, talk, and dress pretty much as she saw fit." Alberro brings this freedom into focus by employing a stark contrast, the standard to which contemporary White women were held. Beatriz's freedom and "naturalness" contrast with the severe restrictions on Spanish and Creole women who, Alberro notes, were meant to keep up appearances and concern themselves with the damaging consequences of hearsay both to themselves and their husbands and lovers.

Alberro's intriguing final statements about this story call for further inquiry. To begin, it is worth considering these notions of freedom and naturalness more closely. By whose definition, and within what limits, did they exist? Did they exist for groups as well as for individuals? What about the norms that Beatriz was judged to have violated so brazenly that she found herself accused before the Tribunal of the Inquisition in Mexico City? It is true that Spaniards and Creoles who flagrantly breached explicit and implicit moral and racial codes might be judged by their peers to be damaging honorable reputations and (especially in the view of eagle-eyed relatives) jeopardizing fortunes, but what dangers did such relationships hold for people from the lower stations of society? Beatriz de Padilla's predicament recalls similar charges made against native Andean love specialists in contemporary Peru (see Selection 35), not to mention many other non-Indians across Spanish America, such as the Mulatto gentlemen of Esmeraldas, Ecuador (Figure 18 in Selection 24), or the settlers of Amapa, Mexico (Selection 40). The interest and significance of Beatriz de Padilla's case seem crowned by the fact that she was not convicted of sorcery by the Inquisition, but it is worth remembering that as Alberro's relation of this particular story draws to a close, the "triumphant return" to a "sleepy town" that she imagines might easily have been different.

In 1650 there was a great scandal in the sleepy town of Lagos, near Guadalajara in western New Spain. The shameless Mulatta Beatriz de Padilla was accused by the royal agent Don Juan Sánchez Vidaurre, an influential gentleman of the country, sixty-four years of age and the owner of several farms and ranches in the vicinity, and by a secular priest and some others, of having caused dreadful and mysterious things to happen to two of her lovers. According to the charges, she had poisoned the first of them, a priest who had been serving as commissioner of the Holy Office of the Inquisition in Lagos; and then, several weeks later, she had driven the lord mayor of Juchipila crazy through the exercise of magic. Informed of this development and alarmed at the possibility that one of its representatives might have been done away with in this cold-blooded fashion with impunity, the Tribunal of the Inquisition in Mexico City summoned the alleged murderess to the capital. In the meantime, it instructed its new commissioner in Lagos to undertake a complete investigation of the case.

In the prisoner's dock in Mexico City, Beatriz informed the inquisitors in spirited language that she was not a Mulatta but a lighter-skinned Morisca, the daughter of a White man and a Mulatta [and a New World usage not to be confused with a new convert from Islam]. She said that she was about thirty years old, unmarried and without any "respectable" means of supporting herself. She had been born in Lagos, the daughter of a Don Lorenzo de Padilla (a descendant of one of the best families of Guadalajara, she was proud to attest, and brother to the late Gaspar de Padilla, who had served for a time as a secular priest in Lagos). Her mother was an unmarried Mulatta serving woman named Cecilia de Alvarado, who had been born a slave in the Mexico City household of the viceroy, Don Luis de Velasco. Cecilia had been an only child whose mother died in childbirth, and as a young woman she had been taken to Lagos to serve as housekeeper to the parish priest there, Don Francisco Pérez Rubín. She was still employed by this priest more than thirty years later, when the scandal broke around her daughter.

Cecilia had borne two other children, younger than Beatriz, by different fathers. They were Francisca Ramírez, who had been legally recognized and declared a free person by her father, a White man of the neighborhood, and Francisco de Alvarado. Francisca was the wife of the administrator of a cattle ranch in Zacatecas, but she lived with their several children in Lagos. Francisco, the unrecognized son of a Basque immigrant long since dead, had been blinded some two years before Beatriz's trial. He was unmarried and also lived in Lagos. Beatriz had begun her life as a slave, inheriting her mother's status, but both she and Cecilia had at length been granted their freedom thanks to the benevolence of their employer and presumably their own satisfactory service in the priest's household. At the time of her arrest and removal to Mexico City, Beatriz had been a housekeeper and mistress in the service of Don Diego de las Mariñas, the lord mayor of Juchipila, for the loss of whose senses she was being held responsible.

Like her mother, Beatriz was a woman who had led an active and somewhat irregular private life. Never married, she had brought two sons and two daughters into the world. The eldest was Agustín Ortiz, then fourteen, the son of the priest Diego Ortiz Saavedra, with whom Beatriz had interacted happily for eight years and whom she was now accused of having poisoned. Seven-year-old María, who was being raised by Beatriz's mother, was the daughter of one Hernando López de Lara, and her children Micaela, five, and Diego, four, were the fruits of her union with Diego de las Mariñas. Asked to provide a little more detail about the history of her life and loves, Beatriz replied that when she was only thirteen or fourteen years old, she had whipped an Indian woman without cause and had been taken to Guadalajara for two months—apparently in an effort to get her away from Lagos until the furor died down. There she had stayed in the houses of Doña María Ortiz, a sister of the priest Diego Ortiz, who was already her secret lover, and of another elegant lady. This visit would seem to have had a great influence in establishing the ideal of a standard of living to which the ex-servant girl hoped to become accustomed.

After returning to Lagos, she had first gone to live with Diego de las Mariñas in the village of Nochistlán. But her friendship with the priest Diego Ortiz was already of long standing, having begun when Beatriz was an adolescent and still lived with her mother in the household of Father Pérez Rubín. It would appear that Ortiz was the man whom she really loved throughout. Two years before his death the commissioner had reversed his earlier policy and determined to make his relationship with her a public one. At that point he had taken her away from Mariñas to live with him at his hacienda of Moya, some two leagues distant from Lagos. It is a powerful testimony to the strength of the affection that Beatriz had managed to inspire in Mariñas in the meantime that after Ortiz's death he was willing to take her back with him.

The witnesses hostile to Beatriz, whose testimonies were taken during the inquiry, were unanimous in declaring that the Mulatta had made life miserable for the lovelorn commissioner of the Holy Office during all the time that she had remained in his house. In their view, she had literally reduced the man to idiocy before finishing him off by placing poisonous powders in his bath. Before entering into relations with her, they recalled, he had been in excellent health, with an indomitable character and an evil disposition. Afterward he had lost his hair and grown very sickly, and he had lost control of his faculties to such an extent that he was often to be seen walking and talking to himself and laughing out loud for no reason at all. Beatriz replied that none of this was true, and that if the truth be known, it was she who had suffered a greater loss than anyone else with the death of Don Diego—because the priest loved her very deeply and had made her the lady of a household where she never lacked for anything. After his passing she had been beset with poverty and persecuted by her enemies. The priest's love for her had grown even more profound after their son Agustín had been born, she recalled. From then on he had often remarked that when he died, the hacienda of Moya would be hers to administer to support their son and another girl whom Ortiz had adopted. This last determination was, as it turned out, to be the chief cause of Beatriz's difficulty with the authorities.

Beatriz confessed that she had been less than exemplary in her conduct while exercising authority in the household of Diego Ortiz. She remembered having been an unduly harsh taskmistress to the slaves and domestic servants, despite the fact that she had served as a slave housemaid herself as a young girl. In particular, she admitted to having been especially cruel toward a lying and gossipy slave named Catalina la Garay—beating her frequently or spattering her with hot grease—and, moreover, that she had had this woman branded. But she denied that Diego Ortiz had suffered any transformations of character or behavior in her company. He had always had the custom of talking to himself, although she had never seen him laugh without reason. He had indeed lost some hair, but only on the face, where two spots had appeared like birthmarks that were free of whiskers. But something none of the witnesses had mentioned was that he had suffered from an illness that caused him to complain frequently of severe headaches and flatulence and colic, and Beatriz believed that it was this that had carried him off.

Certain witnesses testified that the silver chamberpot in which Beatriz prepared the water for Diego Ortiz's bath had turned black on account of the menstrual blood she was in the habit of putting into it in an effort to poison her lover—and that when someone had pointed this out to the faithless mistress, she had replied that the skin of a prickly pear had fallen into the water and given it its red color. Beatriz responded sharply and astutely to this charge that, in the first place, blood would not cause silver to turn black, and, in the second place, she was not so foolish a person as to tell the whopper about the prickly pear skin, since everyone knew that the red color of the prickly pear was not the same as the color of blood. But most of the process was not so easy. The young woman was obliged to defend herself vigorously against the calumnies of her accusers, and in the course of doing so she took pleasure in providing many interesting details concerning life in the town of Lagos.

The folks back home, she pointed out, were green with envy at the fact that the lovers of Beatriz had all been important men who were crazy about her, such as the commissioner of the Holy Office and the lord mayor of Juchipila. Often people had asked her by means of what charms or love potions she was able to attract such admirers, and Beatriz recalled that she would reply with a laugh that the only charms or potions she employed were those she carried between her legs! But public opinion had a hard time accepting the fact that a mere Morisca, and an ex-slave at that, could come to enjoy the devotion of such important men by any such natural means as simply seduction, or youth and beauty, or sincerity in affection combined with a lively intelligence and a sparkling wit. The only convincing explanation for many was that she must be having recourse to magical procedures that were mysterious and dangerous, not to mention illegal.

As the trial proceeded, however, it became clear that something further lay behind the scandal, namely, a complicated situation within the family of the late commissioner, Ortiz. He had lived for years under constant pressure from his mother, Doña Luisa Ortiz, his sister's husband, the drunken but "respectable" royal agent Juan Sánchez Vidaurre, and their daughter María. These envious relatives had woven a veritable conspiracy against Beatriz when they realized that the priest was genuinely enamored of her and that he proposed to leave his entire estate to her and to their illegitimate son. It was they, together with their slaves and retainers, who had plotted to dispose of one whom they perceived as a contemptible upstart in any way they could.

Beatriz maintained that when Ortiz had died, the family had been in such a hurry to bury him that there had been a rumor in Lagos that they had buried him alive. She recalled that on that day the relatives of the deceased had descended on the house like a flock of buzzards, picking through his property and making off with the most insignificant objects. Doña Luisa had gone so far as to make off with a bird cage belonging to Beatriz, which she had gotten from some boys who had gone out looking for birds to snare in the countryside. Not satisfied with this, the greedy sister had later invented the preposterous charge that Beatriz only kept birds on hand so as to be able to use them in the preparation of her love charms.

Ortiz, said Beatriz, had for his part felt a great distrust toward his family—knowing full well that they despised her and would do their best to frustrate his desires in the disposition of his estate. At one point, in an effort to win them over, she had begged Diego to name Luisa and her husband, Juan Sánchez Vidaurre, as godparents of their son. Ortiz had resisted the idea strongly, although in the end he had agreed to her request. But all of this had been to no avail. It was the *compadre* Sánchez Vidaurre and his wife who had first circulated the rumor that Beatriz was a sorceress and then put it about that she was a murderess as well. They simply could not accept the genuine love that Beatriz insisted had existed between the late priest and herself, and much less the certain loss of a prosperous hacienda. Once launched by the envious relatives of Ortiz, the conspiracy had quickly broadened to serve as a channel for the rancor of all the leading citizens of Lagos—people who saw in the relationship between the commissioner and the Morisca the beginning of a dangerous process of social dissolution. Having a colored mistress of low social  standing was no scandal in colonial society; on the contrary, it was a common practice, even among priests. But to demonstrate an exclusive affection for one's concubine in public, to put her in charge of one's household, and above all to make her the heir to one's estate were altogether unheard of. And this was especially hard to swallow when the woman in question was as outspoken as Beatriz and as indiscreet as she in boasting about her amorous and social successes.

The clamor against Beatriz had eventually been joined by no less a personage than the licentiate Andrés López, Don Diego Ortiz's replacement as commissioner of the Holy Office in Lagos. López was called upon to receive formally the depositions of the witnesses who testified against Beatriz. Before she left for the capital, he committed the error of warning her not to speak out against the hostilities that had been directed against her in Lagos if she wanted to avoid being muzzled as she stood before the Tribunal. Andrés López's hatred for Beatriz derived from the facts that at some point she had been the lover of his brother Hernando López de Lara, the father of Beatriz's second child María, and that the sister of these two men, Catalina de Lara, had been abandoned by her fiancé Don Diego de las Mariñas some years before, when he had "lost his head" and decided instead to take the humble Beatriz as his mistress! This intricate web of licit and illicit relations between civil and ecclesiastical functionaries and their female relatives, which seems to have been typical of the society of colonial Mexico, had left a bitter residue in the broken marriages, the frustrated ambitions, and the envies of many people. Beatriz was being made the scapegoat for all of them.

Catalina la Garay, the slave woman who had been so cruelly treated by Beatriz when she lived at the hacienda of Moya, had moved on later to become the servant of Ortiz's sister Doña Luisa. As a resentful ex-servant, she was able to contribute many valuable pieces of information to the preparation of the case against Beatriz, recounting with prejudice the details of the day-to-day life of the couple. All this notwithstanding, the Tribunal of the Inquisition was persuaded by the intelligent and sincere defense of Beatriz de Padilla (if not by her beauty, or by the recollection that she had been the beloved companion of a brother). To be doubly certain, the judges had Catalina la Garay brought to testify in Mexico City. Catalina confessed, apparently after a session in the torture chamber, that she had made up all her accusations. Then, so that her fate might serve as a lesson to all the evil-tongued gossips of Lagos, she was taken home and punished with two hundred lashes administered in the streets of the town. Beatriz, for her part, was acquitted and allowed to return to her hometown without any sort of punishment or reprimand.

At the time of Beatriz's release from the jail of the Inquisition she had returned to her the following items of personal property, which had been sequestered by the Holy Office at the time of her arrest. The list gives some indication of the conditions of material comfort in which the mistress of a leading citizen of the provinces might expect to live:

two sheets of Rouen linen
a pillow with its casing
a white bedspread and blanket
a mattress stuffed with cane leaves
two white shirtwaists
five embroidered blouses
two chambray petticoats
a Spanish woolen skirt
a blue petticoat adorned with Spanish flannel
a used green woolen skirt
one blue embroidered handkerchief
an embroidered linen bonnet
a red cloak
a piece of coarse frieze cloth
an old hat
two pairs of slippers

We may assume that the disgust felt by the respectable society of Lagos toward the beauteous Beatriz was in no way diminished by the sight of her triumphant return—especially in view of the fact that during the trial she had exposed to public criticism all the petty dealings and machinations of her detractors. It seems likely, however, that she returned to the household of the not-at-all crazy lord mayor of Juchipila with her position as beloved and respected concubine enhanced rather than diminished—and that there was little that anyone could do to harm her from that time forward.

The Mulatta mistress as a social type has always attracted the attention of students of colonial society, and it may be that her importance has been exaggerated. There is still a mysterious aura about women of this sort, a lingering suspicion that perhaps they did make use of love potions or other magic that turned their White owner-keepers into their sexual slaves. But without discarding the possibility that there may sometimes have been some basis to these charges, it is worth pointing out that in a colonial society the woman of low caste and swarthy skin, operating in a more marginal position than the White woman, was also less subject to a series of severely restrictive social regulations. A woman like Beatriz had in her favor, in addition to the attractions of her physical person and the color of her skin, a relative freedom of movement, a freedom to walk, talk, and dress pretty much as she saw fit, and an opportunity to give full rein to spontaneity and naturalness in her interpersonal relations. These freedoms were not available to the "respectable" White woman, whether Spanish or Creole, who was obliged to concern herself always with what others might say and to do her best to adhere to the norms of society not only in every social interaction but also, since domestic servants were nearly always present, in the most intimate details of her private life.

The women of color in New Spain, whether of African or Indian extraction, performed—however unconsciously—a fundamental role in the historical development of Mexican society. The vital impulse that led them to join their flesh with the White men's and give birth to the White men's children was the biological response of a social group that found itself despised by the existing social order. What legitimate hopes for helping to mold the future might a Black person or an Indian in midseventeenth-century Mexican society reasonably entertain? Few, if any. But the same people might save some elements of their culture—a rhythm, a musical instrument, an aesthetic ideal, a culinary principle, perhaps a formula of courtesy—if they embraced the partial survival represented by the process of genetic and cultural *mestizaje*.

The Blacks and Indians who lost hope killed themselves, or they allowed their line to come to a halt by means of abortion, amenorrhea, and sterility—the physiological manifestations of a rejection of life. But the Indian, Black, and racially mixed women who had their babies, who struggled so that their fathers would recognize them, free them if they were slaves, provide for them, perhaps provide them with some education—these women were making possible the survival of their own kind over the long period. They were refusing to die. These women, for the most part despised by their contemporaries (and so little understood today), also were those who helped make life a little less harsh than it would otherwise have been for the European immigrants themselves. They forged the details of the domestic culture that gives a unique flavor to the home life of Mexican families even today. And above all they guaranteed the survival of many races in the new humanity that populates most of the Americas in our own time.

 29

Fruits of the Faith in the Seventeenth Century

MARIANO CUEVAS, S.J.

Writing in the late 1920s, the Mexican Jesuit Mariano Cuevas celebrated the seventeenth century as a golden age of religion and social order, a time of peace and unity founded on a pervasive, living faith. He liked Baroque art and the "healthy remorse" of the time that contributed to an exemplary solemnity and religiosity in public life. His essay is a vigorous response to adversaries—he had Protestants, politicians, and schoolteachers particularly in mind—who would see the seventeenth century as a time of dark struggle, disorder, despair, hatred, persecution, and depression. Cuevas's heartfelt ire was obviously influenced by national events then swirling around him, known as the Cristero Rebellion. National governments had gone beyond the nineteenth-century separation of church and state to treat the Catholic Church as an enemy of the state. Churches were closed and all Catholic services were forbidden in 1926, and a three-year civil war ensued in parts of central and western Mexico, with inevitable atrocities and destruction.

Cuevas's vision of the seventeenth century, however, is more than a diatribe against the godless state and "repugnant apostasy" of modern life. He was an accomplished scholar, and he musters intriguing evidence from the time that challenges readers to reckon and respond. His extended discussion of the annual Corpus Christi processions serves as a reminder that such processions were ubiquitous throughout the Spanish empire (and perhaps everywhere in Catholic Europe in the seventeenth century). In honoring the consecrated body of Jesus Christ—resurrected after His crucifixion and miraculously present in the Mass—these processions also celebrated the unity of society as a religious and political body under a Catholic monarch.

With all of its powerful institutions, the repressive as well as those that ease the way, the Mexican Church achieved a society that was steady and firm in its ideas, and generally well balanced in its customs and tendencies, as far as one could hope in this miserable world.

To begin with the fundamental point, in the seventeenth century the faith was a truly enviable social good. This is because it was a tranquil faith, with an absolute tranquillity, which was the source of the great tranquillity that we enjoyed at that time. Our revolutions then (a total of six minor rebellions with some shouting, clubbing, and rock-throwing by the riffraff) did not spread or take root because in one way or another the faith took over as a tree that was full of life, in which friends and enemies were part of the same trunk, partaking of the same root of love and charity.

From this tranquil faith, happiness in households was also well rooted, resulting in their prosperity and harmony, which declines to the extent that its source is lacking.

For the same reason, that class of unfortunates whom we find so numerous today did not exist. I mean those who, because of bad reading habits and essentially corrupting teachers, have thrown their rationality into the abyss of doubt, the moral helplessness of bitter remorse, and the most repugnant apostasy. For this reason alone, all good parents should raise a statue to the Holy Inquisition, which from Cádiz, and with even more determination from Veracruz, took charge of throwing into the sea or the flames the moral poison in the form of books that some tried to inject into the Christian blood of America.

This faith, Catholic to the core and with the royal seal of everything Spanish, was incessant and progressive in the reverence and splendor of its worship of God during that century. The archbishop of Mexico (a peninsular Spaniard) wrote to the king in 1752:

> I often marvel at the zeal with which many things have been undertaken in this Church, things that would have been daring even with greater resources. These people are used to praising and blessing God with magnificence in their worship of Him. In such zeal, this Church exceeds any that I have seen. What is lavished on these churches comes from Europe, and the materials used are the expensive kind. European wax is burned only in the churches, as an offering to the true God. It is used in no other way. . . . I hope that Your Majesty will make a saintly contribution to the completion of the cathedral here, because no project should be more attractive to Your Majesty than the first and most glorious monument to the religion of this new empire. After all, God has given it [the empire] to Spain, and continues giving such riches that the ancient empires seem insignificant by comparison and those that we read about in the Holy Scriptures seem credible.
>
> For me, this Church is worthy of veneration not only because I see it as the source from which the religion of all these vast provinces of New Spain derives but also because of the piety of the Spanish conquerors of this kingdom who, with great care and study, gathered all the idols and filled the foundations with them to show that the Mexican Church was literally built on the ruins of idolatry—a truly religious act and one that is little mentioned by our historians. It does credit to the constant and pure faith of the Mexican nation.

Worship was not a mere formality, confined to the churches; it was a living worship and, even more, it was the very life of society. It provided the nourishment and was the source of much of the high art and skilled crafts.

Life was beautified throughout the year—like the starry firmament—with religious celebrations. However, Corpus Christi was like the sun of them all, and this day was like the center to which the eyes of the devout, as well as artists and builders, were drawn.

As early as 1524 there were Corpus Christi processions in which the city's officials participated. The municipal records of 1529 inform us

> that all the artisans joined the procession, and among them there were disputes over preferential placement among the armorers and the tailors. To resolve these

> differences it was decided that the armorers would march alongside the ark containing the Blessed Sacrament, and directly in front of it would be the tailors, with the other occupations marching behind, one after another, so that, as is customary, no occupational group is left out. Henceforth this practice is to be followed and not broken, under penalty of fifty gold pesos for the occupational group that fails to march.

We can see that from this early date the Corpus Christi procession was growing in importance and solemnity in the capital and in the other cities and towns throughout New Spain. In the capital the procession left from the Escalerillas gate, following the streets of Tacuba to the Callejón de los Bethlemitas, turning left there, reaching the cathedral by way of San Francisco and Plateros streets, and entering the cathedral door. During his term as viceroy, the pretentious Conde de Baños [1660–1663] sought to have the procession pass in front of the viceregal offices, but this pretension cost him 12,000 ducats in fines imposed by the Crown.

The streets along the procession route were covered with a coating of damp sand, tamped down and leveled. On this surface, Indians from Xochimilco and Ixtapalapan spread an abundance of flowers and sweet-smelling herbs.

The procession was interrupted by comical figures called "the great giants" and "la tarasca" (the dragon), and dances and games of the Spaniards, Indians, and Mulattoes. All of these amusements, criticized by some unthinking commentators, had their own important purpose, which was to separate by a good distance the serious part of the procession from the crowd of children and people of little account who otherwise would cause confusion and impede the devotion.

One of the expenses underwritten by the city and not the guilds was the "great giants," allotted 500 pesos for their conservation and repair. Sometimes the cost was less than this sum, but it was often not enough because they took a lot of care. One of the less costly years was 1636, when Don Baltasar de Guevara and the corregidor contracted with the painter Cristóbal Franco to spruce up the giants, giving them new heads and faces, reclothing two of them, adding gold and silver trappings to all of their clothes, giving them new hair, redoing the dragon and giving it a coat of oil paint, dressing ten little devils, and repairing and refurbishing the awning, all for 400 pesos. But on other occasions the cost far exceeded this. In 1638 the directors of the fiestas of the Holy Sacrament, Juan de Alcocer and Cristóbal Velasco, reported in writing that the clothing of the giants was so torn and shabby that it was hardly suitable for lining. They sought to have new clothes made for all of them, from lustrous Chinese silk, decorated with designs and flowers in gold and silver, lining the new clothing with the old for longer wear.

Then came the guilds, each with its own extremely rich banner, patron saints on silver litters, matching lanterns, and silvery staffs for the mayordomos. They were followed by the religious brotherhoods proper, similarly outfitted, their ranks closed by a group of beadles, two or four trumpeters, and two especially privileged members, one to carry an elaborate case with the rules of the brotherhood and the other with the Sine Labe, or emblem, of the corporate pledge to defend the dogma of the Immaculate Conception. There were no fewer than eighty-five of these sodalities in Mexico City alone at the end of the seventeenth century.

A cloth awning reached across the street for the entire length of the procession. To hang it, iron or stone fittings were inserted into the walls of the houses along the route at the time they were built. Some are still to be seen along Tacuba Street. Every family extended itself, according to its means, in decorating the facade of the house. This sort of decoration reached its peak in the seventeenth century. Never since have we had so much silk, gold, Chinese materials, and, above all, such pious munificence as then.

Indians from throughout the valley brought an incredible abundance of flowers, boughs, and sweet-smelling herbs with which to construct showy triumphal arches here and there, replete with a multitude of songbirds and birds of brilliant plumage, which gave the Corpus Christi celebrations in America their stamp and special character among the unequaled ones in Seville, Burgos, and Toledo.

The entire week was filled with spiritual celebrations revolving around the Most Sacred Mystery [the transformation in the Mass of Communion wafers and sacramental wine into the body and blood of Christ], celebrations that the people put on according to their means and hallowed traditions.

In the year 1600 the Conde de Monterrey did not go along with what the city council had prepared according to custom; rather, he wanted an extraordinary solemnity in this fiesta that would exceed every other. To this end, the city agreed to have an excellent theatrical performance about divinity and another during the week, and on these two days the Spaniards, Indians, and Mulattoes would put on their dances. So that everything would be done properly, Don Francisco Escudero Figueroa was commissioned to supervise things. Before the event, as Figueroa described, the viceroy decreed that the theatrical production should be something well worth seeing, even though the costumed dancers and giants were quite ordinary. He thought it well not to stage the dances of swords, among others, and that it would be good to do everything with great solemnity. He had sent out letters to interpreters and other authorities to arrange for young dancers and guitars and other instruments for the fiesta and the week of celebration, as was customary, which he would sponsor. The following year, Don Francisco Trejo Carvajal contracted with Florián de Vargas, dance director, to provide a cartload of dancers and many fireworks and music both inside and beyond the church for the day of Corpus Christi and throughout the week, for a price of 200 pesos. He was to include as a flourish other dances and celebrations; Vargas himself was to organize another dance by twelve men, for which they would be paid another 100 pesos.

There were abuses, as one would expect, in all of these solemnities, but they occurred in spite of the celebrations, not because of them—they were not the acts of many, but of a few. In a word, they are not a fair basis for judging our long history of processions. Only a morbid hypocrisy has wanted to dwell on the abuses as a way of justifying the sacrilegious tyranny of our current laws forbidding religious services.

We only wish to add one thing on this matter: in 1564, when the municipal government of Mexico City decided to have the most solemn celebrations, the council record states that "this city must put on the Corpus Christi procession every year with great majesty and authority and the greatest rejoicing and enthusiasm. It is important and fitting as service to God Our Lord and *to unsettle the Lutheran heretics.*"

Not only was our way of expressing devotion to God and His saints lively and enlivening, it was universal, informing our *entire* life, just as the soul gives life to the body.

For the Protestant God, it is only the God of the church for a while on Sunday who does so. For good Christians, God is God their whole life through, and life seems sad if it is not illuminated by His holy presence.

Thus, our streets were God's streets; the cross crowned the entryways of our buildings; devout niches dedicated to a particular saint—so typical—each with its own little lantern, adorned our corners; our fields were God's, their best flowers were for the church altars and their newly harvested wheat stalks were the classic decoration for home altars to Our Lady of Sorrows, set up (who knows why) right on the stairs. The tillers of those fields would not begin their work without first coming together to intone the admirable "hymn of praise," a precious legacy of the first friars in the sixteenth century. Our military and conquistadores recognized in God their reason for living; they swore by the cross of their sword, they had "their saint and sign," their indispensable chaplain, and, when in agony on the field of battle, like Pizarro they made a cross in the sand in order to die with God.

In the hospitals and even in the jails an atmosphere of the supernatural reigned, and for the prisoners their incarceration amounted to a solid and corrective spiritual seclusion, not a school of crime.

In our very way of speaking, especially in our Mexicanisms, the religious seventeenth century left its mark. For example, we say "Whatever souls may come"; "What a miracle to see you again!"; "Those of Saint Peter left him"; "It's as good as dancing at Chalma"; "Don't break the fast at fifteen minutes to midnight," etc., etc.

The whole society felt very Christian, and the municipal council and others felt a pleasurable obligation to express publicly, before God and society, this official representation of such noble sentiments. For this reason the municipal councils had their special patron saint, their chaplains, and daily Mass in their own chapel. And when in 1618 there was a question about the legality of celebrating Mass in their private chapel (in view of recent pontifical decrees), the members of the cathedral chapter tore down the wall connecting to the jail so that the municipal council as a body could attend their customary Mass in their quarters.

When—as in that century—all of this external religion is in harmony for the moral improvement of the people, and with the Christian formation of families and the various social classes, then that devotion is a true measure of the faith and Christian charity that give life to all the virtues, and refine them.

Another measure of these virtues and of the very circumstances of the time was the generosity of the richest men. By contrast, the malignity of our present age is evident, among other things, in the shameful parsimony of Catholic capitalists, with rare exceptions. This generosity, which was not limited to the rich but extended to the middle class and even among the poor, shone through not only in their faith, but also in the numerous alms collected among the people for the support of the missions among infidels in the north of our country and especially in the Californias, the Mariana Islands, and the windward part of the Caribbean basin.

Apart from this, Madrid was continually requesting—always with great success—alms for various spiritual needs, whether for poor convents in the mother country, for expenses required for the canonization of some saint, or for hospitals or the ransom of captives.

With all of this we do not mean to say that there were no sins or crimes in our country. They existed in all classes and stations, as in any country inhabited by human beings.

And, of course, each of our racial classes had its own particular vices: among Indians, drunkenness seemed to dominate; among Blacks and Mulattoes, robbery and superstition; among Mestizos, libertine propensities, untrustworthiness, and theft; among Creoles, gambling; and among Spaniards, greed. This is not to say that these vices were monopolies in which the vice-ridden of any of the other aforementioned classes did not participate.

Speaking now in general of all classes of sinners in the seventeenth century, there is one characteristic that should be underscored in the field of history, for its roots and consequences are historical. It is that sins were committed with a knowledge of what they were, without attempting to justify them on the basis of twisted principles, leaving the soul (which, thanks to faith, was rarely lost) a healthy remorse and a path that was open to returning to God. Aside from various trustworthy anecdotes which we could cite in profusion, we will present some very significant data from a contemporary source on what we could call the conversion of Guanajuato (with good reason, the most notorious city when it came to customs), due to the mission preached there by Jesuit fathers in 1666:

> Knowing the padres' purpose in undertaking the mission, some people of Guanajuato told them they should go preach among the Chichimecas, not among themselves who were Christians. But these same people would later be the first and most faithful in attending the talks and other exercises of the mission, and fervently requested confession. The servant who accompanied the padres—an Indian neither versed in Spanish nor well educated—noticed that when the padres entered Guanajuato, the Indians observed them and kept their distance without removing their hats; but after the mission began, if one of the missionaries was coming toward them they would stand up, hat in hand, when he was still a block away. . . . The very day that the padres arrived and began the mission, and thereafter, the number of people in attendance was so great that even if the church was very spacious it filled up; and many, deeply disappointed, were left outside, unable to enter the church and hear the sermon.
>
> The owners of the mines had not allowed their servants to come in for confession during Lent, so they had not fulfilled their Easter Duty for many years. But now they couldn't keep them in the mines. In large groups they went to the mission exercises looking for a convenient place to confess. . . . Others called out for the padres to confess them, saying that it had been eight years or more since they had confessed; and one of them said he had not confessed in forty years. Many did not return to their houses at night. Instead, they rested in the street fully clothed waiting for the padres to say Mass for them, passing the time as well as they could while awaiting confession, until the gathering of people was so great that it became difficult to make a good confession and put themselves in grace with God. Since many awaited confession with the missionary padres in this way from the night before, it was not possible to confess them all; and, after the difficult night and morning waiting so as not to lose their chance, they went without eating well into the afternoon, sometimes still not getting their turn. It seems that Our Lord wanted them to endure those difficult days in order to atone for their sins; and they, rightfully, told the padres that it earned them the opportunity to be confessed.
>
> To recognize that all of this mission came from Heaven, one should notice that these people had not been known for their scruples and had lived with little

fear of God, wretched and tied to their passions like wild beasts. Consider this case of a mortally ill man who had received the last rites: an enemy of his, who was convinced that he would not be avenged of some injury which the sick man had done him before he took ill unless he took revenge by his own hand, entered the dying man's house and attacked him with a knife.

On another occasion these people were so entangled in one of their feuds—which they called *sasemin*—that when a priest in full clerical robes, with the Blessed Sacrament in his hands, went out to reprimand them, they had the audacity to show him disrespect. And in front of the Sovereign Lord they proceeded to throw rocks at him and shoot firearms, filled with fury, with the perverse intention of killing him.

Four months ago a priest from one of the regular orders went out with a layman who helped him celebrate Mass in the cemetery. Some men shot at the priest's companion and made a direct hit, so close to the priest that the sleeve of his habit was perforated with shot.

So, when the residents and honorable citizens of Guanajuato saw the great and unprecedented gatherings—even for theatrical spectacles—and the devotion of universal tenderness of those who were present, they said repeatedly that this alone was the greatest miracle of the mission, leaving Guanajuato in a condition that they never thought possible. If they had not seen it for themselves, they would not have believed it, for it always seemed as impossible as slapping the sky.

During the three weeks of the jubilation all the exercises of the mission were carried out; the procession of the Holy Christ, as is customary; and a nighttime function with the Miserere [the penitential psalm beginning "Have mercy on me, O God" ("Miserere mei Deus")]. The mine laborers were the first to know about it, finding their place in the church. They brought various implements with which to flagellate themselves during the duration of the Miserere. And they lashed themselves fiercely, showing the true penitence with which all of them wanted to satisfy God in some way for their sins. Speaking out, and with heartfelt clamoring, they affectionately asked God for mercy. A child of six or seven years, brought up in much luxury, surreptitiously went off to a corner of the choir so as not to be noticed, but his crying betrayed him and the sincerity with which he undertook acts of contrition brought him to notice. And the beating he gave himself was so rough that with his innocent blood he spattered those who were in the choir.

In that mining center there have been continual disputes which pit many of the residents against one another. But, thanks to Our Lord, after one sermon the spirits of those present were reconciled and they came together, providing an example to the rest of the pueblo. After a sermon, publicly, in front of the assembled people, the priests, who were many, knelt down and fervently pleaded with one another for forgiveness for any slight or trouble they might have caused. Moved by this example, the laymen did the same in the church and again just after dark. The gathering was so large and the confusion of people in the streets so great that it seemed like Judgment Day. The only utterances were for pardon as people pleaded, kneeling, facing one another, throwing themselves at each other's feet, crying with vivid feeling over the troubles between them, trying to outdo each other. Moved spiritually by the Lord, even the highest nobles paid no attention to their status and the other human distinctions that cause such impediments to serving God. The greatest offenders among them entered the homes of their adversaries, seeking pardon with all submission, and it cannot be denied that in the flush of their fervent devotion they acted in ways that by the judgment of human prudence could suffer the censure of indiscretion. The great ladies did the same, being even more pious.

The labor bosses are the most responsible for the *sasemin* and the most influential, for good or ill, by their personal conduct. The padres summoned each of them, one by one, calling upon them to make solid peace and be friends. They promised to do so and then embraced as a token of the friendship they had promised.

In order to ensure that these friendships lasted, it was arranged that on the last day of the mission the labor bosses and others who had been adversaries would accompany the padres to the church in the afternoon for the sermon. And so it happened, but upon reaching the church patio, they encountered a great gathering of people who could not enter to hear the sermon. To console them and so that they would not leave deeply disappointed, they were advised that there would be another address in the street. It was impossible for the padres to enter the church with their entourage, and the crush of people was no less great around the sacristy door. But since the padres somehow had to get in with their entourage if they were to do what they had come for, which was so much in the service of Our Lord. So, with great difficulty, the padres and their group made it into the church, and high-ranking persons had to cede their places to the labor bosses.

Once the latter were settled, the Blessed Sacrament was brought in with such a crowd of people that various high-born ladies ended up right next to the high altar for lack of room to get to their assigned seats. The Hail Mary was sung and the sermon began. At the appointed time, priests vested in surplices took the bosses by the hand and led them to the Blessed Sacrament. Kneeling, they embraced and swore to the Sacrificed Christ not to raise another rebellion or allow their supporters to do so; rather, they would work against such a thing with punishments and would do what they could to prevent it. And having embraced and given their word to the Sovereign Lord (who, on another occasion, as we noted, was so boldly treated with disrespect and lack of veneration), they cried copiously, as did the audience, out of tenderness, consolation, and happiness, seeing spirits that had always been opposed come together in agreement. This opposition had caused innumerable souls to be condemned—those of people who had died in the sasemines, including some Indian women who had become so bold that with great skill they had fired carbines, thrown rocks, and used other weapons as if they were the most skillful warriors or unrestrained captains. . . . In the sermons and examples, setting aside the timidity and faintheartedness to which some were accustomed, everyone gave positive demonstrations of great sorrow for having offended God, and no one took note in order to censure them, but only for a saintly emulation. Everyone was so contrite and turned so quickly to acts of devotion that the slightest insinuation was taken as an inviolable requirement to be undertaken with great fervor.

Some among the most observant, noting the momentum that the Lord, in His piety, had communicated to them, remarked that if the slightest suggestion were made to bring stone to rebuild the church there, everyone would immediately pitch in, and the highest-ranking women of the town would be the first among them, as an example to others. And they did not stop there but went on to thank

> God, whose powerful hand brought that change to Guanajuato. And the Mulattoes and other common people, astonished by that movement, said *"the Company [the Jesuits] needed to be established here."*

It is not surprising that certain authors of bad conscience pretend that our best century was a shrunken and sad time: to those of bad conscience, religion and its ramifications amount to repression and remorse. History that follows its true course, without prejudices, declares with abundant documentation that the Mexicans of the seventeenth century were strong and enterprising, just as during that time Mexicans themselves undertook the most extensive conquests and valiant deeds with arms. They were also a hard-working people, the manufacturing guilds being built by their own efforts; a people of conscience, because in that century, more than any other, they looked out for these interests with great efficacy; an artistic people, since it is from that time that our best architectural and pictorial works date; dreamers in the best sense of the word (those literary figures who would take us through the fields of romanesque and courtly legend, with their touches of mystery and their intense religious basis, must turn to the seventeenth century: from that age come Don Juan Manuel and la Monja Alférez, Treviño and la Mulata de Córdoba, la Mariscala de Castilla, and la China de Puebla, etc., etc.).

From all these elements, with their trunk and root in religion, sprang the happiest and most contented Mexico that has existed in this world of the possible and relative. It is living proof for pessimists that in Mexico and with Mexicans there can be happiness.

30

Santa Rosa of Lima According to a Pious Accountant

(1617)

In the early days of the Christian church, news of saintliness spread by unofficial channels, and often after a holy individual's death. Some "saints" remained locally famous, whereas others attracted cults that greatly transcended their beginnings. Saint-making grew more formalized in the eleventh century, when Pope Urban II required witnesses to testify that miracles had occurred and that sufficient virtues had been possessed by the people who were candidates for sainthood. From the thirteenth century, both saints and heretics were to be determined by ecclesiastical tribunals, the procedures of which were dictated from Rome. These "trials" were presided over by judges and included advocates, witnesses, and—in the case of the candidate for canonization (the Church's confirmation of saintliness)—a skeptical officer known as the Devil's advocate.

Yet the implementation of legal procedures at the center did not result in strict centralized control over the posthumous reputations of holy persons or the actions of their devotees in the many corners of Christendom. Written accounts of a saintly person's life, as well as word of mouth among the faithful, continued to ensure that enthusiasm would grow in predominantly local settings, and sometimes in eccentric ways, after the individual's death. Not surprisingly, the veneration of saints attracted criticism and concern from Protestants and Catholics alike during the Reformation. As the great humanist and student of the Church authorities Desiderius Erasmus of Rotterdam (1466–1536) complained, the cult of the saints was "not a great deal different from the superstitions of the ancients." The saints, Erasmus and others implied, were like local heroes whose powers were concentrated in sacred places, and who were regularly worshiped in themselves as well as in return for their mediation with God. The Council of Trent provided a pivotal setting at which Catholic churchmen gathered to debate a comprehensive set of reforms spurred both by reformers within the Church and by the growing critical presence of breakaway Protestant groups in parts of northern Europe. At the twenty-fifth session (December 1563), the participants at Trent clearly demonstrated their preoccupation with the practices by which saints were made. These churchmen effectively presided over the heart of an era of caution with regard to the determination of sainthood. Between 1523 and 1588, while saintly people and reputations continued to live on, no saint was officially canonized.

A revival of official saint-making began in the late sixteenth century, but with even more careful and centralized procedures directed from Rome. By the early seventeenth century, a prudent distinction between "true" saints and *beati* (saintly individuals) grew sharper, with the formal addition of a beatification stage in the certification of saints. Moreover, to guard against the hasty canonizations which were thought to have overtaken the Church in the euphoric moments after the deaths of certain pious persons in the past, it was decreed that no canonization proceedings could begin until fifty years after the death of a candidate.

Santa Rosa of Lima (1586–1617) was one of some fifty-five people (forty-three men and twelve women) canonized by the Catholic Church between 1588 and 1767. She died at the age of thirty-one on August 24, 1617, and was beatified in 1668 and canonized in 1671 (on April 12), judged heroic in virtue more quickly than an extraordinary cluster of certified saints and holy people who were her contemporaries and near-contemporaries in Peru. Most notably, the Franciscan Francisco Solano, who died in 1602 and was beatified in 1675, and the archbishop of Lima, Toribio Alfonso de Mogrovejo, who died in 1606 and was beatified in 1679, were both canonized in December 1726. Rosa's fellow Dominicans Juan Macías (1585–1645) and the Mulatto Martín de Porres (1579–1639) were not even beatified until October 1837. Within the half-century following her death, Rosa's patronal relationship with the city of Lima grew and soon extended well beyond it. Even before she was canonized, she became patron of Peru (1669) and of the Americas and Philippines archipelago (1670). Rosa's cult subsequently spread to pockets of devotion in Europe. Her example sheds light on religion and some of its functions in the period we are studying.

At the request of the head of the Dominican Order, the process of accumulating the testimonial evidence that would determine Rosa's sanctity began promptly on September 1, 1617, only eight days after her death. One source of information about her life and how she was perceived by her principal devotees and promoters just after she died are the declarations that Don Gonzalo de la Maza made between September 16 and October 6 in response to thirty-two questions put by a tribunal of judges to him and seventy-four other witnesses in the first stage (*proceso ordinario*). (Some 147 other witnesses were heard during a second stage—*proceso apostólico*—conducted between 1630 and 1632.) For reasons that will become clear, de la Maza's testimony is perhaps the most substantial of those collected in the first round of investigations. Excerpts from it are collected in the selection that follows.

Soon after his arrival in Lima from Spain in 1601 to take up his appointment as bookkeeper to the Tribunal of the Santa Cruzada, de la Maza made his home a haven for local people of extraordinary piety and ascetic devotion. In 1613, twenty-six-year-old Isabel Flores de Oliva (Rosa's baptismal name), the Creole daughter of a noble Spanish family in the city, was one of those attracted to Don Gonzalo's home. On the strong advice of her confessors and, it was later claimed, with the permission of parents who were "already" edified by their daughter's stirrings, Isabel became a *beata* (a lay holy woman).

De la Maza described her life at a moment soon after her death, as noted, in response to official queries about her alleged sanctity. His answers run in a number directions, frequently doubling back on themselves and, in effect, emphasizing the principal image he wanted to convey—that of a woman voluntarily withdrawn into a world of exemplary piety and for whom the goal of mystical union with God was open and attainable. His "Rosa" was one intimately remembered by him, his wife, and his daughters. Although he was older, de la Maza calls her "his mother," having sought her wise counsel and example, as did many others.

De la Maza was not an ordained priest and did not hear the young woman's confessions himself. Yet he says that they shared confidences, and he clearly learned what he could from her confessors, committed to memory events from her short life, and, in the process, became one of her most ardent promoters. There are strong indications in his testimony, however, that the extent of his personal relationship with her might easily be exaggerated, and that intimacy with the young recluse was enjoyed principally by his wife, Doña María de Usátegui, from whom de la Maza seems to have learned much about Rosa.

Pious writings about those who chose lives of chastity, private penitence, and prayer often conformed to a pattern, as much in early seventeenth-century Lima as in other places and times. De la Maza's testimony vividly conveys how Isabel Flores de Oliva came to see herself, and to be seen by others, in terms of known models of conduct. Rosa's saintliness is one expression of a set of values and understandings that suited her and her admirers, then and later, in the Peruvian capital. The person Isabel-Rosa sought a life of exemplary piety and contemplative devotion, just as her "life" (or saintly biography) was also converted into a series of spiritual feats for the edification of others. Further, inhabitants of Lima, and eventually the colonies of the Spanish world as a whole, sought through her an enhanced and legitimate place in a continuous Christian tradition of sanctity. As in José de Acosta's framing of the evangelization of Indians within the same long history of Christianity (see Selection 18), Rosa's fame and pious example came to sanctify her person, her city, and its people in the wider context of Counter-Reformation Catholicism.

She was said to have emulated the youthful path of the fourteenth-century mystic Saint Catherine of Siena (ca. 1347–1380), who was canonized in the fifteenth century. As Catherine had done, young Isabel adopted the simple dress of a tertiary of the Dominican Order—that is, she made only simple vows, as opposed to formal, more binding ones, and a "profession," which made her part of the Dominican family but not a nun. And like Catherine, she abandoned the distracting comforts of her parents' home. Isabel moved into a room in de la Maza's house and signaled the beginning of a personal transformation by taking a new, religious name, Rosa de Santa María. According to de la Maza, the resemblances between her life and that of Saint Catherine began very early, with special signs occurring in childhood. Like Catherine, Isabel was said to have acted on a precocious resolve to mask and thwart her beauty and to have unsettled her parents' expectations for her.

Her life, as told, was punctuated by a series of spiritual yearnings and tests that became milestones along a known path of spiritual perfection. There was her hunger for seclusion so that prayer and acts of penitence might continue undisturbed. There was the economy of her speech and her impatience with petty preoccupations or imprecision in others. There were her painful vigils of wakefulness, the feats of fasting and resistance to worldly comforts, all in pursuit of spiritual rewards that were said to have taken her more than once to the brink of death.

How much of her do we see in the following account? Rosa, who appears to have wanted nothing more than a private life of devotion and closer union to her God, became much more than a saintly recluse in the minds and hands of her contemporaries. Her Dominican champions made the most of an association between the name "Rosa" and the order's promotion of the Rosary and Our Lady of the Rosary (see Figure 25 in Selection 36 on a chapel in the church of Santo Domingo in Puebla, Mexico). The earliest "life" of Rosa, the *Life, Death, and Miracles of Sor Rosa de Santa María* (*Vida, muerte y milagros de Sor Rosa de Santa María*) of 1619, was written by a Dominican, Pedro de Loayza, in time to be included as evidence in the investigations into her sanctity. She was a seemingly perfect candidate for sainthood in her age and one that was literally seized upon in Lima, as de la Maza's testimony shows. Seeking the widest legitimacy for his account, he presents a "Rosa de Sancta María" who for many years (before and after her death, he says) was fervently discussed by people far outside his family's circle of beatas, including her confessors and the learned inhabitants of Lima dedicated to private spiritual lives. And her life was marveled at by many other contemporaries who had caught a glimpse of her or who had learned something of her from others. The sick flocked to her tomb to be healed, and others sought relics from the places in which she had lived. De la Maza describes many of Rosa's later devotees as "distinguished ladies" and gentlemen of Lima's elite, but he is just as quick to stress how much her example and reputation attracted and edified members of all social groups and stations, bridging earthly class divisions and economic interests.

[We join the testimony of Don Gonzalo de la Maza at his answer to the fourth question.]

Answering the fourth question, this witness explained that he had known the said Rosa de Sancta María for about five years, and he told of the personal contact he had with her. Although this witness had wanted to make her acquaintance years before, knowing the considerable virtue she possessed, he had not done so out of respect for her rigorous seclusion. His first direct experience came on the occasion when the said Rosa de Sancta María wrote to this witness asking him to assist her in a charitable deed, which greatly delighted him. However, he was afraid to disturb her tranquillity, until one day soon thereafter this witness chanced to see her enter his house with her mother, the said María de Oliva, and his wife, Doña María de Usátegui. As strangers, they [the three women] had met and spoken in the Jesuit church, for she [Doña María], too, wanted to meet the said Rosa. And for much of the time between that day and the one on which she passed from this life, he saw a lot of the said Rosa de Sancta María in his house with his wife and daughters due to the special affection they all had for one another. Rosa's taking of a room in this witness's house was favored both by her natural parents and by her spiritual fathers [her confessors], with whom she communicated. Sometimes, it was even by their orders, as this witness learned from her confessors, Padre Maestro Lorenzana of the Order of Saint Dominic and Padre Diego Martínez of the Society of Jesus. Through her stay and his personal exchanges with her, this witness learned of the beginnings of her calling.

Rosa told this witness of an incident that occurred when she was about five years old, while she was playing with one of her brothers, Hernando, who was two years older. Rosa [then Isabel] had grown beautiful blonde hair and [on this occasion] it had been handled roughly and soiled by her said brother. Once she saw the state of it, she started to cry. Her brother asked why she cried. Did she not know that on account of [worrying over] their hair many souls were in Hell? Knowing this, she should not be crying over her hair. [Rosa said] that this retort had so imprinted itself in her heart that in thinking about it she was seized by so great a fear in her soul that from that moment on she did not do a thing, not one thing, which she understood to be a sin and an offense to God Our Father. From this fear Rosa gained some knowledge of the divine goodness, which helped her [understand things about] her grandmother [who had died] and a sister, a little older than her, who died at the age of fourteen. [Rosa was now able to see them] as souls that, in her opinion, had been very pleasing to Our Lord, [and] whose deaths had been a great consolation to her because the things she had seen in them and been given to understand by His Divine Majesty convinced her that they had certainly gone to Heaven.

Thus, the said Rosa de Sancta María said to this witness that at that tender age she had dedicated to God Our Lord the gift of her virginity, with a vow [of chastity], and that, to this witness's understanding, the great outward modesty and purity of life attained by the said Rosa suggested that she honored the said promise not only in her deeds but also in her thoughts, as one of her spiritual fathers expressed it to this witness. And her introspection was such that the said Rosa also revealed to the witness that in her life she had neither seen nor longed for a feast day or worldly celebration, not even a common procession, and that during the time that he knew her he clearly perceived this [to be a true account of] her way of withdrawal [from the world] and devotion. She withdrew not only from direct communication but also from seeing people and [worldly] things in order that they might neither impede nor delay the serenity of her soul, the power of which this witness saw at that time to be so focused that he beheld it with great admiration.

And as much [was true] in other senses, because this witness never saw her tongue move to utter an unnecessary thing. [This was true] in her answers or advice to others, in her praise of the Lord and in her encouragement of others to give praise. Her words were so careful and serious that they demonstrated very well that it was God who moved her. She was so chaste in her speech that if she said something that might be understood in more than one sense, she added, "What I am saying" or "I wish to say." She wanted everyone to do the same, as was demonstrated on the occasions when other people recounted something she had said or done. If [the relation of her words or acts] was not undertaken with absolute precision, she pointed out whatever was wanting with complete courtesy, [noting] that she had said or done this [or that]. And this witness noticed this perfection of the truth in her speech until she died. [In fact, this was] so much the case that on the very day she died, a devoted friar had come and asked one of the people who were attending Rosa in her illness if it would be acceptable for Father So-and-So, for whom Rosa had asked, to enter, at which point the said Rosa, though in very great anguish and pain, spoke up, saying "I said I wished to see him before I die."

The downward cast of her eyes was notable, so much so that this witness said that, in communicating with her so familiarly and with such openness that he called her his mother, it was amazing how few times he saw her lift her gaze. She was so chaste and pure in her sensibilities that in no manner would she attend conversations that were not spiritual and directed toward the good of souls and the service of Our Lord. And if it happened otherwise, or if some person began to speak on secular themes, with very great modesty she attempted to divert them or absent herself from the conversation, as this witness saw in his house on many occasions. Thus, in the time they knew one another, it was very rare for her to go out [or be among] people from outside the house, not counting the times in which some spiritual fathers visited, because the whole of her interest was in retreat and solitude. . . .

The day of her birth is recorded in her father's book and the certificate of baptism. Concerning the day of her death [in order to establish her age at death], it occurred in this witness's house on Thursday, August 24, Saint Bartholomew's Day, one half hour after midnight. And after the said beginning of her calling, the said Rosa de Sancta María told this witness that she scorned the things of this mortal life, such as trying to impress people and be their object of curiosity. To manage this, for some time she had worn the habit of Saint Francis until, at the age of twenty or twenty-one years, she dressed in that of Saint Dominic and Saint Catherine of Siena, her mother, whom she had wanted to imitate since the beginning of her life, and become a nun of her order. And this witness has never heard, understood, or seen anything which contradicts what he has said, nor anything against the virtue, honesty, spiritual absorption, and virginal purity of the said Rosa de Sancta María. This is his answer to the question. . . .

To the sixth question . . . Although they kept secret her mortifications of the flesh and penances until she died, this witness and his family knew of her way of life. This witness said that from a young age she was given to mortify herself with fasts, scourges, and other [self-inflicted] sufferings, and that from early on she had subsisted on bread and water for many days [at a time]. And, from the age of ten or eleven years she kept to her fasts of bread and water, especially on the days that her mother would excuse it, that is, on the Wednesdays, Fridays, and Saturdays of each week. At the age of fifteen and sixteen years she had made a conditional vow to forego meat and to fast on bread and water for the rest of her life. . . .

This witness observed her abstinence when she lived in his house, during which time even when she had a fever and her doctors and confessors ordered her to eat meat, she would not do it. Her fasts on bread and water were continuous. . . . [In fact,] this witness saw that she would go a day or two or more without eating or drinking anything, particularly on the days when she took Holy Communion, because at certain times of the year confessors granted permission for one to take Communion every time one went to church, and this is what she did with much modesty and without drawing attention to herself. During these fasts and abstinences, [when] she left the church or her secluded room in his house, she had such color [in her face] and showed such health [that it seemed] as if she was fortifying herself with plenty of nutritious dishes. Worrying over her stomach pains and all that she suffered, one would ask her why she did not eat anything, to which she ordinarily responded that Holy Communion made her feel full to bursting and that it was impossible for her to eat [even] a bite. . . .

[It often happened that in ill health Rosa would be made to eat meat and other food, especially by her well-meaning mother, but also by doctors and her worried confessors. In this witness's experience, these feedings had the effect of worsening Rosa's condition.] During one of her dangerous illnesses three years ago, the doctors forced her to eat meat, which left her weary and so short of breath that she could walk no more than a few steps for many days. She said that it [her worsened condition] had resulted from her distress at having eaten meat, and she began getting better when she resumed her abstinence. . . . During the time that the said witness knew her, the said Rosa's manner of abstinence was such that the amounts she ate even when she was not observing it [her fast of bread and water] did not, to him, seem enough to sustain the life of a human body, especially one so young. . . .

To the seventh question this witness answered that he knew for a fact that since the beginning of her life the said Rosa de Sancta María performed continuous and rigorous mortifications of the flesh, usually with iron chains. And this witness knew [about these mortifications] from what he had heard from her, her mother, some of her confessors, his wife the said Doña María de Usátegui, and his two young daughters, from whom, even given their tender ages and the love and concern he had for them, he did not deny exposure to [Rosa's] virtuous example.

With the same certainty, this witness learned that for a long time she [Rosa] had worn an iron chain wrapped two or three times around her waist and fastened with a padlock for which she had no key. [At one point when] she was in her mother's house, she developed a very severe pain in her abdomen, and the chain had to be removed in order for her to be helped. She suffered much as the lock was broken because her skin and, at some parts, her flesh had become stuck to the said chain, as this witness saw after Rosa's death.

Because all of this information was communicated to his wife, the said Doña María de Usátegui, on the understanding that it might be told to this witness, he also understood with the same certainty that she [Rosa] had employed different hairshirts, and that she had worn one with very rough bristles [that extended] from her shoulders down to her knees. For a long time she had worn tunics with sackcloth on the inside until, after two years, her confessors noticed her health so diminished that they took them away. This witness had seen them on the occasions when she changed them and hung them out in the sun. By order of her confessors, from that time [when the rough tunics were forbidden] until the point of the illness from which she died, her simple outfits were brought to her, on which occasions this witness also saw that she changed them.

The said Rosa de Sancta María sometimes told this witness and his wife and daughters that from an early age she had greatly detested putting on a good appearance for people and the care taken by her mother in arranging her hair, face, and clothes. Seeing that she was not getting very far [toward the realization of her ascetic designs] with her mother, at the age of twelve years she cut off her very blonde head of hair, at the sight of which her mother scolded her harshly. [But her quests continued.] Feeling that her fasts and mortifications were not sufficient to drain the color from her cheeks, she poured pitchers of cold water over her chest and back even when she was dressed. Because of this, or because of divine will and providence, she contracted an illness at the age of thirteen years and became crippled and [had to be] clamped to a bed by her hands and feet for a long time. [She suffered] a great pain over her entire body that could not be explained, but, in bearing it, a very great relief and comfort came to her, in [knowing] that on account of Heaven her patience and compliance with the divine will had never faltered. She told this witness that on this occasion, as on others, Our Lord had rewarded her with so much pain, of a kind she had not believed a human body could withstand. [It was] nothing like the kind [of pain] He Himself had suffered, [she had said,] yet she was bewildered at having enjoyed so much forgiveness from God's hand, [considering] it was not possible that this [reward] would be bestowed on so wretched a creature as herself.

This witness also understands it to be a certain thing [based on what he had learned] from his wife the said Doña María de Usátegui, and from other people, that the bed in which Rosa slept until the age of one and a half or two years in her parents' house, [eventually] taken by her confessors, was a barbacoa, a small platform of rather coarse canes, like those used for threshing wheat in Spain. [It was] bound together by leather cords, with sharp, two- or three-cornered shards of an earthenware jug scattered over it and between the said canes. . . .

And after the said bed was taken away, and put on a shelf so that the said shards would not fall away, this witness knows that the said Rosa de Sancta María normally slept either on a plank of wood with a blanket, or seated in a small chair, as she did the whole time she lived in this witness's house. . . . This witness also knew that from the beginning of her life the said Rosa de Sancta María had endeavored to punish her body by depriving herself of sleep, and there came a time when in a day and night she slept no more than two hours, and sometimes less. . . .

And, on the matter of her ways and mortifications, from one of Rosa de Sancta María's spiritual fathers this witness has heard [of one of her methods] to be able to keep praying when she was overcome by drowsiness. She set about tying together a number of the hairs at the front [of her head], [hairs] which concealed a crown of thorns that she wore [underneath], [and then attaching these knots] to a nail she had driven into the wall of her refuge. [Thus,] she would be virtually hanging [there], only able to reach the floor with difficulty. And in this way she conquered weariness and continued her prayers. . . .

To the twenty-ninth question he answered that he has heard said that there have been many, and very exceptional, miracles performed by Our Lord God for the greater glory of His name and in demonstration of the virtue and sanctity of the blessed Rosa. [By these miracles] many people with different maladies, [who] entrust themselves to her intercession [by] touching some traces of her clothing and the earth from around her tomb, have been restored to health. This witness defers to the testimonies and proof of the said miracles.

Since the day on which the body of the said blessed Rosa was buried in the chapter room of the said convent of Saint Dominic, every time this witness entered [the chapter room] he has found a great gathering of people of all orders, stations, and sexes, and at the tomb this witness has seen many of the sick, crippled, and maimed.

And in the same way he has observed what is [equally] well known, [namely,] the veneration and devotion which the notables of this city, like the rest of the general population, have for the blessed Rosa de Sancta María and for the things that were hers [and that were associated with her life]. [This is demonstrated] by the number of people of all stations who have gathered at this witness's house to visit the rooms in which the blessed Rosa stayed and died. In particular, there have been very few, if any, distinguished women who have failed to turn up in this witness's house to ask for relics from the clothing and other things that belonged to the blessed Rosa. And the same [close attention] has been paid by important men; indeed, the first one whom this witness saw request relics was Dr. Francisco Verdugo, the inquisitor of this realm, and this witness sent them to him. And [then] there was the judge from the royal Audiencia who has come twice to ask for them.

The demand has been such that if the tunics and habits which she left were many, they [still] would not have been enough to share in very tiny parts among the people who have come with such great affection and devotion. [One notes] particularly the monks from the five religious orders and the nuns in the convents of this city, whose requests [for relics] have not been small.

The flow of people who have visited the house of Rosa's parents in which she grew up and lived has been of no less magnitude. [They visit] the little cell that was her room, taking from it what they have been able to prize away and remove, even the little latch from the door, as this witness has seen, and [even] the threshold and planks are cut out from the room and its door. There was one time when this witness wanted to do the same, and he visited her parents only to find so many people and coaches and horses outside the door and in the street that he returned [home, having been] unable to enter. . . .

What this witness had most noticed were the tears shed by many people [while] talking about the life and things of the blessed Rosa. Some friar-confessors told him of the exceptional conversions of souls and arduous transformations of [people's] lives that had occurred among those who commended themselves to the blessed Rosa after her death. Other people, especially devout women, have told this witness they wanted to receive the habit that the blessed Rosa had worn and to found the convent of Saint Catherine of Siena that she [Rosa] so much desired. A prelate of a religious order, and not even the Dominicans, has told him the same thing. And this witness knew a maiden whom he took to be very virtuous, who now was attempting to imitate the life of the blessed Rosa. And [there are] spiritual people, very devout, among them some friars, who have said to this witness that since the death of the blessed Rosa de Sancta María they have received from Our Lord remarkable favors and rewards, much better than those which they had received before. And this he knows and is his response to this question.

31

Sor Juana Inés de la Cruz's Letter to Sor Filotea (1691)

Perhaps the most celebrated literary figure of colonial Spanish America is Sor Juana Inés de la Cruz (1651–1695), a Jeronymite nun in Mexico City. Her life and writings say much about the Baroque predicaments that were keenly felt, especially in the seventeenth century—a life of struggle toward salvation in a world of troubling contradictions.

The illegitimate daughter of Creole Spanish parents from the pueblo of Chimalhuacán, near the Valley of Mexico, she was identified as a child prodigy and at the age of eight went to live with relatives in the capital. Her beauty, wit, and skill at poetry and her amazing knowledge of books and ideas made her an instant celebrity at court. At age fifteen the admiring viceroy and his wife sent her before a panel of learned professors of the University of Mexico (women were not permitted to study there), who failed to stump her in a probing oral examination ranging across physics, mathematics, theology, and philosophy. Abruptly in 1667, still not sixteen, she entered a Carmelite convent, switched the following year to the less rigorous Jeronymite Order, and spent the remainder of her life as a nun.

Marriage and religious seclusion were the usual lines open to respectable colonial Spanish women. Misogyny was unusually overt among clergy of the seventeenth century, who dwelt on the idea that women were passionate daughters of Eve, temptresses who invited sin and damnation. As an Inquisition judge remarked during an early seventeenth-century investigation, respectable women "are to remain at a distance from the mundane affairs of the public and stay shut up in their houses." So it was not surprising that Sor Juana, with her stated "total disinclination to marriage," would choose this conventional way to remain faithful to her religion and pursue her passion for study. Almost to the end, the secluded life of the spirit for this refined, troubled, and vibrant woman took a very different turn from that of Santa Rosa of Lima, and it met with a very different response from her ecclesiastical superiors.

Nearly all of Sor Juana's writings come from behind cloistered walls, and she remained in correspondence with literary friends and scientists in Mexico City and abroad until 1694. Her poetry offers a rich variety in form and content, including love lyrics, tender Christmas carols, morality plays, allegorical pieces, and the contradictions of her time and all time. Much of it is written in the ornate, rather obscure style that was popular then, but often there is a stunning clarity of meaning and accessibility. Her remarkable intellectual life as the Age of Reason was beginning to unfold in western Europe left her deeply distressed by the prevailing dichotomy of emotion and intellect that was hardly questioned by Spanish ecclesiastical authorities. She was not a rebel at heart, but her joyful, sometimes indignant curiosity and biting wit about the world and the mind trespassed conventional boundaries for women's lives and spiritual activity. Torn by her interior struggles over religion and science, body and soul, passion and reason, and the situation of a woman entering the intellectual territory of men, she found little of Santa Rosa's reported serenity. She finally gave up the struggle in 1694 at the age of forty-two. She gave away her books and scientific and musical instruments and in her own blood wrote out an unqualified renunciation of her learning, signing it "I, Sor Juana Inés de la Cruz, the worst in the world." (With this phrase she cites Paul [1 Timothy 1:15] in making a statement of utmost humility: "Christ Jesus came into the world to save sinners, of whom I am the worst of all.") She died the following year while caring for her convent sisters who had contracted smallpox.

The famous letter to "Sor Filotea" is a spirited, autobiographical response to critics among her ecclesiastical superiors. "Sor Filotea" was not another nun but rather her sometime friend and adviser, the Bishop of Puebla, Manuel Fernández de Santa Cruz (1676–1699), who wrote to her under this pseudonym, warning of her intellectual activities (which he himself had encouraged) and worldliness as threats to her immortal soul.

Although she was celebrated by some leading intellectuals and patrons (including two viceroys' wives), Sor Juana was a troubling example for many of her contemporaries. There would be no sainthood in her future, but she has become something of a heroine for our time. In reading these passages from her letter, we might consider why she speaks to late twentieth-century readers more directly than does Santa Rosa. Part of an answer is that *she* speaks, whereas someone else always speaks for Rosa or claims to have her words. But there is much more. The two young women spent their energies in the service of God in different ways, perhaps expressing Miguel de Unamuno's sense of the difference between mystics and others: mystics "reject science as futile and seek knowledge for a pragmatic purpose, in order to love and work for and rejoice in God, not for the sake of knowledge alone. Whether or not they are aware of it, they are anti-intellectuals." The colonial-era portraits of Santa Rosa and Sor Juana (Figures 23, 24) are as suggestive of the differences as are the texts.

Moses, because he was a stutterer, thought himself unworthy to speak to Pharaoh. Yet later, finding himself greatly favored by God, he was so imbued with courage that not only did he speak to God Himself, but he also dared to ask of Him the impossible: "*Show me thy face.*" And so it is with me, my Lady, for in view of the favor you show me, the obstacles I described at the outset no longer seem entirely insuperable. For one who had the letter printed, unbeknownst to me, who titled it and underwrote its cost, and who thus honored it (unworthy as it was of all this, on its own account and on account of its author), what will such a one not do? What not forgive? Or what fail to do or fail to forgive? Thus, sheltered by the assumption that I speak with the safe-conduct granted by your favors and with the warrant bestowed by your goodwill, and by the fact that, like a second Ahasuerus, you have allowed me to kiss the top of the golden scepter of your affection as a sign that you grant me kind license to speak and to plead my case in your venerable presence, I declare that I receive in my very soul your most holy admonition to apply my study to Holy Scripture; for although it arrives in the guise of counsel, it shall have for me the weight of law. And I take no small consolation from the fact that it seems my obedience, as if at your direction, anticipated your pastoral insinuation, as may be inferred from the subject matter and arguments of that very letter. I recognize full well that your most prudent warning touches not on the letter, but on the many writings of mine on humane matters that you have seen. . . . I want no trouble with the Holy Office, for I am but ignorant and tremble lest I utter some ill-sounding proposition or twist the true meaning of some passage. I do not study in order to write, nor far less in order to teach (which would be boundless arrogance in me), but simply to see whether by studying I may become less ignorant. This is my answer, and these are my feelings. . . .

To go on with the narration of this inclination of mine, of which I wish to give you a full account: I declare I was not yet three years old when my mother sent off one of my sisters, older than I, to learn to read in one of those girls' schools that they call Amigas. Affection and mischief carried me after her; and when I saw that they were giving her lessons, I so caught fire with the desire to learn that, deceiving the teacher (or so I thought), I told her that my mother wanted her to teach me also. She did not believe this, for it was not to be believed; but to humor my whim she gave me lessons. I continued to go and she continued to teach me, though no longer in make-believe, for the experience undeceived her. I learned to read in such a short time that I already knew how by the time my mother heard of it. My teacher had kept it from my mother to give delight with a thing all done and to receive a prize for a thing done well. And I had kept still, thinking I would be whipped for having done this without permission. The woman who taught me (may God keep her) is still living, and she can vouch for what I say.

I remember that in those days, though I was as greedy for treats as children usually are at that age, I would abstain from eating cheese, because I heard tell that it made people stupid, and the desire to learn was stronger for me than the desire to eat—powerful as this is in children. Later, when I was six or seven years old and already knew how to read and write, along with all the other skills like embroidery and sewing that women learn, I heard that in Mexico City there were a university and schools where they studied the sciences. As soon as I heard this, I began to pester my poor mother with insistent and annoying pleas, begging her to dress me in men's clothes and send me to the capital, to the home of some relatives she had there, so that I could enter the university and study. She refused, and was right in doing so; but I quenched my desire by reading a great variety of books that belonged to my grandfather, and neither punishments nor scoldings could prevent me. And so when I did go to Mexico City, people marveled not so much at my intelligence as at my memory and the facts I knew at an age when it seemed I had scarcely had time to learn to speak.

I began to study Latin, in which I believe I took fewer than twenty lessons. And my interest was so intense, that although in women (and especially in the very bloom of youth) the natural adornment of the hair is so esteemed, I would cut off four to six fingerlengths of my hair, measuring how long it had been before. And I made myself a rule that if by the time it had grown back to the same length I did not know such and such a thing that I intended to study, then I would cut my hair off again to punish my dull-wittedness. And so my hair grew, but I did not yet know what I had resolved to learn, for it grew quickly and I learned slowly. Then I cut my hair right off to punish my dull-wittedness, for I did not think it reasonable that hair should cover a head that was so bare of facts—the more desirable adornment. I took the veil because, although I knew I would find in religious life many things that would be quite opposed to my character (I speak of accessory rather than essential matters), it would, given my absolute unwillingness to enter into marriage, be the least unfitting and most decent state I could choose, with regard to the assurance I desired of my salvation. For before this first concern (which is, at the last, the most important), all the impertinent little follies of my character gave way and bowed to the yoke. These were wanting to live alone and not wanting to have either obligations that would disturb my freedom to study or the noise of a community that would interrupt the tranquil silence of my books. These things made me waver somewhat in my decision until, being enlightened by learned people as to my temptation, I vanquished it with divine favor and took the state I so unworthily hold. I thought I was fleeing myself, but—woe is me!—I brought myself with me, and brought my greatest enemy in my inclination to study, which I know not whether to take as a Heaven-sent favor or as a punishment. For when snuffed out or hindered with every [spiritual] exercise known to Religion, it exploded like gunpowder; and in my case the saying "*privation gives rise to appetite*" was proven true.

I went back (no, I spoke incorrectly, for I never stopped)—I went on, I mean, with my studious task (which to me was peace and rest in every moment left over when my duties were done) of reading and still more reading, study and still more study, with no teacher besides my books themselves. What a hardship it is to learn from those lifeless letters, deprived of the sound of a teacher's voice and explanations! Yet I suffered all these trials most gladly for the love of learning. Oh, if only this had been done for the love of God, as was rightful, think what I should have merited! Nevertheless, I did my best to elevate these studies and direct them to His service, for the goal to which I aspired was the study of Theology. Being a Catholic, I thought it an abject failing not to know everything that can in this life be achieved, through earthly methods, concerning the divine mysteries. And being a nun and not a laywoman, I thought I should, because I was in religious life, profess the study of letters—the more so as the daughter of such as Saint Jerome and Santa Paula: for it would be a degeneracy for an idiot daughter to proceed from such learned parents. I argued in this way to myself, and I thought my own argument quite reasonable. However, the fact may have been (and this seems most likely) that I was merely flattering and encouraging my own inclination by arguing that its own pleasure was an obligation.

I went on in this way, always directing each step of my studies, as I have said, toward the summit of Holy Theology; but it seemed to me necessary to ascend by the ladder of the humane arts and sciences in order to reach it; for who could fathom the style of the Queen of Sciences without knowing that of her handmaidens? Without Logic, how should I know the general and specific methods by which Holy Scripture is written? Without Rhetoric, how should I understand its figures, tropes, and locutions? Or how, without Physics or Natural Science, understand all the questions that naturally arise concerning the varied natures of those animals offered in sacrifice, in which a great many things already made manifest are symbolized, and many more besides? How should I know whether Saul's cure at the sound of David's harp was owing to a virtue and power that is natural in Music or owing, instead, to a supernatural power that God saw fit to bestow on David? How without Arithmetic might one understand all those mysterious reckonings of years and days and months and hours and weeks that are found in Daniel and elsewhere, which can be comprehended only by knowing the nature, concordances, and properties of numbers? Without Geometry, how could we take the measure of the Holy Ark of the Covenant or the Holy City of Jerusalem, each of whose mysterious measurements forms a perfect cube uniting their dimensions, and each displaying that most marvelous distribution of the proportions of every part? Without the science of Architecture, how understand the mighty Temple of Solomon—where God Himself was the Draftsman who set forth His arrangement and plan, and the Wise King was but the overseer who carried it out; where there was no foundation without its mystery, nor column without its symbol, nor cornice without its allusions, nor architrave without its meaning, and likewise for every other part, so that even the very least fillet served not only for the support and enhancement of Art, but also to symbolize greater things? How, without a thorough knowledge of the order and divisions by which History is composed, is one to understand the Historical Books—as in those summaries, for example, which often postpone in the narration what happened first in fact? How, without command of the two branches of Law, should one understand the Books of Law? Without considerable erudition, how should we understand the great many matters of profane history that are mentioned by Holy Scripture: all the diverse customs of the Gentiles, all their rituals, all their manners of speech? Without knowing many precepts and reading widely in the Fathers of the Church, how could one understand the obscure sayings of the Prophets? . . .

They [who sought to prohibit me from study] achieved this once, with a very saintly and simple mother superior who believed that study was an affair for the Inquisition and ordered that I should not read. I obeyed her (for the three months or so that her authority over us lasted) in that I did not pick up a book. But with regard to avoiding study absolutely, as such a thing does not lie within my power, I could not do it. For although I did not study in books, I studied all the things that God created, taking them for my letters, and for my book all the intricate structures of this world. Nothing could I see without reflecting upon it, nothing could I hear without pondering it, even to the most minute material things. For there is no creature, however lowly, in which one cannot recognize the great "*God made me*"; there is not one that does not stagger the mind if it receives due consideration. And so, I repeat, I looked and marveled at all things, so that from the very persons with whom I spoke and from what they said to me, a thousand speculations leapt to my mind: Whence could spring this diversity of character and intelligence among individuals all composing one single species? What temperaments, what hidden qualities could give rise to each? When I noticed a shape, I would set about combining the proportions of its lines and measuring it in my mind and converting it to other proportions. I sometimes walked back and forth along the forewall of one of our dormitories (which is a very large room), and I began to observe that although the lines of its two sides were parallel and the ceiling was flat, yet the eye falsely perceived these lines as though they approached each other and the ceiling as though it were lower in the distance than close by; from this, I inferred that visual lines run straight, but not parallel, and that they form a pyramidal figure. And I conjectured whether this might be the reason why the ancients were obliged to question whether the world is spherical or not. Because even though it seems so, this could be a delusion of the eye, displaying concavities where there were none.

This kind of observation has been continual in me and is so to this day, without my having control over it; rather, I tend to find it annoying, because it tires my head. Yet I believed this happened to everyone, as with thinking in verse, until experience taught me otherwise. This trait, whether a matter of nature or custom, is such that nothing do I see without a second thought. Two little girls were playing with a top in front of me, and no sooner had I seen the motion and shape than I began, with this madness of mine, to observe the easy movement of the spherical form and how the momentum lasted, now fixed and set free of its cause; for even far from its first cause, which was the hand of the girl, the little top went on dancing. Yet not content with this, I ordered flour to be brought and sifted on the floor, so that as the top danced over it, we could know whether its movement described perfect circles or no. I found they were not circular, but rather spiral lines that lost their circularity as the top lost its momentum. Other girls were playing at spillikins [jackstraws] (the most frivolous of all childhood games). I drew near to observe the shapes they made, and when I saw three of the straws by chance fall in a triangle, I fell to intertwining one with another, recalling that this was said to be the very shape of Solomon's mysterious ring, where distantly there shone bright traces and representations of the Most Blessed Trinity, by virtue of which it worked great prodigies and marvels. And they say David's harp had the same shape, and thus was Saul cured by its sound; to this day, harps have almost the same form.

Well, and what, then, shall I tell you, my Lady, of the secrets of nature that I have learned while cooking? I observe that an egg becomes solid and cooks in butter or oil, and on the contrary that it dissolves in sugar syrup. Or again, to ensure that sugar flows freely, one need only add the slightest bit of water that has held quince or some other sour fruit. The yolk and white of the very same egg are of such a contrary nature that when eggs are used with sugar, each part separately may be used perfectly well, yet they cannot be mixed together. I shall not weary you with such inanities, which I relate simply to give you a full account of my nature, and I believe this will make you laugh. But in truth, my Lady, what can we women know, save philosophies of the kitchen? It was well put by Lupercio Leonardo that one can philosophize quite well while preparing supper. I often say, when I make these little observations, "Had Aristotle cooked, he would have written a great deal more." . . .

I confess also that, while in truth this inclination has been such that, as I said before, I had no need of exemplars, nevertheless the many books that I have read have not failed to help me, both in sacred as well as secular letters. For there I see a

Deborah issuing laws, military as well as political, and governing the people among whom there were so many learned men. I see the exceedingly knowledgable Queen of Sheba, so learned she dares to test the wisdom of the wisest of all wise men with riddles, without being rebuked for it; indeed, on this very account she is to become judge of the unbelievers. I see so many and such significant women: some adorned with the gift of prophecy, like Abigail; others, of persuasion, like Esther; others, of piety, like Rahab; others, of perseverance, like Anna [Hannah], the mother of Samuel; and others, infinitely more, with other kinds of qualities and virtues.

If I consider the Gentiles, the first I meet are the Sibyls, chosen by God to prophesy the essential mysteries of our Faith in such learned and elegant verses that they stupefy the imagination. I see a woman such as Minerva, daughter of great Jupiter and mistress of all the wisdom of Athens, adored as goddess of the sciences. . . . I see Gertrude read, write, and teach. And seeking no more examples far from home, I see my own most holy mother Paula, learned in the Hebrew, Greek, and Latin tongues and most expert in the interpretation of the Scriptures. What wonder, then, can it be that, though her chronicler was no less than the unequaled Jerome, the Saint found himself scarcely worthy of the task, for with that lively gravity and energetic effectiveness with which only he can express himself he says: "If all the parts of my body were tongues, they would not suffice to proclaim the learning and virtues of Paula." Blessilla, a widow, earned the same praises, as did the luminous virgin Eustochium, both of them daughters of the Saint herself [Paula]; and indeed, Eustochium was such that for her knowledge she was hailed as a World Prodigy. Fabiola, also a Roman, was another most learned in Holy Scripture. Proba Falconia, a Roman woman, wrote an elegant book of cantos, joining together verses from Virgil, on the mysteries of our holy Faith. Our Queen Isabella, wife of Alfonso X, is known to have written on astrology—without mentioning others, whom I omit so as not merely to copy what others have said (which is a vice I have always detested): Well, then, in our own day there thrive the great Christina Alexandra, Queen of Sweden, as learned as she is brave and generous; and too those most excellent ladies, the Duchess of Aveyro and the Countess of Villaumbrosa. . . .

If ever I write any more little trifles, they shall always seek haven at your feet and the safety of your correction, for I have no other jewel with which to repay you. And in the opinion of Seneca, he who has once commenced to confer benefits becomes obliged to continue them. Thus you must be repaid by your own generosity, for only in that way can I be honorably cleared of my debt to you, lest another statement, again Seneca's, be leveled against me: "*It is shameful to be outdone in acts of kindness.*" For it is magnanimous for the generous creditor to grant a poor debtor some means of satisfying the debt. Thus God behaved toward the world, which could not possibly repay Him: He gave His own Son, that He might offer Himself as a worthy amends.

If the style of this letter, my venerable Lady, has been less than your due, I beg your pardon for its household familiarity or the lack of seemly respect. For in addressing you, my sister, as a nun of the veil, I have forgotten the distance between myself and your most distinguished person, which should not occur were I to see you unveiled. But you, with your prudence and benevolence, will substitute or emend my terms; and if you think unsuitable the familiar terms of address I have employed—because it seems to me that given all the reverence I owe you, "Your Reverence" is very little reverence indeed—please alter it to whatever you think suitable. For I have not been so bold as to exceed the limits set by the style of your letter to me, nor to cross the border of your modesty.

And hold me in your own good grace, so as to entreat divine grace on my behalf; of the same, may the Lord grant you great increase, and may He keep you, as I beg of Him and as I am needful. Written at the Convent of Our Father Saint Jerome in Mexico City, this first day of March of the year 1691. Receive the embrace of your most greatly favored,

Sor Juana Inés de la Cruz
Treasurer of the convent

32

Portraits of Santa Rosa and Sor Juana

Santa Rosa's reputation and her association with the city of Lima grew rapidly after her death. We recall Gonzalo de la Maza's words about the stir in Lima, the fervent clamoring after relics and stories. An emerging set of attributes can be seen in almost any of the many early paintings of her: the crown of fresh roses entwined with thorns, a wreath of flowers, the rosary, a Dominican habit, and depictions of her visions (that of the Christ Child holding a golden wedding ring as a reminder of her marriage to God, for instance, appears in one painting from the early eighteenth century).

This posthumous portrait (Figure 23) emphasizes another characteristic feature which, one suspects, Santa Rosa would have appreciated more than all the attributes: a likeness to the classic depictions of her spiritual mother, Saint Catherine of Siena. An understated crown of roses and thorns, a rosary, and the habit make the necessary identification, but the image's most striking feature is its quiet portrayal of its subject's purity and inward focus: the downward, meditating gaze of her eyes. Eyes lowered, hands joined, rosary within reach, Rosa is in another world. We are meant to imagine an inner place of contemplation, and moral and mystical beauty. The elaborate rays projecting from her head and the designs on her habit seem to be the canvas's reply to its decorative silver frame. They are distractions put in place by admiring patrons and successors—not so unlike the associations with the city of Lima, the layers of flowers, or the Dominican Order.

The second image (Figure 24), a painting of the Mexican nun Sor Juana Inés de la Cruz, also completed after her death and said to be a copy of a self-portrait, is different. She gazes straight out at her viewers, engaging us with a presence and an intelligence that recall her letter to Sor Filotea (Selection 31). Sor Juana's right hand rests on a carefully identified volume of her own works, while with her other hand she marks a page in another tome, as if we have interrupted her reading and she would like to know why. She wears her nun's robes and *escudo de monja* (an oval painting on copper that members of her order in New Spain wore on special occasions; hers depicts the Annunciation). Taking the veil, in Sor Juana's words, offered her the "least unfitting and most decent state." Like the "skills that women learn," discipline is endured because of devotion to God and the life that it can bring with it. She cut off her hair as a girl, just as Santa Rosa did, and both decided to leave "the world." But, whereas in Rosa's case the gaze turns inward in contemplation of God, with Sor Juana the withdrawal is meant to serve God and become a refuge for study and writing. She leaves in order to find the time and opportunity to scale intellectual heights denied her and other women outside a convent. Santa Rosa seeks the same time and opportunity, but, for her, different heights are in view. The heavens have opened.

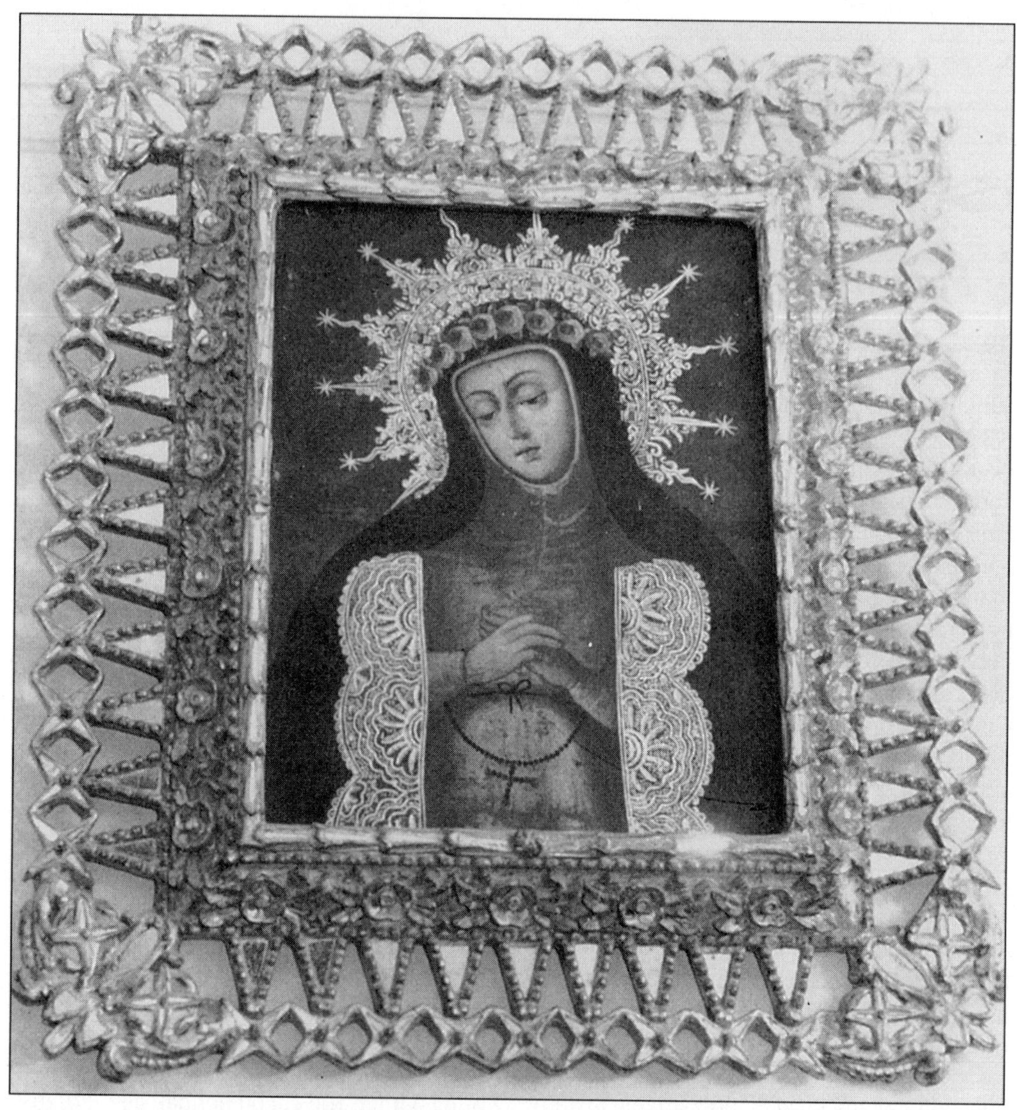

Figure 23. Portrait of Santa Rosa of Lima with silver decoration, artist and date unknown.

FIEL
Copia de otra que de si hizo, y de su mano pintò la R. M. Juana Ynés de la Cruz Fenix de la
America, Glorioso desempeño de su Sexo, Honrra de la Nacion de este Nuevo Mundo, y argu-
mento de las admiraciones, y elogios de el Antiguo. Nació el dia 12. de Nov.e de el año de 1651. à las
onse de la noche. Reciuiò el Sagrado Habito de el Maximo D.r S. S.n Geronimo en su Convento de
esta Ciudad de Mexico. de edad de 17. años. Y murio Domingo 17. de Abril de el de 1695. de edad
40. y 4. años, cinco mezes, cinco dias, y cinco horas. Requiescat in pace. Amen

Figure 24. Portrait of Sor Juana Inés de la Cruz by an unknown artist.
Courtesy of the Philadelphia Museum of Art.

 33

Mutilated Memory

Reconstruction of the Past and the Mechanisms of Memory among Seventeenth-Century Otomís

SERGE GRUZINSKI

Serge Gruzinski of the Centre National de la Recherche Scientifique in Paris has written extensively on Indian life and thought in colonial Mexico. His books and articles make intriguing use of primary sources in which an Indian presence is directly felt: records drawn and painted, as well as those written in the Roman alphabet. The following essay revolves around an anonymous chronicle of events, the *Relación anónima,* that culminated in the establishment of colonial Querétaro (Miguel Hernández's hometown; see Selection 19) from the viewpoint of Otomí nobles originally from Tula and their ancestral hero, Don Nicolás Muntañez. This chronicle is known only in an eighteenth-century Spanish version, but Gruzinski regards it as a "first-hand Indian account," perhaps translated from an Otomí original.

The various groups of Otomí speakers north of Mexico City along the Chichimec frontier had an ambiguous place in the colonial history of Spanish-Indian relations. Some had lived in small, mobile communities—like their Chichimeca enemies and neighbors—and fought incorporation into indigenous states such as that of the Aztecs. They resisted Spanish encroachments in turn. Others became important allies of early Spanish expeditions and settlements that pushed north into the Bajío, the ranching and irrigated farming zone located near the great silver mines discovered in the 1540s. These Otomí allies were settled in or near new Spanish towns like Querétaro and could lay claim to some of the special privileges granted to the Tlaxcalans (see Selection 13).

Gruzinski views this anonymous chronicle as an idealized memory of the past by a group of Otomí nobles living in Querétaro sometime in the seventeenth century, a memory "crystallized" by the colonial act of writing. His understanding of that memory is informed by psychoanalytic theory, centering on "anxieties and preoccupations suffered by an Indian group." Gruzinski tells a story of crisis and negation, dramatic change and decay. He suggests that in speaking of Otomí adjustments to colonial rule as documented in this chronicle, it may be "more appropriate to speak of alienation than of acculturation." While discussing the indigenous authors' use of numerical details, he describes "an acculturated mentality unable to conceive of the past or describe reality without resorting to Western-style methods of quantification."

"This idealized version appears to be determined by present circumstances," writes Gruzinski—that is, memory is affected by the harrowing experience of these people in the seventeenth century and their particular needs for an acceptable past. His provocative discussion opens out to other selections on Indians under Spanish rule in this sourcebook and to other possible interpretations and contextualizations of this particular chronicle. The author acknowledges that Conquest methods varied and were not confined to initial armed confrontations, yet he ultimately finds in the chronicle's failure to mention the Spanish Conquest a denial of "the defeat and degradation of the vanquished," a "blotting out" of the "true nature of the Conquest" by "a group of Indians whose leadership was considerably weakened in the course of the seventeenth century." Olivia Harris (Selection 6) sees a different meaning in Indian historical accounts that gloss over the Conquest period. She finds in them evidence of colonial Indian vitality and a vision of continuity that regarded the Spaniards' arrival as rather unremarkable. The Texupa map of 1579 (Figure 9) seems to catch the spirit of Harris's interpretation. Gruzinski's interpretation may be more appropriate for the seventeenth century and this Otomí group, but is there perhaps more even to this Otomí chronicle than "amputation" and "mutilation" of memory, and more to the interaction of Spanish impositions and colonial native society?

As Gruzinski points out, the chronicle's insistent reference to the Otomí protagonists as Catholics rather than Otomís is particularly arresting. Is this comparable to Felipe Guaman Poma de Ayala's identification with Christianity, which he proceeded to use as a foundation for his criticism of Spanish mistreatment of Indians in Peru (Selection 25)? Is it comparable to Nicolás Ñenguirú's appeal to the royal governor from Paraguay as a Christian subject representing other Christian subjects with special rights and privileges (Selection 38)? Or is it, as Gruzinski says, "no more than a fantasized self-identification with the colonizer," a case of the Tula Otomí leaders casting "themselves in the mold of their conquerors almost to the point of confusing the latter's identity with their own, subsuming themselves under the broad category of 'Catholics' "? As he also notes, Otomís had long distinguished themselves from the enemy Chichimecas, so that their distinction between themselves as Catholics and the Chichimecas as barbarians was partly a reinforcement of an older separation in colonial times. And in its legalistic language, in the prominence, heroism, and exalted titles of their ancestor, Don Nicolás, and in its claims to special privileges that recall the Tlaxcalans of central Mexico or the Cañaris in the Andes (see Selection 37), the chronicle was also a brief of the kind that accompanied formal petitions for favor from the Crown throughout the colonial period.

It is sometimes forgotten that the colonization of the vast territories north of the Valley of Mexico would never have been possible without the indispensable support of native auxiliaries. The urgent need to protect the roads to the silver mines drove the Spanish to seek Indian collaboration. And so it was that Mexicas, Tlaxcaltecas, Tarascos, and Otomís, sometimes singlehandedly and sometimes combining forces with the colonizers, increased their attacks on the Chichimeca Indians, acting not only as soldiers but also as spies, go-betweens, and scouts, before finally settling in sedentary villages. Thanks to their collaboration, the Spanish succeeded in greatly reducing the threat posed by the nomadic group's resistance, during the Chichimeca War, which lasted from 1550 to 1600.

Episodes of less consequence in the areas of San Juan del Río and Querétaro preceded the Chichimeca War. It is worth recalling that shortly after the fall of Mexico-Tenochtitlan, groups of Otomí Indians retreated to the semi-desert regions to the north of Tula and Jilotepec, in the face of the conquistadores' advance. Around the year 1531 a few of them, led by a merchant by the name of Conni, a native of Nopala in Jilotepec province, took up residence in the neighborhood of Querétaro. Conni established good relations with the Chichimecas in the surrounding district. Some time passed, and then a Spanish *encomendero*, Pérez de Bocanegra, made contact with Conni, who agreed to be baptized and to accept the king's sovereignty. From then on, Conni's name was Hernando de Tapia. The new convert managed to entreat the Chichimeca Indians, and they were baptized in their turn by a priest brought in from Acámbaro. Hernando de Tapia was to play a distinguished role, as is known: he became governor of the town of Querétaro, he helped bring about the surrender and conversion of numerous Chichimeca groups, and he founded various towns such as San Miguel el Grande. Another Otomí Indian from Jilotepec founded the town of San Juan del Río after first having attempted to retreat from Spanish domination. Like Conni, he finally submitted and converted to Christianity.

Thus ran the "official" version of the origin of San Juan del Río and Querétaro, toward the year 1582. This is what we shall call the "White memory" of events, the standard account recorded by the chroniclers of the colonial period and reiterated by modern historiography.

The Past Recalled

1. *The* Relación anónima

However, we have access to one text (or at least to a copy of it) which offers quite a different version of the facts. This text took the form of an "ancient and battered notebook," found lodged in the archives of the Colegio Apostólico de Propaganda Fide in Querétaro at the beginning of the eighteenth century. Later evidence tells us that this document constituted an anonymous Otomí chronicle believed to have been translated into Spanish at the request of the Franciscans of Querétaro, who were seeking information about the evangelization of the town and the miraculous origin of the cross worshiped there. I only know a copy of the text, made in 1717, and housed in a collection in Rome. Both its author and its date of composition are unknown. However, there are various indications that the document was probably drafted by Otomí *caciques* in Querétaro toward the mid-seventeenth century. Although only the Spanish version has survived, it remains a historical document of exceptional worth. We need only recall the words of one well-known expert on the Otomís, Jacques Soustelle: "Otomí history was never written down by the Otomís themselves, for they never wrote anything." A detailed examination of the text, its "rude and awkward style," and its content—full of "chimeras and despicable fictions"—at times incomprehensible, prevents it from being considered a piece of writing of European origin. Other observations, which we cannot discuss in detail here, lead the reader to think that a large part of the text was directly written in Spanish, rather than translated from the Otomí.

Briefly, the anonymous *Relación* offers a first-hand Indian account of the facts as they were still preserved in memory by certain groups of caciques over a century after the foundation of Querétaro. It is a version that differs greatly from the one asserted in [Spanish chronicler] Ramos de Cárdenas's *Descripción.*

The *Relación* narrates events that took place during May, June, and July of the year 1502 [a date seventeen years before the actual arrival of Cortés in the Valley of Mexico]. It highlights the part played by one *capitán general,* Don Nicolás Muntañez, in the conquest of the [region known as the] Gran Chichimeca. The account falls into three parts: the first describes the prelude to the conquest, from May 20–31, 1502 (arrival in the vicinity of Querétaro, the proposals made to the Chichimecas, the latter's reply fixing the date for the military encounter); the second part tells of the foundation of San Juan del Río from June 23–26; and the third and final part relates the actual conquest of Querétaro and the origin of the miraculous cross, between July 24 and 30.

This is obviously far removed from Ramos de Cárdenas's version, whether with regard to the identity of the main protagonist (Nicolás Muntañez instead of Hernando de Tapia), the nature of the contact with the Chichimecas, or the absence of any reference to the encomendero Pérez de Bocanegra.

2. Settlement of Accounts?

The emphasis laid on the town of Tula and its cacique Don Nicolás Muntañez, at the expense of Jilotepec and Hernando de Tapia, is of particular significance. Not only is the main focus of attention upon Don Nicolás, but he is also actually featured as the narrator of a large portion of the text. The highest-ranking titles are reserved for Don Nicolás: he is a nobleman, a descendant of the king, capitán general, and even "the" emperor; his name always appears immediately after those of the king and the viceroy. Nonetheless, the account does not ignore the existence of the famous Hernando de Tapia, whose son Don Diego was cacique and natural lord of Querétaro until his death in about 1614. But it consistently assigns him a role of lesser importance: he is named one of the *principales* [Indian notables] who accompany Don Nicolás, he is Don Nicolás's helmet bearer, and he figures as godfather to a Chichimeca chieftain's child. The chieftain then nominates him governor and captain of the future Querétaro, although this information is later corrected to indicate that one Don Alonso Guzmán "was the first governor of the settlement." While Hernando de Tapia's actual role is played down, the *Relación* substitutes for him a protagonist who was by no means fictitious: Don Nicolás de San Luis Muntañez, cacique and nobleman of the town of Querétaro, indeed existed and was the most acclaimed military leader of the first decade of the Chichimeca War in the mid-sixteenth century. He was capitán general and *capitán de las fronteras* of the townships of San Felipe, San Miguel, and Valle de San Luis; he led the "principales and Indians of the town of Querétaro" on military expeditions against the nomads. This is to say that the fictitious part attributed to Don Nicolás is in fact a plausible one, although it is fixed at a date prior to the real period of his activities.

On the other hand, in being twice set on a par with Tlaxcala, Tula appears as one of the political centers of New Spain. According to the *Relación,* both towns were the first to receive the Christian faith, a fact which qualifies Tula as the "first center of Christianity," a center capable of rallying 25,329 Indians in the fight against the Chichimecas. On the other hand, the Indians of Jilotepec—"historically" the true founders and conquerors of San Juan del Río and Querétaro—are assigned an inglorious role. Despised by Don Nicolás's troops, forced to fight against their will, locked up in the garrison at

San Juan or in the caves on the red hill, these so-called "untrustworthies" are punished for reasons that remain as obscure as do the motives for this political manipulation of the past. Perhaps the *Relación* was composed by a group of caciques from Tula who took advantage of the gradual disappearance of the Tapias from the Querétaro scene to impose a version of history less favorable to the founder of the place. They may have deliberately constructed a past that fitted in better with their own ambitions and with the composition of the leading Otomí group as it was by the mid-seventeenth century. This they did by temporally displacing the events recounted, and reversing the roles of the two principal protagonists.

3. Autonomy and Identification

However, far from stopping at a simple manipulation of the past, the work of memory opens up other perspectives that are more complex to explain. For this is a version of history whose actors are almost exclusively Indian. With three or four exceptions (Charles V, Viceroy Luis de Velasco, the Royal Audiencia, Father Juan Bautista), the Spanish are excluded not only from the stage of events but also from the scene of New Spain altogether. And yet we know that they always supervised and often accompanied the native auxiliaries on their expeditions. Even more surprising is the fact that, with one exception, the protagonists are never referred to as Otomí Indians. They are called and refer to themselves as "the Catholics," Catholics whose conversion is alluded to only briefly and is set in a vague, remote past, prior to the [ostensible] date of the events related here, 1502. Although the *Relación* recalls that Tula and Tlaxcala were the first two towns to be evangelized, it never mentions the Spanish Conquest, as if this military and political conflict had been totally erased from memory. The very choice of the date 1502 precludes any need to refer to the real and dramatic circumstances of the Conquest in 1519. This is rather reminiscent of what psychoanalysts call *souvenirs-écrans* [screened memories] which, despite their apparent temporal and spatial precision of detail, are no more than constructs serving to mask key events situated more recently in time.

Once again, the past described here is not a totally fictitious one. The style of the expedition led by Don Nicolás, the objectives attributed to him, the policy of conquest and resettlement, and the strategies developed derive from a real past, that of the Chichimeca War, which took up the second half of the sixteenth century. But the *Relación* projects this set of data and memories into a more distant past which, for us, corresponds to the pre-Hispanic period.

Furthermore, there is a fictitious geopolitical framework to go with the fictitious time frame. The Otomí Indians enjoy a privileged position: their twofold status as conquerors and Catholics allows them certain immutable rights and obliges them to bow to the higher authorities of the king and the viceroy alone. Furthermore, they participate actively and directly in the evangelization of their Chichimeca adversaries, preaching to them "what Christianity is." On the other hand, of course, no detail is given of the precarious conditions under which these expeditions were carried out, no mention made of the real reasons for their emigration, not to say flight from Jilotepec province, and, above all, no word said of their utter subjection to the Spanish invaders and of the abuse and mistreatment suffered at their hands. Instead of this, Otomí memory constructs an idealized image of the past in which, both materially and spiritually, the Tula Otomí cast themselves in the mold of their conquerors almost to the point of confusing the latter's identity with their own, subsuming themselves under the broad category of "Catholics." They therefore manage to identify themselves with the Spanish without losing their autonomy. This memory attempts to combine native military prestige with the achievement of acculturation "without tears," at least as far as the Otomí chiefs were concerned. Without being a flagrant distortion of the past, but rather an imaginary account of what might have been, this idealized version appears to be determined by present circumstances.

Let me explain. Behind the systematic selection of certain details and the suppression of the less flattering aspects of the past, it is possible to decipher the inverted image of a mediocre present reality in which the Indians of Querétaro were living during the greater part of the sixteenth century. The town's one-time founders are now no more than an ethnic group among many: Nahuas, Tarascos, Mestizos, Mulattoes, Negros. Their cultural specificity is reduced to the status of an urban subculture essentially based on language and kinship ties. Caciques and principales hardly lead brilliant careers in a city which is no longer a military stronghold and which has fallen into the hands of rich Spanish herders and traders who have taken control of the best lands. Their agricultural and commercial activities are few, while the power of the Indian governor—a post held by the Tapias during the sixteenth century—dwindles slowly. This is to say, the *Relación* was written in an atmosphere of crisis and social and political decline in which, even for the caciques, acculturation no longer meant access and integration into the dominant colonial class. It is likely that this situation influenced the drafting of the *Relación,* leading its authors to look for a lost and glorious past in which the Otomís would be free of the stereotypical image that dogged them throughout the colonial period and beyond: "These Otomís are held to be the most rustic, incapable, and stubborn Indians in all the land." According to this logic, the present would constitute the reverse of the past: the social and political mediocrity of today would contrast with the brilliance of yesteryear, and present subjection and dependence would be counteracted by the display of military strength and responsibility by the "Catholics" of the *Relación.*

Though it be said in passing, such a representation of the past does no more than draw on the fictions encouraged by the Christian ideology of the Conquest: by becoming Christians and submitting to the king, the Indians could hope to achieve a measure of political autonomy under the protection of the Crown. Although colonial reality became far removed from this principle, the *Relación* seems to draw inspiration from this argument in order to conceive an "acceptable" past, one which associates the acquisition of a new identity (that of Catholics) with the preservation and even the consolidation of an authentic military force. It is very probable that the Otomí group was already so acculturated that to imagine a non-Christian or pre-Christian past was impossible for them, and to adopt an adverse attitude toward Spanish domination more unthinkable still. But perhaps it is more appropriate to speak of alienation than of acculturation, for not only is the primordial episode of the Conquest amputated from memory but the latter is deeply conditioned by colonial ideology. For this reason their identity as "Catholics" is no more than a fantasized self-identification with the colonizer.

4. The Conquest Denied

However, the content of the *Relación* goes beyond reflecting a settlement of accounts between local leaders and providing an idealized image of the past. It includes a further dimension that we shall now examine. The whole text is constructed around a military encounter which we have tried in vain to locate in the account itself. We follow the incursion of 25,329 Otomís into the Gran Chichimeca at four in the morning; we read of their fear ("very fearful were the Catholics, for that day their lives were in danger"), and so to the appearance of a tall cross "about four yards high and shining" in the sky. The "Catholics" lose all fear, "wiping away their tears and sweat." As prearranged, both armies discard their weapons and prepare to fight "man to man." At this point, and without interrupting the story line, the text suddenly describes the baptism of the Chichimeca chieftain. There is not a single word about the battle. However, further on, the *Relación* alludes to "the 25,800 wounded men, covered in the blood of battle, and my (the Chichimeca chief's) 25,800 Chichimecas in the same condition." By this curious sleight of hand the text avoids describing an event while not actually denying it happened. It is true that in order to explain the origin of the miraculous cross and satisfy the Franciscans' demands, it was necessary to invent a bellicose incident which, as we know, never took place. But how to explain why memory and imagination, so prolific on other points of little relevance, suddenly clam up on this issue?

It is as if there were a need to erase all details regarding violent confrontation and humiliating defeat from the account of the conquest. On the other hand, an effort is made to offer a more balanced image of the relations between the conquerors (the "Catholics") and the conquered (the Chichimecas). Otherwise, how to interpret the fact that from the beginning the Chichimecas are the ones who dictate the conditions of the coming battle? They fix the date, decide the number of contestants, and declare: "May the battle be fought man to man!" Better still, the Chichimeca chief and his wife ask to be baptized and married in advance, to the sound of bells "so that my vassals may rejoice," and a cross be placed on the "little hill." In a letter addressed to the Chichimeca chief, Don Nicolás adds this surprising phrase: "Everything shall be as Your Majesty commands!" We might also mention the warm embrace which seals the first encounter with the Chichimeca chief: "He asked for his hand and said 'Let us embrace, we shall be friends.' "

Thus, from the very beginning of the text, the Chichimecas plan the course of events rather than passively suffer the onslaught of their "Catholic" conquerors. At the same time, the *Relación* emphasizes their good nature. Take, for example, the words of the Chichimeca chief: "My sons, the Catholics come in good faith, offering us baptism and marriage and gifts of blankets and clothing to bring us to an agreement with them. . . . I say they come in good faith seeking agreement."

Reciprocity, equality (both with regard to the number of belligerents and the number of wounds received by each party), the "agreement," and the respect for the will of the other are hardly the common practices of conquest. It is true that some pacification expeditions—more frequent at the end of the sixteenth century—also resorted to persuasion, promises, and the offering of gifts and foodstuffs. It is also true that the *Relación* specifies the meaning given to the term "conquest" when it describes the distribution of clothing to the Chichimeca chiefs: "They dressed them finely . . . and they were happy to be at peace because . . . Don Martín, the interpreter, was conquering them that night in the proper way." However, peaceful methods of conquest never involved accepting the conditions of the people about to be conquered. This is a surprising paradox in a text so concerned with emphasizing the greatness of the Otomís and their expansionist military past.

Unless, that is, we consider the following hypothesis, which fits in with the logic of negation mentioned above. Just as native memory succeeded in blotting out the Mexican Conquest from the past, so it endeavored to de-dramatize the confrontation between Indians and Catholics, transforming it into an encounter without real losers. It is as if the aim of the *Relación* were to deny the true nature of the Conquest, and the defeat and degradation of the vanquished, be these the Chichimecas or the Otomís themselves. For although, on the surface of things, the *Relación* concerns the struggle between Otomí Catholics and Chichimeca Indians, it draws on an archetypal image of conquest according to which the category "Catholic" may merge with that of Spaniard, and that of "Chichimeca Indian, barbarian" be applied to the Otomís themselves. This model of conquest is, yet again, to be seen as a contrived effort to reconstruct a past acceptable to a group of Indians whose leadership was considerably weakened in the course of the seventeenth century.

This brief look at the content of the *Relación* leads us to suggest that memory operates in different registers, which correspond in turn to different levels of consciousness: 1) In response to immediate interests and local strategies, it rearranges and modifies the vestiges of a military past for the periods after 1550 and after the foundation of Querétaro. 2) At a more deep-seated level, memory appears characteristically to split in two directions: while on the one hand it cannot forget the episode of the Conquest, on the other it attempts to deny the nature of the latter as an event of war by constructing a fantastical image of it. This contradictory process of "scotomization" [dimming, obscuring] of reality, due to a splitting of the ego—to borrow the terminology of psychoanalysis—results in the definitive alteration of the past, as if it had undergone a process of repression. But above all, this phenomenon confirms that memory is a manifestation of the present, a prime indication of the anxieties and preoccupations suffered by an Indian group living in the mid-seventeenth century.

The Methods and the Forms of Memory

The work of remembering and constructing the past is a complex one, for, in addition to the processes outlined above, much depends on the *form* of the materials that feed native memory, in the elaboration of content. It is not sufficient to idealize or modify the past; it is also necessary to find images capable of expressing and reviving it.

1. Memory and Colonial Festivals

Too little is known of the oral tradition of this group of Otomí caciques for us to explore this field; we shall therefore focus our analysis on more easily observable aspects. First, there is an obvious link with certain features of colonial festivals. The latter appear to inspire various passages of the *Relación,* from the minute description of the processions, troops, arms, costumes, and music to the collective shows of rejoicing and the "dances of the Chichimecas." Both sixteenth- and seventeenth-century chroniclers mention mock battles between Indians "dressed as Spaniards" and Chichimecas "acting the fool and gesticulating." Others recall festive occasions directly related to the festival of the Holy Cross. It is very likely that the spread of the cult of the Holy Cross of Querétaro coincided with the proliferation of the dances of Moors and Christians, or Christian Indians and Chichimecas according to the Michoacán and El Bajío versions. Furthermore, it is known that in 1690 a masque [costumed celebration] was enacted in Querétaro in which groups of "rude Chichimecas," companies of native foot soldiers, pre-Hispanic kings, and musical groups playing *teponastli* [drums made of hollowed logs] all took part. For the festival of the Holy Cross in the same town, "a rowdy celebration was held in which some people dressed up as Moors and others as Christian soldiers and they erected a mock castle in the square, with a cross upon it, to represent the prison for the Turks." Similarly, the account of the Acclamation of King Philip V in 1710 contains descriptions closely comparable to those in the *Relación* of multicolored costumes, hats decorated with feathers and pearls, and a "squadron of coarse Chichimecas." Whether in the urban processions full of learned historical references, in the festivals' "Baroque folklorism," or in the dances and ritual battles performed by the common people, it was easy enough to find spectacular images to awaken imaginings of an already distant past. Neither should we forget that librettos of Indian theatrical works were in circulation at the time. It is not impossible that, rather than being inspired by the urban festivals, the *Relación* was itself such a libretto: a script to guide the steps of the actors through the streets of Querétaro. Its succession of dialogues and scenes, its choruses of Catholics and Chichimecas, its liturgical and military sequences briefly but clearly sketched, the movements of the crowd depicted on various occasions, the expressly indicated timing of the episodes (at 2:00 and 5:00 P.M.) in San Juan del Río—all contribute to evoking the image in the reader's mind of a lavish piece of Baroque street theater whose text would make up a large part of the *Relación.* It is sufficient to quote the reference to Don Nicolás donning Chichimeca regalia to take part in the masque: "He put on Chichimeca costume," and to mention the music which accompanies many of these images, the ringing of bells and the sound of teponastli and trumpets.

2. Memory and Writing

But neither can the *Relación* be reduced to the status of a mere script for a local festival. It is also a set of documents and a source of information like any other historical work. There is no doubt that the Otomí caciques had full access to native archives, official papers such as title deeds, nominations, certified résumés of distinguished individuals, ordinances, royal decrees, writs, and dispatches, as well as various documents relating to the incursions into and pacification of the Gran Chichimeca region. From the early days of the Conquest, the Indian nobility and caciques made efforts to assemble and transmit all documents issued by the king, the viceroy, or the Royal Audiencia, which expressed and protected their rights and property. However, instead of extracting the substance of the information from such documents, the *Relación* makes do with reproducing, if not with plagiarizing them. For example, it begins with the following words: "Mandate delivered by the King Our Lord," and throughout the text fragments of varying length are inserted, crammed with titles, formulae, and stereotypical declarations, extracted from such documents as a petition to the viceroy or to the master architect, or from the license issued by the Crown to Don Nicolás. The first part of the *Relación* is largely built out of such texts, either cited directly or simply referred to: the "*Jecutoria*" [writ] of Charles V, the King's Dispatch, the Viceroy's License, License for the conquest and settlement of Querétaro, summonses to General Assemblies issued by Don Nicolás, the King's License, and so on.

A comparison between these passages and other documents that have survived from the period shows the relationship between the *Relación* and the products of colonial bureaucracy. Nonetheless, we were unable to trace the original documents which might have inspired the writing of the *Relación* in this way. We tend rather to think that such texts were fabricated in order to be included in the account and that use was made, above all, of existing documents as a model for the *Relación*'s framework, rather than as a source of authentic data. This would appear to be the case with the myriad titles so generously bestowed upon the main protagonist, Don Nicolás, in the course of the narration: "Nobleman, descendant of the King, Emperor, capitán general and Settler, Conquistador, Citizen and Mayor, Public Prosecutor and Chief Constable. . . ." Elsewhere, Don Nicolás appears with the titles: "Emperor of Tula, Emperor of New Spain, Governor, Mayor, Chief Public Prosecutor and Preacher of this town of Tula . . . , capitán general of New Spain, Emperor of the great province of the town of Tula. . . ." What is more, Don Nicolás's name often appears at the head of documents incorporated into the *Relación,* occupying the place usually reserved for the king and his viceroy. Such details suggest that the *Relación* is strongly inspired by official rhetoric; the stereotypical expressions and juridical turns of phrase with which it abounds would also be a sign of this. To quote a few: "conduct," "vassals," "protection," "dispatch," "council," "in the name of His Majesty," "to authorize." We might add to these epistolary formulae, fragments of catechisms, and liturgical formulae that invoke the Holy Trinity.

The influence of colonial texts is also to be seen in a marked taste for numerical data, both dates and measurements. The *Relación* manages to accumulate such a quantity of details of this nature that it is difficult to imagine that they were transmitted through any oral tradition. Thus, for example, the first part about making contact with the Chichimecas and the return to Tula unfolds over a period of two weeks: the Otomís leave Tula on a Wednesday, they reach the Chichimeca region on a Saturday, they discuss the conditions of the encounter on a Sunday, they return to Tula on the following Wednesday, where they hold general assemblies on Thursday and Sunday. On the following Tuesday, they draw up the petition to the viceroy. They reach Querétaro at seven in the morning, they await the Chichimecas' reply for a day and a night; they leave at four in the afternoon, they arrive in Tula also in the afternoon, and they hold assemblies in the morning. The procession to commemorate the foundation of San Juan del Río was performed at 2:00 and 5:00 P.M. on the 24th of June and ended at 6:00 P.M. The garrison erected on the square was visited at 7:00 A.M. Similar details are given for the conquest of Querétaro proper, which lasted over eight days.

However, in their zeal for accuracy, the authors' use of numerical details does not always fit with the norms of the Christian calendar. In the first part, although the days of the week are given in their normal sequence, the corresponding dates somewhat miss their mark: Thursday the 28th of May is followed by Sunday the 30th (instead of the 31st) and Tuesday the 31st (instead of June 2). A similar confusion is to be observed in the episode of the conquest of Querétaro in which many liberties are taken with the Gregorian calendar: after the 24th, 25th, and 26th of July, the narration mentions the 25th again, followed by another 26th, which falls on the eve of a 22nd of July (!). The latter day also figures as the 3rd of July, before a correct series is once more established (28th, 29th, and 30th of July).

This obsession with figures is also shown in relation to the numbering of the troops, the building of the garrison at San Juan del Río, the fabrication of the cross at Querétaro, and the planning of the town. Numerical references to the native troops abound (1,007 Catholics, 25,329 men, etc.), and no unit of measurement is spared mention.

We attempted to trace a native logic behind the incoherent ordering of the dates and the choice of particular figures, but in vain. It is true that there is some regularity in the numerical data, but it is the regularity of a decimal system (and its multiples), that is, of a European concept of numeration. Similarly, a preference for sequences of three-day periods of time can be observed, but this is insufficiently consistent to be interpreted as representing some underlying intention or conceptual model. We therefore prefer to take this eagerness for precision as the mark of an acculturated mentality unable to conceive of the past or describe reality without resorting to Western-style methods of quantification.

Generally speaking, the constant emphasis on the role and the presence of interpreters, scribes, and witnesses in certain episodes could be attributed to a considerable familiarity with colonial bureaucracy on the part of the authors. To take one striking example: in the description of the ceremony to sanction officially the foundation of the town of San Juan del Río on June 25, 1502, there are twenty-two occurrences of words and expressions connected with the act of signing: "signature," "to sign," "to sign with a flourish," "to hold the pen," etc. The Otomís have three notaries (Don Vicente, Don Origüela de Vilafaña, and Don Fernando de Tapia), a scribe (Don Pedro de Cristo y Tapia), an interpreter (Don Alonso de Gusmán y Tapia), not to forget an enigmatic character referred to as "Interpreter of Christian Letters," and a "Notary and Scribe": this is none other than la Malinche, Doña Juana Malinzi, that is, Hernán Cortés's mistress.

What conclusions may be drawn from these converging data? 1) That the group was more than familiar with the products of colonial legislation and its administrative apparatus. 2) That it possessed numerous titles bestowed upon it by the colonial authorities. 3) That it used writing as its prime instrument for recording the past. Writing provided the means of validating the account (the dates, the signatures, etc.), and a mnemonic framework (the calendar).

In fact, the entire *Relación* reveals an undeniable fascination with the written text; the latter constitutes the principal means of communication for these Otomís of "1502," who do not hesitate to write to their Chichimeca adversaries in order to announce the foundation of San Juan del Río. This fascination leads the authors, furthermore, to incorporate a large fragment of the dedicatory prologue to a New Spanish literary work. With its rhetorical turns of phrase and its flowery style (in which form takes precedence over meaning), the prologue lends a literary flourish to this section of the *Relación,* which quickly degenerates into confused gibberish and an accumulation of misunderstood and misrepresented formulaic expressions. At this point we are forced to abandon the carefully chosen terms "group" and "caciques," which we have hitherto used to refer to the authors of this text. It seems to us that the inclusion of this dedicatory prologue suggests the presence of a native author who probably wrote the Castilian version: an Otomí author with literary pretensions who wished to address himself to the "virtuous readers" mentioned in the prologue, and who praises Don Martín for being "highly lettered"; an author familiar with the skills of carpentry and bricklaying and who is able to cite Bramante, the distinguished Italian Renaissance architect: "together with an architect of Ancient (Rome?) called Bramante." So the *Relación* not only expresses a collective oral tradition and the interests and mentality of a group of Querétaro caciques, but it is also seen to be the work of an individual whose personality undoubtedly influenced its composition.

This aspect leads us to consider the repercussions of fixing in writing what is predominantly an oral native memory. It would be absurd to forget that the caciques, the principales, and, above all, the native scribes of Querétaro were in constant contact with a dominant culture that used writing as a primary weapon for domination. Through a multiplicity of legal, religious, and commercial channels, alphabetic writing had become a feature of their daily lives. However, we must bear in mind that in all of these cases the Indians were no more than consumers of juridical, economic, and ecclesiastical documents drawn up by the colonizers. They never had the opportunity to create and draft whole texts themselves. The *Relación* would therefore appear to belong to this exceptional category, in which a group and an individual move from the position of "consumer" to that of creator and author, and in so doing are led to impose the techniques and limitations of writing upon oral tradition.

What are some of the possible repercussions of this step from orality to the written text for the native memory? First, memory that once stayed alive in diverse and scattered oral narratives, attached to specific social contexts (family gatherings, religious and civic festivals of different kinds), becomes fixed and immobilized in the lines of a text. Written memory is the crystallization of the past (real or imaginary) and so escapes the vicissitudes, multiplicity, and diversity of culture and oral tradition; for this reason it acquires material autonomy ("an ancient and battered notebook"), and it is transformed into an object with a specific meaning, which we then call "the native version" of the Conquest of Querétaro. The legal terms used in the *Relación,* the oaths and the signatures, all testify to the desire to create a bona fide, authentic document on a par with the title deeds issued by colonial authorities.

The "reification" of memory by means of the written text brings with it a change in stance with regard to the past. It creates temporal depth (from 1502 onward), less easily observable in oral tradition; it introduces a fixed point of reference that facilitates thinking about processes of change and encourages comparison between what is and what was. Perhaps the unfamiliarity for members of an oral culture of this type of projection into a meticulously dated past explains the uncertainty with which the Christian calendar is handled. This is clearly one of the factors that explains the choice of the unorthodox date, 1502.

For the *Relación* to evolve into a standard text necessarily entailed the organization and systematic classification of information. The process of writing down this information both facilitates and demands the elimination of variants, the suppression of contradictory data, the choice of a line of argument. The visual and simultaneous layout of data is far removed from the dynamic and changeable form of oral narrative, more difficult to cross-check by its very nature. The written text allows for backpedalling, it makes room for the cross-comparison of events, it tends to develop closed, parallel, or symmetrical sequences. Writing achieves formal perfection more easily than does oral discourse. To take one or two examples: it appears to be no coincidence that the first part of the *Relación* unfolds between May 23 and 31; this would appear to be the result of a conscious desire for symmetrical form in relation to the two key dates of Saint John the Baptist (June 24, foundation of San Juan del Río) and Santiago (July 25, "battle" of Querétaro). Thus, thirty days separate the first negotiations with the Chichimecas (May 24) from the foundation of San Juan del Río, and another thirty days go by between this event and July 25. Such structuring of time probably owes much to the facilities afforded by the process of writing composition. Similarly, if we look at the overall organization of the text, the *Relación*'s raison d'être would appear to be that of putting into effect the instructions contained in the initial *"Jecutoria,"* and events repeatedly occur as the carrying out of a previously fixed program laid down by other documents of a similar type. Likewise, the event only acquires reality once ratified by an official document. As well as being a source of information and a formal model, the written document also functions as a mechanism for the advancement of the narrative.

A further example of the means employed to manipulate the past is provided by the cunning way in which the true role of Hernando de Tapia is disguised. This attempt is also revealed in the meticulous idealization of the Otomí group. The *Relación* systematically depicts the Catholics as the very antithesis of the Chichimecas on linguistic, social, economic, alimental, and religious grounds. The Catholics—that is to say, the Otomís—are sedentary agriculturalists who live in towns and have skills in town planning and the building of garrisons, whereas the Chichimecas are hunters who live in caves and on hillsides, in ignorance of religious practices. The former are bilingual and trilingual (Otomí, Chichimeca, Castilian), while the latter speak only their mother tongue. In fact, by means of a skillful shift of focus, the *Relación* manages to say of the Chichimecas what is generally said of the Otomís themselves: "They are fond of living in wild and remote places where no one may see them. . . . They are of very low intelligence, very dirty in their dress and eating habits . . . ; their language is barbaric." The artificial nature of this dichotomy is also seen, as we mentioned above, in the Otomís' self-identification with the Spanish, through the category of "Catholics." The Catholics bear Castilian titles and surnames, and their leaders are Knights of Santiago. The names reserved for the Chichimecas reflect the cultural context assigned to them: "Eagle," "Deer," "Archer," or have pejorative connotations: "Bumpkin," "Yokel." Their weapons are quivers "wrapped around with animal skins," daggers with "tips of flint," and arrows, as opposed to the firearms and gunpowder assigned to the Otomís.

In this way, by selecting such complementary data, the *Relación* constructs two ethnic identities, two abstract categories: the Catholics and the Barbarians (or "pagans"). Once again, we believe that writing, with its scope for objectification, provides the native memory with the means of creating a more synthetic, homogeneous, and structured image of the past.

Being all at once manipulation, idealization, reification, and crystallization of the past, there is no doubt that Otomí memory, such as it is rendered by the anonymous *Relación,* throws little light on the origin of Querétaro. But the "anachronisms and inexactitudes" of which traditional criticism accuses it are the very features which make it an exceptional document, a rare display of native literary zeal, and evidence of a memory mutilated in content and immobilized in form by the inflexibility of Western writing techniques. The product of a doubly marginal group—being both Indian and Otomí—the *Relación* reveals a people's attempt to write its own history the way they wish and dream it had been.

34

Francisco de Avila's Christmas Eve Sermon (1646)

In the last years of his life, the office of canon in the cathedral of Lima upon which Francisco de Avila (1573?–1647) had long trained his eye was finally his. Avila was born in Cusco of uncertain parentage, and he may have been a Mestizo whose career was impeded by prejudice and suspicion. In the mid-1640s a new archbishop of Lima, Don Pedro de Villagómez (1641–1671), was working to revive the mechanisms of the Extirpation of idolatry (see Selection 35), a process for which Avila was prepared to take much credit. As canon, he added to his apparent triumph with the publication of the first part of his *Treatise on the Gospels* (*Tratado de los evangelios,* 1646), from which the following selection derives. When the second part appeared posthumously in 1648, the entire work formed an extensive cycle of 122 sermons in Quechua and Spanish that followed the holy seasons and feast days of the Catholic calendar. Avila's *Tratado* was the first substantial new book of sermons for Indians to be published in Peru since the thirty-one trilingual sermons (in Spanish, Quechua, and Aymara), the *Third Catechism and Exposition of the Christian Doctrine in Sermons* (*Tercero Catecismo y exposición de la doctrina cristiana por sermones*) (Lima, 1585), appeared in the wake of the Third Provincial Council. Expounding orthodox understandings of doctrine while paying especial attention to the identification and refutation of native Andean religious errors, Avila's bilingual *Tratado de los evangelios* offers valuable insight into the style and strategies of one of the most knowledgeable evangelizers in seventeenth-century Peru.

It is worth noting that comparatively few Indians would actually have heard Avila preach from these texts. They were collected to assist others, an audience of contemporary priests of Indians in particular. These parish priests were required, most recently by the dictates of the Council of Trent, to preach on Sundays and major festivals in the year as well as daily during the seasons of Advent and Lent. Model collections of sermons such as Avila's were often published late in a noted preacher's career, reflecting the texts used and elaborated upon over decades of thought and practice.

Avila did not, however, live to enjoy much of the new extirpating atmosphere presided over by Archbishop Villagómez. He died in 1647, the year before the publication of the final part of his *Tratado*. He missed, too, the elaborately staged departure of six idolatry inspectors from Lima the following year, the symbolic beginning of Villagómez's new campaign to eliminate suspect native religiosity in the Archdiocese of Lima which had, in effect, already started. And one suspects he would not have been pleased to know that his sermons failed to become the primary texts used by the itinerant inspectors of idolatry to complement their judicial and penal labors.

Another bilingual collection of sermons by Avila's contemporary in the cathedral chapter in Lima, Fernando de Avendaño, overshadowed the *Tratado* at the time and has done so ever since. Avendaño's personal history as a preacher and extirpator was almost as storied as (and considerably less controversial than) Avila's. To Avendaño fell the double distinction of being named the prelate's honorific superintendent of the Extirpation and having his own set of anti-idolatry texts, the *Sermons on the Mysteries of Our Holy Catholic Faith* (*Sermones de los misterios de nuestra santa fe católica*), favored by Villagómez and widely distributed as the pedagogical appendix to the prelate's exhortation and instruction for extirpators of idolatry, the *Pastoral Letter,* published in 1649. Apart from its revealing preface, Avila's book of sermons has not been carefully examined by most students of colonial Latin American history, for whom he is associated principally with the Huarochirí Manuscript (see Selection 1). The official attitude toward the contents of the *Tratado* at the time is more complex and stems from more than the simple fact that Avila himself was off the scene. It is quite possible that his sermons were judged by Villagómez and by others who offered him advice to be less safe in the hands of priests in Indian parishes than the texts of his contemporary, Avendaño.

Avila's *Tratado* signaled some of its differences from Avendaño's *Sermones* with its very name. The contents of a tratado are set in a freer, more leisurely mold than a book of sermons proper. Moreover, the tratado as a form enjoyed a reputation for popular and accessible references rather than argument by logic. The freedom clearly suited Avila's style, allowing him not only to wander between points, unfettered by an initial proposition and the formulaic need to present his proof through contraries (although he, too, would sometimes revert to this basic strategy), but also to enter repeatedly into extended dialogue with Andean religious traditions. This is not to say that Avila, in choosing his form, abandoned structure; in fact, as we have noted, he chose to base his sermons, in an entirely customary way, on the Catholic festival cycle. Yet, even as the sermons expounded on the appropriate biblical texts through the calendar year, these seasons and Scriptures became launching points for a freer discourse. If Avendaño's works are notable for the directness of their argumentation, then Avila's are more subtle in the way that they weave engagement with Indian beliefs and practices into a cycle of close scriptural instruction and elaboration. Avendaño's texts are often predictable, whereas Avila's are full of surprises. The historian Pierre Duviols memorably took his comparison of the styles of the two great preachers of the era of the Extirpation in the archdiocese of Lima to an emotional level. He refers first to Fernando de Avendaño: "That which is probably most lacking in these sermons is Christian charity, or simply a feeling of humanity. The man is without a doubt dominated by his iconoclastic and apologetic zeal; he is skilled and brilliant, but his heart remains cold and hard. Of this we are fully convinced when we compare his sermons with those of Francisco de Avila."

The preface that Avila composed for his *Tratado* in 1645 provided an opportunity to reorder and recall selectively experiences from his early career as a priest in the Indian parish of San Damián de Checa, Huarochirí, from 1597 to 1609. He had been in trouble with his Indian parishioners as early as 1600, when accusations of misconduct were first brought against him. The priest was cleared of guilt on this occasion, yet in September 1607 he found himself accused again, and this time in a far more serious manner. Andean notables from his parish made over one hundred charges, denouncing Avila for behavior that flagrantly contravened the directives of the Third Provincial Council of Lima (1582–83) concerning the activities of priests among Indians. The charges ranged from exploitation of Indians as manual laborers (some of whom were constructing a home in Lima for the aspiring canon-to-be), through frequent absenteeism from his responsibilities in San Damián (presumably while he completed his doctorate in Lima during these years), his collection of exorbitant fees for the performance of sacraments and other religious services, and his involvement in the lucrative trade of agricultural goods for his own profit, to a number of allegations of scandalous sexual relationships with native Andean women in the community. On the orders of the chief judge of the archdiocese, Avila was removed from his parish and incarcerated in the ecclesiastical jail in Lima. Yet Avila had soon rallied some regional friends—native Andean assistants among them—and secured his release. Acting on his behalf, his allies had put pressure on three of his principal accusers to retract parts of their denunciations and thus cast doubt on the veracity of the other charges.

At this point, with the help of native Andean informants and writers as well as Jesuit assistants, Avila began a systematic collection of information on colonial Andean religiosity, part of which became the Huarochirí Manuscript featured in Selection 1. Assisted by the corpus of religious traditions and specific knowledge that he and his agents were assembling, Avila began an ambitious tour of the region, exposing and punishing Indian "idolaters" as he went, and burning or otherwise destroying *huacas* and other religious objects in great numbers. The extent of the Indians' deception, he maintained, had come as a painful revelation. Representing these events in the 1645 preface to his book of sermons, Avila cast himself as a "discoverer" of native Andean religious duplicity, a devoted shepherd who, having recognized the urgent need for reform, had transformed himself into a tireless warrior against religious error in the parishes of Huarochirí and beyond.

He tied his supposed discovery of idolatry into a compelling narrative surrounding one sensational event. Avila wrote that in August 1608 he had been invited by Bartolomé Barriga, the priest in neighboring Huarochirí, to attend and preach at the local celebration of the Feast of the Assumption. But before he arrived, Avila claimed that Cristóbal Choque Casa (one of the native Andean allies who earlier had helped to cast doubt on other parishioners' charges against Avila) had come forward to reveal these Indian parishioners' errors. Choque Casa supposedly informed him that the Christian festival in Huarochirí was nothing but a diversion, and that holy images were sullied by an observance that served to mask Andean dances and rites in honor of the regional huacas, Paria Caca and Chaupi Ñamca (see the introduction to Selection 1). Avila wrote in his preface that, once possessed of this information, he not only kept his engagement in the neighboring pueblo but also used it to deliver a fiery sermon admonishing the Indians for the idolatry that tarnished their Christian devotions, and to begin to stamp out the cults of which he had learned.

Unmasking a persistent idolatry, of course, served his purposes in 1608–09 perhaps even more than it did when he was working out a heroic rendition of his San Damián experiences at mid-century. At the earlier juncture such discoveries allowed Avila to deflect attention from the charges brought against him by his parishioners and to provide himself with a platform from which to claim that through their fabricated lawsuit the idolaters sought to rid themselves of a zealous priest who threatened their evil rites. Avila was certainly not the first, nor would he be the last, churchman in colonial Spanish America to present himself and Indian "deceptions" in such dramatic and manipulable terms. The notion of a native Andean idolatry that was hidden and that had to be discovered and confronted was even being employed at virtually the same time by Archbishop Villagómez. In his *Pastoral Letter,* written by 1647 and published in 1649, Villagómez wrote of "an evil lost to view" in the Indian parishes, exhorting all Christians to join him in renewing a systematic struggle against Andean religious error through the mechanisms of the Extirpation of idolatry. The idea of a recalcitrant bloc of idolaters operating as a uniform evil beneath a guise of Christianity was potent in the intellectual atmosphere of the time, a potency that has not been completely dispelled in scholarly treatments even today.

In San Damián, for instance, both the Indians' charges against their priest and Avila's subsequent decision to unmask their idolatry seem to have challenged relationships and common understandings that were very like those which had developed more gradually between many other priests and their native parishioners. Like the Franciscan Bernardino de Sahagún in an earlier time in central Mexico (see Selection 3), Avila had learned a lot about the complex realities of colonial Indian religion. Although the study of Avila's destructive actions and their timing seems to indicate that he was not much moved to worry over these realities before it suited his interests to channel his knowledge toward Extirpation, there is no reason to stop there. The consideration of his sermons offers wider insights on his thought and methods of pedagogy. Avila was a gifted Quechua linguist who knew as much about colonial Andean religion, and the vital functioning of regional oral traditions within it, as any non-Indian in his day. He used this knowledge when he entered the same oral medium as native Andean ministers and dogmatizers in his efforts to express the Gospel and dispute errors.

The following sermon for Christmas Eve provides an especially rich opportunity to reflect on the imagery and methods of this talented preacher in the action of instruction and refutation. The sermon is often catechetical—that is, it employs questions and answers pertaining to a given religious lesson in the manner of an elaborate catechism. Avila not only preaches on an appropriate biblical text and seasonal theme but also pauses to imagine and counter doubts, questions, and difficulties and even to catch out the mental tricks of his indigenous congregations. He seems confident both that he knows what is going on in the minds of his hearers and that from this knowledge he can persuade them to reform their ways. He assumes that some of them, hearing of the Christian fasts and abstinence to be observed before Christmas, will begin reflecting on and legitimating roughly analogous non-Christian practices that have persisted into colonial times. "There are those of you who are listening to me now who are saying in your hearts, 'Father, in the paganism taught to us by our elders, we, too, fast when the festivals of our idols are approaching.' "

In a text such as this one, we can linger over the changing faces of Avila's Christianity. At times, the preacher is a restrained and patient father, imploring his children to reflect carefully on what is being taught. "Have you understood?" he asks, "Do I not tell the truth?" "Listen a little more," "Have you not learned?" He seems particularly understanding in dealing with the thorny issue of the Immaculate Conception and the unquestionability of Mary's virginity despite her marriage to Joseph. "Do not a man and a woman marry for this reason in order that they might have children?" ask the imaginary Indian interlocutors. "This is true, my children, nevertheless many married people have achieved this feat," begins the reply. And there is a notable patience in the teaching of this Christian moral ideal: "All this, I know, takes some time to understand."

But Avila can also grow more forceful, insisting on attention: "Look here, listen to me." Much of the visual imagery of his words, too, seems meant to inspire awe and fear and to be memorable in a chilling way. The Indian congregations might often have been listening to the sermon in a courtyard similar to the one drawn by Diego Valadés (see Figure 15 in Selection 22), and it was onto just such a group of people—not unlike themselves and in this same kind of space—that Avila asked his hearers to project their thoughts. They are to imagine people who have not heard, or who have not responded to, the word of the Christian God, a patio full of shackled wretches on the night before their executions rather than Valadés's busy but tranquil scene. For Avila, the word of God is a puncturing, burning, and pounding thing—a thorn, a brand, a hammer, a stick. God does not let one rest. Rather, He delivers the beatings that are the soul's only nourishment and correspondingly the only way to escape the Devil's clutches. The body is molded clay or it is a house in which the invisible soul dwells, giving life and requiring no other meal than this forceful divine Word. To have fed one's soul is likened to waking from a bad dream. All this to think about on the night commemorating Jesus's birth.

Like the Jesuit Arriaga, a few of whose views are discussed in our introduction to Selection 35, Avila recognizes a wide definition of "idolatry." He recognizes convergences between Christianity and native Andean religious beliefs and practices as a more prevalent concern in the middle of the seventeenth century than simply persistent traditional beliefs and practices. For Avila, religious mixture and local imitations and appropriations of Christianity offer both danger and opportunity for the faith in the Andes. On the one hand, it is the misunderstanding of Christianity brought on by the false parallel that will lead to Hell. Everywhere, there are dangerous interpretations and Christian concepts not only to define properly but also to seclude from Andean analogies. These analogies are the menacing work of a restless Devil, "God's monkey," who "goes around imitating God." And yet the small convergences and new religious understandings emerging in the Andean parishes need attention and even selective embracing if the evangelizer is going to get anywhere worth going. The convergences and emerging understandings are fraught with heretical danger, and they are Avila's principal points of entry into the imaginations of his hearers. In the sermon that follows, Avila engages colonial Andean religion even as he refutes it. He perceives that even when his Indian audience is made up of people who call themselves Christians, his act of describing a time of abstinence and a vigil will summon a number of charged thoughts. It is the cajoling and coaxing of those thoughts that is this preacher's art.

Mary, the Mother of Jesus, Married Joseph, etc. Matthew, Chapter 1

Neither in the Spanish towns nor here [in the places where you Indians live] is the eve of the feast day an officially observed festival. Yet all of us have come together to hear Mass and to sing for the Baby Jesus and the Blessed Mary, His Mother.

This being so, I will tell you something about this vigil. The first thing to explain is the meaning of a vigil. Why does the Holy Mother Church command that the days before certain of the year's festivals should be vigils?

Then I will read today's Gospel, expounding a little on it, leading finally into the sermon which I shall give with God's help. For this we ask the intercession of Our Lady, the Blessed Virgin Mary, saying *Ave Maria.*

Be attentive and I will tell you what a vigil is. When Christ Our Lord was on this earth as a man, even though He was the True God, He continually prayed to God His Father. Sometimes He separated Himself and went into solitude, or He went out into the countryside, while other times He did it in public; often, He spent the entire night in prayer. He did this to provide us with an example so we would know not to be negligent in praying to God and asking for His help.

And so, He had returned and ascended to Heaven after being resurrected. The saints, following Christ's example, rose from their beds four times each night to pray; and because they passed almost the entire night without sleep, they called this a vigil. To stay awake, in the Spaniards' language, is to perform a vigil.

People customarily performed a vigil in the evening or on the day before the most important festivals. And, beyond this, they would not eat meat on this day or eat more than once. This is called a fast in the Spanish language. This is what a vigil used to mean.

Because it is a very arduous kind of vigil to do without sleep, Our Holy Mother Church directs that in place of not sleeping the night before, we must only fast the day before some festivals. This is commanded in order that we may worship to good effect, and that we might pay closer attention in our veneration of the saint of the given feast day and thus earn his mediation. That, then, is the vigil and the purpose it serves. Have you understood?

From here, then, we come to the festival itself, the day on which Jesus Christ, Our Lord, was born of Our Lady, the Virgin Mary. Today is the vigil on the eve of the festival, in order that we may reach this day with calm, and without offense to God, arriving with much respect and care—for these reasons we fast.

There are those of you who are listening to me now who are saying in your hearts, "Father, in the paganism taught to us by our elders, we, too, fast when the festivals of our idols are approaching."

You speak candidly in this, I know. Here is how I feel about it. Look here, listen to me.

In the time of the Inkas, and even before the period of their dominance in these lands, all of you, according to your *ayllus* and smaller groups, were faithful to your idols. In order to worship them in festivals, you would occupy yourselves in preparations before the feast for one month, or even two months in the case of your principal idol. And the chief priest would give notice to make ready, saying that the festival would fall on such and such a day; and then you made your *chicha* [maize beer] and all the other things because, it was said, the day of Our Great Father was coming.

And you were also ordered to fast, eating neither salt nor *ají* [a hot pepper], and men and women would abstain from all sexual relations. And in this way you say you had to fast. And not to have done it in exactly the prescribed way would be taken to be a great sin, which would cause you to fall ill and suffer labors, and your crops to fail, causing your children to die. Thinking all this was true, you were frightened, and you fasted and kept the vigil without sleeping the entire night. Do I not tell the truth?

Look here, my children, all of this is the deception of the Devil. The accursed Devil does not stop; he is always thinking and wanting desperately to make himself Lord so that people will worship him as they do God, thus he goes around imitating God. Have you not seen how a monkey, when he sees what a person does, copies it? In this way the Devil imitates God, like God's monkey. And since the fathers in the Church sing praises to God, the Devil has himself sung to in the worship of hills, snowy peaks, and rocks. And if Our Holy Mother Church directs us to fast during Lent and at the time of vigils, the Devil in turn wants people to fast and to work for him. He does the same in many other things, too, deceiving those people who know little.

Thus we come to the end of our treatment of the vigil.

Now I am going to tell you the Gospel that Our Holy Mother Church provides for this day of vigil. This Gospel derives from the evangelist Saint Matthew in his first chapter, and what it says is this: Mary, the mother of Jesus, was recently married to a man named Joseph, with whom she had no carnal relations of any kind (and this is absolutely certain, not even once). Yet her womb was growing, and she began to appear to Joseph to be pregnant (and the truth is that she was, but by the work of the Holy Spirit). Joseph knew all this very well in his heart and soul, but being so saintly and not wishing to have her pregnancy be apparent in public, before anything was said, he wanted to go into exile far away from his lands. While he was sleeping with all these worries on his mind, an Angel, a messenger from God, came to him in his dreams and told him: "Joseph, son of David, do not decide to abandon your wife Mary, and do not be burdened with distress and worries, because what she has in her womb is the work of the Holy Spirit, and to you will be born a son whom you shall call Jesus, that is, Savior, for He will save and redeem His people."

So ends the Gospel.

Those words are very appropriate on the feast day of Saint Joseph; in fact, they are the very same ones I repeat to you on that day.

This being so, I have something more to tell you now. When you hear that Saint Joseph was the husband of the Blessed Virgin Mary, you are not to say, nor to understand, that the couple knew each other carnally or that they had sexual relations. Because even though they were truly married, it did not come to this. Our Lady the Blessed Virgin Mary was always a virgin, a maiden who was superior, perfect, without ever knowing a man in that way. You will say ,"But, Father, how could Joseph be her husband if they never came together [and consummated the union]? Do not a man and a woman marry for this reason in order that they might have children?" This is true, my children, nevertheless many married people have achieved this feat. They live as a married pair without coming together carnally; they neither sleep together nor know each other in this way, in order that they might better serve God, loving each other as brother and sister; and from their ranks have come many saints and saintly individuals. Saint Joseph and Our Lady the Virgin Mary were people of this kind. It was God who ordered it to be thus, wanting His mother to be married in this manner. Now all this, I know, takes some time to understand; this being so, we will tell of one other thing, and then we will be done.

We will finish now by speaking a little more about today and your vigil, all the things which precede, and prepare us for, tomorrow.

Imagine a great crowd of people crushed together in a large courtyard, dark and confined, panic stricken, and all condemned to have their heads cut off for their alleged offenses. As they were waiting for the moment of execution, without anyone who could help them, is it not true that they would be very dejected, crying out as they awaited their deaths? And, the situation being thus, imagine that some letters were delivered to them from a powerful lord telling the prisoners not to worry, assuring them that their grief would be over tomorrow, because then, with the help of God, they would be saved from their distress and labors, and properly cared for.

What is more, they themselves would become great lords. *Hodie scietis quia veniet Dominus, et mane videbitis gloriam eius.* [Know that on this morning the Lord will come and you will behold His glory.]

What would those prisoners say after hearing this? What great comfort would this be for them? What cries of happiness would come with such news? They would pass the whole night without sleeping, saying: "Oh, if only the day would come!" wondering if there was perhaps some impediment which might keep their savior from coming, and saying: "May he not be taken ill, may no one have held him up."

Is it not certain, my children, that this would occur? "Yes, father," [you will say], "it is very certain." Well, listen now. Before Jesus Christ, the Son of God, came from Heaven, all humankind were in darkness and in the shadow of death, prisoners in chains and iron shackles.

"Well, Father," [you will say], "if this was so, who farmed the fields in those times? Who tended the cattle, sheep, and goats? Who built the houses?" I am going to tell you, so give me your undivided attention. Look now, do you not know that as men we are made of two different things? One is the soul, and the other is our body. Similarly, life itself has two ways, the life of the soul and the life of the body. And thus, there is sustenance for the soul, and also for the body, and there is the sleep of the soul, and the other of the body, and there is the death of the soul, which is different from the death of the body. Have you understood?

Listen a little more, because it is of great importance that you understand this; herein lies nothing less than your salvation. Are you and I not living? Yes, we are living, and in this life, in this being alive, are we not living in the company of one another, with our bodies and souls together? Yes, we live together, and together we eat and sleep.

This being so [you will say], "Father, I still want you to persuade me that the life, food, and rest of the soul is different from that of the body."

In order to understand this well, it is best that you know first that when the soul is compared with the body, the soul wins out easily. Because our body is a bit of clay, molded clay, and in the end it reverts to clay. But our soul is not like that. Then what is it? It is intellectual, it reasons, and it does not have a body, hands, feet, a head, or eyes. It is immortal, and God created it from nothing in order that He could give life to the body. It was in order that we might live and dwell in Heaven, that God did us this kindness. This is our soul, my children. The soul gives life to our body, and exists in the body, as in a house, for as long as we live; and when the soul leaves, the body dies. Thus, even though the soul leaves the body, it lives and never dies. So, when we eat bread, meat, or any other thing, it is only our body eating, not the soul. And when we drink, sleep, and become sick, these are matters affecting the body, not the soul. Because without a mouth, teeth, or belly, how could it eat or drink? That much said, it is true that the body eats and drinks so that the soul can dwell within it, and for the same reason the body also sleeps and rests.

"So, the soul does not eat?" That's right, brother. "Well, how is the soul able to sustain itself? And whatever it does eat, where does it go if the soul has no teeth, mouth, or belly?" Look, the soul has no food other than the word of God, to which it listens carefully and which it understands well, and with this it lives and gains strength. Now that you have listened, have you not understood me? Have you not learned? And is not your heart and mind made content by what you have heard, as someone feels when he has just woken from a bad dream? Well, this is to have eaten, to have fed the soul; because the word of God brands our soul as a knife makes its mark, and God's word may also destroy like a big hammer. "But, Father," [you ask], "how is the word of God like a brand, and how does it give blows?" In this way: when the father preaches to you about abandoning your life of sin, do not the words bore into you and live in your thoughts as if you had been pierced to your core by a thorn or beaten soundly with a stick? And do you not come to a point at which, in your heart, you say, "What will become of me"? Well, this is God pricking at you and delivering His blows. The very same thing He reveals to us in His Scriptures, informing us that this is the soul's meal.

There is no one who can completely make this meal for the soul, cooking it, preparing it, other than the Son of God Himself. And it is He who tells you, through the voice of the Church: "Await tomorrow, all those who are in sin. I tell you to wait because tomorrow I will be made into a man, born of Mary, in order that I may teach men, light the way for them, and show them the path to Heaven. And I will suffer for you and die, as a man, to free you from the claws of the Devil."

This is what He tells us today: *Hodie scietis quia veniet Dominus, et mane videbitis gloriam eius.* [Know that on this morning the Lord will come and you will behold His glory.]

With which words, with what language, in what sense can I, as an insignificant man, explain to you this great marvel, of God becoming a man?

Look, my children, many years ago, God revealed in His Holy Scriptures that He would come in order that we would know and that we would wait for Him. If He had come without forewarning us, we might claim that it was not Him; thus, we must believe in His coming with all our heart. Because if we do not believe, He will not have come for us; and if this were to be the case, what would become of us? Without a doubt, we would be condemned to the punishments of Hell among the demons; all the things that you have been taught, all that you have suffered, and even your death—all this would occur, yet none of it would be of any use.

Therefore, we must believe that on a night that was very like this one, Jesus Christ was born of the Blessed Mary, and we must love and humbly worship this Child, asking His help. Of the Blessed Mary we are to ask the same, saying "Oh, Our Lady, it gives us the greatest joy to see the precious Son born to you. Plead and intercede for us sinners with the tender Child that He might grant us understanding and the capacity to comply with His will and live in His presence forever." Amen.

35

The Witness Francisco Poma y Altas Caldeas of San Pedro de Acas, Cajatambo, Peru

(1657)

Francisco Poma y Altas Caldeas, a forty-six-year-old native Andean, testified before the idolatry inspector and judge (*visitador*, or by his full title, *visitador general de idolatría*) Bernardo de Novoa in the village of San Pedro de Acas (or Hacas), Cajatambo, in the central Andes. Novoa—a native of Lima, fluent in Quechua, with some thirteen years' experience as a priest in three Indian parishes—was an agent of the process known as the "Extirpation of idolatry." The Extirpation was an effort by the Christian authorities in the seventeenth- and early eighteenth-century Archdiocese of Lima to root out and destroy suspect colonial Andean religiosity through systematic campaigns of investigation and destruction, and the trial and punishment of principal offenders. His investigation in Acas was spread over almost a year and a half (1656–1658). During this time, Francisco Poma, like the other witnesses, responded to a series of questions posed by Novoa and an interpreter. Poma's responses in Quechua were recorded in Spanish translation by the interpreter and notary, and this testimony, now rendered in English, is the document that follows.

The Extirpation's agents employed and adjusted methods drawn from the quintessential arbiter of religious orthodoxy in the contemporary Spanish world, the Holy Office of the Inquisition. After the establishment of the Holy Office in Spanish America in 1570, it was formally determined that indigenous peoples, judged new to the faith and uncommonly susceptible to error and the Devil's wiles, would not fall under its jurisdiction. Thus, the process of the Extirpation in the Archdiocese of Lima was a substitute that Pierre Duviols has accurately dubbed an "Inquisition for Indians," an adaptation with scaled-down penalties and, at least theoretically, an amplified pedagogy of reform.

A judge's path and the duration of his stays were largely determined by the information and cooperation he received from native Andeans and their parish priests. He could investigate leads, but without specific information, in places and among people he often did not know, there was only so much he could force. Trials might last a few days, months, or, as in the case of Novoa in Acas, even years, with a visitador often interrupting proceedings and resuming them later on. Each idolatry inspector's brief was a little different, depending on what he knew or had been led to believe about a given place and its people. But, generally speaking, he was charged to determine a region's principal religious offenders, the people who were thought to hold evil spiritual sway and represent obstacles in the Christianization of others. He was also commissioned to locate sacred places and objects in the local landscape as well as to raise pious work parties so that these places and objects might be efficiently destroyed and publicly reconsecrated with holy crosses and the application of new, triumphantly Christian names. Procedure varied from one visitador and his entourage to the next, but the remoteness of many of the Indian parishes and a general failure by Lima's authorities to enforce existing rules failed to curb the abuse of power. Even so, most information gathered by extirpators came from Indians' confessions obtained without recourse to various methods of torture. Ordeals, however, were sometimes applied if, after an obigatory series of stern warnings, a witness was suspected of withholding vital evidence. A great range of punishments—again, borrowed and adapted to the Peruvian context from the Inquisition's examples—was meted out to convicted "idolaters." Castigations were public and intended as examples to others; sentences were harsher for the unrepentant.

Francisco Poma's testimony before Novoa offers a richly descriptive angle on Andean religion and life over a century after the Spanish had arrived in Peru. Poma tells of steadfastly local relationships between Andean people and divinities, and customs of sense-making which remind us that the ways of Huarochirí (Selection 1) have many other companions. As a member of one of the eight *ayllus* (social, ritual, and territorial units) that made up the resettled village of Acas, and as a self-described participant in religious rituals and practices long forbidden by colonial authorities, Poma knows what he is talking about. He tells of a local and regional religious structure that, while clearly embattled by depopulation, colonial work regimes, and intermittent Spanish Christian pressures, is very much alive. People were resettled not far from ancestral lands populated by *malquis* and *huacas* (on these Andean divinities see Selection 1), gods who were conceived of as parents and relatives and protectors. Every ayllu in the village, he reveals, had its ministers who nourished the gods and mediated between the people and the divine, and its specialists who tended to the community's needs and enforced its codes of conduct. Even the archbishop of Lima, Don Pedro de Villagómez (1641–1671), who was eager to convey the impression that he and his Extirpation were winning a battle against the gravest forms of Andean religious error, found it impossible to deny the great degree and range of traditional religious survival in mid-seventeenth-century Cajatambo, especially with regard to the ancestral dimensions of the religion, the worship of malquis and huacas.

Francisco Poma speaks frequently of Huari progenitors, revealing his own allegiance to the ancestral divinities of one of the two founding peoples who settled in this region at points deep in its pre-Inkaic past. The Huaris' arrival was said to have ended an ill-defined period of chaos and war—a regional, ordering vision of the past that tells much about imaginings of history, recalling the idea of "imperfect time" being set right as conceptualized not only by Andean neighbors, but also by peoples in Mexico (featured in Selection 4 or 33) and by the Spanish theologians and chroniclers who made sense of Iberian history in retrospect (as in Selection 8 or 18). The Huaris were said to be children of the Sun, giants who came either from the sea in the west or from Lake Titicaca to the south. The Huaris were the arrangers of the world, the civilizers and agriculturalists who brought irrigation techniques and built terraces on the mountainsides to maximize the land available for cultivation. They gathered people together into small settlements called *llactas* (hamlets).

The invaders of the Huari domain were austere and warlike pastoralists from the high plateaus known as the Llacuazes, the self-described sons and daughters of Libiac (who made himself manifest as a bolt of lightning), a people "joined to the sky." According to another witness who came before Novoa in neighboring Otuco in Cajatambo, although the conquering Llacuazes killed many of the Huaris and took their lands, at least two of the Huari progenitors survived to maintain the lineage. A number of seventeenth-century witnesses explained that the Huaris and Llacuazes had inaugurated a period of peace and mixing between the two peoples that did not, however, completely erase a distinction that endured through the era of Inka domination and into Spanish colonial times. At least into the middle of the seventeenth century, Huari and Llacuaz divinities were recognized, while local festivals emphasized a historic relationship of complementarity.

Francisco Poma's testimony is packed with interpretative challenges. Like the other contents of this book, the source is a point of view that contains distortions, emphases, and silences generated in and reflecting a specific time and circumstance. The most fundamental challenges in this case are the filters through which Poma's own words have passed, most of which result from the inquisitorial atmosphere in which the evidence was collected. Francisco Poma, a Quechua-speaking Indian witness with some understanding of spoken Spanish, was interrogated by a Lima-educated Creole priest and inspector. As we have noted, Poma's answers were translated by an interpreter and recorded in Spanish by a notary, and an additional filter is, of course, our translation of the Spanish record into English. Each filter muffles the transmission of Poma's original meaning, as do the terms of reference and particular aims and interests which the idolatry inspector and notary could not help but have as they listened to the man, questioned him further, and crafted the translation.

What do some of the common terms in the document mean? "Idolatry," the worship of false gods or "idols," was a familiar crime to a seventeenth-century mind educated in the Judeo-Christian tradition. It was the Devil's work, and it was expected among non-Christians in Peru, as elsewhere in the past and in contemporary times; it was a presumed weakness in the religious systems of Amerindians. Idols were thought to be vile, impotent, and inanimate objects that, among misguided peoples who had not yet received or digested the message of the Gospels, stole reverence due only to the Christian God. The standard manner of refuting idols in sermons before Indian congregations was through aggressive ridicule and denigration. Idolatry, along with related concepts such as superstition, sorcery, witchcraft, and even heresy, increasingly became a blanket term for many perceived wrongs. In the mid-colonial Andes it had come to refer to beliefs and rites persisting since pre-Hispanic times, perceived perversions of Catholicism, moral laxity, and acts of disrespect to Spanish religious and secular authority, although at its base it remained a term that accused people of worshiping false gods. Notaries frequently called huacas and malquis (not to mention a good many other Andean religious concepts and beings) simply "idols," although the official who recorded Francisco Poma's words often takes a middle path and refers to "malquis and idols."

To complicate matters, we can be certain that by the mid-seventeenth century, terms such as "idol" were not descriptions used only by Spaniards. Thus, the notary's "malquis and idols" may in fact be a faithful rendering of the words spoken by a native Andean witness such as Francisco Poma. Indeed, there is considerable evidence to suggest that many colonial Indians had taken on some of the language and were engaging with the ideas that Christian preachers and catechists used to devalue and refute Andean beliefs and practices. At times, Catholic prescriptions for how to understand, and behave before, Holy Images seem taken over and turned around by certain native teachers (the notary who recorded this testimony called them "dogmatizers") as they assembled their own teachings and critical interpretations of Christianity and some of its agents. At other times, native Andeans might combine their appropriations of Christian elements with a dose of the Church's intended skepticism toward the ways of their ancestors. Indian usages of "Devil" and "demon" and, in the Andes, the Quechua loan-word "Supay" are instructive examples of the mutability of language and the challenge of translation (not to mention religious change) in colonial terrains.

For native Andeans and others who were interacting in colonial society, religious and cultural indoctrination became processes that begged participation. Words and ideas became unfixed; what began with one set of meanings could accumulate new ones. Indian witnesses might turn Christian narratives heard in sermons into colonial Andean stories; they might blend some doubt in with their knowledge of Andean practices, and they might employ terms such as "demon" and "Devil" to define gods, ideas, and forces in a religious framework that was less traditionally "Spanish" or "Andean" than it was living, and thus incomplete and transforming. Francisco Poma fits into this atmosphere of gradual mixture and change in which Christian concepts and rituals were not necessarily or purely contamination.

The atmosphere of fear that the trial might generate in a small community, not to mention an individual's dread of torture or the ramifications to be suffered by family members, might induce some witnesses to confess in certain terms or against certain persons simply to secure an escape. And many native Andeans were, by the mid-colonial period, hardened veterans when it came to facing interrogation by Spanish Christian officials. There were times to give details and show the way, and times when specific information (such as a huaca's name or location) could safely be suppressed. People targeted by these proceedings soon gathered, for instance, that the immensity (indeed, the impossibility) of most extirpators' tasks and their bureaucratic and zealous needs to justify their endeavors with material results could lend an imprecise and even desperate character to the process. Out of a mixture of necessity and attempted conformity to standard procedure, extirpators of idolatry frequently focused their investigations on a few offending individuals (conceived of as the corruptors of others) or on the destruction of notorious sacred places. Thus, it became an astute move for a witness who wished to deflect attention away from himself and those whom he wanted to protect simply to meet an interrogator's most urgent needs and expectations. This might be done in a number of ways, not least by further implicating community members who were already under suspicion or by assigning blame to a rival village in the next valley.

Do such sources "poison" the documentary pool, misrepresenting society in their hunger for information about those people who ran most afoul of prescribed laws and customs? And does the information in them support unquestioned assumptions about indigenous responses to Spanish Christianity or colonialism—assumptions of "resistance"—or its usual opposite, "accommodation" and acquiescence? In the present context, are we in danger of being led toward an image of the people of mid-colonial Acas as more or less uniform in their extraordinary adherence to a traditional system of belief and practice?

The answer can easily be "yes" on all counts if certain elements in the documentation are emphasized to the exclusion of others. One can extract solid and various demonstrations of native Andeans' organized resistance and intelligent countering of Christianity in Acas. For Francisco Poma illuminates an atmosphere of religious competition and tension in the village. He tells of the commands and prophesies of doom made by dogmatizers, powerful local religious figures who, within the celebration of regular festivals, besieged the place of Christianity among the people of Acas and its environs. But it is instructive also to consider how the answers can be "no." For it would be a misrepresentation to insist that the ministers and dogmatizers, the people who most embodied resistance, existed alone, or even that their substantial countering of an exclusivist Christian position somehow defied the influence of Christianity on themselves or others.

Francisco Poma's testimony, far from poisoning the pool with information skewed in one direction, offers a glimpse at a number of seemingly contradictory elements within colonial Andean religion. When an idolatry visitador was not present and attentively defining religious boundary lines, would the merging and simultaneous participation in native Andean and Spanish Christian religious practices have been "contradictory" or particularly remarkable to an Indian man or woman who was not a huaca minister and dogmatizer? Poma is a colonial Andean who is difficult to place in a simple category or clearly defined faction within the village. He lives what at first appear to be compartmentalized lives. His testimony reveals him to be a knowledgeable participant in Andean religious rituals, practices, and specializations as well as in native structures of religious authority that had long been forbidden by Spanish Christians. He is also knowledgeable about Christianity. He served as lay assistant to the parish priest and as an organizer of the festival of the patron saint of the community, Saint Peter. Further, by performing his duties as the priest's assistant, Francisco Poma incurred the wrath of Acas's principal native Andean minister and the powerful head of his own ayllu, the memorable Hernando Hacas Poma.

As Poma's conflict with the chief minister unfolds, and as it is resolved, a reader is left to ponder the diverse influences on this person speaking before a Spanish Christian interrogator. What reflects the things that Hernando Hacas Poma said and did, and just what is Francisco Poma's imagining and re-creation? In part, the story might be viewed as a remarkable local distortion upon the kind of narrative example regularly recounted by contemporary churchmen to stir and edify their faithful and correspondents: an evil opponent (Hacas Poma) is identified, a participant-teller endures a time of trial, a vital lesson is learned, and an individual's correction is achieved. If this is the case, what precisely is the lesson, and to whom does it apply? One prospect is that Hacas Poma has been shown to be a great and fearsome instrument of the Devil, an obstacle to Christianity who must be brought down at all costs. But another is that the chief minister and dogmatizer's power has been demonstrated yet again to all who know of him, and that his teachings and warnings pester and even torment new converts to Christianity. Poma's story about his run-in with Hacas Poma does not sit in splendid isolation. It can be examined alongside his description of the cross-cultural actions of the native Andean governor, Don Juan de Mendoza, and especially his words about the villagers' observance of the Christian festival of Saint Peter in conjunction with (not as a disguise covering) the Andean festival of Vecosina. Such information accumulates and combines to suggest a number of possibilities for the study of colonial Andean life—possibilities that complement the conflict and competition of which the witness Poma also tells.

The image of a constraining mechanism of repression (either the Catholic Church or, more specifically, the Extirpation) facing off against a unified but embattled adversary ("idolatry") would seem to oversimplify colonial Andean religious realities. Through the information he provides and through the instance of his own position, Francisco Poma challenges the plausibility of this purely oppositional framework as a full and accurate portrait. He participates in a wider colonial religious culture that, however tentative, disorganized, and variable, did not conform to the strict dictates of either the official Church or the native Andean dogmatizers. The parish priest of Acas mentioned in this document does not, through what little we learn of his actions, appear to have been much known for his negotiated positions within the workings of this emerging colonial religious culture. Yet it seems important to note that Poma, Don Juan de Mendoza, and many other native Andeans like them, who were simultaneously Catholic parishioners and adherents to a complex of transforming Andean religious structures, were not unique, just as clergymen and Spanish Christians in general were not all cut from the same cloth. They, too, occupied an interactive colonial terrain in which the practice of everyday life sometimes made nonsense out of theoretically separate and tidy categories.

We should not (and do not have to) take Francisco Poma's indirect word for it. Some of the most prolific and insightful commentators on native Andean religious life in colonial times were well aware of the complex nature of religious change. A "common error" among native Andeans, wrote the Jesuit Pablo José de Arriaga (1564–1622) in his 1621 manual for extirpators of idolatry and priests of Indians, "is their tendency to carry water on both shoulders, to have recourse to both religions at once. . . . Most of the Indians have not yet had their huacas and *conopas* [personal divinities and sources of fecundity, sculpted or natural in form] taken away from them, their festivals disturbed, nor their abuses and superstitions punished, and so they think their lies compatible with our truth and their idolatry with our faith." Padre Arriaga was a contemporary of Francisco de Avila (see Selection 34), an early mastermind behind the Extirpation and one of its first active agents. His biases are about as clearly articulated as his keen perception of Andean religiosity a century or so after the Spaniards' arrival in Peru. What he saw happening in the Indian parishes of the Archdiocese of Lima echoes in many ways what a similarly observant Juan Polo de Ondegardo perceived about a century before and what José de Acosta noticed after him (see Selection 18). The testimony of Francisco Poma, a witness before an idolatry trial conducted by one of Arriaga's successors over three decades later, adds color and detail to the colonial Andean religious culture only hinted at by the Jesuit's metaphor and Polo's and Acosta's earlier observations.

In the village of San Pedro de Acas in the district of Cajatambo on the 25th of January, 1657, there came before us a very rational and acculturated Indian. He testified that Don Cristóbal Hacas Malqui commands all those in his ayllu to gather offerings for the malquis and idols, and that this same man is the dogmatizer of his ayllu who directs them to worship not Our Lord God, but their malquis. And [he said] that Alonso Chaupis the Blind is the confessor and minister of idols of the Quirca ayllu. This witness stated that on many occasions, when it was time to clear the irrigation channels and plant their plots of land, he had seen the said Alonso Chaupis carry two measures of coca leaves and some two pounds of fat and chicha [maize beer] to the Huari malquis, and that he offered these things to them in sacrifice in order that they might enjoy bountiful crops and that their channels would not rupture. When he went to make these offerings, he was accompanied by everyone in the village; and after these were complete, they began clearing the irrigation channels, and plowing and planting their plots of land.

This witness continued, saying that one time, going as far as the herb gardens and passing the ancients' settlements of Quirca and Yanqui, he had seen Alonso Chaupis the Blind, Hernando Chaupis Condor, Pedro Sarmiento, and Pedro Capcha Yauri making sacrifices, cutting the throats of many cuyes [Andean guinea pigs]—there seemed to be six or seven—burning much coca and fat, pouring out chicha, and scratching off powder from coricallanca shells [collected from the coast for this purpose], all before some huge wooden masks, painted and with large noses that they call guasac. Pedro Quespo and What's-His-Name Guaman Capacha took up the masks in their hands and began dancing with them, and other times they would put them over their faces, and in the same way resume dancing accompanied by small drums; and there they stayed, getting drunk, while this witness passed by on his way to the herb gardens.

And he said that it is a common rite and ceremony in the village of Acas, and in all the other communities of this parish, that when a man or woman dies and before their burial the relatives of the deceased—wife, father, children, brothers and sisters or husband—invite the maestro of the idols or the sorcerer of their own ayllu to make the offerings of a llama, cuyes, and all the rest. Much chicha is prepared, and the relatives of the deceased also invite the whole village. The said minister of the idols does the honors in the following way. A llama is killed either through its side or at its shoulder, the blood is collected, and he [the minister] takes out the entrails and lungs. Then the sorcerer himself, in the presence of the deceased, blows in the windpipe and inflates the lungs, which swell up like a wineskin; and if the sorcerer sees that the lungs have sores [*guarcos*], he tells the relatives of the deceased that they have committed great sins and that the deceased is angered because he has eaten a flawed offering and that it is necessary to make another offering of cuyes, coca, and fat to him, asking the cause of his anger. And then the relatives provide the said offering, and burn the cuyes, coca, fat, and black and white maize before the deceased. And in making the sacrifice they shed blood and burn it, and smear the face of the deceased with the llama's blood. And the said sorcerer then acts as if he speaks with the deceased, and returns to tell the relatives that the deceased revealed that he had died because he had not kept up the rites and ceremonies and had not worshiped his malquis, and that if his relatives do not worship their idols and malquis and if they fail to make their offerings to the deceased himself in order that he might come to rest in his pacarina [place of origin to which one also returns], then they will die very soon. Afterwards, the said relatives gave another offering to the minister of the idols that he might make a sacrifice to the malquis, and then they sat down to eat of the llama that had been killed and to drink before the deceased for a day and a night. And even if there did not appear sores on the llama's inflated lungs, they would proceed in the same manner before the deceased, burning cuyes, coca, fat, the ears of the llama as well as its eyelids and the calluses from its feet, black and white maize, along with the llama's blood and chicha, and they would say that this was the mircapa, that is, the food for the deceased to eat in the other life. And thus, the ashes produced by the burned sacrifice were carried to the church and cast into the grave meant for the deceased.

During the night before the burial, at the first crowing of the cock, the said minister of the idols along with the closest relative of the deceased, such as the mother or father or husband, wrapped their own heads with the clothing of the deceased and took staffs in their hands. Then, followed by all the Indian women, they went through the streets shaking their heads, crying and calling out to the deceased so he would see how they wept over his death and remembered him, and so the other world would not curse his relatives. And with some brushes of guaillapa, which is a coarse straw, they went about brushing the streets and walls with llama's blood and chicha from the jugs they carried. Upon returning to his [the deceased's] house at dawn, the said minister of the idols cut a little of the hair and the nails from the fingers and toes of the deceased and carried them to the machay [cave tomb] of the malquis of his ayllu where they were kept for a year. When the year had passed, the same minister removed the hairs and repeated the said rites and ceremonies already described. If the relative or relatives of the deceased were wealthy, they killed two llamas, prepared chicha from a fanega [about 1.5 dry bushels] or two of maize, and invited everyone in the village. And in the house of the deceased they drank and danced one day and one night to the sound of the small drums. In the middle of the night the hairs and nails of the deceased that the said minister of the idols had brought from the cave tomb were placed on the blanket or shirt of the deceased, and over them he killed cuyes, and cast coca leaves, llama fat, white maize flour, powders from the [white] pasca stone and coricallanca shell, all of which were burned in sacrifice so that the soul of the deceased could go to rest in its pacarina, taking with it the mircapa.

Five days after the death, all those in the house of the deceased cooked him a meal and put out chicha for him to drink, and they say that during those five days he came to eat. And on the fifth day the deceased's old clothes, animal hides, and the straw [from his home] were burnt with powders of pasca stone and white maize flour at a place chosen outside the village, and new clothes were washed with maize flour in the river that runs close to the village. And cross-examining the said witness, the idolatry judge and inspector asked who, and how many Indian men and women had observed these rites and ceremonies and honors in the pagan way for their dead relatives. To which the witness replied that however many had died in Acas, that was how many had had performed for them the said sacrifices and honors, and that this abuse is common in this village of Acas and in the other communities of the parish. They had invited this witness [to attend and participate] many times, and he had found out about the said [funeral] rites.

And this witness told the said inspector that when he was visiting in the village of Mimuchi he had seen that, along with Leonor Nabin Carua and Inés Colqui Maiguai, Alonso Chaupis the Blind was killing a llama and sacrificing it in the herb gardens to the idols and malquis who are in that place. The said llama was given to the ministers for this purpose by Gonzalo Poma Lloclla. And in inquiring of these ministers how they could make that sacrifice and [commit] idolatry, and why they were not afraid when the señor visitador was currently visiting this parish, they responded [to this witness] that it did not matter that the idolatry judge and inspector knew; and, even if he knew of it, what could he do? And the said Gonzalo Poma Lloclla and his brother Bartolomé Chuchu Condor, who are the keepers of the herb gardens, call for the said Alonso Chaupis and give him llamas and cuyes to offer to the idols and malquis of the said gardens.

And in the same way he said he saw with his own eyes that, one time in the village of Cochillas, Hernando Chaupis Condor, Alonso Chaupis the Blind, and Francisco Hasto Paucar were worshiping, and sacrificing a llama to an idol named Macacayan that had been dislodged and burned [some forty years earlier] by the señor bishop Don Fernando de Abedaño [Fernando de Avendaño, the preacher-extirpator noted in the introduction to Selection 34]. This witness asked the said ministers why they venerated that idol and honored it [in the customary way] if it had been taken away and incinerated, and they responded that although it had been destroyed, the soul of the said idol lived and descended for a sacrifice and would receive it. And he said it is well known that Domingo Chaupis Yauri, now deceased, had an idol named Micui Conopa and another idol Colqui Conopa to obtain food and money, and that his nephew, Pedro Chaupis, inherited them and would show them to him.

And this witness, asking mercy of the said señor visitador, showed him a guacanqui [idol usually used for influencing love] that is like a glittering rock or bit of stone marl from the mines. He said that this guacanqui had been sold to him by an Indian man named Don Cristóbal Chauchisac, an important person in the village of j . . . s in the province of Huamalies, who told this witness that by having and worshiping this stone he would have good fortune, money, llamas, clothing, and that this witness [himself] had always kept it for these ends. And in a similar fashion the said witness showed the said señor visitador two idols called llama conopas that were some long stones like pestles, one of which had a head and was in the shape of a person, and he said that the said idols had been passed down through the members of his family since the time of his ancestors and that now he revered them for the increase of his llama herd. And he had seen that at the beginning of the rainy season Pedro Capcha Yauri goes to worship the malqui Hacac, with respect to which he [the witness] is unsure whether it was removed by the señor bishop Don Fernando de Avendaño, and takes llamas to sacrifice to the said malqui, and that for this purpose he keeps close to thirty llamas, [a herd] that, since ancient times, has been dedicated to the worship of this malqui. And the said Pedro Capcha Yauri, as minister of the said idol and having succeeded in his office from his ancestors, watches over and preserves the said herd. It is a well-known tradition among the Indians, and especially the said Capcha Yauri and the other ministers of the idols Hernando Hacas Poma and Hernando Chaupis Condor, that when the said malqui Haca [the same one called Hacac above] was wont to live in the presence of the Indians, he would blow on his hand with pursed lips, and, by the art of the Devil, he caused clumps of potatoes and maize to be born on his palm, at which the Indians had felt great wonder and fear; and they venerated and respected him as a man of great power, and for this reason they adored him and gave him worship, and devoted the said llama herd to him so that sacrifices could be made of them.

And this witness said that one Friday, three years ago, the interim priest of this parish of Acas, Licenciado Ignacio González de Ozerín, seeing that many Indians were failing to attend the doctrine classes, became angry and began quarreling with this witness, who was then serving as fiscal [lay assistant], ordering him to get the people to the indoctrination. Going through the streets and to their homes, urging the people to go to the church, he said that most all of them resisted and told him they could not go to the church because they were observing their fasts and making confessions to their malquis, as was the custom. And the person who resisted him most especially was Hernando Hacas Poma. He argued with the said witness, telling him not to get in the way of his custom or a great illness would come to him. And by pushes and shoves this witness brought the said Hernando Hacas Poma to the church. From that night forward this witness began to sicken seriously, and for six months he was in bed with great pain, withering away and becoming so frail that he was obliged to receive all the sacraments. After these six months the wife of the said Hernando Hacas Poma came to see this witness and said to him: "Give me a llama if you do not want to die, and, with my husband, I will offer and sacrifice it to the idols and malquis, and we will eat part of it without salt or ají [hot pepper], and then you will be well." This witness gave a llama to the said wife of Hacas Poma and she took it to her husband. And on the next day the said Hernando Hacas Poma came to visit this witness and asked him for cuyes, fat, and coca, and told him that six of this witness's hairs would be taken and hidden away. Having provided the cuyes and coca, this witness's wife went with the said Hernando Hacas Poma to see him take the hairs from her husband. [Then,] as both of them arrived at a wall in the ancients' settlement of the Tacas ayllu, near to where the idol Yanaurau resides, she saw that the said Hernando Hacas Poma took from a recess in the said wall a goat-kid's skull, and from the hollow within it he removed some hairs that were mixed with fat, coca, blood, [and shavings from] mollo [or *mullu*, a reddish-colored shell] and llacsarumi [a stone], and he gave them to the aforesaid [the witness's wife]. And the said Hacas Poma cut the throats of some cuyes and performed a sacrifice in that place, burning them with coca and llama fat. The aforesaid [witness's wife] then took the hairs to her husband, and from that day and hour he began to recover from his illness. And when he was better, this witness went to see the said Hernando Hacas Poma to thank him for his health and he told him: "Yayamic [father] and my lord, you are a great wise man and doctor; tell me you made me ill"; and the said Hernando Hacas Poma responded by saying: "I am the one who made you ill because you led me to the church by force and with shoves . . . and [you did the same] to all the Indians at the time when we were fasting for our idols and huacas, and watch that you do not try it again or else the same illness will return to you."

And this witness said that three or four years ago the captain Don Juan de Mendoza, cacique governor [in Quechua, *kuraka* (or *curaca*), hereditary lord] of this repartimiento [regional administrative district] of La Chaupiguaranga de Lampas, came to this village of Acas on three different occasions, and that each time he brought a llama, along with cuyes, coca, and fat, to the said Hernando Hacas Poma. And he [the governor] ordered him to sacrifice those llamas and offerings to the idol Yanaurau so that his son Don Alonso, whom he currently had at the [Jesuit-run] school [for the sons of the Indian nobility] in the Cercado [the Indian sector in Lima] learning to read and write, would emerge well schooled and thus able to take on the office of cacique governor now held by the said Don Juan de Mendoza. This witness saw with his own eyes that the said Hernando Hacas Poma killed and sacrificed the said llamas at the place called Canto that is close to the idol Caruatarquivrauc that is said to have been destroyed by the señor bishop Don Fernando de Avendaño. And when the said Hernando Hacas Poma made those three sacrifices, the said governor Don Juan de Mendoza attended along with Acas's important people, Don Cristóbal Poma Libia, Cristóbal Pampa Condor, Pedro Caico, Domingo Tantayana, Domingo Chaupis Yauri, and many other Indians from the village. The said Hernando Hacas Poma poured llama blood, coca, and chicha and burned fat at the place of the said idol Yanatarquivrauc, and then the said cacique sat down with the Indians to drink and to eat from the llama whose blood they had sacrificed, and he said to this witness and the rest of them: "Observe that we are Indians and although we worship Yanaurau, which is our custom, do not tell anyone of it."

And on another occasion five or six years ago this witness saw that the said Don Juan de Mendoza came to this village of Acas and, accompanied by Domingo Yana Pintor and all the Indians of the village, the curaca [Mendoza] killed a llama in a corral behind the rest house [*tambo*] and said [to the people]: "I am your cacique governor; we make this sacrifice and shed the blood of this llama on this land so that I will know how to govern you and rule in peace and calm, and so that all of us will be in peace and live with tranquillity." And, having killed the llama, Domingo Chaupis Yauri helped to shed the blood on the earth, and so did Domingo Yana Pintor; and then, all together, they ate the llama and spent the entire night drinking much chicha, dancing and performing the cachua [dance], all with their small drums, and they chewed coca leaves and scattered them on the soil.

Some three years ago, a little more or less, the said curaca came from Lima, bringing his son who was very ill. And passing through this village, he [summoned and] took the said Hernando Hacas Poma with him to the village of Rahan [Rajan] where the said curaca lived, and he kept him [Hacas Poma] there for many days, and everyone said that it was to cure his son with superstitions.

And this witness said that all the ayllus of this village, and there are six, have their ministers and confessors. Juan Raura is the minister of the idols and confessor of the Tacas ayllu, and his assistants who help collect the offerings are Domingo Ribera and Chatalina [Catalina] Chaupis Maiguai. In the Chaca ayllu the minister of the idols is Hernando Hacas Poma, of whom he has already spoken, and this man is famous as a sorcerer-healer who draws out spiders from the bodies of the sick, and as the one who dogmatizes in all the ayllus of this village and whom all the Indians consult. And it is equally well known that it is to him that the malqui Guamancama and the idol Yanaurau respond. And [still in the Chaca ayllu] Don Cristóbal Hacas Malqui is a confessor, and Pedro Sarmiento and Leonor Nabin Carua are their assistants who gather the offerings and make chicha. And Cristóbal Pampa Condor is also a confessor, and he holds the office of socya pacha, that is, using spiders he divines what they are to do and what sacrifices [are required], [the location of] lost things, and other incidents and issues. And in the Carampa ayllu, Andrés Guaman Pilpi is confessor-teacher and Alonso Quispi Guaman is also confessor, and Pedro Caico is his assistant who looks after the collection of offerings and is also colca camayo, responsible for the storehouse where the maize is kept to support the service of these idols. Hernando Chaupis Condor and Alonso Chaupis the Blind are the great ministers of the idols, confessors, and dogmatizers from the Yanaqui ayllu, yet they travel as far as the village of Cochillas to dogmatize and make sacrifices to the Yungas' idols and malquis. And Inés Colqui of this ayllu is a sorcerer, while Inés Upiai is a confessor-dogmatizer and holds the office of cauya and who, [through her divinations,] solves thefts and finds lost things. And Francisco Hasto Paucar and Domingo Guaras are also confessors and dogmatizers in the said village.

Pedro Guaman Bilca is assistant in the Quirca ayllu and he gathers the offerings; and because there are no ministers of the idols, [all of them] having died, the said assistant gives the offerings and the rest of the necessary materials to Alonso Chaupis the Blind that he might make sacrifices to the idols of the said ayllu. And Inés Colqui is a sorcerer as well as serving in the office of rapiac ychanioc [or *rípiac,* diviner who consults the fleshy parts of the arms, and confessor]. And from the Canta ayllu, old and crippled Domingo Tatcachi (or Taicachi) is minister of the idols, confessor, and dogmatizer, and the crippled Hernando Poma Quillai serves as his assistant and in the office of socya pacha. In the Picoca ayllu, with those who were the ministers of the idols, Domingo Chaupis and What's-His-Name Vilca, having died, Andrés Guaillapaico, who is religious assistant of this ayllu, and Leonor Llacsa Tanta give offerings to Hernando Chaupis Condor to sacrifice to the ayllu's malquis and idols. And, in the same manner, the ministers have died off in the ayllu of Yacas, thus Bartolomé Chuchu Condor and his brother Gonzalo Poma Lloclla give the said offerings to Alonso Chaupis the Blind in order that he might make sacrifices to the idols and malquis in the herb gardens, as he has already stated above and as is well known.

And this witness has seen with his own eyes that two times each year, the first before they begin to prepare their plots [for seeding] at the first rains and the other at the time of [the festival of] Corpus [Christi] when the maize starts to ripen, all the ministers mentioned earlier collect offerings from their ayllus, and many times this witness has given cuyes, coca, llama fat, and chicha to Hernando Hacas Poma. They [the ministers] take them to the ancients' settlements and offer them to the malquis and idols. The sacrifices made, with a voiced announcement they call the Indians from their ayllus, and they gather in a small open space where the idol Tauris is, and there everyone confesses with the minister of their ayllu, and [in this way] this witness has confessed many times with Hernando Hacas Poma. After the confessions they washed their heads with maize flour and the powders of the pasca stone and they said it left them absolved, and they were ordered to abstain for the next five days, eating neither salt nor ají and not sleeping with women, even their legitimate wives. And on the night of the first day of the abstinence, they were ordered not to sleep during the entire night, because it was said that if they slept the sacrifices they had made would be rendered ineffectual and that the sins they had confessed returned to those who slept. And for those five days of abstinence, the said ministers of the idols ordered that they rest and not work because it was a festival, and that they occupied themselves with drinking, for which effect all the maize from the storehouses dedicated to the cult of the idols was shared out to the Indian women of the pueblo, and each year it was sown for this ministry in the plots of land designated for the malquis and idols.

Don Cristóbal Poma Libia, a notable [*principal*] and the local headman, and Domingo Tantayana, Cristóbal Tanquis, and Pedro Caico, also important local people, commanded the village to make the chicha and seed the plot of land for the said malquis and, during the five days of abstinence, they [also determined] the ways in which some ayllus invited others. And this witness concurred with everyone else in that he saw and heard that before all the Indian men and women, the said ministers taught and preached that the native Indians did not have to worship Our Lord God or the wooden saints who were in the church, that this was for the Spaniards, and that they were their [the Spaniards'] idols and huacas; and that the Indians had other, different camaquenes [creator beings and forces] which were their malquis and idols, and that the Indians had to worship these with sacrifices of cuyes and llamas; and that they had to observe their fasts and times of abstinence and make their confessions, because if they did not respect and adore them, the Indians would waste away and suffer great illnesses and die and lose their crops to frost, and the springs and irrigation channels would dry up. And at the time they do this, they would not eat any other type of meat apart from cuyes and llamas, because the rest of the food, the meat from Castilian sheep, pigs, or goats, was abominable and it was forbidden to eat it at the time of the said abstinence. And in this time they would not enter the churches to pray because that would defile their sacrifices, confessions, and abstinences, and they [the dogmatizers] also ordered that they [the Indians] not confess these rites and ceremonies to the priest so that he did not discover and punish them. And during those five days of abstinence they would make offerings of money, and each person gave from one-half real to one real, and these offerings would be kept by the head steward [*mayordomo*] of the storehouses so that livestock and other materials necessary to the cult of the idols might be bought.

And four or five days before the festival of the Señor Saint Peter, official standard-bearers give llamas, cuyes, coca, and chicha to the said ministers of the idols of their ayllus so that they [the ministers] can make sacrifices and ask [both] for their [the huacas' and malquis'] permission and indulgence that they must hold the festival of Señor Saint Peter in the church. And when he was mayordomo one year, this witness gave the said offerings to Hernando Hacas Poma so that he could ask the malquis for the said permission, and this is a common practice which all the mayordomos respect and maintain, and everyone will confess to it and tell of it just as he has said. And on the night of the festival of Señor Saint Peter all the ministers of the idols come out with the women from all the ayllus, with their small drums; and in groups they pass through the streets dancing and carrying on this revelry until dawn, entering the homes of the standard-bearers and drinking. And if any of these groups goes to sleep before the dawn, they are said to be defeated, shamed, and dishonored because they have not known how to do a proper festival to their idols, nor how to worship them because they went to sleep. And those who dance until dawn without sleep emerge victorious for having stayed awake all night performing the festival to their idols, and this rite they call the Vicochina [Vecosina].

And on those five days of abstinence and confessions this witness saw that the said ministers of the idols taught all the Indians to worship the Sun, because he is the father who created men, and the Moon as the creator and mother of women, and the bright star of the morning that they call Chachaguara because it is the father and creator of the curacas, and [also] the two small stars that travel together [through the night sky] that they call Chuchuicollor because they are the creators of twins, and the seven nanny-goats that they call Uncuicollor so that their crops do not freeze and that there will not be illnesses.

And at the place where the idol Tauris resides this witness has seen all the people of this village of Acas dancing the dance of the Airigua with their small drums and drinking much chicha the whole night long. And on a maguey pole they attach a bunch of many maize cobs that they call airiguasara and misasara. And having performed the dance with them, the said ministers of the idols burn and sacrifice them [the maize cobs] to the malquis and idols. They do this dance, rite, and ceremony after taking up the crops from their lands, giving thanks to their idols and malquis for having provided food that year. And this witness had seen many times that Andrés Guaman Pilpi and Pedro Caico took Hernando Hacas Poma to the Carampa ayllu with offerings to worship the malqui named Caratupaico. And [he said] that, before plowing their plots of land, it was a common thing for all the Indians of this parish to cut the throats of cuyes in the fields themselves, and to burn coca, fat, and chicha; and when the first choclos [ears of maize] began to ripen, even before tasting them, they would give the first fruits to the ministers of the idols so that they would be offered to the idols.

And this witness saw that Pedro Julca of the Yanaqui ayllu had a daughter born with curly hair named Isabel Chaupis, and [when she was born] he made chicha and invited all the villagers; and at the feast and drinking party he cut her hair, and with a cuy, coca, and fat, he burned it in sacrifice to the Sun, and after [the offering] all those who attended the feast gave offerings of silver coins. And Andrés Guaillapaico performed the same rites and ceremonies as described above three years ago when one of his sons was born with curly hair, and he cut it; and Pedro Guaman of the Quica [likely Quirca] ayllu also cut the hair of his daughter who was born with curly hair, and [this witness said] that this is a custom and ceremony that they observe in this village and parish whenever a young one is born with curly hair, which they call pacto or guarca.

And this witness saw with his own eyes that two years ago Hernando Chaupis Condor and Alonso Chaupis the Blind took thirty cuyes, three measures of coca, and a little bag of fat to a plot of land called Tauya where they made a sacrifice to the malquis called Huaris, burning before them the said cuyes and fat, and pouring out chicha. He [the witness] also saw that Pedro Capcha Yauri has some large cups from ancient times and made from the shell of a coconut, and in which they carry chicha to offer to the idols and malquis.

And in the same way this witness said that Don Diego Julca Guaman, an acculturated Indian who has become leader and headman in the village of Santiago de Chilcas, an annex of this parish, and whom the Indians fear and respect, has threatened them and stated that any Indian man or woman who reveals some idolatry to the said señor visitador would have to be whipped and punished severely once the visita [idolatry investigation] passed through. And this the witness knows because his sister Juana Solórzano, who lives and participates in the said village of Chilcas, told him of it. . . . He stated [under oath] and confirmed [that what he had spoken was the truth] and said he was forty-six years old, and because he neither knows how to write nor how to sign his name, the said interpreter and the señor visitador sign.

36

Crossing and Dome of the Rosary Chapel, Church of Santo Domingo, Puebla, Mexico

(1632–1690)

Inside the looming, rather plain shell of the gray stone church built for the Dominicans in the city of Puebla, Mexico, at the beginning of the seventeenth century is a remarkable chapel to the Rosary of Our Lady. Decorated over a period of at least sixty years, it suggests in an unusually concentrated way the Baroque artistic and religious sensibility that was popular in Spanish America during the seventeenth and eighteenth centuries.

By the time of Spanish colonization in America, the Dominicans had attached their ardent devotion to the Virgin Mary to the Rosary—the round of devotional prayers consisting of fifteen sets of ten Hail Marys preceded by a Lord's Prayer and followed by the doxology (Gloria Patri). The string of 165 beads used to assist the recital of the Rosary was the emblem of this special devotion, and images of Our Lady of the Rosary depicted the Virgin holding such a string of beads. Dominican churches in America typically gave special prominence (often in the form of a separate chapel) to this devotion.

Situated on the left side of the church just before the main altar, Puebla's Rosary chapel is in the shape of a cross. Where the two arms of the cross intersect, a dome lit by arched and rectangular windows rises above a gilded tabernacle of twisting Solomonic columns that houses a small statue of the Virgin of the Rosary in its lower story and the statue of a saint (perhaps Saint Dominic?) in the upper story. The dome and upper story of the tabernacle appear in the photograph.

Every available space on the walls, window wells, and dome of this chapel is decorated with gilded or painted high-relief stucco forms. There are recognizable figures. At the top of the dome, golden rays of celestial light surround a circular band with a Latin inscription from Isaiah, "Requiescet Superem Spiritus Domini" (And the Spirit of the Lord shall rest upon her), surrounding the white dove of the Holy Spirit. Below this central element, twisting trunks of sturdy vines rise from bulbous vases like ribbed vaults to define the eight sections of the dome, ramifying in all directions. Within each section a female figure represents a gift of the Holy Spirit, or, in one instance, Divine Grace. The heads and flexed arms of winged cherubs emerge from the foliage above the arched windows to support the female figures. The rectangular windows in an octagonal band below the dome are flanked by statues of sixteen virgin martyrs. And in the inverted triangles

Figure 25. Upper reaches of the Rosary chapel,
Church of Santo Domingo, Puebla, Mexico, 1632–1690.
Courtesy of James Early.

created by the four arches at the intersection of the cross are hefty winged angels holding ribbons with phrases in praise of the Virgin. But these various figures largely dissolve in the undulating and swirling rhythms and dazzling overall effect of the many forms and glittering surfaces, as if this space were alive with the sacred. The center of attention is not so much Mary as the dome itself, the radiant canopy of Heaven, bathed in shafts of celestial light that suggest the transcendent delights of eternal Paradise.

By the late sixteenth century, Mediterranean and Latin American Catholic art began to focus greater attention on the display of sacred *things*—relics of saints and other holy objects; miracle-working images; beautiful (and therefore divinely inspired) paintings and statues of the heroes of Catholic history; medals, crucifixes, rosaries, pilgrimage mementoes, inexpensive prints of saints; chestfuls of fine vestments and costly, precious implements of the liturgy; and other ornaments fit for the House of God. Altars and entire church interiors teemed with gilded forms. These things made church buildings not only places of worship but also models of the Kingdom of Heaven. Like much Hispanic Baroque art, they were intended less to engage the intellect with theological propositions than to provide an experience of the divine, a glimpse of the celestial kingdom. The complexity of rounded forms and angles, the paintings and sculpted figures, the play of light on polished silver and twisting forms coated with gold leaf gave the impression of concentrated preciousness pulsating with life. To be inside a well-furnished colonial church or chapel in the seventeenth or eighteenth century was to approach the heavenly realm, to be transported toward the divine in an atmosphere of worship intended to engage all the senses—the smell of incense, candle wax, and damp earth; the cool wetness of holy water, the feel of a saint's robes and the hard ground or tiles under one's knees; the sound of organ music, the cantors' voices, the priest's mysterious speech and echoes of his footsteps at the altar, the bell that signaled the presence of Christ, and the murmurings of prayers and confessions; and the sight of precious objects, colors, movement, tall arches, and bright domes that drew the eyes up and out.

The contrast to the sixteenth-century altarpiece at Huejotzingo (Figure 16), with its symmetrical vision of Church authority and history so cleanly expressed, is striking. It invites intellectual appreciation, whereas the Rosary chapel is more an escape from history and firm rules about design. It is full of invention and an abundance of details that disguise its symmetry; it is an open, intimate invitation to soaring emotions. But both places convey a sense of order in hierarchy "up there" and affirm the preciousness of objects, seeking to inspire awe through art. Both fit well with the Spanish Hapsburgs' sense of their royal authority in patriarchal terms, utterly inseparable from their Catholicism, although the Rosary chapel's surfeit of details is more in the spirit of the extraordinary elaboration of customary rights and practices that distinguished society and the application of justice in Spanish America under the later Hapsburg kings.

Such highly ornamented religious art as that in this chapel is often regarded as a sign of decadence in Spanish American life, of a Church and society in extravagant retreat, increasingly preoccupied with material wealth and superficial appearances, of elaborate forms emptied of content and order or meant to cover over grim realities. The decoration of the Rosary chapel does correspond to a time when the robust aspiration to a universal Christian state under Spanish leadership had turned hollow, when Spanish power in Europe had ebbed and Europe itself experienced a prolonged economic depression, when troubling contradictions in the world seemed permanently irreconcilable, when the Devil seemed to have gained the upper hand in "the invisible war" for immortal souls. But should the Rosary chapel be taken as a kind of decadence in itself, as one kind of response to these circumstances of decline, or as something largely unrelated to the ideas of decadence and decline? Criticism of this hugely popular and long-lived taste in art in the old central areas of the Spanish empire rarely was voiced during the seventeenth and eighteenth centuries. Rather, it was widely accepted as beautiful and full of meaning, not decadent but a suitable expression of grandeur reaching for pure spirituality. It was a style with beginnings in Italy, developed in a confident spirit of struggle against the Protestant Reformation more than out of disheartened feelings of collapse.

When criticism of Baroque artistic expression did come from within the Hispanic world in the late eighteenth century, it was royal administrators and *peninsular* style-makers who spoke up, favoring a restrained and orderly neoclassicism that was more in keeping with their own exalted sense of themselves as enlightened, modern rulers. Buildings inspired by neoclassicism began to appear, especially those designed for state agencies, such as governors' palaces and royal mining and art schools, or the grand palaces of Spanish merchants and Creole nobles. But popular taste in religious art and architecture still inclined toward exuberant, homemade, inventive Baroque effects in the old centers of colonial life long after Spanish rule ended in America.

 37

Two Paintings of a Corpus Christi Procession in Cusco, Peru

(ca. 1674–1680)

A remarkable series of at least sixteen paintings of a procession of the Blessed Sacrament—the Corpus Christi, the body of Christ, His living presence in the consecrated Host—in late seventeenth-century Cusco is thought originally to have hung in the parish church of Santa Ana in the northwestern district of this city, once the imperial center of the Inkas. The colonial church was erected on Karmenka, a hill that had been significant for solar observations in Inka times and that came to mark the principal entrance to the colonial city. The open plaza in front of the parish church hosted the ceremonial dances and performances with which the native Andeans and others greeted visiting dignitaries traveling into the highland city from coastal Lima and which enlivened the final moments of the annual processions of Corpus Christi.

The parishioners of Santa Ana were predominantly native Andean descendants of a variety of ethnic groups brought by the Inkas to Cusco as *mitmaqkuna*—peoples conquered and resettled in "safe" areas by the Inkas to discourage rebellion and promote integration. Notably, the parish was home to a number of Cañaris, a people originally from the region of modern Ecuador, south of Quito. The Cañaris had been noted guards and fighters in the service of the lords of Tawantinsuyu, a set of roles they only enhanced in privileged alliance with the Spaniards once the tables turned on their Inka ruler-rivals. Also residing in the parish of Santa Ana were another group resettled by the Inkas, the Chachapoyas. Their post-Conquest paths were similar to those of the Cañaris. The positions of these indigenous groups as allies of the Spanish authorities in Conquest and colonial times recall alliances and resettlements of Tlaxcalans and others in New Spain (see Selection 13). Santa Ana's most prominent representatives, Cañaris and Chachapoyas among them, are depicted in the Corpus Christi paintings as highly Hispanicized in their apparel (cloaks, breeches, lace shirts, stockings, and shoes) and comportment.

These works of art are examples of the so-called Cusco School of painting and cultural production (our black-and-white reproductions of two of the canvases do not capture the distinctive predominance of red in the palette of the originals, the gilt brocade, and decorative detail). The series is thought to date from between 1674 and 1680, to have been commissioned by a number of patrons, and to have been painted by two or more native Andean artists within the circles of well-known contemporary painters Basilio de Santa Cruz and Juan Zapaca Inga, and perhaps with the contributions of these artists themselves. Twelve of the sixteen known paintings from the Santa Ana series have been restored and hang in the Museum of Religious Art in Cusco; the other four are in two private collections in Santiago, Chile.

The Catholic celebration of Corpus Christi, transplanted to the Indies by Iberians in the sixteenth century, quickly became the most important festival in the religious calendar in many of the larger urban settings in Spanish America. Corpus Christi fell between late May and mid-June, and it coincided with a pre-Hispanic festive season at the time of the winter solstice and maize harvest. The continuity of certain agrarian and religious rhythms doubtless accounted for some of the Catholic festival's popularity among native Andeans in and around the city in early colonial times. Indeed, scholars have investigated numerous parallels between the celebration of Corpus Christi in Cusco and the Inkaic festival of Inti Raymi, and also that of Capacocha. Yet it is worth considering the effects of focusing investigation on the possible symbolic and practical parallels between pre-Hispanic and colonial festive behavior. Such a focus encourages a kind of questing after a bedrock of Andean religious structures and meanings that somehow survives beneath a convenient but ultimately superficial cover of the Spanish Catholic feast day; as David Cahill shows, this is true whether the focus falls on coinciding festive calendars, shared solar imagery, the use of central spaces and the public roles of dancing and drinking, or certain images and ethnic regalia. What, then, are we assuming about the appeal and meaning of Corpus Christi processions for native Andeans, both initially and later in colonial times? Does the vitality of colonial Andean religious culture depend only on the native peoples' successful camouflaging of a notional pre-Hispanic purity and resistance of foreign influences?

Fundamentally, the festival of Corpus Christi was of European provenance. Nearly all of its organizers and appointed deputies were members of the colonial elite; and, further, the procession was in many ways an expression of the triumph of the Spanish Christian social order that this elite guarded in the former Inka heartland. The Corpus Christi series of paintings had an ethnically diverse set of male and female patrons, but as Cahill convincingly demonstrates, primarily non-indigenous male sponsors from the city's guilds took on the principal burden and honor of funding the elaborate triumphal arches and altars that transformed the processional circuit and that figure so prominently in the paintings. These arches and altars were the pride of the city and drew comments from visitors to Cusco during the Corpus Christi cycle throughout the colonial period. In the late eighteenth century, the author of another document in this book (Selection 41), Concolorcorvo, remarked that "the entire transit of the procession is a continuous altar." Even so, these paintings invite the consideration of more complicated kinds of change in colonial Cusco. This was a place and time in which native Andean notables, like others, might preserve and reinforce their positions through identification with and participation in Christianity. There is also the matter of colonial Cusco's rapidly changing social composition, and the fact that the festival procession became a focus of popular religious life not only for Spaniards and Creoles but also for a multiracial population. Such dimensions can be overlooked if the colonial festival is sealed off as though it were an arena for a winner-take-all contest between opposing symbolic structures that belong exclusively to native Andeans or Spaniards.

The paintings allow us to glimpse the streets, plazas, and edifices of Cusco as they may have looked after the rebuilding that followed a devastating earthquake in 1650. And the procession itself is rendered at the height of its regional popularity and significance, in the years before a 1685 reform of the festival which strictly limited the zone from which its participants might be drawn. Through their ambitious inclusion of subjects and detail, the images are visual delights that suggest a complex society participating in the most important religious procession of the year. Patrons oversaw the creation of these paintings and influenced not only their own placement within them but also the placement of others. Yet their documentary value is only the beginning of their wealth, for the canvases are best approached as purposeful works of the imagination, not simply as ethnographies painted and peopled for our research.

A number of European models informed the artists' "localized" inventions. Carolyn Dean has explored a memorable example of this painterly process of appropriation and localization by showing how in a number of canvases the native Andean artists depict multi-storied processional carriages copied from prototype engravings in a contemporary festival book from Valencia, Spain. Although they became dramatic components in the canvases from the series, there is no evidence that such triumphal carriages ever rolled through the streets of Cusco.

Like the Huejotzingo altarpiece (Selection 23), and also like paintings of other events rendered to be remembered—the paintings of the conqueror of Mexico, Hernán Cortés, watched by an assembly of native lords, abasing himself in welcome of "the twelve (Franciscan) apostles of the Indies" to Tenochtitlan in 1524 is an example—the Corpus Christi canvases were commissioned by patrons, coordinated by churchmen, and created by artists to send certain messages to viewers within society at large. For, unlike so many works of art that adorned private walls within the homes of the Spanish and native nobility, the procession paintings would have been regularly viewed and re-viewed by people attending Mass and entering the church of Santa Ana—members of the very same multi-racial society, including Spaniards, who would watch the annual procession in person. What messages were they meant to take away from the paintings?

Connected to the glorification of a public religious procession in the most symbolic city in the Andes, these paintings offer an idealized representation of society, a consecration of the prescribed social order in an urban center of colonial Spanish America. The canvases offer messages about prestige and participation that call for a comparison with the narrative of the Corpus Christi procession in a contemporary Mexican context by the historian Mariano Cuevas (Selection 29). The communication of Spanish Christian triumph seems firmly present, as are ideas about the potential for the redirection of popular cultural and religious enthusiasms toward reformed Catholic Christian ends.

In the first image (Figure 26), some thirty or so priests and lesser clerical officers in black cassocks under white surplices—three carrying their birettas (three-lobed hats) and others candlesticks—form a line passing under a triumphal arch. The arch is paneled with landscapes and topped by the figure of the archangel Michael defeating Satan, flanked by two helmeted trumpeters. To the right of center, the well-dressed official wearing the Maltese Cross of the knightly Order of Saint John and enjoying the honor of carrying the banner of the Holy Sacrament is thought to be Don Alonso Pérez de Guzmán, the *corregidor* of Cusco (1670–1676). Six paintings—two more landscapes and four archangels—almost obscure a building behind a processional altar devoted to Christ's crucifixion. People fill the background, most of them watching the procession. To the left of the altar is a native Andean man playing an elaborately carved harp, accompanying a group of young singers.

The crowd in the foreground stands in the street. In the center, a bearded European man with his long hair tied in a queue, wearing a large hat and enjoying a cigar, seems oblivious to the solemn procession of clergy and provincial authority. In contrast to him are the three patrons of the canvas—an old Andean woman who made the commission on behalf of her two grandsons—facing the viewer, all with hands raised and clasped in prayer. The woman stands behind the boys, one of whom

Figure 26. Corregidor Pérez and secular clergy in a Corpus Christi procession, Cusco, Peru, ca. 1674–1680.
Courtesy of the Museo del Arte Religioso, Cusco, Peru.

is with her on the far left, while the other is somewhat displaced to the right. The old woman, who dominates the foreground from her corner, wears Andean clothing while both children are dressed in Spanish attire.

This painting, with its focused expression of piety and order, like a number of others in the series does not quite deny the intrusion of more messy and entertaining social realities. But the intrusions are deemphasized or neutralized in ways that were common in European art of the day; the intrusions here function much as the cavorting servants and pets do in paintings of the Last Supper. The distracted man with the hat and cigar in the foreground of the Corregidor Pérez canvas is a good example of a figure whose capacity for trouble seems reduced to inattentiveness. He draws the gaze but seems benign and contained, allowing the artist and viewer to delight in him. The didactic message about order and society is conveyed by contrasting the disruptive or simply inattentive behavior among the diverse commoners in the foreground and outer fringes with the careful and intent propriety of the White elite (see also the background figures on the balconies in the second image, Figure 27), the pious patrons, and the central order of the procession participants.

Even more obviously irreverent behavior is also included according to contemporary artistic conventions, as a useful foil to exemplary behavior. As Dean has shown, in the Corpus Christi series these further "distractions" are often unruly children, confined to the margins of the pictorial space, suitably away from properly restrained and reverential attitudes. To the far right in the first image, just beyond the triumphal arch, is a group of people who unfortunately cannot be seen clearly in our reproduction (or in any others of which we are aware). These people gaze at the next and culminating segment of the procession "outside" this canvas (and depicted in another painting from the series), namely, the bishop of Cusco, Manuel de Mollinedo y Angulo, bearing the consecrated Host in its monstrance. A group of men (seemingly an Andean, a European, an African, and another figure) are about to kneel, and the African has even removed his hat out of respect. Yet just in front of the men, a woman holds a baby while another child seems to aim a peashooter in the direction of the approaching Host.

What does such a rendering achieve? It is unlikely that the artist's discreet sideshows of casual disorder and disrespect are clever messages chanced by native Andean artists who meant to subvert the order-seeking messages of the commissioned paintings. In fact, one possible interpretation following from Dean's work is that the intended messages are entirely opposite to subversion and closer in spirit to routine. Arguably, the placement of the inattentive commoner in the foreground, or the misbehaving child almost out of view (and before the attentive men and beside the reverent mother, all of whom are notably unfazed by the child's actions), assembles in this canvas a Baroque message about the coexistence of opposites, a micro-lesson in what is and is not appropriate in the presence of Spanish Christian authority. By depicting the most destabilizing elements in the paintings as marginal and "childish," are the artists saying that however unfortunate their behavior, they are exceptional and, like children, more or less controllable? How do these messages relate to Cuevas's descriptions of commoners and their behavior during Corpus Christi processions in another region of Spanish America? Building from elite perceptions of "uneducated" and less Hispanicized segments of society as childlike, Dean suggests this insight, arguing that many of the misbehaving children in the series (unlike the praying grandsons in Figure 26) are treated similarly and are "behaviorally analogous" to the more chaotic and talkative commoners in the foregrounds of the Corpus Christi paintings.

How were these paintings seen? One cannot know for certain if the native Andean parishioners of Santa Ana noticed the few disruptive elements in the paintings, much less if they saw them in a prescribed manner. Yet an interpretation that sees ethnic variety and hints of disorder being pictorially "conquered" and rather hopefully set in place in these depictions of Christianity's processional triumph seems strengthened by wider attention to contemporary events and concerns. Although serious and sustained challenges to the social and political hierarchy were rare, churchmen and other authorities recorded that Corpus Christi celebrations were notorious for their public drunkenness, small-scale violence, disrespect for authority, and any number of excesses and disruptions. Even the leaders of Hispanicized groups such as the Cañari parishioners of Santa Ana used the public moments of the dances and demonstrations during the procession to goad rival ethnic groups, sometimes setting off pitched battles in the plaza and streets and bringing ignoble ends (or at least long and bloody delays) to any expression of communal consensus. Colonial officials in Cusco, and in the rest of Spanish America, were not the only ones with such troubles, and in fact shared them with many contemporaries throughout the Catholic world who increasingly lamented that religious festivals, in addition to their financial drain and lost work time, were often occasions for violence and protest. Cusco's patrons and sponsors had these reasons and more to be urgently concerned by the disruptions that marred actual festivals, and they were obviously eager to curb such behavior.

In its use of the pictorial space and in the activity and arrangement of subjects, the second image (Figure 27) is an even more elaborate idealization of a colonial social order that reached downward to the people from the Spanish monarchy itself. At the center is the festive altar before which the procession would pause. It features the young King Charles II, a number of archangels, and a collection of paintings on biblical themes. The eye is drawn toward two resplendent images. On the left is Santa Rosa of Lima, patron of the Indies, carrying her wreath of roses and wearing her customary Dominican habit, crown of roses, and a rosary draped around her shoulders (see also Selection 30 and Figure 23 in Selection 32). Following her is the patron of Cusco, the Virgin locally known as "La Linda" (The Pretty One). The two saints ride on litters carried by members of their *cofradías*, or religious associations.

These native Andean litter bearers are depicted as ethnic non-Inkas; shod in sandals, they wear their hair long, and most are dressed in European breeches beneath tunics covered by darker traditional mantles. They contrast with the noble standard-bearer who wears a modified Inkaic tunic, bordered at the neck (recalling the messages of such dress suggested by Figures 1 and 2 in Selection 2); and they contrast also with his elite companions, who carry their staffs of authority and office and who are dressed in the darker colors of Hispanicized garb, with lace sleeves of mixed European and Andean styles. The red fringed ornamental headgear (*mascapaycha*) that the Sapa Inka had worn on his forehead as one of the symbols of his preeminence, now forming part of the imagery adopted by Cusco's post-Conquest Inka elite, is borne on a pillow in front of the standard-bearer—perhaps, it has been suggested, because wearing (as opposed to displaying) the connotative headdress of his bloodline would confuse his current capacity as head of the Catholic *cofradía* of "La Linda." The castle and elongated rainbow, and other elements of this headpiece, demonstrate a colonial sharing of symbols, most basically that of the Inkaic forehead insignia and the Spanish coat of arms signifying Cusco and its recent history.

Unlike the litter bearers who stare intently ahead, the Andean leaders who walk in front of "La Linda" gaze proudly out at the viewer. The post-Conquest Inka carrying the standard appears an embodiment both of a noble Andean and of an Andean Christian leader. A partial inscription to the lower right on the canvas announces: "Here goes the standard-bearer with his father Don Baltazar Tupa Puma. . . ." On his bright tunic, in addition to the Andean geometric motifs (*tocapu*) and borders, is a solar visage—a round face with its rays projecting outward—suggesting a mixture of Andean solar imagery and the Inkaic divinity Inti with European solar metaphors for Christ and the spreading warmth and light of Christianity, and recalling the sun-shaped receptacle of the focus of this event.

The cofradía as principal patron asserts a collective vision of its members as devoted agents within the order of the procession and a reconstituted civil and religious community. The modified Inkaic dress marks a clear association with the pre-Hispanic past, but one that is not bereft of symbols which seek a reformulated and participating "Christian" Andean authority in colonial times. The depictions of the native leaders and supporting cast seem eager to speak to and gain legitimacy from a mixed audience of viewers. Santa Rosa is surrounded by Indian musicians, while a group of Indian notables with their ceremonial staffs precede "La Linda." Nobles who

Figure 27. Santa Rosa and "La Linda" in a Corpus Christi procession, Cusco, Peru, ca. 1674–1680.
Courtesy of the Museo del Arte Religioso, Cusco, Peru.

descended from the royal line of Inkas, as well as native Andean governors (*kurakas*) from the environs of Cusco, regularly participated in these processions and would characteristically dress in a mixture of Andean and Spanish costumes. Two such men—perhaps the most striking portraits in this painting—are positioned in front of "La Linda," one in a patterned white tunic and the other in dark dress with the lace sleeves of a noble, staring straight back at the viewer. These native leaders, as intermediaries between Spanish authorities and Andean peoples, appeal to a kind of traditional authority that was encouraged by the Spanish rulers, and also to a modified understanding of authority that the Indian elite were obliged to negotiate with their subjects in colonial times. The governors and notables, like the musicians and members of the cofradías, walk as men of local importance, as dignified and exemplary participants in this representation of a central Christian occasion.

What does one make of the use of Inkaic dress and symbols during the Corpus Christi processions? As in their general portrayals, the artists seem to have held a vision of achieved assimilation in mind. Here in the late seventeenth century, it might be said, dressed in their revised pre-Hispanic finery and striding magnificently at the center of the holy pageantry, are ideal representatives of Andean colonial culture, examples to those who watch. Such messages were thought more useful than subversive by officials in the late seventeenth century. Yet, as Cahill has pointed out (and see Selection 43), in the face of the spreading rebellions and signs of an Inka's return to power in Peru, views could change. Colonial officials in the later eighteenth century would grow distrustful of native Andean assimilation and increasingly hostile toward the presence of Inkaic reminders and even ceremonial Andean dancing within the celebration of Corpus Christi. Such festivities were eventually deemed dangerous rallying points as well as extravagantly wasteful of time and money.

The magnificent paintings of Cusco's Corpus Christi are ultimately ambitious works of the mind, imaginings (even instructions) of how an ideal procession would appear in this prestigious and symbolic setting. As such, they seem to signify the hopes and efforts of members of a Spanish and native Andean elite in late seventeenth-century south-central Peru to forge and maintain a social unity, thereby reducing the likelihood of disturbance and rebellion. All of the participants and observers of the popular real event, pictorially represented as people from every social station, were given their parts to play, even as the agents of distraction, who were carefully minimalized. Now, if only everyone would learn their lines and gestures and keep to their places.

PART IV

Bourbon Rules and American Practices in a Short Eighteenth Century

38

Nicolás Ñenguirú's Letter to the Governor of Buenos Aires

(1753)

The province of Paraguay in the interior of southern South America had a singular colonial experience. It was remote from the centers of Spanish colonial activity but was strategically located on the frontier with Portuguese Brazil. Few of the resources that drew concerted Spanish interest were present—no precious metals, no Indian state societies—but there were peaceable Guaraní Indians clustered along the banks of the Paraguay, Uruguay, and Paraná rivers, not far from hostile neighbors in the Chaco region. Many of the Guaraníes accepted a modified *encomienda* system in the vicinity of the colonial capital of Asunción and mission settlements on the eastern fringe of the province.

The Crown and Church would not invest heavily in administering territory that did not at least cover costs, and accounts of Paraguay throughout the colonial period stressed the general poverty and lack of money in the province. Yet it was important to extend and consolidate a Spanish colonial presence in Paraguay as a buffer against Portuguese expansion and other European designs on Spanish territory. The result was that the province had a long military tradition, considerable independence, and poorly defined boundaries.

Lay and ecclesiastical settlers were allowed considerable freedom. From its beginnings in the 1550s, the long-lived encomienda system developed in a peculiar way, with Spanish *encomenderos* residing among their Guaraní subjects, relying on kinship networks and traditions of chieftainship as much as on military prowess for their authority, fathering many children, and speaking both Spanish and Guaraní—the beginnings of a bilingual, Mestizo society. The result is the only country in modern Latin America that is bilingual, with both a European and a native official language. By the 1570s nearly all the encomenderos were Mestizos. The "Spanish" Mestizo residents of little Asunción came to exercise a virtual veto power over the appointment and tenure of royal governors sent out from Lima. And thirty Jesuit missions were founded in the early seventeenth century among Guaraní people to the east in both Spanish and Portuguese territory, distant from provincial authorities in Asunción and Buenos Aires, not to mention Lima and Madrid. Except in these frontier missions, the Church and priests in Paraguay were much less important than in the central areas of the Spanish empire. There was no Pedro de Gante, no missionary "Twelve," no Las Casas looming large in a "spiritual conquest" of the Asunción hinterland. Few priests settled there at all in the sixteenth century, and few of those who did learned the Guaraní language.

The Jesuit missions were important to the colonial state in stabilizing a frontier with the Portuguese and resisting the slaving expeditions of *bandeirantes* (explorers and fortune seekers in the interior of Brazil) from São Paulo, but they were controversial as virtually self-governing armed refuges run by Jesuit priests, which sometimes tipped the balance of political power in the province. In 1750 international politics broke in on Paraguay and its local controversies. The Spanish and Portuguese monarchies agreed to terms of peace in the Treaty of Madrid, which attempted to define more clearly the imperial borders in South America. Lands occupied for Spain east of the Uruguay River in Paraguay were to be turned over to the Portuguese and the settlements there disbanded. Seven Jesuit missions were affected. Guaraní people in these seven communities resisted in various ways their transfer to Brazil, leading to the sporadic fighting and negotiations of the so-called Guaraní War from 1753 to 1756.

The Guaraní settlements were more inclined to fight in the 1750s, when they were faced with removal from their lands, than they were in 1767, when the Jesuits were expelled from all Spanish territories. Recent scholarship by Barbara Ganson and James Saeger indicates that the Jesuits controlled Guaraní lives and loyalties less than suggested by the usual emphasis on Jesuit actions and the regimentation of mission life. Rather than suddenly abandoning the missions, the Guaraní residents participated in the gradual breakdown of the mission system after other religious orders took the Jesuits' place. Guaraní militias continued to play a role in imperial defense, but the Indians began to leave for work on plantations or as artisans in towns, and thereby avoid the tribute tax or escape mistreatment by colonial authorities and labor contractors. Perhaps the heaviest blow to the missions as viable communities was the royal decree in 1800 that freed Guaraní residents from communal labor obligations. In any event, there was no widespread retreat into the forests; most of the former mission Guaraní people continued to find their living within colonial society.

The following 1753 letter was one kind of response by Guaraní leaders in the seven missions to orders from the colonial governor at Buenos Aires to disband their settlements or face a war to the death. Six of the seven mission communities replied in writing to the governor's order. The author of the longest reply was Nicolás Ñenguirú, the Indian *corregidor* of La Concepción (Figure 28). He became the nominal commander of Guaraní mission soldiers in 1756, but he was always more a man of words than an effective military leader. Philip Caraman, a Jesuit historian of the Paraguay missions, regards him as an "ignorant pawn" for not being a more determined fighter, but Ñenguirú enjoyed more prestige and respect in his community than Caraman's view allows, and his letter to the governor suggests that he was no simple tool of the governor (or of the Jesuits).

The Guaraní letters of 1753 claimed a moral right to their settlements that, they said, the Spanish Crown had endorsed. The letters argue for an implicit contract between the king and the Guaraníes: they had not been conquered by the Spaniards. Rather, they had chosen to accept Christianity and the protection of the king of Spain. The king was the representative of God, not just of the Spaniards, and thus the Guaraníes' lands belonged to them by divine right. They had, they said, always been loyal subjects of the king, and it was inconceivable that he could wish to expel them from their lands.

Ñenguirú's letter is worth reading for its elaboration of the case for Guaraní mission rights. It raises questions about how the author positions himself with the governor concerning the likelihood of open rebellion. Does he present himself with hat in hand, contrite and obsequious? Does he presume to speak for "his people"? On the other hand, what are his relations with the Jesuits? Could this letter have been ghost-written by a Jesuit missionary at La Concepción? And in what sense could this letter be read as a colonial communication? Does his stance as a loyal Christian subject calling for mutual responsibility compare with the position of Felipe Guaman Poma de Ayala (see Selection 25)? We should remember that Paraguay was not Peru or central Mexico, and Ñenguirú was not in the same situation as Guaman Poma.

Governor, Sir:

Hearing your letter has given us a great fright. We cannot believe that the saintly heart of our king has ordered us to move—a most troublous thing. And so we say that this is not our king's will. Of course, the Portuguese, we say to you, those enemies of our well-being, want to make us move for their own wicked reasons.

We also have another letter from our king, in which the deceased father of our king lets us understand his heart very well, the love he has for us. He approves of our way of life, our church, even what we have done in war [in the king's service], and he is consoled by what we have so readily done in all matters, according to his wishes. "Well done," his congratulatory letter says to us. His letter also tells us: "I will remember you, I will help you, I will take good care of you, and my governor also will help you; and I have ordered him to free you of all harm." Therefore we say: How can it be that these two letters from our king are so unequal, so different? Our king would not err in his words. Why should he now harass us, burdening us when we have not failed him, impoverishing us greatly without cause, wanting to expel us from our land in order to give the Portuguese our possessions and what we have worked so hard to create? To lose us without more ado? This, sir, we cannot believe, nor do we know how to believe it. So we say: This is not the will of our king. If he knew about this, if he could hear our words, he would be angry, he would not see it as a good thing, and he would not approve of our removal.

Sir, we have never gone against our king, nor against you. You know this well. With all our heart we have honored your commands; we have always followed them very well. For love of you we have given our possessions, our animals, even our lives. This is why we cannot believe that our king would repay our faithfulness with an order to leave our lands. Our Indians, our children speak constantly of this; and, growing angry, they are going to extremes, acting as if they were in rebellion. They no longer wish to hear our words as those of their corregidor and the cabildo [council]. They get angry at us and only their caciques [chiefs] sway them. It is now useless for us to say anything to them about this move. You know very well how the Indians are when they are oppressed by some excessive, harmful demand. If we tell them, with respect to their pueblo, to send away the vassals of our king, force them out into the open country in the name of our king, take away their possessions, impoverish them, beggar them without cause—if we tell them this, you will hear what they say and you will see their anger. Sir, listen, you should also hear the true words of these our children, just as they speak them to us. They say: "In former times our sainted father named Roque González de Santa Cruz, as soon as he arrived, taught us about God and also to be Christians. Not even one Spaniard entered this land. By our own free will we chose to place God above all, and then also our king so that he would always be our protector. For this reason alone we submitted and humbled ourselves. And we chose to do so. The king gave his word to our grandparents to treat us well. And he has always repeated this same promise to us. Then how is it that suddenly he wants to break his promise?"

"This land," say our children, "was given to us by God alone. In this land our sainted teacher Roque González and many [Jesuit] fathers died among us, they raised us, and they labored for us alone. Why, then, are the Portuguese so intent upon this when it is none of their business? The magnificent church, the good pueblo, the ranch for our animals, the maté plantation, the cotton fields, the farmland and all that is needed to work it is a great endeavor that we alone have accomplished. How can they presume to take away the possessions that belong to us, and wrongly mock us? It will not be so. God Our Lord does not wish this, will not stand for it; nor is it the will of our sainted king. We have not erred in anything, we have taken nothing from the Portuguese. They will never pay us anything for what we alone have built."

Never even in the remote past have our [Jesuit] fathers spoken to our children of such a move. They have cared for us, indeed they have. They have always loved us well. Only now do we hear these words from them. Only now do they speak wrongly to persuade us to leave our pueblos and lose our well-being. So, what is this? By chance did they remove our grandparents from the mountains for this? Did they congregate and teach them just to send them away again now? Is this what the padre comisario [the Jesuit delegate, Luis Altamirano] was sent for? He certainly has made our [Jesuit] fathers into something other than what they were. They weren't as they are now. He has bothered them, badly. He certainly is a new kind of father to come to this our land. He does not offer anything that we need. He has not labored for our love. Wrongly he wishes to remove us from our pueblos and lands, suddenly, hurriedly, period. He wants to cast us out to the mountains as if we were rabbits, or to the open countryside as if we were snails, far away, even if it is bad weather or winter. He only wants to impoverish us. He seems to want to finish us off. This is what the Indians say to us: "This is not the will of God, nor does He wish it. This is not Christian conduct. We, too, are Christians, children of the Church, our mother. We have never failed the Church nor our king." The padre comisario does say, in the name of our king: "Send them out in poverty. Go far away, to the edge of the mountains. Look for your livelihood there. Go to the countryside. Take your belongings. Work there, grow tired, experience illness and poverty." This way, they say, you will also achieve our sense of poverty and will learn to have compassion for us. We gain no consolation from him, for he does not know our language. He does not know how to speak to us, he cannot hear our words. So the Indians say to us. After this, our children repeatedly say to us: "Where do they want to send us? And they want us to go suddenly, hurriedly to a bad land. Good land has not been found for even three pueblos, much less for our animals. And our fathers seem happy that two pueblos are to be founded in a bog where we are sure to die, saying that no good land can be found. They have not even allowed us time to move gradually. Therefore they wrongly mean only to see us destroyed."

Sir, I have written these words of the Indians to you, and they are their true words. We, the members of the cabildo, have no more words to calm them, nor to oppose them when they become angry. Therefore we humble ourselves before you so that, in the words of the king, you will help us. In the first place, all of us are your vassals: please let our king know of our poverty and what we are suffering, and send him my letter, wherever he may be, so that he himself will see, that he will hear and understand our poverty and tribulations. Our Lord God made him our king; we chose him to take care of us. We have not erred in anything to justify being abandoned. So we trust in his good heart, that he must take pity and mercy on us, then we will all fulfill his will most willingly. In the second place, Sir, for the love of God, if you do not believe these to be our true words, send someone, even if it be two good Spaniards whom you trust, so that they can hear our words and see with their own eyes. They cannot but help telling you the pure truth. We desperately need you to do this, and since we are in such need, we hope that they will come. Surely God Our Lord hears the words of the poor.

Finally, Sir, this my pueblo of La Concepción is not bad, although there are misgivings here. It is not on the other shore of the Uruguay River. We have two ranchos in that land, two maté plantations. If this land is taken from us, we and the people of this pueblo will be in a very poor state. We have been looking for some suitable land and do not know where to find it. That great cacique named Nicolás Ñenguirú is my true grandfather. It was he who, long ago, at the beginning, allowed the sainted father Roque González to enter. He revered and loved greatly the words concerning faith in God. From this my pueblo Indians, all children and relatives of mine, went to the other shore of the Uruguay River to establish two pueblos. They wanted me (and they asked me to do so) to inform you in this my letter of their poverty and suffering. All of us, every day, pray before God and put our trust in Him. May this same Lord give you a good heart and long life, and may God protect you eternally so that you may help us well. At La Concepción, July 1753. Nicolás Ñenguirú, corregidor.

Plan of the Jesuit Mission at La Concepción, Paraguay

This late colonial plan of Nicolás Ñenguirú's home community shows the standard buildings and configuration of space in a Jesuit mission of Paraguay. The Indian community was arrayed in long blocks (F) around a large plaza, more than a football-field's length on each side. Facing east onto the plaza and dominating the layout is the Jesuits' compound (A to E): the church, cemetery, school, residence patios, and large "garden" plot, presumably worked collectively under supervision by the missionaries. A separate building (G) located close to the school and living quarters of the missionaries was reserved for widows and orphans, or perhaps served as the hospital.

The neat layout recalls the typical grid plan of colonial towns in Spanish America that was inspired by imperial Rome, but there are differences. The church compound with double patios for schooling, the manual arts, and residences for the priests is the principal feature here. There are no town offices or other civic architecture to rival its prominence on the plaza. The residential blocks face the plaza rather than running in many long lines toward it. The effect was to make the plaza and the Jesuits' compound a more interior, protected place. The residential blocks of the mission settlement also have a more standardized appearance than the usual colonial town. Built as one continuous structure, each block was divided into one-room family dwellings with connecting walls and private entrances. The front of each dwelling consisted of a doorway and one window with a long portico running the length of the block. The rear wall of each connected dwelling had another window. In most older, better established missions the buildings were of cut stone with tile roofs. Typically, there was a large cross at each corner of the plaza, and in the center a statue of the Virgin Mary or the patron saint of the community.

Key

A. Church
B. Cemetery
C. School
D. Patios
E. Garden
F. Blocks of Guaraní dwellings with their porticos
G. "House of the needy" (*casa de miserias*)

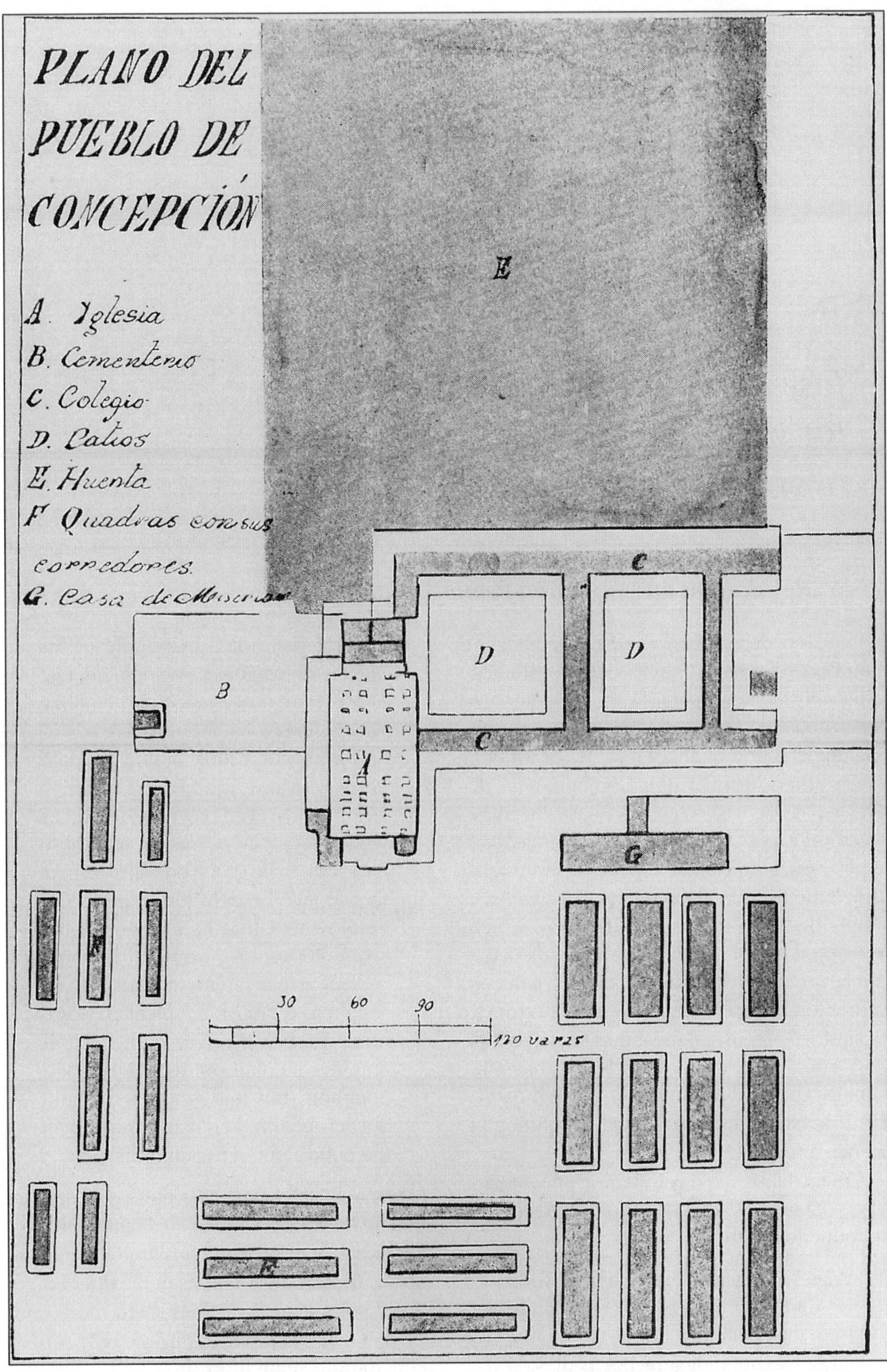

Figure 28. Plan of La Concepción mission, Paraguay, in late colonial times. Courtesy of the Academia Nacional de Bellas Artes, Buenos Aires.

José de Gálvez's Decrees for the King's Subjects in Mexico

(1769, 1778)

Regulations on Wages and Peonage, Sonora, 1769

José de Gálvez was a chief architect of Bourbon reforms in the American colonies, especially for New Spain. As *visitador* for New Spain and then Minister of the Indies, he oversaw the creation of a vast military district for the northern frontier (the Comandancia de Provincias Internas), intendancies for the entire viceroyalty south of the Provincias Internas, and other new administrative offices. He established the first Academy of Fine Arts (La Academia de San Carlos in Mexico City), which promoted neoclassical restraint; tripled the public rents; corrected various abuses; reduced restrictions on trade; and moved to give practical, strictly regulated meanings to "freedom" and "equality," two watchwords of eighteenth-century Europe that, conceived more broadly, became closely associated with revolution in France and the United States.

Wage labor came within his restless regulatory gaze. As Charles Gibson writes in his introduction to this document,

> Wages for repartimiento [corvée] workers had been fixed by viceregal order from the beginning, but wages for free labor had not ordinarily been adjusted to any regular schedule. It was entirely characteristic of Gálvez, and of his eighteenth-century frame of mind, that efforts were now made to systematize wages. Everyone should have a job, and equivalent jobs should be paid equally. Many jobs in the Spanish colonies involved payment of food as well as financial payments, and these also were to be specified. With respect to peonage or debt labor, a type of employment that had begun in the sixteenth century and had become general in many forms of labor, Gálvez sought to establish a typical compromise: that workers in debt to their employers could not renege on their contracts, but that employers could not advance workers' wages more than the equivalent of two months' pay.

Mexican novelist Carlos Fuentes's pithy remark that Spanish Bourbons of the eighteenth century were "modernizing busybodies" may be one of those exaggerations in the direction of the truth. Gálvez's decrees seem more concerned with efficiency, productivity, order, and minute regulation than with freedom, equality, and justice for all.

Don Joseph de Gálvez of the Supreme Council and Chamber of the Indies, intendant of the army of America, general visitor of all the tribunals of justice and royal finance and the treasuries and branches of it in these kingdoms of New Spain, and with His Majesty's approval commissioned with the fullest powers by the very excellent viceroy Señor Marqués de Croix, viceroy, governor, and captain general of the same kingdoms:

In order to make sure that workers needed for the cultivation of lands and the grazing of cattle are not lacking, through agreement with the mine owners and hacienda owners, I have resolved upon a measure that will benefit the poor and promote the public welfare, namely, to set a quota upon salaries and rations of goods that will prevail in the future in the provinces of this jurisdiction, for workers, wage earners, and servants, of the following classifications:

1. The leaders, captains, and heads of mining labors; majordomos of haciendas and ranches, whether for agriculture or for grazing; mule-train shippers; and the overseers of other kinds of occupations equivalent to these, are to receive from their masters the wages and rations so that they may negotiate with them in accordance with the skill and circumstances of each one, with the indispensable requirement that wages must be paid in reales or in silver.

2. Workers in mines and others laboring at equivalent tasks should receive at least seven pesos per month in money, and each week they should receive two almudes [about one-fourth of a bushel] of maize and one-half arroba [a 12-pound measure] of fresh meat or one-quarter arroba [a 6-pound measure] of dried meat, whether they be married or single, and with no innovation for the present in the arrangement commonly granted to mine workers by the owners of mines.

3. The same salary and rations are to be paid to the principal cowboys, farm hands, muleteers, horse guards, and others of similar work in other tasks and occupations, except that carriers are to receive six pesos with the same ration.

4. Subordinate shepherds and cowboys who are aides in mule trains or have other equivalent work are to receive the same weekly ration and are to receive as salary five pesos per month in reales, or in silver if reales are lacking. But if they are Indians under the age of eighteen, they are to receive only four pesos in money, with the same rations.

5. In accordance with the laws, I prohibit vagabonds in these provinces and order that everyone is to have a precise job or office, under penalty of one month in jail for the first offense, whether he be Spaniard or Indian or other non-Indian; and a fine of twenty pesos against anyone who protects him under pretext of refuge and fails to report him to the judge, so that he may be punished and set to work. And with any repetition of the offense, the vagabonds will be assigned to the public or royal works, with rations but without wages for two months.

6. Servants have a natural freedom to leave one master in order to make arrangements with another, but this freedom is used by some with such impudence and to such excess that the matter requires some effective correction; there is also the opposite extreme, wherein servants are forced to work for masters who do not treat them well or do not pay them the wages agreed upon. To remedy both abuses, I declare and order that the worker who is in debt to his master cannot leave him

without first fulfilling the terms of the contract, and no other employer may accept him without having assurance that this is the case, in the form of a written statement by the former employer. And no master may advance the wages of his workers or servants more than the amount of two months' wages; nor may he stand in the way of those who have paid up their debt and who want to look for better employment, at least so long as they are not repartimiento workers.

And so that no one may contravene this regulation, which is useful for all, and so that the masters, servants, and workers may ensure from the government its observance, it is to be published and posted in all the reales [licensed mining settlements] and towns of these provinces, with the corresponding testimonies placed in their archives.

Done in the Real de los Alamos [Sonora], June 2, 1769. Don Joseph de Gálvez, by order of His Most Illustrious Highness.

Royal Cédula *that American and European Vassals Are to Be Equal, Madrid, January 2, 1778*

On the surface, the royal decree that elicited a complaint by the Mexico City municipal council and the following somewhat testy reply by Gálvez (now the king's Minister of the Indies in Madrid), seemed to strike a blow for equality of opportunity between peninsular Spaniards and people born and raised in the American colonies, inspired by the king's abiding love for all his subjects. But Creole Spaniards in New Spain's viceregal capital took it as a move to insinuate more *peninsulares* into high offices of American cathedral chapters. Invoking Enlightenment rationality, Gálvez replied that the new decree merely made Americans and peninsular Spaniards equally eligible for these offices; it did not mean to favor one group over another. Past experience, at least, would have suggested the opposite to ambitious Creole Americans, for few of their ancestors had ever received preferment for important offices in Spain, whereas many peninsulares were selected for prestigious offices in the American colonies, especially in the second half of the eighteenth century. They also might well remember Gálvez's retort as the king's *visitador* to New Spain in 1767 to those who questioned the expulsion of the Jesuits: "Vassals of the throne of Spain were born to be silent and obey, not to debate or discuss the affairs of Government."

Josef de Gálvez to the municipal council and judicial and military branches of the city of Mexico. I have advised the king of your communication of last July 24 in which you complain of His Majesty's order of February 21, 1776, reserving one-third of the places in American cathedral chapters for American Spaniards [Creoles], and another order of September 17 of the same year providing for the nomination of European Spaniards for the vacant post of deacon in the cathedral chapter of the Archdiocese of Mexico and cathedral dignitaries elsewhere in the Indies. Naturally, His Majesty noticed the imprecision with which you refer to the two royal orders and that you either do not understand, or pretend not to understand, the spirit that motivated them and their purpose. It is clearer than light that the spirit of the two royal orders is His Majesty's religious ardor, the motivation is his paternal love for his American vassals, and the purpose is the well-being and happiness of these same vassals. In the first order, His Majesty stipulated that for the purpose of maintaining the splendor of the divine cult in the cathedrals of the Indies and the greatest exactitude in administration of justice in the secular tribunals, and also to strengthen the union of those Kingdoms with these and reward equally the merit and services of his vassals, it was his will that the Council of Castile consider Americans for prebends and dignitaries in the churches and tribunals of Spain, and that the Council of the Indies do the same for the churches and tribunals of those dominions, with the proviso that one-third of the cathedral chapter posts there be filled by American Spaniards. This wording makes it perfectly clear that at least one-third of the prebends must be from the Indies. It does not exclude the possible appointment of many more, as there have always been, are now, and will be.

In the second order, His Majesty directed that for the deaconate of the cathedral chapter of the Archdiocese of Mexico, which was then vacant, European Spaniards be considered and that the same be done for the dignitaries of other American cathedrals. But it did not order the exclusion of Americans for consideration; rather, for that post and for others in the cathedral of Mexico that have been filled lately, Americans as well as Europeans have been considered, and His Majesty appointed the American Don Luis de Torres Tuñón.

Therefore, it is evident in these two orders that His Majesty opened the doors of the churches and the tribunals of Spain to his vassals from the Indies, demonstrating his paternal desire that they and his European vassals be considered equals. It is well known that since the two royal orders were issued, Americans have been considered and appointed as dignitaries. And lately the few Europeans in the Mexican cathedral chapter and other cathedrals of both Americas are conspicuous. So there is no rational or just reason for your communication, especially not for the complaints that figure in it. His Majesty orders me to make this known to you, and advise you that the efforts and care with which his generosity seeks the well-being, happiness, and security of his beloved American vassals deserve justice from the municipal council of Mexico City, not unfounded complaints. They deserve that recognition, love, and gratitude which has always been its [the council's] most glorious keynote and character.

 40

The Foundation of Nuestra Señora de Guadalupe de los Morenos de Amapa, Mexico

(1769)

In the following prologue to a parish register of baptisms (now among the manuscripts of the Zimmerman Library, University of New Mexico), part of the complex history of slavery and freedom for Americans of African descent in this colonial history can be glimpsed. Here, Licenciado Joseph Antonio Navarro, the priest of Nuestra Señora de Guadalupe de los Morenos de Amapa in northeastern Oaxaca, near the southern tip of Veracruz, Mexico, traces events that led to the recent founding of his town and parish. Amapa's residents were descended from *cimarrones,* runaway black slaves, who had taken refuge in the mountainous district of Teutila from the early seventeenth century. These cimarrones reputedly robbed travelers on the road to Córdoba, terrorized nearby valley settlements and sugar mills, and sowed rebellion among settled slaves.

The early colonial history of the Teutila district and this account of the establishment of Amapa in the late eighteenth century reveal a paradoxical combination of motives and responses to the cimarrón problem by Spanish authorities, which contributed to a growing free black population but not an egalitarian view of society. Colonial authorities' treatment of slaves and cimarrones in Mexico varied from exceedingly cruel punishment (including execution, castration, and amputation of hands and feet) to offers of freedom, property, and spiritual care in exchange for loyalty to the Crown and colonial laws. During the early seventeenth century, after punitive expeditions had failed, a policy of conciliation was favored. In 1630 the town of San Lorenzo Cerralvo near the Villa de Córdoba was established as a settlement for peaceable runaways, but few agreed to reside there, and sporadic raids and counterattacks followed. An intensification of unrest among slaves and cimarrones in the vicinity during the mid-eighteenth century led to more repression by colonial authorities. Abortive punitive expeditions by the Córdoba militia were launched in 1748 and 1750 to root out the cimarrones. Shortly thereafter, Teutila's *alcalde mayor,* or district governor appointed by the Crown, also failed in his attempt to negotiate a settlement in his district.

Although their guerrilla activities continued during the 1750s, the runaway slaves of the Teutila area apparently split into two factions: one willing to accept the Spanish offer of freedom and rights to a separate town; and the other preferring to oppose the Spaniards and continue a fugitive life in the mountains. An armed clash between the two factions ended with the victory of the pro-settlement chief, Fernando Manuel, and his followers. Eighteen of the opponents were turned over to their former masters and their leader was imprisoned. In 1762 a group of cimarrones from the Amapa area formally obtained their freedom after serving in the defense of the port of Veracruz against British attack. Finally, in 1767 an agreement was reached between the *alcalde mayor* of Teutila and the cimarrones for the establishment of a town and church services, and a declaration of freedom for its inhabitants. Some of the original settlers of the town of Amapa had been fugitives for as long as fifty years, but most had lived in mountain refuges of the Teutila district for less than eight years, having escaped masters from the Villa de Córdoba who operated sugar mills and plantations. By December 1767 land titles had been secured, boundary markers laid out, and houses and a church were under construction. (See Figure 29.) With this new town the colonial authorities had succeeded in incorporating a group of fugitives from colonial rule who had proven that they could not be subdued by force. (At least this was the idea. As the story behind and beyond that arresting portrait [Figure 18] of the black dons of Esmeraldas, Ecuador, in 1599 suggests, fairy-tale endings were unlikely for anyone in these circumstances.)

That a preoccupation with security underlay the colonial officials' willingness to grant privileges of freedom, municipal life, and spiritual salvation to the cimarrones is suggested by the duties and obligations to the Crown assumed by the *morenos* (dark ones) of Amapa. The townsmen of Amapa were obliged to take up arms in defense of the king of Spain and to undertake expeditions into the mountains every two months to capture runaway slaves and prevent the formation of new cimarrón colonies. The parish priest, identified as a peninsular Spaniard of pious intentions, admitted that "the principal motive" for the establishment of a parish at Amapa was the government's desire to form a *reducción*, or settlement, for more effective administration and law enforcement.

Here, Spanish officialdom found security and control to be compatible with more disinterested motives in dealing with runaway slaves. In 1750 the alcalde mayor saw two potential benefits from the foundation of a town: "The salvation of their souls would be facilitated by instruction in Christian doctrine, which they sorely lack; also the roads they used to terrorize would be safe to travel." In the priest's mind the impossible had been achieved at Amapa: "The Negroes are extremely happy in their town; the countryside is free from the outrages they perpetrated as vagabonds; sugar mill slaves are more secure in their servitude; the king has more soldiers in his service; and the salvation of these souls is more certain." The legal freedom obtained by Amapa's residents was not without strings, nor was it simply an act of Christian conscience. Practical, paternalistic, and religious considerations appear all at once, under the mutually celebrated protection of the Virgin Mary as Our Lady of Guadalupe, New Spain's official patroness since 1754.

Although Black slaves near the end of the colonial period were comparatively few in Mexico—reportedly fewer than 10,000, while Venezuela and Cuba each had more than 60,000, and Peru still had 90,000—the legacy of forced African immigration there since the sixteenth century was substantial. In the 1790s, 381,941 free Blacks and Mulattoes were counted (about 6 percent of the viceroyalty's population), most of them residing in highland mining and ranching districts of the north center and west, as did Miguel Hernández and Beatriz de Padilla over a century earlier (see Selections 19 and 28).

In order to trace the beginnings of runaway Negro slaves in the high mountains of Mazateopam whose consolidation into a town was the principal reason for the founding of this new parish of Nuestra Señora de Guadalupe de Amapa, it is necessary to recall that Negro slaves were brought to this kingdom shortly after the Conquest. According to the post-Conquest histories, Negroes were introduced to work the fields, mines, and sugar mills and to perform other onerous labor considered too strenuous for the weaker Indians. Royal law enacted to preserve the Indian population even prohibited the relocation of Indians in different climates in order to prevent illness.

Thus entered the Negroes, seedbed of the various castes that perverted the purity of the Indians—a painful thought. Disaffected with life in the mines, haciendas, and sugar mills, many slaves deserted their masters, forming small settlements in the mountains of Totula, Palmilla, Tumbacarretas, and Totolinga, presently in the jurisdiction of the illustrious Villa de Córdoba and Veracruz. They assaulted travelers, robbing them of their belongings. Under existing conditions they could not be contained or captured. As a result, residents of the town of San Andrés Huatuxco . . . in 1617 petitioned the viceroy, the Most Excellent Don Diego Fernández de Córdoba, Marqués de Guadalcázar, for permission to found the Villa de Córdoba. The following year, 1618, the villa was established, bearing the viceroy's family name. The founding is described by the parish priest of the said villa, Doctor Don José Antonio Rodríguez Valero, in his sacred historical treatise published in Mexico in the year 1759.

Various measures were attempted to dislodge and subjugate the cimarrones. Since force alone proved inadequate, a policy of forbearance was applied with the thought that by winning the affection of the cimarrones the difficulties could be more easily overcome. . . . The cimarrones were offered their freedom on the condition that they come together in a permanent settlement and parish so as not to lack the spiritual nourishment of which they were deprived in such a licentious and dissolute life. The majority of the runaways accepted the offer. The town of San Lorenzo Cerralvo was founded a considerable distance from the said Villa between 1630 and 1635 during the viceregency of the Marqués de Cerralvo, after whom it was named.

Suspicious of this settlement, a band of Negroes continued to roam the highlands of Mazateopam, venturing into the valleys and sugar mills from time to time to plunder travelers, arouse the slaves, and even carry off women from the small, isolated communities. Taking advantage of the cover afforded by the palenques [protected upland refuges], slaves frequently fled from their masters, continually venturing back in surprise attacks. After considerable expense and effort it was at last sadly realized that the cimarrones could not be subdued by force. On the contrary, armed sorties into the mountains in pursuit of the cimarrones only gave them more reason for revenge to the detriment of the sugar mills, travelers, and the inhabitants of the entire region.

In the years 1725 and 1735 there were slave revolts in the above-mentioned sugar mills of the Villa de Córdoba. In 1725 the greater part of the area in the direction of Xalitatuani to the banks of the Quetzalapa River in this jurisdiction of

Teutila was involved. A large number of slaves fled; some were captured; others escaped deep into the mountains of Mazateopam where they joined the long-established cimarrones, as José de Padilla, Marqués de Guardiola, former alcalde mayor, told me and described in a written account. In 1735 the region was menaced by a nearly general uprising. If the dragoons from the plaza of Veracruz and the provincial militia had not arrived in time to subdue the runaways before they penetrated deep into the mountains and procured arms, the result would have been grievous. As it was, not all were returned to slavery. Many disappeared into the palenques where their comrades were hiding. With the ranks of the cimarrones thus expanded, vigilance had to be increased day by day. The available means were not sufficient to contain or diminish their forays, which resulted in widespread damage.

In 1748 two punitive expeditions into the mountains of Mazateopam were attempted by the militia. One was directed by Don Gabriel de Segura, Don Bernardo de Zeballos, Don Miguel de Leiba Esparragoza, and Don Vicente Tapia; the other in the direction of Xalitatuani was led by Captain Don Nicolás Carvaxal Castillo de Altra. Both efforts failed miserably. In 1750 two more expeditions were undertaken with the same result. Don Andrés de Otañes, alcalde mayor of Teutila, realizing the futility of these attempts, decided to engage in talks with the said Negroes. He met with the captain and some of his comrades on the banks of the Quetzalapa River two leagues from the town of Zoyaltepec and persuaded them to establish a town to facilitate the salvation of their souls through instruction in Christian doctrine. . . . The result would be that the cimarrones would no longer be persecuted and the roads would be free from their frequent attacks. The alcalde mayor offered his complete support for this Christian purpose. He stipulated only that the unanimous consent of the runaway slaves living in the highlands be secured. This seemed agreeable to the leaders, who returned to the mountains to tell their comrades of the proposal, promising to return with a reply. Viceroy Revilla Gigedo was informed of the talks, but for the moment nothing resulted.

In 1750 at this stage in the negotiations another punitive expedition by the militia was made on behalf of the sugar mill owners. The Negroes now became suspicious of the promises made by alcalde mayor Otañes, for they did not return with the reply. They undoubtedly believed that he intended to bait them with deception. From 1750 to 1760 the region experienced various incursions at the expense of the mill owners and travelers. Meanwhile the Negroes had divided into two groups. Some, who were less distrustful, joined the party seeking the formation of a town; others continued to oppose the Spanish proposal. The cimarrones' course of action was decided by formal combat. The part against a settlement was led by Captain Macute, longtime chief of the cimarrones. Fernando Manuel, Macute's lieutenant, headed the other group. Fernando Manuel acknowledged that before firing his guns he made a fervent plea to Nuestra Señora de Guadalupe, humbly seeking protection for the success of his Christian purpose. From that moment he designated her Patroness and Guardian of the town which would be founded by his followers, an admirable recognition for such uncivilized people, worthy of envy by the most enlightened and zealous [Christian]. God allowed that

Fernando Manuel be rewarded with victory over his opponents. He gravely wounded Captain Macute; and after killing many others, he captured eighteen of those still living who were brought to the Villa de Córdoba, where they were turned over to their respective masters. Captain Macute today is still imprisoned in the Córdoba jail. . . .

Having done this, the said Fernando Manuel went to the Hacienda de la Estanzuela where he encountered the owner, Don Fernando Carlos de Rivadeneyra, and Bachiller Don Apolinar de Cosio, his administrator and chaplain. Fernando Manuel sought their protection in establishing the town. Whether or not they agreed to do so cannot be determined because shortly thereafter both men died. The cimarrones settled at sites known as Palacios, Breva Corina, and Mandinga, belonging to the hacienda. These settlements were located near the summit of the mountain leading to the palenques as an escape route should they be pursued. In 1762, on advice given to them, the cimarrones went down to the plaza of Veracruz where they presented themselves to the Most Excellent Viceroy Marqués de Cruillas. They offered to serve the viceroyalty in the current war with Great Britain and requested that he grant them their freedom in exchange. Undoubtedly he agreed, for they were incorporated into the corps of lancers, as we know from the document appointing Fernando Manuel sergeant, authorized by Don Santiago Cubillos, infantry captain. When peace was achieved they returned to their settlements to live with their customary distrust, for they could find no one to protect their communities and they had lost the decree signed by the Marqués de Cruillas. At the same time a suit initiated by the mill owners was pending, which threatened the Negroes' freedom and their town. The mill owners lost the case for lack of a sound legal base. However, the records of this case were maliciously jumbled or abridged on behalf of the mill owners.

In 1767, when Andrés de Otañes was again serving as alcalde mayor of Teutila, the Negroes appeared before him in the town of Zoyaltepec. Remembering the proposal of 1750, he offered to support them in the declaration of freedom and founding of the town. The cimarrones readily agreed . . . and this became the fundamental basis for the good fortune they later experienced. The proposal for founding the town was formalized in a written document relating their former occupations and residence; designating the land where the town would be located . . . ; and fervently imploring the protection of the most illustrious Señor Doctor Don Francisco Fabián y Fuero, most dignified bishop of this bishopric. The bishop, upon whom they depended for judgment and pastoral zeal, joyfully complied. The alcalde mayor ordered that various judicial formalities be carried out and informed the Most Excellent Viceroy Marqués de Croix of the proceedings. An agent was appointed on behalf of the Negroes to expedite the petition. Reports were gathered by various ministers; and finally, on January 12, a decree signed by the señor fiscal [the high court's legal adviser] Don Juan Antonio Velarde C. and the señor asesor [special adviser to the court] Don Diego Cornide declared a list of cimarrones and others still living in the palenques liberated from servitude and perpetually exempt from paying the royal tribute. The decree further granted them the power to found a town in the appointed location and obligated them to destroy completely the runaway bands of Mazateopam; to take up arms in the service of king and country whenever called; to capture henceforth those Negro slaves who fled from their masters with a reward of twenty-five pesos each; to prevent the formation of other marauding bands; to go into the mountains every two months to verify that no bands had formed; to live in obedience to the Royal Justice of Teutila; and to name alcaldes and regidores to govern the community. . . .

On February 5 of the said year a dispatch was drawn up directing Don Andrés de Otañes to oversee the establishment of the town and apportionment of lands. I, Don José Antonio Navarro, native of the city of Valencia in the Spanish kingdoms, was selected for the spiritual guidance of the community. . . . On May 3, accompanied by the alcalde mayor and the Negroes, I went to survey this location known as Amapa. The site chosen is a gently sloping hill formerly occupied by a Mulatto Juan González and his wife Manuela Rodríguez, both natives of the port town of Tamiagua in the jurisdiction of Guauchinango. González was employed in cultivating corn and cotton, carrying travelers across the Amapa River in his canoe, and defending the area against attack by cimarrones. This was a favorite spot for their ambushes. The hill was chosen for its supply of potable water, healthful winds, proximity to the highway, and access to the Amapa River.

On May 6 a town meeting was held at which alcaldes, regidores, and other community officials were elected and presented with the trappings of magistrates. Immediately thereafter the locations of the church and houses were designated. The alcalde mayor ordered that materials be secured for the buildings as soon as possible, to which the Negroes agreed. The alcalde mayor returned to the town of Zoyaltepec and I returned to the Hacienda de la Estanzuela.

On May 31, Don Miguel Rodríguez de la Vega, alcalde mayor of Córdoba, brought an order at the instance of the mill owners to suspect the establishment of the new town. For reasons totally unfounded in fact, it was asserted that the town should be established at Mata del Agua, located between the exposed areas of Totolinga and San Campuz. The order was promptly obeyed. A document opposing the settlement at Mata del Agua was then submitted on behalf of the Negroes, which the mill owners tried to refute with arguments of more bulk than substance. It should be noted here that alcalde mayor Otañes, realizing that further delays would revive the Negroes' distrust, resolved to begin construction at the townsite. At Amapa on August 30 he was joined by the Negroes who had come down from their huts at the edge of the mountains. With the help of more than 125 local Indians, who worked on a rotating basis for a week at a time, the church was begun. On September 17 the church was ready for celebration of the first Mass, which I performed with a happy throng of assistants and communicants. Construction of public offices and private dwellings for the Negroes was then begun along streets laid out in straight lines. As a whole it was a very pleasing sight and in time will be the most resplendent town in the lowlands. The viceroy approved the entire proceeding and extended his congratulations for the efficacy and devotion with which this important matter was carried out. On October 19 the matter of the mill owners' opposition was resolved. In a strongly worded order their petition was denied and the completion of the town approved. The mill owners subsequently failed in an appeal to the Audiencia. The Audiencia refused jurisdiction since the Negroes, as soldiers, were subject to the captaincy general.

On December 5 possession of the land was finalized and boundary markers were set out. The Negroes are extremely happy in their town; the countryside is free from the outrages they perpetrated as vagabonds; the plantation slaves are more secure in their servitude; the king has more soldiers in his service; and the salvation of these souls is more certain. In this, the impossible has been conquered without staining the endeavor with human blood; accomplished in the felicitous and just reign of Our Catholic Monarch Charles III (May God protect him many years!), being Viceroy the most excellent Señor Marqués de Croix, Knight and Comendador de Molinos y Laguna Rota of the Order of Calatrava and Lieutenant General of the Royal Armies, and being Bishop the Most Illustrious Señor Don Francisco Fabián de Fuero. The establishment of this town has not been carried out at the expense of Your Majesty or any other person. The undertaking was supervised and paid for by the said Don Andrés Fernández de Otañes. It seemed opportune to me to recount this as an introduction to this book [the baptismal record of Amapa] so it may serve as a monument to posterity. . . .

Plan of Amapa (1769–70)

Alcalde mayor Andrés Fernández de Otañes, sponsor of Amapa in its first years, had a plan of the town and surroundings (Figure 29) prepared to commemorate its founding. His sense of himself in the project and his vision of its future are apparent in this image and his ebullient description of the place. Here the neatly ordered grid plan of the pueblo dwarfs the landscape, as it never would have done in fact. The little community of twenty-two adults centers on an ample plaza about 200 feet across, defined by the church and eight houses with modest arcades, two of them reserved for the priest and the town office. A road linking Amapa to the Villa de Córdoba and the Indian pueblo of Zoyaltepec enters on the open north side of the plaza and turns off to the west. The plan shows room for expansion of the settlement on a plain bounded by rivers, pasturelands, and woods arranged in orchard-like rows.

Writing in February 1770 of "this great work of settling the Blacks in their own pueblo," the alcalde mayor described the site as "agreeable, even delicious, in a hot climate well suited to this type of people, very healthful and good for raising maize, cotton, vanilla, and other crops—better than other places that do not enjoy these advantages—and with ready access to various towns, which will facilitate commerce." Fernández de Otañes wrote of the good order of the town and the civil life to which the once-naked residents were growing accustomed in their elections, new clothes, farms, and the "yoke" of Christianity. In the town itself he was especially proud of the church, with its freestanding bell-tower and two "beautiful" bells. This wooden structure with a fine thatched roof was more than 75 feet long and 25 feet wide. The high altar displayed painted images of Our Lady of Guadalupe (patroness of the new community and personal protectress of Fernando Manuel, who had led the struggle to make peace with the colonial government and settle at Amapa), Saint Joseph (the Virgin's husband), and Saint Carlos Borromeo (in honor of the reigning king of Spain, Charles III). Facing each other near the altar were a portrait of King Charles and his coat of arms, with inscriptions noting that the foundation of the town was accomplished under the protection and at the expense

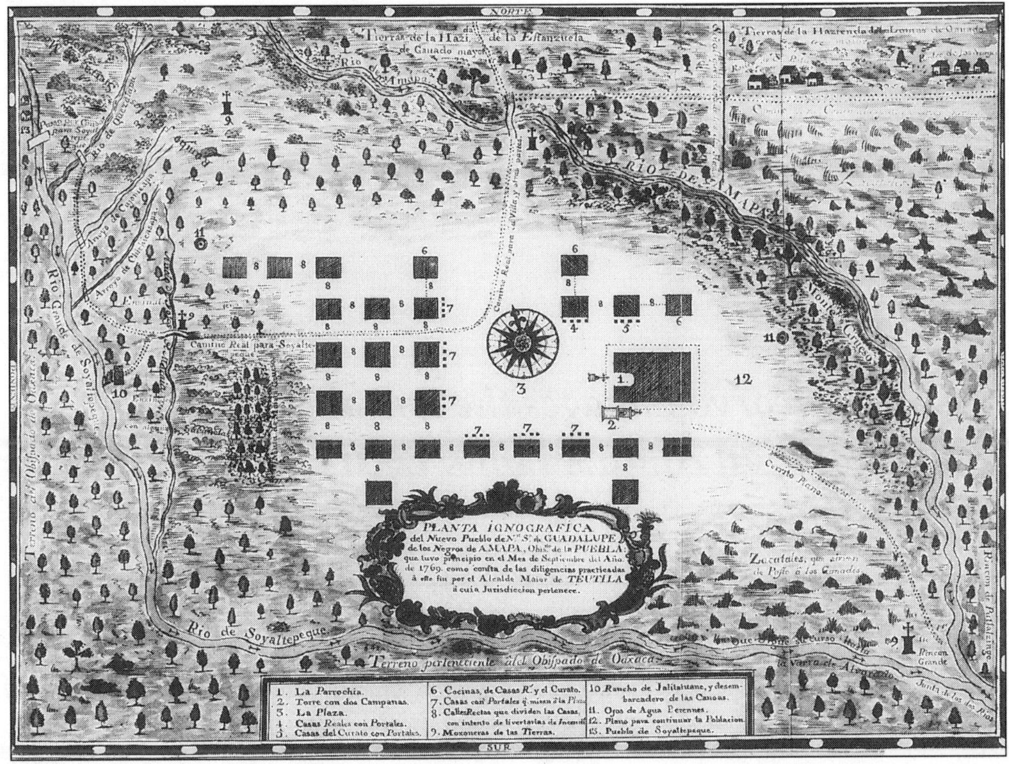

Figure 29. Plan of Nuestra Señora de Guadalupe de los Negros de Amapa, Mexico, 1769–70.
Courtesy of the Archivo General de la Nación, Mexico City.

of Alcalde Mayor Fernández de Otañes. All of the paintings were housed in fine gold frames, he added.

Six years later, the original settlers were still in place, quite contented despite the difficulty of tilling land laced with tree roots, but a different alcalde mayor and interim priest took a dimmer view of the town and its citizens. The priest lamented their drunkenness and torpor, especially when it came to serving the church. The alcalde mayor wanted the town disbanded because the settlers showed little fear or respect for his authority (which he exercised from the distant head town of Teutila); they harbored Indians, *castas* (people of mixed racial ancestry), and military fugitives from Veracruz, usurped lands from a neighboring Indian community, and failed to pay tribute or personally submit their annual elections for his confirmation. They lived, he said, "in complete independence and the pueblo is nothing more that a Castle from which they sally forth to commit outrages."

The viceroy and his legal adviser rejected this 1776 proposal to disband the settlement. The likelihood that the residents of Amapa would return to their mountain refuge and raids weighed heavily in the decision, but the viceroy's adviser also noted that most of the alcalde mayor's complaints were without foundation. The people of Amapa, he noted, had been granted extended relief from the tribute tax and sacramental fees. Moreover, they were only required to submit their election results to the alcalde mayor's lieutenant who lived nearer to their town, and there was no prohibition on non-Blacks settling there if they wished. Nuestra Señora de Guadalupe de los Morenos de Amapa prevailed, at least for the time being.

41

Concolorcorvo Engages the Postal Inspector about Indian Affairs, Lima, Peru

(1776)

In 1776 a book of travels in Argentina, Paraguay, Bolivia, and Peru began to circulate in Peru. In it, a royal inspector of the postal service, Alonso Carrió de la Vandera, and his Indian assistant, Don Calixto Bustamante Carlos Inca, alias Concolorcorvo or "Mr. Inca," described and reflected on what they encountered along the way. Presented as if it had been written by Concolorcorvo and published in Spain in 1773 by the La Rovada ("Something Stolen") Press, it was, in fact, the work of Carrió, fresh off the press of an unidentified Lima printer. Carrió had made this arduous tour across nearly three thousand miles of often forbidding terrain during nineteen months beginning in November 1771.

Born about 1716, Carrió spent most of his life in America, going first to Mexico about 1736 and then to Peru ten years later as a trader. He settled in Lima where he married and entered a series of second-level government appointments in 1750, interrupted in 1762 by service in a cavalry regiment of distinguished citizens of Lima against pirates on the coast of Peru. In early 1771 he received the appointment to inspect the mail service between Buenos Aires and Lima and expected it to be his springboard to some prestigious permanent office in the viceregal capital. But his report and recommendations were ignored by the armchair director of the mail service, and a long, bitter, and ultimately fruitless complaint by Carrió to the viceroy ensued. *El lazarillo de ciegos caminantes,* in the form of a dialogue, was Carrió's way of presenting his side of the dispute without openly offending his superiors (other than the director of the mail service). The postal inspector speaks abundantly, but not as the author, and the printed pages appear as if they came from a different time and place—Spain in 1773, at the end of the inspector's tour, rather than Lima in 1776, when Carrió had lost patience with the formal channels of appeal.

El lazarillo de ciegos caminantes is often described as a satirical work. The author's mocking and ironical wit peeks through in every chapter and dominates several, but who and what were being mocked? If Carrió was angered by the dismissive reception of his efforts as postal inspector, as he must have been, his anger did not turn into a subversive critique of Spanish rule or Bourbon designs for commercial and political reform. His occasional irreverent criticism of Spanish governors in America could be used by others to justify self-righteous rebellion (as could Felipe Guaman Poma de Ayala's forgotten exposé of

Spanish abuses almost two centuries earlier; see Selection 25), but Carrió himself remains a Spaniard in his predilections and prejudices, and something of a super Bourbon.

Ancient Rome and Greece were in vogue in the neoclassical high culture of Bourbon Spain, and Carrió did not miss the opportunity to draw in a story about Alexander the Great and Darius. "Progress" in terms of civilization and commerce was one of his watchwords, as it was for Bourbon policymakers under Charles III. Ever the advocate of improved communications and circulation of goods, Carrió lamented the opportunities missed by Spanish merchants to tap the rich Indian markets and incorporate Indian trade into the imperial economy. His advice to would-be traders in the Indian markets was: learn the ways of Indian petty commerce and apply them, patiently, to sales and profit.

In this chapter on Indian affairs, Carrió had his caustic fun at the expense of virtually everyone except the king. He could be critical of Spaniards' mistreatment of Indians, but he was no Las Casas—no defender of Indian rights on ethical grounds, and certainly not as a reason to question Spaniards' right to rule in America. He recognized different kinds of Indians (his evolutionary categories were much like those of José de Acosta; see Selection 18), but he kept returning to their fundamental barbarity. In their natural state, he concluded, Indians were violators of the Ten Commandments, not innocents. He excused Spaniards from corrupting Indians with their sins, including drunkenness, because such sins were already present "twice over" in ancient America. The Spanish conquerors' failure as rulers was that they "governed themselves [and Indians] according to the custom of the land," not that they behaved as tyrants.

Even when Mr. Inca invites the postal inspector to speak positively about Indians' courage and industry, the response veers off to their cowardice and ineptitude and the foolhardly arrogance of Aztec and Inca leaders. His respect for Indian fighters of Chile and the Chaco region turns into a backhanded compliment, for their fierce cunning becomes another sign of extreme barbarity, subject to no law, ruled by their passions rather than the genteel light of reason.

Like a good reformer, Carrió had some solutions to the problem of Indian barbarity. The subject of "Indian affairs" meant to him subjugation or removal. For settled Indians—the "less crude" who "live from their plantings and livestock"—his answer was to promote mass education in the Spanish language, the civilized tongue of empire. This solution offered him an opportunity to criticize Catholic priests as pastors, a favorite target of Bourbon administrators. He attributed the spotty development of Spanish among Indians to the self-interest of parish priests, with a special swipe at the recently expelled Jesuits who, he claimed, kept Indians in ignorance in order to control them better.

With implacable Indian adversaries on the frontiers, "there is no other way . . . than firm defense and thinning them out with our growing numbers." Carrió was particularly enthusiastic about the string of new *presidios* (fortified garrisons) in northern New Spain that, he said, had transformed Nueva Vizcaya from "forsaken plains" into a zone of bustling towns and trade. (But in Carrió's world of original sin, even this advent of civilization did not bring a simple resolution to disorder. The great landowner, the Conde de San Pedro del Alamo, discovered that Indian incursions had been replaced by the prejudicial conduct of "the multitude of Mestizos and Spaniards who lived off his properties.") Towns and forts, forts and towns: Christian missions are notably absent from this vision of a frontier Indian policy.

There are eighteenth-century twists that emphasize state reforms and commerce and mute the importance of Church and religion, but Carrió told a familiar colonial story of civilization approximated versus barbarism in the extreme. If not a premonition of the Túpac Amaru rebellion of 1780–1783 (see Selections 43 and 47), this panorama of South American life by a longtime resident of Peru at least suggests deep doubts by those who thought of themselves as Spaniards about their ability to control Indians of any kind.

"The first charge I would make against the parish priests [said the postal inspector, or *visitador*] is that they have not thrown themselves into the task of incorporating the Spanish language into their religious instruction. It is only these ministers of doctrine who can achieve this desirable result because the corregidores who are sent out to govern thirty pueblos for five years at a time—often for only two years—have neither the time nor resources to find a way toward something so useful to religion and the State. The parish priests' assistants, who are usually ordained as Indian-language priests and have the most contact with Indians, do not want them to speak anything but their native language. The few Indians who want to express themselves in Spanish are berated for doing so and mocked as degree-holders and men of letters, as the current and most worthy bishop of La Paz confessed to me. These circumstances retard any great progress in the Spanish language.

"The Jesuits, who for 150 years were the principal teachers, pursued a strategy prejudicial to the State by trying to keep the Indians from any contact with Spaniards and limit them to their native language, which they [the Jesuits] understood very well. I make no attempt to defend or attack their principles since they have already been expelled. I need only refer to the general points which their disciples and successors follow. Those good fathers asserted that when Indians had contact with Spaniards and learned their language, they became infected and tangled up in enormous vices that they could not even have imagined before. There is no doubt that these ministers of the Gospel spoke in bad faith about this because all of the accounts written at the beginning of the Conquest describe many abominations that the Spaniards themselves had never imagined (as I recounted earlier). So, these Spaniards can only be held responsible for making the Indians confess in their languages the enormity of their sin and abominate it, such as eating human flesh, sacrificing prisoners of war to their gods, worshiping various monsters or logs shaped into a horrendous figure, and often poisonous insects.

"The polygamy and incest permitted under their laws were not practiced by Spaniards, nor was intercourse between males, which was very common among Indians, as can still be seen among those who have not been conquered. The sixth, seventh, and eighth of the Ten Commandments were and are so commonly violated, as they are among Spaniards and every other nation in the world, that one can infer that they [Spaniards] did not introduce any sin into this kingdom that was not already present twice over. As for swearing, the Indians know how to say Supaypaguagua, which means son of the Devil, which would have offended God in this language as much as in any other, unless one assumes that God only understands Spanish and only punishes those who offend Him in that language. Drunkenness was more widespread among the [ancient] Indians than anywhere else in the world. Spaniards appear to be guilty only of having introduced a more potent version in the form of spirits and wine.

"The parish priests will do a great service to God, the king, and the Indians by eliminating Indian languages from their teaching and replacing them with Spanish, making their assistants responsible and ordering their native constables to carry it out. The corregidores, their lieutenants and accountants, and everyone else passing through their parishes will derive great benefit because the Indians, on the grounds of not understanding Spanish, fail to understand many things, which leads to disputes, unfortunate arguments, and Indian crudities."

"No, for the love of God," I said to him. "Don't leave without saying something about what you mean by their courage and industry."

"As for the former," he said, "they are like greyhounds—in a group they are capable of attacking a lion, but alone they can hardly come up with a hare. Just draw a drop of their blood and they're said to be dead; and in the greatest uprising, unless they are drunk, if they see one of their own struck down dead, the rest will flee even if they outnumber us fifty to one."

"That's why so few Spaniards conquered over seven million Indians," I replied.

"You understand very little, Mr. Inca," the visitador said to me. "The conquest of a civilized kingdom with the loss of control over its inhabitants, which is not aided by other rulers, is achieved with two or three victories on the battlefield, especially if its leaders are killed or captured. The Spaniards, with the defeat of the Otumba army, earned a reputation for courage but they also showed the Indians that they were mortal and vulnerable, like their horses. But with the capture of Mexico City, aided by the Tlaxcalan nobles, they subjected that great empire of more than forty million souls because thereafter every prince, general, or petty lord swore his allegiance out of fear of being attacked and ruined.

"If Darius had opposed Alexander the Great with 50,000 men and one or two good generals, even if he had been defeated, his officers could have gathered at least 20,000 men and Alexander would have had no more than 4,000 or 5,000, and he would have had to use some of them to guard the prisoners and equipment. Darius could have attacked him a second, third, fourth, and fifth time with his remaining army, tiring out Alexander's valiant troops and reducing them in the engagements and strategic garrisons he could capture. But Darius attacked as if victory over Alexander was assured, and not as a fighter. He thought Alexander would be frightened by his powerful, disciplined army and the size and trumpeting of his elephants. With this confidence he entered the battle and in one day he lost a great empire and his life, while his conqueror made off with his treasures, his wife, and his daughters.

"The Chileans knew better how to deal with the Spaniards. Observing that they had always been defeated when their numbers were four times greater, and even many times when they outnumbered them one hundred to one, they changed their plan and mode of combat. They judged the Spaniards more skillful and courageous than themselves, and in possession of better weapons, but they also knew that they were mortal and subject to human frailties. So they undertook to engage them in combat repeatedly until they overcame them and forced them back to their trenches with the loss of some settlements. These reflections show that a large but poorly led army of 200,000 men—even veteran soldiers, if the generals are inexperienced—can be defeated and put to flight by 30,000 well-disciplined soldiers led by wise and courageous chiefs. But these subjects are beyond our conversation and talent, so tell me, Mr. Inca, whether you have more to say or ask about your countrymen."

"Well, I wonder why the Spaniards, who conquered and subjected seven million Indians to their ways, are unable to subject the Indians of the Chaco region and those of the mountains?"

"That question would more appropriately be asked of one of your Inca and chiefly ancestors. But since they have given their account to God for their actions, for good or ill, I will take the trouble to defend them, as well as to disabuse some Spaniards who think the Chaco can be conquered with a well-ordered militia of 1,000 men led by good officers, and that the same result can be achieved in the mountains with the same number more. Of course, I confess that this number of men, at considerable expense, could move through the various provinces and territories. But the barbarous Indians, who have no formal settlements or cultivated fields, would change their locations. They will mock the vain efforts of the Spaniards who, being unable to fortify their strongholds, would abandon them, enabling the Indians to return at their pleasure, at considerable cost to us, as you judiciously observed in your opening thought.

"By barbarous people I mean those who are not subject to laws or magistrates, who in the end live by their own devices, always following their passions. This is the nature of the Indians on the pampas [of Argentina and Uruguay] and the inhabitants of the Chaco. In New Spain, seeing the impossibility of subjecting the barbarous Indians who occupied the forsaken plains of central Nueva Vizcaya [in northern Mexico], including more than one hundred leagues of the royal road leading to the valley of San Bartolomé del Parral, the Spaniards built four presidios twenty-five leagues apart garrisoned with fifty soldiers each and the appropriate officers. The soldiers were to be married and young enough to bear children. Each month they accompanied the great mule trains to the next presidio. The mule train that did not arrive at the next link in the chain by the third day of the month had to wait nearby until the following month. The muleteers were left to their own devices to find safe and fertile pasturage. For this escort no fee was collected because the officers and soldiers were and must be well paid by the king. The soldiers of the first three presidios did not deviate more than two leagues to the left or right from their route to guard the surrounding territory where their horses grazed. But in the fertile and delightful valley of San Bartolomé where a large town by the same name is located, a mobile company is located which goes out in groups to reconnoiter the countryside at a considerable distance, under orders not to engage the Indians unless victory is assured. In case they encountered a large number of Indians together, they were to note the location and advise all the presidios and militiamen so that together they could engage and disperse them with minimal losses.

"Rarely did they take prisoners, and they did not often allow any barbarous Indian into the presidios because the soldiers said that they were good for nothing but eating their bread and robbing their horses if any trust was placed in them. The presidios were not even twenty years old, and they already consisted of a large population of Mestizos and Spaniards of both sexes, with cultivated fields and pastures for livestock. The rural presidio in one place grew so much that the Conde de San Pedro del Alamo, whose great estates were nearby, asked the government to move it or close it down because it was no longer useful in that place since there were no more Indian incursions; and, in any case, Indian incursions were less prejudicial to him than the multitude of Mestizos and Spaniards who lived off his properties. Finally, he wanted them ordered to devote themselves to clearing the countryside and escorting the mule trains—which would save the royal treasury 12,000 pesos a year, the cost to His Majesty of providing for those presidios—on the condition that as those areas were populated and the hostile Indians removed, they, too, would advance. The Conde achieved his aim, and perhaps now not a single presidio exists in that vast region, replaced by many towns of varying sizes, according to the greater or lesser fertility of the land and presence of watering places, for Nueva Vizcaya is a very sterile land. I am going to conclude this point with a notorious public event in Nueva Vizcaya.

"It concerns a certain captain of the mobile company, whose first name I don't remember but whose last name was Berroterán, whom the barbarous Indians called Perroterán. [Changing the "B" to "P" makes the first part of the captain's surname mean "dog."] He was frequently deceived by the promises they made him, for he followed the pious maxim of our kings, who repeatedly ordered that peace be granted to Indians who requested it, even if it was in the heat of battle and they were about to be defeated. They were confident of the generosity of our laws, and he, I say again, having been repeatedly deceived by these infidels, resolved to make war on them without quarter. So, when the Indians asked for peace [*paz*], the good Cantabrian would construe it as bread [*pan*], replying that he would take some for himself and his soldiers. He attacked them with such vigor that he terrified them and forced them out of that entire territory. As the story goes, at the hour of his death, the priest who was helping him to achieve a good death asked him if he repented of having killed so many Indians. He responded that he only regretted having left behind on Earth a rabble lacking in religion, faith, and law, that he thought only of their treachery and deceptions and way of life at the cost of trouble to the Spaniards and the sweat of the civilized Indians. What is certain is that there is no other way to deal with the barbarous Indians than firm defense and thinning them out with our growing numbers. In New Mexico, which is eight hundred leagues from the capital, the Spaniards maintain themselves in a small number, under the command of a governor, among a multitude of enemy nations without taking sides beyond asking the conquering nation to pardon the remnants of the defeated army that sought their protection. With this maxim they make themselves feared and loved by those barbarians who are less crude than those of the pampas and inhabitants of the Chaco."

"From all of this I take it that you regard the Indians as civil people" [remarked Concolorcorvo].

"If you are speaking of the Indians subject to the emperors of Mexico and Peru and their laws, whether good or bad, I say that they have been and are civil, that they are the most obedient nation to their superiors that exists in the world. From the Chichas to the Piuranos, I observed their way of governing. They are assiduously obedient, whether to the regidor, who assumes the duties of constable, up to the corregidor. They live from their plantings and livestock without aspirations to wealth even if they have had some opportunities through the discoveries of mines and tombs. They are content with a little assistance for their fiestas and drinking parties. Some attribute this timidity to concern that the Spaniards will despoil them of those treasures, which usually are imaginary or depend, as in the silver and gold mines, on the industry of many men and great expense. The Spaniards would be delighted if the Indians were rich so they could trade with them and enjoy part of their wealth. But the sad fact is that in the greatest Indian market, which is that of Cocharcas [in highland Bolivia], where over two thousand Indians gather from various provinces, one does not see anyone buying even a real's worth of goods from a Spaniard because they do not like their stinginess. So they go to the Indian women merchants who have the patience to sell them a muleteer's need for a quarter of a real, a bit of string, and so on. The Spaniards' commerce is made among themselves, including the fluctuating numbers of Mestizos and other Castas who are outside the sphere of the Indians. The rare Indian who gathers some wealth is esteemed by the Spaniards, who offer him their goods and gladly offer terms, and do not disdain trade with them and invite them to their tables.

"No Spaniard is capable of deceiving an Indian, and if a Spaniard takes something from an Indian by force, he is pursued in the courts until his dying day. This does not lead me to say (as I have already noted) that there are no tyrannies among them, that they [Spaniards] cannot be regarded as tyrants—since [tyrannies] have a reciprocal basis—because of the bad foundation laid by the first conquerors, who governed themselves according to the custom of the land."

42

Parish Priests and Indian Resistance in Late Colonial Mexico

WILLIAM B. TAYLOR

In Selection 33, Serge Gruzinski writes that "the Indians were no more than consumers of juridical, economic, and ecclesiastical documents drawn up by the colonizers. They never had the opportunity to create and draft whole texts themselves." The Otomí document that Gruzinski discusses is unusual as an Indian-made whole text. (It is not unique: the Maya Books of Chilam Balam, Techialoyan manuscripts, and other "primordial titles" from central Mexico, the Huarochirí Manuscript, and Felipe Guaman Poma de Ayala's report to the king also come to mind as "Indian texts" composed in the colonial period.) But there is another very large body of written records in which Indians were neither just consumers nor sole authors. It is the petitions, judicial complaints, and other litigation records on a variety of subjects that were initiated and often crafted by Indians with the aid of an urban lawyer, supplemented by supporting documentation and the testimony of witnesses. These litigation records are another facet of the power of the written word in colonial Indian history that complicates Gruzinski's attention to subjection and crystallization of thought.

Complaints over ecclesiastical fees—one kind of judicial record generated in great number by Indian petitioners of central Mexico—offer a window onto the relationships of parish priests and native parishioners in the late colonial period. In the following essay, William Taylor describes an especially long record of litigation over fees for the parish of Ozoloapan, Mexico, that began in the 1760s and was closely tied to a new *arancel* (schedule of fees payable only in cash, to which parish priests were entitled). The essay begins to relate this series of disputes to a wider history of priests in their parishes, the politics of religion under the Bourbons, and Indians under Spanish rule.

The Ozoloapan disputes occurred as the Crown was moving to extend its authority over the state religion and church, redefining a narrower role for parish priests as spiritual specialists and completing the "secularization" of parishes, that is, placing them under diocesan priests rather than members of the regular orders who were less subject to royal supervision. The Jesuits were expelled from Spanish territories in 1767, the year of the new arancel, and "regalist" bishops who accepted subordination to royal authorities and embraced many of the Bourbon reforms were arriving from Spain as administrators of key American dioceses.

This arancel became a green light for complaints by Indian villagers against priests who demanded labor service (see Selection 39 for another Bourbon initiative to change labor relations) and other customary charges. But the judicial disputes that ensued were almost always more than contests over the tender matter of how a pastor could earn his living and whether labor service was required. They had to do with changing the place of the priest in public life, local strivings for power (whether among ambitious Indians in the community, a subordinate village against its head town, a district governor or hacienda owner against a priest, or villagers against their pastor), and expressions of local autonomy.

Indians in these disputes expressed their opposition in ways that were neither antireligious nor anticlerical. Their actions expressed both self-government and subordination to colonial rule through intermediaries. But the disputes touched off by the arancel of 1767 could be more unsettling than Bourbon lawmakers and judges seemed to recognize in their bland pronouncements for all parties to obey it. The Crown's intention was to reduce the volume of litigation and establish a "fixed rule" in place of the welter of customary practices and petty disagreements. But the result was fiercer conflict, new estrangements, more litigation, and manipulations of the arancel by parishioners and priests in ways that undermined the "fixed rule."

The relations between parish priests (*curas*) and their Indian parishioners are a richly documented subject for the history of religion and politics in colonial Spanish America. From the beginning of Spanish colonization, curas were royal appointees, located at sensitive intersections between Indian subjects and higher authorities. In the Hapsburg conception of the state, which envisioned two majesties—the Crown as father and the Church as mother—no clear line divided secular and religious life. Until the mid-eighteenth century an energetic cura might operate quite freely as keeper of public order and morals, punishing adulterers, gamblers, and drunkards, and reporting more serious offenses to royal judges. He and his assistants (*vicarios*) also were expected to report to viceroys and other royal officials on agricultural conditions, natural disasters, local disturbances, and other political news; record the population; supervise the annual elections of officers in communities within the parish; and help maintain order in other ways. He could be a patron in times of illness and want. As a moral and spiritual father and healer, and a literate local resident often able to speak the native language of his parishioners, the cura was well placed to represent the requirements of the state to rural people and interpret their obligations, as well as to intercede for them with higher authorities.

One protracted dispute, between the priests and Indian parishioners of Ozoloapan, Mexico, from 1767 to 1776—an important juncture in the high politics of church and state—can serve to illustrate some of the complexity of village Indian resistance and accommodation to colonial pressures in the eighteenth century. The Ozoloapan dispute, which centered on the fees and services that the parish priest could properly collect for baptisms, marriages, funerals, blessings, and the like, was also understood by all its participants to involve his wider authority to direct the public life of the parish. The two priests who served at Ozoloapan over the dispute's nine-year course repeatedly complained about the Indians' refusal to pay the proper fees and perform the customary services, and their disrespect for clerical authority. The Indians, for their part, complained that the priests were behaving oppressively by imposing excessive fees and using unwarranted violence. Both parties appealed to colonial superiors, especially the Audiencia (the high court in Mexico City), to define the limits of colonial authority and local autonomy within the parish.

Located on the temperate-to-hot western edge of the mining district of Temascaltepec and Sultepec, today in southwestern Estado de México, Ozoloapan parish stretched over a wide area, with the farthest of its three subordinate pueblos (San Juan Atexcapan, San Juan Sacasonapa, and Santo Tomás del Cristo), six haciendas, and numerous small ranchos some forty miles away from the parish seat. Most Indians of the parish reportedly spoke Spanish as well as Nahuatl in the late eighteenth century. The population of this large territory numbered only 4,000 in 1792—fewer than at the beginning of the century, perhaps largely because this district was especially hard hit by the epidemic (apparently smallpox) of 1737. Atexcapan seems to have recovered faster than the head town of Ozoloapan, and began to press claims for special recognition. The parish reportedly produced only eight hundred pesos in annual income for the cura, too little to support an assisting vicario.

The record begins with a complaint in 1767 by the cura, Mariano Ruis Coronel, against the Indians of Atexcapan. Father Ruis reported that within a few weeks of his appointment to the parish, in December 1766, the Indians of this outlying village had secured an order from the archbishop's attorney general that the new priest must follow the arancel. The Indians presented the arancel to Father Ruis in a haughty manner, he claimed, saying that they had secured it only for their pueblo, not for the parish as a whole. Now, "under cover of this order" and on the "frivolous pretext of the litigation" and their alleged poverty, the Indians were, said the priest, "behaving in such an insolent and disorderly way that they are paying none of the parish duties" and refusing to perform all of the customary services agreed to in writing in 1758. The cura felt personally wounded by the Indians' "malice": they intended "to do damage to my personal reputation and station" even though he had always acted "in a benign, loving, and impartial way."

In response to the priest's complaint, the Audiencia ordered the *teniente* (deputy) of the district governor in Ozoloapan to see that the Indians paid their fees according to the arancel. Father Ruis replied with thanks but lamented that because of "the isolation of this place, the broken terrain, the insolence of the Indians, and difficult access to the markets," there was no one he could count on to help him hold the Indians to their obligations.

Both the date and the form of this opening salvo are significant. Before 1767 sacramental fees in most parishes were determined by custom and local agreement rather than by the arancel of 1637, with its various amendments. There was great variation from parish to parish, and for a long time there were only occasional formal complaints in which Indian parishioners requested enforcement of the old arancel instead of customary fees and services. During the 1750s, however, uncertainty about the proper fees increased as parishes administered by the regular orders were secularized. The new diocesan curas often were said to have disregarded or revised customary fees, and Indians sometimes responded by withholding payment, refusing to abide by the customary fees, failing to attend Mass, or pressing for division of the old parish territories. Curas sometimes retaliated by withholding services. And both sides went to court in record numbers.

Intended, as Archbishop Francisco Antonio de Lorenzana put it, to "cut the habit of litigation at its roots," establish a "fixed rule," and provide a decent living for curas who lacked other resources, his new arancel, issued in 1767—a few months after the Ozoloapan litigation began—mainly added to the confusion. Indians could ask for the arancel to be applied or could choose to follow customary obligations. Because local interests and customary obligations varied, there was considerable uncertainty over which course would be most advantageous to the Indian parishioners. The revised fee schedule of the 1767 arancel listed little of what villagers customarily paid and none of the labor service they performed. Whatever the cause, formal disputes over aranceles were numerous throughout the period from 1767 to 1810, far more numerous than before 1767. Many were lodged by Indians to force the cura to abide by the published schedule, but others were initiated by curas who complained that Indian pueblos demanding the arancel complied only with those provisions that suited them. Of course, some curas wanted the arancel, too, even if it meant temporary confusion and a small reduction in income, for it produced cash rather than a welter of goods, cash, and services and was easier for the priest to administer. But even where the cura and parishioners both wanted the arancel, bitter disputes could arise. One reason is that curas began pressing to perform more of the services that required fees, especially Sunday Mass outside the parish seat, elaborate funerals, and processions and feast day celebrations in the main church.

Whether the cura preferred custom or the arancel, he was likely to regard his clerical fees as a right, to be defended as the very essence of his authority. As one cura put it in a letter to his Indian lay assistant (*fiscal*) in an outlying village of central Mexico in 1786, "Tell the sons of that pueblo that the clerical fees are by order of natural law, divine law, ecclesiastical law, and royal law. It is not a voluntary contribution, as you and the others seem to think. Just as I am obliged to give you spiritual care, you are obliged to care for my material needs, as Saint Paul says." Verbal intimidation, physical punishment, and ceremonies of deference were familiar instruments of the priest's power. However, in resorting to the power of the written word, this cura found his pen turned against him. His letter survives because the Indian recipient saved it to use as evidence of the priest's unfatherly conduct.

By 1768 the Atexcapan arancel dispute had bubbled over into the three other villages of the parish of Ozoloapan, and the four pueblos together secured a court order that required the cura to follow the new arancel. On December 8, 1768, as Father Ruis was preparing to leave for Atexcapan to celebrate the Feast of the Immaculate Conception, an Indian of the head town died. The priest sent his Indian deputy, the fiscal, to the mourners with a message that the fee would be four pesos for the burial. Before leaving town, he authorized his notary to permit the burial once the fee was paid. According to Father Ruis, on the next day the entire village council, including the fiscal, buried the body in the church with full honors and the cross raised on high—ignoring the notary who had confronted the mourners at the church door, saying that he would allow them to proceed once the fees were paid. On December 13, Ruis wrote a complaint to the Audiencia and added that the Indians of the parish were not showing him or the Holy Church proper respect; for example, Indian officials had pulled a parishioner out of church by the hair during Mass on the eve of the Immaculate Conception feast and whipped him. Ruis repeated that he could do nothing because there was no one to help. He asked for a judicial order that the Indians of the four pueblos must obey the first Audiencia decree requiring the Indians of Atexcapan to pay their fees according to the arancel. The Indian officials of the head town replied that they had waited for the cura's return to start the burial and that after they had paid three pesos he had authorized them to proceed.

Widening application of the new arancel after 1767 moved the relationship between cura and communicants toward being a financial transaction. In a way, this is what many Indians from outlying pueblos, like those of Atexcapan, would have wanted: it reduced or eliminated labor service to the cura and people of the parish seat, as well as other inconvenient and disagreeable acts of subservience that had been customary. The desire of remote villagers to loosen the bonds of such customary service to the parish priest echoes the tension between subject villages and head towns apparent in the late eighteenth-century attempts by many subordinate pueblos to gain the legal status of head towns or parish seats, or at least to get their own resident priest. After the 1767 arancel, which raised the fee for Mass in the outlying villages to twice that of the head town, the cura or his itinerant vicarios could find the church doors locked against them when they traveled outside the parish seat to perform the service of the Eucharist.

In early 1769, Indians of one of the pueblos complained to the *alcalde mayor* (district governor) that his lieutenant for Ozoloapan had arrested two of their officials at the cura's request for not paying the customary fees. The Audiencia responded that the Indians were to be released if the arancel dispute was the only reason for the arrests. It added that the cura was to obey the arancel. Apparently the claims in court were suspended at this point, although the dispute itself had not been resolved. Ruis left Ozoloapan in 1770, having won a more desirable parish in the periodic competitions for vacant posts.

The judicial record picks up again in August 1771, when the Indian *alcalde* (community official) of Atexcapan accused the new cura, Simón de Castañeda, of using "loathsome force" in violation of royal laws and in disregard of the arancel: of whipping Indians, including the fiscal, who was whipped in public with his pants down, and of not permitting confession at Easter until the fees from Mass in the outlying pueblos were paid. The alcalde went on to complain of the villagers' "life of oppression" under this cura who, he said, claimed to be the king of the parish. The Audiencia responded with the standard terse order for all parties to follow the arancel.

In the late eighteenth century, Indian pueblos often greeted new parish priests with a lawsuit—if not over clerical fees, then over local elections or control over the treasuries of lay brotherhoods. This tendency was abetted by the rapid turnover of parish priests, especially after the last round of secularization of parishes starting in the early 1750s. Among other effects, these suits provided a means for village leaders to put some distance between themselves and the cura, show him where local authority was to reside, and assert the autonomy of the local community without challenging the authority of the Crown. These were contests in which there were winners and losers. Both sides used the verb *ganar* (to win) for verdicts that did not obviously favor the other party.

Some curas observed that their Indian parishioners believed that the arancel had freed them from obedience to the priest in other matters. Many suits that began as disputes over clerical fees became more general, looping complaints against the cura. Indian parishioners in these disputes were remarkably reluctant to compromise with the cura and settle with him extrajudicially (when he was intransigent, compromise would have been all but impossible, in any case). In some cases they were simply determined to go directly to higher authorities in Mexico City, bypassing the cura's traditional authority as mediator and judge. The villagers' growing inclination to avail themselves of the high courts in disputes with the parish priest enhanced the mediating role of the Audiencias and the Indians' attorneys in Mexico City and Guadalajara, who often were retained permanently to look after whatever legal actions the community might have pending. Indeed, there were well-known cases of attorneys encouraging pueblos to litigate. And the Audiencia itself must have been aware that by the 1760s the Indians' litigiousness was encouraged by, and took advantage of, the royal decrees secularizing parishes and other administrative attempts to restrict the activities of parish priests.

In August 1772, Father Castañeda wrote a blistering reply to the Indians' complaint, emphasizing what he called their "perverse nature." He knew that trouble awaited him when he first arrived because, although it was "customary for the entire village council to meet me and accompany me to the head town, none of the officials except the fiscal did so." The Indians, he added, resisted the new arancel's fees for Mass in the outlying pueblos, and the Indian alcalde ignored his call for the establishment of a school. During the ceremony in which the cura formally invested the village officials with their staffs of office, he had exhorted the alcalde to fulfill his obligations, to which this Indian retorted: "The cura should stick to giving Mass and confession, and only when he is called. Otherwise he should stay in his house."

The Indian officials' *vara,* or staff of office, was apt to be featured in dramatic confrontations involving both threats and the kind of violence that left bruises and broken bones. Defiant Indians brandished their varas; priests responded by striking out with their own silver-tipped canes and angrily seizing the officials' staffs. One priest who was particularly fond of minatory gestures imprisoned the Indian council's staffs. Such physical conflict involving these symbols of office points to the wider assault at that time on the role of parish priests as judges that was part of the Spanish Bourbons' reformulation of church-state relations in the late eighteenth century.

Father Castañeda went on to recount how the same alcalde came to the parish seat escorted by his village councillors during Easter Week in 1772. The cura rebuked him for his disobedience in not attending church in the head town and not making other Indians from his pueblo do so. According to Castañeda, the alcalde's reply was so insulting that he had to order up twelve lashes. At this point one of the councillors rose to the alcalde's defense, shouting to the other Indians to help him, and "they threw themselves upon me, shoving their staffs of office in my face and saying they would defend themselves with the staffs, for the king had given these to them for that purpose."

In August the alcalde had gone to Mexico City, promising to obtain another cura for the parish. In the meantime the Indians were not fulfilling their Christian duties. They went elsewhere for baptism and did not call him to administer the last rites so that, "thanks to their depraved character and addiction to a brutal licentiousness, they have gone to eternity without the slightest spiritual aid." The alcalde, he had heard, had been collecting small contributions of a *real* (one-eighth of a silver peso) or two from all households to continue the lawsuit against the cura. Castañeda blamed the "malevolence of the Indian alcalde" and the administrator of a nearby hacienda, Don Francisco Maroto. Indians in general were easily taken in by outside agitators, he said, and some of the recalcitrants were Maroto's sharecroppers and thus under his control. The cura continued his litany of complaints against Maroto, especially that he buried Indians in the hacienda chapel without the priest's permission, saying that he was the lord of the chapel as well as of the hacienda and "in both, he alone gives the orders." Castañeda also blamed the Indians' attorney in Mexico City, an "unprincipled defense counsel and source of discord between curas and their parishioners." Castañeda said that he had complained to the deputy district governor but had received no help. Later in 1772 the Audiencia issued yet another short decree for the parish of Ozoloapan: the cura was to follow the arancel, and the Indians were to do their Christian duties.

The record ends with a document dated October 6, 1776, in which the attorney for the Indians of Atexcapan petitioned for better spiritual care, claiming that Father Castañeda had been cruel to his clients, levying excessive charges and not obeying the arancel despite two Audiencia verdicts to this effect won by the Indians. Castañeda, the petition alleged, had imprisoned the alcalde when payments were not to his satisfaction, had failed to confess anyone at Easter, did not celebrate Mass in Atexcapan, and rarely came to confess the dying. When asked to do so, he had allegedly replied, "Let the Devil take them." No reply from the Audiencia or further action by the priest or parishioners is recorded in these files.

After failing to win a clear victory at court, the Ozoloapan curas, previously so energetic in defense of their local interests, withdrew from the fray. Father Ruis Coronel found another post as quickly as he could; Father Castañeda spent less and less time in the outlying pueblos. Both were familiar career patterns: parish priests, and especially their vicarios, often remained in a parish for only a few years, or they became rooted in the head town or stayed away from the parish for months at a time. But for these two curas the prolonged arancel disputes also lengthened the emotional distance between pastor and parish. The formal disputes hardened their feelings of isolation, fear, loneliness, and helplessness as well as their worst judgments of Indians as cunning imbeciles who were adept at using their protected legal position to win unjust orders from the Audiencia. Curas in such circumstances often spoke of Indians as "this ignorant rabble," "Moors without a lord," "deceitful and lazy," and people of "small hearts and lowly spirits." They judged Indian towns to be "seminaries of disputes." The Ozoloapan priests' failure to gain more than minimal support from the district judge when local defiance peaked in 1767 and 1772, and the disappointing verdicts from the Audiencia, added to their frustration over the challenges to their traditional duties as father, judge, and enforcer in the moral life of the parish.

The immediate answer to why so many formal complaints over clerical fees were made by Indian parishioners and priests after 1767 would seem to be the encouragement of the Crown, the archbishop, the Audiencia, and licensed attorneys. But in every parish involved there were other reasons as well. Incoming curas, especially in newly secularized parishes, depended on the sacraments for a living and might well violate local practices in order to increase their income from fees, or parishioners might treat the arrival of a new pastor as a chance to change the customary fees to their advantage. A priest might be opposed for personal immorality, excessive use of force, demands for labor service, business interests, and control over community property and elections during this time of population growth, land shortages, new administrative demands, and declining real wages.

The Ozoloapan case documents two other kinds of brokers and men of influence in late colonial villages who contributed to the suits against parish priests. One was the hacienda administrator, who used his association with Indian sharecroppers to feed the conflict, while the other was the local Indian who took up a collection from fellow villagers to launch lawsuits in the name of the community. In the Atexcapan example he was a village official, but often he was a self-appointed legal agent with connections to a lawyer in Mexico City—a political entrepreneur who had been left off the ladder of community offices. If he succeeded in court at the priest's expense, his reputation soared and the path was cleared for his election to community office and further enrichment. Leaders of this kind often were the product of intense factionalism within villages, and a successful litigation against the cura could signal the rise of a new group to local influence.

But even in this case of estrangement and hostility toward the curas, it is clear from the Atexcapan Indians' desire for a priest and the sacraments that they were not leading a pagan revival or a separatist movement. They accepted the dogma of the Church as it was taught to them; they were concerned with salvation in Christian terms, with the "welfare of our souls," as they put it. Even when their feelings toward him ran more to fear and anger than to love and respect, the cura was clearly an important spiritual figure for them, not an object of indifference or simply an adversary or hired hand.

It would be a mistake to speak of curas in these circumstances only as they described themselves (as isolated, lonely, defenseless servants of God), or only as the Indians described them to colonial judges (as omnipotent tyrants). These descriptions are important social facts in themselves, but they are too much like the bad priest/good priest antinomy that streaks the literature on the Church in Mexican history. Few of the curas documented in late colonial records, including those of Ozoloapan, were poised to be tyrants or martyrs. As intermediaries and specialists in rites of passage for individual believers and the community and in the mysteries of a powerful state religion, they were instruments of influence, well-being, and terror; and their contacts outside the community, their traditional part in policing public life, their economic interests, and their command of the written word gave them added access to power. They were rarely the unquestioned local leaders, however, and their effective influence was under sharp attack in the late colonial period.

The confrontations between the priests and parishioners of Ozoloapan suggest that Indian responses in the Mexican heartland to late colonial political pressures focused on local rule and protection against more demands from Spanish authority without challenging that authority or contributing much to Indian class identity. The assertion of independence expressed in the alcaldes' staffs of office reflects a localized Christian identity that interpreted and adjusted to the received beliefs and expectations of priests and other colonial officials. As Elizabeth Wilder Weismann wrote about popular art in the late eighteenth century, colonial Indian culture was "not so much disrespectful of [official] tradition as untamed by it, surmounting it."

The priest in these parishes supplied the framework for Catholic practice. He was central to rites of the life cycle, weekly Mass, annual confession and Communion, the periodic feast days and blessings, and the administration of church affairs. He also might exercise considerable influence through his economic interests and political activities, but in general he appears to have been a good deal less important to the religious aspects of everyday life, especially outside the parish seat.

The litigiousness of the Ozoloapan pueblos and Indian officials shaking their royal staffs of office at the cura marked resistance to the acts of one kind of colonial official while validating colonial authority at a higher level. This chain of disputes over clerical fees and election procedures took its cue from recent royal and archiepiscopal decrees to standardize the schedule of fees and limit the curas' local authority in favor of royal governors. While expressing a determined opposition to labor service, externally imposed alterations of clerical fees, and other perceived injustices, these late colonial lawsuits and protests were framed as supplications for the king's favor. Their petitions and complaints to the colonial courts more often began with "Venimos a pedir" (We come to request) than "Venimos a contradecir" (We come to object). And the Audiencia's mechanical rulings that all parties must follow the arancel seem to have been a sufficient victory for most Indian litigants.

Although these lawsuits were always presented in the name of the community, resistance of this kind did not simply express communal solidarity against intrusive outsiders. They could also express personal ambitions, factional divisions, and other kinds of local dissension. This is true even though written evidence of religious and ceremonial practices tends to highlight corporate community behavior, whether directed from above or originating from below, leaving the misleading impression of little conflict within communities.

In the Ozoloapan disputes, colonial Indians did not regard themselves as enemies of the colonial state and its religion. True, where Indians who believed that they were chosen Christians went on to make invidious comparisons to their social betters and distinguish between Christianity and the Church, millennial dreams of a new order could have revolutionary possibilities. Such dreams rarely were acted upon in New Spain—rarely, at least, beyond the local level, where they had helped define a colonial identity.

The Indian resistance and accommodations documented for Ozoloapan suggest that the political disunity and unstable authoritarian regimes of Mexico in the early nineteenth century had less to do with popular submissiveness, Indian absolutism, and a lack of political mobilization than with the long-standing strength and experience of localities and regions. Political participation was greater than is often imagined. The curas of Ozoloapan certainly felt the weight of local political initiative that was not simply the product of a petty tyrant's machinations. The observation of David Wells, a late nineteenth-century North American commentator, that a "native spirit of independence" and the decline of state and national courts of justice were the principal sources of Mexico's disunity comes closer to the militant myopia of districts and pueblos such as Ozoloapan and Atexcapan in the political circumstances of the late eighteenth century.

 43

Taxonomy of a Colonial "Riot"
The Arequipa Disturbances of 1780

DAVID CAHILL

The work of David Cahill, a historian at the University of New South Wales, examines the social and cultural history of the Andes in the eighteenth century in a manner that digs deep while consistently extending the relevance of his subjects beyond the study of colonial Peru. The following reading is excerpted from an article illuminating "four days of political violence" in the highland city of Arequipa in southern Peru. It offers a valuable perspective on events that transpired to the side of the more dramatic contemporary rebellions led by Túpac Amaru II and Túpac Catari during the years 1780–1782.

The essay brings to light some of the local effects of the reforms initiated in Peru by the *visitador general* José Antonio de Areche, in connection with the wider "rationalizing" enterprise undertaken by José de Gálvez (see Selection 39). Cahill's analysis of the implementation of a more comprehensive tribute system and a range of new taxes—and, in some cases, only the fear of their implementation—by Bourbon administrators and their officials in Arequipa uncovers the limits of this late colonial society's tolerance for economic hardship brought on by new rules and practices of execution. The essay shares some of the concerns seen in William Taylor's investigation of *arancel* disputes in contemporary Ozoloapan, Mexico (Selection 42), in that Cahill ponders the points beyond what he calls the "acceptable ambit and level of authority and its exercise," the moments when authority or its abuse was commonly deemed to have become "excessive."

Cahill finds undercurrents of fierce antagonism, distrust, and fear within this society, brought to the surface by the immediate threats of the new fiscal implementations. The antagonism is most sensibly reduced, he says, to "a notion of class expressed in its most simple terms between those who have and those who have not." But he also demonstrates how the new fiscal regime threatened many different people in similar ways and created a fleeting situation in which common understandings and organized action became possible. A multiracial group of people suddenly found themselves about to be required to pay tribute and contribute to work projects as manual laborers. There were, of course, gradations of effect, but Cahill argues that almost every social group in Arequipa and its environs either had felt the bite of the new customs tax or perceived that it might soon feel it.

The essay combines an analysis of the structure of the riot and its participants with a narration of the people's actions. Warnings and provocations come in the form of written satire and grievances, often composed in verse, and pasted or tacked up in conspicuous places. "Non-elite men of substance" become crucial actors, and they are joined even by some members of wealthy families and the *corregidor*'s own circle. All, for their own reasons, opposed the changes in the fiscal system in Arequipa and were to be counted among the participants in the riot. Cahill calls many of them by name and traces their connections and situations, arguing that "there was every reason in the world for everyone to join an insurrection."

New taxes and threats to existing patterns of doing business might be resented and even hated in themselves, but Cahill asks us to consider matters even further. Referring to the manner in which the new fiscal system was introduced and carried out, and the much-noted self-importance and cruelty of a new set of prosecuting officials, he asks: What were the ramifications of cold rigor and arrogance? The administrators of the customshouse in Arequipa after 1779, Juan Bautista Pando and Pedro de la Torre, come particularly under Cahill's lens. Their demeanor, pronouncements, general attitude toward the place, and their treatment of people whom they openly regarded as their social inferiors are viewed by Cahill as crucial both to their own fates and to the violence that ensued. He also considers the effects of a well-developed local hatred of outsiders. This is not simply a case of Arequipan Creoles resenting peninsular Spaniards, but a quarrel with impositions that seems more like a quarrel with Lima and visiting officials from there than with exploitation and indifference from Spain.

Cahill also raises issues that reflect on the place of religion in this riot and, more generally, in this late eighteenth-century city. The first of many written critiques and satirical attacks on the impending customshouse was nailed to the doors of the cathedral, and an unnamed and frequently drunken friar was said to have been among the authors of these pieces. In an argument that recalls the violence and distraction that sometimes interrupted Corpus Christi processions and other festivals in other parts of Peru and Spanish America (see Figures 26 and 27 in Selection 37 and Selections 29 and 35), Cahill suggests that some of the riot's instigators would have seen the coinciding Sabbath and upcoming patronal feast day in Arequipa as a providential "opportunity," an "overture" for violence and protest. He argues that plotters capitalized on the "widespread drunkenness" among the people—what Cahill calls "the 'profane' side to Andean religion." Participants in the riots included members of an impoverished religious association (*cofradía*) that Cahill proposes had become something like "a revolutionary cell," seemingly confirming, he also notes, Bourbon administrators' characteristic suspicion of the extra-religious functions of these associations. The same rioters are said to have engaged in the "invocation of patron saints to help or guide . . . [them] in their political ventures."

Religion is clearly not to be trusted; and, under Cahill's scrutiny, these feelings are not reserved to officialdom suspecting "popular" religious eruptions, but took other forms even among the rioters. There is mention of a "Dominican [friar] famed for his virtue" threatened by protesters: when he twice raised an image of Christ "to pacify the multitude," rocks were thrown and shots fired. Cahill views the incident (and another like it in Urubamba), and the crowd's failure to obey religious calls for calm during the riots in Arequipa, as evidence of "a drastic cessation of normality," part of the mood that would see an entire "establishment" assailed. And he challenges us further, making a point about popular hostility to the clergy that again recalls Taylor's litigious parishioners of Ozoloapan. "In the Andes," Cahill writes, "profound religious sentiment often exists with equally profound anticlericalism."

There is a rich corpus of historical literature relating to riots, rebellions, and sundry disturbances in pre-industrial Europe that focuses on the composition of the crowd, its political culture, and the capacity of the plebeian strata to organize themselves politically in defense of traditional rights and conditions and even to seek some increment in those very rights and conditions. This approach—associated above all with the names of George Rudé, Edward Thompson, Eric Hobsbawm, and Michel Vovelle—has in the past decade been applied with notable success to the study of the North American Revolution, and its influence is evident in recent publications on Latin America by William Taylor, Scarlett O'Phelan Godoy, and Anthony McFarlane. The approach consists essentially of the simple device of lending an ear to the testimonies of the numerous lower-class witnesses and defendants buried within the voluminous depositions generated in the wake of the incessant riots, rebellions, and protests that so characterized late colonial Spanish South America. . . .

This essay . . . will treat but one of a series of political demonstrations [across late colonial Peru] that collectively have been viewed as a kind of vestibule to the uprisings of Túpac Amaru and Túpac Catari. It will focus on the eruption of political violence in the city of Arequipa in January 1780, the best known and best documented of this constellation of antifiscal protests. These demonstrations—in Arequipa, Huaraz, Cerro de Pasco, La Paz, and Cochabamba, and some less spectacular disturbances in the Diocese of Trujillo as well as an abortive conspiracy in Cusco—have thus come to be seen as what one author [Francisco A. Loayza] has called the "prelude to the conflagration." Others have stressed, rightly, that the protests were a response of local society to the fiscal reforms initiated by the visitor-general José Antonio de Areche and implemented in the viceroyalty from mid-1777 onward.

An assumption, though, pervades most such accounts that the riots were a natural, even mechanistic, response to Areche's reforms, much as if Peruvians shared with their North American analogues a belief in the putative right of "No taxation without representation." This essay will analyze the manner in which the new fiscal system was implemented and examine how and why increased taxation led to political violence. It will then address questions that have been left fallow or only partially treated in existing accounts: the level of popular versus elite participation in the protests; the extent to which the events were spontaneous or controlled—or, put another way, the degree to which the crowd was the instrument of patrician elements; the participation of rural inhabitants in what was an urban phenomenon; the degree to which the events constituted a transient fiscal protest or bore witness to a more durable popular ideology. An attempt will also be made to uncover a structure within the apparently anarchic disturbances and to detect political fault lines in colonial society and the ways or mechanisms by which a colonial crowd could either mobilize itself or be mobilized politically.

The Fiscal System: Old and New

A lengthy report written soon after the four days of political violence in Arequipa (January 13–16, 1780) expresses the view that the new administrator of the customs house (*aduana*) in the city, Juan Bautista Pando, had commenced where he should have finished in implementing the new system, and that had he undertaken his task with more skill, he would eventually have achieved his goal. This opinion was just one of many, of course, but it does indicate the radical difference between the old and new systems of customs. For the threat to *arequipeño* [resident of Arequipa] interests consisted not merely in a 2 percent increase in the *alcabala* (sales tax) as well as new imposts of 12.5 percent on *aguardiente* [brandy] production (*nuevo impuesto*) and the fifth (*quinto*) [reserved for the royal treasury] on minted and worked silver and gold, but quite as much in the rigor with which the exercise was undertaken, its differential social impact, and, not least, the arrogant manner in which Pando and his lieutenant, Pedro de la Torre, whom he had brought from the Lima customshouse, set about complying with their responsibilities. To comprehend the seriousness of the threat posed to arequipeño interests by the establishment of the customshouse, however, we first need to assess the nature of the fiscal system in Arequipa before Pando's arrival in late 1779.

The alcabala had been charged at a rate of 2 percent from its inception in the viceroyalty in 1591 until 1772, when Viceroy Amat y Junict raised the excise to 4 percent. In spite of Areche's belief that customs officials had failed to implement the Amat reform in Arequipa, it is clear that arequipeños had been obliged to pay at a rate of 4 percent at least since 1775, well before the implementation of Areche's reforms, though this percentage had never been collected with the rigor that the visitor-general's appointee was to introduce in 1780. Under the regulations Amat introduced in 1773, *hacendados* [owners of large landed estates] and merchants had been conceded a year of grace in which to make good the sales tax and, to judge from the surviving customs records, were accustomed to "rolling over" their debts from one year to the next. It was Pando's express intention to do away with such practices instituted by the royal officials who had been responsible for the alcabala collection and who, he alleged, had exercised their office "to acquire friends, establish a good name, and a fortune."

A royal decree of July 6, 1776, had provided for a further increase in the sales tax from 4 percent to 6 percent, and Areche was sent to the viceroyalty to oversee, inter alia, the implementation of this measure. The new rate of 6 percent began to be charged in the Lima customshouse in mid-1777, snaring among its earliest victims José Gabriel Túpac Amaru [the soon-to-be rebel leader] and his cousin Diego. In Arequipa, the alcabala was collected at the rate of 6 percent at least from the end of 1778, and the new aguardiente excise had begun to be collected sometime in 1777. That is to say, the new measures were implemented in Arequipa at least a year before Pando established the customshouse in that city; all collections were the responsibility of the royal officials of the provincial treasury, aided by minor functionaries who manned customs posts on the outskirts of the city. For this reason, the *pasquinades* [satirical compositions and lampoons posted in public places] that accompanied the political turmoil of January 1780 leveled threats against those very officials and other lower-level functionaries. Nonetheless, when one looks at how the alcabala was enforced before 1777, the wonder is that anything was collected at all. There was a profusion of exemptions from which the muleteers, merchants, hacendados, *caciques* [native Andean governors], *corregidores* [district administrators appointed by the Crown], and assorted travelers could choose, with apparently little need actually to prove their rights to exemption. Excise collection appears to have relied upon something like an honor system.

The surviving customs invoices for Arequipa do not, unfortunately, record exemptions, but those for the Cusco region record not only the exemption but also its ostensible justification. . . . Custom as well as legal privilege had determined that distinct social categories [especially people designated "Indians"] were exempt from the sales tax, while those who stood outside such privileged groups might choose from a phalanx of excuses or loopholes to avoid payment in full or in part. Failing that, there was always graft. Again, in Cusco in 1780, two of those executed for their role in the abortive conspiracy of that year, Eugenio Cárdenas and ringleader Lorenzo Farfán de los Godos, were employees of the customshouse. The implementation of the new system threatened the livelihood of those who had cooperated in, and profited from, the informality of the old one. Among the targets of the pasquinades in Arequipa in 1780 were two *peninsulares* employed by the customshouse—a doorman and a lower-level official—as well as the *limeños* [Lima natives] Pando and De la Torre. In the anti-peninsular sentiments of the time is implicit the slogan, "Local jobs for local people."

From the first, Pando vigorously defended his role in the establishment of the customshouse, laying the blame for the disturbances on the corregidor of Arequipa, Baltasar de Sematnat, his commercial connections, and the treachery of the local patriciate, pointing out that the first pasquinade directed against its implementation had appeared even before the new customshouse had begun to function. In so doing, however, he unwittingly focused on his own personality and maladroit methods as causal factors in the disturbances. For several months prior to the establishment of the customshouse, Pando had startled, angered, and finally instilled fear into all arequipeños who had anything at all to lose. In late 1779 he had commenced a visitation of neighboring valleys and the provinces of Camaná and Moquegua. Many witnesses attested that in those two provinces and the nearby Valley of Tiabaya he had publicly boasted that he would leave their denizens in their undergarments; in Tiabaya, seeing the inhabitants dressed with "considerable decency," he had exclaimed that he would yet see them clothed in the coarse cloth customarily worn by the urban and rural poor.

Such arrogance seemed to find its echo in his very actions in those provinces, for in Camaná and Moquegua he took a detailed inventory of all haciendas, lands, houses, taverns, occupations, and shops and market stalls. It appeared that no one, not even a humble housewife, was to be exempt from some new form of taxation. Word of this filtered through to the city of Arequipa, where he began a similar inventory upon his arrival. It was believed, at any rate, that he intended a tax "on the wage of the poor artisans, bakeries, taverns, and street stalls." Accordingly, sometime before dawn on December 31, 1779, the first pasquinade, threatening violence if the customshouse was established, appeared on the doors of the cathedral, scarcely days before the inauguration.

That event encapsulated all of the fears of the arequipeños, and then some. If citizens had expected the new taxes to be implemented with rigor, they had not anticipated the notion of indirect taxation. Indians had always been exempt from the alcabala, but now that custom—indeed, existing legal privilege under the 1773 regulations—was summarily revoked by Pando. This served as a provocation to arequipeños not because of any nascent *indigenista* spirit [sympathy for, or identification with, the condition of indigenous peoples], but rather because the Indians of the sierra and the surrounding villages were the principal purveyors of foodstuffs, handicrafts, and fuel to the city. The custom was either for the Indians to bring their wares for marketing or to send them with small traders, or for the Indians of the city itself to set out each day to procure produce, which they would then sell upon their return. In this way the city was supplied daily with fresh produce. The opening of the customshouse vitiated this mutually satisfactory marketing arrangement in several ways, abrogating "that right [of exemption for] the grains and seeds for supply sold in the markets and public places for the provisioning of the towns." Indians were immediately charged a sales tax on the goods that they brought to market and, at the same time, were subject to maltreatment by leading officials.

The almost instant effect of such treatment was that many, perhaps most, Indians ceased to bring their merchandise to market; and where they continued to do so, they sold it at inflated prices. The effect on the small retailers of the city was that they either could not obtain the provisions from which they earned their livelihood, or else they were forced to pay higher prices, which they perforce passed on to their customers. Overall, the principal result of the opening of the customshouse was that when servants sallied forth from the houses at daybreak to purchase the daily provisions, there were none to be had. Even where foodstuffs had reached the market at an elevated price, they tended not to be available much before noon because of the habit of customs officials of detaining goods inside the customshouse until that hour. Moreover, on Sundays and feast days none at all was available, as Pando had ruled that on such days the customshouse was to be closed and no one permitted to bring goods into the city, travelers and muleteers being obliged to camp outside the city. The entire population of the city, whether merchant or not, was thus immediately and deleteriously affected by the establishment of the customshouse in Arequipa.

All social classes felt the arrogance of the new officials of the customshouse, but the Indians bore the brunt of such high-handedness. When they claimed that they had never paid a sales tax, Pedro de la Torre, said to be even less pleasant than Pando, treated them as fools. None of their goods, be they foodstuffs, cloth, fuel, or carpets, passed muster; and where they lacked the wherewithal to pay, as they usually did in that only partly monetarized local economy, their goods were impounded. Moreover, they, in common with other travelers, were obliged to remove their hats and spurs upon entering the customshouse. De la Torre's racial contempt reached such a pitch that on one occasion he set upon a group of Indians who were passing through the customshouse. When a longtime employee of the customshouse reminded De la Torre that the alcabala was not charged on the merchandise of Indians, the latter flew into a rage and began to charge the Indians with even more rigor. In the two attacks on the customshouse on the nights of January 13 and 14, the only official to be injured was De la Torre, who received a lance through his face and for some time was thought to be on the brink of death.

As with the Indians, the Mestizos, Cholos [Hispanicized Indians and other dark-skinned people], and other castes were likewise the victims of such imperious treatment. Perhaps more crucial, however, for subsequent developments was the rigor to which hacendados, merchants, and other members of the patriciate found themselves subjected. There are numerous cases of such luminaries having to pay the excise on goods [especially wine, but also grains, fruits, and firewood] for which they had previously been exempt. . . . The surviving customs records for the 1770s indicate, however, that many prominent hacendados were accustomed to paying the impost, so that such claims may well represent little more than frustrated hyperbole. Of equal annoyance for landowners were the refusal of Pando to allow them the twelve months of grace that the regulation of 1773 permitted them and the probability that, for the first time, their word as to value, volume, and weight of merchandise was distrusted and goods would be measured and weighed. It was significant that, in the wake of the "riots," the corregidor held a meeting with prominent hacendados to patch over differences and, it is likely, to obviate any conflicting testimonies in the face of forthcoming investigations.

The new aguardiente excise was just as damaging to the interests of this social group because Arequipa was the leading wine producer in the viceroyalty and the major exporter of wines to Upper Peru [what is today Bolivia]. This impost meant that wine producers were paying the property tax and a further 12.5 percent, a considerable erosion of their profit margin. The new tax had a wider impact in that it forced an increase in the prices in popular taverns throughout the province. An indication of the attitude of hacendados to the new excise charges was revealed by a peer of Domingo Benavides, one of the more prominent patrician landholders. Benavides, attested this witness, had suggested in high dudgeon that because "there were so many *gravamens* [exactions], the haciendas didn't give [profit], and that it was more worthwhile to revolt [*levantarse*]." Benavides's son Diego was later to be identified by several witnesses as the leader of the attacks on the customshouse on January 13–14, as indeed was the son of the mayordomo of Domingo Benavides's inn, where goods stolen from the corregidor's house on January 15 were also to be found. The late colonial haciendas in Peru were characterized by heavy mortgage or lien burdens and high turnovers of ownership. Clearly, a key to the success of such an operation lay in minimizing the tax burden payable to the treasury, the adroit avoidance or limitation of which might well prove to be the difference between survival and bankruptcy, whatever the position of the owner in the social pecking order.

If the alcabala affected the urban poor and the peasantry quite as much, in relative terms, as it did hacendados and the more comfortable urban dwellers such as merchants, it was also the case that the extension of tribute liability to Mestizos, Cholos, and Zambaigos [sons of African mothers and native Andean fathers] embodied in Areche's circular order of November 16, 1779, might, in the worst of all cases, reach into the urban and rural patriciate, some of whose members conspicuously lacked *limpieza de sangre* ["purity of blood," implying not Jewish or Muslim, but rather native Andean and African ancestry]. Here, again, our anonymous chronicler avers that those who came within the ambit of the new tribute regulations included "the plebeians of the city and rustics and even many who, being Mestizos, etc., are considered patricians because their circumstances have elevated them." Moreover, it is clear that this new tribute provision had been made immediately and widely public, with copies having been distributed to all the parish priests of the region. Even more so than in the case of the sales tax, the tribute question was a matter of fear of future developments rather than resentment at anything yet implemented by the Crown, though Sematnat had undertaken a census of the residents of Tiabaya in November 1779 that had been abruptly canceled when social unrest there and in Cailloma became evident. Such attenuation was, of course, an abrogation of the corregidor's fiscal responsibilities. The chronicler noted that the designation of "tributary" was heard with revulsion, but a lowered social status and the monetary contribution itself comprised only a portion of the burden that such a designation implied. . . . [Generally speaking,] to be categorized as a tributary thus signified not only an instant loss of social status but also a financial devastation and the possibility of forced-labor service. In Arequipa, however, the correlation between tributary status and financial loss was rather more blurred, as Sematnat had included in his *repartos* [(*de mercancías*), the forced sale of goods to Indians by a corregidor] many mixed-race individuals.

The third impost that drew forth protests and pasquinades was the royal fifth affecting primarily miners, traders in silver and gold, and the guild of silversmiths, though at a lower remove the customer was, of course, also affected. Gold and silver were non-essential goods for the wider society, but not for the clergy and confraternities who were regular purchasers of silver vessels and silver and gold thread for the ongoing work of ornamentation and embellishment of the numerous churches and chapels in the diocese. The new measure implied a 20 percent increase in the cost of such devotional activities. Moreover, silver plate appears to have been, in the absence of savings banks in colonial life, an item in which the more comfortable sectors of society invested in order to safeguard their savings. Two of the seven conspirators executed in Cusco in 1780 [after plotting there] were silversmiths, and another two were goldsmiths, one of whom was the mayordomo of a confraternity. Several of the organizers of the political demonstrations of January 15–16 in Arequipa appear to have been members of the confraternity of San Antonio Abad who had been unable, several days before the feast of their patron saint, to complete a chapel for the fiesta owing to lack of funds.

The injection of Bourbon efficiency into excise collection in the Arequipa region thus affected not only those more conspicuously involved in the marketing of bulk foodstuffs, aguardiente, and cloth, but the lower strata of urban and rural society as well: Indians, artisans, petty merchants, and consumers of whatever social provenance. . . . However, the rebarbative personalities of Pando and his henchmen have tended to obscure the fact that colonial officialdom's exploitation of Indian carriers and street traders had antedated the arrival in Arequipa of those fiscal adventurers. A city councilor testified that, before Pando's arrival, the lower orders had been "terrorized" by the employees of the provincial treasury as they entered or left the city and were forced to pay excise on whatever goods they carried with them, however trifling, which were impounded at will. There is, too, testimony that city councilors also made a tidy living from such extra-official practices, charging each street trader two reales for the privilege of setting out his or her goods and four reales for each carcass sold to meet the city's provisioning requirements. So, too, the corregidor was said to receive four pesos from each tavern for the privilege of not being forcibly sold wine, in a region that was the major wine producer in the viceroyalty. In the colonial period, exploitation usually begins at home.

Added to the effects of fiscal measures new and old, legal and illicit, the meticulousness of Pando's inventorying threatened some barely imagined new form of taxation on houses, occupations, shops, taverns, market stalls, haciendas, and even the street-corner sites from which local government officials already garnered bribes. All had lost something, directly or indirectly, as a result of the opening of the customshouse, and all stood to lose more as Areche's underlings developed their fiscal rhythm. The proposal—indeed law, which the corregidor had as yet failed to implement—to widen the tribute net was calculated not only to reap for the Crown vast increases in revenue from this source but also to enrage a large proportion of the existing non-tributary population. How, indeed, could it be otherwise after some 250 years of miscegenation? Many might see generations of social climbing and economic consolidation evaporate when they found themselves, with the designation of "tributary," forced to meet biennial payments and *repartos* as well as liability for personal service. If this constellation of gravamens represented the worst-case position, the designation itself constituted adequate offense in a racially and status-conscious society. A host of other people, less socially prominent, were similarly affected by the measure: the urban masses, the artisans, the mayordomos and cowboys employed on the haciendas, and the smallholders, who played a vital role in local production but who appear only infrequently in the historical record. There was every reason in the world for everyone to join an insurrection.

The wide-ranging social impact of the new taxes constituted what may be called the structural cause of the civil disorder that was to follow. But there were, as there usually are, contingent factors that exacerbated the already highly charged political atmosphere in the city. Aside from the uncivil manner of the collection of the new imposts, such factors tended to center on the figure of the corregidor. Social unrest in Tiabaya and Cailloma had accompanied his attempt to draw up new tribute lists, unrest that provided something of an overture to the establishment of the customshouse. The officials of the provincial treasury had requested its erection, and in late 1779 considerable bad blood existed between these officials and the corregidor, though the precise reasons for this are lost to us. In any case, Sematnat's own financial interests were not served by the opening of the customshouse, and a rivalry was quickly established between the corregidor and Pando.

Sematnat seems to have chosen for himself the role of local hero, and indeed many saw him, or conveniently chose to cast him, in such a light, notwithstanding the general odium in which he was held in Arequipa. Others, however, to judge from many among the pasquinades, accredited the corregidor as well as local treasury officials with being the joint authors of their misfortunes by bringing the customshouse there in the first place. A flurry of pasquinades and reports of suspicious nocturnal movements in the city and suburbs induced Sematnat to call Pando to order, advancing the thesis that the administrator's activities constituted a threat to the peace of the realm. The latter's prompt response revealed his contempt for the self-serving corregidor, and a breach was thereby established, with both vying for preeminence: a conflict of jurisdiction rooted in irreconcilable personalities. This exchange of correspondence took place on January 12. Pando's rejection of the corregidor's overtures became known at once, and on the next night the first of the attacks on the customshouse took place.

The Events

In his appeal to Pando, Sematnat had referred to "bands of masked persons" passing through the streets "at strange hours" of the night, on foot and on horseback. On the nights of January 5 and 8 the city guards reported such movements in various parts of the city. On January 10 there was a discernible increment in these bands, evidently calculated at this juncture more as a threat than as an intent. A cleric reported that at 1:30 A.M. on January 11 he saw some sixty horsemen "wearing ponchos and with white caps that almost covered their entire faces," riding in good formation. After having thoroughly and intentionally frightened one of the customs officials living on the outskirts, they set out for the center of the city, riding slowly two by two, at an interval of a block between each pair. These demonstrations were obviously intended to drive home the message of the pasquinades, which were by now multiplying rapidly.

That message was not confined solely to the abolition of the customshouse, as the activities of the nocturnal rangers might have suggested. One functionary reported that, before the outbreak of violence, many persons (whom he was unable or unwilling to identify) passing by his post had said that if the Cholos and Zambos [people of African and native Andean descent] were to be charged tribute, then "they have to revolt (*alzarse*)." Again, on the night of the tenth, the cacique of the villages of Chimba and Tiabaya, Colonel of the Militias Esteban Condorpusa, was visited by two of those mysterious horsemen, now armed, who demanded details of the new tribute list that the corregidor and Condorpusa had undertaken in the previous November. When the cacique denied that such a register existed, they riposted that they had been reliably informed that it did, and that not only Cholos but also *españoles* [Spaniards] had been included. Both horsemen were Mulattoes. The message had, however, already been well taken by Sematnat, who had refrained from taking any further census and who now made concentrated efforts to deter Pando from his potentially destructive course. Yet on the thirteenth, in spite of such overtures, there was a disturbance (*alboroto*) at the customshouse when a group of peons belonging to a client of the customshouse, together with another group of *muchachos* [young men], Cholos, and *indios* [Indians] [totalling between five and six hundred people], assailed an employee with sods of earth, accompanied by whistles, shouts, and general pandemonium; the protest was against Pedro de la Torre's ill-treatment of some Indian carriers. The intransigence and arrogance of Pando and De la Torre thus served to ignite the steadily deteriorating political climate in the city. That night the customshouse was attacked. . . . This crowd retired, almost evaporated, in good order, apparently convinced, as one chronicler of the event asserted, that they had achieved by their actions either a complete abolition of the customshouse or at least a diminution in the level and nature of the imposts henceforth to be charged. The naïveté of that illusion became apparent on the following day.

After reviewing the damage at dawn on the fourteenth, Sematnat called a *cabildo abierto* [emergency meeting of local officials and notables] that demanded the lifting of all fiscal innovations, at least until representations could be made to Lima, and at the same time avowed to defend the customshouse to the death. A delegation accordingly met with Pando, who gave it to understand that he was in favor of such a course of action, but on that very day he proceeded to collect the excise with even more temerity than hitherto, even forcing some interregional traders to pay the excise twice on the same item of merchandise. The reply of the victims was swift. That night a horseman was seen to ride toward the customshouse, whereupon, approaching his goal, he gave a whistle. This signal was immediately answered by a rocket fired from behind the nearby Convent of San Francisco, at which the block was filled with some six hundred horsemen, riding, again, "in such good order." Several versions attest to an overall number of some three thousand participants in this protest, all of whom were armed, after a fashion, with pistols, lances, sticks, and stones. This multitude destroyed and selectively looted the offices, stealing some three thousand pesos but leaving other sums untouched, and most notably refusing to violate the sanctity of the considerable merchandise that had earlier been interned in the customshouse. As one commentator put it, "They had no mind to rob but rather to kill or terrorize the administrator." Pando and other employees made good their escape by scuttling over a back fence and into hiding. On the following day, Sematnat formally abolished the application of Areche's innovations in the region, permitting local hacendados to remove their merchandise from storage without even paying the excise at the old rates. It had been a skillfully executed "riot," a resounding success. The matter should have rested there, at least until such time as recriminations from the authorities in Lima could reach the city. . . . [Similar crowds, demanding a cessation of all tribute innovations, had also assembled in the nearby villages of Cayma and Yanahuara.]

The nights of the fifteenth and sixteenth bear witness to a spirit of iconoclasm loosed in the city. This is not to say that there were no clearly defined targets: on the fifteenth, the corregidor's house was attacked by a large crowd, and men were posted in the back gardens of adjoining houses to kill Sematnat as he fled. He had, though, already done so in the early evening, when he took refuge in a monastery after being tipped off by a faint heart among the multitude. He had taken the precaution of removing his prized possessions, but left the rioters some sixty-seven Crown rifles. His house was despoiled of its remaining contents and then set on fire, whence the crowd moved to the house of a prominent merchant, rumored to be the financier of the corregidor's commercial interests, whom they robbed of approximately thirty thousand pesos in money and cloth. Then it was on to the royal jail, the heavy doors of which were broken down, Bastille-fashion, releasing the prisoners, who then joined forces with their liberators. By now it was nearing dawn, so the leader—at least he who wielded the trumpet that marshaled the throng—ordered everyone to disperse, convoking them for a further assault the following night on the provincial treasury and on the house and persons of prominent members both of the corregidor's inner circle and the urban patriciate generally.

There now occurred a general exodus of families and their prized chattels to the convents and monasteries of the city, where, indeed, the corregidor had been the first to take refuge, despite his function as guarantor of law and order. The political demonstration directed against the establishment of the customshouse, which in part at least had been organized by disaffected members of the elite, had clearly run out of control. On the sixteenth the corregidor convoked the numerous militia companies of the city and surrounding districts, infantry and cavalry, to protect life, limb, and loot from the attack they knew was to come. At this gathering, Sematnat was able to confirm what all had suspected, that "the suspicion was vehemently against those persons who form the infantry and cavalry militias." . . . All the cavalry companies were said to be composed of Mestizos and Cholos of the city and environs. It was not surprising, then, that the corregidor and his dwindling band of supporters, mostly the patrician elements based in the city itself, felt that they could rely only on the infantry company of nobles and "some soldiers" chosen from the company of grenadiers.

The attack came in three waves between 10:00 P.M. and 2:00 A.M., from the countryside, and comprised Indians, Mestizos, and other castes armed with lances, sticks, and the classical weapon of Andean warfare, the sling. . . . [The first two waves drove back five companies of cavalry toward the center of the city they defended. It was largely the superior arms of a company of nobles that turned the people back.] After some four hours of fighting—much of it hand-to-hand—the third and final wave was dispersed. Having seized the initiative, the two patrician militia companies embarked on a policy of exemplary reprisals. That very night they set out on a punitive expedition and searched, looted, and burned the houses and huts of the Pampa of Miraflores [from which the main thrust of protesters had come] and took prisoners in droves. Particular care was taken to destroy all of the *rancherías* [settlements and possessions] belonging to *indios forasteros* [or *forasteros*, itinerant Indians absent from their places of origin]. Five cadavers of luckless invaders were hung in the Plaza de Armas [central square] on the seventeenth as a preventative warning, and on the following day six prisoners went to the gallows. Who were all these rioters, and how had they been organized?

The Composition of the Crowd

If the attacks of the thirteenth and fourteenth were in a certain measure distinct in character from those of the succeeding two days, there does appear to have been some continuity of personnel, though a change of leadership is evident, perhaps a seizing of the baton from the erstwhile organizers by some involved as participants during the first two days. The events of the first phase appear to have been organized, at least in part, by disaffected patricians, to judge by the presence of Diego Benavides, but also by militiamen, who continued to involve themselves during the final two days. In the first phase, the presence of the militia appears to be attested by reports of large groups of well-disciplined horsemen riding in good formation. Their involvement on the fifteenth is similarly suggested by a report that when the corregidor's house was sacked, the surrounding streets were guarded by armed horsemen. On the sixteenth the Tiabaya militia, encouraged by its officers, publicly boasted that they would join the attack on the city that night, an intention underscored by the fact that the city was then defended by no more than two companies and a handful of volunteers.

One chronicler of the events asserted that the bulk of the militia of the province was composed of Mestizos and other castes. This explains the attitude of the Tiabaya militiamen, for they also protested against their heavy reparto debts. It also helps to explain the action of the corregidor, who, on the eve of the violence, entrusted police powers not only to city magistrates but also to the cacique Condorpusa and men of his confidence, though not, apparently, in his capacity as a militia colonel. Another report had it that, on the night of the sixteenth, the Tiabaya company had allied with Indians and castes of the Pampa to attack the city and avail themselves of the wealth of the patriciate. The militia, comprising as it did such racial categories, was to be subject to the new tribute regulations in the same manner that it was already the victim of reparto.

All of the *plebe* [commoners] of the city and countryside were identified at various times by many witnesses: the racial composition of this designation included "Cholos, Mestizos, Sambos [or Zambos], Negros [Africans], and Indios." Of the crowd of the fifteenth, several witnesses distinguished the prominent role of women—"various little mobs of young women, Cholas, Indias, and Mestizas"; or [in] another [designation]—"little girls and boys, Cholos, Mestizos." There is here some accent on youth, reports that prompted the corregidor to issue a circular asking citizens if they really knew where their adolescent children were after lights-out. Again on the fifteenth, in the assault on the house of the corregidor were identified "Cholitos and Cholitas" as well as mounted rustics. Responsibility for the disturbances was never really established, as the Crown, in issuing a general pardon, was apparently willing to let the matter rest.

Nevertheless, some evidence of the ringleaders exists, especially regarding the events of the second phase of the disturbances. Domingo and Diego Benavides, father and son, appear to have been the principal organizers of the demonstrations of the thirteenth and fourteenth; the latter was the street leader, and the former was reported to have made insurrectionary suggestions before the disturbances. More incriminating was the disclosure that an inn owned by Domingo Benavides had been the point of reunion for the participants on the fourteenth, that the signal rocket had been fired from the same inn, that the son of its mayordomo had been identified among the rioters, and that booty from the sacking of the customshouse had been discovered in the very same locale.

We are on firmer ground regarding the leaders of the fifteenth and sixteenth since a virtual cascade of names was revealed during the investigations. All of those inculpated appear to have been residents of the Pampa of Miraflores on the edge of the city: Pedro and José Alarcón; their brother-in-law, Antonio Figueroa; a tenant farmer, Lorenzo Cornejo; the "lieutenant of the Pampa," Tadeo Mantilla; an anonymous "collector" of the Pampa; three tailors, two of whom were Mulattoes; another Mulatto, "Pechito"; a stonemason (*cantero*); the innkeeper, Antonio Sanabria; and a "rich Indian," Huamán Vilca. Most of these participants appear to have been members of a confraternity; the sixteenth was the eve of the feast day of the patron of the Pampa of Miraflores, San Antonio Abad, and one witness testified that insurrectionary talk had started several days before the disturbances at a reunion at which the group was attempting to complete a chapel for the feast. Lacking the necessary funds, Pedro Alarcón had inveighed against the "shoeless paupers" who had come to Arequipa to enrich themselves from the "blood of the poor." He wanted to proclaim, "Kill the corregidor and all *chapetones*" ["tenderfeet," derogatory term for Spaniards born in Spain] and rob them so as to provide the "money and alms" that were necessary to complete the chapel. At a time when the Bourbons were moving to control the confraternities, then, we appear to have an arequipeño confraternity doubling as a revolutionary cell.

The undisputed leader of this group—possibly mayordomo of the confraternity or other informal religious association—was Pedro Alarcón, identified by several witnesses as the convoker of the crowds on January 15–16. Alarcón appears to have been an acknowledged community leader of the less-than-genteel society of the Pampa. He also appears to have been, notwithstanding his protestations of poverty to his fellow religious devotees, a man of substance. He was said to have financed one of Sematnat's repartos, and was held to have paid the corregidor eleven thousand pesos for his freedom when slated as the organizer of the disturbances. Other participants had similar connections to officialdom. . . .

Among the organizers of January 15–16, the "rich Indian" Huamán Vilca merits our attention. In 1781 the cacique of Yanahuara, Ambrosio Quispe Cabana, attested that one Fernando Huamán Vilca, described as a butcher of the Pampa, was, according to "all the Indian butchers" of the Pampa, one of the troop leaders of Túpac Amaru. In January 1780, Huamán Vilca fled the Pampa in the face of the avenging militia. He was never captured, as his "woman," described as a "nun," was alleged to have paid the corregidor some four thousand pesos to leave things well alone. . . . More generally, residents of lower-class boardinghouses in the city itself were discovered to be in possession of goods stolen from the corregidor's house, as were Sanabria and Huamán Vilca. The Indians who invaded the city on the sixteenth were said to have comprised a confederation of those of the city parish of Santa Marta together with those of the village of Cayma, Yanahuara, Chiguata, and "other nearby parishes."

The authors of the pasquinades were variously identified as a young seminarian, Pablo Zárate, who fled to Cusco after he had been apprehended, evidently fearful that all the pasquinades would be attributed to his hand; Lorenzo Rendón, an occasional errand boy and informer of the corregidor, said to have "some knowledge of poetry . . . having no other means, with which to gain his living"; an unnamed friar who was held to be perpetually inebriated; and the *escribano* [notary] and *éminence grise* of Sematnat, Pedro José Salazar, and his army of scriveners. Some witnesses even testified that on one occasion a pasquinade, not yet public, dropped from the corregidor's pocket, though this was after the four nights of rioting. As to Sematnat and Salazar, the theory offered was that they continued to foment trouble so as to ensure the arrival of a battalion from Lima for their own protection and to prevent the possibility of a reestablishment of the customshouse, which competed with their own financial interests.

Apart from the Indians, Mestizos, and other castes, then, there were present an urban underclass of artisans, minor officials, those who lived in rental accommodations, and non-elite men of substance, such as Alarcón, Sanabria, and Huamán Vilca, who were prominent in the organization of the demonstrators of January 15–16. These men were able to take leading roles because, apart from the immediate issues of the day, a subterranean class antagonism existed, which they themselves shared, due to the arrogance of the customs officials, the hatred of outsiders, and the crippling financial impositions of the corregidor and his cronies, all of which flowed into the fear that such exactions would become insupportable with the coming of a more comprehensive tribute system and the range of new taxes that Pando had seemed about to implement.

The new aguardiente excise had affected not only innkeepers but their lower-class customers as well by raising prices, and there is also the report that the corregidor received a tax or bribe from innkeepers for the privilege of not being forcibly sold aguardiente. This helps to explain Sanabria's involvement in the events of the second phase. The Alarcóns, Sanabria, and Huamán Vilca all lived on the Pampa and all appear to have been community leaders there. These instigators had been presented with the opportunity of the sixteenth being not only the Sabbath but also the eve of the feast of the patron saint of the Pampa, San Antonio Abad; that is to say, there was widespread drunkenness among its residents—the "profane" side to Andean religion—a phenomenon that is often an overture to Indian riots or uprisings in the colonial period.

Finally, an intriguing note on *agents provocateurs.* At the outset of the Túpac Amaru rebellion, a nephew of José Gabriel, Simón Noguera, was hanged by the corregidor of Lampa. Shortly before his death, the nephew confessed or bragged to his jailer that he and his illustrious uncle had been in Arequipa at the outbreak of violence, which the Inka had actually fomented. The records of the customs invoices that would enable us to test for the presence of Túpac Amaru in Arequipa at that date are not extant, presumably having been destroyed in the attack on the customshouse on January 14.

Ideology and Political Culture

We are afforded entry to the political consciousness of this racially mixed crowd—or, best to say, crowds—by way of both the import of the pasquinades and the shouts and slogans of the crowd as it went about its business. The pasquinades are our best source, but are fraught with interpretative difficulties. Although some prose versions exist, on the whole they belong to the free verse tradition known as *décimas,* which survived well into the twentieth century in Peru as a form of literary expression and, indeed, even now are not entirely extinct. Now, décimas ranged from elegant, witty verse to jaunty doggerel and plain graffiti. It is tempting to divide pasquinades on the grounds of literary quality, with the more unpolished being held to represent the popular mentality. Within the corregidor's immediate circle, however, it was believed that at least one of the early pasquinades posted in the city "was of no rustic despite its style being disguised." Even where such a pamphlet did indeed derive from a lower-class group or individual, chances were that it had been composed by someone of a higher social rank, thereby probably distorting, if not the message itself, then the form and idiom in which it was expressed. . . .

The rejection of "bad government" with its fiction that a benign monarch is surrounded by "bad ministers" is a common denominator of popular protests across Europe. . . . It is never really quite clear what is subsumed under the rubric of "bad government" in the popular consciousness, and it is frankly not any use in adverting to Spanish juridical tracts to ascertain this context, for original formulations become mediated through the existing popular consciousness and may be tempered by cultural and even geographical variants until they acquire a new content in the process. The concept obviously refers to an acceptable ambit and level of authority and its exercise, beyond which limits such authority becomes excessive. This excess describes physical violence, for example, corporal punishment either gratuitous or meted out without due process; arrogance in the exercise of office—a certain fraternal spirit seems to have been expected from functionaries; and, most of all, graft and corruption in the exercise of office, with the emphasis on the lining of pockets at the expense of the lower orders. . . . Colonial Americans of all social classes knew only too well what comprised corruption, which they denounced frequently. The following slogan, uttered on the night of January 15, neatly captures all of these components of "bad government": "Die, these thieving dogs, they and not the king are the cause of our woes." The four elements are here: corruption expressed as thievery, bad officials, the exculpation of the monarch, and, implicit here, the parish-pump [local] xenophobia, directed against peninsulares and all other outsiders (in this case the limeño customs officials). The mutinous Tiabaya militiamen's chanting of "Long live the king and death to bad government" on the afternoon of January 15, however, has a ritualistic, even legalistic dimension; one of their officers told them to chant clearly, so that later they could not be accused of *lèse-majesté*. . . .

There is, too, an invocation of patron saints to help or guide a people in their political ventures. Santo Domingo is invoked twice; San Francisco once; Jesus, Mary, and Joseph are called on individually and collectively; and even Santiago is called upon, though in which of his manifestations it is not clear. One pasquinade asks the Virgin Mary for "divine grace" to achieve the popular "designs," while another, even more remarkable, asks Jesus to intercede with God the Father for "license" to behead the corregidor and his henchmen. This is popular religion with a vengeance. No real reason exists to doubt that such invocations were sincere; before the establishment of the customshouse, there were reports of what sound like apocalyptic expectations in the city. A public argument between the corregidor and the officials of the provincial treasury, whose grounds for contention are lost to us, gave rise to wild rumors in the city that various of the convents and monasteries would have to "be extinguished" and that "much blood had to run." . . .

[Turning back to the concept of "bad government" and notions of kingship,] among the authors of the pasquinades, some rejected the monarch as well, perceiving, rightly, that the king himself was in great measure responsible for what ailed arequipeños that year. What, then, did they propose to do about it? In fact, they scratched around for alternatives, suggesting either an alliance with Great Britain—whose king, in contrast to Spain's Charles III, "loves his vassals"—or the coronation of an Inka. The Inka nominated was a certain Casimiro, also called Casimiro III in one pasquinade (to provide a witty counterpoint to Charles III), "to whom we swear as king." This personage was identified as an Indian noble of either the Huaraz or Tarma; quite how he came to be known and nominated by arequipeños is not entirely clear, especially when the nearby Cusco, Puno, and Charcas regions were awash with indigenous nobility. However, the "rich Indian" of the Pampa, Huamán Vilca, was alleged to have been in contact with "Indians of Tarma and Jauja." The sales tax records of this time also provide us with the name of Casimiro Condorpusa, possibly a relative of Colonel Esteban Condorpusa, and, if so, an Indian noble. The pasquinade of Cayma mentioned both Inka and Inglaterra [England] in the same breath, while another in the city was said to refer to the possibility of rule by "a confederation of the Indians of Cusco." . . .

What is evident is that in Arequipa in 1780 there were glimmers of a search for a political alternative to the colonial state, however rudimentary these might have been. . . . It is now clear that, at least at some point in his rebellion [soon after these events in Arequipa], if not perhaps at the beginning, José Gabriel Túpac Amaru conceived the reimposition of an autocratic Inka state. But for this to take root among Creole elites was perhaps another matter. . . .

The defensiveness of the political stance of most of the rioters in Arequipa in 1780 is evident from their frequent shouts that they only "wanted" to pay the old rate of excise, but no other pension. But what is to be made of the many threats and imprecations against not only the officials of the customshouse but also against the corregidor, his cohorts, and all those families "of honor and affluence"? E. P. Thompson suspected that the incidence of such rebellious phrases in eighteenth-century England was "usually . . . to chill the blood of the rich with their theatrical effect." Something of the kind is probably in evidence here, but it nevertheless remains true that blood was spilled and that an ambush was prepared behind the corregidor's house to kill him when the main body of rioters flushed him out from the front. The first two days of rioting also appear to have activated a class envy, even class and racial hatred, which then made possible the final two days of calculated assault—two days that threatened the whole fabric of the polity in that provincial city.

In spite of the threats to the town worthies, the events of January 1780 came to be a source of much pride to arequipeños, perhaps the germ of that rebellious spirit for which the city came to be renowned in republican Peru. Its children are our guide to this spirit. One of the Crown investigators of the disturbances reported that, by 1781, the children of the city had developed a popular game based on the assault on the customshouse. Two children seated themselves on chairs acting out the roles of Pando and De la Torre, while others brought them parcels, representing merchandise subject to the excise. At a signal, another crowd of children would rush the two seated figures and beat them to a symbolic death, all the while chanting the slogans that their elders and betters had shouted during the actual attack on the customshouse of January 14, 1780.

The political disturbances in Arequipa of January 13–16, 1780, were made possible in the first instance by the uncanny manner in which the fiscal reforms of the alcabala, tribute, nuevo impuesto, and quinto managed to affect detrimentally all classes in the city as well as the surrounding countryside, an effect exacerbated by the arrogance of the customshouse officials. The temporary cross-class alliance thus generated a springboard from which the underclasses of the city and countryside were able to protest that most hated of imposts, the reparto, which affected not only the Indians, the conventional victims, but Mestizos and other castes as well. If the events of the thirteenth and fourteenth were to some degree directed or inspired by aggrieved members of the patriciate, those of the succeeding two days of violence signified the traditional elite's loss of control over both the city and the surrounding countryside. From that moment, the rioters, who had had at least the blessing of those patricians who wished to see the customshouse banished once and for all from the region, perceived that the city was undefended. That it was undefended was due to the folly and avarice of the corregidor, who had included Mestizos and castes in his forced distributions, precisely those racial categories that constituted the bulk of the militia of the region. On the sixteenth, the city was defended by two companies of patrician militiamen, now fearful for their families and wealth, and fearful, too, of the designs that the lower orders had on their very own White skins. Had they remained solid with the bulk of their brother militiamen, the city would surely have fallen.

The events certainly represent much less than an attempt at revolution, but surely, too, something more than a mere antifiscal protest. The attacks of the fifteenth and sixteenth bore witness to considerable class antagonism, a notion of class expressed in its most simple terms between those who have and those who have not. . . .

There is here, though, something more than class antagonism. All of these prisoners were from the Pampa of Miraflores, as indeed were those who convoked and directed them. An antagonism existed between the city and the countryside, especially between the city and the curious society of the Pampa, where indios forasteros had made their home and where the community leaders were wealthy traders and storekeepers whose lack of breeding and gentility, their relative rusticity, precluded their acceptance among the racially conscious patriciate of the city. The bitter Pedro Alarcón epitomized this socially marginalized subclass. He and his companions, in convoking the poor denizens of the Pampa to the assault, relied on lust for gain and class antagonism to win their recruits, rather than on any more overt political terms. Nevertheless, this latter aspect must remain open to some doubt, inasmuch as there is testimony that the attacks of the sixteenth were in part an expression of a confederation of the Indian parishes of the surrounding countryside, and the attack clearly came not only from the Pampa but from other directions as well.

The attacks of the thirteenth and fourteenth were organized around the companies of militia, judging from the considerable numbers of well-disciplined horsemen and, indeed, from the sheer numbers of armed assailants. The militia also appears to have involved itself on the final two nights, though with less solidarity than hitherto. At least on the first two nights, the crowd probably included peons and other employees of haciendas, drafted especially for the event. The network of haciendas and the distribution of the militia companies provide the two obvious means of communication and recruitment of large numbers of individuals acting in concert. The taverns represent a third possible network: the presence of Sanabria among the organizers of the fifteenth and sixteenth and the use of Domingo Benavides's inn as a staging point for the attack of the fourteenth suggest that this network was used to conscript a crowd. In 1777 and early 1780 the taverns of Cusco were so used in an attempt to spread sedition and recruit aggrieved citizens.

The alienation of the militia through its liability for reparto and possibly tribute provides one explanation of why the traditional means of social order had ceased to function, but it is evident that the social control exercised by the clergy had also broken down. The clergy was, of course, also deleteriously affected by the fiscal innovations, but on the two occasions when the Crown sought their intervention, the rioters peremptorily rebuffed it. On January 15 the confraternities of the convents and monasteries were on the streets with their rosaries in response to a plea from the corregidor; when they attempted to soothe and disperse the rioters, they were abruptly told to get out of the way. Moreover, when a Dominican famed for his virtue held aloft the image of Jesus in this attempt to pacify the multitude, the crowd responded by firing rifles and hurling stones at the sacred image. That same Dominican friar was sent to Cayma to disperse a gathering; but not only were his entreaties ignored, he himself was personally threatened. In Urubamba in 1777 the bishop of Cusco similarly sought to quell a revolt by holding aloft the Sacred Host; he, too, was stoned and later died from his wounds. In the Andes, profound religious sentiment often exists with equally profound anticlericalism, yet attacks on an effigy of Jesus and on the Sacred Host point to a drastic cessation of normality.

Yet, overall, the movement had its own momentum. When the lower-class rioters perceived that the city was undefended, class and perhaps even racial hatreds repressed in quotidian life flared to the surface. The events in Arequipa in January 1780 demonstrated all too clearly that Spanish power in the Americas rested on fragile foundations that, if challenged by a cross-class alliance, might easily crumble. That cross-class alliance was vitiated not only by racial fear and distrust, but also by a yawning gap between the material conditions of the life of the rich few and the many poor.

 44

Juan Francisco Domínguez's Discourses on the Ten Commandments, Mexico

(1805)

Catholicism remained the state religion of Spanish America throughout the colonial period, but there were notable changes both in the place of the Church as an institution in public life and in the religion promoted from Spain and cathedral cities in the colonies. Especially during the eighteenth century, these changes had at least as much to do with developments in Europe as with American circumstances.

Many of the late colonial changes gave the appearance of a lighter, gentler Christianity. The old metaphor of fear and love as the two wings of flight toward Heaven fell out of favor in Church teachings, replaced by a heavy emphasis on love. The bishops' pastoral letters and urban religious art presented God less as a remote and stern judge than as a loving Father, and the crucified Christ less as a wounded figure in agony than as a sublime human form anticipating the Resurrection. The sky in fashionable paintings of the Virgin Mary grew pink with the backsides of frolicking baby angels. There were fewer references in learned theological treatises to the Seven Deadly Sins, less preoccupation with the Devil, Adam and Eve's Fall, and the innate sinfulness of humanity; less of the somber solemnity, mystical strivings, and endless war between body and soul that pervaded seventeenth-century beliefs and practices (see Selections 29, 30, and 31). With the glass half full rather than half empty, a more optimistic view of human nature pointed toward education for salvation and the potential for growth in "la felicidad pública" (public happiness and welfare). The Ten Commandments and the epistles of Saint Paul grew in prominence as positive guides to improvement through love, charity, and sociability. And, as in the sixteenth century, the early centuries of the Church were recalled as a model of Christian values in practice.

This apparently softer, more loving religion did not emerge in a vacuum, nor did it capture the imagination of most Church members. The late eighteenth-century redefinition of the parish priest's role in public life as the loving teacher and spiritual specialist had less to do with a sea change in religious sensibility than with the politics of religion. Bourbon policymakers were intent upon enhancing the power and prestige of royal governors by removing priests from their customary position as moral judges who oversaw the family life and public affairs of communities in their parishes. With a more forgiving and approachable God, there should have followed—as there apparently did in Spain—a decline in the veneration of saints as intercessors. But no such decline seems to have occurred in the old centers of colonial Spanish America. On the contrary, the growing veneration of Mary there in the eighteenth century suggests that her intercession was needed more than ever.

A lighter version of Christianity was preferred especially by educated city people, colonial administrators, bishops, and other Spanish immigrants. It could be used to reduce religion to an individual matter in a realm of its own, and relegate the Church to a subordinate bureau of the state instead of a partner (even instead of the wife and mother in the old family metaphor for the political hierarchy and social order). It tended to root more deeply in emerging regions such as Argentina, Venezuela, and Cuba than in rural areas of the old centers in Peru and central Mexico.

This selection by a prominent Mexico City priest is in keeping with these changes, but it also expresses deep worries about their ramifications for the Church, public virtue, and political order. When it appeared in 1805 in the opening pages of a lengthy treatise on the Ten Commandments, the author, Juan Francisco Domínguez, was an eighty-year-old senior pastor of the cathedral parish who had served eighteen years in Indian parishes of central Mexico. Before his death in 1813 he produced a small string of publications on devotional subjects and moral issues including the virtues of the Virgin Mary, the renowned image of Our Lady of Guadalupe, and sermons on pure love and proper relations with women.

The emphasis on love, charity, the teachings of Saint Paul (the "Apostle" whom Domínguez keeps mentioning), and a loving God who is the essence of generosity and goodness are here in abundance, along with an optimistic view of human potential for virtuous conduct, "felicidad pública" in this world, and salvation in the next. In this passage, as in several others within the treatise, Domínguez turned the negative injunctions of particular commandments into positive statements about Christian virtues. Even the Fifth Commandment, "Thou shalt not kill," is presented as an affirmation of God's love for humanity by forbidding acts of hatred and violence against others. This view follows Christ's positive reflections on the Ten Commandments in Matthew 19, more than that of the thundering Old Testament God in Exodus 20, but Domínguez balanced his optimism about the potential for virtuous behavior with stress on the prohibitions embedded in each of the commandments and the rampant selfishness he saw around him. He did not forget "the terrible sting of the Almighty's hand" or the Virgin's gift of forgiveness when she might well have "raise[d] the lash of her justice."

Despite his disclaimer that the treatise was not directed toward Bourbon governors and councillors, it is hard to avoid the conclusion that they were his intended audience, the group whom he wanted most to persuade. The title itself—"Religion and the State Conjoined"—and the way that Domínguez developed the political implications of reducing religion to a separate, secondary place in public life make this clear. He sees religion being removed from the center of human affairs and replaced by the "happiness of the state" ("la felicidad del estado"). Yet how could the two be made distinct in this way, he asks, when the irreplaceable foundation of a just and happy state is the divine law embodied in the Ten Commandments? The state cannot achieve maximum peace, order, and happiness unless it actively supports religion (and its priests), he keeps saying. There is more than a subdued warning in his repeated thought that justice and the common good are the state's only purposes, and that "in God dwells all justice and truth." True to form, he ends on a positive and loyal note, with a ringing endorsement of common cause between state and religion in order to breathe life into the Ten Commandments, "which will bestow upon us honor, peace, and glory."

From the first discourse [on the First Commandment: You shall love God above all else, and your neighbor as yourself.]

The point of my discourses will be to persuade with evidence that if we yearn for good order, the exceedingly useful harmony of souls, innocence in our customs, peace with everyone and victory over foreign enemies, help for the unfortunate, the blessings of God over the fruits of the Earth, abundance and equity in trade and commerce, [and] essential provisions—in a word, a reasonably abundant fulfillment of needs, made up of the foregoing, which make for a fortunate state—we must obey the commandments of God.

By "the state" we mean consonant harmony between the principality and the people for a political government that establishes kingdoms with good customs, preventing the divisions that have desolated many kingdoms. From such harmony, true peace springs. By "religion" we mean that first among moral virtues, which has as its object the worship of God, not only in sacrifices and offerings or the furnishing and magnificence of its churches or awe for these buildings and their altars and ministers. Although religion has especially to do with the [officials] of the Church, [we mean] also the wholehearted observance of its commandments. Each of the commandments reflects on some special virtue: almost all of the Ten Commandments have to do with charity and justice. But they all share the injunction to do what God commands, which is the object of religion.

The words of Ecclesiastes 12:13, which I have chosen to give spirit to my own [words], say it concisely: Fear God, and obey His commandments. This applies to all people, as if the passage said: the entire being of a contented person, and his entire well-being consists of obeying the commandments, animated by the holy fear of God. Everyone is obliged to do this. No vassal, king, great person or small, poor person or from the high reaches [of society], or even the lowliest of the low, no one is human who has not absorbed this respect for what God commands. For the very destiny and purpose of human creation was to serve God. Thus, if the sun no longer shone, it would cease being the sun; and humans would cease to be human if they did not serve God because they would no longer be taken for humans, but for donkeys. All this the wise Ecclesiastes wished to tell us in this pithy warning, with which he closed his loving and salubrious sermon. I infer from this: if every person by his very being should keep the commandments, he who does not observe divine law lives outside human society. And with such a multitude (for the number of stupid people is infinite) living outside the law, how can there be a society? And without society, how can the state exist? Let us go on to reflect on each of the commandments, and it will be lucidly clear that the observance of all those [commandments] that religion prescribes is utterly necessary for the well-being of the state. And if it [the state] is not based on religion and religion is not called upon by the state, if they do not come together, everything will be ruin and desolation for the kingdoms. . . .

Section 3

This commandment [You shall love God above all else, and your neighbor as yourself] is not two separate commandments, but one that the Divine Master subdivided in two because of its distinct objects, God and one's neighbor (in which the Supreme Legislator orders us to love the neighbor as we love ourselves). Even though the beloved objects are infinitely distinct and distant from each other, the motive force of love is the same. Let us love God through God and the neighbor through God. So our standard theology teaches, according to Saint Thomas Aquinas.

This powerful motive force softens the inclusion of love for one's neighbor in this commandment, without which [neighborly love] would seem extremely hard. Considering the vices, bad tempers, perverse opinions, and ingratitude of people that make them unworthy of love of any kind, to love them as ourselves even if they were lovable would seem an impossible thing. Self-regard ranks high in our hearts as we covet our own well-being, preferring our own welfare above all that can be done for others. But with God in the picture, what God wants and commands must be fulfilled even at some personal sacrifice. This is a commandment that Jesus Christ took as His own, so that it is not only from a God who, being God, must be obeyed, but from a God become human, from a God who became human and died for us in order to give us the supernatural state of grace. That He gave His life for us obliges us, as the Apostle says, to give our lives for others.

Taken all together, not much is required of us. Our self-regard is left intact when we are ordered to love our neighbor as we do ourselves. This does not require us to love others as much as we love ourselves, only [that we love them] in the same way as we do ourselves. This amounts to wanting the good things for others that we want for ourselves, and not wanting the misfortunes for others that we would not want for ourselves, as in the advice that Tobias gave to his son. But we shall not fulfill our duty simply by wishing others well and causing them no harm in a detached way, as if we did not really love them. Beyond not doing harm to anyone, we must seek out the opportunities to influence and contribute to their well-being. This is not simply a negative precept not to hate or wish misfortune upon others, but a positive one to love and do well. Of course, it does forbid hatred, envy, pretense, the scandals that cause spiritual ruin, and the hardness of heart that keeps us from helping those in great need.

Section 4 [the final section in Discourse 1]

There is no need to reflect deeply to be convinced that nothing suits the happiness of the state so much as the love of God above all else and [the love] of our neighbors as ourselves. This is one of those truths that is evident in its very terms. If we love God above all things, we shall never violate justice because of selfish motives of honor, life, or property. This is the moral fiber of the Republic. With its observance alone good Order is preserved, rights are respected, and good government operates. Justice gives to each what is his, not only in material terms but also in personal rights. Justice requires that the constituted authorities be obeyed, that they govern with equity, that they do not lack humanity either in guiding or collaborating toward what is just, that crimes are punished and merits are rewarded. Justice directs the tribunals, arranges business transactions, and attends to the public interest. The only thing that threatens it is self-interest, which causes merit to be ignored in public officeholding, the worthy and best-suited to be left out of these offices, [and] subjects to disparage the public authority granted by

God to those who govern us. It [self-interest] causes the impious to prevail against the just, leading to perverse judgments, as Jeremiah lamented. In short, iniquity upsets everything, confuses everything, ruins everything. Therefore, justice is the epitome of the law, and our law in the Ten Commandments is, as Saint Thomas teaches, the law of justice. Everything is maintained and fortified by the love of God alone, above all things, and everything can be lost if it is neglected.

The state is strengthened just as much by mutual love among ourselves. Just as a building cannot stand if the stones are not well joined, the Republic cannot last without the bond of charity uniting its people. If everyone only wants to live for oneself, against the maxim of the Philosopher [Saint Thomas Aquinas], not caring for one's neighbor, no one will contribute to the common good and everyone will perish for lack of assistance. Some may help others because they fear the governor's authority, but [they serve] badly and not for long if they do not help because of love. With chains of gold, love binds subjects to their prince, servants to their lords, [and] children to their parents. Under the soft and efficacious influence of love, elders and superiors look out for the well-being of minors and inferiors. Through love, difficulties that stand in the way of the welfare of others are surmounted because love conquers all. No doubt the entire foundation of a happy Republic depends on peace. But how can there be peace where there is conflict? And how can there be harmony where mutual charity is lacking?

The Apostle [Saint Paul] calls charity the bond, because it ties people to each other. With this charity everyone moves with equality toward the target of universal happiness. The unfortunate person, because of illness or unemployment, cannot support his poor family. He has many companions in his misery, and they cast a shadow over the happiness of the people. You who have an abundance, give them a hand, relieve their poverty with your abundance. Do the same for other unfortunates who are worthy of equal compassion and they will no longer live in misery.

Husbands and wives are not working together under the yoke of matrimony. They live in continual disagreement. Despite being yoked together, one goes off in one direction, the other in another. The result is furious arguments, which is scandalous for their children. This family falls apart and, since there are many in this unfortunate situation, many homes do not contribute to the beauty of this city [Mexico City]; that is, many [do not contribute to] the beautiful edifice of the Republic. The [family of the] Church was never better governed than in the first centuries when all believers formed a single spirit and heart, according to the accounts of the Apostles.

And how does religion influence this reciprocal charity? Beyond its role in the observance of all law, as already said, it directly inspires charity among brothers and sisters. Such is the character of Christians, and consequently the spirit of religion, that in the first centuries when persecution prevented them from congregating and communicating among themselves, they were known for this [reciprocal charity]. Look (said the pagans) how they love each other, how they are quick to give up their lives for others. Religion has joined us in a baptism in which we were remade as children of God; a single Father unites us in a single faith, at one table where we eat of the same bread, the bread that Our Father sent us from Heaven, the bread that gives us life. Christ dwells within us, and thus we are animated by His spirit. How can we not declare ourselves Christians and, through our religion, be united by love? This is characteristic of Christianity. Those who do not love, who put their vile self-interest before the preciousness of their character [as Christians], do not belong.

We are in urgent need (I say again with the Apostle [Saint Paul]) of the charity of Christ. Can we be Christians if we do not follow Christ? Of course not. If we are to follow Christ, who loved us all, we must love each other. Religion inspires this love, and by this love (for the reasons mentioned) the Republic lives and the happiness of the state is preserved.

45

Two Castas *Paintings from Eighteenth-Century Mexico*

Through most of the eighteenth and into the early nineteenth century a number of artists in New Spain produced sets of portraits collectively known as "*castas* paintings." These sets sought to portray different racial combinations in late colonial Mexico. The term "castas" referred specifically to those people thought to be of "mixed race" and excluded Spaniards (*españoles*) and other Europeans, Blacks (*negros*), and Indians (*indios*) even if, in the eighteenth century, it was common enough for anyone who was not Spanish to be considered a casta. Many of these canvases were not signed or dated, but the bulk of the works on the castas theme appears to date between 1750 and 1800, with the earliest series currently believed to have been painted about 1725.

Some of the painters of castas were obscure and anonymous, and some created series that were copied (at times crudely) from earlier castas groups. But the theme also attracted the likes of the master Miguel Cabrera (1695–1768), a Mestizo from Oaxaca who had moved to Mexico City in 1719 and was painting at the viceregal court by mid-century. Between 1761 and 1766, Cabrera produced portraits of a number of the most powerful secular and religious personalities in Mexico. And it was roughly at this time that he executed a striking series of castas portraits (not all of which have been found) from live models. Other known artists of castas include Ignacio de Castro, Luis de Mena, José de Páez, Ignacio María Barreda, and two painters whose work is featured here: José Joaquín Magón (Figure 30) and Andrés de Islas (Figure 31).

In idealized ways, the castas paintings depict people in a variety of trades and occupations, in their homes and customary dress. A few of the pictures consist of a single canvas or panel on which the different racial combinations were compartmentalized and classified. Many others are separate compositions, commonly showing a mixed-race couple with at least one child, within a series of paintings (usually about sixteen) meant to be viewed in succession. Some, but not all, castas series included a final painting depicting not racial mixture at all but "savage" Indians, sometimes identified as Mecos (Chichimeca) or Apaches from northern Mexico. It became customary to inscribe a number and an identifying explanation on each canvas. The inscription described the racial mixture being portrayed and sometimes (as in Figure 30) included a short descriptive phrase.

Many sets of castas paintings have been found in Europe. Others have been discovered in Mexico, with their frames removed and rolled up in preparation for shipment. These castas were commissioned as souvenirs by

Spaniards returning home after a time in America. Other Europeans who had never crossed the Atlantic sought them as exotic curiosities, both decorative and in some sense descriptive of the many racially mixed people of Mexico. Still other sets appear to have been undertaken for members of the Spanish and Creole elite within New Spain. The paintings can be viewed in part as another dimension of the increased regard for scientific inquiry in an "enlightened" and order-seeking Bourbon era, a general interest in descriptive classification and rationalization here delivered with a blunt message of Spanish racial superiority. The urge to classify seems particularly pronounced in images such as Figure 31, in which the castas vignette with its careful description is accompanied by American fruits and vegetables similarly indicated and labeled.

The first image (Figure 30), without a precise date but from the second half of the eighteenth century, was painted by José Joaquín Magón, an artist from Puebla, Mexico, who approaches the level of Cabrera in his skills. This is the first of sixteen canvases, and an inscription at the top of the painting introduces the series: "In America are born people of diverse colors, customs, temperaments, and languages." The painting offers a peaceful and sentimental domestic scene in a household of some means. A bright red bird perched on the back of a chair to the far left is the American marker, reminding the viewer that this locale is an exotic place. A young Mestizo boy, dressed as elegantly as any contemporary adult in his French-style coat and white shirt, exhibits the results of a recent lesson in letters to his father. His expression is expectant and proud as he receives his father's praise.

Figure 30. Castas painting featuring the Mestizo, child of a Spanish man and an Indian woman, by José Joaquín Magón, Mexico (second half of the eighteenth century).

Light falls on the white paper that the boy is holding, on which he has written the word *parco* (meaning temperate and moderate), and on his father, an extraordinarily pink-cheeked, doe-eyed Spaniard seated at a desk on the left. The man wears an unbuttoned cutaway coat over a richly embroidered vest. His clothing and demeanor suggest that he is a professional man of some standing. He is at home; and thus in place of the white wig he would wear in public, he sports a cloth cap of the kind commonly worn by nobles and professional men to keep their heads warm when their wigs were off. The father is shown just closing Miguel de Cervantes's masterpiece, *Don Quixote de la Mancha*—further emphasizing the benefits of the education that his son is beginning to receive. (In another painting in this series, a Spanish father sits within reach of bookshelves upon which the labeled works of Virgil are prominently displayed.) Figure 30 seems to suggest that literacy in the Spanish language is the key to civility and refinement for the Mestizo (as it is for the Indian in the opinion of many of Magón's contemporaries in Spanish America, not least Alonso Carrió de la Vandera; see Selection 41). The father is only too pleased to receive his son and looks affectionately into his eyes. The boy's mother, a demure Indian woman to the right, dressed in a delicately embroidered garment and with glittering earrings and a necklace, regards the boy's exhibition with a tender smile as she points out a practice page of repeated letters. But the moment occurs mostly between Mestizo son and Spanish father. The Indian mother is painted in a shadow, framing the main action with her smile.

Here is a picture of a harmonious union, a successful fusion of European and Indian resulting in a new "American" racial type, the Mestizo. A second inscription beneath a Roman numeral "I" (for the first class of race mixture) reads: "From a Spaniard and an Indian woman issues a Mestizo, who is commonly meek, tranquil, and straightforward." The Mestizo might be found wanting in a number of the qualities possessed so effortlessly by his Spanish father, the painting seems to say, but he is sober, obedient, and well-meaning. And, within certain limits, he is able to learn. There are worse qualities for a colonial subject to have. The Mestizo is imagined as an ideal servant.

Magón's portrayal of the Mestizo is a determined step away from the ways in which Mestizos and many other castas were usually described in contemporary literature, drama, and chroniclers' accounts. Especially in the sixteenth century, Mestizos were often the offspring of illicit unions. This illegitimacy contributed to their negative image among privileged Spaniards as rootless and disruptive figures. Like the Zambos (people said to be of Indian and African ancestry and often identified as "Mulatto" in seventeenth-century Mexico), Mestizos by their very existence demonstrated that official attempts to keep Europeans, Africans, and castas out of the Indian communities had failed, and failed rather spectacularly.

Mestizos were perceived as floating uncertainly between Spanish and Indian cultures, the very agents of chaos within a cultural and racial framework that colonial law defined in simple terms that did not go far beyond the idea of the "two republics" of Spaniards and Indians. Mestizos were said by their detractors to make cruel use of their acquaintance with the Spanish language and ways to victimize gullible Indians. Not that Mestizos could be much trusted by anyone else, either. The caricature of the Mestizo serves up a rash and absurd upstart who brags incessantly, a pretentious and uneducated half-breed, anything but "parco." By keeping such derogatory stereotypes out of this picture, Magón paints a new world in which Spaniards and Indians marry and live in peace and in which Mestizos are accepted, tutored, and supported—even if, in an imaginary world as in the real one, there were limits to what a person supposed to be "meek, tranquil, and straightforward" would be judged capable of achieving.

The second castas portrait (Figure 31) was painted by Andrés de Islas about 1774. It is the fourth picture in a series of sixteen. This work departs sharply from the realm of domestic bliss and literacy of Figure 30. Life for this family is seen as closer to basic matters of food, clothing, and shelter, with less room for luxuries and refinements. Whereas the Spanish father in Figure 30 seems to preside over a productive calm, the Spaniard in Figure 31 has no control and the family threesome is embroiled in a fierce quarrel. An African woman, gritting her teeth, has flown into a rage and grabs her Spanish partner by the hair. With her free hand she is about to strike him with a cooking utensil. The man's eyes are wide open as he tries to restrain her. The child of their union, a Mulatta, looks up and screams in fear as she grabs her mother's skirts.

At the foot of this domestic strife, fourteen carefully numbered "fruits from this country" seem an absurdity to the modern eye, except that the results of scientific classification fold into this painting's message and distance the

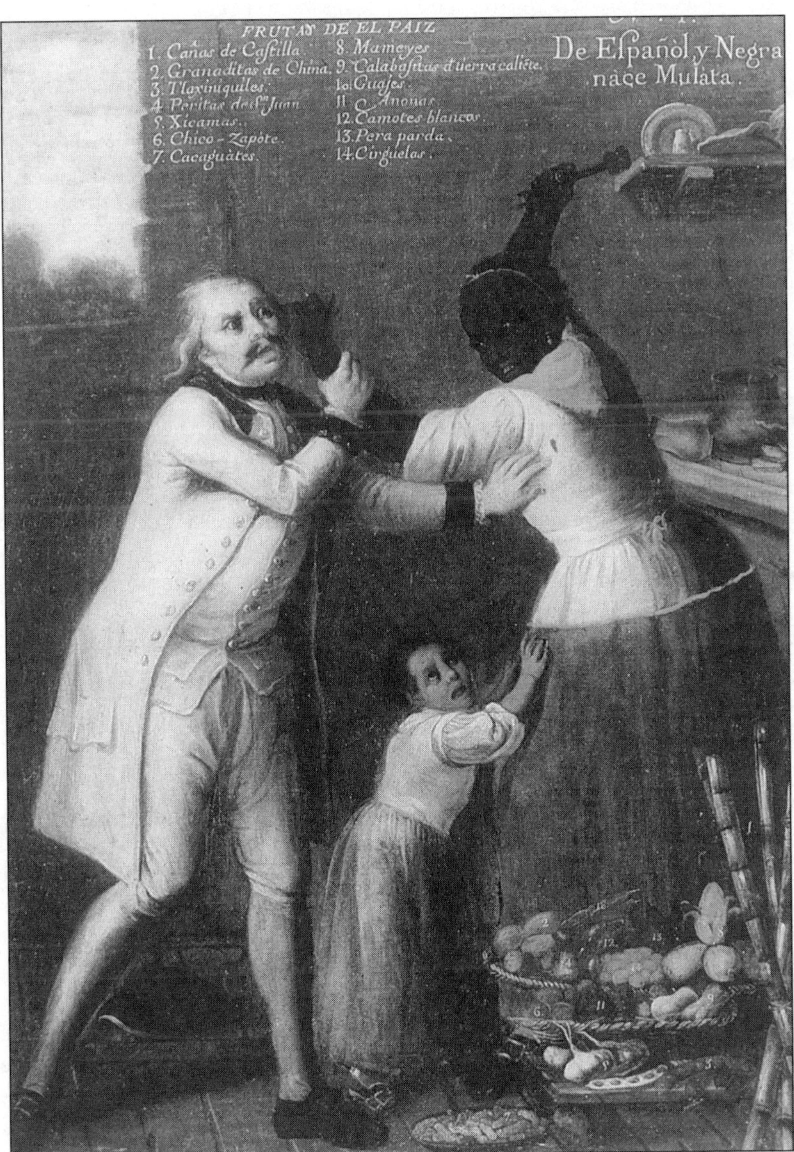

Figure 31. Castas painting featuring the Mulatta, child of a Spanish man and an African woman, by Andrés de Islas, Mexico, ca. 1774. Courtesy of the Museo de América, Madrid.

scene from its presumably European audience. The painter and his patron have a negative view of Blacks, and the image warns Whites against unions with them. (See also the controversy surrounding Beatriz de Padilla's family life with several distinguished Spanish men in Selection 28.) The African woman is portrayed as violent, and her union with a Spaniard has descended into an unhappy mess for both parents and the child. (Another canvas from the same series, not reproduced here, seems to underscore the point. In it, an industrious Mulatta is seen participating in a peaceful and shared task with her Spanish male partner, while their Morisco boy, lighter-skinned than his mother, looks on. The tension felt in Figure 31 is lifted as the artist seems to say that a further stage of miscegenation in the right, or White, direction is a good thing, altering a person of part-African extraction for the better.) Considering Figure 31 with Figure 30 (not to mention other depictions in the castas genre), the viewer is informed that Spaniards do not fare as well in their relationships with Africans as with Indians.

In making such statements or in taking on such commissions, Islas and Magón confirmed general opinions. In many learned as well as popular circles, *mestizaje*—miscegenation or racial mixture—was perceived as detrimental, bringing about the deterioration of human character, ability, and intelligence. Yet segregation laws and official warnings did not prevent it, nor did they eliminate miscegenation anxiety. And by the time most of the castas paintings were executed in the second half of the eighteenth century, the old racial classifications of early colonial times—Spanish, Indian, Black, Mestizo, Mulatto, Zambo, Castizo (offspring of Spaniard and Mestizo), and Morisco (offspring of Spaniard and Mulatto)—no longer sufficed to identify and order society. Most supposed "Mestizos" and "Mulattoes" were themselves the children of casta parents. Thus the categories grew considerably more elaborate, as the contemporary castas series and classification lists show. The more elaborate they became, the more impossible they became to distinguish visually.

A *tente en el aire*—a localized Mexican expression meaning "suspended in air"—was the offspring of six possible racial mixtures (a *torno-atrás* man and a Spanish woman, a *cambujo* man and an Indian woman, a *salto-atrás* man and an *albarazado* woman, a *jíbaro* man and a Mulatto woman, an albarazado man and a jíbaro woman, or a cambujo man and a *calpamulo* woman). Most of these castas themselves were the products of a comparable number of alternative unions. To consider only one of the parents of a tente en el aire for the purposes of illustration, a cambujo man (derived from the name of a reddish-black stallion) might himself be the offspring of some nine possible parental combinations.

Most of the elaborated classifications amounted to mental puzzles, exhibitions of pseudoscientific precision. They tell far more about an eighteenth-century elite's refined sense of racial privilege and order in society than about social realities. For people in Mexico and other parts of Latin America had long been spilling beyond, and defying, the bounds of even the extended ideals of race and privilege. And many racial categories (cambujo, for instance) effectively referred to a dark-skinned person who, in practice, might have sought and been identified by other terms—and perhaps by even more than one in the course of his life.

The castas paintings offer insight into the eighteenth-century elaboration of attitudes and prejudices toward miscegenation which, to some extent and from different points of view, would have been shared by painters and patrons. Racial categories were more than abstractions, and they mattered to and for people beyond the various officialdoms and before the eighteenth century. The compartmentalized renderings and imaginings within the castas paintings capture only parts of these colonial realities—parts that might seem strange or simply amusing on a wall in Spain. As a number of selections in this book demonstrate, individuals and their actions could usually be depended upon not to conform perfectly to their officially designated categories. The image of the passive and dutiful Mestizo boy in Figure 30, for instance, is challenged by the prevalence of Mestizos among the militiamen who led the 1780 attack on the customshouse in Arequipa, Peru (Selection 43). People from among the so-called castas were sometimes able to live beyond the limits set on their activities, whether in separate communities, through their intelligence and charm, or by "passing" as Spaniards thanks to wealth, education, and personal connections.

46

Late Eighteenth-Century Inscriptions on Fountains and Monuments in Mexico City

Some important changes in politics and culture were promoted from the top of Spanish and colonial American society after the War of the Spanish Succession (1700–1713), when a French Bourbon dynasty replaced the Hapsburgs on the Spanish throne. Administrative and economic reforms were introduced, aimed at material improvement and a more centralized authority for an "enlightened" monarch and his *peninsular* advisers, but these reforms were not often achieved in lasting ways or with the intended results. "Fixed rules," strict obedience to law, reason, and applied science became the new watchwords, while customary practices of Baroque Catholicism were often discredited as irrational and dangerously tangled in confusion. Bourbon administrators hoped to restrain the elaborate, high-spirited, and costly religious festivities of virtually every community in the old heartlands of the empire, and channel that energy and wealth into more sober, productive activity. For the new Spanish monarchy, ancient Rome became, again, a revered model of greatness and order.

These aspirations and values of Bourbon leaders—a somewhat pale, top-down version of the great Enlightenment changes becoming evident elsewhere in western Europe by the late seventeenth century—were expressed in some ordinary, overlooked ways. By the reign of Charles III (1759–1788), the kingdoms of Spain were more conspicuously personified in the current occupant of the throne. The king's visage now appeared on silver coins of the realm in place of the royal coat of arms, his head in profile with a laurel wreath, like some Roman emperor. The point was driven home in a larger-than-life equestrian statue of the reigning monarch Charles IV commissioned for Mexico City at the turn of the nineteenth century. The king, again, appears in the dress and posture of a Roman emperor. The cool, restrained monumentality of the neoclassical style of art and architecture, also inspired by Roman models, appealed to the Spanish Bourbons' obsession with orderly, rational grandeur (which often meant massive, symmetrical, and austere). An official academy of art in its own neoclassical building was established in Mexico City during the 1780s to teach the properly "regal" aesthetic.

The many public works undertaken during the late eighteenth century—bridges, paved roads, waterworks, parks, fountains, municipal buildings, jails, and the like—were characteristic of the Bourbon program.

And, unlike earlier construction initiatives, every new work seemed to merit an inscription for the public's edification. Here are three examples from late eighteenth-century Mexico City that convey more about their time and sponsors than just names and dates. But even dates on buildings were not "just" dates. The vogue of dating the beginning and completion of new works and of commemorating centennials and other anniversaries with inscriptions on buildings in the late colonial period suggests a heightened historical consciousness that was more alert to change.

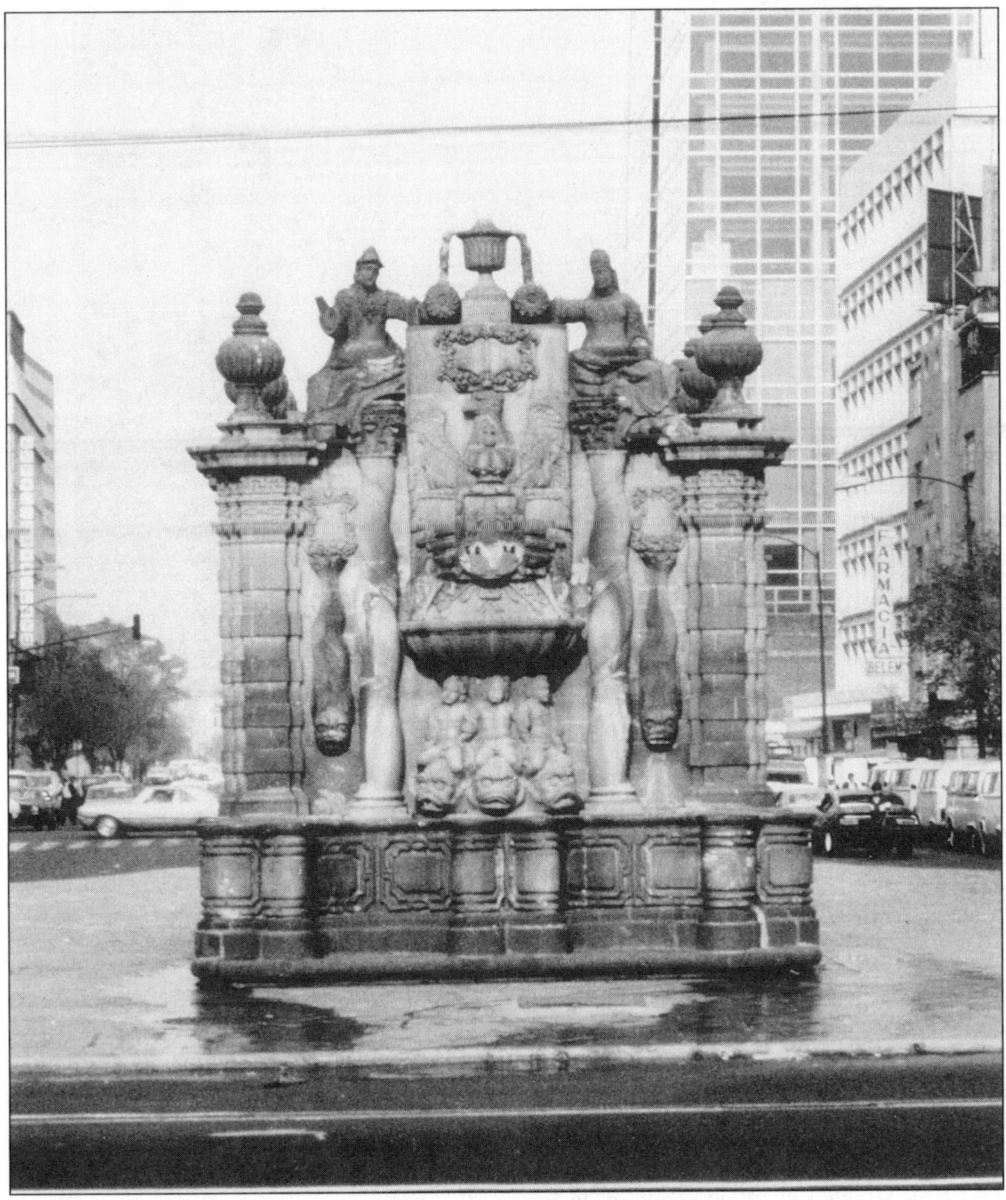

Figure 32. The Salto del Agua, Mexico City, 1779.

Figure 33. Inscription on the Salto del Agua, Mexico City, 1779.

Translation of the inscription on one side of the Salto del Agua (Figure 33), the great fountain at the terminus of the newly built aqueduct that brought water to the city from springs at Chapultepec:

> From the reservoir to this receiving station
> is a distance of 4,663 *varas* [13,056 feet, or about
> two and one-half miles], and from the Chapultepec
> bridge there are 904 arches [in the aqueduct].
> And having made various experiments to achieve
> the greatest elevation and water pressure, the
> height of this new aqueduct was raised another
> one and three-quarters varas [nearly 5 feet],
> while the previous governors had raised the
> water channel by just over one vara [2.8 feet].
> The results of this new construction are clear:
> a height of two and three-quarters varas [7.7 feet]
> over the original aqueduct has been achieved
> by (as already stated) various prolix and
> exquisite experiments.

On the opposite side of the Salto del Agua is another inscription in an identical frame (not illustrated here), translated as follows:

> This aqueduct and receiving station were completed on March 20, 1779, in the reign of His Catholic Majesty Charles III (may God protect him); being Viceroy, Governor, and Captain General of this New Spain and President of its Royal Audiencia the Most Excellent Baylio Frey Antonio María Bucareli y Urive, Knight-General, Descendant of Military Leaders, Commander in the Order of Saint John, Gentleman of His Majesty's Council, soon-to-be Lt. General of the Royal Armies; being Judge-Conservator of Ways and Means of this Most Noble City Don Miguel de Acedo, member of His Majesty's Council and Audiencia judge in the city of Mexico; and being the magistrate in charge Don Antonio de Mier y Terán, perpetual alderman of this Most Noble City.

Figure 34. Monument for the New Roadway to San Agustín de las Cuevas, Mexico City, 1787.
Courtesy of the Archivo General de la Nación, Mexico City.

Translation of the inscription on the Monument for the New Roadway from Mexico City to San Agustín de las Cuevas, Mexico City, 1787 (Figure 34):

> Stay a moment, Traveler, and listen carefully
> To the Great Conde de Gálvez about the care
> Taken by this Royal Mexican consulado [the powerful merchant guild]
> Their concern for [American] development.
> For the greater embellishment of Mexico
> And to ease the lives of beggars and the needy
> They have built this beautiful roadway,
> Emulating the splendor of Rome:
> The Via Stabiana, the beautiful Via Cornelia
> The famous Via Salaria of Sabinius [and]
> The one that goes between Capua and Rome.
> Claudius built the Via Appia for the traveler;
> All others acknowledge the glory of this famous road.
> Now continue on your way, Traveler.
> This roadway, which begins here, ends
> at the town of San Agustín de las Cuevas.
> It is four leagues and 1,141 *varas* long
> [about fifteen miles], partly with a crushed
> stone embankment and partly paved; and along
> its course three bridges have been restored,
> seven new ones have been added, plus six
> underground drainage channels. The work was
> begun on April 29, 1786, and completed on
> December 31, 1787.

Translations of the inscriptions on the four fountains of the Plaza Mayor, Mexico City, 1794 (not illustrated here):

On the fountain in front of the cathedral:

> In the glorious reign of Charles IV, being Viceroy
> the Most Excellent Juan Vicente de Güemes Pacheco
> de Padilla, Count of Revillagigedo, this plaza was
> lowered in the years 1790 to 1793 and its four
> fountains were erected. The atrium of the Holy
> Cathedral Church also was lowered and redecorated,
> and its façade was completed and beautified.

On the fountain in front of the main entrance to the viceregal palace:

> In 1790, during the glorious
> reign of Charles IV, being Viceroy the Most Excellent
> Juan Vicente de Güemes Pacheco de Padilla, Count of
> Revillagigedo, public lighting in the streets of this
> city was introduced, as were the most useful lantern-
> keepers who attend to them and to the public safety.

On the fountain in front of the entrance known as that of the viceroy:

> In the reign of Charles IV,
> in the viceregency of the Most Excellent Juan Vicente
> de Güemes Pacheco de Padilla, Count of Revillagigedo,
> the street plan of the city was laid out, glazed tiles
> to mark the name of every street and plaza were set in
> place, the houses were numbered, annexes were marked,
> the façades of many buildings were painted, and a
> regimen of general cleanliness was undertaken.

On the fountain in front of the municipal offices:

> In the glorious reign of Charles IV, being Viceroy the Most Excellent Juan Vicente de Güemes Pacheco de Padilla, Count of Revillagigedo, between 1790 and 1794 the principal streets of this city were paved: 545,039 square *varas* [4,273,106 square feet] of paving were laid, 16,535 square varas [129,634 square feet] of drainage canals, and 27,317 square varas [214,165 square feet] of sidewalk with piping underneath; and the plazas for markets were formed and arranged.

47

Túpac Amaru I, Remembered

(eighteenth century)

This painting by an unknown artist in the eighteenth century carries on a colonial tradition of idealized Inka kings' portraits and an interest in portraying Inka history. Yet the person depicted here is not one of the line of pre-Hispanic Inkas whose Tawantinsuyu was invaded by the Spanish in 1531–32. Rather, this is a depiction of Túpac Amaru (d. 1572), the last from the dynastic line of Inkas which established a royal court and government in defiance of the Spaniards from a mountain fortress in the region of Vilcabamba, north of Cusco, between 1537 and 1572.

Manco Capac was a son of Huayna Capac, the last Inka to rule over a united realm. In 1534, after one half-brother, Atahuallpa Inka, had been garroted and another half-brother, Topa Gualpa (the first of the Spaniards' puppet Inkas), had died, Manco Capac was crowned Manco Inka by a hopeful Francisco Pizarro. However, Manco soon defected and led Indian forces in rebellion in 1536. After a siege of Cusco that lasted over a year and nearly culminated in his retaking the imperial city from the Spaniards and their Andean allies, Manco Inka retreated with an entourage to Vilcabamba. Here the group, dubbed the "neo-Inkas" by George Kubler, built their capital-in-exile (in counterpoint to Manco's rival younger brother, Paullu [d. ca. 1550], who became the Pizarros' next Inka in Cusco). The early Quechua interpreter and chronicler Juan de Betanzos, who accompanied a Spanish embassy to Manco Inka's young successor, Sayri Túpac (or Saire Topa, d. 1560) in 1556–57, wrote of a "town in the image of Cusco" that had emerged in the "wilds," a rugged country of mountain passes where horses soon became useless, where "even the Indians go up arm in arm on ropes and tree roots and vines." In 1610, Captain Baltasar de Ocampo wrote a narrative of the events surrounding Túpac Amaru's capture and execution, at a remove of almost thirty years and at a time when this aged eyewitness was seeking recognition and favors for the settlers in the region where he was now an official. He said that the fortress-city in Vilcabamba possessed "an extensive level space, with very sumptuous and majestic buildings, erected with great skill and art." Manco and his successors exacted tribute from loyal groups in the region and organized raids against areas under Spanish rule.

After a succession of entreaties and promises, the Spanish embassy to Sayri Túpac persuaded the Inka to leave Vilcabamba and accept extremely advantageous terms in Cusco. Sayri Túpac's elder brother Titu Cusi Yupanqui Inka (d. 1571) spurned the palaces and an Inkaic noble's life in conquered Cusco, however—and he knew something of what he was rejecting. As a young child, Titu Cusi had been captured by Spanish troops and taken for three or four years to live in the home of the Spanish noble Fernando de Oñate, until 1541 when Manco bargained for his return to Vilcabamba. Titu Cusi remained in Vilcabamba, usurping power from a legitimate heir and younger half-brother, Túpac Amaru, in about 1558–1560. Titu Cusi's strategy of hostilities and negotiation, along with his professions of interest in Christianity, were increasingly suspect in Lima and Cusco.

The newly arrived viceroy of Peru, Francisco de Toledo (1569–1581), abandoned the luring and negotiating tack of his predecessors and acted decisively and swiftly in the matter of the rebel Inkas. He ordered an assault on Vilcabamba from Cusco in 1571–72. For the expedition, he augmented Spanish troops with some two thousand Indian auxiliaries, among whom were a large contingent of pacified Inkas and a company of Cañari guardsmen (the same native Andean allies discussed in Selection 37). By this time, Titu Cusi had died; and his Mestizo secretary, Martín Pando, and an Augustinian friar named Diego de Ortiz had been killed at court in Vilcabamba, on the suspicion that they had poisoned him. The assault led by Toledo's captains proceeded as planned, and perhaps with even greater purpose once this intelligence was known. On October 4, 1571, after a battle and a chase, the youthful new Inka, Túpac Amaru, was seized along with his elite guard.

Túpac Amaru had been a largely neutralized younger half-brother after Titu Cusi's assumption of power by 1560. He appears to have kept up hostilities against "pacified" regions and to have repulsed Spanish efforts to communicate with Vilcabamba in 1571. But his reign as rebel king was above all short and tragic; he took power as if only to preside over the dissolution of early colonial hopes for the survival of an independent Inka state. After Túpac Amaru Inka was captured and marched off to Cusco, the Vilcabamba over which he ruled so briefly was officially transformed: it was reconsecrated in memory not of thirty-five years of heroic Inka resistance but of conquest and domination achieved. The Spanish town of San Francisco of the Victory of Vilcabamba was founded with much pomp and fitted with a Spanish garrison, just in case.

According to Ocampo's narrative of events, the triumphal party stopped at the entrance to the city at the archway of Karmenka (in the parish of Santa Ana, again see Selection 37) to put the troops in order and chain together Túpac Amaru and the members of his court and guard. The Inka was said to have been wearing a brilliant crimson tunic and the fringed headpiece, or *masca paycha* (see Selections 2 and 37). He was marched through the streets, presented before Viceroy Toledo, and then imprisoned in a palace. The Inka's "captains" were sentenced to hang, although, according to Ocampo, after much mistreatment only two made it to the gallows. As if in reenactment of what had happened before Atahuallpa's judicial murder forty years earlier, Túpac Amaru was instructed in the tenets of Christianity for "two or three days" and was said to have been baptized in his prison by two Quechua-speaking Mercedarian friars. Túpac Amaru was then led from his prison to a scaffold erected in the central square in front of the cathedral and beheaded by a Cañari executioner before a crowd of thousands who filled two plazas and the streets and watched from balconies, windows, and rooftops. The Inka's head was put on a high spike in the main plaza, intended as an example to anyone contemplating defiance of the Spanish will. However, the head was removed when, it is said, Indians were observed in what appeared to be nocturnal worship of it.

Figure 35 is no great work of portraiture, yet the rather wooden image is strikingly deliberate with its storytelling. What does one make of the expression and the stance of the young prince in the painting? With a serious expression, gazing upward as if awaiting a higher justice, he wears links of chain around his neck and arms, but the bonds appear more like reminders or props—the symbolic attributes of a hero or martyred saint—than devices of restraint. He stands erect and dignified with

Figure 35. "Don Felipe Tupa Amaru" by an anonymous artist (eighteenth century). Courtesy of the Museo Nacional de Bellas Artes, Buenos Aires.

his arms crossed in front, seemingly more out of choice than because the chains hold them thus. The plaque in the lower left corner, amid its basic identifying information, gives a reason for his stoical attitude to any viewer who cared to read it. This is "Don Felipe Tupa Amaru, last Inka of the Pagan Kings of Peru," it announces, proceeding to tell of his royal marriages and children, his public decapitation on the orders of Viceroy Toledo, and the burial of his body. The plaque carefully notes that Toledo's summary action was disapproved of by King Philip II, a piece of information perhaps gleaned from the claim by Mestizo humanist and historian El Inca Garcilaso de la Vega (1539–1616), whose *First Part of the Royal Commentaries* (Lisbon, 1609) and *General History of Peru* (Córdoba, 1617) were widely read. Garcilaso had written that, upon the viceroy's return to Spain, the monarch rebuked Toledo for his actions in the case of Túpac Amaru and banished him from favor.

What were the expectations and needs of the late colonial audience of the painting? What kind of past is being drawn, and then drawn upon, and why? Why, some two centuries later, the survival, and even mounting, of concern over the treatment of a rebel and obstacle to Spanish dominion? Why the preoccupation with the justice of Toledo's decision?

Remarkably little is known of Túpac Amaru. Yet this short-term rebel was the last Inka of Vilcabamba, and, in being so and in dying as he did, he has become as evocative a symbol as one is likely to find in Andean Peru—with time, often merging in the collective Andean imagination, as Alberto Flores Galindo has shown, with Atahuallpa, the last Inka executed by Pizarro at Cajamarca. The many local revolts, uprisings, and conspiracies in the Andes through the eighteenth and early nineteenth centuries (the events in Arequipa treated by David Cahill in Selection 43 are no exception) frequently played upon the "Inka's head" and on the theme of beheadings, along with the transforming memory of Túpac Amaru and the expectation of an Inka's resumption of power. For some, natural catastrophes such as floods and earthquakes seemed to herald an overturning of a corrupt order in Andean Peru.

Critical reflections on the way that Túpac Amaru died in Cusco in 1572 were popular among late seventeenth- and eighteenth-century Peruvian Creoles and well-to-do Mestizos, the people who would have formed this painting's principal audience. At least until the great rebellion of 1780–1782 dampened many Creoles' enthusiasm for things Inkaic and "Indian," members of the eighteenth-century elite in Cusco even allowed spoken Quechua and the chewing of coca leaves in their intellectual gatherings. And they commissioned and collected paintings that featured indigenous themes and motifs, paintings like this one and the earlier examples from the Corpus Christi series (Figures 26 and 27 in Selection 37). José Gabriel Condorcanqui, the *kuraka* (regional native governor) from the south-central Andes who adopted the name Túpac Amaru II (d. 1781), became the most memorable, but not the first, Andean rebel leader to present himself successfully to a multi-ethnic audience as a disinherited descendant of the Inka Túpac Amaru I and to reclaim rightful authority in the land. Critiques such as those which seem to appear in this image could merge with hopes and plans for the coronation of a late colonial Inka who might rule over a new confederation, a reborn Tawantinsuyu, which might remedy any number of abuses that people perceived as embodied in the practice of Bourbon rule.

The prisoner in the painting seems to touch his viewers' discomfort and their dreams. He wears a glittering crown adorned with feathers and a tapestry tunic with a circular design (a stylized sun?) on his chest. His dress and accoutrements, his dignity, suggest royalty, yet now in a vague and patterned way. The details of a post-Conquest Inkaic tunic and a distinctive masca paycha, so carefully rendered in many earlier paintings and chroniclers' accounts, seem to have grown either less important or more dangerous. This Túpac Amaru seems depicted more as a legendary hero than as an actual Inka rebel. Artists and viewers deemphasized certain details and recast the rebel, and events from the sixteenth century, for their own purposes. The painting's message about *peninsular* outrages in America seems clear. Viewers might attach this image of the heroic rebel Túpac Amaru, wronged and murdered without a proper trial by a peninsular viceroy, not only to similar depictions of the death of the Inka Atahuallpa but also to a general brutality that, according to some views, characterized Spanish treatment of their American subjects, not least the Creoles.

The colonial memory of this sacrifice in Cusco in 1572 did not depend on a sense of grievance about Bourbon reforms. And it was well remembered by a wider set of observers and subsequent tellers than the early generations of disgruntled Creoles or native Andean eyewitnesses within the crowd in Cusco's center (who are said to have wailed and groaned at the sight of Túpac Amaru's death). Both Garcilaso's and Ocampo's early seventeenth-century descriptions of the execution of Túpac Amaru precede the messages in this eighteenth-century canvas with similar feelings. In particular, they treat the subject as Toledo's serious, criminal blunder. A higher verdict seems required and awaited. Ocampo lists the heads of the religious orders in Cusco by name and claims that before the execution each of them pleaded with the viceroy to spare the Inka and send him to Spain to be properly tried by the king. El Inca Garcilaso, whose projections on the Inka past inspired a multi-ethnic elite readership in the eighteenth century that perhaps included Túpac Amaru II, implied even more about justice and legitimacy—explosive messages to many late colonial readers who reflected on his account of the death in Cusco's central square in 1572: "So ended the Inka," wrote Garcilaso, "the legitimate heir to the empire by the direct male line from the first Inka Manco Capac to himself."

 48

"America Nursing Spanish Noble Boys," Peru (ca. 1770s)

Art historians George Kubler and Martin Soria identify this as a painting from the central Andes (perhaps Lima) in the late eighteenth century. They write, "Toward the end of the century, perhaps during the rebellion of Túpac Amaru II (1780), an anonymous painter showed America nursing Spanish noble boys. Negroes and Mestizos are pressing around her throne, while naked Indian children weep, abandoned. Two richly dressed Indian couples present their gifts in a beautiful park crowded with different animals."

The sense of movement of the figures, the informal posture of the Inka lord with crossed legs, and the swooping lines of the decoration around the inscription place the painting well into the eighteenth century. But perhaps it was done shortly before the Túpac Amaru rebellion rather than during that violent and complex Andean struggle of the early 1780s, which pitted Indian communities against each other or against their leaders in alliance with Creole (American-born Spanish) elites, as well as Indians against colonial elites of all kinds. The painting expresses a popular Creole elite identity and a standard lament during the Bourbon reforms of the second half of the eighteenth century: invoking their Americanness through a glorious Indian past, and decrying the privileges of *peninsular* appointees at the expense of sons of America. Judging by their costumes and complexions, the children looking on as the two peninsular boys in fashionable European outfits nurse at America's breasts are Creoles as well as Mestizos and Afromestizos.

These sentiments of indignation and Americanness were expressed with particular vehemence by Creoles in Spanish America during periods of *visita*—the inspection tours carried out by high peninsular officials appointed by the king to raise revenues and otherwise reform administrative procedures in the name of good order and efficiency, largely to the Crown's advantage. Criticism of this kind and scattered rebellions accompanied the visitas to New Spain in the 1760s and to New Granada in 1780–81. The notorious visita to the Viceroyalty of Peru headed by José Antonio de Areche during this period began in 1777, thus making 1777–1780 a likely date for this painting—before Peruvian Creoles were jolted from their comfortable association of America with the Indian past.

Figure 36. "America Nursing Spanish Noble Boys" by an anonymous artist, Peru, ca. 1770s.
The inscription at the bottom reads in part:
"Where in the world has one seen what one sees here. . . .
Her own sons lie groaning and she suckles strangers."

49

José María Morelos's "Sentiments of the Nation," Chilpancingo, Mexico

(1813)

The two great leaders of the early, unsuccessful struggle for Mexican independence in 1810–1815 were parish priests from the Diocese of Michoacán: Miguel Hidalgo and José María Morelos. Hidalgo, a Creole Spaniard, held a doctorate in theology and was a leading figure in the cathedral city of Valladolid (modern Morelia) before running afoul of ecclesiastical authorities. He was charged with mismanaging funds of his diocesan seminary and was mistrusted for his eclectic intellectual life; there was some suspicion that he held unorthodox views about Christian doctrine. On the eve of the struggle he served the prosperous parish of Dolores in the modern state of Guanajuato. Morelos, the priest of a poor parish in the hot country of lowland Michoacán, had studied briefly with Hidalgo in Valladolid but was not as well educated—less well read and less bold in his ideas. His baptismal record identifies him as a Creole Spaniard, but he was evidently a Mestizo, or perhaps an Afromestizo. In any case, he came from more modest roots and relied on experience and studies of moral theology and pastoral manuals for his sense of political ethics.

Hidalgo's insurrection in 1810 did not openly declare for independence, but it was clearly opposed to colonial government and the immigrant Spanish elite (*peninsulares*) in Mexico. He was captured and executed in 1811. Morelos had joined Hidalgo's forces some weeks after the insurrection began; and, after Hidalgo's death, he became the outstanding military leader in the first years of struggle against colonial rule and privileged Spaniards. But he did not succeed in overthrowing Spanish rule, and, unable to hold any important provincial cities for long, he operated mostly on the edges of the heartland of colonial Mexico—in lowland Michoacán, Guerrero, Oaxaca, and Puebla. He, too, was captured and executed in 1815.

Nonetheless, under Morelos's nominal leadership, a declaration of independence was finally issued and a congress was convened to plan for a new national government in 1813. Morelos was not a political philosopher, and his ideas for an independent nation emerged slowly. They are most clearly expressed in the following document known as "Sentiments of the Nation," presented to the opening session of the Chilpancingo Congress on September 14, 1813. Usually regarded as a homegrown "liberal" document enshrining popular sovereignty, liberty, and equality, the "Sentiments of the Nation" offer Morelos's growing belief in liberty and elements of equality without giving up a preference for hierarchy, precedence, status, and religious exclusivism. And he did not lightly refer to his words as *sentiments*. For Morelos, ideas expressed passions, longings, and frustrations, not just Enlightenment rationality. Religious sentiments and the social values behind them pervade the document, giving it the character of a pastoral lesson and a connection to the past, while critiquing the present and breaking with colonial rule and its hereditary inequalities.

Morelos's thinking in this text can seem contradictory. He opens with a clear call for national independence from any other sovereign power, but the second, third, and fourth of the original twenty-two articles turn immediately to religion in ways that seem to confuse the liberal cast of the document: Article 2 declares Catholicism to be "the only [religion], without tolerance for any other"; Article 3 provides for the financial support of the priesthood; and Article 4 affirms the responsibility of the Church hierarchy to keep Catholic dogma pure.

Yet, to simultaneously affirm hierarchy, religious intolerance, popular sovereignty, and equality before the law would not have been a contradiction to Morelos, the parish priest. A unifying idea behind this mixture of apparent opposites was the old regard for moderation and balance. Morelos could speak of liberty and equality among Americans without accepting these principles as absolutes or abandoning his conviction that hierarchy was essential to social order, that the poor and humble—like Indians in the colonial conception—required parental care, and that salvation was the highest purpose of human activity. Liberty for Morelos still centered on the freedom to fulfill a Catholic Christian destiny, and it still centered more on freedom from unjust restraint than on freedom as an absolute good in its own right. It was not freedom to practice false religion. Nor was it, in J. H. Parry's words, "freedom to be idle, to be left to one's own devices, to refrain from making any contribution to the well-being of society."

---

1. That America is free and independent of Spain and every other nation, government, or monarchy, and thus it shall be proclaimed, informing the world why.
2. That the Catholic religion shall be the only one, without tolerance for any other.
3. That the ministers of the Church shall live only from the tithes and first fruits, and the people shall not be required to pay for services, except as true offerings and expressions of their devotion.
4. That the dogma of the religion shall be upheld by the Church hierarchy, consisting of the Pope, the bishops, and the parish priests, because *every plant that God did not plant should be weeded out*. . . . Matthew 15.
5. That sovereignty flows directly from the people, and they wish it to be lodged only in the Supremo Congreso Nacional Americano, composed of representatives of the provinces in equal numbers.
6. That the legislative, executive, and judicial powers shall be divided among those bodies that are established to exercise them.
7. That the representatives shall serve for four years in rotation, the old ones leaving office so the newly elected can take their places.
8. The representatives shall be paid a sufficient but not excessive salary. For now, it shall not be more than 8,000 pesos.
9. Government posts shall be held only by Americans.

10. Foreigners shall not be allowed to enter the country unless they are artisans who can instruct others and are free of all suspicion.
11. States alter the customs of the people; therefore, the Fatherland will not be completely free and ours until the government is reformed, replacing the tyrannical with the liberal, and also expelling from our soil the enemy Spaniard who has so greatly opposed our Fatherland.
12. Since the good law is superior to any man, those [laws] that our Congreso issues shall be so, and shall promote constancy and patriotism, and moderate opulence and poverty so that the daily wage of the poor man is raised, his customs improved, and ignorance, preying upon others, and thievery removed.
13. That the general laws shall apply to everyone, including privileged corporations except as applies directly to their duties.
14. To draw up a law, there shall be a gathering of the greatest number of wise men possible, so that the deliberations may proceed with greater certainty. [These men] shall be exempt from some of the duties that might otherwise be demanded of them.
15. Slavery shall be forever forbidden, as shall caste distinctions, leaving everyone equal. One American shall be distinguished from another only by his vices and virtues.
16. That our ports may admit [the ships of] friendly foreign nations, but they cannot be based in the kingdom no matter how friendly they are. And only designated ports—ten percent of those that exist—shall be used for this purpose. Disembarkation in any other is forbidden.
17. The property of every individual shall be protected, and their homes respected as if they were a sacred asylum. Penalties shall be assigned for violators.
18. That the new legislation shall not allow torture.
19. That the new legislation shall establish by constitutional law the celebration of December 12 in every community of the land in honor of Our Most Holy Lady of Guadalupe, patroness of our liberty, and every community is to practice monthly devotions to her.
20. That foreign troops or those from any other [Spanish] kingdom shall not set foot on our soil unless it is to come to our aid, and then only with the authorization of the Suprema Junta.
21. That no expeditions outside the limits of the kingdom shall be made, especially not overseas expeditions; but others not of this kind are to be encouraged in order to propagate the faith among our brothers in the interior [*tierradentro,* or northern Mexico and the American Southwest].
22. That the plethora of tributes, fees, and taxes that weigh us down shall be eliminated. A five percent charge on grains and other produce, or a similarly light tax, shall be levied on every individual. It shall not oppress us like the alcabala, the tobacco monopoly, the tribute, and others. With this light contribution and good administration of property confiscated from the enemy, the cost of the war and the salaries of employees can be paid.

Chilpancingo, 14 September 1813.

[appended Article] 23. That September 16 also shall be solemnized each year as the anniversary of the beginning of our struggle for Independence and our holy Freedom, for on that date the Nation spoke, demanding its rights with sword in hand so as to be heard. Thus the distinction of the great hero, Señor Don Miguel Hidalgo, and his companion, Don Ignacio Allende, will be remembered forever.

50

The Argentine Declaration of Independence, San Miguel de Tucumán

(1816)

Several great areas of South America that had been on the margins of Spanish colonial history in the sixteenth and seventeenth centuries, with smaller populations and a weaker colonial administrative presence, developed rapidly in the eighteenth century. Modern Venezuela and Argentina are the most striking examples. It was from these two areas in which the centralizing institutions of the Catholic Church and the imperial state developed late that the movements for liberation from Spain gained an early hold and spread. Priests and ideas from moral theology (Christian principles applied to everyday life) were less evident in the independence movements of Argentina and Venezuela than in Mexico. Insurgent leaders there expressed themselves more clearly in the modern language of the eighteenth-century revolutions in France and the United States: individual rights and freedoms, popular elections, the will of the people, representative government, separation of powers, and other democratic institutions. The brief Argentine declaration printed below hailed democracy and representative government as natural rights of American peoples that the Spanish monarchy arbitrarily cancelled; it condemned as artificial such a forced connection between American peoples and Spanish kings. These words of political liberation from Argentina differ from Morelos's "Sentiments of the Nation" for Mexico (Selection 49) in their debt to the United States' Declaration of Independence, their vision of democracy, and their way of invoking God and religion. But this Argentine document is not in all ways a clean break from traditional Spanish American ideas about political rights and organization.

Decreed in the meritorious and very worthy city of San Miguel de Tucumán on July 9, 1816. Having terminated its ordinary session, the Congress of the United Provinces continued its earlier discussions on the great and august subject of the independence of the peoples that form it. The clamor of the entire territory was universal, constant, and decided for a solemn emancipation from the despotic power of the kings of Spain. The representatives nevertheless dedicated to this crucial issue all the profundity of their talents, the rectitude of their intentions, and the interest that requires the sanction of their destiny, their represented peoples, and their posterity. Finally they were asked if they wished the United Provinces to be a nation free and independent of the kings of Spain and the metropolis. Filled with the holy ardor of justice, they first acclaimed, and one by one successively repeated, the unanimous and spontaneous vote for the independence of the country, setting forth accordingly the following determination:

Declaration: We the representatives of the United Provinces in South America, reassembled in General Congress, invoking the Eternal One who presides over the universe, in the name of and by the authority of the towns that we represent, protesting to Heaven and to all nations and men of the globe the justice that governs our votes, declare on the face of the Earth that it is the unanimous and unquestioned will of these provinces to break the forced chains that have linked them to the kings of Spain, to recover the rights of which they were despoiled, and to invest themselves with the high character of a nation free and independent from Ferdinand VII as well as from his successors and metropolis. In consequence they remain in fact and by right in possession of full and ample power to provide themselves with the forms which justice requires and which the sum of their present circumstances demands. All and each one of them thus publishes, declares, and ratifies it, and we thus commit ourselves to the fulfillment and preservation of this our will, under the security and guaranty of our lives, our property, and our reputation. Let this be communicated to the appropriate persons for publication, and in recognition of the respect owed to the nations, enumerating in a manifesto the very serious and basic motivations of this solemn declaration. Given in the Legislative Chamber, signed by our hand, sealed with the seal of Congress, and authenticated by our official notaries.

GLOSSARY

Afromestizo—person of mixed African, Indian, and European ancestry, a term not used in the colonial period.
Albaicín—sector of Granada, Spain, in which many Moriscos lived.
alcabala—sales tax.
alcalde—community official, member of the cabildo; a secondary officer in a head town but often the chief local officer of a subordinate town.
alcalde mayor—district governor appointed by the Crown; also *corregidor.*
alcalde ordinario—community official, member of the cabildo exercising judicial authority.
algarabía—local dialect of the Arabic language spoken in Granada.
arancel—schedule of fees; here, payable to a parish priest.
atrio—atrium or church courtyard.
audiencia—colonial high court, consisting of a president and judges; also refers to this court's jurisdiction. There were ten Audiencias situated in provincial cities, including Lima and Mexico City, by the end of the sixteenth century; two more were added in the eighteenth century.
auto-da-fé—public ceremony at which sentences of the Inquisition were announced and where processions of the repentant and condemned took place.
ayllu—Andean social, ritual, and territorial unit.
Aztec—common term for the Tenocha-Mexica people of the island city of Tenochtitlán (now Mexico City), who embarked on territorial expansion outside the Valley of Mexico in the decades before the Spaniards arrived.
Baroque—term from the art history of Catholic Europe from the late sixteenth century. It suggests religious devotion radically separated from the workaday world, engaged less with the intellect than direct, emotional experience of the heavenly realm through dazzling displays of holy objects and the fine arts.
beata—lay holy woman.
cabecera—head town of a region or parish.
cabildo—annually elected town council.

cacao—chocolate, or the bean or plant from which it comes.

cacique—hereditary Indian leader. The term is Hispanicized Arawak used generically by the Spaniards to refer to a local ruler of an Indian polity.

Cañaris—a resettled Andean people originally from the region of modern Ecuador, south of Quito. The Cañaris had been noted guards and fighters in the service of the Inkas, a set of roles they continued in privileged alliance with Spaniards in the Cusco of colonial times.

casta—person thought to be of mixed Indian, African, and European descent and hence not pure-blooded; in late colonial records the term more often distinguishes a non-Indian from an Indian than a non-European from a European. The plural *castas* refers to a genre of late colonial Mexican painting featuring racial mixture (see Selection 45).

cédula—written authorization; here, usually short for *real cédula*, or royal decree.

Cercado—walled district of colonial Lima in which many native Andeans lived.

chacra—Quechua term for a plot of cultivable land.

chicha—fermented beverage made from maize, the most common alcoholic drink in the colonial Andes.

Chichimec—term of Nahuatl origin for barbarous invader and looter. It was used by Aztecs and colonial subjects of New Spain to identify enemies in the Chichimeca region, a floating zone defined mainly by rainfall belts separating sparse, semi-nomadic groups of part-time farmers and hunter-gatherers from denser, stable farming communities to the south.

coca—low tropical bush, the leaves of which are among the common offerings to Andean divinities and which are chewed as a stimulant during work and travel.

cochineal—small insect that thrives on the native nopal cactus of central and southern Mexico. The females were collected, dried, and crushed into a deep red dyestuff coveted by Europeans.

cofradía—religious association or confraternity established to promote a particular devotion.

colegio—residential college; here, established and run by a religious order.

coloquio—dialogue; exchange of speeches.

conopa—personal divinity and source of fecundity in the central Andes, the natural or sculpted form of which often depicted its creative function.

converso—"new convert" to Christianity from Judaism.

convivencia—"coexistence," or the living together of Muslims, Christians, and Jews within medieval Iberian society. The term has often stressed creative interaction and intercultural borrowing.

Corpus Christi—term for a principal feast of the Roman Catholic Church in honor of the Holy Eucharist, the body of Christ, His living presence in the consecrated Host, celebrated in the period between late May to mid-June. The Corpus Christi procession, in which the Host in its special vessel is carried through the streets before the whole community (as featured in Selections 29 and 37), became a prominent part of the feast days in western Europe from at least the middle of the fourteenth century.

corregidor—district governor appointed by the Crown; also *alcalde mayor*.

Council of the Indies—royal tribunal that governed Spanish American affairs and advised the monarch from Seville.

Council of Trent—the nineteenth ecumenical council of the Roman Catholic Church held between 1545 and 1563 in Trento, Italy, the principal purpose of which was to order and clarify Catholic doctrine in the face of the challenges raised by Protestant reformers. The twenty-five sessions brought compromises between radical and more traditional delegates, much legislative reform of discipline and bishops' duties and powers, and the strengthening of seminary education and papal authority. The reform decrees of the Council became the centerpiece of a Catholic revival in the sixteenth century (usually referred to as the Counter-Reformation, or Catholic Reformation) that saw, among other things, the renewal of piety, prayer, mysticism, and the emergence of a Baroque art and culture in Catholic Europe.

Creole—or *criollo*, an American-born person of, or claiming, Spanish ancestry.

cura—pastor; parish priest.

cuy, cuyes—Andean guinea pigs raised in homes, important for blood offerings to divinities and for healing rituals.

demonio—demon or the Devil. The term was often applied to indigenous gods themselves in colonial times, and/or to the evil force said to be behind them.

doctrina—elementary Christian dogma that parishioners were to be taught repeatedly and expected to commit to memory. The term may also refer to a parish of Indians, technically a temporary or proto-parish administered by regular clergy in which the newly converted are to receive indoctrination.

dogmatizer—literal translation of *dogmatizador*, a Spanish term for an Andean teacher, guardian, and teller of sacred histories as well as a minister and ritual adept.

Dominicans—common name for the Order of the Friars Preacher, a religious order of the Catholic Church founded especially to preach against heretics in the early thirteenth century by Saint Dominic. The Dominicans became known for their devotion to preaching and study, and in Spanish America they sought to combine the contemplative life with their apostolic endeavors and the administration of Indian *doctrinas*.

don—an honorific title indicating high status, used sparingly in the early colonial period but more widely in the eighteenth century as a term of respect or standing as a Spaniard or Indian notable.

encomendero—the possessor of an *encomienda*; a Spaniard to whom a group or groups of Indians have been "entrusted." He might demand manual labor and tribute from the Indians in exchange for payment, protection, and religious instruction.

encomienda—a grant of labor and tribute rights from the Crown to an *encomendero* over a specified group of Indians.

escribano—notary; scribe.

español—Spaniard, whether born in Spain or America.

fanega—unit of dry measure, about 1.5 bushels.

fiesta—community feast-day celebration.

fiscal—lay assistant to a parish priest; chief legal counsel to an *audiencia*.

forastero—*indio forastero*, an itinerant or migrant Indian who lives away from his place of origin.

Franciscans—common name for the Order of the Friars Minor, a religious order of the Catholic Church founded in the early thirteenth century by Saint Francis of Assisi. The Franciscans pursued an ideal of complete poverty, but successive reforms led to the development of distinct branches within the order. In the early fifteenth century, a division hardened especially in the Spanish kingdoms and in France between a reformed (Observant) branch committed to extreme poverty and missions, and a more moderate one (Conventual) that did not adhere to the reform. The friars who arrived in Mexico in 1524 at the request of Hernán Cortés were from a reformed group within the Observant ranks.

hacendado—owner of a *hacienda*, a large landed estate.

hacienda—large landed estate engaged in farming and ranching.

huaca—local or regional sacred place and divinity in the Andes; sometimes a physical object; often, but not exclusively, conceived of as an ancestor being and "founder" in the landscape surrounding a community, regularly nourished with offerings and given reverence.

humanist—a classical scholar, devoted to the study of the literature or "humanities" associated with the mostly fifteenth- and sixteenth-century revival of interest in ancient Rome and Greece.

idolatry—literally, the worship of a false god represented by an idol; in Christian terms, a grave sin in violation of the First Commandment. Here, idolatry is a judgmental term or charge applied by Spanish Christian authorities and commentators to the most serious religious errors, especially those of Indians. It refers to surviving pre-Hispanic beliefs and practices but also to the many aspects of colonial Indian culture, including alleged perversions of Christianity, believed to be subversive to genuine conversion and Christian life. *See* superstition

Indian—*indio*; a major social and ethnic category in colonial law; a blanket term for descendants of the indigenous population living under Spanish rule. Indians were tribute payers, legal minors, and usually associated with a home community or pueblo. The term derives from Columbus's mistaken belief that he had reached India or east Asia in 1492.

Inka or **Inca**—The common term for the people from the Valley of Cusco in the south-central Andes whose rapid conquests mostly in the course of the fifteenth century extended their power over much of western South America. The Inkas referred to their "empire," which comprised many peoples, as Tawantinsuyu, Land of the Four Quarters. The usage of Inka derives from the Spaniards' mistaken assumption that the Quechua term for the supreme ruler or king applied to an entire people.

Jesuits—common name for the Society of Jesus, a religious order of the Catholic Church founded in 1540 by Saint Ignatius of Loyola. The Jesuits began as a missionary order embodying the discipline and ideals of the Counter-Reformation and soon emerged as leading teachers, scholars, and spiritual directors in Catholic Christendom. After earlier missions, and a number of martyrdoms in Brazil and Florida, the Jesuits established themselves in Peru (1568) and Mexico (1570) and the rest of Spanish America. Jesuits were known not only for their schools, seminaries, and urban ministries (among slaves and in prisons), but also for their missions and "reductions" among indigenous peoples such as the Guaraní (see Selection 38).

kuraka or ***curaca***—hereditary native governor in the Andes. *See also cacique*

league—variable measure of traveling distance in colonial times, about three and one-half miles, or 5.57 kilometers.

llactas—small Andean settlements.

malqui—Andean ancestor whose body has been mummified; a divinity of regional significance, and, like the *huaca*, regularly nourished with offerings and commemorative, festive attention.

masca paycha—Inka ornamental headpiece.

Mass—"the holiest of holy things," the ritual event performed by an ordained Catholic priest in which the bread and wine of the ceremony become Christ's body and blood.

mayordomo—overseer, or chief steward; here, a rotating position as chief attendant of a religious association.

mendicant—member of one of the religious orders in the Catholic Church committed to living without possessions through work and alms alone; here, especially a Franciscan, Dominican, or Augustinian.

mestizaje—racial, but here also cultural, mixture; miscegenation.

Mestizo—person of mixed Spanish and Indian ancestry, sometimes applied more generally to a person of mixed race.

Mexican—term used by Spaniards for Aztecs; also a colonial term for people from Mexico City, thus not "Mexican" in the modern national sense.

mita—Spanish adaptation of a labor rotation system employed by the Inkas, the *m'ita*, to gain workers for large projects. An Indian away from his home area for purposes of work was known as a *mitayo*.

Morisco—a new convert to Christianity from Islam in the Spanish kingdoms. A second meaning occurs in Selection 28, in which the New World usage of Morisca refers to a daughter of a white man and a Mulatta.

Mulatto—person of mixed, but part African, ancestry, often taken to be of roughly equal European and African descent, but a term that might also refer to a person of Indian and African ancestry.

Nahuatl—the language of much of central Mexico at the time of the Spanish occupation.

neoclassicism—art style promoted by the Crown in the late colonial period, inspired by the buildings and sculpture of ancient Rome. Austere, massive, and symmetrical, it promoted a vision of rational grandeur.

New Spain—the viceroyalty of northern Spanish America with its capital at Mexico City. It included modern Mexico, the American Southwest, and much of Central America and the Caribbean islands.

notarial records—legal documents recorded by, or certified as authentic by, licensed public notaries. Much of the voluminous written record for colonial Spanish America was officially taken down by notaries for courts and governors. A notary's archive (in contrast to a court's or governor's archive) consisted especially of records of wills, property transfers, and other legal agreements.

pacarina—place of origin, venerated by native Andeans, to which one also returns.

palenque—protected refuge for runaway slaves.

peninsular—person born in the Iberian Peninsula who has come to America.

Peru—the viceroyalty of southern Spanish America with its capital at Lima. Until the creation of the viceroyalties of New Granada and La Plata in late colonial times, the Viceroyalty of Peru included most of South America with the exception of Portuguese-controlled Brazil.

pintura—literally a painting, but in colonial usage a map or picture.

plaza mayor —central square.

posa—"stopping place," the chapels sometimes built at the corners of a church courtyard.

presidio—fortified garrison on the frontiers of colonial settlement.

principal—local notable or important person; here, often a member of an hereditary Indian elite in a community.

pueblo—town.

pueblo viejo—old town; Spanish term for the settlement of Andean ancestors before the colonial "reduction" of peoples into towns and villages, frequently within walking distance of the resettlements.

pulque—fermented beverage made from the maguey plant, the most widely consumed intoxicating drink in Mexico during the colonial period.

Quechua—the language (or group of related languages) of the Inkas and many of their subjects in the Andean highlands at the time of the Spanish arrival.

real—one-eighth of a silver peso.

reconquista—the centuries of war by Spanish Christian kingdoms against Islam in the Iberian Peninsula.

reducción—town resulting from the forced resettlement of groups of Indians in colonial times; also, a mission community among indigenous peoples established by the Jesuits.

regidor—community official; a secondary member of the *cabildo*.

regular—from *regula* (rule or law), referring to regular clergy, the special groups of Catholic priests, nuns, and aspirants who live by a separate set of rules, for example, Jesuits, Franciscans, and Carmelites. *See* secular

religious—member of a regular order of the Catholic Church; also, a devout person. *See* secular

repartimiento—distribution of anything; here, a labor draft from Indian pueblos.

reparto—*reparto de mercancías*, or *repartimiento de mercancías*, a monopoly trading privilege of a *corregidor* or *alcalde mayor* within his territory.

secular—from *saecularis*, referring to a member of the secular or diocesan clergy living in the world (*saeculum*) under the authority of a bishop, as opposed to living according to the rule of a religious community; also, more generally, a person or thing that is worldly or non-religious. *See* regular; religious

Supay—native Andean force with good and evil properties, sometimes described as the flying soul of a relative. Appropriated by some Spanish missionaries and lexicographers as a gloss for the Christian idea of the Devil.

superstition—broad term applied, here, by Christians to religious behaviors and attitudes believed to be contemptible and inherently irrational, the result of ignorance, misinformation, the inventions of sinful people, and fear of the unknown. Like "idolatry," superstition was an impediment to "true religion," yet, by the sixteenth and seventeenth centuries, superstition came to signify an abject, less serious, and thus more easily surmountable kind of error. *See* idolatry

Tawantinsuyu—"Land of the Four Quarters"; the Inkaic term for the Inka empire.

teniente—deputy or assistant.

Tlaxcalans—people of Tlaxcala. A central Mexican people who had maintained a measure of independence in the face of Aztec expansion, the Tlaxcalans became the Spaniards' valuable allies in their military takeover of Tenochtitlan. The leaders and communities of early colonial Tlaxcala successfully argued for a privileged place in the colonial order on the basis of their people's alliance, early embrace of Christianity, and participation in various Spanish colonizing expeditions on the frontiers of New Spain.

tradición—tradition; here, the common colonial gloss for an Andean sacred history regularly told by a native minister-dogmatizer and sometimes performed in dance and song.

tratado—treatise.

vara—short for *vara de justicia*, or staff of office, especially of an Indian official; also, a unit of distance of about thirty-three inches.

vicario—assistant to a parish priest.

viceroy—the monarch's chief representative with extensive executive and judicial authority and more limited authority to issue laws. The capitals of the two viceroyalties—territories governed by viceroys—in the sixteenth and seventeenth centuries were Lima and Mexico City. Two more viceroyalties were added in the eighteenth century, New Granada and La Plata, with capitals at Bogotá and Buenos Aires.

villca—demigod-like human in native Andean traditions; a favorite of a *huaca*.

Vira Cocha—a principal creator-divinity in the pre-Hispanic Andes. It became a term applied to White people in colonial Peru.

visita—a general tour of inspection, often of a viceroy's or *alcalde mayor*'s administration, commissioned by the Crown.

visitador—a commissioned inspector; an administrative official conducting a tour of inspection (*visita general*). Here, a *visitador general de idolatría*, an idolatry inspector and judge who is a priest commissioned to investigate "suspect" Indian religiosity (Selection 35), or a postal inspector (Selection 41).

Zambo—person of African and native Andean descent.

NOTES ON SELECTIONS AND SOURCES

1. Selection 1 is excerpted from *The Huarochirí Manuscript: A Testament of Ancient and Colonial Andean Religion,* edited and translated from the Quechua by Frank Salomon and George L. Urioste, © 1991 (Austin, 1991), pp. 41–54. Courtesy of the authors and the University of Texas Press. Readers wanting more of this source are encouraged to consult the paperback edition noted above and Salomon's fine introductory essay, which informs the present introduction. On the context out of which the document derives, see especially Karen Spalding, *Huarochirí: An Andean Society under Inca and Spanish Rule* (Stanford, 1984); and the interpretation of Antonio Acosta Rodríguez, "Francisco de Avila, Cusco 1573(?)–Lima 1647," in *Ritos y tradiciones de Huarochirí: Manuscrito quechua de comienzos del siglo XVII,* edited and translated by Gerald Taylor (Lima, 1987), pp. 551–616.
2. Our opening to discussion of the two tunics in Figures 1 and 2 is indebted to an essay by R. Tom Zuidema, "Guaman Poma and the Art of Empire: Toward an Iconography of Inca Royal Dress," in *Transatlantic Encounters: Europeans and Andeans in the Sixteenth Century,* edited by Kenneth J. Andrien and Rolena Adorno (Berkeley and Los Angeles, 1991), pp. 151–202; and to pioneering work by John H. Rowe, "Standardization in Inca Tapestry Tunics," in *The Junius B. Bird Pre-Columbian Textile Conference,* edited by Ann Pollard Rowe, Elizabeth P. Benson, and Anne-Louise Schaffer (Washington, DC, 1979), pp. 239–64, and Ann P. Rowe, "Technical Features of Inca Tapestry Tunics," *Textile Museum Journal* 17 (1978): 5–28. The Inka key checkerboard tunic (Figure 1) is in the collection of the Textile Museum in Washington, DC (no. 91147) (Andrien and Adorno, 173, 9d). Courtesy of the Textile Museum. Figure 2 is the so-called Poli uncu from the Poli collection in Lima, Peru (Andrien and Adorno, 176, 10b).
3. This selection is translated from Bernardino de Sahagún, *Coloquios y doctrina cristiana,* edited by Miguel León-Portilla (Mexico, 1986), fols. 34r, 35r, 36r, and 37r (facsimile), pp. 86–89 (Spanish transcription). Courtesy of the Universidad Nacional Autónoma de México.
4. Much of the discussion for Selection 4 is adapted from Richard F. Townsend, *State and Cosmos in the Art of Tenochtitlan* (Washington, DC, 1979), pp. 63–70. The photograph of the stone (Figure 3) comes from Jay A. Levenson, editor, *Circa 1492: Art in the Age of Exploration* (Washington, DC, and New Haven, 1991), p. 503. The drawing of the stone (Figure 4) is taken from Antonio de León y Gama, *Descripción histórica y cronológica de las dos piedras . . . ,* 2d ed. (Mexico, 1832), plate 2.
5. Selection 5 is excerpted from *Christians and Moors in Spain* (Warminster, Eng., 1992), vol. 3, *Arabic Sources (711–1501),* edited and translated from the Arabic by Charles Melville and Ahmad Ubaydli, pp. 28–31, 52–55, and 110–15. Courtesy of Aris and Phillips, Warminster, Wiltshire, England. Melville's and Ubaydli's short introductions to these texts inform our own, as does their glossary

on religious and legal terminology. Also of particular help has been the approach to *convivencia* in the work of Thomas F. Glick, as well as recent formulations on the interdependence of violence and tolerance in related settings by David Nirenberg in *Communities of Violence: Persecution of Minorities in the Middle Ages* (Princeton, 1996). Américo Castro's *España en su historia: Cristianos, moros y judíos* (Buenos Aires, 1948), with modifications and additions, exists in an English translation by Edmund L. King, *The Structure of Spanish History* (Princeton, 1954).

6. Olivia Harris's essay was first published in the *Bulletin of Latin American Research* 14:1 (1995): 9–24. Notes have been omitted. © 1994, Society for Latin American Studies. Reprinted courtesy of Elsevier Science Ltd., Oxford, England.
7. This translation first appeared as the first part of Appendix 1 in *The Oroz Codex: The Oroz Relación, or Relation of the Description of the Holy Gospel Province in New Spain, and the Lives of the Founders and Other Noteworthy Men of Said Province, Composed by Fray Pedro Oroz* [1584–1586], translated and edited by Angelico Chávez, O.F.M. (Washington, DC, 1972), pp. 347–53.
8. Selection 8, an extract from an anonymous original manuscript in the collection of the Biblioteca de Palacio in Madrid, is excerpted from Francisco de Vitoria, *Political Writings,* edited by Anthony Pagden and translated by Jeremy Lawrance (Cambridge, Eng., 1991), Appendix B, "Lecture on the Evangelization of Unbelievers," pp. 341–51. Courtesy of Cambridge University Press. Our introduction to this reading is assisted especially by Pagden's "Introduction," pp. xiii–xxviii; Lawrance's "Biographical Notes" and "Glossary," pp. 353–81; and Quentin Skinner, *The Foundations of Modern Political Thought,* vol. 2, *The Age of Reformation* (Cambridge, Eng., 1978), pp. 135–73.
9. Figures 5 and 6 are from Hugh Honour, *The New Golden Land* (New York, 1975), p. 10. Numerous editions and translations of Vespucci's letters on his voyages exist. An original of the Strassburg edition of 1509, the German translation that includes Figures 5 and 6, is in the collections of the British Library in London. The letter is reproduced in facsimile in Americus Vespucius, *The First Four Voyages of Americus Vespucius: A Reprint in Exact Facsimile of the German Edition Printed at Strassburg, by John Grüninger, in 1509,* with a prefatory note by Luther S. Livingston (New York, 1902). Among numerous English translations are *The First Four Voyages of Amerigo Vespucci translated from the rare original edition (Florence, 1505–6); with some Preliminary Notices, by M. K.,* edited and translated by Michael Kerney (London, 1885); and *Letters from a New World: Amerigo Vespucci's Discovery of America,* edited and translated by Luciano Formisano (New York, 1992), pp. 57–97.

   The circuitous path of Vespucci's letter to Soderini, even within the confines of the five years after it was written, tells us something of the diffusion and reproduction of documents and books of great interest in contemporary western Europe. The original Italian "Lettera di Amerigo Vespucci delle isole nuovamente trovate in quattro suoi viaggi" was written by Vespucci in Portugal on September 4, 1504. It was carried to Soderini in Florence by one of Vespucci's fellow seamen and published there. The publication bears no date, but it was probably printed in 1505 or 1506. The letter found its way to France and was first translated into French by an unknown hand in Saint-Dié in Lorraine, and this version has never been found. But from it, Jean Basin de Sendacour, a member of the college at Saint-Dié and one of a group who had just set up a printing press, made a Latin translation. The letter from "Vespucius" was published in 1507 at Saint-Dié as an appendix to the *Cosmographiœ Introductio* by Martin Waldseemüller (1470–1521?), and it was in Waldseemüller's book that "America" was suggested as the proper name for the new lands beyond the Ocean Sea. The German translation of the Grüninger edition, of which these two images were a part, was thus made from a Latin edition, which itself was translated from a lost French translation of the Italian original.
10. Figure 7 is from Christoph Weiditz, *Authentic Everyday Dress of the Renaissance: All 154 Plates from the "Trachtenbuch"* (New York, 1994), plate XVIII (sheet 1). Weiditz's manuscript is held in the German National Museum in Nuremberg. It was published in a trilingual (German, English, and Spanish) edition by Theodor Hampe as *Das Trachtenbuch des Christoph Weiditz von seinen Reisen nach Spanien (1529) und den Niederlanden (1531/32)* (Berlin and Leipzig, 1927), with forty-one of the plates in color. Dover Publications has printed a paperback edition of the *Trachtenbuch,* retaining Hampe's introduction and contextualizing first chapter along with a slightly revised version of the 1927 work's English text. The plates are in black and white, collected two to a page. Courtesy of Dover Publications.

11. Figure 8 is from Christoph Weiditz, *Authentic Everyday Dress of the Renaissance* (New York, 1994), plate LXXX (sheet 100). See note to Selection 10 above. Courtesy of Dover Publications.
12. Gante's letter is translated from *Cartas de Indias (publícalas por primera vez el Ministerio de Fomento)*, editor unknown (Madrid, 1877), pp. 92–102.
13. This selection was published as "The Evils of Cochineal: March 3, 1553," in *The Tlaxcalan Actas: A Compendium of the Records of the Cabildo of Tlaxcala (1545–1627)*, edited by James Lockhart, Frances Berdan, and Arthur J. O. Anderson (Salt Lake City, 1986), pp. 80–84.
14. The text in this selection and the image in Figure 9 come from *Papeles de Nueva España* (Madrid: Sucesores de Rivadeneyra, 1905), 4:53–57 (relación), between 52 and 53 (map). Both images in Figure 10 are from John M. D. Pohl and Bruce E. Byland, "Mixtec Landscape Perception and Archaeological Settlement Patterns," *Ancient America* 1 (1990): 120. Courtesy of Cambridge University Press. For Dana Leibsohn's interpretation of indigenous maps, see "Colony and Cartography: Shifting Signs on Indigenous Maps of New Spain," in *Reframing the Renaissance: Visual Culture in Europe and Latin America, 1450–1650*, edited by Claire Farago (New Haven, 1995), pp. 264–81, on the Texupa map especially pp. 278–79.
15. Selection 15 is translated from Pascual Boronat y Barrachina, *Los moriscos españoles y su expulsión*, facsimile reprint of 1901 original (Granada, 1992), 1: 522–24.
16. Selection 16 is translated from Enrique Otte, editor (with the collaboration of Guadalupe Albi), *Cartas privadas de emigrantes de Indias, 1540–1616* (Seville, 1988), p. 81.
17. Selection 17 is excerpted and translated from Archivum Romanum Societatis Iesu (Rome), *Epistolae Hispaniae* 104, fols. 129–129v: Hieronymo de Benarcama to Francisco de Borja, Granada, September 25, 1566. Helpful to our introduction and suggestive on Benarcama is Nigel Griffin, " 'Un muro invisible': Moriscos and Cristianos Viejos in Granada," in *Medieval and Renaissance Studies on Spain and Portugal in Honour of P. E. Russell*, edited by F. W. Hodcroft, D. G. Pattison, R. D. F. Pring-Mill, and R. W. Truman (Oxford, 1981), pp. 133–54. On the early Society see John W. O'Malley, *The First Jesuits* (Cambridge, 1993), and the first section of essays by Terence O'Reilly in *From Ignatius Loyola to John of the Cross: Spirituality and Literature in Sixteenth-Century Spain* (Aldershot, Eng., 1995). A concise and up-to-date introduction to the experiences of Nahua collegians in New Spain appears in Louise Burkhart, *Holy Wednesday: A Nahua Drama from Early Colonial Mexico* (Philadelphia, 1996), chap. 2, esp. pp. 55–73.
18. Selection 18 is excerpted and translated from José de Acosta, *De Procuranda Indorum Salute*, edited and translated by Luciano Pereña et al. (Madrid, 1984), vol. 1, *Pacificación y colonización*, chaps. 14, 15, and 18, pp. 199–209 and 231–43.
19. John C. Super's essay was first published as "Miguel Hernández: Master of Mule Trains," in David G. Sweet and Gary B. Nash, editors, *Struggle and Survival in Colonial America* (Berkeley, 1981), pp. 298–310. Courtesy of the Regents of the University of California and the University of California Press.
20. Figures 11 and 12 are from *Pintura del gobernador, alcaldes y regidores de México. Códice en geroglíficos mexicanos y en lenguas castellana y azteca, existente en la Biblioteca del Duque de Osuna* (Madrid, 1878), fols. 501v, 470v.
21. Figures 13 and 14 are from the *Códice Sierra. Fragmento de una nómina de gastos del pueblo de Santa Catarina Texupan*, facsimile edition (Mexico, 1906), pp. 16 (Saint Peter, 1555) and 42 (the arm, 1561). Courtesy of the Marquand Library of Art and Archaeology, Department of Rare Books and Special Collections, Princeton University Libraries.
22. Figure 15 is from Diego Valadés, *Rhetorica Christiana* (Perugia, 1579), facing p. 206 (misprinted as "106"). Courtesy of the John Carter Brown Library at Brown University.
23. Figure 16 is a photograph of the Huejotzingo altarpiece from *Retablos mexicanos*, Artes de México series, no. 106 (Mexico, 1966), preceding p. 21. The schematic drawing (Figure 17) is adapted from *Retablos*, p. 27. On pp. 26–27 this source has a helpful short essay on the symbolism of the altarpiece by Francisco de la Maza.
24. This painting by Andrés Sánchez Gallque, Figure 18, is courtesy of the Museo de América, Madrid. The 1606 document comes from the archive of the Duque de Infantado, Madrid, on microfilm in the E. William Jowdy Microfilm Collection of the Montesclaros Papers, DeGolyer Library, Southern Methodist University.

25. Felipe Guaman Poma de Ayala left his *Nueva corónica* with a viceregal official in Lima on the understanding that it would be read and viewed by Philip III. Although the manuscript was taken to Spain, there is no evidence that the work received the attention of the king or the Council of the Indies. A Danish ambassador to Spain is thought to have purchased it, thus explaining its eventual home in the Royal Library in Copenhagen. It was found there by Richard Pietschmann in 1908. The two excerpts forming the text in Selection 25 are translated from Felipe Guaman Poma de Ayala, *El primer nueva corónica y buen gobierno,* critical edition by John V. Murra and Rolena Adorno, with Quechua translations by Jorge L. Urioste (Mexico, 1980), 2: 533–39, 570–73. Within vol. 2, Figure 19 appears at p. 602, and Figure 20 at p. 571. Courtesy of Siglo Veintiuno Editores, Mexico City.
26. This selection is excerpted and translated from *Descripción del virreinato del Perú. Crónica inédita de comienzos del siglo XVII,* edited by Boleslao Lewin (Rosario, Argentina, 1958), pp. 55–63. We have not been able to include the marginal titles from the original manuscript of the "Discriçión general del Reyno del Pirú, em [*sic*] particular de Lima" (Bibliothèque Nationale de France, Paris), which Lewin included. For contemporary population figures and other information, we are informed especially by Buenaventura de Salinas y Córdova, *Memorial de las historias del nuevo mundo, Piru: Meritos, y excelencias de la Ciudad de Lima, Cabeça de sus ricos, y estendidos Reynos, y el estado presente en que se hallan, para inclinar a la magestad de su Católica Monarca Don Felipe IV, rey poderoso de España, y de las Indias, a que pida a Su Santidad la canonización de su patrón Solano* (Lima, 1630), and by Frederick P. Bowser, *The African Slave in Colonial Peru, 1524–1650* (Stanford, 1974), Appendix A: The Colored Population of Lima, pp. 337–41. On the author of the "Description" we are indebted to Guillermo Lohmann Villena's deductions in "Una incógnita despejada: La identidad del judío portugués autor de la 'Discriçión general del Pirú,'" *Revista de Indias* 30 (1970): 315–87; on Don Nicolás Vargas (or Corso), see Manuel de Mendiburu, *Diccionario histórico-biográfico del Perú,* 2d ed. (Lima, 1932), 4: 228–29. Figure 21 is reprinted from *Chronicle of Colonial Lima: The Diary of Joseph and Francisco Mugaburu, 1640–1697,* translated and edited by Robert Ryal Miller (Norman, 1975), p. 184. Courtesy of the University of Oklahoma Press.
27. Figure 22 is from Fray Miguel Suárez de Figueroa, *Templo de N. Grande Patriarca San Francisco de la Provincia de los doze Apostoles de el Perú en la Ciudad de los Reyes arruinado, y engrandecido de la providencia Divina. En panegyrico historial, y poetico certamen* (Lima, 1675), foldout page preceding fol. 1. Courtesy of the John Carter Brown Library at Brown University.
28. Selection 28 is reprinted from the translation of Solange Alberro's essay by David G. Sweet in *Struggle and Survival in Colonial America,* edited by David G. Sweet and Gary B. Nash (Berkeley, 1981), pp. 247–56. Courtesy of the University of California Press.
29. This selection is translated from Mariano Cuevas, S.J., *Historia de la iglesia en México,* tomo III, libro 3 (El Paso, Texas, 1928).
30. This reading is excerpted and translated from "Declaración de don Gonzalo de la Maza (o de la Masa) año 1617. Procesos de beatificación y canonización de Santa Rosa de Lima," published in *Una partecita del cielo. La vida de Santa Rosa de Lima narrada por Don Gonzalo de la Maza a quien ella llamaba padre,* edited by Luis Millones (Lima, 1993), from the answers to questions 4, 6, 7, and 29 at pp. 149–52, 153–56, 156–59, 207–8.

    Recent essays that inform our introduction and a deepening understanding of Rosa and her historical context include Ramón Mujica Pinilla, "El ancla de Rosa de Lima: Mística y política en torno a la patrona de América," in *Santa Rosa de Lima y su tiempo,* edited by José Flores Araoz, Ramón Mujica Pinilla, Luis Eduardo Wuffarden, and Pedro Guibovich Pérez (Lima, 1995), pp. 53–211; the chapters by Luis Millones and Fernando Iwasaki Cauti in *Una partecita del cielo* (with Iwasaki's also appearing in *Hispanic American Historical Review* 73:4 [1993]: 581–613); Luis Miguel Glave, "Santa Rosa de Lima y sus espinas: La emergencia de mentalidades urbanas de crisis y la sociedad andina (1600–1630)," in *Manifestaciones religiosas en el mundo colonial americano,* edited by Clara García Ayluardo and Manuel Ramos Medina (Mexico, 1993), pp. 53–70; and Teodoro Hampe Martínez, "Los testigos de Santa Rosa (Una aproximación social a la identidad criolla en el Perú colonial)," *Revista del Archivo General de la Nación* 13 (1996): 151–71, which includes a catalog of the witnesses heard at both stages in the determination of Rosa's sanctity. Our thanks to Jodi Bilinkoff for her comments.

31. Sor Juana's letter is taken from the English translation by Electa Arenal and Amanda Powell, *The Answer/La Respuesta* (New York, 1994), lines 98–123, 210–346, 723–795, 825–844, 861–884, and 1368–1397. Courtesy of the Feminist Press, City University of New York.
32. Figure 23 is a painting of Santa Rosa of Lima with silver decoration whose artist and date are unknown. From Bertha Kitchell Whyte, *Seven Treasure Cities of Latin America* (New York, 1964), p. 229. Figure 24 is a posthumous portrait of Sor Juana Inés de la Cruz, also by an unknown artist, from the Robert H. Lamborn Collection of the Philadelphia Museum of Art. Courtesy of the Philadelphia Museum of Art.
33. This selection is adapted from the English translation by Rosaleen Howard of Serge Gruzinski's essay in *History and Anthropology* 2 (1986): 337–53. Notes have been omitted.
34. Selection 34 is excerpted and translated from Francisco de Avila, *Tratado de los evangelios que nuestra Madre la Yglesia nos propone en todo el año. Desde la primera dominica de Adviento hasta la última Missa de Difuntos. Explicase el Evangelio, y en cada uno se pone un sermón en lengua castellana y la General de los Indios deste Reyno del Perú, y donde conviene da lugar la materia se refutan los errores de idolatría* (Lima, 1646–1648), "En la Vigilia de la Natividad del Señor," fols. 45–53. This sermon comes from the first part of the *Tratado* and was published in 1646. A shorter second part was published in 1648, the year after Avila's death, by his executor Florián Sarmiento Rendón. The principal biblical text for Avila's sermon is Matthew 1:18–25.

    The comment by Pierre Duviols is from *La Lutte contre les réligions autochtones dans le Pérou colonial* (Lima, 1971), pp. 43–44. Informative recent interpretations of Avila's life, intellectual influences, and aspects of his preaching, respectively, are the essay by Antonio Acosta Rodríguez noted above in our reference for Selection 1; Teodoro Hampe Martínez, *Cultura barroca y extirpación de idolatrías: La biblioteca de Francisco de Avila (1648)* (Cusco, 1996); and Juan Carlos Estenssoro Fuchs, "Les Pouvoirs de la Parole: La prédication au Pérou de l'évangelisation à l'utopie," *Annales HSS* 6 (November–December 1996): 1225–57.
35. Selection 35 is translated from the "Denuncia que hace don Juan Tocas principal y fiscal de la dicha visita contra Hernando Hacas, Cristóbal Poma Libiac y muchos indios del pueblo de San Pedro de Hacas, 15 agosto 1656–11 enero 1658," in *Cultura andina y represión: Procesos y visitas de idolatrías y hechicerías, Cajatambo, siglo XVII,* edited by Pierre Duviols (Cusco, 1986), pp. 182–91. Pablo José de Arriaga's 1621 work, *La extirpación de la idolatría en el Perú,* in *Colección de libros y documentos referentes a la historia del Perú,* series 2, vol. 1, edited by Horacio H. Urteaga (Lima, 1920), has been translated into English by L. Clark Keating: *The Extirpation of Idolatry in Peru* (Lexington, KY, 1968).
36. Figure 25 is a photograph of the Rosary chapel by James Early. Courtesy of James Early. The description of the dome draws from Early's *The Colonial Architecture of Mexico* (Albuquerque, 1994), pp. 79–88.
37. Reproductions of some of the Corpus Christi series, and much else on the Cuzco School of artistic and cultural production, can be seen in José de Mesa and Teresa Gisbert, *Historia de la pintura cuzqueña,* 2d ed., 2 vols. (Lima, 1982), esp. 1: 177–80; and 2: plates 229–42. Figures 26 and 27 are from the Museo del Arte Religioso in Cusco, Peru. Our thanks to Carolyn S. Dean.

    Our introduction is informed especially by Dean's Ph.D. dissertation, "Painted Images of Cuzco's Corpus Christi: Social Conflict and Cultural Strategy in Viceregal Peru," University of California, Los Angeles, 1990; and by the same author, "Who's Naughty and Nice: Childish Behavior in the Paintings of Cuzco's Corpus Christi Procession," in *Native Artists and Patrons in Colonial Latin America,* edited by Emily Umberger and Tom Cummins, a special issue of *Phøebus—A Journal of Art History* (Arizona State University) 7 (1995): 107–26, and "Ethnic Conflict and Corpus Christi in Colonial Cuzco," *Colonial Latin American Review* 2:1–2 (1993): 93–120. See further instruction taken from two essays by David Cahill, especially "Popular Religion and Appropriation: The Example of Corpus Christi in Eighteenth-Century Cuzco," *Latin American Research Review* 31:2 (1996): 67–110; and "Etnología e historia: Los danzantes rituales del Cuzco a fines de la colonia," *Boletín del Archivo Departamental del Cuzco* 2 (1986): 48–54; also Thomas B. F. Cummins, "We Are the Other: Peruvian Portraits of Colonial *Kurakakuna,*" in *Transatlantic Encounters: Europeans and Andeans in the Sixteenth Century,* edited by Kenneth J. Andrien and Rolena Adorno (Berkeley, 1991), pp. 203–31; and

Juan Carlos Estenssoro Fuchs, "Los bailes de los indios y el proyecto colonial," *Revista Andina* 20 (1992): 353–89.

38. Selection 38 is translated from Martin Lienhard, editor, *Testimonios, cartas y manifiestos indígenas (Desde la conquista hasta comienzos del siglo XX)* (Caracas, 1992), pp. 332–35. Courtesy of Biblioteca Ayacucho, Caracas. The plan of La Concepción, Figure 28, is from *Documentos de arte argentino, Cuaderno XIX: Las misiones guaraníes* (Buenos Aires, 1946), illustration "E." Courtesy of the Academia Nacional de Bellas Artes, Buenos Aires. See Barbara Ganson, " 'Like Children under Wise Parental Sway': Passive Portrayals of the Guaraní Indians in European Literature and *The Mission*," *Colonial Latin American Historical Review* 3:4 (1994): 399–422; James Schofield Saeger, "*The Mission* and Historical Missions: Film and the Writing of History," *The Americas* 51:3 (1995): 393–415; and Philip Caraman, *The Lost Paradise: The Jesuit Republic in South America* (New York, 1975).
39. The first decree was published in Charles Gibson, editor, *The Spanish Tradition in America* (New York, 1966), pp. 231–33. The second is translated from Richard Konetzke, editor, *Colección de documentos para la historia de la formación social de Hispanoamérica* (Madrid, 1953–1962), 3:434–35. Courtesy of the Consejo Superior de Investigaciones Científicas, Madrid.
40. Archivo General de la Nación, Mexico City, Ramo de Tributos, vol. 43, expediente 9, folio 8r. According to this count, free Blacks and Mulattoes were distributed in the following numbers by intendancy district: Guadalajara, 63,009; Zacatecas, 58,317; Potosí, 49,140; Valladolid, 48,768; México, 46,813; Guanajuato, 42,868; Mérida, 29,036; Oaxaca, 17,767; Puebla, 11,304; Arispe, 10,070; and Veracruz, 5,849. "Mulatto" is often thought to identify people of mixed African and European descent, but it was regularly used in the colonial period for people of mixed African and Indian descent (see also Selection 24). Selection 40 was originally published with a different introduction in William B. Taylor, "The Foundation of Nuestra Señora de Guadalupe de los Morenos de Amapa," *The Americas* 26 (1970): 439–46. Courtesy of *The Americas.*

    The map in Figure 29 is located in the Archivo General de la Nación, Ilustración num. 2455; originally in Ramo de Tierras, vol. 3543, exp. 2, from which additional information was drawn for our introduction. Courtesy of the Archivo General de la Nación.
41. This selection is translated from the first edition of *El Lazarillo de ciegos caminantes desde Buenos-Ayres, hasta Lima con sus Itinerarios según la más puntual observación, con algunas noticias útiles a los nuevos comerciantes que tratan en mulas; y otras históricas. Sacado de las memorias que hizo Don Alonso Carrió de la Vandera en este dilatado viage . . .* ("Gijón: Imprenta de la Rovada, 1773" [Lima, 1776]), unnumbered pp. 16–39 of the 58-page Tercera Acusación.
42. This selection is adapted from the second half of William B. Taylor, "Santiago's Horse: Christianity and Colonial Indian Resistance in the Heartland of New Spain," in William B. Taylor and Franklin Pease G. Y., editors, *Violence, Resistance, and Survival in the Americas: Native Americans and the Legacy of Conquest* (Washington, DC, 1994), pp. 162–73. Notes have been omitted. © 1993 by the Smithsonian Institution. Courtesy of the Smithsonian Institution Press. Wells's observation is from David A. Wells, *A Study of Mexico* (New York, 1887), pp. 84–85.
43. This selection is adapted from David Cahill's essay of the same name in *Reform and Insurrection in Bourbon New Granada and Peru,* edited by John R. Fisher, Allan J. Kuethe, and Anthony McFarlane (Baton Rouge, 1990), pp. 255–91. Notes have been omitted. © 1990 by Louisiana State University Press. Courtesy of Louisiana State University Press.
44. The discourses are excerpted and translated from the Princeton Theological Seminary Rare Books Library's copy of Juan Francisco Domínguez, *Conveniencia de la Religión y el Estado. En diez discursos sobre los Mandamientos de Dios* (Mexico, 1805), pp. 3–7, 16–27.
45. For Figures 30 and 31 featured in this selection, see María Concepción García Sáiz, editor, *Las castas mexicanas: Un género pictórico americano/The Castes: A Genre of Mexican Painting* (Milan, 1989). The series by José Joaquín Magón (in a private collection in Mexico) is no. XI, pp. 102–11; and that by Andrés de Islas (in the Museo de América, Madrid) is no. XV, pp. 124–33. Figure 30 is at p. 103 (a), while Figure 31 is at p. 127 (d). Figure 31 is reproduced courtesy of the Museo de América.

    Helpful on the *castas* genre are García Sáiz's "Introduction" to *Las castas mexicanas,* and the illustrations and short essays within a special issue of *Artes de México* 8 (nueva época) (Summer 1990) on "La pintura de castas." García Sáiz identifies over fifty surviving groups of *castas* paintings.

The series thought to date from 1725 hangs in Breamore House in Wiltshire, England. Other groups are in the Museo de Monterrey, Monterrey, Mexico, and in private collections in Mexico, the Museo de América in Madrid, and the Musée de l'Homme in Paris.

46. The photographs and transcriptions for the Salto del Agua (Figures 32 and 33) are by William B. Taylor. The roadside monument drawing (Figure 34) is in the Archivo General de la Nación, Mexico City, Ilustración num. 268, removed from Ramo de Historia, vol. 118, exp. 5. Courtesy of the Archivo General de la Nación. Inscriptions on the four fountains in the Plaza Mayor were published in Francisco Sedano, *Noticias de México desde el año de 1756 . . .* (Mexico, 1880), 1:138–40.
47. The painting shown in Figure 35 hangs in the Museo Nacional de Bellas Artes in Buenos Aires, Argentina. From Carmen Bernand, *The Incas: People of the Sun* (New York, 1994), p. 53. Courtesy of the Museo Nacional de Bellas Artes. A number of key sources for Inka history, and on the Inkas of Vilcabamba and the figure of Túpac Amaru in particular, are now available in English translation. Informing and pertaining to our discussion are Juan de Betanzos, *Narrative of the Incas* [1557], translated and edited from the Palma de Mallorca manuscript by Roland Hamilton and Dana Buchanan (Austin, 1996), pp. 276ff.; Baltasar de Ocampo, "Account of the Province of Vilcapampa and a Narrative of the Execution of the Inca Túpac Amaru" [1610] in *History of the Incas by Pedro Sarmiento de Gamboa and the Execution of the Inca Túpac Amaru by Captain Baltasar de Ocampo,* translated and edited by Sir Clements Markham (Hakluyt Society, second series no. XXII, 1907) (Millwood, NY, 1967), pp. 203–47; and El Inca Garcilaso de la Vega, *Royal Commentaries of the Incas, and General History of Peru* [1609; 1617], translated and edited by Harold V. Livermore (Austin, 1966). See also Alberto Flores Galindo, *Buscando un Inca: Identidad y utopía en los Andes* (Havana, 1986); and George Kubler, "The Neo-Inca State (1537–1572)," *Hispanic American Historical Review* 27 (1947): 189–203.
48. Figure 36 is from George Kubler and Martin Soria, *Art and Architecture of Spain and Portugal and Their American Dominions, 1500–1800,* Pelican History of Art (Baltimore, 1959), plate 179(b).
49. The "Sentiments of the Nation" is translated from Ernesto Lemoine Villicaña, editor, *Morelos: Su vida revolucionaria a través de sus escritos y de otros testimonios de la época* (Mexico, 1965), Document 110, pp. 370–73. Courtesy of the Universidad Nacional Autónoma de México. The quotation from J. H. Parry is found in his *The Spanish Theory of Empire in the Sixteenth Century* (Cambridge, MA, 1940), pp. 174–75.
50. Selection 50 was originally published in Charles Gibson, editor, *The Spanish Tradition in America* (New York, 1966), pp. 239–40.

INDEX

References to definitions and identifications found in the Glossary are printed in boldface type.